The Road to Parnassus

Artist Strategies in Contemporary Art and the rise of Douglas Gordon

by Diego Mantoan

Vernon Press

www.vernonpress.com

In the Americas:
Vernon Press
1000 N West Street,
Suite 1200, Wilmington,
Delaware 19801
United States

In the rest of the world
Vernon Press
C/Sancti Espiritu 17,
Malaga, 29006
Spain

Library of Congress Control Number: 2014948701

ISBN: 978-1-62273-029-2

D188: Zugl. Berlin Freie Universität, Diss.2015

TO DOUGLAS, HE KNOWS WHY

TO GIULIA, SHE SHOULD KNOW WHY

TO MARILENA, SHE MUST KNOW WHY

TO ANNA AND ANTONIO, THEY MIGHT KNOW WHY

TO ANTONELLA, SHE HAD ABSOLUTELY NO CLUE

Table of Contents

Introduction

Building a career in the visual arts

Is it possible to plan one's own career in any professional field, as, for instance, visual arts? The answer to this query would likely depend on the specific sector one is interested in. Prospective doctors seem to follow a path starting with medical school and leading to hospital employment, while aspiring lawyers usually enter training at law schools to be followed by an apprenticeship at an established solicitor. Something similar appears to be the case for visual arts, although the ways to enter durably the art system often appear very enigmatic – sometimes even to insiders. How may then a young art student effectively gain recognition or even fame commencing at zero point? There can hardly be a universal rule that applies to everyone, but examining the career of successful people may help finding useful advice. Looking at a specific example, the following chapters thus try to uncover what a good start in today's art world may be. The explicit aim is finding a framework of feasible explanations that should reveal who are influential players in this field and which career strategies could apply best. The swift career improvement of Glasgow artist Douglas Gordon – one of today's leading visual artists – and of the broader movement of Young British Artists that rose into worldwide prominence in the 1990s – Damien Hirst and Sarah Lucas among the best known – serves as a convenient case study to analyse artist strategies in contemporary art.

Both intended as a specialists' textbook as well as a discovery journey for a broader audience of art enthusiasts, this research is supported by a constant multidiscipline approach – spanning from traditional art history, to sociology and economics. Along the track, this book pursues the reconstruction of the field of forces that preside over the visual arts, as intended by French sociologist Pierre Bourdieu. Compared to previous publications on art system dynamics, such as Thompson's "The $12 Million Stuffed Shark", this reading aspires to offer an enhanced understanding of the factors that allow a young artist to enter the arena of contemporary art, further becoming a recognized author. Reconstructing the career path of a successful artist – proceeding step by step – aims at uncovering the seemingly mysterious logic of the art system. Indeed, analysing the biography of those who made it would easily reveal that artists are aware they need to consider global trends, beat competitors and meet the demands of dealers, collectors, curators and museums. Having chosen a topic referring to the British art boom that occurred in the late 20th century, this book further offers innovative conclusions on the subject theme. Previous studies on the so called YBA generation, such as Stallabrass' "High Art Lite" for instance, have hardly grasped the duality between London and Glasgow at the time, as well as the harsh gender opposition among emerging artists – not to mention the clear predominance of the most resourceful authors in the end.

Due to its original methodological approach to the study of contemporary art, this contribution means to deliver a more complete understanding of the intrinsic dynamics of the art system. Apart from offering an unprecedented insight into the art world to non-experts, this book should also be useful to scholars of various disciplines (art historians, sociologists and economists) as well as to prospective artists or other professionals who are interested in entering the artistic field and prompting their individual career. Almost a handbook, this research may help students and teachers – as well as artists, dealers, curators, critics and collectors – to gain a deeper knowledge of the mechanics of the art system, possibly helping them to outline their own action plan and strategies with more self-awareness or even success.

Chapter 1
Unveiling successful artist strategies

1.1. Way upwards in the field of art: a career start in contemporary art

How can one become a successful artist? Where should one start a career in the art world? Which is the right path to follow? What are useful strategies to achieve recognition? Is it feasible to imagine and carry out a precise career plan step by step? When does one make a real breakthrough? Who can one get advice or support from?

These are some of the questions all young students may be haunted with ever since entering art school, or at least at some point in their education. Albeit there is no easy answer, the quickest reply is that there are as many ways as there are successful artists in the art world. Which aren't so many, in fact, since just a few artists can earn a living solely out of their production and even less rise to fame. Everyone has found his or her own path: some late in their life and some earlier than others, some at home and some abroad, but all with great commitment and endurance. One must be definitely stubborn to start a career as an artist, being prepared to tackle resilient entry barriers set by the contemporary art system. From a dealer's point of view, for instance, launching a new artist is indeed a risky business: the art world is a tight place, the channel of trade is relatively narrow, the costs of promotion and marketing are very high and it generally takes years for unknown authors to reward the initial investment. Not to talk about the future trends in style and taste, which often seem unpredictable and ever changing. The mechanisms and logic of the art system appear pretty enigmatic to those who look out onto it as artist candidates, not to mention total outsiders and non experts who frequently raise doubts on the transparency of the art market.

However discouraging it might seem, this is the situation aspiring artists are usually confronted with. Depending on the evolution stage of the local art system, as well as on global trends, would-be artists need to find a way for putting their specific offer onto the market. Doing so means trying to beat competitors and meet the demand set up by dealers, collectors, curators, museum directors, critics and the public. Hence, as in every market, the artist is to be seen as an active player of the system – at least he or she should better act as one. The artist is no truffle for others to dig out, even though literary tradition and collective imagination may still share the romantic view of a painter isolated in the studio who awaits to be unearthed by others. On the contrary, in the last few decades the art system has experienced a wave of particularly engaged artists, who didn't want to wait to be discovered. Even though entrepreneurship may be a valuable asset, there is no straightforward answer as far as the right features that make a real difference in the art system are concerned. A future soccer player has to score to be effective, while an aspiring pop musician needs a prospective audience to hope for a recording contract. A young artist must likewise reveal some attitude to the job, but it's hard to foretell, whether he or she will pay off one day. In such matters, keeping an economic perspective on the art world may seem useful, since it considers the dynamic interaction between subjects exchanging goods and services on the marketplace. These could well be symbolic objects and meanings, thus also artworks and contents: an economic way of thinking, as part of broader social sciences, may explain human behaviour in the frame of how people make their choices in a set of countless needs and restricted means[1]. In fact, such an approach to art doesn't necessarily point to its sole monetary value, which is in reverse the consequence of a shared cultural view – that is a paradigm (Mankiw, 2009). The artist looks for appreciation – both artistic and financial – in exchange for his or her contribution to the art world and, more broadly, to society and history. A give-and-take logic might prove efficient and has been adopted lately by many scholars attempting to describe how the art system works, among others Benhamou (2000), Caves (2000), Frey (2000), Galenson (2001-2009), Jyrämä (2008a+b), Mossetto (1993), Santagata (1998), Thompson (2008), Throsby (1996), Towse (1998). However, to explain artistic success one cannot avoid examining a tangible case set in a specific historic and geographic context. The economic perspective may illuminate mechanisms and strategies of various system agents, but it can hardly grasp the specific set of preferences – as well as the evolution of taste – that trigger triumph or failure in the artistic field in a given time and place. A sole economy-centric approach would leave the initial queries unanswered for contemporary artists. So, what assets should an artist get hold of in order to emerge from obscurity? How may he or she boast chances of being noticed? Which degree of awareness concerning the art system, its key players, its mechanisms and trends is really necessary? Do aspiring artists at all care about planning their career and perform strategic actions at all? Unless one is inclined to wait forever, such thoughts are everyday concerns for candidate artists. Given art economical implications and art market dynamics, the best way to find a likely answer is investigating the path of a successful artist considering its historic and social contingencies. The chosen author should possibly be someone who stands out of his or her own generation and whose frame of reference is comparable to one's own situation. This task needs then to be set in a complex framework, rather than exposing the elusive historic context, but pursuing a specific reconstruction of the field of forces and relationships in the art system, as intended by Bourdieu (1993).

Early career strategies in contemporary art will thus be investigated by means of a specific case study that is the swift rise of Glasgow artist Douglas Gordon in the late 20th century. The Scotsman is considered today one of the top ranking artists worldwide, deserving particular appreciation for his video-installations and neo-conceptual works. Born in 1966, Gordon belongs to a generation of British artists who went through art education in the Eighties and gained success soon after, truly establishing the trends of the following decade while still very young. His career start and rapid success occurred at a time of a new UK art boom on international scale. The case of Douglas Gordon is to be set in the frame of events in British art and society during the Nineties, but on the other hand may itself be useful to highlight several aspects of this period. In fact, he belongs with the resourceful and engaged young artists who rapidly made their breakthrough thanks to their particular awareness of the mechanisms and key players of the art system. Self-promotion and entrepreneurship are distinctive features of the Scotsman, as much as they are common to the majority of British artists rapidly rising in the decade under investigation. Furthermore, Gordon's career progress seems particularly attention worthy for his apparent role as an outsider, both in respect to London art scene and in respect to dominant art trends. Indeed, albeit London was then at the centre of artistic turmoil, he preferred to steer his profession from Scotland and decided to walk the road of video art, which at the time was slowly taking off but didn't represent a mainstream choice for immediate commercial success. Another reason to study this peculiar case relates to Gordon's hometown: once an industrial stronghold where, in the aftermath of Thatcherite recession, a vibrant art community emerged for the first time ever on the River Clyde. Douglas Gordon played a substantial part in the so called "Glasgow Miracle"[2], the city's artistic bloom during the Nineties, which has since put this peripheral town on the mind-map of todays art system. His role could even be considered somehow pivotal for the local artist milieu, being the first Scottish artist to achieve the Turner Prize in 1996 and leading a long row of several Glasgow-based authors to win the most prestigious British art award in later editions. This unexpected and apparently unpredictable victory – when he had just turned thirty and still lingered with a loose gallery connection – was a striking success indeed. The irresistible rise at a very early career stage, though commencing from the art world outskirts, make Douglas Gordon a feasible case study seeming reason enough to examine the path that led him upwards looking for successful early career strategies.

1.2. From aspiring to established in Swinging Britain: timeframe and research scope

In order to approach the chosen research topic accurately, its historical context is of particular relevance due to the concurrent rise of many other artist peers, marking a substantial generation shift in British art over just a few years. In the first half of the Nineties, the UK experienced the gradual emergence of an entire new group of artists that is and was referred to as young British artists – short YBA. Rather than a coherent movement, it was more of a trend in art production proper to a varied grouping of English and Scottish authors, that had recently graduated from art school and were still in their twenties or thirties. At a glance, common features of these artists were irreverence and coolness (Cohen, 1997), irony and humour (Bush, 2004), as well as the visible sensationalism of artworks and direct references to pop culture (Stallabrass, 2006b), instead of an elitist attitude. Many of these young artists reached immediate notoriety due to high media exposure, awareness of marketing strategies, many provocative works and some that involved everyday topics or objects. The YBAs dominated the British art scene throughout the Nineties and played an important part in restoring London's lead role in the international art market (Galenson 2005b).

YBA mythology sets the beginning of this season in Summer 1988, when a bunch of young students and recent graduates of the prestigious Goldsmiths College in London[3] gave birth to an entirely self-organized group show in an abandoned warehouse of the city docks. Titled *Freeze*, the exhibition consisted of three different exhibitions and was primarily conceived, curated and promoted by the twenty-three-year-old Damien Hirst, who had already proved to be a charismatic young leader amongst his peers. Born in Bristol and grown up in working-class Leeds, he was destined to celebrity of international range before the age of thirty. The 1988 warehouse show by the Goldsmiths' was one of the first to settle in a disused industrial building and paved the way to many future exhibitions by aspiring artists in similar areas of the British capital. In 1989, after a decade of Thatcher's eleven-year rule, recession hit badly, so these art ventures counted as efforts to overcome the country's social and economic situation, while they were originated in principle as a means for artist candidates to beat entry barriers of the particularly stiff British art system. Albeit such shows apparently opposed the art establishment, the young exhibitors lived on the fringes of the system just for a short time, carving out a niche for themselves in the guise of a new avant-garde. Besides warehouse shows, there were several causes that contributed much more to this progressive generation shift. The issue of *Frieze* in 1991 may be listed amongst others, a new London based art magazine founded by Matthew Slotover and Tom Gidley, who were also in their twenties at the time. *Frieze* rapidly gained importance and rose to the rank of official house organ for the new trend. Furthermore, it is impossible not to mention the substantial twinning of many YBAs with Charles Saatchi, probably the most unscrupulous yet influential British collector. His official stance on the young artists from 1991 onwards credited a lot of them in the face of the art system. One last reason to be mentioned is definitely the growing importance of the Turner Prize due to its reformation in 1991 determined by Nicholas Serota, recently appointed Director of the Tate. During the Nineties the shortlisted artists and the award ceremony were in the limelight, causing a massive media coverage and consequently a heightened public attention to contemporary art. These, as well as other key factors will be explored further on, especially because some young artists decidedly understood how to play along with them.

As regards contemporary art in the Nineties, the British boom can't be overlooked nor underestimated, especially for its worldwide repercussion boosted by several national players. Twenty-five years from now, those days seem at a safe distance to be taken under examination and to determine their impact on the advancement of the arts, as well as on the development of the local and international art system. Regardless of any possible artistic legacy of the YBAs, no doubts London took advantage of the art fever that excited the whole nation, developing into a crucial hub for the international art system (Galenson, 2005a). In those same years, Glasgow underwent a similar transformation earning a stable reputation worldwide as a preeminent centre for young creativity – a challenging one especially for art market rules. As far as Douglas Gordon is concerned, his personal fate appears then particularly meaningful. Apart from winning the Turner Prize in 1996, being the first Scotsman to do so, he previously went to art school in both cities constituting the actual bond between the artist milieu of London and Glasgow. Thus, his key role in the period under examination can hardly be underrated, on the contrary deserving peculiar attention for one more reason.

The Nineties' art scene in Britain was characterized by true excitement and an immense variety of people, shows and venues. At the same time, the career of several artists who emerged in those days has been going very far and very fast, as in Douglas Gordon's case. Thus, while his example may well serve to detect early career strategies, one must define the research scope clearly, in order to avoid getting lost in the multitude of events and players of that period. What seems of real interest for the given purpose is retracing the single steps in a specific artist biography that lead from aspiring to established. Set against the background of YBA frenzy, Gordon's early career will be searched for the people who proved crucial for his profession, the circumstances and artworks that determined his rise, the general context he had to deal with, the strategies he employed to emerge. Early enough it will occur, that Gordon's take on life is intimately connected to artistic production (Sinclair, 1993a), thus making it virtually impossible to separate his biography from the work catalogue or exhibition list.

A rising art star's life and deeds in late 20th century UK seem an appropriate scope definition so far. However, it is necessary to point out, what should exactly be defined as an artist's early career. In fact, there are different strategies for different career stages, as there are diverging action schemes for enterprises according to their ripeness and competitive position. At first sight, what marks the difference in the artist milieu is, whether one lives from his or her own artistic outcome. Whenever an artist durably sustains his or her own life and production by means of selling works, he or she should be considered as an established artist. At earlier stages, one may find aspiring artists, new entries and rising authors in the art scene. The former are still students, the second are newly graduates, the latter are emergent artists – hence those who have been able to draw initial attention on their work – but in each case they are all busy financing their production by other means rather than selling it. The gap from beginner to establishment is bridged with a breakthrough, being possibly a single event or work, more often a progressive rise due to increased critics' consideration or media exposure. More appropriately, the above-mentioned career situations should be considered as separate stages, in particular the latter two. On the one side, immediately after art education, the artist candidate would generally be defined to enter his or her career start, thus being at the kick-off stage. On the other side, one who already managed to get going with some exhibitions – possibly a proper solo show – and good reviews, as well as a talent scout dealer representation – formal or factual – is definitely on a developing stage of his or her career. The borderline between the two levels described above is often very difficult to be drawn clearly. The British Nineties are a good example of how things in real life can get mixed up for young artists. Thanks to warehouse shows and artist run spaces, newly founded magazines and peer critics, all of a sudden it seemed possible to have a career bypassing the art world establishment and constrictive profession schemes. Examining an artist's early career should better comprise both kick-off and developing stages, thus embracing the whole path that goes from art education to the ultimate breakthrough.

These reference points may help identifying the approximate career section to be examined thoroughly in the case of Douglas Gordon, hence defining the research scope needed as a starting assumption. However, as with every initial hypothesis, this may give birth to lingering inaccuracies or even compel the research in a prejudicial manner. To avoid this risk, the premises will be checked at every step along the way. Factual evidence further requires constraining the period under examination, since Gordon started very young to be active on an international basis and has since reached a considerable career length. Commencing with his first performance at Transmission Gallery in Glasgow together with art-schoolmate Craig Richardson, which occurred in 1987 at the age of 21, he has participated in more than 450 group shows up to now and held over 100 solo exhibitions worldwide[4]: an impressive number for a 27 year-long career. The analysis intends to focus in particular on the period that goes from 1985 to 1996, which may be defined roughly as his early career. These time limits match with two peculiar events that hold factual relevance for his life and profession. Despite entering Glasgow School of Art in 1984, the real turning point in his art education occurred later, when he opted in favour of the Environmental Art Department after the first comprehensive year. In fact, this choice resulted also in a very premature, as well as idealistic and strategic stance for a non-medium specific art practice. Furthermore, by way of the Department he was allowed into precocious shows and performances, while still a student. Thus, the temporal coordinate for his kick-off in Glasgow lays in the middle of art school experience. 1996 as the outer limit of Gordon's early career seems rather feasible too, considering the success in late autumn at the Turner Prize. The undisputed prestige the award had gained during the Nineties, as well as its pervasive media effect, left an indelible mark on every winner of that decade. It proved a decisive moment for Gordon's career too, especially in light of the previous edition who had been won by Damien Hirst. Indeed, in 1995 YBA's "enfant terrible" had been awarded with a much-debated piece, *Mother and Child Divided* (1993), a work consisting of a cow and a calf cut in half and put into formaldehyde filled showcases. Hence, anticipation for the 1996 edition was extremely high, for both the public and the critics waited to learn about Hirst's successor (Beckett, 1996). Eventually, it was a year of complete artistic breakthrough for Gordon, even before the Turner Prize, as regards to media exposure and participation in shows at renowned international venues. On the occasion of cinema's 100th anniversary, falling that very year, he found himself involved in several international shows and touring exhibitions, which raised his position considerably. Further came another important award from Germany that comprised a grant plus residence in Hannover for the following year. 1996 appears to be a major turning point in Gordon's career, possibly proving to be the final limit of his early moves in the art world. What came next was rather the reinforcement of the acquired position, as well as the attempt to climb some more stairs up the way to celebrity status. The following years projected the Glasgow artist in a completely different arena, winning more and more awards[5], producing larger works[6] and finally ending up in the gallery of Larry Gagosian, probably the most influent living art dealer[7].

1.3. A "vie raisonné" in recent art history: methods and sources for Douglas Gordon's kick-start

To win the Turner Prize at thirty Gordon had necessarily shown some potential in his debut years. His early career may thus be defined as a story of professional success in the art system of the Nineties. First of all, retracing his personal path aims at revealing the possible reasons, which determined his steady climb towards an established reputation. Specific attention is paid to professional and personal occurrences in his life, rather than only to artistic outcome, thus driving at a sort of "viè raisonné" of the Scottish artist. Of particular interest seem the connections he built in the local and international art milieu, which gradually unfolded into a large network of relationships to peer artists and famous authors, dealers and curators, critics and collectors. Besides recognizing those who sustained or even promoted his career both the works he produced and all exhibitions of the period are under detailed examination, especially relevant group shows he was involved in or solo shows he carefully planned. This analysis aims at focusing on all crucial factors for his career, evaluating the different influence each one had. Going back over Gordon's early years might prove useful even to trace the roots of his peculiar art production. At a first glance, in fact, his work seems to combine several distinct veins of inspiration: as a proper identity matrix he appears to draw on conceptual art, whose language and procedures are interpreted by means of new media in a minimalist-like setting, all put together to achieve an impressive sensation on the viewer, which spoils a good resemblance to the broader YBA trend. The various influences and experiences in his early career may thus illuminate the deriving artistic choices. All the above intentions must be pursued by means of a thorough archival research combined with a close examination of the artist's studio practice and interviews, which in fact lie at the basis of the present work. Apart from assisting Douglas Gordon for several years, the writer of this research has recently been in charge of the complete renovation and first time organisation of the artist's personal archive[8], thus being allowed an unprecedented insight over preparatory material, documents, correspondence, reviews and further belongings collected in over two decades. This investigation uses a strict chronological order, intended as an overall framework, which suits the purpose of following Gordon's career improvements in a historical perspective, as well as of examining broader developments in the art system of that period. As regards the applied research approach, it stems from a sociological tradition in art studies, in the wake of Hauser (1958, 1983, 1987) – and more recently in its rephrasing by Bourdieu (1993, 2003) and Heinich (1999, 2001) – as well as from cultural history following Burke's (1998, 2009) and Wolff's (1981, 1999) method. Rather than cultivating a mere aesthetic perspective on matters or, on the contrary, exceeding with an overall economic interpretation overlooking specific contingencies, this work is set for comprehension of historical and social issues to explain both the occurrences in Gordon's career and the broader developments in British art. Setting his biography and production in social and art-historical context drives at an expected outcome of deeper understanding than previous publications on the Scottish artist, such as various catalogue essays or Katrina Brown's useful monograph (Brown, 2004), which all rather point at a mere art-critical view on his major pieces. For the sake of objectivity, the opinions expressed by critics and journalists writing for magazines and newspapers at the time of his early moves are necessarily taken into appropriate account, thus allowing to evaluate the critical reception of Gordon's work along the path. The present research takes further advantage of a previous analysis conducted by the writer, who could reconstruct the entire list of artworks produced by Gordon in the years of his career start, as well as the exhibitions which he took part into, thus partially allowing to set stage for a much more thorough study of the Scottish artist's success (Mantoan, 2012).

Furthermore, the present research will resort to several accounts on the YBA generation, both in England and in Scotland, but using them also as documents that witness the different positions in the art field in that period, since they have been written mainly by people directly involved in those events, hence lacking sometimes a sufficient critical distance. In this perspective, it may be useful to mention already some of the most important sources on recent British art that will be scrutinized. Among the first and foremost counts the work of art historian Julian Stallabrass, which appears very rigorous and scientific, but perhaps too critical and humourless as regards to the provocations of works by some young British artists, as well as deficient in drawing a clear distinction between different groupings inside that generation (Stallabrass, 2004, 2006a+b). Another crucial study is the one conducted by Neil Mulholland, who focusses on the cultural devolution that ran through recent British art involving the indeterminate relationships between institutions and practical/theoretical issues, thus interpreting the development of visual arts in the UK in the light of a competition for power over the production and interpretation of art (Mulholland, 2003). Various accounts by former artist and then art critic Matthew Collings contribute to a valuable survey on the London art scene in the last decades of 20th century, which is not centred solely on YBA and gives a good insight in the situation of young artists of the time, revealing opinions about players and institutions of the local art system (Collings, 1997, 2002). Other insider accounts, on the contrary, tend to be less objective, though they hold nevertheless particular relevance to crosscheck data and information on specific subjects or people. Jeremy Cooper's study on several *Freeze* artists takes a celebratory drift – often poor of rigour in reporting facts and figures – but is anyway helpful for fixing relationships and connections between several YBA characters (Cooper, 2012). The books and essays by curator Gregor Muir instead usually hold a gossip-like approach, as they were written by a main character of the London alternative art scene, hence they appear useful to draw anecdotes, place them in chronological order and grasp the more general YBA atmosphere (Muir,1995, 2011; Cat.2004). Concerning the Scottish counterpart, probably the most complete study is the one conducted by former Glasgow artist and now professor Craig Richardson, which is extremely scientific in its approach and presents a thorough reconstruction of Scottish art since 1960 (Richardson, 2011). At time it may appear even too academic in the references made, but it is truly fundamental to understand the developments in Scotland's art scene, as well as to identify the people and institutions involved. The only problem with Richardson's work, however, may arise regarding his statements on Douglas Gordon and artist colleague

Christine Borland, since the author was directly involved in the Glasgow art scene and apparently left the emerging group of artists, with all of whom he is well acquainted with. Sarah Lowndes has conveniently gathered many recollections on the rise of the Glasgow art scene in a book that offers an interesting and detailed reconstruction of the vibrant alternative Glaswegian milieu from its birth in the late Eighties (Lowndes, 2010). Albeit it presents dozens of interviews with various protagonists of that period, it sometimes lacks accuracy and rigour in reporting or interpreting facts and statements – which might have been avoided with a double check – hence risking to be excessively based on verbatim or hearsay. The overall information resulting from these sources appears crucial to crosscheck further material such as interviews with artists, exhibition catalogues, essays and reviews, hence detecting the possible intentionality or self-referentiality of statements and accounts.

An obvious template of this research is represented by the Nineties' British art, which was apparently dominated by YBA fever and the frantic London art scene. However, choosing the case of a Glasgow based artist should help to extend the view beyond the narrow margins of the emerging artists in the English capital. Avoiding a London centred perspective may help to recognize the diversity of trends and approaches by young artists during the period under examination, which partly stem from the peculiar geographical context they were living in. It cannot be neglected, that at the end of the 20th century both London and Glasgow have played a crucial role at in promoting the upswing of British art abroad, though in different forms and with varied relevance. Hence, a major aim of this research consists in detecting resemblances, as well as distinctions between the two cities' art scene. Although young artists in Glasgow and London applied similar strategies and partly reached homogeneous aesthetic outcomes, discrepancies still remain untouched as regards to the art market approach or artist peer groups' internal relationships. These aspects must be analysed thoroughly to avoid any superficial conclusion, especially concerning centre and periphery dynamics, which appear somehow distorted in this specific case. The archetypical path of cultural innovation usually irradiates the outskirts proceeding from the main geographical heart of a given region, though finding locally dissimilar ways of absorption and reception depending on domestic traditions and needs (Burke, 1998). However, as regards to Scotland, Glasgow's rise to an international centre of the art system went at the expenses of Edinburgh, which – for the visual arts – decidedly regressed to a parochial town. Furthermore, Glasgow emerged quite in opposition to the London art scene, drawing inspiration from very different sources and advancing an alternative development to the British capital. The peculiarity of the Glasgow art scene is stressed so far only in Scottish authors' versions, such as previously mentioned Sarah Lowndes and Craig Richardson. On the contrary, most publications on British visual arts in the Nineties rely on a decided centripetal narrative – such as Matthew Collings' patchwork on the London art world – or even concentrate on the mere YBA phenomenon as a comprehensive and exhaustive movement – so for instance reports by Gregor Muir and Jeremy Cooper. Even the imposing study of Julian Stallabrass on the YBA generation – by now the most accurate and detailed critical analysis on the subject – treats the few mentioned Scottish artists as mere subordinate affiliates of the general trend of those years. To avoid such lack of consideration, the Nineties' art scene in Great Britain should be appraised especially for its variety, both inside London and outside. The case of Douglas Gordon appears to be very significant in this regards, because he basically operated as a Glasgow outpost in the English capital. In fact, he could bring back to Scotland most connections he acquired during his study period at the Slade School of Fine Arts.

Retracing Gordon's steps, thus, demands a constant comparison to the situation in London, especially to its obvious leading artist Damien Hirst. It has been observed, indeed, that the Glasgow born artist somehow acted as a Scottish counterpart to Hirst. Both artists must be put on the background of their peculiar context, but there are definitely similarities and the two crossed their paths on several occasions, especially in 1996 at Gordon's turning point. On the heels of Hirst's Turner Prize victory, the Glasgow artist became his successor for the award in part due to a blockbuster group exhibition they both participated in at the Hayward Gallery in London earlier that year. An intense work on original sources – involving interviews and catalogues, newspaper articles and art magazines – must be carried out, in order to compare the two distinct cases. However, it might not suffice to look at those two artists, despite their leading role in the respective cities. In fact, isolating Hirst and Gordon would cut off another vital aspect of the British art scene in the Nineties that is many women artists truly bursting on the art scene. Compared to the previous decade – as well as to the entire development of Western art history by then – a considerable number of female authors came to the fore and several were indeed capable to achieve wide recognition, some even uttermost success. Due to its quantity, the presence of a large part of women in the artists' milieu at the end of the 20th century appears to be a major feature of the YBA generation. Besides affecting trends and themes expressed by peer artists, this circumstance even raised a harsh gender issue at some point, as the art system still seemed to favour male participation. A good example may be the unexpected opposition of media and public opinion at the disclosure of an all male shortlist for the 1996 Turner Prize, which was then restored the following year with an all female award final. A complete analysis of early career paths in the British Nineties shouldn't neglect the case of women artists, since they often seem to differ from male model both at the debut and on the long run. Other two accounts might thus be examined for a comparison, one from London and the other one from Glasgow, in order to discuss possible differences for female authors at an early stage. The chosen cases are those of Sarah Lucas, for the English capital, and Christine Borland, for the Scottish city. Both are successful artists of their generation and lay at the heart of their respective peer groups from the very beginning. Sarah Lucas graduated at Goldsmiths a year before Damien Hirst and was selected to take part in *Freeze*. Besides, she was close at the time to many other main characters of the YBA generation, such as for her relationship with painter Gary Hume and later with Angus Fairhurst, or again her fellowship with Tracy Emin. On her part, Christine Borland attended the newly founded Environmental Art Department at Glasgow School of Art together with Douglas Gordon, later her boyfriend, and after graduation they sat together on the committee of artist-run Transmission Gallery. In the early Nineties both Lucas and Borland started their careers as outsiders, struggling hard for the appraisal their male colleagues achieved more swiftly. At the end of the decade, they were eventually considered for the Turner Prize: Borland was on the final in 1997, while Lucas always refused to be shortlisted. As a term of comparison to Gordon and Hirst, they appear to be a good example of successful women artists of their generation, contributing to a tale of two cities and opposite genders on the background of YBA explosion.

1.4. Beginners strategies, step by step: uncovering early career moves in contemporary art

The comparison of success stories set in the art world context may help to define some reasons of the UK art boom in the late 20th Century. However, as a major contribution, this research focuses on various key players besides artists, thus describing the complete dynamics of the art system, mainly by means of an economic perspective on matters. In fact, it wouldn't be sufficient to look at the fortune of single authors to understand what happened in Great Britain during the Nineties, their career must be set in the dynamics of the art market. Although the YBA generation claimed to bring about a revolution, its impulse was carefully steered and soon absorbed by the art establishment. The true change this period brought about was rather young artists' new attitude towards the system, fuelled with pragmatism and initiative. Thus, the case of Douglas Gordon is instrumental for examining early career strategies in the art world, at least for the last decade of the 20th Century. The final aim is studying the role of the artist in contemporary times intended as a self-conscious player, who is aware of the art system's clockwork. At the heart of this work there is the purpose of identifying and classifying the various strategies that lie at hand for artists to gather the necessary resources and start a successful career. The entry strategies to climb up the first few rungs of the art market ladder seem particularly interesting, which are those from the end of art education to an established position. On the contrary, strategies, which point at stabilisation and improvement of an already achieved high status – that is for middle or late career stages, are beyond the scope of the present investigation. The overall research approach on artists' strategies derives from widely accepted theories in arts economics – for instance those by well appreciated scholars such as Benhamou (2000), Galenson (2001-2009), Mossetto (1993, 2003), Throsby (1996, 2005) and Towse (1996a+b) – though many will be challenged to prove their consistency with factual evidence. Furthermore, by now there have not been proper studies in the academic field uniquely dedicated to artists' strategies. In this regards, artists' awareness appears particularly significant, concerning both the dynamics of the art system and the efficiency of possible entry paths.

An essential part of this research is carried out thorough a study of Gordon's complete interviews, in order to measure – at least to some extent – the degree of intentionality an artist might put into strategic actions to foster his or her own career. The collection of Gordon's interviews with critics, curators and journalists span from 1991 to 2001, covering the first ten years after completion of his art education. The aim is avoiding conversations that were conducted too late in his career and might project a distorted view on his earlier stages due to possible afterthoughts. On the contrary, opinions and ideas caught in the middle of his professional rise may prove extremely useful to reveal the genuine – or even unconscious – attitude of the Scottish artist towards the art system. However, a greater accuracy is achieved by means of several private conversations with the author conducted between 2008 and 2010, as well as a long interview session held in July 2011. People and venues he came across, as well as artworks and actions adopted in those early years of his professional path, should hopefully lay out several strategies and devices at hand to try a successful career in contemporary art.

A short summary of the following six chapters highlights the logical structure this book has been built upon, in order to retrace the initial professional path of the chosen artist and analyse artist strategies devised for the kick-start of a successful career in the art system.

The starting chapter is entirely dedicated to refine a proper methodology useful to conduct the overall study of the career of Douglas Gordon, especially comparing perspectives and theories on the art system and its mechanics. The scope of this research clearly requires defining the concept of art to draw on, which in this particular case stresses the relevance of institutional processes and structures in the development of visual arts. Hence, it will be argued that the artwork shall be intended as a cultural product, which emerges from ideological, institutional and social contingencies set in a specific historic moment. Furthermore, the artist is considered an active player in establishing his or her role model in society, the self-projection as an artist and the position in the art system. Consequently, the chapter will pledge for such an idea of the art system, in which several political and social forces interact as if they were in a space of positions, where cultural meaning and predominance are at stake. Three variables thus emerge and need to be analysed in order to understand artistic success, which are players who constitute the art system, key resources that determine one's position in the field and strategies, which can be activated to improve an artist's career. Given this perspective, Gordon's professional path will be studied comprising all actions, events and players that mutually contributed to his gradual rise. Indeed, the chosen theoretical model highlights the existence of several career stages any artist must go through – either slowly or swiftly – and which constitute the basic structure this research is based upon: starting as an artist candidate in art school, becoming a new entry in the art system after graduation, possibly making it to be considered a rising artist with good chances, finally achieving the position of an established artist.

The following chapter starts retracing Gordon's first steps in childhood and adolescence, hence seizing his family and social background for early sources of influence on his future artist career, furthermore considering possible auto-biographical reference on which to draw on. Three major issues concerning the broader generation the Scottish artist belongs to will particularly be highlighted, as they hold relevance also for his peculiar case. In fact, the British generation born in the Sixties and who went to art school in the Eighties experienced some crucial transformations, the first one related to demographic development, the second being dependent on reforms of the university system, the third concerning the increased attendance rate of women in higher education. Indeed, Gordon belongs to the second British baby boom generation, which profited from higher education gradually opening up to working class and female students. Emphasizing class differences or gender discourse will appear to be related also to the issue of the artist's self-image, possibly becoming powerful devices to interpret one's own role as an artist in society and to promote one's peculiar artistic production in the art system.

Hereafter, the book will analyse the period Gordon spent in art education between his hometown Glasgow and later in London, spanning from 1984 to 1989. Several issues will arise along the research path, since in the Eighties the UK higher education system was characterized by a major transformation. Especially art theories and its pedagogy were fundamentally reformed, which had relevant consequences for the new generation of artists that would graduate from art schools across the country. The so-called *ethnographic turn*, which prompted the conversion of the artist's role into a researcher, gave indeed rise to comprehensive visual arts courses. The newly founded Environmental Art Department at Glasgow School of Art, lead by conceptual and public art inspired David Harding, will prove a crucial event for the Sottish city, as well as for Gordon and many of his peers, who would later gather around the artist-run Transmission gallery. Meanwhile in London a comparable group of young students at Goldsmiths College would try to tackle the local art system by organizing one first warehouse show, the renown *Freeze*, and mimicking the upcoming art trends form the USA. This chapter will highlight the differences and affinities between London and Glasgow, as well as their influence on young Gordon for the start of his artistic production, as well as for the acquisition of profitable connections in the art system.

Following the accomplishment of his art education, Gordon's debut period is comprised between 1990 and 1992, which was characterized by his production of text-pieces and instructions, as well as by the dedication to a collective experience with several Glasgow peers, which allowed him to participate into some relevant group shows and to start refining his artistic proposal. Indeed, coming together as a group with fellow countrymen at the artist-run Transmission gallery helped these new entries to foster communal chances to seek early recognition, feeding the alternative art scene and starting exchange programmes with likeminded venues all around Europe, though keeping away from commercial establishments.

Meanwhile in London a comparable experience was represented by numerous warehouse shows sprawling in abandoned industrial areas that would soon become emblematic for an entire generation of new artists. While Glaswegians were looking for endorsement of relevant mentors and godfathers, such as from established artists and curators, the Londoners were already seeking dealers and collectors that would foster their career in the art market. The chapter will demonstrate that Gordon and many of his peers – both in Scotland and in the British capital – were resolute to define their artistic production, as well as to increase relational capital. As a matter of facts, several events in the considered years would bare progressive signs of breakthrough for the new generation of artists, such as the appearance of new dealers, art magazines and collectors.

The years that span from 1993 to 1995 mark a relevant period both for Gordon's career, as well as for the general rise of the new generation of British artists. Indeed, several events would signal the progressive acceptance of the so called YBSs on national and international level, proving that established institutions started to appreciate the ferment originated by the alternative art scene in London and Glasgow. Thanks to the backing of several influent players of the art system – both old and new ones – many young artists were gradually included in institutional exhibitions, which toured both in Great Britain and abroad, bearing witness of the growing strength of British art worldwide. As regards Douglas Gordon, he was granted the first few solo shows in relevant venues such as influent galleries and renowned museums, which definitely turned him into a rising artist. Thanks to a thorough research process, the Scottish artist reached a more complete thematic and stylistic maturation that coincided with more general developments in contemporary art, especially having adopted video installations as a crucial means to spread his artistic propositions. In fact, the outcome of his new production would finally impress the critics and even grant Gordon some very controversial media exposure. Furthermore, together with several Glasgow peers, he could profit from the British art sprawl fostered by homeland institutions and thus he would start to be permanently present at international venues.

Finally, the last chapter of this research focuses the attention on one particular year in Gordon's early career, as it will be argued that 1996 holds particular relevance for the artist's definitive legitimation as an established author. Indeed, the year 1996 proved a momentous period, which delivered several opportunities for enhanced visibility, that Gordon exploited by means of his acquired ability to re-use filmed material and create captivating video installations. On the occasion of the worldwide celebrations for cinema's centennial jubilee, it will be discussed how the Glaswegian artist could take advantage of the visibility of a few particular group shows, which would eventually lead to his designation in the Turner Prize shortlist and later to the victory of this prestigious award. The events of 1996 would permanently project Gordon into a new stage of his career, having succeeded to climb up all steps towards establishment with a rapid ascent.

After drawing some conclusions about artist strategies in today's art system, which emerged from the thorough reconstruction of Gordon's swift rise to international success, a table of images set in chronological order offers a glimpse of the Glaswegian’s early career with unprecedented pictures taken from the artist’s own archive. An index of names in alphabetical order allows further to enumerate the particular players of the art system be it institutions or people that the artist came across in these years and possibly influenced his career. Again following a strict chronological order from 1987 to 1996, two separate lists keep track of all works produced by Gordon in this period and all exhibitions he participated into, distinguishing solo and group shows. Furthermore, besides the bibliography included in this book, an index of relevant reviews for the year 1996 will be listed on the publisher’s website in chronological order, since presenting the complete press coverage should help to stress the importance of this particular year for the Glaswegian artist.

Chapter 2
A cultural producer in the art system

2.1. Who is an artist: the artist and the art system

Dealing with the kick start of an artist's career, especially a contemporary artist's, requires defining the actual research subject in the first place, which is in turn obviously a problem related to the more general concept of art that one proposes to draw on. Philosophers, art historians and sociologists – recently even economists – spilled gallons of ink on paper to find an exhaustive answer. It would appear, that two centuries ago a swift reply might have been easier, given the control over art validation implemented by Academia. Especially since the various strains of avant-garde around 1900, art's boundaries have been constantly challenged and broadened, not to mention the last five or six decades that apparently opened up the field to all sorts of artistic production. The days in which aesthetics ruled over whatever was called art seem now long gone, although the presumption of art's constitutional timelessness and universality is still a deep rooted commonplace. So far, it appears rather useless to study an artist's first steps purely concentrating on ideological aspects of his or her artworks, as it would indeed be impossible to determine how his or her production came about to be considered as true art objects. Surely art can be seen to hold a transcendent value, nevertheless an artist is rooted in the society he or she lives in and acts as a supplier of the art system. One may even observe, that artists play an active part in establishing their own position in the art system and their role model in society, as well as their ideological self-projection as artists. Clearly these remarks arise from a sociological approach that has widely interested the field of art studies in the second half of the 20th Century, for the most part setting aside the critical revision of art's categories of analysis, while insisting instead on the relevance of institutional processes and structures in the development of the arts (Wolff, 1999). Minimizing the importance of atemporality and value-freedom which insists in art critics and art history, art sociology helps to understand the social and cultural construction of art, of artists, products, institutions and of its public (Wolff, 1981, p.201). Hence, the artwork is intended as a cultural product, for it loses any transcendent value, which emerges in turn from ideological, institutional and social contingencies set in a specific time and place (Hauser, 1983, p.622). Likewise art practice and institutions, this happens also with both critics and art historians, whose conclusions are necessarily constrained by those very conditions, which would thus invite to demystify creativity and analyse aesthetic paradigms in their specific social, historical and geographic period (Wolff, 1981, p.199). In fact, even considering art from an ontological perspective leads to the awareness that the peculiarity of every artificial object consists in the intentionality of its production, conversely to natural objects (Margolis, 2000, p. 125). Intentional properties can thus be interpreted, since they are determined due to a consensual process within society, such as for any kind of linguistic, semiotic and symbolic property (Carroll, 2000, p.18). This intentional essence, proper of cultural and artistic products, claims for the necessity of a history-aware interpretation, since they emerge from mutual agreement in a specific society. Both producing and describing a cultural entity are interpretation procedures in themselves, hence every propriety that is objectively conferred to an artwork could be altered in time due a constant revision process, which counts as a distinctive feature of human societies (Margolis, 2000, pp.120-127). For the above reasons it would be unthinkable to separate the meaning of a given artwork from the historic moment and place that cherished it. Far from maintaining absolute relativity in cultural discourse, these arguments place art in the field of social and institutional theory. The art world would thus be a group of assorted spheres, which members of a given society have collectively bestowed with artistic value (Dickie, 2000, p.100). In this perspective, art emerges as a cultural product consequently holding arbitrary features derived from the development of social consensus over centuries.

If art is intended as the cultural product of a determined society, then this may become much clearer at times of artistic change, which often depend on shifting paradigms due to social, political or economic turnings (Hauser, 1983, p.100). Nevertheless, transformation in the economic and social field takes a long run, thus revealing the importance of structural continuity in habits and institutions[1]. Such a notion of art requires understanding the artist as a cultural producer; hence the development of this profession demands to be observed over several centuries. At large, the artist needs to be someone who is aware of the general idea of art in his or her own society and who has acquired the necessary knowledge of the means for artistic production (Dickie, 2000, p.98). However, both his role model and status within society have experienced different stages in time, along with changing art practice and institutions. Considering Western tradition, visual artists have progressively gained social importance since late Medieval Times, while their conventional education and professional profiles have changed as well. Shifting standards for artist training (from workshops to academies), for artistic labour (different types and profiles of artist) and for artist's intercourse with art demand (starting with the artist-client-relationship) had indeed a substantial influence on art production over history (Previtali, 1979). Thus, being an artist holds various meanings and features depending on the specific geographic and chronologic field under observation. Already for the period that ranges from late Middle Ages to the early 19th Century, five different types of artist may be counted at least, as suggested by Peter Burke: artisan, courtier, entrepreneur, bureaucrat and rebel (Burke, 1979). These archetypes are of course theoretical models and hardly existed as pure forms, but they adequately describe the variety of an artist's professional attitude, role model, social status and pace of mind. Furthermore, they are consistent with examples drawn from art history and seem to move along a timeline, as if they were subsequent stages of a linear forward push. For each type there are specific political, social and economic premises that made its appearance possible and favoured it over others. Nevertheless, all five types coexisted at some point in Modern Times, thus they must be regarded as typical for European Art in the considered period. Besides these major archetypes, two more should be counted, although less frequent: the purely religious artist and the woman artist. Speaking of the main categories, each one had a different way of producing and marketing works, as well as a peculiar role he or she was credited with in society. The artist as a craftsman dates back to medieval tradition, when labour was organized in small workshops and constrained by guild's ruling. Artisans usually worked on a local basis for small commissions, possibly moving from place to place in order to engage in bigger commissions. Quite every late-Medieval artist would make a good example, even some who were well recognized in their own lifetimes like Duccio di Buoninsegna, Cenni di Pepo or his pupil Giotto da Bondone, all of whom had occasionally touring workshops. In the Renaissance period a growing number of visual artists were allowed into the homes and palaces of rich noblemen and became part of their private courts. Even though courtesan-artists were usually paid higher wages then artisans, not many reached a stable position and had to move around from court to court, eventually yielding to the pressure of their patrons – sometimes even aesthetically. Courtesans would count for instance Leonardo Da Vinci, who stayed in Milan at Ludovico Sforza's side for over twenty years, or Cosmè Tura, hired as official painter by the Este family in Ferrara and lodged in the lord's mansion, the likes of Hans Holbein for the Tudors decades later. At the beginning of the 16th Century the art market became more and more international with painters travelling all over Europe and some celebrity artists earning big money. The art boom allowed a few famous artists to open huge workshops, some becoming true enterprises that fed the richest courts on the Continent with pieces of art. Venetian painter Titian and German Lucas Cranach the Elder used their talent and broad appreciation to establish very successful businesses based on big workshops that almost worked around the hour. Due to the predominance on the European continent of large nation-states such as Spain and France, which came about gradually in the 17th century, several artists gained a stable position inside newly founded institutions – such as academies – or even hold influent posts in government. This is often true for architects, but also in the case of visual artists such as the sculptor Antonio Canova who was appointed as the superintendent of cultural heritage in Rome. Hence, artists became part of a nation's bureaucracy and were drawn into a high ranked lifestyle. Finally, there have always been some artists who didn't want to play by the rules and were already considered rebels in their epoch. Notably Michelangelo Merisi da Caravaggio or the Neapolitan painter Salvator Rosa lead a wild life, often on the run due to disrespectful behaviour towards some powerful notables of their times. However, for the centuries before the French Revolution the term rebel holds a different meaning from the *bohémien* attitude of anti-burgoise, typical of many late 19th century artists. In fact, rebel-artists didn't cut all ties to society, since they also needed the appraisal and protection of at least one influential client or patron to thrive on, the likes of courtesans and bureaucrats (Haskell, 1989, p.3-23).

Considering the five categories exposed above, one can see there has never been a time when artists were not influenced by social relations and duties. The quest for success has always implied some sort of acceptance of society's pressure, either willingly or reluctantly (Burke, 1979, p.112). An artist may try to force these constraints, sometimes even succeeding in subverting the normal order, but he or she will always remain an expression of their own personality strictly within the frame of allowances society is ready to make to artists (Marcone, 1998). However, playing by the rules doesn't mean an artist becomes conventional – in a pejorative way – or less creative. One may think of Andrea del Verrocchio's very traditional Florentine workshop, where some great masters apprenticed, amongst others Domenico Ghirlandaio, Pietro Vennucci also known as the Perugino, Lorenzo di Credi, Filippino Lippi and even an absolute genius as Leonardo da Vinci. Despite the five different archetypes, the true issue for artists in Early Modern Time was rather the rise in status they wanted to establish for themselves in society, seen as the only key to gain more creative freedom.

Besides personal success, an increased social status was a major concern, since visual art was neglected in the Middle Ages due to its exclusion from the *septem artes liberales.* Autographing works had been an important step for visual artists out of Medieval Times, in order to emerge from obscurity and assert their own personality. The next stage was the claim to benefit from a greater social standing, alongside growing commercial and cultural success. Self-portraits make a good example for a decisive gain in artists' confidence over their own social role. One may recall Albrecht Dürer depicting himself wearing expensive fur coats or Tiziano Vecellio who didn't miss a chance to tell the world he was the Emperor's official painter, portraying himself grabbing for the Golden Fleece on his neck received from Charles V of Habsburg.

So far, the historical development of art appears to rely extensively on the social and economic circumstances, as well as on the ideological strain implied in every cultural product. The latter depends in turn on the economic situation, the social position, the political predominance and the spiritual attitude of a determinate class, group or community of interests that influence the artist. However, the complexity of an artwork goes beyond materialistic constraints, as it is also related to the specific field of aesthetics, as well as on the individual characteristics and biographic aspects of a given artist. Although aesthetics may again be explained resorting to social and ideological paradigms, its theoretical dimension dwells autonomously and should be drawn into art discourse as an additional means of interpretation (Wolff, 1981, pp.199-200). Hence, an artwork lays at the overlap of three separate conditions, which are psychology, sociology and history of styles (Hauser, 1958, p.13). Hardly one may find a psychological or sociological equivalent to aesthetic value that would make considerations about styles, forms or ideas completely useless. In fact, artistic quality appears to be dependent on the certification of a minimal aesthetic amount. Hence, art would be what counts as such or consequently what those people reckoned as artists produce (Hauser, 1983, pp.57, 341, 746). Relying on an implicit agreement, art must be the result of a negotiation amongst those players that hold some sort of determination right over artistic judgement. The creation of an artwork would thus be comprised in a broader field, based on a collective foundation rather than being an individual activity (Boime, 1990). Recognizing two separate, though mutual necessary kind of productions for an artwork reveals itself as a crucial aspect: on the one side lays art's material production, which is up to the artist, while on the other side there is the production of its symbolic meaning, that is the creation of its value based on institutional and social recognition. The idea of an art system emerges, in which several political and social forces interact, going far beyond the existence of a singular patron or institution, on the contrary focussing on the merge of individuals into a community characterized by the predominance of political and cultural elites (Bourdieu, 1993, pp.12, 36). The ruling class as a whole would then appear to hold the post of art system certifier or gatekeeper, rightly declaring artistic value. However, this system hardly is a unified set and should be defined appropriately as a space of positions where cultural meaning and predominance are at stake. In fact, the art world involves numerous players, each with different means and intentions, and depends on the particular power relations between them. Lending the words of French sociologist Pierre Bourdieu, it can be described as "a force-field as well as a field of struggles which aim at transforming or maintaining the established relation of forces" (Bourdieu, 2013, p.15). The particular conformation of this arena depends on the distribution of specific capital amongst all participants, which consists of those properties that determine success in the considered field. The agents who hold stronger power are in a dominant position due to the accumulated cultural capital – which may be prestige, influence over other key players, opinion leadership, network assets – and usually try to thrive on their revenue of position, opposing competitors that challenge it. The true struggle, however, is over authority inside the field, which means conquering the role of legitimate and acknowledged decision maker of the arena. The position everyone is fighting for holds the typical advantages of oligopoly, awarding the rare ability to sanction symbolic meaning in the artistic field. Typically the struggle is over the definition of the field limits. The main concerns are, what should be legitimately considered as art and who should be counted as a field player. Studying the career of a particular artist, hence, should be comprised inside the broader artistic field, therefore considering all agents that contribute to the meaning and value of his or her works: dealers, museum directors, collectors, critics, publishers and all other players who mutually determine artistic value (Bourdieu, 1993, pp.30-36). Hence, it wouldn't be sufficient to take the social, psychological and biographical conditions of the direct producers into account – speak, of the artist – but it is necessary to consider also the conditions of production defined by the different agents involved in the field. Widening the scope even more, cultural production in turn is inscribed in the more general economic and political filed, thus being affected by its laws and forces (Stallabrass, 2006a). It may be understood as a dominated position and its players as a dominated fraction of the dominant class. However, the art field and its agents may decide to fluctuate between two opposite attitudes towards the broader arena: a more market oriented position prone to the dominators, on the one side, and a rather detached or even opposing position on the other side, which relays on the claim of creative freedom and autonomous principles for aesthetic development (Bourdieu, 1993, pp.40-42).

In any case, the most difficult position appears to be that of new entrants, because they start with a very low capital level and must find strategies to break entry barriers. From their starting point they can only try to get the pulse on the situation – which may happen instinctively or more deliberately – in order to understand how to gain access to the arena. Membership of the field will rather be granted to those aspiring agents who possess a vast amount of information on the trends and force relations of the field itself: one should better know the field's past, understand its present state and be capable of imagining its future developments. Furthermore, it is advised to identify influential institutions and people, to comprehend the nature of their relationships to one another – harmonic or at odds – and to gather information about ideas and issues which are "in the air" (Bourdieu, 1993, pp.31-32). This is also what should be done to retrace the first steps of a successful artist, as it would be insufficient to concentrate on his or her sole biographic, psychological and social background. A thorough research on the artistic field of his or her time is inescapable, in order to recognize the various players, their peculiar position in the arena and the network of relationships between them. Furthermore, it is necessary to go beyond the mere description of the field and try to understand the intrinsic aims and motivations that may explain the different player's behaviour, in order to understand the specific decisions taken in terms of art trends (Heinich, 1999, p.26). Although dominant agents tend to maintain the acquired position setting up entry barriers, in fact this doesn't mean that their artistic choices are inherently conservative and that only artists who follow major trends stand a chance. Powerful players would usually try to thrive on the revenue of their position, but this could also involve progressive change in taste that leads to new artistic developments, in order to be ahead of times and lead the line. Thus, entry barriers are not insurmountable, but one needs to understand the ideology and preferences of the gatekeepers. Consequently, listing the most important people and institutions of the art system must be understood as the first step to investigate the historical development of art trends. Beyond the mere identification of crucial agents, it is necessary to consider the criteria adopted by these players for their peculiar definition of art, as well as for their actual choices. The issue of individual preferences of influential players – such as ideologies, theories, motivations and taste – may be linked to an understanding of art considered as a cluster concept, an idea derived from Wittgenstein's language philosophy (Carrol, 2000, p.16). A cluster concept is formed by a set of mutually sufficient properties – e.g. several characteristics that an artwork should possess – none of which is actually necessary, neither jointly nor individually. This would mean, that an artwork could lack any of the supposed properties that are usually conferred to its status[2]. As a matter of facts, the list of criteria adopted might not be exhaustive to explain why an object is considered a piece of art, but this would only mean that new items should be added to the list. New criteria might even contrast previous criteria: an artefact may for instance distance itself form natural beauty (such as for Cubism), disregard emotions (as in the case of Minimalism) or lack any technical skill (such as *ready-mades*). The cluster concept should simply pinpoint a variety of factors, which define what art is, but the real focus should be put on the subset of criteria adopted by a determined agent. Every player in the art field chooses his or her own subset, which is a possible combination of criteria. Hence, an object or an action may or may not be considered art, depending on the subset considered by the assessor. This approach allows one to understand the existence of a variety of opinions about art, which can all be legitimate at one and the same time although showing harsh discrepancies. A mere institutional, social or historic interpretation of art may be deficient in understanding certain developments in trends and tastes, if not combined with an investigation of individual preferences and opinions among agents who hold a strong position in the art field – such as influential critics, museum directors, dealers, collectors (Gaut, 2000, pp.27-37). Once established that gatekeepers are no coherent group, stressing individual preferences shouldn't lead to the idea that they all are independent individuals. As a matter of facts, dominant agents may feel mutually sympathetic or even form some sort of alliance, thus creating interdependent sub-groups or factions that take the same side against other groupings (Vettese, 2007, p. 21). Consequently, an artist who is seeking affirmation must not only be aware of the general art trends, but also create a production pertinent to the reference system or specific sub-set of gatekeepers he addresses, in order to hope for their endorsement (Vettese, 1998, pp.116-117).

Cultural capital and historic feel, field of forces and struggles, dominant position and individual preferences, alliances and connections: entering the art system doesn't seem at all an easy game for a young man or woman, who intends to be reckoned as an artist. However, more than a few find a way to gain access to the field and some are even able to master the situation to their own advantage. Being amongst the most successful artists of his generation, Douglas Gordon makes a good case study to identify strategies and moves – both deliberate and unaware ones – which helped in the specific historic context and should supply general directions for the artistic field at large. In order to unveil his early career stages, it could be useful first to recognize the current position the Scottish artist has reached in the art system.

2.2. What an artist: Douglas Gordon in the art system

Glasgow born Douglas Gordon has been active now for more than two decades in the art system at international level and is regarded as one of the most successful living artists, usually set in the upper positions of various annual artists rankings[3]. Succeeding in establishing himself as a markedly international artist, today he is regarded among several art scene celebrities, though his personal attitude and media exposure make him a quite tempered artist, who usually aims at escaping the public glare of stardom. Over the past two decades his impact on recent art developments has been highly significant, especially as far as installation art and the use of new media are concerned, becoming one of the most influential authors of his generation. The peculiar works, techniques and genres which ensured his position in the art system are videos, projections, installations and films – the following two standing among his best known works: the most celebrated *24 Hour Psycho* (1993), a slow motion screening of Alfred Hitchcock's famous Hollywood thriller which was recently purchased in a revised edition by Kunstmuseum Basel at a record price for video art[4], and the documentary film *Zidane: A 21st Century Portrait* (2006) shot with Philippe Parreno on the great French football champion, which premiered at Cannes Film Festival that same year. His career has been distinguished by several international awards granted by notable institutions such as Tate Britain (Turner Prize 1996), Venice Biennale (1997) and New York Guggenheim (Hugo Boss Prize 1998), as well as other significant prizes such as Berlin DAAD Stipendium (1997), Hannover Central Kunstpreis (1998) and Zurich Roswitha Haftmann Prize (2008). As regards to the media applied, Gordon's distinction is essentially due to his choice to abandon traditional techniques, primarily painting and sculpture, favouring instead the use of language and performance, of video images and environmental installations. The four categories mentioned are useful to classify the various types of works he makes, tough two in particular stand out among them: on the one hand the production of texts, words or phrases circulated by different means – either attached on walls, ceilings, floors, and similar surfaces or broadcasting them via print, phone or mail – and on the other hand the creation of video works, both by means of using existing material, such as movies and footage drawn from various sources, and of original shots. Both kinds of works are usually displayed as installations that conceptually involve the exhibition space in which they are positioned. His most significant production will be briefly reviewed in order to outline the Scottish artist's distinguishing features on the international art scene. For now, those works which date back to the exact scope of this analysis – being the decade 1986-1996 – are described very concisely, since they will be analysed in detail further on.

Concerning his textual works, the very early ones include *Meaning and Location* (1990), which was conceived and first installed at the graduate exhibition of London's Slade School of Art. It consists of a biblical quote, repeated twice with distorted punctuation, applied on the edge of the circular opening on the ceiling of the Octagon Room at London University College, the phrase being: 'Truly I say to you, today you will be with me in paradise. Truly I say to you today, you will be with me in paradise'. Another work, *Above all else...* (1991), was shown at the Serpentine Gallery in London on occasion of the group show for the Barclays Young Artist's Award that same year. It is a Bembo font capital letter text declaring 'WE ARE EVIL', which again had been fixed on the central room ceiling, emblazoned with a fake blue stain. Since 1991 his textual works also include a long series of autograph letters, containing either quotations or the artist's original words, which were sent to friends and acquaintances, but above all to art world professionals and often even celebrities. The first letter dates back to an exhibition held in Nevers, France, featuring the sentence 'I am aware of who you are and what you do'. Text works also include *List of Names* (1990), which records thousands of names on the wall, looking like a sort of war memorial and quoting – at random – the names of all the people Gordon could remember having met so far. The first installation listed 1440 names and was created in 1991 for the exhibition *Self Concious State* at Third Eye Centre in Glasgow. His telephone pieces, defined as *Instructions* by the author himself, are midway between text works and performances. For these projects Gordon asks the organizers of the exhibitions to make several phone calls to strangers, who are unaware to be involved in an artistic situation. The caller has to utter a short sentence, written by the artist, that may be interpreted by the receivers as a disturbance into their private lives, aimed at getting their secret feelings exposed. The first telephone piece,

Instructions (Number 1) (1992), was devised for a small group show at the Cafè Picasso in Rome and the sentence was 'You can't hide your love forever'.

In 1992 and then permanently from 1993 on, Gordon started to adopt video for his works, at first he employed existing materials: on the one hand his production made use of more or less well known cinematic movies, on the other hand he created video installations exploiting medical or amateur footage. His first and most celebrated video installation is *24 Hour Psycho* (1993), shown at the Tramway Gallery in Glasgow in 1993. As already mentioned, it is a dramatically slowed down projection of Hitchcock's famous thriller, in order to last one full day. It is displayed as a double side projection on a screen hanging mid-air from the ceiling in the centre of a darkened room. As a result the orthodox cinematic experience is wiped out, since the viewer will never see the film in full. However, the audience share the same physical space as the movie, while the stop-motion frames bring about a state of hypnosis and can trigger mental associations induced by both personal and collective memory (Verzotti, 2006, p.18). Similarly, still by means of the appropriation of Hollywood film footage, Gordon created various other works, as for *Confessions of a Justified Sinner* (1996), a double video projection he displayed at the 1996 exhibition of the Turner Prize finalists. A clip is shown of Dr Jekyll's transformation into Mr Hyde drawn from an 1930ies movie, though the scene is slowed down and projected onto two separate screens, one projected in negative photography – on the left side – and one in normal positive – on the right side. As another example counts *Between Darkness and Light* (1997), exhibited in an underpass in the German city of Münster for *Skulptur Projekte '97*. The work stages a simultaneous confrontation of two films on the same screen, which belong to two contrasting genres: the famous horror movie *The Exorcist* and the religious biopic *The Song of Bernadette*. Finally for the video installation *Through a looking glass* (1999), installed the first time at the Gagosian Gallery in New York, Gordon resorted to a famous scene from *Taxi Driver*. The title is borrowed from Lewis Carroll's novel, that sequels *Alice in Wonderland*. The work features the projection onto two perpendicular screens of the clip in which actor Robert De Niro, playing the title role, is rehearsing his new personality in front of a mirror, revealing first signs of a developing schizophrenia. However, the displayed frames differ on the two projections, as they are mirroring images run at a slightly different pace, hence losing soon coordination and tending to confuse and disorient the viewers.

Employing found footage, instead, from 1994 on the Scottish artist has created various video installations, three in particular being *Trigger Finger*, *Hysterical* and *10ms*$^{-1}$, which all exploit clinical shootings that focus on physical disorders caused by psychological traumas. *Trigger Finger* (1994) and *10ms*$^{-1}$ (1994) were shown in his first solo exhibition at Lisson Gallery in London in 1994. They were both produced using materials from World War I military archives and play upon sequence loops. *Trigger Finger* shows on a single screen the take of a male hand repeating the gesture of a shooting gun, while *10ms*$^{-1}$ features a young man laying on the floor unable to get up on his feet, being constantly pulled to the ground by his own weight. *Hysterical* (1995), the first video installation projected onto a double screen, was made for the group exhibition *General Release*, featuring the selection of younger British artists for the 1995 Venice Biennale. On two screens, black and white frames are shown of a schizophrenic woman given a medical sedative treatment by two doctors. For the series called *Bootleg* (1995-96) the Scottish artists drew from illegal shootings taken at rock concerts in the Seventies. *Bootleg (cramped)* (1995), *Bootleg (stoned)* (1996) and *Bootleg (bigmouth)* (1996) were displayed as video installations for a comprehensive solo exhibition at Zurich's Museum für Gegenwartskunst in 1996. Each of them features a clip from three different rock concerts showing a brief sequence in which the lead vocalist pretends a hysterical attack on stage, as if possessed by the music. Finally, the last work to be mentioned for the use of bootleg material is *Black and White* (*Babylon*) (1996), created on the occasion of the touring exhibition *The British Art Show 4* in 1996. This installation manipulates an amateur clip of a striptease performance secretly taken in a nightclub of the Fifties and projects it on two screens hanging side by side: the first screen shows the actual image, while on the second one the clip is projected upside down.

Gordon later moved on to shoot also original videos, beginning with a series of clips featuring his own limbs, hands and arms, legs and feet. The most significant achievement of this type are two videos entitled *A divided self I* and *II* (1996), which were shown at the Turner Prize nominees' exhibition in 1996. The two monitors, on which the two clips run, show the sequence of two incessant fighting arms, one hairless and the other hairy, as if they were staging a struggle between opposite principles, between good and evil. They are actually the artist's own arms, having shaved one of them, in order to enact the struggle of two different personalities within the same individual. In 1999 he shot his first full-length movie, entitled *Feature Film*, which was produced by London's Artangel foundation and supported by the Kölnischer Kunstverein. The movie is about conductor James

Conlon's performance of Bernard Herrmann's score to Vertigo with the Paris Opera orchestra. For the entire shoot the camera insists on Conlon with takes of hands and head, movements and expressions while conducting the thrilling soundtrack of this other Hitchcock movie. Another movie already mentioned is *Zidane: A Twenty-first Century Portrait* (2006), that hold much in common with *Feature Film*. It is a sort of documentary which insists on the moves of the French soccer player, assembled from footage shot in real time over the course of a single football match by seventeen synchronized cameras placed around the playground. Other original videos, though intended as more complex video installations, include *Play Dead, Real Time* (2003), shot inside the Gagosian Gallery in New York, where it was later premiered. Two slightly leaning screens and a small monitor, all positioned in the middle of the room, play the video of an elephant in the gallery striding and tumbling around to mimic his own death. The footage causes a little dizziness to the viewer, as the camera lens constantly rings around the big animal in a swift and circular motion.

Over the years Gordon has also created several series of photographs or of physically manipulated photos and posters, each as an individual piece. They were produced mainly on occasion of solo shows for commercial galleries that acted as his dealers, such as Lisson Gallery in London, Yvon Lambert in Paris or Gagosian Gallery in New York. The photographs include for instance the series *Three Inches (Black)* (1997), which comprises eleven colour C-Print photos, showing a hand whose index has been totally blackened by a tattoo[5]. The series was realized for Yvon Lambert in Paris on occasion of a solo exhibition in 1996 and was displayed inside a room with pitch-black walls. *Croque-Mort (2000)* is another series of about ten photographs installed in a room that had been painted red, instead, for a solo exhibition at the Gagosian Gallery in New York in 2000. The photos feature close-up details of a baby grabbing its little foot and nearing its mouth, as if to bite it[6]. For Gagosian Gallery Gordon produced several other series, but in this case he manipulated existing photographs and posters of Hollywood celebrities and pop stars. In 2002 he made the *Blind Star* series, which are pictures portraying several cinema stars of the past, whose eyes he had cut out and replaced by mirrors on the background. In 2006 he started the series of so-called *Self-Portrait of You + Me*, which are again celebrities' photos and posters, but partially burnt by the artist, then installed on a mirror and finally framed altogether.

The Scottish artist has further developed a peculiar strain of environmental installations, making use of a varied range media, which include among the best known *Something between my mouth and your ear*

(1994), *30 Seconds Text* (1997) and *From God to Nothing* (1997). *Something between my mouth and your ear* can be considered one of his first installation pieces, other than the environmental performances belonging to his school years in Glasgow in the mid Eighties. Created in 1994 for the exhibition *The Reading Room* at Dolphin Gallery in Oxford, the work consists in a room painted dark blue with dimming blue light, where a HiFi station on the floor plays incessantly 30 pop songs. The music pieces belong to the British top list of the period January-September 1966, which were the months of Gordon's mother's pregnancy, so the room should recreate the visual, acoustic and aural sensations that the foetus had likely felt before birth. *30 Seconds Text* is another mixed media installation, a fragment of a bigger piece formerly made in Uppsala castle in 1996 for a solo exhibition within an broader group show of Scottish artists in Sweden entitled *Swan-off*. The original work is called *...head* (1996) and was displayed only once, consisting of two separate installations: a text about medical experiments projected onto the wall and a double screen video projection in an adjacent room. The text was shown underneath a ruined stuccoed decoration, which is an angel's body whose head had been severed due to the lowering of the ceiling. The two videos, instead, were shown in a suitably darkened room and featured black and white frames of a severed head and its headless body. For the Venice Biennale in 1997 Gordon rearranged the piece extracting the text and reworking it as a mere environmental installation without videos, changing also the title. This new version consists of the same text applied onto the wall of a pitch-black room, lit by a small lamp that is switched on and off every thirty seconds. The story tells about the experiments carried out by a French physician on prisoners sentenced to death and executed in the early 20th Century. The scientist tried to interact with the severed heads and wrote they remained conscious for about thirty seconds on average. The time to read the whole text is exactly thirty seconds, which is also the time the light bulb stays on before leaving the viewer in the dark. A black room and light bulbs hanging from the ceiling are again used in *From God to Nothing*, which he conceived during his stay in Germany subsidized by the Deutscher Akademischer Austauschdienst (DAAD) and was later installed at the Galerie Micheline Szwajcer in Antwerp that same year. On the four walls Gordon applied continuous a line of text at eye height that recorded all of the artist's one hundred and forty-seven fears. In ascending order, the words start with the fear of God and finish with anxiety over nothingness, hence elucidating the title of the work. The room is set in a dim atmosphere thanks to three light bulbs hanging at different heights, coinciding with three human pivotal points being the mind, the heart and the genitals.

In view of the means predominant in his production, it would appear reasonable to regard Gordon as a media and performance artist. However, circumscribing his action to a specific category of art could possibly lead to underestimate the impact of his work on the general development of contemporary art. What emerges from this quick survey over his production, demonstrates instead that Gordon has not switched to new media to conduct a mere media-centric discourse, which is to thematise formal or stylistic problems pertaining solely to new media. Considering the wide influence of Gordon's video works beyond video art itself, for instance, he doesn't appear to be a mere video artist, because that medium does not necessarily define all results of his creativity. Furthermore, art categories and genres – as for every kind of heuristic classification – are devices conceived for the organization of learning and knowledge; hence they don't represent adamantine truths. Rather Gordon makes use of any possible media such as video, language, performance and installations as they are adequate means of expression to focus on topics and issues he is concerned about (Stemmrich, 1995). Hence, the neglect of traditional techniques derives from their unsuitability to express the subjects Gordon intends to treat and should not lead one to think that the author fully identifies himself with the new media[7]. As a matter of facts, the true common denominator of his production appears to lay in the contents and in the underlying creative process that leads to the works subsequent realization. In order to outline the traits that characterize Gordon's role on the international scene, his art should better be approached from the viewpoint of the issues dealt with and of the peculiar working method, rather than starting from the media he applies. Even if sentiments often differ, critics' opinions will also be expounded to learn about Gordon's stance in the art system and identify the main features of his contribution to the development of visual arts in recent years.

At a first look over Gordon's production the overall poetics of his efforts appear to be epitomized by the word unsettlement[8]. As a matter of facts, the Scottish artist consistently seems to employ an approach leading to the alienation of apparently consolidated meanings, a result that is achieved by handling the context and perceptive conditions of their very presentation (Brown, 2004, p.107). By altering conventional patterns of visual and psychological perception, Gordon's strategy aims at undermining the foundations of any certainty, which usually rests on broader social acceptance (Verzotti, 2006, p.20). To achieve this goal, the author tries to involve viewers in an active process of visual and mental reception of the work, often enthusing them to make use of collective memories or of their personal recollections. Rather than referring to viewers, it would be more appropriate to define the public as 'recipients', since experiencing Gordon's work – as for many other contemporary artists – is never a merely visual occurrence. All of his works should be regarded as incomplete from a linguistic or heuristic perspective, although completed in their formal appearance. The artist voluntarily aims at a sort of indeterminacy, which in his view leads to a process of reflection and possible discovery triggered by the work itself, instead of reaching a final climax in the work (Stemmrich, 1995, p.26). For this very reason it may be eventually apparent why Gordon's production cannot be constrained within the tight limits of a specific medium, which is in fact rather used as a means to convey ideas and carry possible consequences (*Scream and scream again,* Cat.1996, p.14). This circumstance is consistent with the utter importance of the titles of Gordon's works, which often serve as an extension of the piece itself and prove crucial to grasp the associations of ideas the artist is implying (Bush, 2004, p.66). Still it should be underlined that Gordon does not intend to interfere with the viewer's ultimate interpretation of his works, which function as a potential for evocation. Being convinced that human experience is essentially subjective, he intends to let the viewer alone come full circle about the meaning, even if moving away from the artist's original intent (Sinclair, 1992, p.43).

Reflecting on the uncertainty and fallibility of human nature and, thus, of social order led Douglas Gordon to rotate around several themes, being specifically: language ambiguity, good vs. evil correlation, double-self, the blurred difference between reality and fiction, the difficulty in distinguishing right from wrong (Sega and Tolomeo, 2002, p.72). Two key concepts distinguish the author's peculiar path through the issues mentioned, which are context and dialogue (Van Assche, 1995). Context should be understood as the field of potential connections to draw from in order to attain evocative power and trigger mental associations. Dialogue should be conceived as a necessary relationship between different standing points – be it conflicting principles or else – that can bread a third way, where opposing perspectives overlap causing the original premises to collapse or to be rethought. Gordon finds the material for his works in familiar contexts, in order to verge on the labile borderline that separates good from evil, right from wrong, truth from fiction. He exploits the evocative power of images, words, sounds and situations that should be familiar to the viewer, but then relocates them in a completely different context, hence enabling a range of possible mental and physical associations which are rooted in the receptors' memory – be it subjective or collective (Verzotti, 2006, pp.15-16; Sega and Tolomeo, 2002, p.73). Drawing on mass culture is a suitable strategy to Gordon's set goals: on the one hand, products such as pop songs or Hollywood movies are phenomenal conductors of psychological affection and mental associations, so the artist may use them to evoke a specific state of mind; on the other hand, such products constitute a pre-existing topical storyline the viewer is already accustomed to, hence to which correspond precise expectations and behavioural models (Brown, 2004, p.32). Furthermore, the artist for the sake of a dramatically altered experience of reality mixes up the chosen products of popular culture. To this purpose the author makes frequent use of para-scientific instances or psychological aspects that modify even the perception of the space where the material he has tempered with is set (Verzotti, 2006, p.17). These are all planned strategies that are aimed to question our ability to perceive time and space, as well as moral issues, hence leading the viewer to doubt the stability of the human psyche and even of his personal identity. Gordon provokes a constant clash between appearance and reality, good and evil, right and wrong. Far from acknowledging a winner for these conflicts, the opposing concepts seem instead to fade into one another becoming interchangeable (*Scream and scream again*, 1996, p.13). The works of the Scottish artist set the viewer in a twilight zone where every familiar notion and its very opposite appear to be equivalent.

There are several artistic strategies Gordon employs to achieve the described results, which are strategies that stem from his education, as well as from his personal inclination and from a thorough research carried out during his early career. The main procedures he adopts are quite recognizable and now define his peculiar style in the art system, the first and foremost being a sort of estrangement effect obtained by transferring materials from a specific context to a completely different one. The work titled *Above All Else*, which has been mentioned earlier, proves a paradigmatic case in point. In fact, it consists of the words 'WE ARE EVIL' applied onto the ceiling, which is really a phrase taken from a hooligan banner seen at a football match. These very words installed at the Serpentine Gallery in London on the occasion of the Barclays Young Artist Award appeared to have two different meanings, at least: on the one hand they could refer to the awareness of the original sin – to which the blue stain on the ceiling might allude too – while on the other hand it sounded as a generational claim of a new group of fierce artists that had to make their way breaking out with forerunners (Verzotti, 2006, p.16). Another process which Gordon frequently resorts to is manipulating the narrative pace, that allows him to muddle reality and fiction, as well as to change the conventional perception of space and time. The most obvious example in this regard is *24 Hour Psycho*, where the extreme act of slowing down the film causes the cinematic fiction to collapse on itself, since the moving image should instead be obtained by a projected sequence of twenty-four frames per second. Many works by the Scottish artist make use of another technique which could be described as 'splitting and mirroring', such as in the case of simultaneous visions Gordon provides, but each seen from different points of view due to rotation or reflection. The result is small, but very efficient: although being different, the images look identical and it is impossible to distinguish the right ones from the wrong ones (Brown, 2004, p.32, 47). This concept may be clarified with the identity relationship between an individual's right and left hands: the two human limbs are equal but different at the same time (Lebovici, 2000, p.166). Several of the artist's works exploit this process, such as *Through a Looking Glass*. Mimicking Lewis Carroll's novel, the title clearly refers to a mirror vision, in fact the same sequence extracted from *Taxi Driver* is shown on two screens, but as a reflected projections run at slightly different speed. Unsettlement is to be understood as the last major strategy Gordon employs and that is particularly recurrent in his textual works, in order to distance his production from that of previous conceptual artists' such as Lawrence Weiner and On Kawara. At odds with the dry and factual sentences typical of several artists in the Seventies, the Scottish artist instils dramatic and sinister meanings in these pieces (Stemmrich, 1995, p.18). Always including words that could be read as a direct intrusion in the addressees' lives, he intentionally aims at upsetting the viewer, in order to have a reaction triggered by the artwork itself. Gordon used to send such text pieces to people he was somehow in relationship to, e.g. dealers, museum directors, collectors, curators, fellow artists, friends and relatives. This method allows him to be conceptual and visceral at one and the same time, as if he played a game involving body and mind (Brown, 2004, p.86).

Having rapidly reviewed the major production and the working method of Douglas Gordon, critics' opinions may help to focus on how the Scottish artist has been received over time by crucial agents of artistic legitimation and what position he has carved out for himself in the field for contemporary art. Opinions diverge alright, since the art system is divided into factions, each of which adopts peculiar criteria for determining what real art looks like and which artists are the most influential (Vettese, 2007, pp.21-22). Hence, it is necessary to discover the different theories and narratives used to describe art by its contemporaries, in order to understand the actual choices and evolution of visual art in a particular period (Danto, 2008). As to Gordon's work, several critics have taken the Scottish artist into consideration mainly for his relevance in video art. Michael Fried values his videos and movies for the ability to dramatize reality, succeeding in portraying his subjects' psychological state of mind and, at the same time, catching the viewers' mind (Fried, 2008, pp.226-233). While praising the production of original films and videos by Glasgow born artist, Michael Rush rather focuses Gordon's personal relevance for video art on the procedure of appropriation and praises his pioneering role in the practice of exploiting existing video material from different sources (Rush, 2007, pp.214-222). Other authors highlight the iconoclastic features in the Scottish artist's production grounding their judgment on Gordon's creative methods, first of all the alteration of borrowed material. Stuart Comer believes that Gordon's manipulation aims to dissect the chosen material until it loses its familiar aspect, thus leading viewers to look beyond external appearance and to implement the work with their subjective experience (Comer, 2009, pp.91-92). Francis McKee points out that exploiting and altering iconic images – Hollywood celebrities, rock stars or famous movies – ends up investigating the relationship that society and the media hold to celebrities: sometimes icons are worshipped, some other times they are rejected and tormented (*Douglas Gordon: self-portrait*, Cat.2007, pp.7-10). Gordon's appropriation of idols may, however, be construed as a reflection of the mass culture permeating our society. According to Gregor Stemmrich, this practice proves to be very useful to render Gordon's procedures both visceral and attractive, while still grounded in the conceptual front of the Seventies consciously resumed by the Scottish artist (Stemmrich, 1995, pp.12-26). Hans Ulrich Obrist also includes Gordon's work among the new conceptual trends of the early Nineties, as he specifically stresses the relevance centred on communicating ideas – hence highlighting the creative act, rather than the physical and material outcome (Obrist, 2003, pp.317-326). Drawing attention to the wide range of media used and the rejection of traditional techniques, Klaus Biesenbach includes Glasgow artist in the branch of media and performance art as one of its most prominent authors. Gordon's enrolment in this classification would be justified by the bulk of his production, which focuses on articulate video installations and other kinds of installation art (*Douglas Gordon: Timeline*, Cat.2006). Richard Dorment fully agrees with this stance, crediting Gordon even with setting media art free from the constraints of the past. Comparing his production with those of video artists' of the Sixties and Seventies, Dorment maintains that earlier artists were obsessed to reproduce eyesight, while Gordon would rather try to investigate the psychological experience of vision (Dorment, 1996c, p.5). Finally, some critics relate Gordon's career more generally to the success of the young British artists that rose to prominence during the Nineties. Julian Stallabrass, for instance, asserts the affiliation of the Scottish artist to so-called YBAs, especially since his works share many characteristics that proved quintessential for that generation. In the critic's opinion, such common features would be the drift towards shock art, represented by cheap provocations and bulky installations, as well as the focus on trivial content, often leaving absolute freedom of interpretation (Stallabrass, 2006b, pp.141-142). As far as these various opinions go, three different trends appear to be recurrent in Douglas Gordon's production and to define his position in the art system. Perhaps the most obvious one, in view of the techniques adopted, is media and performance art. Another tendency is related to conceptual art, whose benchmarks for Gordon seem to be Lawrence Weiner, On Kawara and Joseph Kosuth, as well as the collective Art & Language (Verzotti, 2006, p.15). All in all, the Scottish artist belongs also to a specific British art season, which was dominated by the YBA trend, to which he is often affiliated as one of the most eminent representatives (Muir, 2011, p.130). Setting aside any question of accuracy of these assumptions or to the possible predominance of one of the trends mentioned above, the critic's opinions on Douglas Gordon have aided to set his production in the broader context of the artistic field. They outline the position he is likely to have reached after his successful career, so they may help to follow up the strategics and moves he has consciously or inadvertently adopted in order to achieve the goal of establishing himself as an internationally recognized artist.

2.3. What does an artist do: players, key resources, strategies in the art system

Having looked at Douglas Gordon's main production over the years, as well as at different strains of interpretation by critics and art historians, several features have emerged which define him today in the art world. The peculiar arrangement of these features, in turn, describe the career stage he is in – as they would for any prominent artist – and are derived from resources gradually acquired, which are crucial in the art system. These may be called a proper artistic capital, as they are relevant for determining the force and position of a player within the art field. Thus, these key resources can be improved through specific strategies that necessarily involve the other agents of the art system, since they affect the overall balance of forces and positions. Depending on the starting point of the artist – or of any other player of the system – a set of different behavioural models can be activated to gain more artistic capital. The provided description of the operations in the art system could appear rather mechanical, however it epitomizes three variables that must be analysed in order to understand artistic success, which are players, key resources and strategies. Players – as economists would call them – are the agents, which constitute the art field (Bourdieu, 1993, pp.30-35), thus being necessary in their specific role for the system to work. Key resources are those stock elements, which determine artistic capital in the field, hence establishing the relative force and position of a player. Strategies are behavioural models turned into actions that aim at an individual capital gain. The outcome of strategies based on key resources in connection with the other players are finally represented by the peculiar features that describe an artist's position in the system. Albeit seeming very mechanical, even in practice any aspiring artist needs to find an answer to the following questions: Who are the relevant agents in the field? What capital or resources must be possessed to enter the field? Which strategies could gain me more key resources? What features should better define my peculiar production and myself as an artist?

So far, only Gordon's present features have been described, so one needs to study how he got there, thus detecting the players, key resources and behavioural models that took him there, as well as his specific choices over artistic production. In order to do so, the above exposed variables may offer a useful description model to analyse the specific case. First of all, then, it is necessary to identify the players on the field, the crucial features and the possible strategies on a general level. At the same time, it is essential to establish a correct terminology for the adopted description model, thus validating the exact choice of words used for its different elements. Starting with the context in which the artist is operating, one should better opt in favour of the term 'art system', that was coined by art critic Lawrence Alloway on the pages of *Artforum* and is now generally preferred over 'art world' (Vettese, 2007, p.19). The notion of system, in fact, conveys the idea of a set of interrelated people, as well as that of an articulated process that can confer the status of art to candidates for aesthetic appreciation[9]. Furthermore, the notion of 'art world' implies an idea of unity, while it is now generally accepted that within the art system strives a large variety of reference groups, some even at odds with one another[10]. Following this interpretation, aesthetic appreciation is formed through common understanding between individuals of a specific reference group, thus representing the outcome of a process of social legitimacy which attributes art status by means of the coordination of various relevant players, the artist being only one link in the chain (Danto, 2008). Furthermore, 'art system' is an all comprehensive notion compared to 'art field', since the latter would describe solely the arena of agents and positions, taking individualism and personal advantage as the true driving forces of art evolution, rather than acknowledging the existence of other motivations, such as ideological attitudes and collective stances (Heinich, pp.27-28). Hence, the art system is rooted in a community of factions and individuals who interact according to their specific role, which must be identified in order to outline the process of art certification. The players of the system comprise a wide range of professions or functions, the artist and the public appearing as the most obvious and necessary[11]. It is important to stand by the definition of 'player', since the term 'agent' might be misleading: for economists the latter refers only to the possible intermediaries between demand and supply, while 'players' are all subjects involved in a determined production or marketplace. Between the artist and the public a large number of players – both individuals and institutions – are hoarded, among them curators, dealers, museum directors, critics, historians, theorists, philosophers, scholars, collectors, investors and other buyers, as well as art schools, academies, galleries, museums, auction houses, fairs, temporary exhibitions such as biennales, magazines, newspapers etc. All of these players take part in the process of art validation, that is claiming and finally establishing the legitimate value of an artist or a work of art by means of a number of steps: provided that it is an author's intention to make a work of art – hence to be an artist – his or her proposition or product will undergo the examination of players trusted with the capability of legitimate artistic discourse, which will decide whether accepting or rejecting the author's proposal (Vettese, 2007, p.21). As a matter of facts critics, curators, dealers, collectors, museum directors and anyone else who is entitled to acknowledge artistic value will judge the work of an aspiring artist – but even of an established one. Each player will react according to his or her own ideological, theoretical and art historical opinion – though provided they appear subjective – as well as along individual taste or even personal mood. Considering the art system as a heterogeneous aggregate, which includes several groups and factions with different visions and interests, an artist candidate could even be cast off by some players, but embraced by others. The system outlined so far appears to be ruled by specialists and it is a little unclear what criteria may be used for artists selection, while the general public seems consigned to utter exclusion from artistic choices – both in influence and understanding. The claim of contemporary art being inaccessible to the masses almost counts as a constant criticism nowadays, especially if compared to cinema, pop music or literature. In this regard, however, on may suggest a distinction between the entertainment industry and high culture[12], although some artists frequently cross the line: in the former, audience is a relevant variable – though popular taste is often steered by corporations or opinion makers – while the latter is definitely controlled by a smaller elite, as was the case in past centuries, thus setting up one more field of specialized human knowledge.

Unless the above strain of explanation is to be judged the mere outcome of social and institutional superstructures[13], one more reason is needed to clarify the existence of players between artists and the public, which may be found in the economic model underlying the art system. Economics of the arts is now an established discipline committed to systematic analysis of the interaction and behaviour of players in the art market (Frey, 2000, pp.1-6). Although psychological aspects are relevant, neoclassical methodology is useful to clarify the mechanics of the art system intended as an aggregate of players (institutions and individuals), where the supply side (artists) matches art demand (museums, collectors, public etc.) by means of intermediaries (dealers, curators, critics etc.). The neoclassical approach to economics consists of a comparative view on individuals and institutions, whose behaviour is supposed to be rational; hence all choices made by players of the market can be influenced by incentives or constraints (Foglio, 2005, pp.51-52). This doesn't appear to be the case of art, since it has been argued previously that the selection of artists depends on a variety of preferences, which are even at odds with one another sometimes. In fact, economists have adopted an 'irrationality axiom' for goods that are qualified by aesthetics and meaning, such as art: hence, the structure of relationships in the art system is non-consequential, as there is a possible qualitative or informative asymmetry among agents due to differing evaluations – based on the value of their different aesthetic information and bias, such as taste (Mossetto, 1993, pp.79-80). Visual arts are thus afflicted by information asymmetry due to the true essence of the goods in question, which are qualified by symbolic qualities: these need to be recognized inside a specific reference group that can understand and appreciate the peculiar value of its meaning and aesthetics (Santagata, 1998, p.22). Information asymmetry in the art system drives in particular to a situation that economists call adverse selection[14], since the differing level of information in the market makes it difficult for prospective buyers to ponder the criteria for choosing one particular artwork or artist (Trimarchi, 1993, pp.86-87). The knowledge gap between seller and buyer would normally lead to the circumstance that a specific artwork is valued differently by the supply side and the demand side, thus compromising the possible transaction. As a matter of facts, if the buyer's estimation of the artwork differs from the seller's one, the former would be ready to pay only a smaller sum than the latter expects, hence failing market equilibrium. Usually, the marketplace sets prices on goods which function as symbols of shared evaluation, hence conveying the information that is necessary to assure quality and make transactions effective. However, information asymmetry caused by aesthetic or symbolic qualification cannot be solved by taking price as a substitute for lacking information, because the buyer would risk a wrong choice being completely in the dark about the true quality of the good at stake: the only possible solution are specific institutional certifiers which are entitled with the authority and legitimation for quality assurance in the art system (Mossetto, 1993, pp.111-112). As regards the art system then, certification is a proper alternative to traditional market information – which would normally be the price – to go beyond information asymmetry among players originally caused by symbolic and aesthetic qualification of cultural goods. In other words, a buyer or audience will be ready to acquire or enjoy an artwork, if he acknowledges its value or trusts its evaluation, hence being assured as to the cultural value of the good before the purchase or fruition. For this reason the art system needs agents who connect the demand and supply sides, which means legitimate intermediaries such as dealers, galleries, curators, critics etc. On a practical level, they function as players that preliminarily select the artists to be introduced to the art system, hence acting as gatekeepers that constitute an entry barrier for any candidate artist (Caves, 2000, p.25). Considering the self-validating nature of legitimacy inside the art field, even the certifiers' reputation is largely founded on self-selection by the cultural establishment, as well as on the individual stock capital a specific player has been able to acquire. Hence, the art system is to be intended as a self-certifying monopoly that supplies a service of 'quality-validation' to consumers, who on their part turn to the cultural establishment in search of someone to trust in, given uncertainty over true artistic products (Mossetto, 1993, p.163). As the art system is made up of several groups and factions, actually every reference group operates as a small monopoly in its own range constituting a sub-field, thus transforming the art system in a kind of monopolistic competition where several producers or groups of producers are struggling for presenting a peculiar production and having a loyal audience[15]. In fact, the specific characteristics that micro-economics ascribes to monopolistically competitive markets seem to fit perfectly the art system: (i) there is a variety of producers and consumers, but none of them is completely tenure of the market; (ii) products are differentiated and consumers are capable to perceive these distinctions, especially thanks to interpretation offered by certifiers; (iii) there are entry barriers for new producers, since they must show their product is different or new; (iv) producers have some control over price definition, as they can claim their product to hold unique peculiarities (Mankiw, 2009, pp.329-348).

The above economic approach has helped to sort out the different players of the system, dividing them into three main categories according to their peculiar function: producers (supply side, e.g. artists), certifiers or gatekeepers (intermediaries, e.g. dealers, curators etc.) and consumers (demand side, e.g. buyers, audience etc.). On a practical level the distinction is not so clear-cut, as some players could intermingle their role, such as a curator substantially leading an artists movement, or an artist becoming curator of a peer group to help all of them to access the market, or again a collector acting as a dealer for the artists he buys. However, the division into three separate categories constitutes a feasible model to analyse the art system and identify the necessary features a specific player must possess, as well as the actions to improve one's own position. To detect those key resources an artist had better work on, aiming at their gradual increase to enhance his or her status in the field, it appears useful to start from the criteria generally adopted to measure artistic success. In fact, ranking methods in visual arts are useful to focus on the outcome an artist is expected to produce, not just as regards to artworks but also for his or her wider appreciation. Several convenient criteria can be found in Kunstkompass, probably one of the best-known contemporary art barometers, developed by the German art and economics editor Willi Bongard and first published in 1970 on the magazine Capital to be published every year on occasion of the Art Cologne fair. Although some specific aspects of the ranking have been criticized over the years for being arbitrary or excessively centred on German institutions, the general parameters represent a valid choice to feel the pulse of the art system. In fact, the philosophy of Kunstkompass is to look at the repercussions of artistic success, since artistic quality would be impossible to measure otherwise. The true guiding light appears to be the degree of visibility acquired by an artist, that is his or her exposure and standing inside the art system, which can be assessed by the number of solo exhibitions in important museums, the participation into relevant group shows, the extent of monograph articles or reviews in leading art magazines and newspapers, the purchase of artworks by influent collections. Kunstkompass doesn't take artist quotations into account, a feature that corresponds to economic theory that considers price irrelevant to understand market mechanics in the case of trust goods such as artworks, as argued before. Other artists rankings define artistic success by means of similar quantitative criteria including a few more – such as the number of academic papers or monograph catalogues – or combining them in a slightly different way. However, several of these methods regard price as important, because it signposts the buyers social status – if artworks are taken as consumer goods for aesthetic and symbolic appreciation – as well as the artist's asset value – if an artwork is meant as an investment (Foglio, 2005, pp.210-211). The real complication with price in the art system is to learn about it, since most transactions are kept private being direct purchases from dealers or artists themselves, while only the most prominent acquisitions are laid bare in auction houses. A minor parameter to classify artists may also be their origin, meaning the training they received: having studied in a renowned institution or worked as an assistant to a famous artist can make a big difference in terms of access to the art system, but such circumstances are not necessarily taken into account in official rankings (Caves, 2000, p.26). Though again rarely considered, one last criterion to define an artist's career stage is his or her dealer or gallery representation, which can disclose the approximate market positioning of an artist. As a matter of facts, galleries and dealers have themselves a reputation in the art system, which depends largely on the success of artists they represent – or have represented in the past – and on the standing of loyal collectors (Thompson, 2008, pp.46-47). Given these circumstances, it is possible to work out a vertical and geographical differentiation, hence a dealer's position can be determined in respect to the average career stage of the represented artists and to the range of his or her commercial influence in the art field (Jyrämä, 2008a, p. 89). These two ways of differentiation outline several kinds of businesses that go on one side from starting galleries for newcomers to big promoters of superstar artists, on the other side from small local or regional galleries to huge international enterprises. Traditionally there would be another kind of differentiation, which is bound to the end market of the gallery, being primary (only new production) or secondary (only second time purchases). However, this distinction has been blown up in the last few decades by means of several influent players such as dealer Larry Gagosian who started to merge the two business branches in one and the same gallery, selling historical Warhol pieces together with fresh artworks by cutting-edge authors. Even auction houses, which were generally dedicated to the secondary market, have recently contributed to blow up this separation starting to pick up sales of latest production by living artists (Thompson, 2008, pp.173-184). In any case, the vertical differentiation still gives an insight on the varied career stages an artist might be at, according to the market position he or she has acquired. Though the boarders may not be clear-cut, one can make the following distinctions as regards to the status of an artist: (i) art student, which would be during art education or training; (ii) artist candidate, usually an aspiring artist at the end or shortly after art education; (iii) new entry, one that has drawn the attention of a talent scout or is already represented by one of the newcomers' dealers; (iv) rising artist, one who has sold several pieces, had at least one important solo show and some reviews in important magazines; (v) established artist, one who steadily manages to live from his or her art production, being represented by a main gallery, and has a stable presence in relevant group shows and specialist magazines; (vi) celebrity, one who has definitively reached the Parnassus of the art system with record prices, several award victories, wide media exposure and frequent features in art history books. The above classification can be questioned as to the parameters used for sorting an artist into one of the specified categories or even criticized in a bulk for being to deterministic, given the various paths that an artist career may take. As a matter of facts, adopting the product's life cycle perspective would generally demonstrate that the advancement of an artist or a movement follows four steps: introduction, growth, maturity and decline (Vettese, 1998, pp.186-189). However, practical examples show a variety of possible career developments, usually with one or two major creative climaxes, while the remaining time is rather characterized by routine. Furthermore, there can be harsh ups and downs, since success is very ephemeral and oblivion always lingers for those who didn't reach an untouchable reputation. One last observation is concerned with the trade off between commercial success and artistic approval, since they don't necessarily go hand in hand: the former may be acquired moving from the fringe through the media lacking a good consideration by the institutional establishment, while the latter could earn an artist many prizes and honourable mentions but scarce financial resources (Jyrämä, 2008b, pp.108-109). All in all, the proposed classification of artists holds anyway the advantage of sketching the various stages of a career development: whether one takes slow steps or rushes through every stage, any aspiring artist must find a way to get some sort of training, enter the system, rise into prominence and finally establish an enduring career at regional, national or even international level. It may happen for an artist to live comfortably with local sales, but a totally different strategy is necessary to become a truly established author with an international reputation, participation in important group shows, exhibitions in relevant museums and representation by a professional dealer.

All aspects mentioned so far represent the measurable traits that describe an artist's career stage altogether, intended as outcome of the crucial resources he or she has been able to accumulate and activate. These features may eventually be summarized in the following categories of quantitative and empirical parameters: (i) origin, hence one's art education and training; (ii) exposure, which is the artist's public standing due to the relevance of featured venues, group and solo shows, catalogues, reviews , awards etc.; (iii) type of clients, being buyers and collectors – both private and public, individual and institutional; (iv) scope, which signals the possible range of an artist's reputation being local, regional, national or international; (v) market positioning, referring in particular to the sales stage of an artist, which comprises the type of dealer representation, as well as the presence on the primary and secondary market (auction house purchases); (vi) price, being only regarded as the last feature given the mentioned problems of its formation in the art market. If these parameters measure the results of an artist's action in the system, which are then the key resources he or she should better possess or gather? What is the capital an artist can draw on inside the art field? The terms capital and art field obviously refer to the sociological theory of Pierre Bourdieu (1993), but could even be interpreted as capital stock with its economic implications: capital refers to the fixed input of production, which is constituted by the fundamental assets that allow the production itself to take place. Hence, it seems a feasible term to describe the key resources, which have been proposed as the second relevant variable to influence artistic success. Ranging from art historians to sociologists and economist, scholars have taken various assets into consideration, though everyone stressing some in particular. However, a few of these are now widely accepted and comprise above all the following: artistic project (art capital), connections (network capital), reputation (social capital) and wage (financial capital). An artist's specific proposition is probably the most obvious resource to foster one's own career, because it constitutes the principal product supplied to the art system. Particular attention should be payed to the basic components of an artist's project, which are represented on one side by talent, of course, but on the other side also by his or her peculiar aesthetic, ideological and systemic choices (Towse, 1998, p.98). In fact, an artist needs to be pertinent to the reference system he or she addresses and must furthermore define – or at least be aware of – how to spread his or her artistic production. This would mean understanding the art system, identifying a demand to satisfy (e.g. a cultural niche), building an offer proposal (aesthetically and ideologically specified), determining the segments to attract, positioning in the art market (Foglio, 2005, pp.128-131). Considering the role of gatekeepers, the second key resource for the artist is represented by network capital, hence the connections he or she is capable of building, in order to obtain support by influent players, gain access to the system and become a legitimate member of the art world (Sacco, 1998, p.47). The crucial contribution of network and relationships cannot be underestimated in visual arts, since they preside over entrance in the field, as well as over reputation. However, the latter should be treated separately, because it properly refers to the personal image and social status of an artist (Jyrämä, 2008b, p.108). This kind of social capital becomes a crucial aspect in the art system, given that artworks are trust goods and that trust is enhanced by reputation. In turn, personal image may even become part of the art capital, especially when the marketing mechanism of branding is exploited. The last key resource that matters for every artist – both aspiring and established ones – is wage, which is the financial capital that can support his or her activity. As a matter of facts, pursuing an artistic career is a particularly risk-taking choice, even though it is frequently done with little awareness (Towse, 1996a, p.321). Candidates to enter the art system come truly in hoards, hence increasing the level of competition among emerging artists and sensibly lowering the wages of new entrants. In addition, at the beginning an artistic career is hardly remunerative and one's own efforts must therefore be intended as a mere individual investment for starting a successful path (Caves, 2000, pp.36-37). Usually an artist candidate takes the risk, because he or she considers chiefly the prospective earnings of celebrities instead of short term evaluations, which is also the reason why most aspiring artists need a non-artistic work to support their production (Benhamou, 2000, pp.38-40). Financial capital is a major concern for every beginner and the most likely solution is to maximize the time spent making art by means of a non-artistic job, which generally doesn't fit one's own education level, but is useful to earn a living and keep on producing art.

All four mentioned forms of capital – art, network, social and financial – can be singularly or mutually increased for leveraging the position of an author inside the art system. Actions on the capital stock may be performed inadvertently, however artists are usually aware of the fact, which they need to take some choices to hope for a career improvement. Furthermore, as soon as one is set to try a profession in the visual arts he or she is immediately faced with necessary decisions, such as what to produce, which reference group to point at, where to live and work, how to earn enough to keep on trying. The answers given to these and other questions design a proper plan of actions, though the final outcome of its application may differ from its expected results. In this regards, one may maintain that even artists do apply specific strategies, for instance used to emerge, to thrive on or to increase their position in the art system. A strategy is not a mere plan or program, but rather an articulate process that combines intentions, decisions and actions (Mintzberg and Waters, 1985). Its beginning is set at the revealed intentions of a player, which are represented by the artist's purposes and ambitions for his personal career. The initial intentions must then be conveyed into an effective plan of actions, which would be called the deliberate strategy, being the decisions taken to foster one's own capital. Finally, the plan has to be carried out and gets confronted with factual circumstances, thus letting diversions and changes arise along the way, which would be called altogether the emergent strategy. This pattern of explanation establishes the concept of strategy as the behavioural model that is used to translate one's own intentions into voluntary actions, hence it may differ according to an individual's characteristics and preferences, which is true even for business managers[16]. In fact, the drive to a particular strategy lays in the aspirations, attitude and personality of the given player, while the final outcome is influenced by circumstantial factors and by the response to their emergence. The general question concerning artists strategies should then be about the possible options they have to leverage their capital stock, rather then if they are at all conscious of acting strategically, since a strategy may also be originally mistaken or fail in the end. So far, only general suggestions can be made, which must later be analysed against factual evidence of the chosen study case. Concerning artistic capital, for instance, an author needs to determine his or her art project making choices on the following issues: (i) select the research themes, as well as a certain media or technique, while working to forge a particular style; (ii) chose a stance in the trade off between cutting edge and tradition, hence trying innovative paths (risky, but with a possible long term gain) or mimicking an already successful trend (safe, but likely to ephemeral success); (iii) think of the possible target or reference group to produce art for, thus defining the product features and one's own market position by means of a coherent distribution channel; (iv) decide on the production model to follow, e.g. whether serial and repetitive or innovative and sporadic, being committed to few iconic pieces or abundant artworks for the broad collectors market. For improving network capital and arouse the attention of gatekeepers again artists have to pick on several strategies, such as: (i) creating alliances, which may be peer groups, ideological movements, style collectives, artist unions etc.; (ii) seeking mentors or godfathers who would offer support and legitimacy; (iii) get in touch with the art market, presenting oneself to dealers and collectors; (iv) communicate with opinion leaders such as curators, critics, art historians or magazines. Social capital depends on reputation and personal image that an artist builds for him- or herself and corroborates by different means, for instance through individual mythology, self-entrepreneurship, branding, celebrity status, opportunities for media exposure (Kerring, Fraser, Özbilgin, 2004, p.136). Financial capital can eventually be drawn too along different strategic moves – apart from artistic production – among which count family support, non-artistic jobs, other art-related jobs such as teaching in art schools or writing reviews, gaining scholarships for residencies, monetary awards and prizes, a patron's backing. All these sort of strategies increase an artist's wage and offer the opportunity to pursue a proper artistic career, provided that one can also minimize the time spent earning a living and dedicate as much as possible to art (Throsby, 1996, p.345). So far the strategies have been divided in respect to the four identified key resources they have influence on, though an integrated perspective would be preferable. In fact, the mentioned strategies often overlap and intertwine, while the total capital stock should be balanced between the four different strains mentioned. Networks, for instance, are most important for success, but would be nothing without a consistent artistic project – however, also the opposite is true. Likewise, choosing a particular art trend that meets one of the influent gatekeeper's taste and ideology is both an artistic and relational strategy. An aspiring artist – more than anyone in the art system – must work on all four key resources together, because they are all mutually necessary and of real advantage on the difficult path to the final breakthrough.

Art system, players, gatekeepers, legitimacy and entry barriers, capital and key resources, strategies and actions: the scene is set to start retracing the first steps of Douglas Gordon's very successful career.

Chapter 3
Family, society, religion in the Scottish Sixties

3.1. Working class, baby boomers, gender issues: of storytelling, family and education

Douglas Gordon was born in Glasgow on September 20th, 1966 from a local working class family – or so it is told. Indeed, on approaching his personal history it is important to stress first and foremost the difficulties – rather than the support – provided by the autobiographical vein in Gordon's production. As a matter of facts, every biographic account of the Scottish artist relates a slightly different tale, frequently blending facts with fiction, a strategy that doesn't appear to be solely limited to his artistic production. Gordon has recounted his own life story himself many times in interviews, speeches and private conversations, but he has also had it told by others, as in catalogue essays, on the occasion of exhibitions, in public letters or in unpublished correspondence to be found in his archive. In general, anyone who has had the opportunity to meet the Scottish artist in person is well acquainted with his natural drive towards intimate storytelling, rather than detached reasoning. This attitude is rooted in a long tradition for Scotland, of its Western area in particular, where people are quite used to tell each other stories, so for instance in extended families or in crowded meeting places such as pubs:

> *"I think that my whole family background was always about story telling." (Gordon in Obrist, 1996b, p.167)*

The artist also asserts the influence of Glasgow social context, where oral narration is widely practised having an essential socializing purpose. In fact, it is worth noticing that the stress is never put on the contents, but on the action performed. As suggested by Gordon himself, the focus shouldn't be set on the reported tale, since the true aim of storytelling is establishing a relationship between the narrator and the listener:

> *"That has surely to do with the political and social context I found in Glasgow, where there is a strong tradition for story-telling. To tell a story is a means of establishing a relationship between people – the story does not need to be particularly interesting in itself, but it*

illustrates your vocabulary. It enables people to know who you are, and if they want to interrupt and encourage communication, it's just fine. I mean, that's what art is all about." (Gordon in Sheikh, 1997, p.17)

A good story doesn't necessarily need to be a true one, it must rather arouse the listener's interest and transmit feelings or ideas. In order to do so, the storyteller usually adds details to the description, which by no surprise could be exaggerated, sometimes even invented. The beginning of a long biographical interview given to Graham Fagen in 1999 epitomizes Gordon's approach to his own life story:

"There's funny stories and there's also the truth of it. The two mixed together actually seem to make some sense." (Gordon in Fagen, 1999, p.71)

This peculiar kind of storytelling attitude, which clearly stems from the Glasgow background, would appear to make the personal accounts on Gordon's biography rather unreliable. Nevertheless, the sources mentioned above, such as interviews and catalogue essays hold great importance to exploit information on Gordon's biography. Caution is required only to sift historical information from factual inaccuracies that apparently fit the storyline, a task to be carried out by means of several conversations with the artist, which then had to be crosschecked with the documents and material preserved in his personal archive. Sometimes it isn't as difficult as it seems, especially in the presence of quite obvious fantastic supplements, so for instance in the case of Gordon's reported encounter with the devil in a Berlin pub at the peak of a wild night-life. These sort of accounts are very useful to discover the artist's psychology, but they shouldn't be considered glaringly false: they are simply untrue – at least in some details – where the term is understood as the opposite of true, or rather its reflection. These stories hold the same relationship to truth as does the left hand with its right pair – one couldn't tell which is the *right* one. The indistinguishable combination of truth and untruth is of course the result of a controlled revelation strategy Gordon applies to his artworks, as well as to his biography. What he displays is an undistinguishable mix of reality and invention – true and untrue at the same time, image and mirror image, positive and negative – capable of questioning acquired certainties on visual reception and moral acceptance (Van den Boogard, 1997, p.38). It is not uncommon for artists to have autobiographical topics permeating their own artistic production, as well as it frequently happens for authors to embellish or readapt their biography for the purpose of self-representation. This is not different in Gordon's case, where autobiographic aspects often pervade the artworks or – the other way round – the creative process influences his public image (Page, 2000, p.7). However, the authentic peculiarity of his personal accounts is their underlying tendency to become artworks in their own right, being conceived as autonomous and completed the same way his pieces are. Hence, the issue is not about drawing inspiration from real life or transforming real life things – even stories and experiences – into art objects, but rather about ceasing to see any distinction between art and life. As far as this goes, Gordon made his point to a curator, who once invited him to join a group exhibition dealing with real life in arts:

> *"I told him that it was impossible for me to differentiate art and real life. As an artist, everything is 'real life' for me. I am not taking anything out of my life and placing it in a museum, as if museums were not part of my life. They belong to my reality [...]. The distinction between art and life is not clear-cut." (Gordon in Sheikh, 1997, p.20)*

Having considered the possible sources for reconstructing Gordon's biography, as well as their utter peculiarity, facts about his childhood and adolescence can be now exposed, in order to investigate his background. A few conclusions might thus be drawn about the way his future choices were influenced at such an early stage by various conditions and circumstances he grew up in – both at family level as well as in the broader social context. Douglas Gordon was born to James Gordon and Mary McDougall, the former a skilled carpenter for the naval industry in Glasgow, the latter a housewife. As the eldest of four children – three sons and a daughter – the artist had lived all the disquiet of a growing Scottish working class household, living in council houses and gradually moving towards the outskirts of the city high on the heels of the last few shipyards that hadn't closed down yet. From the artist's early childhood to the end of primary school the Gordons lived in Maryhill, North of Glasgow, relocating on the Western periphery near the coast in Dumbarton, at the birth of their third child. Originally they were a conservative Calvinist family, and in fact their first born attended Protestant schools rather than Catholic ones: in Maryhill he went to Gilschochill Primary School, then to Dumbarton Comprehensive School. Hence from the beginning young Douglas experienced Scottish society's inner conflicts driven by religious distrust between Protestant and Catholic culture, which at that age resulted in frequent fights amongst opposite students' groups. A major disruption on a psychological level was his mother's conversion to Jehovahs's Witnesses, which will be addressed later on, however Gordon's social and cultural background can be considered absolutely average for a Glaswegian. Both his name and surname are among the most widespread in the nation – and so his family situation or education wasn't any different from that of thousands of his peers. The artist himself is well aware of having grown up in an absolutely ordinary milieu and claims a strong sense of belonging to the working class. In his interview with Graham Fagen, Gordon is very upright – at times even harsh – in describing his origins:

> *"I had a bog standard education, I'm from a standard, probably in some ways very typical Scottish, west of Scotland family, and we've been through all the shit like every other family from that background, and been displaced like everybody else, and had to find another set of values like everybody else also. So within the turmoil that is working class life in Scotland to be an artist didn't feel like anything extraordinary. It was just another wee bit of nonsense in the world." (Gordon in Fagen, 1999, p.78)*

The environment he grew up in could have hardly encouraged him to start an artistic career or given him superior incentive compared to other people from the same background. A significant motive to approach the art world must rather be sought in a powerful individual predisposition, stimulated by his teachers and supported by his parents. Although his family and social background would appear utterly irrelevant as far as art was concerned, Gordon believes his straightforward disposition of Scottish working class temperament did assist in his professional choices. As a matter of facts, he is persuaded that proletarian upbringing and standard education never presented him with elitist ideas on art: quite the opposite, in his mind they granted him a sense of ease he still tries to convey into art, avoiding to take his profession too seriously and refusing the idea of the artist as an exceptional person. Indeed, Gordon described the relation of his family to art with a mix of class-pride and self-abnegation:

> *"So I'm normal, my family's normal, [...] because they have no [...] real sense of sophistication; what we would see as sophisticated because we're educated that way, they probably think is just a bit weird. So they don't have any sense of art snobbery or anything like that." (Gordon in Fagen, 1999, p.78)*

If one opens up the view on the broader generation the Scottish artist belongs to, which would be the children born in the Sixties and who went to art school in the Eighties, the working class narrative can be appreciated as a major issue for the UK. Indeed many of the young authors who aroused some interest the Nineties art world came out of working class families. This is true for instance for the other three artists, who will be repeatedly mentioned as a comparison with Gordon's case. Damien Hirst (1965) was born in Bristol, but was brought up in Leeds by his single mother, who worked for a citizen's advice bureau, after both his father – a car mechanic – and later his stepfather had left them (Holmes, 2007). With a milkman father and a part-time gardner for a mother, Sarah Lucas (1962) grew up in Islington, at the time an overcrowded London council houses area with a strong working class background dating back to the early 19th century, when almost half a million people lived there (Edamariam, 2011). Christine Borland's parents (1965) both worked in the local lace factory of Ayrshire and they expected her to end up in the same manufacture (Bredin, 1997). All of their families would be classified as unskilled workers or having routine jobs, while Gordon's father instead rather belonged to the skilled manual workers category, however still falling into working class. At this point, it is important to determine which social classes account as working class, considering that social division in the UK is something of a national trait. Since 1997 up to 2001 classes were divided into five main categories plus one sub-category, being: i) professional; ii) intermediate; iii) skilled [iiin) non manual and iiim) manual]; iv) partly skilled; v) unskilled (Bolton, 2010, p.2). The last three categories, starting with iiim, would be definitely comprised as working-class[1]. According to this definition, several other young artists who became eminent in the Nineties fall into working-class families, amongst them Patrick Caulifield and Gillian Wearing in London or Roderick Buchanan, Ross Sinclair, Martin Boyce and Suzanne Philipsz in Glasgow. Boyce even grew up in the working-class area of Maryhill as young Douglas did. Far from being the majority, students from lower class families did however enrol in big numbers during the Eighties in art schools across the country, mainly coming from abandoned industrial areas such as the Northern part of England and West Scotland. Remembering that period, then art student and now curator Gregor Muir highlights how the working class students often stood out for their dedication:

> *"Most of the northerns I was meeting on the art circuit came from working-class backgrounds and had strong affiliations with the kind of politics spun out of Marxism. [...] At art school, to be middle or upper class had little cachet and set you apart as being a bit of a*

nonce. [...] By the time I left college, the very idea that art could come from a Conservative position, as it has done occasionally, was unthinkable. For a brief moment it was entirely desirable to be an artist with a northern working-class background. It came with the right credentials and dovetailed neatly with the image of the rebel, the 'enfant terrible'." (Muir, 2011, pp.51-52)

Art critic Matthew Collings (1996, p.8) was another attentive observer of that period, as well as himself an art student at the time, and divides college students in London into two main categories. The first were working class kids trying to climb up the social ladder, while the second and biggest group were actually middle class people who already had an artistic family background – that's what he would call Bohemians. To the latter belong artists such as Gary Hume, Angela Bulloch and Rachel Whiteread in London, while – roughly compared – there appear to be less in Glasgow, save for instance Jackie Donachie and Julie Roberts among the well known ones. Whereas it might be the reason for entering higher education, social promotion doesn't seem to be the only drive for working class kids to pick up art school. In fact, students from lower social class backgrounds are used to take account of a lot more issues than counterparts in higher social class groups when deciding to enter college or university, for instance emphasizing on the expected outcomes in terms of prospective wage, which seems rather uncertain for artistic professions (Connor and Dewson, 2001, p.1). On the contrary, choosing art education appears to be in the middle position between dropping higher education and going to university, since the practical skills involved in visual arts tend to relate it to manual work. This was the case of Christine Borland, whose parents accepted to have her going on studying beyond compulsory school only because she enrolled in the Mural and Stained-Glass Department. Eventually, it would later be transformed into the Environmental Art Department attended by Gordon and many others of the future Transmission generation. Although she had revealed a strong interest in drawing and crafting early in her life, Sarah Lucas started to work after finishing high school, then practiced applied arts at the Printmaking College in London and finally applied a year later for the much more prestigious Goldsmiths College. A total rascal in his adolescence, Hirst started foundation courses in Leeds, but later moved to London to work on a building site and only then tried to enter Goldsmiths. His choice too was supported by a strong personal interest in art, though he couldn't really imagine making a profession out of it, as he would later confess in an interview with Tate Director Nicholas Serota:

> *"I knew I wanted to make art, but I never really believed you could get paid for doing it. I was having a lot of fun, but I needed to work out what I wanted to do with my life." (Hirst in Serota, 2011, p.91)*

Whether by chance or firm belief, lower social class students are hardly aided by family in decisions involving higher education, hence relying mainly on reasons related to both cost and personal interest in specific subjects (Connor and Dewson, 2001, p.3). Individuals from higher social class, on the contrary, are more likely to be aesthetically active due to family exposure and childhood learning experiences, as shown by psychology researches suggesting that art interest stems partly from home environment, as well as through formal education (McManus and Furnham, 2006, p.580). Considering Gordon's family background, he could have hardly received stimulus from his parents to choose an artistic career, while he maintains having rather been encouraged by art teachers in his school years (Fagen, 1999, p.72). Indeed, in his last year at primary school Gordon remembers having an art teacher, Mr. Jamison, who rode a motorbike, listened to rock music and wore what were considered transgressive clothes at the time – jeans trousers and a leather jacket. Jamison exhorted his pupils to be exceedingly creative and adopt any possible means of expression. He noticed young Douglas' penchant for art and decided to write a note to his parents urging them to encourage their son to follow his predisposition. James and Mary Gordon were so inspired by this letter that they still keep it to show to visitors. From that day on they stood by any decision Douglas would take for his art career, so for instance in 1982 when sixteen-year-old Douglas was offered a job in his father's business. Realizing the utter reluctance of their son, they encouraged him to pursue his artistic inclination, rather than push him to make a choice he was averse to. Again in high school Douglas was so lucky as to meet charismatic art teachers, who were specially dedicated to art print. Towards the end of his school years, Gordon was decidedly considering higher education, but he was not sure about what course he should take. He was certainly in favour of creative professions, but still unsure regarding three possible options: architect, writer or visual artist (Finn-Kelcey, 1995, p.109). After spending one morning in an architect studio, he gave up the first alternative. However, he was also reluctant to choose visual arts, because he feared to finish up drawing still lives forever, as was the case in his previous art classes. In 1983 he remembers expressing all his doubts to his art teacher, whose response to such uncertainties came with the gift of two books: the first was on Marcel Duchamp, the second on Andy Warhol. In the artist's own words, this discovery convinced the young man to choose the local art school after completing compulsory education:

> *"When I was 15-16 years old, making drawings of stuffed animals and rotting vegetables, like every school child does, I remember one of my teachers, coming up with two books and saying, 'I don't really like these guys [Marcel Duchamp and Andy Warhol] very much, but I think they are probably quite important for you to look at'." (Gordon in Obrist, 1996b, p.169)*

Such stories of early inclination are true for most artists – such as the cases of Hirst, Lucas and Borland, as well as for others from different class categories – hence suggesting that social class origin might not be the decisive drive towards an art career. Evidence from in-depth statistics and analyses conducted in recent years concerning UK education in the second half of the 20th century confirm there is no direct influence in subject choice from social class (Bolton, 2010, pp.11-12). Data set rather appear to bestow a major role to different individual or family characteristics, so for instance parenting quality, school and teachers' quality or students' motivation and ability. What's more, the study of higher education enrolment in the period 1981-1991 for the UK shows no evidence at all of statistically significant differences in the probability of picking a specific degree subject due to social origin, hence proving that the tendency to chose art education is comparable for students of every social class (Bratti, 2006, pp.19-20). However, accounts on art students' life in the Eighties – such as those of Gregor Muir and Matthew Collings – seem to set working class rhetoric in the centre of discourse at the time. Quite often working class students made the point even in their artistic production, drawing inspiration directly from their milieu, such as in some socially engaged photographic series of Roderick Buchanan (*Work In Progress*, 1995[2]) or Gillian Wearing (*Signs that Say What You Want Them To Say and Not Signs that Say What Someone Else Wants You To Say*, 1992-1993[3]), which were all first shown in independent spaces – not by any chance[4]. Such pieces don't conceal class identity, but rather make an explicit claim of it, which is confirmed by Buchanan himself speaking of another similar work (*Legacy*, 2011):

> *"My attraction to working with these communities was a recognition that this was an expression of working-class identity. It often seems to be distasteful to a middle-class agenda; people would like them just to go away." (Buchanan in Mansfield, 2012)*

Besides rhetoric and identity, however, higher education for working class kids was a unique opportunity of social promotion, hence causing often a stronger motivation during art education, as well as immediately after in order to avoid downward mobility (Wakeling, 2009, p.290). This might be the true reason for them to stand out – or at least to try harder than others – as compared to students with different social backgrounds, which is confirmed by Gordon's competitive attitude:

> *"Most of us are coming from working-class, or lower middle-class background, and the experience of higher education is not a tradition to us; it was something new, something to get your teeth into and get a lot out of it." (Gordon in Van Assche, 1995, p.81)*

As a matter of facts, some decades before no working class child would have considered studying beyond compulsory school, since higher education did not belong to the lower classes' customary choices, especially in economically depressed areas as 1960s and 1970s Western Scotland. Had he been born twenty or thirty years earlier, Gordon like many of his peers would hardly have gone for an artistic career. There are indeed two circumstances that made a difference for his generation, the first one related to demographic development, the second being dependent on reforms of the education system. The Scottish artist belongs to the second British baby boom generation, which took place in the Sixties (Easton, 2011), and profited from the breach in higher education that gradually opened up to all social classes in the late Seventies. This double occurrence led to a downright explosion of university enrolment in the Eighties, which was directly proportional to the increased birth rate two decades earlier. Regarding population growth, the birth rate in the UK has declined throughout the 20th century, but was interrupted by two rapid post-war peaks after each World War and – most of all – by a prolonged acme that lasted for a whole decade in the 1960s, clearly related to the economic boom period (Hicks and Allen, 1999, p.6). The large number of so-called 'late boomers' completed secondary education in the late Seventies and early Eighties, causing an immediate and massive enrolment rate of students at British universities, polytechnics and academies. Entrance features more than doubled in two decades, recording an increase of overall participation in higher education from 8.4% in 1970 to 19.3% in 1990, which of course granted also a higher access for working class people (Bolton, 2012, p.14). Gradual removal of social barriers had already started with the 1944 Education Act, when the doors of higher education – including art schools – had officially opened to students from lower-income backgrounds (Fox,

2013). However, as statistic evidence suggests, over the second half of the 20th century there was but little difference in the proportion of university students coming from lower social classes. As a matter of facts, between 1977 and 1992 higher and middle classes (i, ii and iiin) covered the average of 80% of candidates accepted to higher education degree courses, leaving a poor 20% to the other three lower social classes (iiim, iv and v) (Bolton, 2010, p.11). Hence, the increasing participation in higher education of working class students is rather due to the overall growth of university enrolment that characterized the last three decades of the century. Although the social composition of university students had not changed a lot in the Eighties, deeper analysis demonstrate that the British education system was nevertheless capable of granting equal access to every possible degree subject, whatever social background a student might have had. Taking social class as a measure, statistics show little variance in subject choices for the years comprised between 1981 and 1991: the likelihood to pick up art courses was exactly the same for students of any possible social background, thus being independent from class discourse (Bratti, 2006, p.38). Equal opportunities were possible in the Eighties thanks to the absence of tuition fees for undergraduates, as well as due to the provision of means-tested maintenance grants for lower-income students. These two features – which were later abandoned in the Nineties – indeed lessened differences across social classes, because they made subject choice as well as the decision for enrolment in higher education independent from economic considerations. Looking back, critic Dan Fox emphasizes the relative openness of the UK system for higher education to all social classes during the period that ranges from the Seventies to the early Nineties – as compared to the present situation:

> *"Class solidarity, and upward and downward mobility – through professional success or class drag – was a topic for work and a target of criticism, sometimes both. The range of economic backgrounds represented in British contemporary art was perhaps wider back then. Recession, cuts, the introduction of higher university fees and a Tory party ideologically bent on marginalizing arts education, are today closing the doors to working-class students." (Gordon in Van Assche, 1995, p.81)*

So far the considered data set depicts UK society as deeply class-separated, but events have set the 1980s at the crossroad of demographic expansion and of an access blast in higher education. The two circumstances combined have been decisive for the future of people like

Douglas Gordon. Being aware of his class situation, the artist is very conscious of the fortunate coincidence to belong to the second baby boom generation, which experienced the consequent higher education expansion and openness:

> *"I think that for my generation, growing up through an education 'boom-time' in Britain, the art schools and universities were opening doors to the working class [...]. If this hadn't been the case, then someone like me would never have had the chance to think about further education [...]. And this is the case for a lot of my friends in Glasgow, and in London." (Gordon in Van Assche, 1995, p.81)*

Besides the greater inflow of working class students, during the Eighties UK higher education system was actually rocked by a far greater occurrence, being the dramatic increase of women participation. Female attendance of higher degree courses was below 10% in 1962, little above 15% ten years later and finally around 25% in 1982 and 36% in 1992, while women students obtained 37% of all first degrees by 1980 and 45% in 1993 – thus the trend has been finally heading towards equalisation over the last half of the century (Hicks and Allen, 1999, p.11). The massive access of women to higher education during the 1980s was much more disruptive than the participation of working class students, clearly causing the burst of numerous women artists in a men-dominated art world in the following decade and determining the rise of gender related issues. While one can hardly name a bunch of successful women artists of the Eighties – Barbara Kruger, Cindy Sherman, Sherrie Levine and Roni Horn among the best known and all American, by the way – during the Nineties dozens can be named for the UK only: Rachel Whitread, Fiona Rae, Gillian Wearing, Sarah Lucas, Tracy Emin, Julie Roberts, Jackie Donachie, Angela Bulloch, Christine Borland, Anya Gallaccio, Abigail Lane, Gerogina Starr, Sam Taylor-Wood, Fiona Banner, Tacita Dean, Jane and Louise Wilson just to name a few. Gender awareness was definitely growing in women art students, representing a major identity issue, but often becoming a powerful means of distinction in reference to the feminist movement. As regards to this, Sarah Lucas maintains a very straightforward position:

> *"One of the reasons I was interested in the feminine was that I wasn't successful." (Lucas in Collings, 2005, p.22)*

The first few tabloid cut-outs of Lucas, such as *Penis Nailed To A Board* (1990) or *Fat, Forty and Flabulous* (1991), make the same violent point about female condition in Western society as do her words, while Christine Borland rather refers to feminism in a more idealistic as well as fatalist way:

> *"The feminist tradition really helped me get where I am today. When I was a student, I was looking at the work of women artists, all basically American women, and it really meant a lot. There weren't that many other examples around if you wanted to look at strong, successful women artists who were actually dealing with something." (Barclay Morgan, 1999)*

Bursting enrolment figures for art schools together with self-aware working class kids and women students decidedly put enormous pressure on aspiring artists of the late Eighties and early Nineties in the UK. Hence the number of candidates for entering the art system was growing at such a rate as to exacerbate competition, even if economic recession had not hit so badly in 1989. In these circumstances, emphasizing class differences or gender discourse was definitely an issue about questioning one's own identity, but also turned out to be a quite convenient strategy to arouse attention. A socially or politically engaged art production could indeed help to emerge from the multitude of artist candidates by differentiating oneself from competitors. Not by any chance, the last decade of the 20th century would later be experiencing a renewed focus on the artist persona, though along different lines from the past, so for instance following the economic paradigm or complying with the gender-issue (Pütz, 2010). At the turn of the millennium, hence, the new artist role-model in society would be fluctuating between two opposite poles: on the one hand lay the quest for differentiation of the artist self-image tainted with non-artistic activities, while on the other hand came the discourse about creativity and genius that reached far beyond the sole field of art (Fasten, Joachimides and Krieger, 2011, pp.11-26).

3.2. Myths, religion, media culture: of reputation, self-image and early influences

The mixed sense of understatement and class-pride that characterizes Gordon's professional attitude appears to be rooted in his family milieu, as well as in his Glaswegian origin, since being an artist in Glasgow wasn't any different from other ways to earn a living and giving one's life some meaning. Even throughout art classes in primary and secondary school no one ever assumed they were doing something special or unruly, though the atmosphere was stimulating and creative. This disposition definitely helped the artist to be humble enough not to take himself too seriously, however he soon learned about expectations and desires projected by contemporary society onto the artistic self. Every aspiring artist is soon confronted with his or her specific function in society and with a definite position in the art system. As debated in the previous chapter, there have been and still are different role models for artists and they need to take a stance, possibly adopting a specific one or developing new intermingles. Furthermore, the question is also about the artistic self-image, which would be how an artist understands it and which options he or she is granted by society, how he or she decides to interpret his role and function and which plan of action might be adopted to pursue a specific kind of public reputation. Beatrice von Bismarck, for instance, insists on the strategic employment of the artist persona since the 1960s, which consequently challenged the stability of previous role models for the artist. In her opinion, the essential trait of the artist self-image today is embodied as a constant struggle to create one's own identity out of the merger which combines personal as well as alien components (von Bismarck, 2011, pp.147-156). Attention should thus be paid to a new sort of mystification of the artistic profession, which leads to a clear conceptualisation of the artist's image. Following this stream of thought, to be considered an artist, staging as one appears to have become much more crucial than actually making artworks. Enactment being the point, there are several strategies one can adopt to pursue an expected result in terms of character building. Without reaching back too far, in the last two decades of the previous century several artists headed directly for celebrity status – Jeff Koons being one of the most successful at that. Acting like a star is probably considered the most effective scheme, though one may change parts if required, just like in the case of Julian Schnabel who went from macho-painter to moviemaker (Berger, 2011, pp.73-88). Damien Hirst has tried a similar trajectory, performing first the role of a devilishly rock star dedicated to death, then trying to move on towards several other business branches, like luxury objects, elite restaurants and film industry, however with alternate acceptance. He is the perfect example of an artist who went for the branding strategy by turning his media image into art, hence his persona becoming inseparable from his production – whichever that might be – rather than being the origin of it (Stallabras, 2006, pp.31-32). Tracy Emin on another instance has placed comparable importance on her self-image, though intended as a means for market positioning through permanent media exposure. Offering herself to British penny press as well as to sophisticated art collectors as a postmodern primitive, constantly on the edge between a patient in rage therapy and a straightforward swearing drunkard, she has become a popular character by exploiting her wrecked life experiences (Fortnum, 2007, pp.60-62).

The mentioned cases make good examples of various strategies that support the improvement of an artist's social capital. While Koons and Schnabel understand their celebrity status strictly inside the art field, Emin is rather a popular figure akin to the entertainment industry and Hirst finally converts his persona into a most complete brand name that spills over to different sectors of luxury business. Douglas Gordon chose a different path that is quintessential for most successful artists, which is going for a kind of individual mythology that fosters artistic reputation. As a matter of facts, he attempts to create a personal image by adopting the method of myths, whose truthfulness is based on belief, being the extent to which the myth is trusted in and spread across a given community. Referring to process art and performances in the second half of the last century, for instance, Hans Ulrich Obrist maintains that a good deal of that art has reached us only through word of mouth, often relying completely on narration passed on by art system players without any kind of documentary proof:

> *"Sociology has this term 'oral history', many sixties performances – lots of different events which only five people may have witnessed – through their testimony the whole world today knows about them, so it's almost like a chain letter." (Obrist, 1996b, p.166)*

Myth building is considered an essential social praxis for transmitting and processing stories, even if done unconsciously, and doesn't need material evidence to be efficient. The relevant feature for myths to work indeed lies in the level of trust granted by a specific social context, hence allowing the myth subject matters even to be totally invented, though plausible. Gordon appears to be well aware of the way myths are conceived and how they can evolve, even without factual support:

> *"I think the idea or the mechanism of mythology is one of the most important social mechanisms. To understand that mechanism, I think, is absolutely critical. It's like you say, all these things that happened in the sixties like some Joseph Beuys performances. As an artist from a different generation one has a relation to it only through second, third, fourth hand oral history. I think that this is just an incredible social mechanism, where people who have no experience of the object, of the action can have a dialogue about*

> *something which maybe did not even exist in the first place. And I think this is a beautiful, fundamental aspect of human relationships." (Gordon in Obrist, 1996b, p.166)*

Individual mythology is a useful strategy to exploit social interaction and the power of community trust to one's self-advantage. Even though the initial sparkle may still lay in the artist's self-image, unlike branding mythology is not imposed upon people, but rather derives from independent social dynamics that can be activated through specific means. Triggering communication is probably the best method to start the transmission of an artist's self-image, hence letting reputation grow out of circulating stories and slowly evolving into myth. Gordon has been able to employ this logic in his artworks and in his biography, eliciting interaction among the viewers. His artworks as well as his personal accounts, whether true or extraordinary, simply aim at starting a reflection process, which should lead to dialogue between people. Gordon would thus intend art as a pretext or detonator for discussion:

> *"Because for me art in any circumstances, whether it's in the museum or outside the museum is for people to go home or to a bar and talk about it. [...] because then art has acted as a trigger to social dynamics." (Gordon in Obrist, 1996b, p.167)*

This attitude towards art, considered as a social interaction catalyser, apparently stresses the viewer's response rather than the art objects themselves. The essential trait of such an approach appears to be the reaction caused, rather than the actual form displayed, while the content conveyed is merely the trigger of this process. Consequently, the receiver is granted a certain amount of freedom concerning interpretation; hence the meaning of the artwork would finally emerge from the context of social interaction between receivers combined with individual viewer's psychology. Far from being fragile, Gordon's production is intentionally set for variability and ambiguity in meaning, because that makes the process of receiving far more interesting. In his opinion, the stream of ideas that flows in his works and around his works renders art alive, becoming an instrument for social dynamics:

> *"Eventually, a work of art is absolutely uninteresting in itself, it is merely a thing which can bring about a discussion. It should be a starting point, never its end. [...] Art is merely an excuse for communicating. What is important is communication. [...] Being static, it is somehow irrelevant, because it is the flow of ideas, either*

political or psychological, circulating around the work of art that is essential." (Gordon in Sheikh, 1997, p.18)

On the one hand the Glasgow artist exploits the mechanism of myth building, which is based on faith and social transmission, on the other hand he challenges that very process by combining reality and fiction in his works, as well as in his biography. In a number of pieces and personal accounts Gordon plays with the trust relationship that usually supports social structures, apparently confirming rational expectancies at a first glance, but then doubting their assumed objectivity. Hence the deriving disorientation on the receiver's part is to be understood as the true expected outcome for the Scottish artist, especially concerning his public persona. Gordon intentionally destabilizes any anticipation referred to his role hiding his true identity and fabricating an ambiguous self-image. The indistinguishable combination of truth and untruth is the result of a controlled revelation strategy Gordon applies to his biography to compel the public to reflect on the actual distortion of reality that any sort of its representation brings about, since reality is normally processed through individual psychology or developed from mass media fiction. Books and catalogues by and about Douglas Gordon abound in this controlled revelation, in which the artist expounds reality and fiction together in order to create a fantastic or mythic halo around himself. Renate Berger (2011, pp.293-302) maintains this attitude is not at all uncommon for the 20th century, considering that many artists have started to experiment with self-fiction finishing up in an intermingle of facts and phantasy, as well as breaking barriers between trustworthy biographies and mythical autobiographies. Besides (auto)-biographical material, analysing self-portraits is probably the best method to approach an artist's fictional self-image, since they materialize the way the artist sees his or her public persona or wants to have it displayed. The pictures of oneself as an artist, whether produced as visual works or textual pieces, can indeed be used as a strategy to steer one's own reputation. For comparison, Andrea Gottdang (2011, pp. 43-56) has convincingly described the case of German painter George Grosz, who adopted a two-tire strategy at the peak of the Weimar Republic. On the one hand, he fed the media with self-representations as a proletarian hero, a true master craftsman, while on the other hand his more private pictures – though still very much enacted – showed an eccentric and nob persona who wanted to stand out of the masses. Among the generation of YBAs, Sarah Lucas has definitely become known for exploiting self-portraiture as a means to define her artistic self, markedly that of an angry woman artist of working class origin. In fact, the photographs of herself basically function as an instrument of self-promotion, because they encompass all themes that run through her production, such as gender and sex, death and smoking, everyday crudeness and popular subculture. She started the series in 1990, first being portrayed while swallowing a banana by her then boyfriend Gary Hume, and was immediately aware of the strength those pictures had in terms of self-representation, as she told Matthew Collings in an interview:

> *I never liked being in photographs and I avoided it if at all possible. I thought I looked masculine in a way I didn't always find palatable. But in that picture with the banana, the first of those photos, you can see that those considerations of whether you looked particularly good that day, or whether or not you look a bit more masculine than you like to look, were in the service of the picture. They weren't in the service of vanity." (Lucas in Collings, 2002, p.72)*

Back to Gordon, his best-known self-portrait dates from 1996 and represents a splendid instance of his attitude towards representation of a disguised artistic self. Titled *Self-Portrait as Kurt Cobain, as Andy Warhol, as Myra Hindley, as Marilyn Monroe* (1996) it is a mere photo booth snapshot the size of a passport picture[5]. The photograph shows the artist wearing a blond bob-shaped wig with a melancholic expression on his face. This is the image the artist sent to Tate Gallery after being selected for the Turner Prize final exhibition in 1996 and which was thereafter used as official photo for the press release. Sending an *en travesti* picture – unlike the other three shortlisted artists who sent their best takes – definitely questioned public expectations over his persona. Gordon decided to hide himself, when in fact he should have sought maximum exposure, which also functioned well as a strategy to stand out against the other finalists. However, this self-portrait doesn't want to disguise the viewer, it rather challenges archetypal preconceptions about the artistic self. Dressed up as various celebrities, Gordon has been able to embody at once all stereotypes that are traditionally bestowed onto celebrities. As a matter of facts, each of the characters quoted in the title is a public icon and they share the same iconographic appearance, a blonde bobbed hairstyle. Furthermore, their personal experiences express different qualities that are usually associated with celebrities, such as drug addiction, disturbed sexuality, criminal attitude, insanity and depression. In a sense, it is as if Gordon had created a composite picture of himself interpreting the atavistic icon of a doomed celebrity (Brown, 2004, p.70). Gordon applies the same strategy of controlled revelation in numerous biographic accounts, thus interpreting them as another means of self-representation, which he is particularly fond of, rather minimizing photographic portraiture as compared to Lucas' case. Three from the many examples stand out because of their temporal comprehensiveness, embracing the artist's whole life span up to the day they were published. Another common feature of these three biographic texts is that an unknown third person narrator has written them, though it is easy to detect Gordon himself being the writer. However, the choice of an alien storyteller of his life is very significant, because it refers to a theme of his artistic production that characterizes the entire 1990s decade, which is schizophrenia. The earliest episode, which reveals the artist's interest in the field of personality disorders, which will be accomplished especially in his video-installations in the years 1993-1998, is a letter sent to friends and colleagues at Glasgow School of Art[6]. Undated though clearly written in autumn 1990, when he picked up teaching at his former hometown institute after completing the Masters of Arts in London, the letter contains an unsettling warning to the addressee: Gordon informs that someone on the campus pretended to be himself, but was in fact his identical *Doppelgänger*. The three supposedly autobiographical texts referred to above were instead all published on occasion of solo shows in important European museums. The first is a letter by an unspecified brother of the artist's – he has several younger ones – sent to the curator of Gordon's exhibition at Van Abbemuseum in Eindhoven in 1995. The second account is a short biography by a nameless friend included in the catalogue of the personal exhibition *Words* organized by Eckhard Schneider at Kunstverein Hannover in 1998. Finally, Fiona Bradley and James Lingwood edited his private memoirs on occasion of *What have I done*, his solo show at London's Hayward Gallery in 2002[7]. The title of the latter text is *Ghost: The private confessions of Douglas Gordon*, which apparently refers to a well known 19th century Scottish novel that is very dear to the artist, being *The private memoirs and confessions of a justified sinner* by James Hogg. Gordon had already borrowed one part of this book's title for a piece on show at the 1996 Turner Prize exhibition, which is *Confessions of a Justifies Sinner* (1996). Of the three, the text for the Hannover catalogue is worthwhile discussing at this point, as it presents the artist's narrative technique as well as his tendency to mystification. Entitled *A short biography: By a friend* it can be found in the very last pages of the catalogue, which is rather common for biographical notes in an artist's exhibition publication. However, what is truly remarkable appears to be the fact that the pages don't follow the correct order. In fact, the text is to be read starting from the last one and then turning the pages backwards, which seems to hint that the content is – in some ways – the mirror image of the truth. The storyline is unravelled by short accounts of real or imaginary single episodes in Gordon's life, which appear to be organized as a mosaic with a lot of intentionally missing tiles. Thus telling some stories and hinting at others, as well as compelling the reader to ponder on facts and fiction, reality and imagination expose his strategy of controlled disclosing. At the end of the reading the truth out of the artist's biography is not easily determined, such that the final sentence consistently asserts,

> *"I don't know what to believe anymore." (Douglas Gordon: Words, Cat.1998)*

Katrina Brown (2004, p.70) maintains that the texts produced by Gordon aim at failing the expectations of a conventional biography reader and work as a mechanism for restrained revelation in order to achieve a mythical self-image. Quoting a passage of this short biography can be revealing, starting with the first page, which is in fact the last page of the catalogue, were it flipped through in the usual manner. The excerpt presented below refers to childbirth as an upsetting event, comparable to the discovery of truth, while another emerging topic is guilt, a feeling which is deeply rooted in the artist's soul and which was later the Leitmotiv for some of his works such as *Tattoo (For reflection)* (1997):

> *"Douglas Gordon was born in Redlands Hospital, Glasgow, in September 1966. He was the first born of four children to James Gordon and Mary McDougall. The birth was not an easy one. From what he can remember, or from what he can remember being told by his mother, the labour lasted @ twenty-four hours. It was clear that he didn't want to be out in the world. Eventually he had to be pulled out, by doctors using forceps. This may account for the odd shape of his head, and the small scar at the base of his skull, where the spine joins the cranium. The event was a traumatic experience for both child and mother. Mary McDougall, his mother, died during the birth. But she came back to life again, after a few moments. Douglas feels guilty for all the trouble he caused his mother during this time. Perhaps this is why he is constantly travelling and putting off his return to Scotland. Maybe he doesn't like having to face the guilt he feels when he sees his family." (Douglas Gordon: Words, Cat.1998)*

The following quotation instead belongs to the last page of the Hannover biography and touches on Gordon's assumed encounter with the devil, which appears to be an explicit reference to James Hogg's main character of the previously mentioned novel *Confessions of a justified sinner.*

> *"I tried to ask some friends of his, and one of them told me that he always spoke about life in Berlin as some kind of "vampire" existence – that life would go on until quite late in the night, or early in the morning, and he would only return home just before the sun came up, then sleep until the evening, and start the whole day all over again. His friend told me that between November and late January he was extremely pale and it seemed that he never saw more than one hour of sunshine in any day. It was around that time that he started telling people that he had actually seen the devil in a café in Berlin. But that's another story for him to tell." (Douglas Gordon: Words, Cat.1998)*

Except for these three biographic texts, most of the others tell only specific incidents in his life – true or allegedly true ones – and are related to circumstances that associate them directly to the target reader. For instance, Gordon used to mail such stories to curators and dealers who had asked for his works for an exhibition. In general, the plot is connected to the artist's first encounter with the addressee or to some event related to the show in context. One of the many examples is the letter in response to Berlin based curator Gerti Fietzek, who had invited him to install *24 Hour Psycho* at a group show held in Leipzig railway station in 1995, which even included works by Lawrence Weiner. Gordon's letter, of which the following piece is an extract that focuses on the artist's first trip to Berlin, was included in the catalogue together with the curator's initial mailing:

> *"Liebe Gerti, One day, soon, I will write the short story for you (as was promised) about my first visit to Berlin. However, at this moment in time, that story does not want to be told. [...] My first Berlin trip was memorable because it has become almost a total blank. I can barely remember anything. The whole trip, lasting about 7 days, is a clouded head punctuated only by a few films, some bad German, and some very strong pain killers. [...] I had left Glasgow with a mild throat infection which was on an upward curve. [...] Berlin was worse. By the time I arrived there my throat infection had travelled into my ears and I was completely deaf. I experienced the city in total silence, and of course, as you know "Ich spreche kein Deutsch"; so, not only I was unable to hear anything but I was lost in being unable to hear that which I was not able to understand." (Kopfbahnhof/Terminal, Cat.1995)*

Whether true or untrue, the various biographic fragments quoted so far reveal several of the recurrent themes of Gordon's production, as seen in the previous chapter. Such are for instance guilt-feelings, consubstantiality of good and evil, splitting personalities, which the artist appears to ascribe to his personal or social background. In fact, in order to fully understand these topic choices one should take religious conditioning into account, as well as due to other peculiar aspects of the Scottish cultural tradition that influenced his childhood. It should be noticed, that inventing or adapting childhood episodes, as well as stressing the relevance of family background are useful devices to find inspiration and widespread means to create an effective self-image. Even though significance of such factors could be artificially claimed or overemphasized – being truly part of a cunning strategy of self-representation – the particular religious circumstances Gordon grew up in might definitely have affected his creativity, at least to some extent. The chasm between Protestant and Catholic Church in Glasgow, for instance, shouldn't be underestimated, because it brings about a basic division in Western Scottish society that is still enduring. Clydeside area has more in common with divided Ulster than any other part of the British isle has, because over the whole 19th century Irish immigrants have progressively crowded the territory bringing about a hostile reaction from Protestant Scotland which lasted for another century (Gallagher, 1987, p.4). At the start of the last century tension mounted between two separate working-class communities, divided by religious belief, but was partially released by soccer rivalry. Known as the Old Firm, the enmity between Glasgow Rangers supporters proudly wearing their Union Jacks and Celtic Glasgow fans, who believe in Scottish independence, is truly epic (Borden, 2012). Back in the 1970s no Catholic school child would have dared to cheer the Rangers, while the opposite was the case in Protestant institutions for the Celtics. Hostilities between the two religious communities may have softened, but they left a state of general mistrust behind that is chiefly palpable in children's interaction. Parents usually urge their kids to make friends only within their own religious group, hence young Douglas experienced a situation of harsh conflict in his school years. These contrast is likely to be the origin of Gordon's sense for artificial antithesis shaping social dynamics, which he is resolved to spoil in order to expose their irrationality and utter insignificance (Fagen, 1999, p.72). However, rather than social pressure, even greater influence on personality was established by his own family's choices in religious matters. Originally both the Gordons and the McDougalls were followers of the Scottish Calvinist Church, hence professing a strict deterministic life view. His father James was always a very critical believer, while his mother and her relatives always had a very rigorous and sympathetic conduct. Calvinist school education significantly affected the idea of guilt and sin the Scottish artist still displays in his works, as if he was still trying to re-elaborate them. In particular, it is the theory of Predestination that shaped Gordon's understanding of the above concepts. According to a very strict interpretation, predestination would divide mankind in two distinct groupings: on one side all who God has selected for eternity, on the other side all others that won't experience His mercy. The chosen ones will receive salvation through Christ, while the others need to suffer a just and necessary wrath for their crimes against the Lord. Considering that the distinction is not rooted in individual virtue, personal merit nor proved faith and good deeds, the doomed ones cannot find a true reason for being guilty, since the answer is unconditionally grounded in God's mercy alone. In various interviews and biographic accounts, as well as in some of his artworks, Gordon discloses a personality haunted by guilt-feelings, oppressed by the burden of sin, which he wants the public to understand as constant discomfort that shape human life (Van den Boogard, 1997, pp.41-42).

Far from being a concern solely to the considered artist, the problematic issue of predestination together with guilt are truly characteristic features of Protestant culture in Scotland, at least for the last two centuries. Gordon grew up in an environment where those features were deeply rooted in people's conscience and have been themes for literature and art since 19th century (Brown, 2004, pp.117-118). One of the best known example – even if virtually unknown to central European readers – is the previously mentioned novel by James Hogg. The complete title is *The private memoirs and confessions of a justified sinner: Written by himself: With a detail of curious traditionary facts and other evidence by the editor* and the book was published in 1824. This work is often considered one of the main inspirations for Robert Louis Stevenson's far better known *The strange case of Dr. Jekyll and Mr. Hyde.* Hogg's novel discloses the invented memories of Robert Wringhim, an observant Calvinist who belongs to the elect people predestined to be saved by God, hence awaiting heavenly reward regardless of how their lives are conducted. Careless of his destiny, the main character is tempted by the devil to challenge predestination and thus performs any type of mischief – even attempting to kill his own brother – but finally commits suicide seized by guilt. When Gordon read the book still a young man, he was struck by it so much that it became a major source of inspiration, further even using Hogg's main character name as an internet pseudonym. Talking with the Dutch dealer and writer Oscar van den

Boogaard, the artist enthusiastically recalls the novel plot showing its deep influence on his imagination:

> *"That is a fantastic story. Unbelievable! It's about a young Scottish man who encounters the devil. The devil challenges him to kill his brother. Finally the young man goes crazy, and you don't know whether the devil exists in his imagination or in reality. Shortly before he kills himself, he writes his memoirs. His manuscript is buried with him somewhere far outside the village. A publisher who hears of the story exhumes the body and steals the manuscript. Everyone is guilty, everyone does something wrong!" (Gordon in Van den Boogard, 1997, p.38)*

The Calvinist environment thus had a strong impact on young Douglas, however it wasn't the only religious influence that marked his early life. Indeed, when he was six years of age, Gordon's family undertook a change of creed steered by almost all McDougalls, who were particularly supportive with each other in religious matters. It occurred that some McDougalls emigrated to the United States where they met the community of Jehovah's Witnesses. After a visit to these American relatives, Douglas' mother and her sisters mutually joined the cult, except for one of them which stayed an outcast Protestant and for their father – Gordon's grandfather – who became instead Catholic after a nearly fatal accident. Religious turmoil shook the entire family and as soon as 1972 his mother Mary started to attend the neighbourhood Jehovah's temple where, together with most of the McDougalls, she took part in all communal activities. She immediately initiated her children to the cult too causing a dramatic change as to young Douglas' attitude to religion with unsettling results. The artist still remembers with mixed feelings of anxiety and fascination the times when – still a very young boy – he was compelled to learn long Bible excerpts by heart and then deliver them standing in front of an adult audience. Owing to his mother's strict observance, Jehovah's cult has influenced the young artist in a crucial way, especially as regards to the idea of evil and the fear of Satan. Gordon was induced to believe in the devil's physical and psychical ubiquity in the world, such that his mind should be shielded against the perils of malice in order to avoid corruption. He was imparted by his mother to arrange for self-defence by means of unconditional trust in his creed. Growing up with an overwhelming sense of the devil's presence and the belief he can plague people's body and mind, this religious education has most likely induced the artist to investigate the struggle of good and evil. The root of Gordon's interest in the issue of the divided self and schizophrenia, regarded as the struggle between different personalities to possess the same body, can as well be attributed to his upbringing in the community of Jehovah's Wittnesses (Obrist, 1996b, p.171). Then again the subject of split behaviour was extensively dealt with in the Scottish cultural context, as Kathrina Brown (2004, pp.119-120) recalls, especially in the form of a sinister alter-ego such as Stevenson's celebrated double character of Dr. Jekyll and Mr. Hyde. Although nowadays Gordon is fundamentally agnostic, still his idea of evil and the possibility of its physical materialization are very much alive in his psyche. The artist sincerely believes that evil is real and that it can take hold of an individual's body and psyche, causing the split personality typical for schizophrenia. On the contrary to Calvinist predestination, however, Jehovah's Witnesses has caused him to care about individual responsibility, in particular concerning accountability for on's own deeds which will be pondered on Judgment Day for salvation. Gordon sometimes recalls upsetting sensations of his religious life during childhood:

> *"I was raised with a very strong, almost corporal belief in the devil. My mother told a lot of stories about him. It was like the devil was everywhere. I learned that you had to protect yourself mentally, physically and spiritually against the devil. [...] I was forced to think about concepts like fate, trust and guilt. [...] I was raised to believe that it is your own responsibility to be good." (Gordon in Van den Boogard, 1997, p.38)*

Choice of topic can become an artist's trademark, something he or she are known for in particular and that contribute in a deciding manner to the fabricated self-image. It is in some way a question of packaging, which is the features that are used for self-promotion, thus creating a significant though artificial distinction from competitors on the art market (Thompson, 2008, p.90). As argued before, Tracy Emin has become renowned for the disclosed sexual confessions of her initial works combined with a media-appealing bad-girl behaviour. Whether she did it on purpose or simply let her natural disposition stroll about isn't really the point, it is instead fundamental to understand, if she was aware of this feature being relevant or even strategic for her career improvement. Commenting on *Everyone I Have Ever Slept With, 1963-1995* (1995[8]), a tent with the names sewed on the inside of all people she had slept with so far and which first drew substantial attention on her work from the art world and the mass media, Emin seems quite conscious about the importance of her topic and formal choices for brand distinction:

> *"The thing about the tent in 1995, it was just a woman that nobody knew or cared about, making a record of part of her life which a lot of people do, consciously or subconsciously, except that I was the first person to do it in that way and that's what made a difference." (Emin in Fortnum, 2007, pp.56-57)*

Damien Hirst's childhood obsession with death has been comparably exploited as a trademark by Bristol born artist and as a marketing means to arouse much discussion. Persuaded that his early works in college were lacking impact due to an excessive minimalist strain, he consciously started digging for something meaningful and impressive. In describing the conception of *A Thousand Years* (1990), his first piece with rotten flesh and dying insects which was displayed at the warehouse-show *Gambler* and immediately purchased by collector Charles Saatchi, Hirst reveals a hang-up for death supposedly rooted in childhood experience and intentionally employed to be significant:

> *"I remember thinking over and over again, 'I've got to make something that's about something important.' [...] There was need for some sort of darkness as well. And I remember struggling with that for a long time. And then I just came up with the life cycle. [...] I'd always thought about death since I was seven years old. I remember when it first dawned me that it was inevitable, and I could never stop thinking about it, from a gruesome point of view. [...] I'd lost my grandmother. [...] I remember saying, 'What happens', 'What happens when you die?' I actually thought there was a way you could avoid death, and when I was seven I realized you couldn't." (Hirst in Serota, 2011, p.95)*

Likewise, both Christine Borland and Sarah Lucas trace their interest in peculiar topics – which later happened to characterize their artistic production – right back to specific childhood experiences. Born and brought up in the country at Darvel, South of Glasgow, the Scottish artist was very much accustomed to wildlife as well as natural history museums, while her parents taught her much about flora and fauna – taxonomy included. She directly ascribes her keenness for anatomical specimens and her tendency towards a scientific-classification-wise display to the environment she was brought up and the frequent contact she had to naturalistic collections:

> *"As a child I was given the gift of being taken round museums and botanic gardens by my parents, and I always remember the*

experience of looking at the collections of stuffed animals and relishing that. My parents really knew a lot about nature, but just in a very matter-of-fact way – you know how to kill an animal and cook it – and that was just a part of day-to-day existence." (Black, 2006)

Sarah Lucas, on her part, vividly remembers the daily encounter with the kind of popular and sexual imagery paraded on British tabloid newspapers. The feminine nudes nonchalantly concealed in the inner page seemed a violent comment on women's subordinate position. Partly fascinated and half-guilty at the sight of naked women she learned duplicity, which is proper of a moralistic society. Lucas later found out that exposing voyeurism could be the strongest means to assert gender issues:

"When I was a kid we used to get the Daily Mirror every day. It came through the letterbox. And there was always a topless image in there somewhere. I'd sort of look at it but if my Dad or Mum passed by I'd probably turned the page or something – so I was aware of that element of it being a very different thing between looking at that stuff privately and making it public." (Collings, 2002, p.23)

Besides emotionally intense experiences in religious matters, the environment young Douglas grew up in his childhood and teenage years was distinguished under another aspect that apparently made a big impression on him and is related to mass media, as in the case of Sarah Lucas, but on a different level. In fact, although the West of Scotland was considered a really deprived area in the late Seventies and early Eighties, yet the artist recalls his home district to set a curious record:

"I always remember the statistics, [...] that although the West of Scotland could be one of the most depressed areas of the world, the big example was always Drumchapel had the highest number of video recorders per family in the world, and to be brought up in a culture where you have control over images [...] was incredibly interesting." (Gordon in Fagen, 1999, p.82)

Set in the Western outskirts of Glasgow towards Dumbarton, it is difficult to say whether Drumchapel really had the highest rate of VHS recorders per family in the industrial world. However, may it be true or not, this figure is relevant to understand the rise of a new mental disposition in society, which started to house and privately consume visual products that had been originally realized for a shared experience in a cinema. Possessing a video recorder in private households hints at a complete change in attitude towards the cinematic experience and celebrity system. The audience had gradually acquired intimacy with Hollywood movies and film stars, who were not appreciated anymore on large size screens in dark crowded rooms, but in a much more comfortable and familiar environment on 4 to 3 television format. It must be highlighted that this type of audience approach to cinema is fundamentally different from that of earlier decades, that is before television spread in Western homes outdoing cinema-goers (Moisdon-Trembley, 1996, p.128). It isn't only a matter of screen size, but a question of different environment, habit and familiarity to the moving image, which gradually transformed into a daily affair that everyone could have an individual relationship to. Gordon himself recalls to have first experienced audio-visual products in a home context and even remembers a great number of films seen in childhood, which he later dealt with in his works. Lulled in familiar surroundings, he watched only the movies he was allowed to, but this is why he asserts they were impressed in his memory:

> *"I think that this story doesn't relate only to Hitchcock or to myself. But his films I remember best, especially from my childhood. When I was seven or eight years old, I watched films like 'North by Northwest' or 'Strangers on a train'. I discovered 'Psycho' when I was a little older [...] because it was said to be frightening, too intense. So I keep memories of films I was allowed to watch, and of those, I wasn't. Maybe that's why they keep coming back to my mind." (Gordon in Haase, 1999, p.138)*

As many other Scottish families, the Gordons had a number of VHS appliances in their home. As a child the future artist was used to consuming a large amount of taped films and as a teenager he was allowed to hold his own video recorder in bedroom. As most children of his age, thus he grew up in a milieu that was very familiar with movies – holding an important role in collective imagination – but in a much more domestic and personal way than what the previous generation had experienced. Gordon's approach to cinema – mediated through television – is the same as that of a great number of people, especially those belonging to his same age group, who share equal recollections and visual imaginary. Rather than cinema taken as a whole, single movies have become a source of memories, desires and values, which are related to the actual occasion when an individual has watched them. They are mass culture products to which he had been exposed as a child together with millions of other people, hence constituting both a personal recollection and common ground to communicate with others. This is the reason why Gordon maintains he is interested in popular movies such as westerns and thrillers or even comedy shows:

> *"[...] it's a fact that we can sit down in any pub in Scotland with anybody who's educated around the same generation as us and talk about [...] 'Star Trek', OK I'm not that interested in Leonard Nimoy [Star Trek's Spock], but I am interested in the fact that it's become such a common denominator, and the only reason that a common denominator is important is that it makes people talk, it's a shared thing." (Gordon in Fagen, 1999, p.84)*

Besides enhancing home cinema consumption the proliferation of VHS technology also changed the interaction of audience and cinema industry. The viewer ceased to be a passive consumer of the film shown in theatres and all of a sudden could choose how to view the moving images. As a matter of facts, the video recorder allows one to decide whether to see some scenes again or on the opposite to skip them, to freeze the pace of the story or to accelerate it. It certainly is a limited power, but it started a process of personalization of the medium and highlighted the conquest of closeness to cinema (Fricke, 2000, p.133). Gordon's generation grew up developing a new approach to pictures and moving images from the media industry, finally taking limited control over them such as repeated view and manipulation by means of an appliance at everybody's reach. Thus the practice of processing filmed materials wouldn't result from academic consideration, but rather from the kind of everyday experience typical for teenagers obsessed by their favourite celebrities, as will be further discussed with regards to the genesis of *24 Hour Psycho* (Moisdon-Trembley, 1996, p.129). In conversation with Graham Fagen, Gordon himself is very clear about this issue:

> *"OK a lot of people never ever use them [video recorders], but a lot of people certainly did, and whether they were using them as an auto-erotic thing or whether they were using them for academic purposes didn't make any difference to me, if there is a cultural fact, in that images were being manipulated by [...] ordinary people, by people who had no education about why they were necessarily manipulating them." (Gordon in Fagen, 1999, p.82)*

Shocking childhood events, as well as apparently irrelevant features of ordinary life, can be turned into sources for artistic inspiration and experimentation, while being simultaneously exploited as convenient means of representation for the artist's self-image and connected reputation.

Chapter 4
Art education between Glasgow and London

4.1. Going for art school in the Eighties: of ethnographers, public artists and education reforms

Whatever the reason, if one was up for a career in visual arts, as a young British man or woman of the 1980s one would need to pick art classes and there was no way around art school. The true choice for aspiring artists was and still is between different institutions and the specific courses or departments inside them. One's decision might be steered by the particular notoriety of an art school due to its history, teachers or successful alumni, as well as by the level of tuition fees and possible entrance examinations that should select the most promising students. As argued in the previous chapter, however, back then in the UK there were no serious economic barriers to hold students off higher education, which appeared to have truly opened up to young Britons in that decade. The explosion of university enrolments during the Eighties – which brought about a varied constitution of gender and social provenance in the students' body – was definitely a crucial feature for artists born in the second baby boom generation, but by far not the only relevant one to involve the British higher education system. As a matter of facts, artistic outbreaks of the late Sixties and Seventies, especially those informed by process and performance art or by libertarian movements, had started to question the traditional model of art schools and soon spread throughout the United Kingdom, eventually influencing the whole system. Some isolated experiments of reformed art education took already place in the Seventies, yet they became widely institutionalized only in the following decade. Although higher education had opened up to all social classes, at the same time Margaret Thatcher's liberal policy also hit hard on university budgets, with structural fund cuts and severe personnel reductions that resulted in a number of negative aspects for art schools (Harding, 2001b). Teachers' wages were reduced, so that spending time in art school was less attractive for successful artists who could have been influent on young artists. Furthermore, teaching hours were increased so that it was almost impossible for a professor to exercise his or her own profession as an artist. Finally, combined with the enrolment boom, the rate of students per teacher in art schools swell from 10 to 1 in the Seventies to 40 to 1 in the Nineties – which goes from workshop-type lessons to overcrowded classes. Despite the latter organizational problems, the philosophy and pedagogy of art education was fundamentally reformed in the Eighties holding massive consequences for the new generation of artists that would graduate from art schools across the country. The importance of the educational framework can hardly be minimized, as it constitutes one of the distinctive features of the art system in every historical age, far beyond mere practical training. As a matter of facts, the institutional form of art education holds crucial influence on the artist's professional attitude and role model in society, as can be said for the period of apprenticeship in a Medieval and Renaissance workshop or for the years spent at the Académie des Beaux-Arts in Baroque France (Burke, 1979). At the same time institutions for art education – regardless of their peculiar historical structure – act as the primal entry barrier to the art system. Be it a practical workshop, a traditional academy or a modern university, such institutions carry out an early selection between talented and non-talented artists, or at least they try to pick artist candidates who show some potential (Caves, 2000, p.26). Nowadays art school still may set two principle hurdles for young people interested in making a career in visual arts: the first one at enrolment, provided there are entrance exams, and then the last one at graduation, taking the final mark into consideration. Art education is definitely to be regarded as the first institutional gatekeeper to the art system, choosing those who will rightly be claimed artist candidates. Furthermore, these institutions deeply affect the art concept over a prolonged period of time, because they are usually cradle to several generations of artists, as well as of a strain of different players of the system, so for instance art critics, curators, dealers and others. Although institutions are accountable for affecting the system, these are made up by individual actors who can influence on their part an institution's course and development, hence contributing to establish new trends (Frey, 2000, p.28). It is not uncommon for art professors to openly interact with the art system and try to steer some of its choices, for instance in the guise of theorists, critics, curators or even artists themselves (Galenson, 2005a, p.22). Concerning their own students, on the other hand, art schoolteachers are instrumental to establish the basis for artistic and network capital of every single artist candidate they teach. They assign cultural value to particular trends or techniques and can later help their students to enter the field or get in touch with influential players, at least on a regional level. For those who enter a proper art school, some teachers in particular might prove far more relevant and influential than the institution as a whole. As will be explored further on, this appears to be the case of Edinburgh born public artist David Harding, who founded the Environmental Art Department at Glasgow School of Art which both Gordon and Borland attended. Another instance is that of charismatic Irishman Michael Craig-Martin, who taught and passionately promoted most of the future YBA stars trained at the exclusive Goldsmith's College in London (Sherwin, 2007).

Despite the influence of individual teachers, however, the 1980s are indeed the decade in which a major pedagogical shift can be observed. In fact, as far as the educational approach is concerned, it is the time when comprehensive visual arts courses or departments spread both in the USA and Great Britain, as opposed to the more conventional model of European Fine Arts Academies. The fundamental difference between the two examples is represented by the core aspect art education is credited with: while traditional courses are still focussed on training in specific techniques, the new curriculum in the Anglo-American world opened up to much more theoretic and inter-disciplinary subjects of teaching (Vettese, 2007, p.30). Still today the true trade off in art education is between learning a technique and stimulating creativity, depending on the artist role model set by the education system: the former being a skilled craftsman, the latter an overall talent. The emergence of this new pedagogical approach in America and Britain was clearly determined by previous as well as pervasive changes in visual arts trends that occurred in the Seventies and Eighties, which the American critic and historian Hal Foster (1996) defines as gradual conversion of the artist into an anthropologist or ethnographer. As a matter of facts, the US scholar argues that one of the most remarkable transformations of late 20th century art could be epitomized by what is to be considered an *ethnographic turn*, which also prompted the conversion of the artist's role and work procedure (Gravano, 2007). Highlighting the convention held in Santa Fé in 1984 around James Clifford and George Marcus, which marked the transition of academic research to cross-curricular cultural studies, Foster acknowledges this transformation didn't only influence humanities and anthropology, but also current visual art trends. The debate in Santa Fé reached the conclusion that any study about cultural events purports at least three actors: the object produced, its creator and the writer/critic who analyses the cultural product. As a consequence, describing culture would be an essentially analytical process, actively involving the critic with his or her limits and preconceptions. Hence the observer appears to be unavoidably biased, his or her opinions on ethnographic truths being inconsistent, because intrinsically partial, subjective and incomplete (Clifford, Marcus, 1986, p.32). However, Marcus and Clifford argue that the ethnographic approach is effective to research cultural events precisely owing to its partiality. They maintain that analysing individuals who are different from us brings about a practice of mirroring and self-description on the researcher's part. This aspect had been previously highlighted also by French historian Michel Foucault, who argued that Western civilisation's true trait in the 20th century was to be found in the tendency to seek the truth in what is unexpected, unconscious and different (Foucault, 2004). No wonder then, if psychoanalysis and anthropology rose into prominence as the main prevailing research methods for developing self-knowledge. Foster explains the artist has taken this very procedure into artistic labour, favouring theoretical research and becoming a self-aware interpreter of cultural facts. So far, culture is considered as a text the artist needs to read according to his or her own predisposition and knowledge about society, politics, history, economy – which is in fact what an ethnographer does when describing alien cultures. In the American critic’s opinion, the transformation of artists into ethnographers would have taken place as a reaction to the wave of liberalism and capitalistic influence on culture which had its climax in Regan’s and Thatcher’s administrations. Substantially this new role model for artists replicates Walter Benjamin's vision of the artist as a cultural producer who should always confront the prevailing economic, political and cultural system. In such a perspective, the artist's only possible reaction would be system criticism as well as self criticism, which originate when faced with those who differ from us (Foster, 1996, pp.171-172). The application of the ethnographic approach to the field of visual arts was probably favoured by emerging trends such as minimalism, performance and conceptual praxis, taking for instance *Homes for America* (1966-67) by Dan Graham which lays at the crossroads of journalism and anthropology investigating new aesthetics and social influences of suburban housing in the United States (Stemmrich, 2008). However, Foster particularly highlights the inner features of ethnography as a discipline, which appear to match the purpose of art perfectly. First and foremost, ethnography is the science of differences, regarding culture both as its outcome and research topic. Furthermore, it takes the context into consideration and resorts to inter-disciplinary approaches, staying open by definition to self-criticism and self-analysis. Finally, the existence of two opposed epistemological visions in the field of ethnography would be reflected in as many diverging procedures even in visual arts. The former school of thought envisions culture from a mere symbolic viewpoint, thus intended as a linguistic paradigm that can be exploited or subverted in art praxis, while the latter epistemological approach is bound to pragmatism, leading at the appreciation of artefacts in their broader context which constitute material culture of a given society. All in all, Foster explains that trends in contemporary art were clearly affected by the same change of disciplinary perspective, which influenced humanistic disciplines, as outlined by Clifford and Marcus at the Santa Fé convention. Adopting the view of cultural diversity as well as the method of field study, contemporary art would thus bear the marks of this epochal shift towards ethnography (Lusini, 2011, p.93). In fact, Foster asserts that the focus of art practice, as well as the conception of the artwork, has been crucially affected, especially in the last two decades of 20th century. Concerning artistic procedure, one may observe a clear twist from *medium-specificity*, which acts in vertical and diachronic sense, to *discourse-specificity* being horizontal and synchronic. Hence, visual artists would have finally embraced a working method centred on topics that involve different disciplines and explore diverse themes, rather than remaining confined within the inner development of one single technique, confronted solely with previous art historical examples. Consequently there would have been a switch from the 'natural' paradigm, which regards the artwork as a window and the visual image as a necessary representation of the world, to a 'cultural' paradigm conceiving the artwork as a text and the visual image as an information network. Following this stream of thought, visual arts become part of a cultural continuum, as Lawrence Alloway had already remarked about Pop Art. However, this transition of artistic procedure from a vertical to a horizontal insight could cause the loss of temporal perspective over art development and, as a consequence, miss the opportunity for an intra-artistic comparison (Foster, 1996, p.202). The danger has to be avoided, according to Hal Foster, by means of constant art-historical awareness and firm critical stance to the concrete themes and objects dealt with in artworks, which is true both for critics and artists.

One of the driving forces behind this epochal shift in the visual arts must be found in the much more general turmoil that had inspired the 1960ies and 70ies. A huge wave of idealism and democratization prompted by libertarian movements soon affected the entire art system, crucially influencing the debate on the meaning of art and the artist's role model in society. Though such issues were treated with reluctance by the art establishment, in the Sixties and gradually more in the Seventies a sense of crisis permeated the art world driving criticism towards the traditional art praxis. Reacting to abstract expressionism, those two decades were in fact cradle for new directions and radical experiments, such as minimalism and conceptual art which progressively conquered the backing of academia. With reference to art developments, some authors went even further completely abandoning the idea of art for art's sake and refusing individualism or self-expression as art's final aim. A new drift towards public and community art stressed social relevance of artistic activity, replacing traditional procedures with collaborative methods cantered on process and context (Crickmay, 2003). Such a vision of socially engaged art spread across the United Kingdom thanks to the support of some art critics among whom, foremost, Lucy Lippard and Caroline Tisdall, who valued the attempt to bring art back to society and change the artist role within it. Scottish conceptual artist and writer Su Braden, who participated in this debate, analysed the different experiences referring to public and community art on British soil in an important study titled *Artists and People* and which was published in 1978. In her research on this phenomenon, she asserts that during this period the real need likeminded artists felt was to change their work practice, in order to reach a socially aware production. Assuming that moving artworks from a gallery to the street would not be enough, the only alternative approach was to reconsider the aim and scope of art, as well as its methods, in order to keep social context and structures into account. At this point, it is necessary to define the concepts of community art and public art, which must be differentiated, though they hold strong similarities as regards to social engagement. In fact, the former refers to a kind of art, which is produced by minority groups, either ethnic or social ones, such as for instance the production linked to the feminist movement. Community art relies on the vision that it is in everyone's right to express their own group identity, objectives and aspirations through art. Public art is instead rather focussed on interactive methods, which should allow the public to get involved in the process of art production and its subsequent appraisal. By this means art should echo the features of the specific place and people the artwork is meant for. Edinburgh born David Harding, the future mentor to many of the Glaswegian off-springs in the Eighties and Nineties, was deeply involved in public art during the two previous decades and keeps a vivid memory of those days:

> *"The democratic urge and idealism of the Sixties moved a number of artists to question their role in society. Individualism, self-expression and 'art about art' began to be replaced in their practice by collaboration, social relevance, process and context and the whole panoply of galleries, dealers and the art market was deemed antithetical." (Harding, 1995, p.1)*

Restricting the geographic field to Scotland, the rise of social sensibility in art and further conceptual innovations is considerably linked to foreign authors who influenced the local scene. Scottish art historian Craig Richardson (2011, p. 55-69) maintains that visiting artists in the late Sixties and early Seventies played a pivotal role in the development of contemporary art on a national scale, but foremost they were able to transfer international trends. The engagement with the Scottish context by artists such as David Hall and Blinky Palermo proved crucial together with many other artists who held exhibitions in that period. However, the two artists who apparently had the biggest sway on Scottish art back then, especially if seen on a long-term perspective, were Joseph Beuys and John Letham. The German art shaman came to Scotland in 1970 thanks to Richard Demarco's enlightened activism, an Edinburgh-based dealer and all-around impresario who run the recently reborn New 57 Gallery. The latter did in fact represent the true avant-gardist venue that tried to foster artistic innovation during the Seventies, while other institutions in Scotland's capital such as the Scottish Arts Council and the Scottish National Gallery of Modern Art at Inverleith House were still lingering in doubts about the direction they should take. The New 57 Gallery originated from a previous artist run experience, the 57 Gallery from 1965 to 1969, which was chaired by an artist committee and had tried to put every young Scotsman on show who revealed some genuine ambition (Lowndes, 2010, pp.40-41). Among the committee's last year was painter Alexander Moffat, who would later become an influent teacher at the Glasgow School of Art. Other cities around Scotland still had to wait a few years for pivotal galleries to be opened, such as the Third Eye Centre in Glasgow in 1976 or the Pier Arts Center in Orkney in 1979. However, although Demarco tried to build an infrastructure for the promotion of innovative trends relaying on public funding, his position in Seventies' Scotland was definitely marginal, while similar experiences in London had taken off rapidly. This is for instance the case of the gradual rise of Anthony D'Offay and Nicholas Logsdail which had started two comparable avant-gardist galleries – though commercial ones – in the British capital at the end of the previous decade. Despite various problems, Demarco succeeded in bringing some of the most relevant international artists to Scotland, as happened with Beuys in 1970 on the occasion of the exhibition *Strategy: Get Arts* at the Edinburgh Art College. This exhibition has been cited as the most important post-war event in Scottish visual arts, because in presenting the vibrant Düsseldorf art scene it provided a fresh and plausible alternative to the regressive practices which still found institutional backing (Richardson, 2011, p.69). Beuys presented three works, among them his celebrated installation with an open Volkswagen van and a trail of sledges, which he created the year before but was here displayed for the first time under the title *The Pack (Das*

Rudel) (1970). Furthermore, together with composer Henning Christiansen he engaged in an almost static performance, *Celtic (Kinloch Rannoch) Scottish Symphony* (1970) which was planned for the occasion and had filmed images of Rannoch Moor running alongside Beuys' action. The German artists' ability to match fine art practice with social awareness and everyday materials, as well as his claim that everyone could be an artist, had a deep impact on the younger generation of Scottish artists, increasing their interest in conceptual and performance art. It must be mentioned, though, that Beuys' works were able to speak back to the Scottish audience because of the encounter with a yet fertile ground. In fact, John Letham, a very controversial English conceptual artist who taught at St. Martin's College between 1965-67, but also operated in Scotland during the Sixties, had previously turned over the soil to some extent. His pieces often consisted in an extrapolation from contextual features, making it hard to discern between the final artwork and its creative procedure. He aroused a huge debate and was finally dismissed from teaching, when he exhorted his students to chew and spit Clement Greenberg's book *Art and Culture*[1]. Besides such extremes, in Letham's philosophy context and procedure held the primary place, while he was genuinely convinced that everybody was an artist in their own right. His aphorisms, such as "the context is half the work" (Letham in Harding, 1995, p.1), made a particular impression on young artists that were interested in the social dimension of art. As far as Scotland is concerned, Letham can rightly be considered a primary source for a public and interactive art form, especially thanks to the establishment of the so called *Artist Placement Group* (APG) founded in 1965 together with his wife Barbara Steveni and later presented in Edinburgh (*Out in the open*, Cat.1990). APG's intention was to assign artists to venues, situations and institutions, which did not usually pertain to the art domain, such as industrial activities, dockland authorities and residential areas. The true aim was for the artists to instill a sense of place and well-being in social contexts that usually lacked the intervention of artistic sensibility. Some of the employment locations APG found for artists were for instance healthcare offices, factories and public transport companies, but foremost the so called new towns which spread all over the country due to the fast growing population. Graham Steven, one of the first artists to be placed in this venture, recalls his experience resolving that the project pursued a context cantered art concept:

> *"This might have been called 'contextualism' since it is founded on the recognition that an artwork changes fundamentally in*

connection to where, who with and how it is made." (Stevens in Harding, 1995, p.1)

A similar experience taking place in Scotland in this period, even though it wasn't directly linked to the APG, was the official employment of David Harding in the position of town artist at Glenrothes, a typical Scottish new town, which will be dealt with in the next paragraph. Another important event as regards community and public art was the start of Craigmillar Festival in 1967, located in the namesake run-down district of the Scottish capital to stand out against the well-known Edinburgh festival, since the latter did not affect the most wrecked areas of the city. Mary Boowir e Helen Crummy successfully created a small concern, that is a Festival Society, which organized all cultural activities getting the locals involved both as workers and as creative artists. In a decade's time the area was completely redeveloped encouraging the adoption of shared actions in organizing art events. In 1979 these achievements were awarded by the European Union that granted 750.000 pounds to the project. The success of such projects throughout the Seventies induced the British Arts Council to foster artist placement as a valuable option for social advancement, however transforming it into a less effective artist-in-residence program. While APG or likeminded ventures let artists work in close contact with people and their issues, artist-residences often ended up lodging young authors in state subsidized studios with no real social interaction (Morgan, 2003). Hence the art establishment did not fully understand the opportunity offered by community and public art procedures as employed in direct artistic production, financing such programs only occasionally rather than systematically. However these new principles found instead their way in art education having a decisive impact on art school reforms. In fact, some unprecedented approaches and innovative teaching methods started to be introduced in traditional education across the UK and soon succeeded in becoming entrenched, as happened in the case of Glasgow School of Art with the institution of the Environmental Art Department in 1985. Most of all the structure of courses and choice of subjects were affected by the new wave of reforms. The first important and extensive example in such terms, which later influenced the renovation of other schools including Gordon's hometown institution, can be found in Darlington College of Arts. Located in the Cornish countryside, this school was originally founded to circulate art in all social classes and different age groups amongst rural population. Despite being at the very outskirt of the British art system, in the years between 1977-1991 a pioneering course called *Art and Social Context* was taught, the first of its kind in Great Britain to introduce a new curriculum.

Indeed, it was sketched on innovative guidelines based on the artistic sensibility and many other ideas raised in the previous decade, such as: favouring process rather than output as well as enhancing communal work; expounding environmental consciousness and planning projects which involved the local community; introducing topics such as semiotics and anthropology, in order to provide more appropriate methods of art creation in contemporary society (Crickmay, 2003). The course at Darlington College openly referred to the idea of context, regarded as a necessary means for art to get closer to everyday life and relinquish the traditional cultural venues. Furthermore, the curriculum was based on a vast range of methodological approaches – including community and public art – while students were driven to a kind of critical praxis aiming at an extensive cultural investigation, often differing from acknowledged theories. Their personal commitment was crucial, since creative development had to be individual, which implied that each student was supposed to analyse his or her own life experience in the wider frame of contemporary trends as would be typical for cultural studies. The choice of topics was meant to offer diverse perspectives on art that would fit into one homogeneous curriculum, hence combining artistic competencies with production strategies capable of keeping the cultural and geographic context into account. Finally, a student residency was the essential and decisive feature of education at Darlington College, conceived as a period for each student to dwell in a non-artistic venue and create an artwork, which could be defined as context-specific. Some of its founding teachers were the true backbone of Art and Social Context including Paul Oliver, the head of department and course planner, as well as Chris Circkmay and David Harding. The latter taught in Darlington from 1978 to 1985, where he could refine an art education model consistent with the principles of public and community art. All in all the course's biggest flaw consisted rather in its rural location, which in fact appeared to weaken the possibility of providing an explicitly context-addressed artistic curriculum, since it confronted the students with less opportunities and variety of situations as would have been the case in an urban setting (Caves, 2000, pp.33-35). However the countryside peace and quiet allowed this new art education approach to go through a trial stage, which would then soon be picked up across the nation. In the late Seventies, similar courses were launched at East London Polytechnic, Newcastle Polytechnic and Bradford College, while in the early Eighties comparable projects were founded in Glasgow, Wolverhampton, Sunderland, Exeter (in the form of student residency) and Birmingham, as well as in Cardiff, Canterbury, Wimbledon, Dundee and in London's St. Martins College as a master in public art. A similar path was followed at

Goldsmiths College, which was one of the most influent institutions in the British capital and where its Dean Jon Thompson had abolished the necessity for students to choose a specific discipline, hence leaving room to inter-curricular experiences. During the Eighties this transformation towards an open art education came to maturation in several colleges across the country, thus becoming a major factor of influence on the next generation of artists who were just entering art school.

4.2. A tale of two cities and their art schools: the 1980's art scene in London and Glasgow

UK Art education reforms throughout the Eighties hit on a country that had almost completely lost its relevant position in the international art system. London being Britain's prevailing centre hardly stood the competition against the New York-Cologne axis, which substantially ruled global art market at the time. Supported by the strong national economy and art institutional backbone, only German artists who had grown up in the Rhine area appeared to keep pace with United States superpower on the international art scene. The British pop-boom of the Sixties characterized by the worldwide success of UK visual artists and music groups seemed long over and forgotten. Great Britain's image in the Thatcher era was that of a wearily conservative country, where art novelties tended to be marginalized. All in all, the United Kingdom was no longer thought capable of producing something trendy or cool, as if this was simply alien to the national character. Grouped around the galleries located between Cork Street and Oxford Street, the heart of Britain's art system was still centred on London, but its outputs apparently matched the social and cultural expectations of the mere national elite, rather than trying to stand a chance against US and German competitors. According to Julian Stallbrass (2006a, pp.56-57), the local art market was mainly attracted by branded international artists, who were already highly appreciated abroad, while prevailing national production looked back to the past and was fairly narrow-minded. The galleries covering the primary market of the capital city usually preferred to bet on safe products, sometimes even mixing up with secondary market items. Firmly recognized dealers in the city were still focusing on 20th century great masters or on recent stars on the international scene, which are either branded artists or established trends that would presumably retain their value for decades (Thompson, 2008, pp.31-32). To give some examples, the Waddington Galleries sold Matisse and Picasso together with Patrick Caulifiled and Peter Blake, while Anthony

D'Offay exhibited works by Warhol and Beuys as well as the latest pieces by Anselm Kiefer and Gerhard Richter (Muir, 2011, pp.14-15). As a means to overcome the risk of uncertainty in the art market, London galleries in the Eighties rather expounded stardom strategy than investing in young artists. Considering the existence of information asymmetry for aesthetic goods, as proved by Gianfranco Mossetto (1993, pp.79-80), purchase decision of artworks is really about minimizing insecurity. Quality assurance provided by the cultural establishment works best, when artistic value appears to be unquestionable to everyone, which is the reason why celebrity status is a convenient strategy to be employed on the art market. As a matter of facts a star has reached this status once he or she is acknowledged as such by most art system players – or at least by the most influent ones – leaving little doubts around. Branding is the most efficient way the art market has to vouch for cultural appreciation of a specific author and justify the economic value of his or her artworks, possibly once and for all. Even though branding is considered a marketing strategy more suitable for widespread consumer goods, celebrity status in the art system works the same way by adding a recognizable surplus value which people are willing to pay for over a similar non branded item. The same stratagem doesn't work only for artists, but even for any other player of the art system such as dealers, museums, curators, collectors, auction houses, fairs and magazines. A branded private gallery, once it has acquired such status, can expect that any of the artists it picks up will likely be considered rising stars, if not celebrities yet: star artists go with established dealers which sell recognized high art (Thompson, 2008, pp.31-32). On the other hand, flattering superstars can lead to appreciation of artworks that are culturally questionable, but it is worth the risk, since successful branding is very difficult to oppose. As a matter of facts, in a system based on trust and self-validation, as in the case of the art world, it is difficult to question players who have achieved the status of opinion leaders or gatekeepers. However, star system and branding should not be regarded as a detrimental effect on visual arts caused by greedy 20th century capitalism, since both exist as a means to market artworks since the very existence of art. In times long past, an artist such as Tiziano Vecellio acquired a dominant position in the system thanks to Emperor Charles V's consideration and of many other monarchs of 16th century Europe, which legitimated the Venetian painter's preeminent status and the high prices of his works. Branding simply functions as a certification strategy to solve information asymmetry typical of trust goods, hence being a device for conferring meaning and relevance in order to create cultural and economic value (Mossetto, 1993, p.163). The choice of some London dealers to focus primarily on the great masters of early 20th century or on international celebrities depends therefore on the urge to exploit a favourable position. It is a safe move, though a very expensive one as well, to bet on the winning horse, when the race is already over. As a consequence the Eighties art scene in Britain was mainly inspired by a quite conservative type of neo-expressionist figurative technique, as in Frank Auerbach's and Lucien Freud's paintings or in Richard Long's and Hamish Fulton's sculptures. There were some exceptions of course, as for instance Tony Cragg, Julian Opie or Gilbert and George, but all in all British art was turned a deaf ear to the newest international trends. Stallabras (2006a, pp.56-59) maintains that the UK art system was entrapped in a sort of autism, as well as completely indifferent to anyone who did not belong to the cultural and political establishment, thus removing art from everyday life experience. Attending art school together with many future YBA celebrities, curator Gregor Muir would not mince words to describe the flatness of the London Eighties' art world in the eyes of an aspiring artist:

> *"But despite the blue-chip glamour of Cork Street, at the end of the day there was no escaping it. The London art world of the 1980s was fusty, parochial and dull. Artists and galleries were divided along lines of politics and class [...]. Snobbery was rife, with experimentation occurring in corners of the art world that could no longer support it, and amateurish conservatism flourishing in parts that could. In all of this there was little of a guiding light. Nor was it just the art world that was suffering; the whole nation was in the doldrums." (Muir, 2011, p.16)*

If the London art scene plodded on in the Eighties, holding relevance merely on a national level, Glasgow virtually lacked any sort of contemporary art system and stood its worst decade in a century from an economic point of view. The Scottish city is no metropolis, but the Strathclyde Region it belongs to has almost three million inhabitants, that is half the population of Scotland. It is a densely inhabited area, which boasts a simple and friendly mentality, typical of a provincial town. This district had enjoyed an imposing economical development in the first half of 20th century due to maritime trade and port facilities, above all, as well as thanks to a hefty industrialization. Despite its economic fortune, Glasgow hardly played an important role in Scottish culture staying a mere subordinate to Edinburgh. The only exception may be found in the first decades of the 20th century, when the city boasted Charles Rennie Mackintosh, a painter, architect and designer who was one of the most important British representatives of Art Nouveau. From World War I to the early Eighties nothing really changed in Glasgow's art scene, since artistic innovation and international trends apparently had not reached this very parochial Scottish town (Richardson, 2011, p.115). Furthermore, in the Seventies manufacturing activities took a rapid downturn, which caused progressive unemployment and consequent impoverishment of the area. Not much later industry collapsed almost completely without finding adequate balance in the development of the tertiary sector and leaving the West of Scotland in bitter need across the Eighties (MacInnes, 2010, p.75). The situation was worsened by Thatcher's liberal reforms, which caused extensive cuts in the public funding of the private sector and put an end to full employment policy. These measures crashed on Glasgow's fragile economic structure forcing numerous manufactures to close down, thus further increasing unemployment at a much higher rate than the national average of the time (Brodie, 2011, p.5). Thinking back, the *Scotland on Sunday* columnist Moira Jeffrey (2011a) considers it almost a miracle that at such a hopeless point the city could nourish a bunch of aspiring artists who in the following decade would succeed in permanently putting Glasgow on the chart of the international art system. Indeed, at the beginning of the Eighties, few people would have imagined that Glasgow could become a magnet for the international art system. Besides the dire economic situation, until the early Eighties Glasgow's art system lacked most of the features and institutions necessary to gain relevance beyond the city boarders and launch a few good artists on an international level. Virtually there were no important art facilities such as private dealers or a true artists community, while the few museums in town were extremely conservative and provincial (Fagen, 1999, p.86). The same applies to the local art school, which didn't have a good reputation at all, unable either to attract students from out of region or to catalyse the creation of a broad artists milieu. Edinburgh painter Alexander Moffat, who picked up teaching at Glasgow School of Art in 1979 to become a reference for young Glaswegian artists, recalls the situation at the institution for being stuck on traditional techniques, haunted by bad teachers and uncaring of pupils who were never requested to be creative neither exposed to international art trends:

> *"In the sixties and seventies Glasgow School of Art wasn't very good at all, and that's because the people who were teaching actually believed they could teach art." (Moffat in Jamieson, 2008, p.20)*

For all economic regression and cultural underdevelopment of the area, the city and its art school started a progressive transition to create the right conditions for Glasgow to emerge as a lively art centre. In the early Eighties, for the first time since very long, Glasgow School of Art attracted international consideration and the town was suddenly under the spotlights. The cause was the success of a rather disconnected group of young figurative painters who came to prominence under the unitary name *New Glasgow Boys* (Chapman, 2003). Steven Campbell, Ken Currie, Peter Howson and Adrian Wiszniewski – all graduates at Glasgow School of Art – were the four artists linked to this movement, although it cannot be considered a proper grouping. In fact, they had never really worked together nor was there a particular bond between them, they rather happened to have a common reference in art teacher Alexander Moffat and took advantage of the new realism upturn in Western art markets across the Eighties (Richardson, 2011, p.111). Moffat encouraged his students to pierce through important exhibition catalogues, to study the work of earlier German and Latin American painters involved with social issues such as George Grosz and Diego Rivera, as well as to attend important exhibitions in London and all over Continental Europe. He was also a mentor to them, helping to participate into exhibitions in relevant venues such as Fruitmarket Gallery in Edinburgh and later even Hayward Gallery in London. Moffat met on these four extremely focused young men who were eager to go abroad by strategically learning international trends on catalogues and magazines. Among the four, Steven Campbell was the most successful as he could read the changes under way on the art scene – being a revival of figurative painting – and exploit the ever-present Scottish keenness over traditional artistic values which were overtly promoted by its institutions. Due to his strategic mindset Campbell immediately decided to go to New York after winning a scholarship, believing his production would fit the new hail for painting. In fact, his understanding of the situation was correct and he soon found broad success in the US, his achievements giving confidence to Glasgow School of Art and fostering proudness over Scottish art (Jamieson, 2008, p.21). High on the heels of Campbell's international success came two very surprising exhibitions – *New Image: Glasgow* (1985) at the Third Eye Centre and the broader review on Scottish art at the Scottish National Gallery of Modern Arts (SNGMA) called *The Vigorous Imagination* (1987) – which together with the four New Glasgow Boys were being hailed in the media earning positive coverage. However, the comprehensive show at the SNGMA was somehow exemplifying what Scottish art was all about in that period. Craig Richardson maintains that *The Vigorous Imagination* demonstrated how national artists were just mimicking international trans-avant-garde, hence displaying a parody of established trends which merely relied upon Scotland's retrogressive attitude to figuration (Richardson , 2011, p.115). The New Glasgow Boys came to prominence due to Scotland's backwardness, which appeared to fit perfectly the necessary Zeitgeist of the international art scene (Lowndes, 2010, pp.81-82). According to Richardson, this unripeness was exactly what attracted international attention on Scottish art – to Campbell in particular, who exported a disingenuous display of Britishness matched with seedy, tweedy ruralism. Whatever the cultural interpretation of the New Image wave in Glasgow, as regards artistic strategies the New Glasgow Boys chose to go for upward trends, behaving as followers rather than trendsetters. The result was an immediate success, because they were able to get on a fast running train, but its journey didn't last long. As a matter of facts, figurative enthusiasm of the Eighties as represented by painters such as Julian Schnabel and Sandro Chia crashed at the same time as the Japanese bubble burst at the end of the decade. Led by financial speculation, the art market had fostered high prizes, which didn't stand the sudden breakdown of global economy (Benhamou, 2000, pp.69-71). The problem with following already branded trends is that it may prove a good strategy to score fast, though it often has a very short run and it is difficult to recover from its possible failure. True change in Scotland – and in Glasgow particularly – had yet to come and was rather dependent on a series of features that fully matured in this decade, revolving around Glasgow School of Art, but which belonged to a completely different set of values: on one hand the ferment created by the debate on public art, on the other hand UK art school reforms inspired by conceptual and process art (Richardson, 2011, p.121).

Even for London this appears to have been the case in the Eighties, since colleges were much more keen on experimenting with adopted novelties than public and private galleries, which favoured instead a type of conservative art with little regard for the latest developments on international scope. For young art students who tried to escape the parochial art scene of the capital there were just a few landmarks left which included the Anthony d'Offay Gallery, where Damien Hirst worked as a receptionist in his first art school year, and the Lisson Gallery owned by Nicholas Logsdail. Both counted amongst the most established dealers in town and were known since the late Sixties for their particular appreciation of conceptual art and minimalism. D'Offay had started his first premise in 1965 in a small flat in Piccadilly, while former Slade student Logsdail had started his gallery in 1967 in a run down building near Marylebone Station with the help of friends like film director Derek Jarman. Since then they have been associated with art trends that were considered on the edge of innovation and sophistication, rapidly rising to prominence as key figures in London's art milieu. By the Eighties they were well-established dealers housing international stars such as Gerhard Richter or home-grown celebrities like Julian Opie. Although art establishment tends to be generally conservative and retrospective, Lisson Gallery and d'Offay make it clear that dealers may try to pick up the newest waves in art and promote innovation, if they directly participate into it (Frey, 2000, p.15). However, the true exception to the local establishment was the Saatchi Gallery in the elegant Saint John's Wood borough, which occupied one of the first industrial buildings to be reconverted into an art facility. The place was actually all about the personality of tycoon Charles Saatchi, a man who had made a real fortune together with his brother in the field of advertising, furthermore having played a crucial role in the election campaign of Margaret Thatcher. Laying somewhere in-between a private collector and a determined art dealer, Saatchi was known for promoting the artists he liked and bought, while in the second half of the Eighties his gallery had become renown for exhibiting trendy and provocative American artists. A two part exhibition organized in 1987-1988 was called *NY Art Now* and presented the British audience and art establishment especially with the works of Jeff Koons, which had an incredible impact on a whole generation of art school students such as Damien Hirst himself and a lot of his college-mates (Bush, 2004). In their eyes the Saatchi Gallery represented all that the other dull British institutions could not even come close to: it was an enormous sophisticated space, suitable for sensational installations which were being created in the United States. Hirst still remembers the genuine shock effect provoked onto himself by these exhibitions at time:

> *"Saatchi was just there at the perfect point with a huge fucking space. [...] And then Saatchi did the New York Show. I remember walking in and going, >Hey, my eyes!< The whiteness of it! It just blew me away. And it was so not British. And that just totally inspired all the students. We wanted to show at the Saatchi Gallery immediately. And then we started making work really to fit in there. And that's when I realized we wouldn't fit into the art world the way it was. So I just went and got a warehouse, and we did that show." (Hirst in Haden Guest, 2008, p.155)*

By no surprise many aspiring artists suddenly hoped to attract Saatchi's attention, so for instance by deliberately trying to duplicate the tycoon's exhibition venue or by adapting to the style of the works he seemed to like (Stallabrass, 2006b, p.57). As a matter of facts, these were the explicit objectives of *Freeze*, the independent warehouse show for which Hirst gathered a dozen Goldsmiths students to debut in the summer of 1988. The direct influence of Saatchi's activities on young art students in the capital is confirmed by Gregor Muir, who was himself in art school at the time:

> *"It would be difficult to underestimate the impact of the Saatchi Gallery and its effect on all those who attended exhibitions such as NY Art Now [...]. The Saatchi Gallery was everything that the boring institutions were not. It provided an excellent space for the display of fresh talent while being such awesome that it literally took your breath away." (Muir, 2011, p.19)*

After his personal turnaround from neo-expressionist painting, selling off almost his entire collection of figurative painters such as Italian Sandro Chia, Saatchi opened up the London art world to the newest developments of the US scene. The art he displayed in his gallery revealed a direct association to mass media, together with a wholehearted opening to popular culture and a massif employment of everyday objects, which soon became some of the distinguishing traits of the newer British generation artists. However, these features must be delved into, for they typify a general attitude, taste and trend of the late 20th century art system. Scholars such as Paul Wood (1996), Julian Stallabrass (2006a), Joseph Koerner and Lisbet Rausing (1996) have strived to define the role, function and progress of contemporary art within mass society, capitalist system and consumerist culture. Their contribution to academic and critical debate revolves around the concepts of commodification, value and artistic drift, which appear to be the distinguishing features of late 20th century. The choice of terms directly hints at an interpretation of the art system stigmatizing its tight link to global economy, hence exposing the real assumptions and internal contradictions of contemporary art. Beyond doubt over the last three decades major museums and galleries around the world have truly adopted business strategies to position themselves in the art system. On the other hand, several industrial sectors have come to rely on structural intersections with high art, such as fashion and lifestyle industry. Meanwhile after the breakdown of the Soviet Union global barriers have dissolved in culture too, but often ensuing a kind of standardized amalgam rather than enhancing differences. According to these scholars, today's art system would be defined in its inner structure alongside the beliefs and methods of neoliberalism, which has shaped globalization (Stallabrass, 2006a, p.10). In order to understand this process, Wood starts from the earliest effects of free market on the art world and introduces the concept of commodity. Indeed, it is a very useful and central term to describe the advent of Fordism, the kind of production system that aims solely at the mass production of objects for the marketplace. Soon after involving economic thought and industrial development, this commodification process would have progressively contaminated other fields of society in the second half of the 20th century, hence including visual arts. However, the course of art commodification discloses a twofold aspect: on the one hand the incorporation of its production mechanisms in artistic creation, on the other hand the cultural reaction to its pervasiveness. As a matter of facts, the way art is produced and marketed has been commodified, since art must follow the rules of any commodity in the free market, but there has also been an ever growing number of artists concerned with commodities, as it is almost impossible for contemporaries not to reflect on the meaning of a commodified reality that appears to pervade human everyday experience (Wood, 1996, p.257). As regards to artworks, Marxist theory maintains that their commodification occurs when the relevance of an artist's creation shifts from its cultural and intrinsic value to its mere commercial value. Indeed, the concept of commodity is related to goods, which are produced for being exchanged on the marketplace, hence their value depending on a transaction between supply and demand rather than for being useful at all. Commodification reduces art to a state of reification – what Mark would define object fetishism – and artistic value would thus be determined only by trade disposition (Koerner and Rausing, 1996, pp.300-302). The historical context that bred art commodification coincides with the long economic boom that commenced after World War II and quickly recorded high rates of goods production as well as of its consumption. It would indeed appear impossible for artists to overlook the fact that Western world was being flooded by consumerist objects. Quite the opposite, art makers had to decide whether they should deliberately ignore or enthusiastically embrace capitalistic reality, whether criticize or celebrate it. In this perspective, the true driving force behind industrial production is consumerism, which ends up steering the preferences of the whole society. In addition comes the impact of mass media, which have definitively influenced the representation of contemporary reality, thus substituting one's empirical experience with a constructed set of values and necessities.

The beginning of massive art commodification truly characterized the Eighties, especially in the United States, so it can be observed that it constitutes the progressive framework into which aspiring artists started to act even in Great Britain for the period. Despite some isolated dealers and collectors such as D'Offay, Logsdail's and Saatchi who already picked up the new trends the art system was challenged with, however the London art market did not appear to offer great chances for aspiring artists. Nevertheless, due to the education boom time which transformed British universities, the various colleges and art schools of the capital were crowded as never before with students hoping for a career in the visual arts, amongst them especially young women and many working class children who quickly represented the true backbone of the last generation artists (Muir, 2011, p.77). Those who pursued an art education were spoilt for choice in London where numerous institutions offered comprehensive courses, but prospective students were well aware of the quality and reputation each school was renown for. Among the best known and favoured ones in the city were the Royal Academy, the Slade School of Fine Art at the University College of London, St. Martin's School of Art, as well as two more in the South of London being Goldsmiths College at the University of London and Camberwell College of Arts. To name some example of perceived reputation, the Royal Academy was considered a very conservative and rigid institution, although being one of the most representative (Stallabrass, 2006a, p.7). Camberwell College instead was known for the vivid social life among students offering brilliant Friday parties, which resolved to be wonderful opportunities to make acquaintance with other aspiring artists and some more established ones. Although very snob and much to close to London gallery tastes, Goldsmiths was regarded as being edgy and definitely possessed a strong image having abolished the partition among different art disciplines thanks to its illuminated Dean and former abstract painter Jon Thompson. In fact, students were encouraged to take up a creative course moving freely around the different techniques available, while given a detailed knowledge of the art system and its mechanisms. This school didn't even request the ability to paint or draw, because no one was expected to become an artist, but could eventually decide to become a curator, critic, journalist or an art business professional such as future dealer Gavin Brown. Goldsmiths educational context certainly influenced its students – among whom were most of the early YBA stars such as Damien Hirst, Tracey Emin, Sarah Lucas, Gary Hume and many more – but some teachers in particular had a deep impact on the prospective artists. Richard Wentworth counted among the best known, but a true inspiration to students was charismatic Michael Craig-Martin, an Irish conceptual artist who looked up to the most recent progresses in the United States, where he was brought up and graduated at Yale University. The Irish teacher encouraged his students to tackle everyday life aspects and objects, particularly applying strategies that would impress visual morality and challenge social acceptance. At the time he was concentrating on painting, but among his students he was still famous for his engagement in the conceptual art scene of the previous decade. The piece Craig-Martin was particularly famous for is *An Oak Tree* (1973), which might be defined as a harsh conceptual sculpture consisting only of a glass of water put on a glass shelf high above on the white gallery wall. The work's first display in 1974 at Rowan Gallery in Bond Street remains a major event for London conceptualism challenging the viewer's belief in art and highlighting the necessity of trust for the identification of artworks. In the artists own words:

> *"[...] belief underlies our whole experience of art: it accounts for why some people are artists and others are not, why some people dismiss works of art others highly praise, and why something we know to be great does not always move us." (Craig-Martin in Muir, 2011, p.19)*

Damian Hirst himself declared once he believed *An Oak Tree* to be the greatest piece of conceptual sculpture ever, but it was particularly the attitude Craig-Martin revealed beyond such artworks the illuminated his pupils. His dedication to art, professional seriousness, personal connections, successful career and abiding faith in pushing individual abilities were a constant stimulus for receptive students such as Hume, who tried to emulate Craig-Martin as a painter, or Hirst, who was instead fascinated by the capacity to declare the art status of a piece (Cooper, 2012, p.20). For his part, the art teacher on working with these students was convinced he had encountered the most talented and determined artist candidates he had ever met, hence he pushed them to get ideas out of art school and stood by every time they tried to do this.

David Harding, whose arrival in Glasgow during the Eighties marked a crucial event in view of the city's artistic development, played a similar pivotal role as Michael Craig-Martin's at Goldsmiths. The Edinburgh born art teacher proved a fundamental player for the renewal of Glasgow School of Art and indeed helped creating a group of exceptional young people that fostered a thriving artist community of international relevance in town. Arriving in 1984, among his students were most of Glasgow's future protagonists such as Roderick Buchanan, Craig Richardson, Louise Scullion, Ross Sinclair and Claire Barcley, two Turner Prize finalists, Nathan Coley and Christine Borland, and even two winners, Douglas Gordon and Martin Boyce. The activities he promoted, but even more his particular art vision, were crucial for turning the art institution around and supporting the evolution of the city into a dynamic and productive centre open to the global art system. Harding's human energy and captivating appeal, not to mention his stout appearance and the Che Guevara shaved beard, possessed a true gravitational pull which was hard to resist, as recalled by several alumni of Glasgow School of Art such as David Bellingham and Ross Sinclair:

> *"You know, it's a lesson in a way that came about directly, or was drawn to my attention directly from being here and studying in Glasgow I mean we have David Harding's line of 'the context is half the work' which no-one who has studied at Glasgow School of Art in the [80s ans] 90s could avoid and was so clear [...]" (Bellingham in Bellingham and Sinclair, 2007)*

As a student Harding attended the local art school in Edinburgh during the early Sixties and after graduation moved to Nigeria, where he lived from 1963 to 1967, whilst his involvement in the field of education drove him to understand the relevance of context for creating meaningful art. African art schools were used to teach young Nigerian pupils to sculpt works in a Marino-Marini-like style, so Harding encouraged his students to draw their inspiration from their home experience purged of European institutional influences. When he got back to Scotland, Harding contacted different city councils proposing to share his art skills and expertise for the town's aesthetic and social improvement. His intention was to breach the pretentious aura enshrouding the contemporary artist role model, recovering instead the crafts-work-dimension of his job, considering artists as part of the workforce endeavoring to enhance society and everyday life. In 1968 he was effectively employed in the Glenrothes' Planning Department, one of the so-called new towns in the shire of Fife, where he stayed for a decade working in architectural and urban advancement by means of the involvement of local residents. In such capacity he promoted a long and varied series of activities very close to public and community art procedures, which revolved around the participation of both young and adult population in art projects, which aimed at making the town distinguished. Due to his position as town-artist, in this period he came in touch with conceptual and wider environmental art considerations, especially thanks to the influence of the Artist Placement Group and soon absorbing Latham's vision that context represents half of an artwork's meaning (Richardson, 2011, p.82). During this period, Harding started to question the features of community and public art in Scotland, resolving that it needed to be not mere decoration, but something much more fundamental for people, capable of touching their inner feelings. For this reason he moved towards context-specific practices that would resort to any possible medium, being accessible to artists whatever their formal training. At the end of his experience in Glenrothes, he entered Darlington School of Art as a teacher of the newly founded course *Art and Social Context*. His practice as a public artist was soon a crucial feature of the curriculum reform carried out in the art school, imparting a very pragmatic tendency to its teaching methods (Crickmay, 2003). In an essay on public art evolution in Scotland, Harding is very clear about inspiration and goals of his working philosophy which matured in the course of his career before making landfall at Glasgow School of Art:

> *"My own concern for the importance of the context in art making developed from working in Nigeria between 1963-67. [...] On my return to Scotland in 1967 I wrote to towns suggesting they might employ me as an artist. [...] My intentions were to try to demystify the artist and to emphasise the notion of the artist as artisan and as part of the workforce building the town." (Harding, 1995)*

Back to Scotland, in 1985 Harding was officially appointed Head of the newborn Environmental Art Department at Glasgow School of Art. As opposed to the traditional disciplines such as painting, sculpture, printing and photography, the new department was not focussed on a particular medium, but rather open to experimentation requiring consideration of the context of an artwork (Higgins, 2011a). Following Letham's vision, Harding wanted his students to practise different languages, but foremost to understand the symbols proper of the places an artist intends to interact with. Indeed, Christine Borland sums up the basic philosophy of the department, that significantly is the same maxim of the Artist Placement Group and which did effectively stay in all Harding's early students:

> *"The ethos of the department was that the context is half the work - an idea which is ingrained in my work." (Gordon in Spector, 1997, p.82)*

The new department's core idea was the suspension of any difference between art institutions and the external world, because art was indeed to be considered as any other occupation. The students were discouraged from shutting themselves up in a studio and instead convinced they were absolute normal people, hence fostering their relationship to the surrounding society. It is notable that Douglas Gordon didn't possess a proper studio until very late in his career, roughly up to his recent relocation to Berlin in 2008. Harding exhorted students to make pieces for unconventional venues, so that they learnt to recognize the correct artistic strategy in relation to a peculiar context: if some ideas could seem good ones, if applied to museums and galleries, they may not work in alternative spaces – or the other way round. The art teacher introduced idea-based art to students that had no clue about Marcel Duchamp and Allan Kaprow, but who had never even seen a real piece by Andy Warhol or Claes Oldenburg if not as a reproduction in books. Together with Borland, Richardson and Buchanan, Gordon enrolled in the first year of the department's existence and in conversation with Nancy Spector still recalls its guidelines:

> *"I was a student in the so-called Environmental Department at Glasgow School of Art, between '85 an '88. There was a group of artists who thought that there was no difference between the art school and the rest of the city. It didn't matter who you were or what you did in life; art was a job like any other. The ethos of the department was that the context is 50 per cent of the work: it meant that we had to think about and respond to the various languages, vocabulary, and signs in the places wherever we wanted to make our work. If we wanted to do things in galleries, then we could probably work best by recognizing what the language was and trying to use it. If we wanted to work in the street, then we had to recognize what kind of street it was, who the users were, and identify their language to see if there was a way to communicate." (Gordon in Spector, 1997, p.82)*

Following the unofficial motto that "context is half the work", Harding actually transferred to Glasgow all that he had experimented at Darlington College and tried to introduce an interdisciplinary principle that corresponded with the seminal transformations in the art world internationally (Lowndes, 2010, pp.86-87). He found full support of Sam Ainsley, another teacher who worked full time in the new department for its first five years. She had the crucial role of helping students and teachers to interact and socialize, so that a very compact group form around Harding's ideas. One of the distinctive features of the Environmental Art Department was the genuine friendship that bonded students with teachers, which soon became such a strong relationship the new students looked forward to as a sort of ritual. This deep connection among the department's community was not at all planned, but simply a by-product caused by different circumstances dependent on the first cohort of students. Indeed, teachers and students first of all shared the keenness for amusement, as they liked to spend time together talking, partying, singing and getting drunk in the city's pubs. Such activities truly contributed to create an adamantine bond between students and teaching staff, which has lasted to the present time as David Harding recalls:

> *"We partied a lot. Drank a lot. And with people like Douglas [Gordon], Martin [Boyce], Nathan [Coley], I'd go to their weddings, their children's christenings, birthday parties, and still do." (Harding in Higgins, 2011a)*

Another reason for socializing was the small number of the first students' cohort, which in Harding's opinion conveniently matched with the teachers' requirement to work full time at the department due to recent reforms in higher education prompted by the Thatcher government:

> *"I do regard this as an important contributing factor in that a small group of staff works with the same group of students for three years. We get to know each other well. We also, from time to time, get drunk together, party and travel together. That certainly was the feature of the Environmental Art Dept, at Glasgow. Socialising came to be seen as an important part of the education and became an expectation, a tradition of the department."* (Harding, 2001a)

Finally a significant feature was also the new department location, which was set apart of the central establishment of Glasgow School of Art, since there was no more room inside the well known building designed by Mackintosh in the city's heart. Hence, until 1994 the Environmental Art Department was housed far away on the abandoned premises of a former Victorian school on the top of a hill near central Glasgow. The so-called Girls High School was a perfect spot to experiment with environmental installations and interdisciplinary performances, as the students soon burst into the off-limit areas of the decaying building to get hold of new reusable space and objects. What is more, secluded from the main school, this location created a sort of department identity which convinced new course members of being different, which again for Harding helped them to got really close:

> *"It was an amazing place. There were basements with 50 children's sinks in them, history books lying around in piles. There were attics, strange, devious, different rooms. An Escher-like staircase. One half of the school was locked off and forbidden. Of course, the students broke in." (Harding in Higgins, 2011a)*

In the Environmental Art Department there was a strong cooperative spirit as well as a network of relations between students and teachers, marked by the belief in reciprocal support and help. This atmosphere soon spread beyond the limits of the old Girls' High School and permeated the Scottish city, which revealed itself to be truly vital for Glasgow, at a time when the local contemporary art scene was neither privately nor publicly supported. In this special context, far from market pressures, the members of the Environmental Art Department were able to find different incentives and ambitions, presenting city with an appropriate response to its peculiar situation. Emphasis was never placed on producing objects or items that had to be sold, but rather on art as breeding ground of ideas, as a project catalyser that should involve and interact with society (Lowndes, 2010, p.88). The driving force behind this new approach wasn't just Harding's persona, but the group of young students who attended the department and grew into a cohesive, supportive party used to interacting and helping one another, well aware that they would not find support elsewhere, as stressed by Gordon himself:

> *"The culture of discussion and mutual support is carried on outside of the education establishment and into the art centres, galleries and so on. Besides, it's in everyone's best interest to support each other because it's not going to come from anywhere else." (Gordon in Van Assche, 1995, p.81)*

The first wave of graduates from Harding's department indeed created a stable network among local artists, which after leaving art school was mainly transferred to the Transmission Gallery. Founded back in 1983, it was the city's first ever artist-run space, which had the goal of drawing international attention to Glasgow and promoting contemporary art into community life. In the Eighties the gallery was organized by the Committee for the Visual Arts, a group of artists that gave birth to some heavily politicized shows and marked the predominance of New Image style throughout Glaswegian artists, involving directly painters such as Peter Howson, Adrian Wiszniewski and Ken Currie. By the late Eighties, the first graduates of the Environmental Art Department had breached through and soon took over the gallery. Transmission thus became the cradle of the city's conversion into an ubiquitous art district, but this development was successful also due to the funding Glasgow was awarded as European Culture Capital for the year 1990. The environmental art group was crucial for enhancing the role of Glasgow School of Art, since at the time most people involved in the in the city's artistic life belonged to the school or were somehow related to it, whereas many of the Harding graduates proved particularly ebullient. Gordon himself is aware of the relevance that Glasgow School of Art had on the city's cultural explosion and described the artistic milieu of his hometown in similar terms:

> *"Most of the artists in Glasgow, and the organisers and administrators, have some connection with the School of Art; either as former students or in some capacity as teachers or visitors. This means that the educational environment plays a huge role in the art activity of the city." (Gordon in Van Assche, 1995, p.81)*

Other former students such as Ross Sinclair e David Bellingham, for instance, confirm further this aspect explaining the complexity and framework of the city's artistic situation:

> *"[...] if you look at an institution like the Glasgow School of Art there are things that happen officially; there's a hierarchy, there's a directorship, there's courses and there's head of courses [...] and there's this body of people who pass through it, the student body, and then there's this body of people that decide to stay in town [...] and there's this kind of floating body of the population in and around the environment of Glasgow School of Art that have an affiliation with the school but aren't the school." (Sinclair in Bellingham and Sinclair, 2007)*

In the early Nineties the educational situation that had matured in the previous decade influenced the city's art events in a decisive way, finding Glasgow Art School graduates who managed exhibition centres and galleries as well as workshops that opened in various districts of the Scottish city. The changes brought about by David Harding's Environmental Art Department were amongst the most relevant in promoting the development of a widespread young, innovative art scene, which was able to focus the art world's interest on Glasgow.

By the late Eighties, recession had hit hard on overall British economy because of the Japanese bubble burst in 1989 and terribly affected the London art world. It abated the number of galleries and caused a general impoverishment in art, owing to the reduced funding and the decrease of collectors' willingness to purchase artworks. This caused a crash of quotations for a lot of well known artist, so that the main effect was for the British art market to hibernate, slowly turning away from the work of expensive international stars to young local talents (Stallabrass, 2006b, p.5).

In Glasgow its effects were less detrimental as there had never been a proper art system, but somehow recession had affected London to a point that its situation was comparable to that of other British city's: from an artistic point of view, almost everything had to be built anew. At the beginning of the Nineties, the different art market players started to devise possible survival strategies. On the one hand dealers and collectors stopped to trade expansive international artists' works keeping an eye on much cheaper young locals. On the other hand some freshly graduate students from London art schools, as well as in secluded Glasgow, understood they could succeed only forming collectives and giving a try to group self-promotion (Muir, 2011, p.28). Some young artists started acting as self-entrepreneurs and organizing exhibitions, which were refined and glamorous enough to compete with the most appreciated international venues. The press has often attached this resourceful spirit to neoliberal ideas prompted by Thatcher rule over Great Britain, however these strategies which were employed by emerging artists should rather be considered last resorts conceived to break the art market stalemate and bypass the rigid access barriers set by the cultural establishment. As a matter of facts, the main private galleries and great public institutions were quite slow to acknowledge the contribution of the newer generation artists, which made the action of those who trusted the work of these young artists more important than ever. According to Stallabrass, recent events of British art would demonstrate the bond between art and economy, which goes far beyond consumerism grounding stylistic choices and art trends on the evolution of economic cycles. In a short reconstruction of the last two decades of the 20th century, the art historian highlights that economic growth usually fosters artists that flatter the capitalistic system, since investors are keen on buying what celebrates their power condition. On the contrary, recession tends to narrow the selection of artists leaving many behind, but on the other hand it offers new and independent room for those authors who overtly criticize capitalism or want to offer an alternative (Stallabrass, 2006a, pp.14-15). Focusing on the end of the last century Stallabrass observes two major phases of economic expansion, which were both immediately followed by a pervasive crisis. The long boom of the Eighties was caused by a combination of growth in the tertiary sector and extensive liberalization policies, but crashed in 1989 owing to the Japanese bubble burst. The recovery in the Nineties was driven on financial markets by a zest for new technologies, which on their part deflated with the crack of the information technology stock market at the turn of the century. Michael Craig-Martin confirms the dire prospect young art graduates were confronted with at the end of the Eighties:

> *"In a country that had few contemporary galleries and even fewer collectors, generations of young artists had survived through art-school teaching, the dole, various enterprise schemes, odd jobs. By the end of Margaret Thatcher's reign, these options had more or less dried up." (Craig-Martin, 2012, pp.38-39)*

If Thatcher deregulation had compelled great museums to find private sponsors to survive, there was no reason why artists themselves shouldn't ask to be founded to organize their shows. The key to promoting their production was organizing exhibitions in unusual spaces, such as deserted buildings or vacated offices. Among the first of many was *Freeze*, organized by a group of Goldsmiths students, which resulted in an important event that helped artists to understand they could bypass traditional establishments. Furthermore, recession made it easier to find facilities, as the crush of real estate market had caused a lot of spaces to be available at a very good price, if not for free. In the Nineties it was possible to rent big deserted buildings in the city centre without spending too much money, which in turn could be used instead to print a trendy catalogue, send out invitations and mount installations. A boom of collective temporary exhibitions in *do-it-yourself* style marked the late Eighties and early Nineties, which contributed to enliven London art world dramatically, despite the severe recession. These events were nothing more or less than attempts to endure the bleak situation, authentic survival strategies conceived for the difficult economical conditions to help young artists to start a career by their own means (Stallabrass, 2006b, p.55). Thus London and Glasgow had completely different backgrounds and art systems, which aspiring artists were well aware of, but at the turn of the decade the circumstances young art school graduates were confronted with appeared absolutely comparable.

4.3. Training, but trying already: of environmental art, *Freeze* and early mischief

In 1984 seventeen-year-old Douglas enrolled at Glasgow School of Art, as he was convinced at that point he wanted a career in the field of art. At first he did not find the courses particularly exciting, because the beginners' classes for the primary year were crowded collective lessons, undifferentiated for all students and aiming at giving some basic information about traditional art techniques. It is important to stress that Gordon's reaction wasn't out of the ordinary, since most students who finally ended up in David Harding's newborn institute felt the inadequacy and averageness of teaching topics and methods at Glasgow School of Art. As a matter of facts, the Environmental Art Department had not been founded yet and came as a welcome novelty for those students who were not satisfied with conventional art education. Christine Borland confirms this feeling for she had entered the school of art into the Mural and Stained-Glass Department, which looked at least to her parents as if she would learn a specific skill (Bredin, 1997). However a year after enrolment to her surprise this unreconstructed department was converted into the more trendy-sounding Environmental Art:

> *"The friends that I still have from that generation, Roddy Buchanan, Ross [Sinclair, Borland's partner], Douglas [Gordon], Craig Richardson and all of these people – they were actually in the year below me, so for a year and a half at college before I got to know them, I sort of thought art school was rubbish! Until they came into the department, and that was a big defining moment." (Borland in Black, 2006)*

During his introductory year Gordon became aware that the media applied in conventional art practice appeared inadequate for his objectives, since he felt to be surrounded by a world full of sounds, images and commodities produced for everyday use which the traditional means could hardly capture. Though very young, he already had the firm belief these sensations, media and issues should be dealt with in what he himself intended to present as art. Seeing no reason to stop at traditional techniques or at the most common subjects of artistic debate, Gordon believes his unrest was a distinctive trait of his development as an artist:

> *"You know, we live in a world that is not silent. Sometimes this seems like a tyranny, I admit, but this is phenomenal that every moment of every day is filled with sounds, visuals, and smells that have been processed for our consumption. My generation is naturally (if not consciously) literate in the vocabularies of technologies that only 50 years ago would have seemed impenetrable to most people. [...] It comes quite naturally to incorporate these media and techniques into whatever it is that we want to present and call it art." (Gordon in Van Assche, 1995, pp.78-79)*

At the end of the first year for summer vacation Gordon travelled extensively in Italy with a few new Glasgow School of Art acquaintances, peers who would later become dear friends and form the core of the group who grew inside the new Environmental Art Department. He set on the journey by chance, reading a notice on the school board posted by some students attending the same classes. They invited anyone who was interested in visiting Italy to join them, hence young Douglas left for the Mediterranean country with a small party, which included Roderick Buchanan e Iain Kettles (*Desire Lines*, Cat.2009). As backpackers with an inter-rail ticket the group travelled all across Italy, in order to see the great Masters of both past and contemporary art, among the latter especially the ones of Arte Povera[2]. The three young students grew close friends and on their return they all decided to attend the new Environmental Art Department. The artist remembers with relish the three years spent at Harding's department and believes they were absolutely crucial for his artistic growth. Indeed, his particular awareness to context and specific capability to respond to metaphorical significance or aesthetic peculiarities can be credited to this period (Brown, 2004, p.11). What was taught at the old Girls' High School was creative freedom, though inscribed within the basic philosophy that context is half the work. As a matter of facts, this kind of responsiveness to the relevance of an artwork's framework and circumstances is deeply rooted in all students who attended the Environmental Art Department in those years (Bellingham and Sinclair, 2007). Gordon himself still recalls the relevance of his years at the Environmental Art Department:

> *"In my art education in Glasgow [...] we were given free reins to do almost anything under the basic philosophy that' context is 50 percent of the work'. [...] it was a good environment to work within and I think that the philosophy has stayed with me, to some extent. As long as one can understand the context in which one is working then there is no reason why an artist needs to limit his/her self to the confines of traditional media or traditional subjects for discussion." (Gordon in Van Assche, 1995, p.78)*

The department situation was quite special: an area of relative freedom from space and time, where life and work were kept together. Under the direction of Harding, the young students transformed everyday problems into artistic matters, as it is still apparent in their production. A case in point is Ross Sinclair, today the partner of Christine Borland, who has made the words 'Real Life' the autograph mark of many of his works, which appears to be converge with Gordon's opinion:

> *"There's no big difference between time spent 'working' and time spent 'living'. So, all problems in life are also problems in art." (Gordon in Van Assche, 1995, p.80)*

The course had been planned to focus on the artist's need to have a precise procedure in order to provide meaningful artworks for society. The students were instructed to interact with the context they intended to work in, developing relations with the place and people who would benefit from the piece. Harding taught his students that the cornerstones of a social strategy were on one hand the planning of a work, establishing a connection with its perspective venue, on the other hand exploring one's own personality, simply applying common knowledge of people belonging to a specific environment (Sheikh, 1997, p.17). As a matter of facts Gordon remembers how, at twenty years of age, his own personal and family life story was his only source of inspiration, as if self analysis and self knowledge were his fundamental necessities at that stage. In the years he spent in the Environmental Art Department, the artist says he experienced an autobiographical frenzy that compelled him to build on aspects of his past, as well as of his social and religious background. Living and working together with fellow students who all felt like outcasts added constant questioning of one's own identity, as well as lively debate on edgy art issues, as Christine Borland recalls:

> *"It was a place [the Environmental Art Department] where people who didn't fit in ended up, so there was lots of discussion, film projects and installation. It was a really live, fantastic place!" (Borland in Fortnum, 2007, p.9)*

The first group of students at the Old Girls' High was capable of seizing the local context in an exceptionally proficient way, possibly because most of them came from the Strathclyde region, an occurrence which allowed them to identify with their milieu and enhanced their sense of belonging. However, such a localized situation could have caused some degree of narrow-mindedness that was luckily avoided thanks to the strong awareness these students had as regards the latest progresses of contemporary art. David Harding and his colleagues soon realized that those young men and women had knowingly chosen to reject traditional techniques and to explore new domains, which would relate them with art language at an international level:

> *"I do not know how all this came about, but the dominant forces in these early groups of students were well aware of contemporary art*

> *practice and had all already, at the age of 18 or so, rejected the other traditional disciplines of the School of Fine Art, Painting, Photography, Printmaking and Sculpture. This was an informed political gesture repudiating what they perceived as the limitations of such art forms. They did not want to be bound to a single medium [...]." (Harding, 2001a)*

Such a firm stance on contemporary trends is confirmed in many statements of some Environmental Art Department graduates already in the early Nineties. A convincing instance is an interview on the then newborn London review *Frieze*, published in September 1991, on occasion of a European-wide group exhibition called *Windfall 91* and organized by Nathan Coley, Martin Boyce and Gordon himself. In the talk with interviewer Matthew Slotover the three emerging artists – all to be on the Turner Prize shortlist one day – defined the New Glasgow Boys of the previous decade as worthless painters, who had failed to grasp the changes in the new artistic languages and media:

> *"People also ask us if we were reacting against artists like Stephen Campbell and Adrian Wiszniewski, who were prominent when we were at school. But really, nobody could be bothered. They were so far away from what we were trying to do, we didn't use them as a reference point at all. They were just a tiny, unimportant part of the international art world." (Gordon in Slotover, 1991)*

In a long interview with Graham Fagen, Douglas Gordon gives very sound reasons for his choice to conform to an international language of art, instead of being bound inside the limited Scottish views and habits. Comparing the function of style in the art system to the function of currency on the market he explains:

> *"It's a simple analogy, but it's like trying to identify the common currency for people, you're travelling through the world, making art, you are showing it to different people, if you're just a professional traveller, what's the currency you want to travel with? [...] Being Scottish we get this all the time, we try an pass off a Scottish pound note, and people won't accept it, because that's not the common currency." (Gordon in Fagen, 1999, p.111)*

This was the spirit common to the young students of the Environmental Art Department, that is to acquire an international language which could be applied to articulate problems – tough sometimes local ones – becoming meaningful and presentable. Christine Borland is also sure about the awareness they had at the time in adopting such references:

> *"I'd say that most of my friends or artists I hung around with were also working like this. I suppose earlier on we used the language of conceptual art an minimalism more self consciously. Often I was dealing with complex issues with different ethical dimensions but I wanted the presentation to be simple, so I also borrowed from the formal language of minimalism or conceptual art, although the basis of the work was more politicised."* (Borland in Fortnum, 2012, p.11)

Most of the students in Harding's department were children of Glasgow working class, hence they had grown up in circumstances with neither value for rareness or beauty nor did they consider objects as fetish, since the prevailing items to be found in their households were rather functional appliances. On the contrary, the ethics deriving from their social background included the importance of human relationships and preserving a sense of belonging. The lack of fetishism is a very important aspect to be taken into account, as it may explain to a point at least these students' common drive to ephemeral works or, in any case, to succeed in focusing their creative process on ideas as requested by the department ethos. Douglas Gordon's words on this topic are unmistakable:

> *"I didn't grow up in a house full of artworks. I come from a household with functional objects like a kettle or a toaster. We owned no antiques. I never thought about the value or status of an object as object."* (Gordon in Van den Boogard, 1997, pp.40-41)

At the Environmental Art Department Harding's artistic belief, as well as his teaching methods favourably blended with the student's social background and personal disposition. Hence these young men and women were imparted with a procedure they could apply to their individual investigation, rather than pretending to be taught a specific style or language. In their years in the environmental art course they experimented and experienced strategies useful to respond to a specific context and create an effective interaction with the intended audience. Social intervention and deep involvement were indeed two key elements that Borland still keeps in mind, like many of her peers:

> *"People just went out and did things, either in public situations or sit specifically. On the Environmental Art course, we had a project*

> *every year where you had to realise an ephemeral piece outside the art school. You had to negotiate how to do that and it became a modus operandi. You can't do that without getting engaged with people." (Borland in Fortnum, 2007, p.11)*

Harding's students were thus constantly encouraged to name new ideas or plan projects with a certain amount of complexity. He taught them to interact with a perspective public, to practice storytelling and even to sing. When asked in 1995 by the curators of Amsterdam Stedelijk Museum what he had acquired at Glasgow School of Art, Gordon indeed answered he had learnt to sing. On the contrary, producing objects was never the aim of the environmental art course, but a mere possible outcome, though at times even an unnecessary one. This ephemeral approach to art has deeply influenced Gordon and his colleagues, both in the understanding of artistic creation as well as in its practical realization, as he once expressed to Hans Ulrich Obrist:

> *"As I don't collect art I make art. And as a maker of it, it's the ideas which are important. I know I don't really care about the objects." (Gordon in Obrist, 1996b, p.169)*

Despite the woeful imbalance among teachers, another major issue in the department were gender topics due to the strong presence of Sam Ainsley, who would have several women artists over for workshops and conferences about sexuality and body politics which were attended both by male and female students (Lowndes, 2010, p.102). The discussions that came about had a great meaning for Borland who could find a direct reference to question her role as a woman artist and draw some inspiration from early feminist aesthetics of the Seventies (Borland in Fortnum, 2007, p.10). At first her pieces were sculptural and looked at the production of Judy Chicago or Georgia O'Keeffe, but later she moved over to environmental installations that tried to deal with the female body in its absence. For a female art student in the Eighties, gender was unquestionably a defining feature, since women artists were finally starting to gain some recognition after the feminist movements of the previous decade had raised the question of equality (Vettese, 1998, p.103). Without asking for permission, women were experiencing open credibility and success by looking beyond the art world and leaving male artists alone, such as in the case of Roni Horn. Most noisily during the early Eighties, a generation of photographers like Cindy Sherman, Barbara Kruger, Laurie Simmons and Sherrie Levine turned the camera into a consciousness-raising tool (Smith, 1992, p.2939).

In this decade there were lots of examples for young female students to look up to, but especially in Glasgow the situation was still dominated by men and many female cultural workers in the city felt to be under-represented. For this particular reason Adele Patrick, one of the first female graduates at Glasgow School of Art, called an open meeting in the late Eighties dubbed *Women in Profile* which claimed representation for female artists and developed the idea to replicate Judy Chicago's Womanhouse community. This ferment in and around the art school proved crucial to overcome the widespread sexist attitude of the local art scene, which reached its peak with the success of the New Glasgow Boys and was epitomized in 1995 by broadcaster Muriel Gray:

> *"There was always this real macho attitude at GSA [...]. There was this idea that the real artists were the guys from the shipyard." (Gray in Lowndes, 2010, p.102)*

The Environmental Art Department was rather different from the rest of the school even in this respect, with both male and female students involved in gender issues. This derived from a general openness that brought about a human fellowship among the group of young aspiring artists at the Old Girl's High, even before establishing a true artistic cooperative which later resulted in the formation of the Transmission gallery committee. During their study years the students spent most time of the day together, thriving on in the guise of a small community based on values such as communication, discussion and reciprocal support. The ability to communicate was considered pivotal for art to make things meaningful, while the communal spirit and group solidarity were the basis on which each member could develop his or her activities in difficult geographical circumstances (Debbaut, 1998, p.117). The special relationship among the environmental art peers turned into a solid network of connections, their friendship bounding them together like a family, which offers reciprocal appraisal and support, sometimes even love such as between Gordon and Borland. Dubbed as "Scotia Nostra" by Douglas Gordon, this generation of artists resisted the uneasy path of art education and then starting an international career by means of a continuing sense of community, which led them to enjoy global recognition. As most members of this grouping, Borland is very upright about the importance of this union for her individual success, being the only true resource in a city with small dealers and little art facilities:

> *"I attribute that to being part of a really special and supportive group of friends and artists who are working in Glasgow, and to*

> *having a network of support that didn't necessarily rely on institutions or structures or commercial galleries – it just relied on people, peer groups, and a lot of support, a lot of friendship, and a lot of really good artists keeping each other going. It wasn't that we were going into a private gallery structure, nothing like that." (Borland in Barclay Morgan, 1999)*

Some of the students might have found public appraisal sooner than others, as happened with Gordon and Borland, but they were always to help their friends who were still thriving to draw attention. Nathan Coley has summed up the essence of this aspect:

> *"[...] if a curator comes to Glasgow to see you, there's an unwritten rule that you introduce them to someone else, too." (Coley in Higgins, 2011a)*

During the three years he spent at the Old Girls' High, Gordon definitely stood out among other students as one of the most impassioned minds, being addressed towards producing ideas for people rather than tangible objects. In fact, in this period a primary feature of his creations appeared to be a propensity to establish a relationship with the public – or better, with the people around him, since he considered artists to be part of their own audience, hence acting on the same level of the public. In his opinion, art's final aim is to set about an interaction to transmit sensations, to rekindle common memories, to arouse thoughts or to find a pretext for having a conversation. It appears to be significant that this attitude is shared also by other of his peers such as Ross Sinclair, thus deriving probably from the educational background at the Environmental Art Department:

> *"I want my art to be like meeting someone new in a bar, and they might be from a whole different situation and culture but surely you have all these things in common, shared histories you never shared with anyone before. Sure you won't agree about everything but that's what makes life interesting. I guess it's called conversation." (Sinclair in Lowndes, 2010, pp.162-63)*

Considering this strain of thought, it appears no surprise that Gordon's very first works, created while still a student at the Environmental Art Department, consisted principally in durational performances often on cooperative basis together with some course peers[3]. From 1987 onwards, and until the end of his training period between Glasgow and London, the artist worked with Craig Richardson, Roderick Buchanan and Euan

Sutherland. Some of these performances allowed them to take part in important art events before they even completed their courses, chiefly at Transmission gallery or at the Third Eye Centre. The main partnership was with Richardson, together they started a series of performances in their last years at Glasgow School of Art which showed a definite procedural influence due to environmental art examples. Their pieces usually consisted in collections of objects, found items, sounds, sensations and minimal movements, obsessively repeated in a circumscribed space to arouse memories or nostalgia (Bain, 1987). The actions of the two young artists consisted, for instance, in sorting out loads of clothes, peeling hard boiled eggs, circling newspapers piles, car wrecks and old hospital tools. It is rather difficult to retrace early works by Douglas Gordon, since they consisted chiefly in performative works that left little material evidence, for instance rare newspaper reviews or exhibition leaflets. Furthermore, they might happen to be repeated in various places or adapted for different venues, so one must rely on stories reported by direct witnesses. Besides Gordon himself, his peers Craig Richardson and Ross Sinclair have related about these early durational pieces, being directly involved as performers or as audience. Richardson's testimony is particularly revealing, as he participated with Gordon into all these performances, especially as regards to concepts and ideas that were at stake. Now an academic, Richardson has published a comprehensive account on Scottish art since 1960, which has been previously mentioned and where he devotes a few pages to the pieces realized with Gordon (Richardson, 2011, pp.140-42). Since the former was part of the performances and doesn't have a close friendship with the latter anymore, these accounts should conveniently be compared with the other mentioned testimonies. In spring 1987 Gordon and Richardson were working on a series of collaborative performances together with Euan Sutherland under the collective name of *tradition:dehabilitation*, which started with several experiences at the Third Eye Centre and once even reached the National Review of Live Art in London's Riverside Studios. Only a few months later, Sutherland left and the two remaining artists went on changing their collective name into *Puberty Institution* and that same year had the chance to take part in the 4th AVE Festival in Arnhem. In fact, they were given the opportunity to perform in the Netherlands at an experimental audio-visual event, as they were asked to fill in for other young artists who had cancelled their performance at the Ocean Gallery. Though very worried about presenting *AntehyperaesthesiA* (1987) abroad, Gordon and Richardson felt lower pressure than in Scotland, because they were unknown to the Dutch public – hence free from meeting particular expectations. The outlines of the performance revolved around a major piece of furniture, a large table in the centre of the room, with several focal materials such as linseed oil, coal or clothing. The two young artists acted onto the various items, while the Bridge song was played in loop. The construction intended to evoke a melancholic feeling of nostalgia, very much attached to British imaginary, that they tried to replicate in their next piece back in to Scotland. In Glasgow they soon made another big hit at the Third Eye Centre on 21st October 1987, when their project *Experiments under nostalgia's umbrella* was staged earning a very good review on the *Herald*, the most popular Scottish newspaper:

> *"It's not often theatre smells. Experiments under nostalgia's umbrella does. Part of Third Eye Centre's New Work No Definition series, these environmental studies students from Glasgow School of Art [Gordon and Richardson] call on all your senses. [...] they have grasped the challenge of concentration such as performance demands. [...] In their first piece together, they isolate the triggers of nostalgia." (Bain, 1987)*

To the purpose they had realized a durational performance inside a small room, entered via a drop cloth. Inside the installation space they had arranged a large number of objects and pieces of furniture, so to recreate the typical features of a Scottish sitting room. Some freestanding fires marked off the space and gave the viewers an acutely hot feeling. On the table in the middle of the room there were some glass vases filled with an oily substance, which emanated a strong sweet smell, a blend of honey and whisky. The room was lit by the fires and by dozens of candles on sticks, while loudspeakers released the sound of bagpipes alternated with a recording of *Lili Marlene* by Marlene Dietrich to evoke British wartime music. One performer kept handling the fires, the other alternated two movements: first he dipped his hands into the vases and then he walked around the room. Both of them looked completely absorbed by their activities and persisted in their minimal movements without being disturbed by the onlookers, who could move around to inspect the different materials on show. In Gordon's and Richardson's intention, the sounds, the smells and the heat were to revive the spectators' remembrances of their past, referring to their home and a typically Scottish context.

Again in 1987 Puberty Institution made it into the program at Transmission, where Stuart Brisley had recently enacted a performance called *Red Army II* (1986). The latter piece had drawn attention to Transmission by the young students at the Environmental Art Department who were inspired by the site specificity and durational aspect of the work

(Richardson, 2011, p.138). Gordon and Richardson were allowed by Transmission to present the performance *Antehyperaesthasia* (1987), which again exploited British performance art – for instance Brisley, Alistair MacLennan, Gilbert and George – and Italian arte povera, however playing on a kind of physical coldness that tried to shift nostalgic gloom towards meditation on illness and destitution. This very event – as well as the good feeling of physicality with the space that Gordon and Richardson were able to bring about – started a durable connection with the prospective Environmental Art graduates, which would later bring them to replace the Transmission committee (Lowndes, 2010, p.111; Richardson, 2011, p.146). The tendency of the next performance pieces by Richardson and Gordon held during 1988 was going further in the direction of progressive decay and risk-taking, for instance by choosing abandoned spaces that could bring about dangerous situations. Such features let emerge a direct inspiration to Joseph Beuys and to some works in particular, like the project for *Skulptur Projekte Münster* in 1977, which used a deserted underpass of the German city. The influence of Beuys of the durational pieces on the young artist couple, as well as an awareness for the ethnographic turn, becomes clear especially when looking at the subject of their undergraduate thesis: Richardson wrote about "Joseph Beuys – the Sphere of Crisis", while Gordon's dissertation was titled "From Anthropology to Performance Art". Two major performances in their graduation year were *Refuse Consumption Decay Survival* once more at the Third Eye Centre and an untitled piece for their final art school project, which was fostered by Transmission but held in an abandoned car park basement underneath the Central Station, which has now become *The Arches* theatre and nightclub in Midland Street. In search for unloved spaces of the city, Gordon and Richardson looked also for objects, clothes and furniture found at second-hand markets, in order to place them in the selected venue and unveil a forgotten past as well as a hidden present, marking the transitory nature of human experience. In the badly lit car park with scattered light bulbs placed over the place, the two artists performed moving between piles of clothing, hoards of mattresses, tons of newspaper bundles, hundreds of eggs and sometimes even wandered around blindfold, when they turned out the lights at selected moments. Low lights and smoke, the sound of passing trains above and the view of innumerable empty car boxes created a sense of danger and unease that permeated and unsettled the audience (Dickson, 1989, p.7). The only non-performative piece by Gordon and Richardson was a commission by the Society of Scottish Artists, who invited them in 1988 to produce a site-specific installation at the Royal Scottish Academy in Edinburgh. Referencing the anniversary of Britain's National Health

Service, *40 Years from Cradle to Grave* was very much a work that followed the guidelines of environmental art procedure, since the artist couple had to negotiate with the Scottish institution the use of the large picture elevator, which usually was not accessible to the public. Furthermore, featuring a wheel chair and dozens of matchboxes with handwritten diseases on them, the installation showed a deep involvement in the social sphere, which the performances did not. Thanks to an open-minded and proactive attitude, Gordon and Richardson had succeeded in initiating important projects and performing at relevant venues still in their early twenties. Even though many of their peers watched them already as successful new entries in the art system, they always tried to bring back the new connections they made to their peers at the Environmental Art Department. Richardson (2011, p.9) maintains that Gordon was nonetheless convinced that an artist had better opportunities, if supported and part of a like-minded group or community.

When in Arnhem back in 1987, Gordon had made acquaintance with several contributors to the AVE Festival, amongst whom some boys from London Slade School of Art. These guys encouraged him to apply for a graduate program at their institution the following year, because they were sure he could pass the entrance exam and promised London would be crucial for his prospective career. The idea tempted him for a while and for the first time he was seriously thinking about leaving Scotland, even though he intended to keep in touch and come back soon to Glasgow. Asking David Harding for advise, the art teacher invited him to go for the capital city, as he believed such an experience in the London environment would definitely bring about new sources of inspiration, not to mention the connections he could make. Gordon finally decided to apply for the Slade and indeed was accepted, so he moved to London in summer 1988 waiting to start classes with inspiring teachers such as Stuart Brisley, Susan Hiller and Bruce McLean (Lowndes, 2010, pp.113-114). Gordon still remembers Harding's guidance and his personal struggle over leaving Scotland for the capital, which in the end turned out to be a very successful strategic move:

> *"David Harding said it will triple your chances of ever doing anything outside of Britain if you go to London. A lot of people in Scotland have a pipedream that you don't have to go through London to do anything, and some people have been successful with that, but going to London definitely helped, there's no doubt about it." (Gordon in Fagen, 1999, p.74)*

When Gordon arrived in London, Hirst and a bunch of Goldsmiths' peers were just trying to climb the ladder of the art system as rapidly as they could organizing a surprising three part exhibition in an abandoned warehouse of the city's docklands. The Glasgow artist met on an extremely competitive artist milieu, where already in art school students were struggling to arouse attention and competing for the consideration of important dealers. Although he was only two years into his Bachelor degree, Damien Hirst had started to make his first moves in the London art scene together with likeminded friends who wouldn't wait to be discovered by private galleries. He had arrived in London three years earlier after attending an art foundation course in Leeds, but worked on a building site first since Goldsmiths wouldn't accept him before 1986. Marcus Harvey, a friend from Leeds and a student at the famous London college, had had him over for several times, but Hirst became interested in applying there only later on. Once at Goldsmiths, he met on people that shared the eagerness for travelling by train to visit museums all around Europe, hence revealing a common attitude of British youth that could take advantage of the inter-rail system. Hirst's early production consisted in collages that combined various materials and leftovers recalling the Merzbau sculpture by German artist Kurt Schwitters. However, these pieces were rather inspired by the young artist's personal experience, as well as by realizing he wasn't that good at painting. As a matter of facts, Hirst himself has told in a number of interviews he had been crucially influenced by the encounter with the forsaken home of Mr. Barnes, his then neighbor in Leeds. The man appeared to have suddenly ran away leaving everything behind in the apartment, but most strangely there was a perfectly sorted collection of ordinary objects such as used toothpaste-tubes that Mr. Barnes had patiently catalogued (Morgan, 1997, p.68). Fascinated by the variety of material remains pertaining to human existence, Hirst explored a kind of Surrealist way to collage with found items (Serota, 2012, p.91). Picking up a job as receptionist at the Anthony d'Offay gallery, the Leeds boy had the chance to encounter top ranking artists and see what was considered high art at the time, hence starting to be confronted with newer trends. Furthermore, this experience helped him to gain some understanding of the true mechanisms which move the art system, thus developing a strong interest in wider strategies for riding or outflanking the establishment (Robecchi, 2007, p.8). His teacher Michael Craig-Martin soon noticed that young Hirst had grown a particular awareness for the operating principles in contemporary art, which he was able to turn into an advantage for his own career building, as well as a peculiar feature of his production:

> *"By working at the D'Offay he gained an understanding of how the art world worked at that level. Over the years, his ability to understand, tease, mock and exploit the art world has been one of his defining characteristics. As an artist, he takes the role of provocateur, playing with the art world's self-image, assumptions, pretentious and rituals." (Craig-Martin, 2012, p.38)*

Meanwhile, at Goldsmiths Jon Thompson and Craig-Martin were teaching a revised version of conceptual art that borrowed a lot from minimalism and looked sort of cool. They were constantly encouraging their students to devour art history books and explore edgy trends, in order to reference the art establishment. For those who studied at Goldsmiths, art education helped them to experiment with all sorts of styles, as well as to focus early on the particular tastes of London dealers. Hirst was still trying to find a way between painting and sculpture, when Charles Saatchi presented the two part exhibition *NY Art Now* in his huge new gallery in Boundary Road, which had a massive impact on most aspiring artists in London. Jeff Koons' works in particular, as displayed in the collector's gallery, taught young authors the relevance of a dramatic presentation for an artwork, considered both as an artistic value and as a way for effective self-promotion. As a matter of facts, the scale of the venue and the kind of art which was displayed had nothing in common with traditional galleries in Cork Street, causing a spark that set Damien Hirst and other young Goldsmiths students on fire:

> *"I remember realising that you can't just have a studio and paint, and put the paintings in a corner and wait to be discovered. [...] And I just wanted things that were irresistible, things that you couldn't ignore, that you couldn't avoid and you couldn't challenge. [...] Saatchi was doing that in advertising, I remember thinking, 'I want to make art that does what that does'. [...] Once the gallery had opened, I was making art for there." (Hirst in Serota, 2011, p.92)*

The second part of *NY Art Now* had not closed yet, that three young Goldsmiths students decided to repeat the art trends and exhibition circumstances as shown at the Saatchi Gallery. At the beginning of 1988, Damien Hirst indeed came across Angus Fairhurst and Abigail Lane, who revealed to be very likeminded about courageously starting on their own even before graduation. The three college peers could get better acquainted during a small group show that Fairhurst had curated in the rooms of the Bloomsbury Gallery, in Bredford Way School just a few steps off Russell

Square in the heart of London. The young students showed their works together with another Goldsmiths colleague, Nottingham born Mat Collishaw, and on this occasion Hirst displayed some early pan works, which were pans of different sizes painted with bright colours and hung up the wall. They soon became close friends and started to plan a much more important event for the summer of the same year, which in Hirst's mind needed to be organized like a professional exhibition that could compete with ultimate trends in art production and display, although the marketing of the exhibition almost took a more significant part than the actual attempt to achieve a unitary curatorial approach (Bush, 2004). In June 1988, then, came the traditional graduate exhibition at Goldsmiths, which for the first time in a number of years drew remarkable attention, since the press highlighted several surprisingly good creations on display (Muir, 2011, p.18). Furthermore, before the opening Craig-Martin had invited Karsten Schubert for a preview, who after assisting Nicholas Logsdail at Lisson Gallery had opened his own space in April 1987 and was gaining relevance day by day on the London art market. The German born dealer snapped up three young graduates who appeared most promising and offered them an exhibition later that year: they were two painters, Gary Hume and Ian Davenport, and the installation artist Michael Landy. Meanwhile, despite the excitement about the last graduate show, at Goldsmiths there were rumors that Hirst, Fairhurst and Lane were planning to curate a group show for the second half of the summer, although they were only starting their third bachelor year. Many college students felt somehow uncomfortable about this project, as the three curators had been very reticent about naming the prospected contributors or revealing the intended venue, which would be a disused London Port Authority building on Surrey Docks (Stallabrass, 2006a, p.54). All in all, it was Hirst who did everything to mount the three part exhibition: he chose the artists and provided the curatorial principles, as well as suggesting which works to put on display; he then found the exhibition venue and secured a substantial sponsorship from the London Docklands Development Corporation to mount the show, send out invitations and produce a stylish catalogue (Cooper, 2012, p.24). The exhibition had been titled *Freeze*, a name that seems to refer to a type of salad which Abigail Lane had once left on the kitchen table where the three young curators held regular meetings. An alternative interpretation, however, could be the technical meaning of this term understood as a still image, hence the title would rather refer to the piece by Mat Collishaw they intended to exhibit. In fact, that work was truly a video still derived from the medical footage of an autopsy and the three curators thought it might cause broad sensation (Muir, 2011, p.23). From August 6th to September 29th 1988 about twenty Goldsmiths students belonging to different age groups were finally divided into a three parts exhibition and displayed in a deserted storage location of the Surrey Docks. Some of young artists were already graduated, such as Sarah Lucas and Anya Gallaccio, others were about to get their BA, for instance Fiona Rae, Angela Bulloch, Ian Davenport, Michael Landy and Gary Hume, while most were only at their second BA year as Hirst, Fairhurst, Lane, Collishaw, Simon Patterson. Coordinated by Hirst, the students didn't just concentrate on the works to display, but put as much effort as they could in painting and fitting the exhibition venue, so that the overall installation would appear on a professional level that might equal the Saatchi Gallery. The result was brilliant, indeed, with the interiors resembling the aesthetics of a proper German Kunsthalle, while the catalogue had been edited with a smart design. Thanks to a good mailing list they had drawn up from different London galleries – in which some of them worked as receptionists – the Goldsmiths boys and girls succeeded in attracting all the important art people in town. The standard of the works shown and the quality of the exhibition space were surprisingly good for a mere students show, but it was as well the entire organizational machine that seemed absolutely unprecedented. What's more, the curators concentrated on a proactive fund raising strategy, hence being able to fund the event especially thanks to building contractors that led the ambitious redevelopment plan of former industrial areas in the British capital. Even without queues at the exhibition entrance, *Freeze* was certainly a crucial event which established a new standard for young artists and showed there was an effective alternative to established institutions. Even in Julian Stallabrass' (2006b, p.53) opinion, the success was not mere luck, since the organizers had intentionally seized to mount a professional-looking exhibition with an impressive catalogue, as well as to get the people who mattered to attend. Michael Craig-Martin effectively contributed to the success of *Freeze*, both assisting the three curators and doing his best to attract important personalities, among whom Nicholas Serota who had been recently appointed director of the Tate Gallery. Even when recession started, the art teacher would stay close to many of his former students whose production he appreciated. As he realized that artist-run-shows made a good survival strategy for aspiring artists, Craig-Martin supported his students' initiatives, not least through his articles on newspapers and specialized magazines:

> *"I had always tried to help my students in any way I could, particularly in those first years after art school. I knew from personal experience how difficult it was – I never had things come easy. I did*

the same with Damien [Hirst] and Freeze. I encouraged people to go and see the work. I would never have done this, if I hadn't believed the show was of exceptional interest [...]. It amuses me that so many people think what happened was calculated and cleverly manipulated whereas in fact it was a combination of youthful bravado, innocence, fortunate timing, good luck, and, of course, good work." (Craig-Martin in Sherwin, 2007)

Considering some of the pieces presented by the selected artists, it is very helpful to understand the influence in style and genre these students had been exposed to in their art education at Goldsmiths[4]. Indeed, most of the works included in the show already revealed some of the main features, which would later be pivotal for the generation of Young British Artists, as they were later epitomized. It is important to note, though, that Hirst took his curatorial role very seriously and substantially advised his colleagues about the pieces to show, often setting tight restrictions but in a constant flow of discussion. Anya Gallaccio recalls the situation she bumped into at the installation of *Freeze*, especially the directions that Hirst imposed as well as the support he provided, which helped her to adjust and find maturity in the work she proposed at the warehouse:

"I was feeling pretty despondent, but then I started to work on Freeze with Damien [Hirst] and all of a sudden I had a space and a set of parameters, so I had another opportunity. [...] I was showing with Gary [Hume]'s paintings. And he was making door paintings and they hung very low, virtually on the floor. I knew that I couldn't make anything high that would interfere visually with what he'd done. The more restrictions Damien imposed, the clearer my choices became." (Gallaccio in Fortnum, 2007, p.2)

Going back over the three parts of *Freeze*, Mat Collishaw presented *Bullet Hole* (1988), an enlarged colour photo drawn from a picture in a pathology manual showing the deadly wound of a man who had been shot in the head. It consisted in an interlocking grid of fifteen separate framed images neatly organized along three lines and five columns on the wall. Because of its oversize, the image is not immediately recognizable as a bullet hole, since the head wound suggests rather the form of female genitals, while at a close observation hair and scalp can be distinguished. Gary Hume displayed *Mint Green Doors I-III* (1988), which were three so called door paintings belonging to a series he had started that same year. The pictures replicated the exact pattern of hospital doors and were painted in household gloss paint on medium density fiberboard, that is the very material hospital doors are in fact made of. These works make a good example of the kind of cool conceptual art that Goldsmiths was famous for in the late Eighties: they were the reproduction of true doors, such as *One and Three Chairs* (1965) by Joseph Kosuth displays three possible versions of a chair, but on the other hand Hume's door paintings used a traditional and acceptable medium, hence being much more marketable in the gallery system. Anya Gallaccio conceived her contribution to the show by working directly in the space that Hirst had assigned to her and responding to the restrictions that were set, which were specifically the presence of Hume's pieces that hung almost at floor level. Acting on site introduced the young sculptor to a completely different set of variables, which she had to react to, in order to make sense of the spatial circumstances. Finally she found the solution to pour a lead mold into a rectangular structure on the floor and left it to cool down naturally, hence leaving a stirred and monochrome surface behind that restituted an inner dynamics very close to Jackson Pollock's dripping method. Gallaccio proceeded with several attempts and once poured the hot metal by mistake on her foot causing a severe burn and a subsequent hospital recovery accompanied by her colleagues. Another woman on the show and Hirst's partner at the time, Angela Bulloch participated with a luminous installation, which consisted of large coloured light bulbs stuck on the wall and lit at casual intervals. Bulloch picked standard colours for the bulbs, such as those, which could easily be found on sale, and the piece was very similar to the series of *RGB Spheres* she later produced in the Nineties. All artworks described so far appeared to have been devised properly and indeed proved convincing to commentators, while ironically Damien Hirst and Sarah Lucas were those who struggled most to find a satisfying proposal for *Freeze*. Hirst felt that many of the Goldsmiths peers he had chosen were doing a brilliant job and perfect up-to-date pieces, while he was still trying to make sense of his Schwitters-like collages, which caused him a lot of frustration in the months before Freeze. Indeed at the first part of the exhibition the Leeds born artist presented *Boxes* (1988), which were a bunch of colourful boxes of various dimensions set up in a corner above eye sight to create an amalgam of rectangular forms. Nicholas Serota on visiting the exhibition remembers seeing the boxes and considering that their arrangement and bright colours, which were against the prevailing aesthetics, appeared like an assault to Minimalism. However, *Boxes* did not satisfy its author at all and furthermore some the boxes fell off every day, so he then tried to display one of his pan pieces again using standard gloss for the frying pans attached to the wall. But it wasn't until Hirst came across a work by celebrated German painter Gerhard Richter in a catalogue at Anthony d'Offay that he realized what could be working for *Freeze*. The young student was struck by an image of *1024 Colours* (1973), which simply is the display of a geometric colour chart organized in 32 columns per 32 rows for a total of 1,024 rectangles of different colour units divided in a white grid, as if they had been taken from the catalogue of a hardware store. The encounter with Richter's work inspired the very first *Spot Paintings* of Damien Hirst, which were canvasses depicting geometrical arranged circles of all different colours, neatly set against a white background and painted with average household gloss. These pieces were a kind of transposition of the German artist into a series that was cool and repeatable, but open to infinite variations. For the third part of *Freeze* he applied the spots directly on a whitewashed wall, arranging them as two squares of ten circles per side and titling the piece *John John* (1988), however converting soon to pharmaceutical names for future creations. Hirst was finally content with the spot paintings, which were reminiscent of the simplicity and yet coolness of the pieces shown by Simon Patterson, another student included in the show. In the course of the three parts he presented two pieces: on the one side two white canvasses with the names of Richard Burton and Elizabeth Taylor impressed on them, on the other a mural text-piece titled *The Last Supper Arranged According to the Flat Back Four Formation (Jesus Christ in Goal)* (1988) in fact showing the names of the apostles written with a standard typewriter typeface and organized in a football team system. Almost puns, his works drew from conceptual art praxis, but had a minimalist aesthetics that fitted the gallery system very well. Sarah Lucas was probably the one who really missed the point in *Freeze* remaining on the sideline, although her companions considered her the most promising of the group. First she created a floor sculpture lying down a large aluminum sheet she then crumpled up, afterwards she had a discrete brick sculpture positioned against the brick wall of the warehouse, playing with artifice and reality, but both pieces remained in the shadows. It appeared as if Lucas had been caught unprepared, while her then boyfriend Gary Hume seemed to have absolutely hit the nail on the head and seriously started to take off by means of dealer Karsten Schubert. The failure at *Freeze* caused Lucas serious disappointment and anger, almost completely dropping the aspiration of a career in the visual arts and inducing a period of prolonged experimentation with new means, as well as with totally different subjects that would make a fresh start such as the gender issue:

> *"I lived with Gary Hume. I was reading a lot of feminist writings and that led to arguments, because I was angry with him for being*

> *so successful. And not just him, but lots of other people, most of my good friends – but him, being my nearest and dearest, he really got the worst of it. I don't get so aggressive when I'm drunk now – but I used to come home furious from openings and fancy dinners, and he'd get the brunt of all that anger." (Lucas in Collings, 2002, p.22)*

The common trait of the pieces featured in *Freeze* consisted of a comprehensive conceptual aura – hence placing ideas at the core of the creative procedure – with a touch of sensationalism devised to impress the viewer, finally putting everything together in a minimalist framework (Stallabrass, 2006b, p.107). As a matter of facts, the works displayed by Goldsmiths students in the abandoned warehouse presented all characteristics in a nutshell that would later be defining for YBAs. The critic David Cohen (1997) shares with other scholars the opinion about the essential quality of this generation of neo-conceptual artists, that is conveniently summed up in the term *coolness* described as a cold, ironic, nihilistic, disrespectful and impersonal attitude. Furthermore, the art historian maintains that *Brit Pop Art* – such is the name he uses for Hirst and his generation of artists – would be characterized on one side by a particular attention to presentation, as if it were the packaging of a mass produced commodity, while on the other side the artwork's contents rather aim at immediate recognition by means of direct reference to media icons and ironic divertissement. In Cohen 's opinion this peculiar kind of artworks appear to be cannibalistic as regards to established trends and quite hedonistic in respect to aesthetic choices. Julian Stallabrass (2006b, p.4) agrees on the above features, however dividing them in three distinct categories which all proved pivotal for the new generation of emerging artists: the connection to international trends – namely US tendencies – meant to pull British art out of insularism; the use of objects and images drawn from mass media and from popular cultural products; finally the presentation of conceptual works in dramatic environment, at easy reach for the general public. Concerning proper artistic sources, Goldsmiths students were definitely inspired by recent American celebrities such as Jeff Koons, whom they had discovered at the Saatchi Gallery, but also by some examples of British art that had been considered outrageous for prudish UK in the Eighties. In particular Gilbert and George had paved the way to YBA generation: the art duo played on the contrast between their deliberately conformist look – wearing striped suits and bowler hat, while holding a cane – and the subtle insertion of features that were thought vulgar or improper such as homosexuality or rude language (Stallabrass, 2006a, p.56). The two artists were among the first ones in Great Britain who included swear words in their works, especially *fuck* and *cunt,* or who showed themselves naked hinting a gay attitude. Furthermore, it was them who discovered London East End as a working place before it became an unconventionally chic and arty neighborhood. The true reference for most installations, photos and paintings of *Freeze* artists was however a sort of New York/Cologne international normal style, as commentator Matthew Collings (1997, p.31) put it, which meant that young students were trying to approach Conceptual Art forms but redoing them with humour and mystery, instead of class issues and philosophy. The rediscovery of Conceptual art in London goes together with the re-appropriation of its methods in Glasgow, whereas the intention there was much more referencing the intellectual ambition of the style in order to address ideological and historic themes, sometimes even localizing it. For different reasons and with different aims, the conceptual art practice was helpful both to young Goldsmith students and to those at the Environmental Art Department, hence providing at a first glance a sort of common ground for the artworks they intended to present. As regards to the situation in the Scottish city, Craig Richardson (2011, pp.9, 147) confirms that Glaswegian artists were in fact clearly referencing a style that was at the same time post-Conseptual, post-Minimal and post-*arte povera* in a way. Christine Borland herself recalls how she and her peers were particularly aware of artistic examples they were looking at for their beginnings:

> *"I'd say that most of my friends or artists I hung around with were also working like this. I suppose earlier on we used the language of conceptual art and minimalism more self consciously." (Borland in Fortnum, 2007, p.11)*

In a way, it was a conscious attempt to get closer to the latest and most promising global trends, since London was rather at the border of the art system at the time, Glasgow being completely out of the map. The new generation of aspiring artists was rapidly understanding it had to get out of periphery and the best way is appropriation of international paradigms, which means employing the language of established trends or acquiring its pathos. There are different means to translate new styles at local level and these students were trying several of them to find convenient strategies for their personal artistic project (Dantini, 2012, pp.72, 99, 119). With the spot paintings Hirst was taking advantage of what may be called a *back-up-artwork* which in this case clearly was Gerhard Richter's *1024 Colour,* that is a recognized and celebrated piece of international art as a direct reference. In a way it is one of the most dangerous paths to go along, since the artworks that result could look like mere copies of the original. Another course was taken by Douglas Gordon, whose durational performances may be considered an *appropriation game* used to make the poetics and methods of Joseph Beuys his own, but without formally copying the style. Such a strategy is quite difficult to operate, since one needs a profound understanding of the artists or styles referenced, risking to be seen as a mere follower and not a proper innovator. A third way to be practiced is that of mocking the referenced style or artist, hence displaying a sort of *critical parody* such as in the case of Simon Patterson, who evidently made fun of Conceptual art practice with his football-team-designed last supper. The high risk here is to end up in a complete joke, which can't be taken seriously by the art system and stays at its margins. Such kind of reception strategies are very similar to what institutional theorists have demonstrated by studying behavioural models of acceptance and transfer of organizational innovation. American management scholar Alfred Chandler (1969) has indeed observed that solutions for labour organization that appear successful are soon received in the wider industrial system. Hence, even corporations would copy each others' institutional structure – especially of those enterprises that are considered up-to-date – in order to keep up with latest trends, taking their relevance for granted. However, the decision to apply specific organizational models doesn't necessarily involve functional or economic advantages, since it is rather based on their reputation as well as on moral obligation. As an example, research and development departments spread throughout corporations in the second half of the last century, because they were thought to represent necessary features for any innovative industry, even though setting research functions apart from other organization units might prove less helpful to the overall improvement of an institution. A similar case is the adoption of marketing departments in museums, which seemed an unavoidable unit in the Nineties and propagated quickly in every organization that wanted to be considered sufficiently modern, although marketing functions are more effective, when kept as a transversal attitude of the institution (Mantoan, 2008). Thus even in organization studies the adaptation to novelties has very much to do with psychology and social pressure that is following latest trends to preserve or expand reputation in the institutional field. Back to the art system, what Hirst and his colleagues were doing in London, as well as Gordon with his peers in Glasgow, were nothing but early and courageous attempts to receive and absorb international styles, aware that artistic reception moves from centre to periphery and constitutes the first step to speak a global language. Although the exhibition didn't really have many visitors, Hirst and the other young Goldsmiths rascals had apparently hit the target and were conscious of this result, according to the impression that *Freeze* made on art experts at the time:

> *"All of us lot, we caned the art world. Absolutely totally phenomenal. We caned the art world as kids." (Hirst in Cooper, 2012, p.27)*

Indeed, most of the works on display in the abandoned warehouse were finally sold and many exhibitors got an immediate offer by some London galleries, even though they had recently graduated or were still college students. Angela Bulloch found the support of Maureen Paley, the American manger of Interim Art Gallery, while German dealer Karsten Schubert picked Gary Hume, Michael Landy and Anya Gallaccio. Both were rising dealers in London's art scene, arousing much attention for being dynamic and trendy, but the big hit was painter Ian Davenport who was chosen by a much more established and traditional gallery such as Waddington, soon to be followed by another *Freeze* painter, Fiona Rae. Rumors were that Craig-Martin, who had just organized an exhibition at the gallery, introduced Davenport to Leslie Waddington. It goes without surprise, that both Davenport and Rae were nominated for the Turner Prize already in 1991, having the backing of one of the most influential London establishments. This situation emphasizes the ambiguity of *Freeze*: originally conceived as an opportunity for the aspiring artists to be heard and spoken of, with a distinct opposition character to the current yet parochial art system, it finally resulted in an explicit attempt to get in direct touch with the establishment which they had tried to bypass (Bush, 2004). Rather than criticizing the motionless British art Gotha of their times, Hirst and his peers aimed at gaining access to the London art scene by means of updated trends, which could wink at popular culture and in particular at mass media, while at the same time being shocking and appealing. This goal was reached so efficiently that the Goldsmiths College teachers themselves were struck by the promptness of some London galleries in absorbing *Freeze* students, sidestepping the long and impoverished apprenticeship that young artists were expected to serve before gaining such deals (Stallabrass, 2006b, p.53). With the exception of Michael Craig-Martin, who had profusely contributed to the exhibition's success, the teaching staff felt obliged to summon a school assembly in the aftermath of *Freeze*, in order to reprimand students and persuade them an art career needed a long apprenticeship, rather than premature self-promotion (Muir, 2011, p.25). Matthew Collings (1997, p.31), Julian Stallabras (2006b) and other commentators argue that *Freeze* and similar warehouse shows were far from being rebellious, but in fact extremely system-friendly and quite conventional as regards to the artworks that were presented. The true aim was to enter the establishment as soon as possible, only bypassing a few barriers and gatekeepers, rather then confronting the art world as such. On the contrary, Michael Craig-Martin has always opposed the idea that Hirst and his peers were just winking towards the establishment to be granted easy access, in fact considering that artist-run-shows were a high risk for newcomers and later became their only resource in recession-hit UK. Although warehouse exhibitions were cleverly devised as entry strategies, artists hardly noticed what was really at stake and succeeded thanks to a little foolishness, which conferred enough bravery to centre the target, as Craig-Martin credits:

> *"I always find it laughable that people think that the YBAs were cynical careerists. [...] Their attitude expressed in their work of that time, was the take-no-prisoners, hellbent stance of those who genuinely have nothing to lose. [...] They made work that was unmistakably British in content, but which spoke to the international art world with irreverent fluency. Hirst said to me recently that he is now amazed by the risks the took in his early career. [...] Freeze felt fresh and exciting, announcing the arrival of a new and very different generation of artists, not afraid to assert themselves or willing to wait for an invitation to the table." (Craig-Martin, 2012, p.39)*

Such a spontaneous and thoughtless attitude is apparently confirmed by Anya Gallaccio, who maintains there was a complete lack of sophistication in the contributors to *Freeze*:

> *"The original energy of Freeze was not cynical. It was a genuine enthusiasm to make work and get seen. I don't think anybody at the time realised how much was at stake." (Gallaccio in Cooper, 2012, p.25)*

Sincere or cunning, unconscious or premeditated, more likely *Freeze* was a bit of all these attitudes mixed together, but in the aftermath Hirst and his colleagues were persuaded they had done the right thing and pursued on the set path, despite admonishments of certain teachers at Goldsmiths. Furthermore, in the advent of 1989 recession self-organization seemed the only realistic way to seek material survival for young artists. As a consequence, self-promotion turned from means for arousing attention into a basic strategy for outliving the economic crisis, hence many aspiring artists started or kept on promoting themselves with growing competence and true entrepreneurial inclination. Fortunately the real estate crash came as a resource, because it made exceptional exhibition venues and working spaces available at very low rates, initiating an era of artist run spaces and do-it-yourself shows. In 1989, while the first few Environmental Art graduates took over Transmission in Glasgow, London saw the birth of City Racing, an autonomous gallery that would later stage early important solo shows by Sarah Lucas and Gillian Wearing. In 1990 Damien Hirst, Carl Freedman and Billie Sellman set up *Building One* in a disused industrial building in the Docklands, where they could mount three crucial shows during the three months of free space assignment, being *Modern Medicine*, *Gambler* and *Market*. These were also the exhibitions when Hirst finally took on the role of artist, dropping his commitment as curator for good. In the same year, Sarah Lucas and Henry Bond took up another building on the London docks mounting the now famous *East Country Yard Show* on an area almost sixteen thousand square metres wide. The crisis would thus inaugurate a new season of do-it-yourself group shows staged in former industrial spaces that fuelled the myth of YBA as both oppositional and entrepreneurial.

4.4. Glasgow outpost in London, London spirit in Glasgow: Gordon in the Capital and the initiation of Transmission

Christine Borland had finished her BA in Glasgow in 1987, the year before Gordon, and was resolute not to go to London for further studies, for she thought she didn't need the kind of commercial and competitive emphasis she would find in the Capital city. Her then companion, instead, had opted for the Slade School of Art and his first impact with London in 1988 was exciting, as the dimension and turmoil in the young artists' community were intoxicating, so different from his quiet and unsophisticated hometown. However, this impression soon faded into unease, caused by the marked differences between the two cities, especially in view of a completely different attitude of aspiring artists. Even if London offered a lot of new acquaintances, Gordon felt a solitary man among a hoard of budding peers that showed traits of strong individualism and were focused chiefly on art market dynamics. The spirit permeating London's art schools and students was well different from what he had experienced at the Environmental Art Department. Gordon's roots were in a city lacking any art market influence, so that in order to survive young artists had to resource uniquely to genuine group solidarity. On the contrary, London's art system was well structured and guaranteed success to the artists who could gain access, although at the time it was definitely minor to the United States and Germany. As a consequence, the milieu of aspiring artists was highly competitive and congregating with other peers appeared to be rather aimed at to one's individual interests, more than to share art projects. There certainly were reliable students communities, such as in the case of Goldsmiths College, but Gordon felt the group spirit was quite different to Glasgow. In his experience, London would grant a chance only to the most resourceful ones and he personally resented economic difficulties due to the high cost of living in the capital, while some of his college peers would be driven around by chauffeurs. At odds with London, at the Environmental Art Department he was used to debate themes such as visual democracy, art's social dimension, getting the public involved, the artist as a mere professional and the necessary plainness that goes with it. Claire Higgins in a resume on British art in the Nineties finds an interesting metaphor to highlight the essential difference between the two cities, which would indeed lie in the primacy of art market concerns in London and its total absence in Scotland. Accordingly, while the Londoners were entrepreneurs with the quick-fire cheerfulness of billboard advertisements, the Glaswegians were rather scavengers, their work being more lyrical and less immediate (Higgins, 2011a). Indeed, there may have been common social backgrounds and shared thematic issues, but Londoners and Glaswegian aspiring artists lived in two worlds apart. The professional approach that Hirst and his colleagues had demonstrated in the organization of exhibitions such as *Freeze* was a significant change in attitude that affected even their Scottish counterparts, but Glasgow-based artists didn't have access to a comparable infrastructure of influential media contacts or commercial galleries (Lowndes, 2010, p.131). The outcome of Hirst's graduate show is explanatory of the distinctive context in the two cities, since the works he displayed were seized by Charles Saatchi himself who intended to purchase them in a bulk, but Goldsmiths tutors preferred a dealer as a buyer, so everything went to Karsten Schubert and immediately passed to future gallery owner Jay Jopling. Such a progression was unthinkable for Glaswegian artists, who instead had to rely on public funding from social security after completing their art education, thus turning it into an exhibition theme at Transmission in April 1990. Even though family background and working attitude among art students across the nation was analogous, since higher education underwent the same demographic and structural transformation in the Eighties overall the UK, London environment produced dissimilar results from Glasgow. This difference was marked by the focus on art market and indeed influenced even London art school curricula, such as at Goldsmiths and at the Slade, which laid miles apart from Scottish art education. As argued before, there was a comparable reference to Conceptual art and Minimalism, but for diverging reasons and with different aims. In London the target was meta-artistic rather than socially engaged, pointed at understanding the art system and strictly referring to it in order to replicate its mechanisms and procedures[5]. The typical concerns of London artists were generally self-referential and elitist, while in Glasgow such a meta-artistic debate would have been pointless due to the underdevelopment of the local art system. For these very reasons Gordon found it difficult to adjust to the new environment, but nevertheless succeeded in making the most from his period at the Slade. In particular he realized how important it was to get to know the art system, to exploit the mentality of different players and to employ the right strategies to relate to different gatekeepers. However, staying in London helped him to improve even his artistic production, as he decided he should combine meta-artistic concerns with the kind of context-centrality he had been taught in Glasgow. For all his troubles and the difference from home, Gordon's experience at the Slade proved pivotal in order to mature his creative strategies and focus the employment of the right art tools, as the artist himself would later confess to Simon Sheikh:

> *"While I found myself in a kind of autobiographical 'muddle' in Glasgow, people's concerns were rather meta-artistic in London, more related to the mechanisms of the artistic system itself. It is somehow logical that such preoccupations were not to be found in Glasgow since they do not correspond to a real necessity. As for me, I think I have chosen the best of both worlds, so I work with a meta-artistic vocabulary while having developed a rather autobiographical language." (Gordon in Sheikh, 1997, p.17)*

In London Gordon's progress was mainly supported by teachers and students of Scottish origin, as if nationality were the common ground on which sound associations could be formed within such a hyper-competitive context. Among the teachers of the Slade School of Art, Bruce McLean and Susan Hiller proved to be true reference points for the young Glaswegian artist. Born and grown up in Glasgow, McLean was the supervisor of painting courses at the Slade and had established himself both as a painter as well as a performance artist. In some way, his personal path resembled that of young Gordon so far, as he had come to London in 1963 after completing his studies as a sculptor at Glasgow School of Art and enrolled at St. Martin's getting to know John Letham prior to the latter infamous dismissal. At the time the college was at its climax for performance art and this is where in 1967 Gilbert & George started their collaborative performance works. McLean would reveal himself very supportive for network resources, helping Gordon to make connection with many important people who orbited around the London art scene, especially with some fellow countrymen such as Alan Johnston. On the artistic side, instead, US artist Susan Hiller definitely proved the most influential teacher in Gordon's education at the Slade. Born and raised in Florida, in fact, before moving to London she had had the opportunity to get directly involved in the great art season of the Sixties in the USA and had achieved a doctorate in anthropology in Louisiana. Consequently in her personal art practice she had drawn both from Minimalism and Conceptual Art, however espousing a clear ethnographic tendency and a straightforward multimedia commitment as experienced with Fluxus (Foster, 2003). It comes to no surprise that Hiller would encourage her students to resort to a variety of media, applying video and photography in particular, but creating complex environmental installations rather than letting small works stand alone. The combination of new media into installation art was indeed a major source of inspiration and artistic growth for Douglas Gordon, going a step further from mere performance art. Among the Slade students Gordon became close friend with Martin Creed, who was English but had grown up in Glasgow and would later be Turner Prize winner in 2001. The two young men shared a similar view on art, especially the love for ephemeral artworks and music which were rather uncommon for art students in London, and would later support each other during their early career such as getting involved together in group shows or exchanging relevant connections.

On the contrary, in Belfast Christine Borland met an environment that was soaked with evanescence, which played an important role for her growth and quest for revealing stories, in order to come to terms with her surroundings. She had opted for the North-Irish town, because charismatic Scottish artist Alastair MacLennan, known for his extreme durational performances and perilous installations, led the arts program at the local university. The loaded political context of the city induced her to opt out sculptural works as she had done in Glasgow, so she rather started to work on temporary installations as most of the Belfast students did, but she could really take off only after leaving that powerful situation at a distance on her return to Scotland. Affected by the leading mood at the University of Ulster, in fact, she tried to reverse her sculptural approach, for instance trying to represent the female body in its absence. This was also an attempt to come to terms with feminist aesthetic and reflect on her work as a woman artist, as she was reading a recently published anthropological history of female art-crafts, *The Subversive Stitch* by Roszika Parker (1984). Furthermore, the Ulster period proved crucial for she focused on museums and archives as an endless source for artistic inspiration, particularly to exploit objects and extract hidden stories. On a visit to the university anatomy museum, she was struck by the pieces she saw and quickly understood she wanted to take that kind of aesthetics and themes in her works. A month-long residency at Stevenage Museum further put her in touch with social history objects, such as domestic items and working life tools, that preluded to a kind of anthropological and archival research which she would subsequent apply to her overall artistic procedure. For her graduate show she displayed various manufactured materials interwoven with found objects from personal or domestic background, loosely referencing gender issues as well as autobiographical topics.

Analogous to Borland's MA experience, also Gordon's Master studies at the Slade as well as the specific London situation helped him to further shape his peculiar working method, advancing from the kind of education he had been imparted at the Environmental Art Department. As a matter of facts, in the Capital city he was faced with material problems both of economic and logistic nature, which seriously hindered him to produce works or embark in articulate projects. While in Scotland he had been able to exploit the old Girls High School's deserted rooms and even get access to some relevant public venues such as Transmission and Third Eye Centre, in London it was almost impossible to find opportunities to exhibit, even to gain admittance in independent spaces, if not acquainted with the right people. Since he could not afford to rent a studio and was often barred from accessing exhibition premises, Gordon needed to work out a solution as regards to the kind of production he wanted to make. For this reason he chose to focus on text pieces that could be adapted onto varied items or surfaces, hence being relatively free from the necessity of a working space or displaying venue. In order to produce still meaningful artworks, he understood well to set *site-specificity* aside in favour of a process that would bring about a psychological space, rather then a physical one, as he once told in an interview back in the Nineties:

> *"I had been involved in performance work and quite large scale installations, but when I was based in London there was a literal problem with the amount of space I had available to work with. I got interested in manipulating a certain space by using only text (I*

should say that this was a pretty much pragmatic decision, to begin with). Eventually I felt that I wanted to work much less with the idea of 'site-specificity' and much more by engaging in the ambiguities of the 'psychological space'." (Gordon in Moisdon-Trembley, 1996, p.120)

At the time he was also attracted by the idea that words – though seemingly factual and unbiased – could acquire a different meaning depending on the place, moment and person who upheld them. He decided to try to exploit the intrinsic ambiguity of language and relate it to a given context, in order to develop an actual psychological state of mind in the audience:

"I always liked the idea that words which are supposed to be concrete, when spoken by a different person at a different time can have a completely different meaning." (Gordon in Obrist, 1996b, p.164)

In a way this approach appeared also to be the best solution to cope with the situation in London, without abandoning the principles he had acquired at the Environmental Art Department in Glasgow. This deliberation resulted in producing his first text pieces, which consisted in short or incomplete sentences at first applied as wall texts on various surfaces. Subsequently the artist developed some projects to release these works by means of anonymous letters and phone calls, but only after completing his art education. His friend and fellow Environmental Art Department colleague Ross Sinclair (1993a, p.9) ascribes the birth of Gordon's text pieces to the scraps of performances held with Craig Richardson from 1987-1988. As a matter of facts, in preparation for those events the artist used to write down incomplete sentences in block capitals on large paper sheets, as a means to think about the actions to be carried out. Purged from the physical context and from the actions performed, these text pieces were the remains of his earlier period and summarized the basic state of mind Gordon intended to evoke, fitting perfectly the economic difficulty and space deficiency in London (Moisdon-Trembley, 1996, p.120). His very first textual work was installed on occasion of an independent event near some friends' studio in the town of Reading back in 1989[6]. The location was old army barracks partly converted into art studios, while the old prison cells had been converted into shelter for the homeless. On the brick walls fencing the yard Gordon posted a quotation from Naum Gabo, a Russian constructivist sculptor and a pioneer of kinetic art. Alternating block and small letter words the sentence was: 'A BUILDING IS MORE THAN a dwelling place... AND HAS INFLUENCE on the emotions OF HUMAN BEINGS'[7]. Gordon already recurred to Bembo font, which is the most common typeface in publishing, but here combined with another one. At the beginning of his text pieces he used different font types and only in 1991 opted mainly for Bembo style, which became since then a sort of trademark for his creations[8]. Still in 1989 he also had further occasions for exhibiting his wall texts, the first one for an independent group show mounted in a deserted industrial plant in Bremen, Germany. The exhibition had been called *Windfall 89* and was a follow-up of an event staged in Hyde Park the previous year and organized by Scottish artist David McMillan that Gordon got acquainted with in the capital due to the shared national origin. The German artists who had taken part in the London group show wished to reciprocate the invitation and set up the Bremen event. Gordon was invited through McMillan and displayed two text pieces conceived on the occasion of the show after an inspection visit at the exhibition site. Both works were written in block Akzidenz Grotesk font, the first one being *Forget Facts and Figures* (1989) posted on a glass panel of the abandoned factory and spelling the title in German 'ZAHLEN UND FAKTEN VERGESSEN'. The second piece was *Now Time* (1989) and it consisted of the words 'JETZTZEIT 1946' placed on a sort of bunker located in the yard of the industrial plant, that the artist had pierced through in various places of the ceiling. These two works intended to refer to the important historical landmark in German history, marked by the shattered past and yet moved by a presentment of the oncoming fall of the Berlin wall. Another good chance to display his early text pieces was in Scotland for the *Smith Biennial* held at the Smith Museum in Stirling, for which Gordon worked out *Rotting from the inside out* (1989). The work consisted of the title sentence presented as a wall text in capital black letters posted at the bottom wall of a small room, while two more items hung on the contiguous partitions: on one side there was a framed photography extracted from a police manual, showing a housing building on which the trajectory of a falling body had been drawn, on the other side a round segment of the wall had been removed in order to reveal a portion of the brick wall, which again had been pierced through in several points. The Stirling Smith Biennial of 1989 was something of a turning point in Scottish art, showcasing the forthcoming schism between the older figurative painters and the new generation of post-conceptual artists. Curator Nicola White was on the selectors' committee at the time and remembers the art scene in Scotland was starting to get vibrant. The prize for that edition was split in four going to Douglas Gordon, Jane and Louise Wilson, Julie Roberts and Steve

Dilworth, most of whom would soon become associated with the YBA generation. White recalls that the verdict felt an outrage for many traditional painters and sculptors of the area:

> *"A lot of the slightly older artists were absolutely up in arms about it. In fact, one of them wrote to the Stirling Smith and said that a 23 year old – meaning Douglas – should not get a prize when there were much more experienced artists there showing work. [...] The age difference wasn't even that big but the difference in terms of outlook was vast." (White in Lowndes, 2010, p.119)*

At the beginning of 1990 Gordon participated with his fourth text installation in the public art project called *Sites/Positions*, which started year of Glasgow as European Capital of Culture and was the first of a number of shows that brought together a loose grouping of likeminded young artists. The title of his work was *Proof*, which consisted in a series of dates (1787, 1812, 1820, 1916, 1922 e 1932) applied on the facade of the long gone Glasgow Green Station, all of them commemorating the building's historical turning points. These first examples of text pieces seem to refer to the tradition of Conceptual Art and are rather different from those that Gordon would later become famous for, which hold a rather ambiguous and visceral character. For instance, the 1989 untitled work in Reading reminds of the neutral and objective sentences created by Lawrence Weiner, the famous American artist who would use language in very factual manner and counted among to the original conceptualist authors that gathered around dealer Seth Sieglaub. The project for *Sites/Positions*, instead, could somehow recall another conceptual artist, the Japanese-American On Kawara, for his *Today Series* that were newspapers put into boxes onto which the release date was imprinted. Gordon's resort to text pieces is definitely to be observed in the light of Sixties and Seventies Conceptual Art, which achieved important results in the employment of language in Anglo-Saxon countries. One of the most relevant cases is certainly *Art & Language*, some sort of collective artist group and intellectual circle founded by British artists Terry Atkinson and Michael Baldwin, who were teaching at the Coventry College of Art. It was a group constantly elaborating their program that focused on theory and philosophical topics. Art historian Thomas Dreher (dreher.netzliteratur.net, 2011) maintains that the main intention was to emancipate art from external theories upheld by critics and philosophers, that is to say by people who were not professional artists. Consequently, their firm proposition was for artists to develop an art theory that should be presented as an artwork in its own right. Atkinson even suggested exploiting art venues in order to display the group's theories on art instead of proper artworks. As early as 1966 Atkinson and Baldwin showed an enlarged picture of their piece of writing titled *print (2 sections A and B)* (1966), where the two authors themselves wondered whether the paper on which the text was written could be considered an artwork. Starting from 1969 the group's considerations were published in the review *Art & Language*, which involved the articles of many British and American conceptual artists, such as Joseph Kosuth, Dan Graham, Lawrence Weiner, Ian Burn and Mel Ramsden. In the Seventies the debate was gradually focused on art system criticism, especially as far as the art market was concerned, radically opposing art reification and mystification (Hunt, 2005). Baldwin and Ramsden, for instance, conceived some resilience strategies to art market pressure with the use of language, especially in the form of texts to be displayed in museums and art galleries as a means to mock the art system and expose its intrinsic faults. The similarity between Gordon's first textual works and some *Art & Language* artists is not fortuitous, since in an interview to Simon Sheikh (1997, p.19) the artist reveals that he drew from the lexis coined by some of those authors of the Sixties and Seventies. However he maintains that he intended to borrow the methods and technique devised by *Art & Language*, as if they finally were an acquired artistic language, rather than feeling obliged to apply it to the same aims and contents favoured by the original grouping of Atkinson and Baldwin. Gordon's intention was to grasp their procedures in order to convey them to his projects, which often focused on extra-artistic themes. Hence, although he wouldn't underplay the importance of *Art & Language* for his own practices, the Scottish artist rather experienced this legacy as one to be processed and adapted to the needs of a new generation:

> *"I think it was necessary for artists, particularly in the sixties and seventies, to study the mechanisms of art production in relation to the museum or of language versus reality, like Art & Language. People did it then and this work will always be needed. [...] But it is also interesting that, while studying such mechanisms, these people set up a vocabulary, an aesthetic, which our generation has carried on with in the way we present our ideas – even if they are completely different form those Atkinson, Baldwin and Ramsden were interested in. But this is something positive, because it means that the vocabulary is not static, that it changes with the generations." (Gordon in Sheikh, 1997, p.19)*

The first text works created from between 1989 and 1990 confirm that Gordon did not spend the two years at the Slade in London exclusively; on the contrary he kept coming back to Scotland. Besides his personal bond with Christine Borland, he kept cooperating with a lot of his colleagues from the Environmental Art Department during his master's period and, as a matter of facts, his most important activities stemmed from his Glasgow connections. In his Slade years, Gordon completed the long performance series in collaboration with Craig Richardson, while on the other hand he started to exhibit his own text pieces. In 1989 he took part with many of the Environmental Art graduates in a show at Transmission Gallery, on occasion of the *Fifth Festival of Plagiarism*, and in the same year he also showed at Tramway for a collective exhibition called *Glasgow Group* as well as at the above-mentioned *Stirling Smith Biennial*. The constant link with his Glasgow peers got him involved in the project of re-opening Transmission Gallery, since its previous management had passed the activities over to some Environmental Art graduates including Craig Richardson, Christine Borland, David Allen, Peter Gilmour, Roderick Buchanan and Martin Boyce. In the summer of 1989 the gallery was completely renovated by Harding's former students and became the venue for group and exchange shows, as well as for meetings and debates with foreign artists (Lowndes, 2010, pp.118-119). The Transmission Gallery soon became a vital centre for Glasgow growing art community, comparable in relevance to London's *Building One* and close to City Racing Gallery, as it was a free association, however of a much more international scope than all possible London alternatives. Gordon recalls those days of the start of a new artist-run space in the heart of Glasgow:

> *"I had a relationship here, so I kept coming back. I'd already been doing some performances with Transmission when I was at college, and I was always into what could lead to within Transmission. Then in '89 I think, I came back for the summer holidays, Transmission was rebuilding in King Street I got involved with banging up walls and sanding floors, all that stuff, and I painted the Transmission sign, so for me that was a really big important thing, so I had a kind of physical investment as well as a spiritual one, I suppose." (Gordon in Fagen, 1999, p.74)*

Gordon maintains that in autumn 1988 he already understood that he had to keep firmly in touch with Scotland, while he was driving from Edinburgh to Glasgow together with David Harding on their way back from a performance with Craig Richardson and suddenly a cloud in the shape of his fatherland appeared in the sky. However poetic it might seem, this feeling of emotional attachment to the hometown was common to most of his former Glasgow peers and was rather directed to very pragmatic features such as the existing mutual support between the people that had studied at the old Girl's High School. Indeed most of them kept coming back and planned to start their career together, hence all experiences abroad were useful to bring in new connections and build up a shared capital of network resources. Christine Borland for instance had originally intended to stay in Belfast after completing her MA, but she soon realized she couldn't find there an art infrastructure such as the one in London, as well as a mutual support network like the one in Glasgow. Hence Richardson and Gordon finally convinced her to return to her hometown and participate into the renovation of Transmission. Almost all members of the new gallery committee had gone away for some time or would leave for a period, encouraged by the others, in order to make experience and extend their communal links: Christine Borland and Roderick Buchanan went to Ulster, Douglas Gordon to London, Ross Sinclair and Martin Boyce to California (*Nettverk-Glasgow*, Cat.1998). The cohesion of a like-minded grouping appeared to them as a powerful means to foster their reciprocal careers and this was more likely to happen in Glasgow, where they were all well acquainted with the local context. Outside of their hometown they knew how difficult it was to find exhibition opportunities alone, in fact both Borland and Gordon had managed to participate only in their own graduate shows so far. During his Slade years, Gordon was indeed given this sole occasion to exhibit in London, since tradition required students in their last year to provide a final piece for their graduation. Installed in the central building of the University College of London, of which the Slade was a department, the featured artists could choose at their free will where to locate their works, because a proper exhibition venue did not exist on campus[9]. The Glaswegian artist chose two quite unusual locations for his contribution: one was a seemingly insignificant room at the Slade, which was used as a storeroom, while the second spot was the circular opening in the ceiling under the main dome of the University College library. Gordon displayed two works that had been conceived particularly for these venues and thus can be defined site-specific or even context-specific. For the first spot he created *The Archive Room* (1990) positioning a billboard on the storeroom threshold that boldly announced a group show with legendary 20th century artists Marino Marini and André Minaux, who had both recently passed away[10]. As a matter of facts, on the inner walls Gordon had found two charcoal doodles which had allegedly been drawn by the Italian and the French artist during their stay at the Slade, or so he claimed. The

Scottish artist had the storeroom refurbished to look like a museum room: the space was emptied, the red carpet cleaned and the walls whitewashed, while the two drawings were finally covered with transparent glass sheets. This project reveals clear meta-artistic references as well as a good amount of humour, very similar to that of Goldsmiths graduates and aimed at enhancing one's own self-mythology. On the contrary, the second piece designed for the graduate show rather bore the mark of context-specificity acquired at Glasgow School of Art, however blended with the requirements of the London situation which was the lack of space. As a matter of facts, *Meaning and Location* (1990) is a text piece in Bembo typeface put on the edge of the ceiling skylight of the University lobby that gives sight to the central dome of the building and to the enormous library of the upper floor. Gordon chose a quotation from the Bible, repeated twice but repositioning a comma: "Truly I say to you, today you will be with me in paradise. Truly I say to you today, you will be with me in paradise". The sentence is taken from St. Matthew's gospel and was supposedly said by Jesus Christ on the cross to the Good Thief. The simple act of shifting the comma causes a disruption in the meaning of the phrase, hinting at language ambiguity by means of theological disputes. However, if one takes into consideration the chosen location for the installation, the work acquires a new and much more specific meaning. London University College was indeed one of the first an oldest lay institutions for higher education in the city. As a consequence religious books and theological treatises had been banned from the library, a circumstance that had not changed at the time of the 1990 graduate exhibition. In addition, the font used for the sentence is Bembo, the most commonly used in industrial publishing, so it evokes printed words in books. *Meaning and Location* is not a mere and self-referential conceptual piece, as it can be related to its physical and psychological context, which enhances the work's impact. Gordon's critical intervention appears to highlight the inconsistency of an instruction method and a supposedly free institution, such as the University College of London, which were in fact based on censorship. Comparing this particular artwork with the pieces displayed by Simon Patterson at *Freeze* is useful to observe up to a point the difference between the artistic procedure imparted at Goldsmiths and the method of the Glasgow artist. Patterson had attracted the critics' attention by employing language in his works, but unlike Gordon he conceived it as a signal system contrived to refer to empirical experience (Beckett, 1996). His procedure consisted of separating an original meaning from its verbal sign and substituting it with a new one, in order to maintain the logical and organic structure of a system. Hence the inner meaning would be modified with a lot of irony and using elements drawn from common imagination or popular culture (Shepherd, 1996). If Gordon played on the ambiguity of word meaning, Patterson would rather aim at manipulating a word's significance thus overturning a system of shared meaning. In *The Last Supper Arranged According to the Flat Back Four Formation (Jesus Christ in Goal)* Patterson simply overwrites a system for knowledge organization – being the particular scheme for soccer teams – with an unexpected content – the twelve Apostles. Similarly the two white canvasses placed side by side and overprinted with the words *Elizabeth Taylor* and *Richard Burton* were adopting the pattern of both Conceptual Art and Minimalism, but overplayed with the memorable Hollywood couple. The final effect of both pieces was eased by a sort of impertinence towards the art system and its consistence with mass media collective imagination. These works plainly resort to popular culture, in order to sound familiar to the viewer without inducing deeper thought, even though they arise from self-reference within the field of visual art. In Gregor Muir's opinion the works Patterson exhibited at *Freeze* were quintessential for the Goldsmiths' standards:

> *"This particular work bore all of the hallmarks of the Goldsmiths standards, referencing conceptual 'high art' while at the same time being somewhat irreverent and down to earth." (Muir, 2011, p.22)*

Despite various difficulties Gordon encountered in London, the time spent in the Capital was crucial for improving his network of connections among the students milieu as well as amongst much more relevant players of the local art scene. In pubs or at parties he came across several young artists that would become defining for the YBA generation, such as Damien Hirst, Simon Patterson and Gary Hume whom he met in a bar next to the British Museum where Goldsmiths students used to hang out. Notably Gordon run into young conceptual artist Liam Gillick, who had graduated at Goldsmiths in 1987 and then very quickly penetrated the London art scene, for instance exhibiting at Karsten Schubert gallery in 1989. Gillick introduced the Scottish artist both in the capital city and to many friends he had in the international art world, amongst whom a number of artists such as Angela Bulloch and Henry Bond in London, Philippe Parreno and Pierre Bismuth in Paris, Rirkrit Tiravanija and Elizabeth Payton in New York. The most important acquaintance Gillick introduced to Gordon was probably Jack Wendler, who had been a prominent dealer and was still an important art collector. In his life Wendler had been a key player for the rising Conceptual artists between the United States and Great Britain. In 1967 he associated with Seth Sieglaub, the famous dealer/curator who started promoting Conceptual Art in the Sixties and succeeded in pushing some American artists to prominence, such as Joseph Kosuth and Lawrence Weiner (Alberro, 2003, pp.13-14). Wendler and Sieglaub founded an association for assisting enterprises, which wished to enter art projects or collecting, in order to improve their corporate image, thus gaining advantages on the marketplace. On returning to the UK he opened the Jack Wendler Gallery holding almost thirty exhibitions in five London venues between December 1971 and July 1974, including many American Conceptual artists such as Robert Barry (Herbert, 2009). In 1976 he finally was among the co-founders of the now prominent magazine *Art Monthly*. Wendler appreciated young Gordon's friendship and often invited him to the dinner parties he threw at his home. On an occasion, the Scottish artist exceeded in drinking and was accommodated in one of the guest rooms. When he woke up Gordon saw one of Marcel Broodtheaers' posters hanging from the facing wall – which depicted cows labeled with car names – and was deeply struck by it (Obrist, 1996b, p.175). He was instantly persuaded that art experience could be but strictly personal and decided to create works that would stimulate individual memory, so that each viewer would go through a personal experience. From this point on the artist started to devise strategies to bring art experience – namely the moment of art consumption – into private lives. Speaking to Thomas Lawson, Gordon openly refers to this function his works should have:

> *"The piece proposes a very direct, but secret intervention in your private life [...] by bringing the moment of consumption of art into the private lives of unwary consumers." (Gordon in Lawson, 1993, p.63)*

After completing his courses at the Slade, Gordon was determined to return to Scotland, as he didn't feel the London environment had given him any opportunity. However, he had in fact developed new strategies and approaches, as well as having had significant experiences and made relevant connections. Thus the period he spent in London proved crucial on the long run, for it helped to ripen his style and establish suitable contacts to start his art career beyond the borders of Glasgow. Years later, Gordon himself would admit the two years he spent in the capital city were crucial for his profession:

> *"On finishing up in London, it seemed like the best thing to do was to go back to Glasgow. The atmosphere in London, at that time, felt like things were closing down, rather than opening up. In retrospect*

this looks like it was the right decision made in response to the wrong reading of a situation." (Douglas Gordon: Words, Cat.1998)

Gordon's frustration with the Slade period in the very aftermath of his graduation reflects a widespread discrepancy between the expectations of art students and the concrete benefits of higher education for a successful career start. Economist Ruth Towse claims the existence of a true "diploma disease" in the case of artistic professions, since aspiring artists would appear to be unaware of the real opportunities provided by art colleges or formal training (Towse, 1996, pp.307-321). The assumed value of art education, as well as the chances of artistic success, is far less than what most prospective artists are willing to believe. As a matter of facts, those who embark on a career in the arts take a very high risk, even if they don't realize it, because they seek an occupation in a sector in which risk is endemic. Hence, artists don't behave as rational agents and tend to underestimate the real chances of success, mostly because they are extremely focused on their aspiration and blindfolded about the probability of its fulfillment. The fact that only a few art school graduates will eventually succeed causes a deadweight loss for society, due to the amount of wasted resources, which have been provided to all other failing students. Describing the selection process of mandarin bureaucrats in imperial China, economist Gordon Tullock has argued that social costs of any specialized training with narrow success probabilities – such as in the case of art education – are far larger than its direct benefits because of the high failure rate (Mossetto, 1993, p.159). Hence it is debatable that any art college can turn a student into a true artist, even branded schools only provide a higher success rate but no absolute certainties. It may sound obvious, however it is very much up to the individual student to make the best out of the various training opportunities he or she is able to pursue. Besides financial backing by means of scholarships, the account of UK art education during the Eighties demonstrates there were – and still are – at least three specific resources that art students can draw from higher education. As regards to social capital, an art school confers an indelible imprint on its students according to the institution's reputation on the local, national or international art scene. A college's standing indeed signals the likely quality of its graduates to gatekeepers of the art system, serving as a sort of preventive selection to beat the first entry barrier (Thompson, 2008, p.68). This is the reason why branded art schools such as Goldsmiths in the Eighties or earlier St. Martin's in the Seventies could be defining for a successful career kick-start, since they would offer more opportunities to aspiring artists due to the institution's recognized image. Relevant dealers such as Anthony d'Offay and Nicholas Logsdail, as well as new gallery managers like Karsten Schubert and Maureen Paley, would in fact visit graduate shows at these institutions around town. The comparison between London and Glasgow, however, has clearly shown that in terms of art skills and paradigms particular teachers tend to be far more influential on students than the school itself (Vettese, 1998, p.96). In fact, the compulsory or optional courses a student attends determine his or her understanding of art, as well as the particular style or procedure he or she intends to apply. While Goldsmiths students were drawn towards a specific trend, Gordon and his colleagues at the Environmental Art Department in Glasgow rather adopted a shared approach. As regards to style and methods it is most relevant that students are capable of looking for upcoming trends, like Hirst and Gordon did, instead of lingering on with old gone techniques or languages. Women artists usually have one more barrier to overcome during art education, which is finding an understanding of themselves as female authors in an originally male dominated profession, hence opting often in favour of gender issues to be treated in their early works, such as in Borland's case for instance. However, art school may not be ultimately defining for every graduate, as in the case of Sarah Lucas who had further extended her personal research to find a way that would meet her ambition. Maybe the most important feature of the time spent in art school is about the network capital that a student is able to acquire, because it is an environment which gives first access to the art system: teachers can provide some influent connections, while educational institutions may offer early chances for public exposure. Nevertheless, the considered examples highlight that the peer group is probably the most relevant resource at this stage for any aspiring artist: this is the true mutual source of necessary confrontation, support and incitement to a young man or woman who embarks on such long and risky journey as a career in the arts.

Chapter 5
Southern flames and Northern lights

5.1. Life after art school: self-entrepreneurship and artist-run-spaces for the seminal period

Immediately after graduation, aspiring artists stand before the most difficult period in their career, as the next few years will reveal which one of the many former students will succeed in turning into a proper artist, one who makes a living from his or her profession. Entering art school already operates an early selection, especially for those who are picked by influent art schools or branded colleges, however it only constitutes the first level of the art world which is relatively protected and free from particular concerns. Indeed, art students have the possibility to concentrate on gaining artistic capital as well as some good connections, while in the aftermath prospective artists rather need to accelerate the increase of individual reputation and network resources. Hence, the value of training for artistic success is not self-assured, but needs to be developed further in the period which follows graduation, especially with regards to relational aspects with gatekeepers for entering further stages of career (Towse, 1996, p.307). But the chief problem on finishing art school is represented by financial capital, since it takes time for any artistic profession to pay off and meanwhile artist candidates must find some sort of job to earn a living, which on the other hand reduces the time spent on working for their career. Australian economist David Throsby (1996, p.345) has thoroughly studied the labour market of visual artists, finding that the wage function of every author is divided into three separate compartments: first of all, there is the obvious dichotomy between arts and non artistic jobs, last there are also arts related activities such as teaching or commercial applications of creative practice. At the kick-start of an art career, the wage deriving from direct artistic creations is rather low, thus the candidate needs to have an art unrelated job to finance his or her aspirations, however finding the latter very time-consuming. Aspiring artists usually favour art related jobs by large – for instance writing for art magazines, working for galleries or exhibition premises, tutoring students or teaching at their former school – because it feels like being in the art world and sometimes even helps to build new connections, although it tends to become very distracting for the time properly spent creating artworks. In any case, after finishing art education one is either extremely motivated for a career in the visual arts, taking the high risk of failure, or one needs the backing of close friends and family for financial support, while thriving on for success. Without a sufficient drive to the arts, it is hard to endure the many difficulties and likely rejections that one may find at this early stage. Furthermore, one's artistic project usually needs still some time to ripen and may hardly find acceptance by relevant gatekeepers. Damien Hirst recalls for instance that the influent London dealer Nicholas Logsdail told him in the aftermath of *Building One* in 1990 that he would keep watching the young artist's developments for three more years, before agreeing to represent him at Lisson Gallery. This anecdote is informative about the low risk attitude of established gatekeepers – be them galleries, curators, collectors or critics – who are usually very careful in promoting new artists or movements, in order to avoid possible drawbacks on their own reputation, if they fail to pick the right authors. Such a prospected trial period can be discouraging thus leading to drop chances for good, but the privileges enjoyed by celebrities are so remarkable that most aspiring artists don't acknowledge the narrow possibilities of success (Throsby, 2005). Ideally both artist candidates and gatekeepers wish to have the shortest early career period as possible, in order to capitalize immediately the promotion costs of a new entry by exploiting the star system mechanics. As a matter of facts, information asymmetry on the art market affects young artists heavily, because the lack of reputation virtually nullifies their starting quotation (Santagata, 1998, p.38). As a consequence, the inclusion of young artists on the art scene depends on the progressive increase of the four fundamental features, which can determine their success. The huge number of artist candidates compared to the small size of the art market, the high access costs and the scarcity of public exhibition venues determine a high entry barrier to the art system. What is more, as contemporary art is extremely specialized, there is a relatively small community of gatekeepers, which hold influence over successful trends and they are difficult to access. According to Italian economist Pierluigi Sacco (1998, pp.43-47), who has analysed access routes for young visual artists, the kick-start selection would in fact be largely based on a self-referential approach of the art élite, even if some objective features may be considered. In the scholar's opinion, in order to meet the art system requirements artist candidates would have to draw on their autonomous and consistent artwork resumed in a coherent proposal or art project, on the one side, as well as on the relational capital they are able to build up, on the other side. As far as artistic capital is concerned, in principle new artists should be able to situate their contribution strictly in the field of current trends, however succeeding also in showing its crucial and original relevance for the future progress of visual arts. On the other hand, network resources are critical in order to be recognized and supported by the most influential gatekeepers, so as to be become a rightful member of the art system. Sacco maintains that both features are fundamental for artistic success, but they must be evenly balanced, since one-sided strategies could lead to serious inefficiency, for instance barring promising candidates who have no connections, while launching others with better acquaintances but lesser talent. Thus in Sacco's opinion (1998, pp.50-75) investing one's efforts solely on the art project or only on the improvement of relational capital could cause an incorrect selection of new entries. To avoid such failure he offers two solutions: either granting young artists easy access to connections by means of opportunities for them to meet relevant gatekeepers, or granting scholarships to offer young talented artists financial support to develop their individual art project. Sacco's propositions appear to go together with the opinion expressed by Ruth Towse (1996, p.98), whose research on art market values and artists' earnings conclude that talent makes up the true difference between failing and successful artists. Although these findings are of great help, they don't give an adequate explanation for the specific reasons that favour the entrance in the art system of one artist or another. Furthermore, they don't consider sufficiently the fact that talent is not an objective feature, but is rather credited by gatekeepers as shown in Bourdieu's theory of the artistic field. Strategies to increase artistic capital or network resources should definitely be balanced, as Sacco supposes, but this is not enough. As a matter of facts, the two aspects cannot be taken separately at this early career stage: every artistic choice is also a means of connecting with a given art system, while relationships in the art milieu may bring about certain options as to creative stances. What's more, after art school an aspiring artist must connect his or her artistic and relational capital with growing social and financial resources, which are reputation and wage. It comes to no surprise, hence, that many successful new entries of the British Nineties have applied similar strategies, which tried to integrate all various resources necessary to increase their position in the art field. Seeking the attention of an influent dealer or curator, coming together as a group to foster communal chances, seeking mentors among gatekeepers and other influent players, working as assistants at galleries or for already successful artists are just some of the most recurrent strategies of the last few decades, if not in general for the entire history of Western art. Taking the latter for instance, many artists have started their career with an apprenticeship for older authors: referring to British contemporary art, Dinos and Jake Chapman worked for Gilbert & George and Marc Quinn for Barry Flanagan, while Liam Gillick was Michael Craig-Martin's assistant and Anthony Caro was Henry Moore's. Any research perspective that focuses only on one of the mentioned aspects, especially those who consider only the artistic production of an aspiring artist, tend to isolate the author from his or her concrete surroundings, thus missing to envisage the whole picture and understand the complexity of conditions that bring about specific outcomes. Any young art graduate is faced with difficult choices that go far beyond mere artistic decisions and need an answer altogether, as well as with the right timing. At this stage the importance of concentration and location proves crucial, since proximity to like-minded artists as well as local infrastructures may favour the creation of a critical mass and enhance individual visibility, however financial circumstances often constitute an insurmountable condition (Caves, 2000, pp.33-35). As underlined by Gregor Muir (2011, p.27), at the beginning of the Nineties London could not provide the best premises for the majority of graduates that came out of the city's academies. In fact, the local art system did not offer much institutional space or resources to support and promote younger generations. After completing his courses at the Slade, the high cost of living in London was one of the main reasons why Gordon immediately went back to Glasgow. As happened to a lot of his London peers, he couldn't find the means for either creating new relationships or focusing on his work and was rather disappointed by his experience in the Capital as far as opportunities and milieu are concerned. On the occasion of his Turner Prize nomination in 1996 he didn't hide his disillusion towards his London period on various media reports, such as the following on *The Independent*:

> *"Douglas Gordon, who prefers Glasgow ("fewer arseholes"), studied at the Slade between 1988 and 1990. It was not, however, a happy time. Marooned in Crouch End in north London, barely able to buy a Travelcard – other students were "being dropped off in chauffeur-driven cars" – Gordon missed the rising tide of new art." (Beckett, 1996, p.19)*

Although abandoning the capital in 1990 proved ill timed as regards the forthcoming YBA turmoil, the Scottish artist was able to keep contact with his friends and acquaintances in London, who would later prove fundamental – for himself and for the wider Glasgow art milieu – to approach the international art system. What really drew him back to his hometown was love to his then-partner Christine Borland and peer support, as he could count on the former colleagues from the Environmental Art Department, while he didn't find a comparable grouping in London that would let him in. Collectiveness is indeed the best way for new entries to arouse attention of influent gatekeepers, such as critics and dealers, but the group must not necessarily share common ideas or style. Mostly it is just a loose grouping of art school mates that keep on hanging out together in order to help each other, as in the case of Hirst and other Goldsmiths' graduates, but there may also be a coherent ideology or method that all members collectively partake such as for the young people that experienced Harding's classes at the Old Girls' High. As a matter of facts, the head and founder of the Environmental Art Department had truly instilled to his students the importance of socialising as a key factor for emerging at an early stage, as he would later comment:

> *"One need only look to the various art movements and groupings of the twentieth century to see how important socialising has been because it offers also the opportunity for the exchange of ideas and information and lends mutual support. This is exactly what this particular network of Glasgow artists did. After art school the Transmission Gallery then became the focus for this." (Harding, 2001a)*

Faced with the difficulties of an almost impermeable art system, groups of young artists act as guerrilla squads to strengthen their position as a collective rather than individually and break entry barriers together, but as soon as they have reached some critical success, they loosen up and every individual proceeds alone. This strategy may in fact prove rapidly helpful, as in the case of the *Freeze* exhibitors who were immediately picked up by various London dealers, but those who stayed behind had to keep on lingering with self-entrepreneurship and autonomous group shows. The most secure way to start a career, which avoids new entries to rush to the market and takes collectiveness a step further, is founding an artist-run space that gives room to the alternative art scene. Relatively free from art market pressure, these enterprises are open to experimentation and thus very interesting for discovering new talents, as well as representing phenomenal means to arouse dealers' attention – although artist run spaces are often born in contrast to current trends (Vettese, 1998, pp.124-130). The founders of City Racing properly expressed in the aftermath the drive that usually leads young artists to open an artist-run space, such as the one they had contributed to launch and which had represented a major spot of the alternative scene in London throughout the Nineties:

> *"Artist run ventures are a valuable way of demystifying the business of art. They promote a sharing of information, skills and experience*

> *while simultaneously nurturing relationships between artists which can often lead to a more genuinely horizontal and organically developing infrastructure of cultural activity. Often they provide resources that are outside the reach of individuals." (Burges, Coventry, Hale, Noble and Owen, 2002, p.6)*

The Transmission gallery in Glasgow fulfilled exactly the purpose of giving a chance to young artists in town, feeding the alternative art scene and thus being very far from the business attitude of private galleries, as well as from the typical art market concerns[1]. This artist-run space was opened following the previous example of Edinburgh's Fruitmarket Gallery, with painter and Glasgow School of Art teacher Alexander Moffat among the chief founders of the new premise, in order to provide the Clyde-side area with a venue for newer generation artists and overcome the lack of exhibition opportunities in town. Very much like a free association, Transmission was open to all artists resident in the city who would apply and be accepted as members by paying a small entrance fee. Furthermore, the articles of constitution provided for a board of directors, who stayed in charge for two years and were responsible for each exhibition organized or for inviting outside artists. However, the statute required to change the directors after they had served one term, while the new committee members had to be younger than the previous ones. The aim of this provision was keeping constant generation renewal and brain turnover, in order to avoid undue personal influence on the gallery policies. Thanks to the performances by Gordon and Richardson of the late Eighties, of which some were held at Transmission, the first cohort of graduates at the Environmental Art Department got involved in the gallery activities. In the summer of 1989 the occasion presented itself that Transmission had to move premises and at the same time renew its direction committee, hence it was passed over to some of the recently graduated students of Harding's department, who also physically renovated the new artist-run space in Merchant city. Dave Allen, Christine Borland, Billy Clark, Douglas Gordon and Craig Richardson served on the new board of directors, although Katrina Brown, Roderick Buchanan and Elsie Mitchell were soon involved in the gallery activities. The six young artists caught the chance to use the gallery as a means to approach the international art system, rather than lingering on in the local and alternative art scene. Their policy was to present works that wouldn't normally find place in the city and to avoid an excessive focus on Glaswegian productions, fearing a parochial drift as had been the case of the former committees. In order to do so, they decided to alternate invitations to young Scottish art graduates with calls of much more famous artists, who still agreed with the visual democracy and public art principle the Transmission directors valued. Each exhibition was then followed by a panel discussion with the guest artists and a smaller show of young Scottish authors commenting on the celebrated author's works. Christine Borland sums up the new committee philosophy, which set Transmission at the margin of the art system, but very conscious of upcoming trends:

> *"These activities remained within a slightly broadened alternative scene of self-initiated projects, artist-run-spaces and work outside of galleries. On comparing ourselves with 'mainstream' initiatives locally we knew our activity was at least equally important, if 'other'. [...] private galleries, dealers, the market all seemed too alien to comprehend since no equivalent existed in Glasgow. 'They' were simply not addressed. [...] The remit of the gallery remained 'to show work which otherwise would not be shown in Glasgow'." (Borland in Guilt by Association, Cat.1992, p.7)*

Richardson still recalls that early discussions among the six new directors brought about a studied decision to abandon neo-Expressionism in favour of what art magazines such as *Artforum, October, Art Monthly* and *Variant* were promoting. The 1989 group exhibition at the Centre Georges Pompidou *Magiciens de la Terre*, for instance, had a fundamental impact on the young artists, convincing them that future developments in the visual arts were moving away from late modernism. This artistic stance towards neo-conceptual art practices was further strengthened through a fundamental shift in attitude that favoured the increase of relational capital; such was their commitment of inviting older and renown artists. Furthermore, the gallery soon became a sort of open workshop all members used for their daily work, since no one had a personal working space because of financial limitations and rather preferred to hang out together exchanging views with peer artists. Thus the true reason why Gordon did not have a studio of his own in Glasgow was in fact a strong belief in socialisation, finding it better to be confronted with his friends at Transmission, in order to ripen his art practice and projects, as he told in an interview with Graham Fagen:

> *"Yeah, a studio I suppose in the traditional sense is where an artist goes to have a singular and exclusive dialogue between himself or herself and the practice, whatever that might be, so I suppose if you isolate the place from that and actually don't have a singular and exclusive dialogue so you have a dialogue between peers about ideas*

> *then that constitutes pretty much the same process [...]. Working at Transmission there was a lot of dialogue between visiting artists, a huge debate between people who were on the committee and the people who were helping on the committee." (Gordon in Fagen, 1999, p.75)*

The people serving on the new Transmission committee intentionally tried to create a coherent grouping, both in attitude and possibly also in style; one, which could appeal to an international audience. As a matter of facts, artist and later Turner Prize winner Richard Wright maintains that the gallery board headed by Gordon and Borland consciously used the premises as a strategic means to foster a leading group for the city, finally making something happen in Glasgow and drawing people from outside to the Scottish town:

> *"In the early '90s what really changed, when Douglas Gordon, Christine Borland and Dave Allen were involved, was that there was a much more conscious attempt to engage with an existing art world. [...] That was a really new thing, and I think the model of Transmission being an agent of attraction and a bridgehead into other situations is still in place." (Cit. Wright in Lowndes, 2010, pp.138-139)*

Curator Nicola White, who had just come back to Glasgow, recalls that the new Transmission committee was amazingly successful in turning the gallery into a showcase for the international art world, rather then remaining in the alternative scene, hence starting exchanges and alliances with likeminded spaces all around Europe (White in Lowndes, 2010, pp.118-119). Thus the committee members learned to work together providing mutual support, discussing each other's works and planning all exhibitions on a joint basis, as well as sending invitations to artists and trying to bring initiatives abroad. This reading of the situation is shared by Christine Borland, who herself recalls that the way the new board managed Transmission proved particularly effective for spreading new ideas and works, as well as for overcoming obstacles that new entries are usually faced with:

> *"I think the Transmission Gallery is a key part, and it continues to be. It's a gallery, so of course it's structured, but really it's about empowerment of artists; they're working and curating shows, going abroad, having exhibitions, telling people about Transmission in Glasgow, asking people to come over – just spreading the wave,*

spreading the circle of friends wider and wider. No doubt about it, that's what's kept me going." (Borland in Barclay Morgan, 1999)

Hence, the six directors didn't simply use Transmission as a premise to show their own works or to exchange it with other artist-run spaces around Europe, but instead exploited the gallery as a chance to get in touch with established artists that could become mentors or even agents of the young Glaswegian artists. While serving in the Transmission board Gordon, Borland and Richardson could indeed approach several older Scottish artists that had achieved a relevant international career, such as Alan Johnston and Thomas Lawson, or even an American star as in the case of conceptual artist Lawrence Weiner. An art writer and himself an artist, Lawson had settled in New York since 1975 and soon become an influent commentator of the American art scene. Imbued with egalitarian socialism typical of his Scottish working class background, as soon as 1982 he was aware of the turn the art market had taken, describing the works of Barbara Kruger and Jeff Koons as sophisticated hoaxes, which plainly valued appearance over substance. Returning to Glasgow in 1990 for an exhibition of his own paintings at the Third Eye Centre, Lawson was contacted by the Transmission directors and remained baffled by their attitude and competencies to stay already on an international art scene, despite the young age and the parochial size of Glasgow. He couldn't believe that these young Glaswegians were so ambitious for their hometown and strategically prepared to interact with relevant players of the art system. In fact, the committee members didn't shy away from occasions to make important acquaintances and never avoided exhibition opportunities that might consequently arise. Some of them presented their works on occasion of two major exhibitions which drew the critics' attention on the so-called 'Transmission Generation': these were the group shows *Self Conscious State* at Third Eye Centre in Glasgow, which took place in late 1990, and *Guilt by Association* at the Modern Art Museum in Dublin only two years later.

The roots of the mentioned exhibitions laid entirely in the events and connections around Transmission, sometimes arising in a fortuitous manner, but chiefly due to a very straightforward strategy of exposure and relation building. The birth of *Self Conscious State* paradigmatically depicts the method of the Transmission people, who never missed a chance to bring new connections home[2]. In order to make a living, many aspiring artists in town were busy installing exhibitions of established artists at the main premises in town, being Tramway and the Third Eye Centre. So did the young members of the Transmission committee, however immediately exploiting the professional connections which they could obtain by working at important institutions, although for unskilled jobs. They made acquaintance with Andrew Nairne, curator of the Third Eye Centre, and asked him for the possibility to organize a show of their own in October 1990 on the occasion of Glasgow's year as European Capital of Culture. During the summer, as soon as he was back home, Gordon got involved with four other Transmission peers for a comprehensive group show to be organized autonomously. *Self Concious State* was entirely conceived by Christine Borland, Craig Richardson, Roderick Buchanan, Kevin Henderson and Gordon himself, which were also included as sole exhibitors. All of them were graduates of the Environmental Art Department, except Kevin Henderson who was from Edinburgh and had attended Gray's College in Aberdeen. He had met on the Glaswegians while presenting a work at the Third Eye Centre in 1988, when he also became part of the earlier Transmission grouping. *Self Concious State* revealed itself a good opportunity to cement the association of the five aspiring artists and directly led to the following exhibition in Dublin two years later. However, this was foremost the starting point of a thriving artists' community that had settled in the Scottish city and was inspired by a solid team spirit. Although being in charge of the cultural program of this prestigious venue, Nairne didn't chose the contributors nor the works for *Self Concious State*, which were instead picked by the Transmission board. It may appear surprising that the Third Eye Centre curator would grant so much free rein to these young artists, however the show followed soon after *Scatter* in 1989, an exhibition that had served Nairne to present a range of different practices emerging in Scotland and moving away from Glasgow Painting. In a way, he had already announced his favour to the neo-conceptual strain and simply sanctioned the decisions made by the Transmission committee, after discussing the general terms of the project to be carried out. This achievement is in fact linked with the ability to negotiate of the young Environmental Art graduates, which was a crucial part of any public art project they learnt at Harding's department, thus constituting a proper working strategy that combined artistic capital and relational resources. The five young artists defined even the title of the exhibition, which appears to suggest they were well aware of their own means as well as of the quality of their ideas. In a way, they wished to present post-conceptual works by young Scottish authors, which resulted from a cooperative practice, though not in a strict sense, but from constant debate and mutual review among the five of them. Furthermore, as they had helped out installing previous shows at the Third Eye Centre, Gordon and his colleagues had a good knowledge of the exhibition premises, hence they tried to take advantage of this condition when mounting the installations in order to set the pieces appropriately together on a visual basis and from a conceptual point of view. Again, in his contribution to the catalogue for *Guilt by Association*, Craig Richardson went over the circumstances that generated the previous group show at the Third Eye Centre two years earlier, which showcased the inclinations and ambitions of a whole local community of young artists:

> *"In our case it was the presentation of what we would have termed post-conceptual art by young artists from Scotland that we wanted to address collectively. [...] In the end the gallery became a type of studio, and the two-week installation period a time for investigation. Self Conscious State was contemporaneous with ideas of interest to the locale at the time. [...] that it was appreciated as a group event made its necessity all the clearer – at the time in Glasgow artists' initiatives were continuing to grow in ambition and self critical success. The identity of a work is different when generated from within a self-generated group. All the competing ideas offered up by the artists in the group supply a context as dynamic as place or site. In this climate works completed and still-planned are always under discussion, responses requested and negotiated." (Richardson in Guilt by Association, Cat.1992, p.9)*

For the exhibition at the Third Eye Centre, Gordon's first in his hometown after the London period, he decided to make a post-conceptual work which combined the disparate methods he had learnt at the Slade and at the Glasgow School of Art, though trying to remain consistent with the specific location. He was determined to avoid bland site-specificity or whatever could go along the lines of a self-referential analysis of the Glasgow situation, maybe to be repeated exactly the same in some other venues and revealing a stereotyped Scottish character. On the contrary, he devised a cognitive survey on historical memory very much in the sense of Roland Barthes, which resulted in an original contribution that heightens time and place awareness. This deliberation was indeed the source of *List of Names*, a wall text displayed as an endless inventory of all the people he could remember to have ever met in person, starting from a maternal uncle and going on in a crowd of acquaintances, friends and relatives. The list included 1440 names, which were applied in the form of black vinyl letterings onto the long white wall of the main exhibition room, thus visually recalling a war memorial. This is a work that clearly leans on conceptual practices, though Katrina Brown (2004, p.15) maintains that Gordon went far beyond its basic notions: as a matter of facts, the piece is truly based on the fallacy of human memory, as well as on the specific relationship of the artist with a significant time and place. *List of Names* is a sort of research on the act of recollection, serving as an empirical demonstration of how human memory system works: sometimes it proves accurate and limitless, some other times it is weak and unreliable. In a way, this work was the practical development of a previous text-piece, in which Gordon simply announced the applied procedure, that was him trying not to *Forget Fact and Figures* (1989), the work presented at the *Windfall* group show in Bremen. At the same time, rather than evoking the memory of the named people, the piece instead gives account of the author's biography being a proof of his life based on the fact that he spent his time – at least for a moment – with all the people mentioned. Exposing the futility of remembering and the vanity of being remembered, Gordon once recalled the creative process that led to *List of Names* in discussion with critic Stéphanie Moisdon-Tremblay:

> *"There were 1440 names at the time, and the work is ongoing. It functioned quite honestly and as much as possible as a mirror of the actual mechanism of memory that most of us use all the time. This meant that on the one hand the system was impressively large, and on the other hand it was unbearably oppressive. It was an accurate and honest statement but it was full of small mistakes (like forgetting the names of some friends etceteras), so there were some embarrassing elements in the work, but that all seemed to be quite close to the truth of how our head functions anyway. Sometimes it works and sometimes it doesn't." (Gordon in Moisdon-Tremblay, 1996, p.121)*

Christine Borland presented a piece titled *Supported* (1990), which the author herself considers her first mature work and derived from a marked forensic interest, especially about the representation of the human body throughout the history of medicine. After frequent visits to the anatomy museum of Glasgow University, she finally started to work with skeletons which were later to become a true trademark of her production, although the actual piece for *Self Conscious State* featured only dust. In fact, *Supported* consisted of a glass shelf onto which a skeleton had been laid on and later removed, in order to sketch its outlines with falling dust[3]. Gordon's and Borland's contributions express the common denominator of the Transmission generation as regards to artistic strategies, being a method based upon thorough investigation as well as on a drive towards negotiation with the prospective venue or public. In his academic review on Scottish contemporary art, which he compiled over twenty years from the exhibition at the Third Eye Centre, Richardson holds that the contributions of the five young artists were far more interesting in theory, while the actual form they resulted in was rather of medium quality, save *List of Names.* Nevertheless, he maintains that Self Conscious State represented a major turning point in the Glasgow art scene for a strain of different reasons. Indeed this exhibition sanctioned the early breakthrough of the kind of self-entrepreneurial spirit represented by the Transmission committee and which had progressively permeated many independent initiatives in town. Gordon and his peers had managed to exploit the heightened visibility brought about by the Glasgow Capital of Culture Year to their favour, but in doing so helped to turn the light on the wider alternative artists milieu in the city. Putting aside the discussion on the quality of the featured works, *Self Conscious State* was the result of a truly masterful operation, which sanctioned the new course of Transmission gallery. Finally, the five young artists obtained the backing of influent players of the local art system who would also become their mentors for future exhibitions, such as curator Andrew Nairne and writer Thomas Lawson. The scene was set for the takeoff of a new generation of Glaswegian artists that demonstrated an improved strategic awareness as well as the intention to address an international audience, hence reaching far beyond the narrow borders of Scotland.

In parallel to the Third Eye Centre exhibition, a much larger group of former students from the Glasgow School of Art started the first widespread public art project in Glasgow's East End. The *Bellgrove Station Billboard Project* reached from September 1990 to August 1991 and was looked after by two young art teachers, Bohemian Pavel Büchler and American Alan Dunn. They chose sixteen graduates who were invited to occupy in turns the empty Bellgrove station advertising spaces. The experiment was not really ground-breaking, still it was interesting considering the hard recession period: art was trying to set the passengers' imagination free, taking hold of the advertising spaces that were generally used to persuade consumers to buy commodities (Rolfe, 1991, p.6). At the beginning of 1991, Gordon was called to contribute to the project and installed the text-piece *Walk a million miles* (1991). The inscription in block italic capitals was applied on the wall at the backend of the station, in order to be seen by all travellers waiting on whichever platform for their train. As far as this work is concerned, there are two important issues to consider, the first being the definitive option for Bembo typeface in his text-pieces, the most employed one in the publishing industry. The second aspect, instead, is represented by the first-time choice of a text aimed at direct communication with the viewer, hence abandoning any sort of descriptive or factual content such as in the tradition of Conceptual Art. It was indeed the first time that Gordon intentionally planned a text, which fosters public involvement, because the sentence clearly addresses to the reader, abandoning once and for all the kind of word plays such as in *Meaning and Location* or descriptive phrases like that for the Smith Biennial.

While artists at Transmission Gallery gave birth to a lively art community which focused international interest on Glasgow, various former Goldsmiths' students and *Freeze* contributors were doing the same in London, even if their means and aims were quite different. Nevertheless, the events in the capital city should better be dealt with together, because the media ferment stirred by the young London authors between 1990 and 1993 came to the general advantage of a new generation in the UK. Douglas Gordon is emblematic in this regard, because he could make the most of both cities from the artistic and relational point of view, bringing back to Glasgow a lot of acquaintances in the art system. At the time the relevance of the London alternative scene was paramount, specifically events such as the *East Country Yard Show* by Sarah Lucas and Henry Bond or the three exhibitions held at *Building One*, curated by Carl Freedman and Billee Sellman. Nonetheless, while London colleagues focused on exhibition venues and installation quality, Glasgow artists valued works and ideas even more. In order to understand the progress of the events in the British art world, it is worth to trace back some crucial points set in the capital city in the year 1990. As the economic recession caused by the Japanese bubble burst of 1989 started to bite, even for the newer generation in London it was artist-run spaces that would assume a fundamental role (Fox, 2013). As regards to self-initiated exhibitions, Goldsmiths' graduates had already tested a successful example, being the warehouse show in the London docklands. Considering that only a few of the *Freeze* contributors had conquered an almost stable entrance in the local art market, such as Fioana Banner and Ian Davenport, the remaining hoard had to keep on producing their own shows to draw attention again. The advantage was however that they didn't have to do it anew, since the working procedure of *Freeze* proved consistent and easy to replicate. In fact, to stage a warehouse show all that was necessary was finding an empty industrial building – which the Docklands were overabundant of at the time – negotiate a free rental period, then find a few thousand pounds to produce the catalogue, put together some talented friends and send out the invitations. This is indeed the exact method applied to *Building One* and to the *East Country Yard*

Show, the former staged in the disused Peak Freans Factory in Bermondsay, the latter in the immense area of the East Country Yard building in the South Docks[4]. Both venues were quite close to one another as well as to the Surrey Docks offices that had been used for the three part exhibition of *Freeze*. Following the latter example in every detail, *Building One* became home to three separate group shows curated by Carl Freedman and Billee Sellman, which were *Modern Medicine* commencing on March 1st 1990 and with Hirst still in the curatorial part, *Gambler* starting on July 1st of the same year, and finally *Market* still in October 1990, although it was a solo exhibition of Michael Landy. A writer and anthropologist, Freedman was an old friend and age peer of Hirst's from Leeds, as well as a fundamental character to help his companion at such a delicate stage. At the time, they lived in the same flat and frequently exchanged opinions on the mechanics of art market, in order to work out how art acquired monetary value. Ambitious and strategically minded, the two young men from Leeds set out to conquer the London marketplace fostering the city's reputation on an international scale again by emulating the particular aesthetic of the Saatchi collection. However, this partnership didn't last long, since Freedman was quite critical about Hirst's tendency to turn into a branded artist for himself:

> *"I think we shared the same goal – to make London a place where contemporary art could thrive and have the same vitality as cities like Cologne and New York (at that time London was somewhat of a backwater). We went different ways when Damien decided he wanted to spend more time making Damien Hirst the centre of the international art world – which on some levels he has achieved." (Freedman in Berens, 2008)*

Despite such diverging visions between the two, Hirst and Freedman together were able to raise corporate funding for *Building One*, including one-thousand pounds from Charles Saatchi who kept on following every single move of the Leeds artist since *Freeze*. Again all participating artists were students or recent graduates, being Mat Collishaw, Grainne Cullen, Dominic Denis, Angus Fairhurst, Damien Hirst, Abigail Lane, Miriam Lloyd and Craig Wood for *Modern Medicine*, while *Gambler* counted among the contributors Dan Bonsall, Dominic Denis, Steve di Benedetto, Angus Fairhurst, Tim Head, Damien Hirst and Michael Scott. As with *Freeze* the catalogue for *Modern Medicine* was designed by Tony Arefin and included writings by Angus Fairhurst, while the one for Gambler featured over 500 colour images and interviews by Liam Gillick with each exhibitor. The third show, *Market,* was mounted by Michael Landy alone and consisted of empty market stalls, as well as various stacks and creates, some covered with fake grass carpets. It looked as if the venue had been once a lively marketplace full of any sorts of goods, but now depleted by recession, which made a social comment that impressed even a severe critic such as Julian Stallabrass (Cooper, 2012, p.28). The *Building One* exhibitions were able to replicate the success of *Freeze* and attracted even more art experts, helping another bunch of young artists to access the art market or at least to sell some of their pieces. Furthermore, such warehouse shows would become emblematic for many aspiring artists, inspired by a sort of do-it-yourself ethos which was incredibly attractive and appeared to be the best strategy to get their voices heard. For the first show in March 1990 Hirst displayed some of his early *Medicine Cabinets,* the first works he declared to be ever content with and which directly referred to the particular installation mode of Jeff Koon's hoovers (Serota, 2011, p.93). They were small white cabinets – either open or shut in glass cases – which had the shelves full of various pharmaceutical bottles, boxes and containers placed in absolute random order to fit Hirst's own aesthetic choice. Some pieces of this series were immediately bought by Charles and Doris Saatchi, who didn't get the chance to buy the works of Hirst's graduate show the year before faced with the refusal of Goldsmiths to authorise the purchase. For the second part at *Building One,* however, the young Leeds artist felt some need for darkness and spectacular installation, thus he switched to a totally different kind of work, as he wanted to make significant art both for its meaning as for its space dimension (Reckhenrich, Anderson and Kupp, 2009, p.42). Hirst maintains that, having recently lost his grandmother, he was struck by simplicity of transition between life and death, hence progressively coming up with the life-cycle theme, which would since then become a trademark of his production. On the occasion of *Gambler* he finally decided to drop any curatorial obligation and concentrated on his first-ever animal installation, titled *A Thousand Years* (1990). It was a large glass case divided into two adjoining parts, the first with a white box filled with breeding maggots and the subsequent flies entering the second compartment, where they would feed themselves with a rotting cow's head and were finally electrocuted by a fly incinerator. In seeing this installation for the first time, Charles Saatchi is said to have stayed open-mouthed and completely astonished. As a matter of facts, the collector immediately purchased the work and offered to fund the next major animal installation by Damien Hirst, thus openly declaring the beginning of a relationship that can be rightly defined a true patronage (Thompson, 2008, pp.68-69). Thanks to *A Thousand Years* the young Leeds author had finally found a collector and patron – even before having a dealer representation – and started on a path of provocation and notoriety that would be profitable for many other artists of his generation.

On the contrary, neither for Sarah Lucas nor for her Goldsmiths peer and co-curator Henry Bond the *East Country Yard Show* resulted in an immediate career launch, even though the group exhibition counts today as a seminal moment for the YBA generation. In fact, this show is being remembered especially for the huge dimensions of the chosen venue, which left almost sixty square metres for every exhibitor to work with (Lillington, 1990, p.55). The impressive East Country Yard building laid vacant for over twenty years in the South Docks, hence Bond approached the competent property development company Skillion and obtained to stage the exhibition from May 31st to June 22nd 1990. In addition to Lucas and Bond, the featured artists were all Goldsmiths' graduates of the late Eighties including Anya Gallaccio, Michael Landy, Virginia Nimarkoh, Tom Trevor and Gary Hume, the latter still being Lucas' partner at the time. The memorable pieces of this show were installations by Gallaccio and Hume, as both managed to deal with the huge exhibition space though staying by the style they had explored in the previous two years. Lucas' boyfriend hung the textile equivalent of his door paintings on a laundry line stretching across the venue, while Gallaccio produced *Tense* (1990) which stayed in tune with her plants and fruits tendency: the installation consisted of a rectangular sweep made up of one ton of oranges that were left rotting, while the walls were decorated with a wallpaper featuring an oranges-motif. Mastering the exhibition venue and revealing a well-defined aesthetic, this artwork spoke out to the London gallery system, expressing the genuine attitude of a young artist that didn't want to wait to be invited in. Both Hume and Gallaccio were already represented by an emerging London dealer, German Karsten Schubert, and such warehouse shows were perfect opportunities to feed their individual reputation, sometimes spilling over to some other peers included in the show. Lucas wasn't one of them and this caused an ongoing rivalry with her then partner Gary Hume, finally braking up when the latter was invited to work in New York the following year. However, after the *East Country Yard Show* Lucas was persuaded to shift to photography as a prevailing artistic means starting a very intense period of creativity that resulted in pieces later recognized as truly iconic, such as *Eating a Banana* (1990) and *Divine* (1991) inspired by the readings of cult feminist writer Andrea Dworkin. Furthermore, on her return from the USA she started a period of thorough experimentation, assembling cut outs from various tabloids that would later lead to collages such as *Penis Nailed to a Board* (1992). Another major achievement for her in 1990 was to get acquainted to Sadie Coles, at the time an assistant for Anthony D'Offay and still a long way from becoming one of London's principal dealers. The two women recognized each other's talent and agreed on waiting for their respective growth, starting to cooperate only in 1997 when Coles founded her own gallery and picked Lucas for her first ever dealer representation. Lucas had worked meanwhile with Jay Jopling and Anthony D'Offay, but she had always resisted entering an established gallery, even though she was seeking public recognition. In her opinion, thriving to enter in a big gallery could only put a young artist at the bottom of the hierarchy, while the real strength of her generation was in numbers and in self-initiated events which would eventually attract some dealers (Robecchi, 2007, pp.9-12). As a matter of facts, the professional care and aesthetic expertise these Goldsmiths graduates had put in mounting the warehouse shows did finally draw the attention of the London art world. Their attempts to enter the system were progressively supported by several critics such as Sacha Cradock from the *Guardian*, Sarah Kent from *London Time Out* and Andrew Renton from the weekly review *Blitz*. Even influent contemporary art magazines – *Artscribe* and *Art Monthly* to name a few – started to take a closer look at these initiatives thanks to British columnists Kate Bush, David Batchelor and Adrian Searle. The latter would become chief art critic of the Guardian in 1992 and since then keeping an eye on the various artists belonging to the newer generation. Maybe one of the most authoritative examples of the early support by several critics is an article written in the summer of 1990 by renowned art critic Andrew Graham-Dixon on the *Independent*:

> *"Goldsmiths graduates are unembarrassed about promoting themselves and their work: some of the most striking exhibitions in London over the past few months – The East Country Yard Show, or Gambler, both staged in docklands – have been independently organized and funded by Goldsmiths graduates as showcases for their work. This has given them a reputation for pushiness, yet it should also be said that in terms of ambition, attention to display and sheer bravado there has been little to match such shows in the country's established contemporary art institutions. They were far superior, for instance, to any of the contemporary art shows that have been staged by the Liverpool Tate in its own multi-million-pound dockland site." (Graham-Dixon, 1990)*

Besides proving autonomous initiative and a good deal of impertinence, the *Building One* exhibitions and the *East Country Yard Show* bore the fundamental traits of the art style and strategies adopted by young British artists. However, numerous art historians and critics have challenged the collective definition coined for this new generation of artists, as it is rather inaccurate to include the broader assortment of individuals or groupings active in that period. Furthermore, it doesn't describe at all the specific trend associated with these various actors, nor does it hint at the main characteristics that were common to most of these authors. This collective name appears to be directly connected to the title chosen for the exhibitions held at the Saatchi Gallery from 1992 to 1996, which was in fact *Young British Artists*, thus it would seem to constitute a successful marketing stratagem exploited by the influent London collector. Ever since then this has become the leading definition to name the new generation of artists that burst on the British art scene in the Nineties, though other attempts of rendition have been made. While critic David Cohen has suggested the name *Brit Pop Art*, which points at the mass market appeal of this art as argued in the previous chapter, art historian Julian Stallabrass (2006b], pp.2-4) has coined a much more judgmental definition, that is *High Art Lite* – meaning a lighter version of engaged art. According to the latter, the common trait of this generation of artists was indeed that of rendering art more appealing, easy-going and popular, quite the contrary to the Eighties, when contemporary art was accessible only to a privileged intellectual and economic élite. Stallabrass maintains further that, in order to achieve such goals, the strategy applied by these young artists consisted in simplifying the contents of their artworks, on one hand by avoiding any sort of meta- or intra-artistic consideration, on the other hand by ironically introducing features linked to popular culture or everyday life experience. As a matter of facts, Stallabrass has always criticized the lack of art theoretical discourse in the production of YBA adepts, as well as the inconsistency of their attitude towards social engagement. The critic is in good company in believing that many of these artists had abandoned any sort of truly artistic aspiration, in favour of plain accessibility to the masses as a highway to success. In this regards, Cohen (1997) agrees on referencing the art of young British artists to high culture, like one would consider the relationship that pop music holds to classical music. Although some of these arguments are extremely harsh and fail to see the ability of this generation to go beyond accepted artistic themes and means, it is true that Goldsmiths graduates for instance were well aware that true popularity needed the intervention of mass media, in order to emerge from the obscurity of small art circles. The two chief strategies to obtain quick and broad notoriety are aimed at improving one's own artistic and social capital, as in the case of Damien Hirst. In fact, on one side with *A Thousand Years* he decided to produce sensational installations, whose content should be immediately recognizable and often shocking, while on the other side he started to build on a personality cult aimed at becoming a celebrity. Because of this attitude, the production of single artworks progressively stopped being the principal purpose of his action, as they were intended to become expressions – almost trademarks – of the artist's persona. Stallabrass (2006b, p.18) properly underlines the way that Hirst has achieved to make himself appear like a rock star, thus expanding the personality of the artist, which would take up the preeminent role in the art system on the expenses of artworks.

Warehouse shows of the early Nineties thus proved a valuable strategy to turn on the lights on a new generation of aspiring artists that was lingering on the outskirts of the London art world. However, it is questionable whether such exhibitions expressed the quintessential spirit of the capital's alternative art scene, since they directly appealed to the various gatekeepers that could grant access to the next career level. Many critics of the YBAs have often pointed out, that initiatives such as *Freeze* and *Building One* were intended to intercept influent players of the local art system, convincing them to pick up some of the young exhibitors. Far from being in opposition to the establishment, Hirst and his peers didn't want to subvert the system, but rather take a quick lift upwards. Artist Mark Wallinger, himself a Goldsmiths graduate and a tutor at this institution in the late Eighties, has consistently criticized warehouse shows maintaining that they were the most elitist of exhibitions which only aimed to attract influent people, "money, ladies who launch, collectors and big shots who were air-lifted into east London" (Cooper, 2012, p.28). Matthew Collings, another young artist and curator that has been associated to the YBA generation, is less cynical about this early attempts of Goldsmiths graduates to cane the art world, though still minimising their apparent contribution. In his collection of anecdotes and opinions on the London art scene of the last two decades of the 20th century, he asserts that the London youth-quake of the early Nineties was due to the fact, that it was the only lively event happening in the city – while everyone was confused and recovering from recession – hence these new entries were thought to be more exciting than they perhaps really were (Collings, 1997, p.35). It must be said, though, that the art presented in those warehouse shows was also a very self-conscious attempt to go further than what local galleries were showing, catching up with spreading trends on an international level. Michael Craig-Martin has always defended the bravery of Hirst and his peers, convinced that although they may have adopted a cunning strategy, it still was a very hazardous path to go and almost the only one left to react to a disastrous situation:

> *"Hirst exemplified their uncompromising, high-risk attitude. In a country that had few contemporary galleries and even fewer collectors, generations of young artists had survived through art-school teaching, the dole, various enterprise schemes, odd jobs. By the end of Margaret Tatcher's reign, these options had more or less dried up." (Craig-Martin, 2012, pp.38-39)*

Self-entrepreneurship was indeed the last resort for this generation; however warehouse shows were only one tool that young artists could activate, the second being organizing an artist-run space. The two means differ from one another for the temporal scope and specific aims: while warehouse shows have a sporadic character and thus need to attract immediate attention, artist-run spaces prove long lasting and need to develop their reputation by unfolding various activities on a wider period of time. To be effective, the *Building One* shows had to be played as one-shot opportunities that referenced the local art system, while autonomous galleries such as Transmission in Glasgow could work only on a thorough and persistent commitment of its initiators, set to build a stable point of attraction. Consequently, artist-run spaces are to be considered proper alternative spaces to established venues, building their own network of relationships, while warehouse shows of the early Nineties rather tended to mimic the latter, in order to gain access to the upper league. Scottish art historian Neil Mulholland (2003, p.4) agrees on this perspective, pointing out that artist initiatives of the early 1990s, which were breaded in Glasgow were usually looking further afield than the UK, seeking a more reciprocal relationship with the European context. One must notice, although, that the Scottish city didn't offer any gallery system or art establishment at all, hence local artists were necessarily drawn to build up relations ranging far abroad. However, constitutional differences between London warehouse shows and Glasgow artist-run spaces are further confirmed by Will Bradley, founder of The Modern Institute in Glasgow in the mid Nineties. When he landed in the Scottish city at the beginning of 1991, after leaving London, he was indeed struck by the energy and determination of Transmission members to uphold the gallery's principles as a means to forge a new direction in the visual arts:

> *"I'd just come from Damien Hirst at the ICA in 1991, and I came to something completely different, different ambitions, different pace and different forms [... a] seriousness and immediacy." (Richardson, 2011, p.167)*

Although several artist-run spaces were initiated throughout the UK already in the Seventies and Eighties, such as Transmission Gallery itself, as the Nineties recession started to bite many more spread as they would assume a crucial role for the survival of rising artists or groups, especially when they were founded far off from London. Such venues were much more than sole exhibition spaces; they often acted as catalyst for a thriving community, a place of relative freedom where to exchange opinions and mature new artistic proposals, though some critics would label them as useful research laboratories for the art market. Despite any sort of criticism, one couldn't underestimate the importance artist-run spaces held in the early Nineties to foster a new generation of British artists that would build a network of relationships among artists' communities, far beyond the influence of sporadic yet effective warehouse shows. Besides Transmission in Glasgow, among the most important artist-run spaces of the time one may count also the Collective and New 57 in Edinburgh, Catalyst Arts in Belfast, Locus+ in Newcastle-upon-Tyne or The International 3 in Manchester, while venues in London included City Racing, Clove near Butler's Wharf, Milch Gallery in Bloomsbury, Cubitt near King's Cross, Matt's, Infanta of Castile and Nosepaint (later Beaconsfield). One of the most interesting examples in the capital was certainly City Racing, which stayed active from 1988 to 1998 in a former betting shop and housed a significant number of first ever solo shows for women artists such as Sarah Lucas, Fiona Banner and Gillian Wearing. It might be helpful to compare the genesis of this artist-run space in London to Transmission in Glasgow and find validation to the common logic of such alternative venues for rising artists. Founded by five young London based artists – Matt Hale, Paul Noble, John Burgess, Keith Coventry and Peter Owen – the space was the straightforward result of the founders' utter exclusion from available exhibition venues in the capital, hence they decided to provide themselves premises to host shows of their own or of friends they liked:

> *"None of us would have even considered running a gallery on our own but as a collective we found the strength to do it. [...] That we did was because we created opportunities out of the little that we had – a bit like turning our cul-de-sacs into a roundabout!" (Burges, Coventry, Hale, Noble and Owen, 2002, p.1)*

Like any newcomer, the five artists had a strain of different jobs such us decoration and painting activities that they directed to raise financial capital for the gallery activities, but in 1993 they managed to get City Council funding which helped for the remaining five years of City Racing's existence. What had started from utter conviction that they were producing valuable though unrecognized artworks, finally resulted in an inevitable career plan for the five gallery founders. In fact, Hale and his colleagues soon understood that an artist-run space can be much more than a place to show one's own pieces. It can become a valuable asset to make durable relationships with other local artists, as well as for cross-country links with similar ventures. Critic Stuart Morgan has cynically, but effectively described the basic logic of artist-run spaces in the horizon of the alternative art scene, in which many artists linger at the beginning:

> *Setting up as a curator to 'curate' friends so that in due course they may 'curate' you or you will be able to curate yourself into an exhibition you have curated. In retrospect these were all ways of trying to look like Mother Theresa whilst secretly wanting to be Anthony d'Offay." (Stuart Morgan in Burges, Coventry, Hale, Noble and Owen, 2002, p. 76)*

The geographic extent and number of artist-initiated spaces in the UK during the Nineties suggest that they were a common and very effective means to contrast the market driven art system, which had by then stopped offering opportunities to aspiring artists due to the prolonged recession. They probably didn't constitute a radically new idea, but they were nevertheless a very helpful venture to start a collective path and engage with other artists' communities in the UK and abroad. The story of City Racing, for instance, is directly linked to that of Transmission, because the two galleries exchanged shows and exhibitors from 1992 onwards creating a stable relationship. The key difference between the two ventures was however their attitude towards such exchange-programs which were constitutional for the Glaswegian artists, whilst their London counterpart embarked in this project rather accidentally. As a matter of facts, the Transmission committee led by Gordon, Borland and Richardson had consciously decided to exploit the artist-run space model as an opportunity for establishing an art scene outside of London and for creating favourable connections with the European continent (Lowndes, 2010, p.161). On the contrary, City Racing's main partner-venue was Transmission and the link was created through Douglas Gordon over some German friends from the *Windfall* Project that managed the *Galerie Gruppe Grün* in Bremen, where he had exhibited with Simon Patterson in 1992. Ross Sinclair and Roderick Buchanan then took over contacts with City Racing leading to a number of exchange shows which included Glaswegian artists such as Annette Heyer, Andrew Lockhart, Julie Roberts and Sinclair himself in early 1992, then Richard Wright in October 1992, Dave Allen and Buchanan in March 1994 and Jonathan Monk in 1996. Hence the members of Transmission kept on following the very self-aware path drafted by Gordon and the first new gallery committee, who had intended the running of an autonomous space as a confident strategic move to systematically raise network capital for their collective career kick-start, but which had to go along of course with the production of good artworks.

5.2. Early signs of breakthrough: of patrons and dealers, mentors and godfathers, prizes and media

The year 1990 will probably be recorded in British art history for the excitement around the numerous artist-run spaces that began to dwell throughout the country, as well as for the mentioned warehouse shows held in the London Docklands. The following two years, instead, bare clear signs of the progressive breakthrough of the newer artists' generation, which was later labelled YBA. Especially in the months spanning from summer 1991 to summer 1992 a number of coincident events took place that should be rightly considered as the true turning point for this hoard of new entering artists, which was by then far greater than the mere group of original *Freeze* contributors and even reached beyond the London milieu up North to Glasgow. As a matter of facts, several relevant gatekeepers of the British art system started to pay attention to these young artists and some critics, collectors or dealers completely shifted towards the new trends they were proposing. Furthermore, in this period there were new players entering the arena also for the other roles of the local art world, such as newly founded art magazines, recently opened commercial galleries and young curators. These actors came to form a sort of alliance with this likeminded next generation of British artists for numerous reasons, especially since they all belonged to the same age group and hence had a comparable urgency to gain artistic, network, financial and social capital in order to climb up the art system ladder. Among the most important events in the biennium 1991-1992 one should take the following into account, as they proved a crucial influence on the development of the entire decade (Stallabrass, 2006b, p.183). Following a strict chronological order, the first relevant novelty was the birth in summer 1991 of the art magazine *Frieze*, which would soon become a sort of house organ for the upcoming wave of new artists. In the same year Nicholas Serota, the recently appointed director of the Tate Gallery, reformed the annual Turner Prize – now broadcasted by Channel Four – and on the first new shortlist three out of four artists were still in their early twenties. Meanwhile, the influence of newer commercial galleries started to grow, since they proved more dynamic than older establishments, and dealer Jay Jopling entered the scene – initially building a network and later opening the White Cube, which would soon become the defining London gallery of the Nineties. Furthermore, in 1992 Saatchi held the first show of the *Young British Artists* series displaying Hirst's celebrated tiger shark in formaldehyde called *The impossibility of death in the mind of someone living* (1991), which resulted in a general uproar starting a decade of art scandals and media sensationalism.

In the summer of 1991 the first issue of *Frieze* was published, a new monthly art magazine that intended to investigate the latest international developments of visual arts, focusing on younger generations. The reason for this specific generational concern can be explained with the age of the magazine's founder and editors – Tom Gidley, Matthew Slotover and Amanda Sharp – which were age peers of the *Freeze* contributors and knew many of the Goldsmiths graduates since the late Eighties. Supervising the design for *Frieze*, Gidley was himself an artist and a close friend to the Chapman brothers, the artist duo constituted by Dinos and Jake Chapman which had been his former colleagues at the Royal College of Arts and soon became among the best known young authors of the London scene together with Damien Hirst. Matthew Slotover instead chose the contributors and selected as such several young authors from the local artist milieu, including Gregor Muir and James Roberts, who would then become prominent critics and habitual curators of some major YBA exhibitions throughout the Nineties. Amanda Sharp worked for the public relations and advertising of the pilot issue, but then immediately hopped in as a co-editor of the magazine. Thanks to its attractive design and fresh authors, among whom the most celebrated London critic Stuart Morgan, *Frieze* rapidly rose to prominence among art magazines in the United Kingdom and abroad. The true masterminds behind this editorial success were Slotover and Sharp, both Londoners with a bourgeois background and university mates at Oxford, where the former of the two had edited a couple of editions of a cultural magazine, titled *Folio*. Slotover's tendency to publishing was likely the result of his family experience, being the son to Robert, a manager for classical musicians, and Jill, a children's book manager, while his maternal grandfather had been a relevant American publisher. His interest for contemporary art, instead, was born out of the genuine encounter with the exhibition *Modern Medicine* at *Building One*, which he visited together with Amanda Sharp. The feeling of amazement and excitement at the sight of the installations curated by Sellman, Freedman and Hirst convinced them to launch an editorial project in this sector. The pilot issue overtly declared its stance for the rising London art scene and this was visually apparent from the magazine cover, which depicted a dead butterfly stuck on a plain blue canvas, a detail taken from the recent series of *Butterfly Paintings* (1991) by Damien Hirst. At the sight of the first *Frieze* cover, artist and writer David Batchelor noticed its design was so different from any other art magazine at the time, especially of established ones such as *Artforum* or *Artscribe*. The bright colours of the yellowish typeface as opposed to the distinctive blue background paint, which enclosed the dead butterfly in the centre appeared to be the manifesto of the aesthetic on which the new generation of British artists had chosen to endeavor. Hirst had just presented the first eight pieces of this Butterfly series at his first comprehensive solo show, called *In and Out of Love*, which had taken place in June inside a temporary exhibition space at Woodstock Street, a few yards off Oxford Street. The paintings were shown at the ground floor of the building, while the main attraction for the exhibition was the title work at the upper floor, which featured live chrysalis and butterflies. Hirst had filled the room of the extemporaneous gallery with hundreds of free-flying exotic butterflies: large monochrome canvasses hung from the walls, sprayed with a sugar solution that fed the butterflies, while at their foot stood rows of vases, whose flowers were covered with chrysalis, from which new butterflies were born. Right after the *Building One* experience, the young Leeds author had felt the need for light after the darkness brought about by the installation with rotting flesh and electrocuted flies, so the butterflies made a perfect choice to persist on the lifecycle theme in a gentler way (Serota, 2011, pp.95-96). Planned to have the first generation of chrysalis opening up at the vernissage, the perfect timing of this piece allowed these wonderful insects to be born, live, feed, breed and finally die in the presence of guests and visitors. Hirst's work showed several of the typical features of the new wave of British art: rather than using objects commonly related to fine arts, he created a sensational installation that partly drew from mass media culture. So for instance, *In and Out of Love* was also the title of a well-known Bon Jovi's rock music piece dating back to 1985, though in this case it referred ironically to the entire lifecycle of the imprisoned butterflies. Julian Stallabrass (2006b, p.131) highlights the quintessential trend that emerged from *In and Out of Love*, since the artwork was easy to understand on a basic level and also very photogenic, both fundamental traits to become popular media targets – a strategy that was further exploited by the relevance of the sensational display mode and the importance of the vernissage as key event to draw the art system's attention. The pilot cover featuring a detail from Hirst's *Butterfly Paintings* went together with the very first interview with the Leeds artists, as well as with a dedicated project conceived by Angus Fairhurst, which punctuated the thirty-two-page issue at regular intervals. It was the so-called *Gallery Connections* (1990) that ironically exposed the closed circuit of established institutions and influent gatekeepers of the London art system. Fairhurst published the transcriptions of cross-lined calls he had made to several commercial galleries of the city: he simultaneously dialed up two opposing dealers and placed receivers next to another, so that responders were led to think their competitor had called. The project read like a humourous sketch about the interlinked structure of today's art system, which already mixed up dealers and experts, private collections and museums, auction houses and art fairs (Fox, 2013). Hence, Hirst's and Fairhurst's involvement for the pilot issue of *Frieze* wasn't accidental at all, instead it was a programmed decision that placed the new venture by Slotover and Gidley on the side of upcoming trends (Muir, 2011, p.41). As a matter of facts, Stallabrass stresses that right from the start of the decade the monthly magazine basically acted as an endorsement tool for YBAs, systematically criticizing the conservatism of London art market and the trends that dated back to the Eighties (Stallabrass, 2006b, pp.100, 267). *Frieze* contributors manifested a determinate vis polemica and a vigorous style, which were far removed from traditional British *politeness*, however consistent with the new trend in national press resulting from Rupert Murdoch's onset on the British media world. Although the new magazine attacked established trends and players, it was not characterized by a clear-cut art theory – quite the opposite, progressively the theoretical aspects were thought superfluous and were generally ignored. This aspect appears to pair with the attitude of several YBA exponents towards art theory, that was rather left aside in favour of a middle ground in which everything was made possible – removing artifice and illusion, often leaving the meaning of artworks to the individual viewer's opinion[5]. In Graham-Dixon's opinion, the lack of ideology may also be due to the fact that these young London artists didn't share a common aesthetic and were basically individualistic creators, though they spent much time together and mounted group shows to support each other (Cooper, 2012, p.40). Stallabrass (2006b, p.100) altogether criticizes this seemingly apathetic and cynical approach of many YBA artists, which he believes tried to escape the responsibility of creating meaningful art and rather relied on marketing strategies fostered by comrade-critics and journalists. The pilot issue had been a true gamble, a personal investment to try a breakthrough in the art-publishing arena, but already at the second issue Slotover and Sharp had managed to get Arts Council funding. The editors' personal ambition and managing skills, blended with Gidley's artistic sensibility and affinity with the YBA scene, proved crucial. Right form the start *Frieze* aimed at becoming one of the most influent magazines in the British art system, a true opinion leader capable of shaping upcoming trends, and indeed it succeeded in doing so pretty quickly rising to prominence even on an international level. Twelve years after launching the magazine, the editors tried another path which led them to establish a new international art fair in London, *Frieze Art Fair*, which counts today among the most important appointments for the art market.

The successful parable of *Frieze* is definitely a unique story in the British case, but in the Eighties and Nineties there existed many comparable experiences in editorial matters, such as the *Edinburgh Review* and *Variant* in Scotland, though these magazines decisively didn't have commercial ambitions at all and stayed rather an important platform for intellectual debate (Richardson, 2011, p.8, 125, 138). On the contrary, these grassroots initiatives in Glasgow and Edinburgh very much contrasted the ideology of Thatcher governments and neo-liberalism as a whole, giving free range to the alternative art scene (Lowndes, 2013, p.90-95). *Variant* for instance had been started in 1984 as a brochure funded by the Glasgow students union and was intended to give voice to those artists who were denied an exhibition space or that were critical of the mainstream directions taken by contemporary art. Malcolm Dickson, a painter but then video and performance artist, was among the founding party of Transmission gallery – as well as its assumed leader in the early Eighties – and after leaving the committee in 1987 he devoted to the re-launch of *Variant*. Under his direction the magazine turned into an example of Scottishness in its outspoken critical independence and soon became an important mirror for the fast growing new generation of artists catalysing in and around Transmission. Craig Richardson and Ross Sinclair were featured as frequent contributors, while on issue 10 in winter 1991 Douglas Gordon published an interview with celebrated American conceptual artist Lawrence Weiner (Gordon, 1991, pp.36-41). The ideology of *Variant* stayed with the new Transmission committee and is expressed in Dickson's word about this editorial venture, funded with a mixture of private donations and advertising subscriptions:

> *"Variant gave expression to a range of non-mainstream views on the arts, culture and politics – it included dissenting views and supported a diversity of creativity. Like the culture and scene it was part of, it was non-parochial, while still very much rooted in the place from where it emanated." (Dickson, 2002)*

While *Variant* provided a useful platform for debate in the alternative Scottish art scene – being namely that of Glasgow rising artists – real publicity in the international art system came instead with *Frieze*. As a matter of facts, already the first official issue of the new London based magazine provided a wide coverage and warm review for the comprehensive group show *Windfall 91*, which was inspired and organized by the Transmission artists together with many foreign contributors[6]. It was the third station of an on-going cross-national project, which set together various artist-run initiatives in Europe. As mentioned in the previous chapter, the first group exhibition of the series had been prompted by Scottish artist David McMillan and was held in London in 1988, while the second one was staged in Bremen the year after, where Douglas Gordon had participated thanks to his acquaintance with McMillan. In the summer of 1991 the Transmission members occupied several deserted buildings of the former Seamen's Institute in Clydeside, in order to host a few dozen young artists who had been invited to Glasgow for the *Windfall 91* project and to return the favour to their German colleagues. Most contributors were actually Glasgow-based, hence it was the perfect opportunity to finally crystallize and exhibit the energy of the new local art milieu. Although the group show didn't have a common theme, all exhibitors were indeed inclined to bypass the gallery system and to focus on dead spaces, hence leaving any commercial concern out of the creative process, as recalled by Roderick Buchanan. The final result was a number of ideas and installations, rather than completed works, which could however well represent the unrest and vitality of young artists in Glasgow's rising underground scene. The general trend was clearly informed by new conceptual practices, Gordon for instance displayed for the first time a number of idea-based paintings, which were grey monochrome canvasses that showed the titles and dates of great late 19th century paintings in black font lettering. His intention was to treat the traditional painting technique in the framework of the specific medium, but with a loose contextualist procedure, hence inviting the viewer to meditate on the paintings which were referenced rather than on the actual canvasses displayed. However, this type of conceptual strategy applied to the pictorial medium did not arouse much interest in the critics and was more successful on occasion of a later exhibition in New York called *Walk On*. Despite Gordon's specific contribution, the overall initiative he had curated together with Martin Boyce and Nathan Coley was extremely successful and gained much critical appraisal. Considering they were all in their mid twenties and basically at the kick-start of their career, they had been able to draw the attention of the specialized press and could claim a positive review of the show on influent magazines. *Windfall 91* was particularly favoured by *Frieze*, which accorded seven full pages to the group show at the Seamen's Institute, including a long interview to the three artists who had curated the event, plus the very encouraging opinions of several London dealers and critics. On the glossy magazine the exhibition was described as the Glasgow reaction to the young artists initiatives in London of the previous year, namely warehouse shows such as *Building One*. The title of Matthew Slotover's leading article for the mentioned issue was interestingly "Northern Lights", presenting the *Windfall* project as the true and only response to the fast rising art wave in the capital. On the pages of *Frieze*, Andrew Cross from James Hockey Gallery and James Hall from the *Independent* appraisingly remarked the different approach they had noticed between Glasgow artists and London ones, especially as regards to the liberation from art market concerns, as well as to the existence of a sincere and supportive team spirit. In their opinion, *Windfall 91* expressed a kind of freshness and ease, which would have been unthinkable in London, where on the contrary mannerism and sophistication appeared to rule the setting. A further difference was the attitude towards the exhibition space, since the various venues at the old Seamen's Institute had been left in their desolate condition, while the buildings exploited by Hirst and his fellows were unfailingly refurbished and whitewashed to look like a commercial gallery. Gordon was very aware of this contrast, which was pursued on purpose in order to cut free from the London model, as he explained in the *Frieze* interview:

> *"We were encouraged by events like Building One and the East Country Yard Show, but at the same time, attention was placed on the spaces and the events more than the work. We wanted to get away from that by choosing a bland space." (Gordon in Slotover, 1991, p.40)*

Cross and Hall shared the same opinion, agreeing that Glasgow artists really appeared not to be troubled about the art market, rather transmitting the feeling that they were less concerned about their career and much more willing to prove themselves in team work as well as in cross-European connections. In this regards, Andrew Cross' words in *Frieze* were unmistakable:

> *"What I liked about the Windfall project is that although the work individually may not have been the best pieces by each artist, the whole event had a freshness, a relaxed attitude which I found very positive. Dare I say it, in some of the most recent initiatives in London there has been an over-emphasis on presentation. Which there wasn't in this case. [...] Up there, there was a greater willingness to all work together." (Cross in Slotover, 1991, p.41)*

Stuart Morgan, one of the most influential British critics at the time and a regular contributor for *Frieze*, ascribed such a different attitude from London to the Transmission committee, who seemed to him really interested in interacting with artists from abroad, rather than pursuing instant success:

> *"A much better question would be to ask why the energy the Scottish artists had to do this is not present in London. It has to be said that the core members of Transmission make very good links with the artists abroad – links which are not made here [in London]." (Morgan in Slotover, 1991, p.41)*

Far from being a rhetorical question, the answer to Morgan's query is to be found in the different aims and strategies the two geographical groupings were applying for their career paths. Indeed, commercial concerns were out of the picture for Glaswegians, simply because they didn't have any access to structured facilities at home, hence the best way to get to the art market was first of all to bring ideas and works out of Scotland by building a network of international relationships that might later prove a useful asset. On the contrary, though parochial and conservative at the time, in London a local art market existed – full of the various gatekeepers such as dealers, collectors and curators – whom young artists needed to intercept in order to rise into prominence. If influent players didn't prove responsive enough, Hirst and his fellows simply tried harder to find in London those who would give them credit and indeed there were new actors entering the scene also on the art demand side, for instance new commercial galleries which needed fresh proposals to conquer their market share. The fundamental difference between rising artists in London and Glasgow appears then to be what they were looking for to start their career: in the capital they were seeking dealers and patrons to enter the local art market, while in the Scottish town they badly needed mentors and godfathers who would help them approach the international art scene. Hence in London an effective strategy for new entries was to build one's own reputation for public recognition, working on impressive creations or on the artist's self-image, while in Glasgow the best way appeared to be the construction of a solid network of connections which could provide potential endorsement. Indeed, Damien Hirst was fully aware of the way mass media portrayed British society, hence he aimed at mirroring these strategies and behavioural models. Together with Tracy Emin and the Chapman brothers, he is an outstanding example of how to exploit the star system for personal popularity through provocation and sensationalism, indulging on a kind of bad-boy self-representation that would attract media attention. However, this strategy needs commercial backing, meaning that someone must be capable of marketing the artist's self-image in order to draw financial profit out of it. In the case of Damien Hirst this person went under the name of Jay Jopling, a young and ambitious aristocrat that wanted to become an influent new art dealer. He was the son of Jay Jopling Senior, an eminent landowner and minister in the Thatcher governments, and thus had attended the best schools in Edinburgh and then Eton College. As an aspiring dealer he possessed two of the ideal prerequisites to launch a successful gallery, which are financial means and a portfolio of clients, as he was perfectly acquainted with the milieu of potential collectors, though still lacking the right artists (Muir, 2011, pp.36-37). Since *Freeze* he had tried to keep track of its various participants, especially trying to meet Hirst on several occasions, as he considered the Leeds artist the most promising of the Goldsmiths grouping. In 1991 Jopling and Hirst did finally get in touch and agreed on a fairly aggressive media campaign to foster the artist's reputation[7]. Similarly Tracey Emin had shaped a strong self-image of herself as a derelict, primitive woman who drew inspiration from adversities, and indeed her personality also appealed to British tabloids. Even the vicious attitude and uninhibited violence displayed by Dinos and Jake Chapman fitted the media stereotype of rebel pop stars. Not by any chance, all of them found big support in Jopling's White Cube, the gallery he opened later in May 1993 on the first floor of 44 Duke Street and which soon become the defining gallery of the London Nineties. Exploiting celebrity system was a crucial aspect for YBA breakthrough, but these young artists would hardly have succeeded alone, if they had not found various new dealers in town that would be ready to cooperate and conquer together the local art market. Besides Jay Jopling, three more galleries had already invested on the contributors of *Freeze* and other age peers, though curiously none of them was managed by a British dealer – as if the national establishment was unwilling to accept the new generation. German Karsten Schubert, American Maureen Paley and Swiss Laure Genillard had picked numerous Goldsmiths graduates as well as other promising young authors from the best art schools in London, such as Rachel Whiteread from Slade Schhol of Fine Arts. Maureen Paley for instance managed Interim Art Gallery and represented Angela Bulloch among others, while Laure Genillard had opened a gallery in Foley Street in 1988, which soon became a showcase for young generations. These galleries acted mainly as starting galleries, are those that concentrate on discovering young artists who still need to build their own reputation and value on the art market (Santagata, 1998, p.38). Usually such players invest in numerous new entries and will earn their remuneration from the huge increase of the few ones that will later reveal themselves to become extremely successful, while more established galleries instead represent only well-known artists and rather get a percentage of their high price sales. This situation is typical of vertical differentiation inside the art market, which divides commercial galleries according to the level of establishment of the artists they represent (Caves, 2000, p.60). Nonetheless, unlike traditional starting galleries, Jopling and Schubert did not limit their work to mere promotion of new and unknown entries, as they intended to launch their protégés much higher by means of employing aggressive media strategies and disrupting the established vertical differentiation of galleries. In fact, they wanted to exploit the star system mechanisms already for emerging artists, hence trying immediately to raise the appraisal of young artists by means of calculated decisions on media exposure, sensational production and outstanding artist-personality. However, it must be noted that this course of actions does not guarantee a stable financial value for investors, because artists may be unable to keep the position they reached so quickly, as was later the case for many after the crash of the financial market in the late Nineties which again cleared up the art world like the previous Japanese bubble. As a matter of facts, art economist Gianfranco Mossetto (2003) and art historian Julian Stallabrass (2006a, pp.14-15) both argue that the early success of young authors in the decade under observation, can easily be compared to keenness for *new economy* firms that characterized the financial market – hence, it appears no coincidence that in the early 21st century the internet market bubble burst was immediately followed by a general crash of art market quotations.

Given the support of collectors such as Charles Saatchi, as well as the commercial backing of some new art dealers on the London scene that matched the ambitions of Damien Hirst and other young authors, it appears that this generation was predestined to a swift ascent. This favourable situation still didn't pave the way to all *Freeze* contributors or Goldsmiths graduate, not to mention that of the innumerable quantity of aspiring artists based in London at the time. Only those who fitted perfectly in the role model and aesthetics of the current or upcoming international trends could aspire to be picked by gatekeepers, old an new (Renton, 1991, pp.17-18). Besides Damien Hirst and the Goldsmiths grouping, in 1991 many more young people stood out for they matched the new requirements of the various art field players, even if they had attended different London schools: among them one may count Rachel Whiteread and Marc Quinn, the twin sisters Jane and Louise Wilson and the brothers Dinos e Jake Chapman. In Stuart Morgan's opinion, 1991 finally marked the end of Goldsmiths hegemony over the rising generation of British artists, especially thanks to two crucial initiatives that took place in London: the first was the group show *Broken English* curated by celebrated critic Andrew Graham Dixon at the Serpentine Gallery, while the second was the publication of *Technique Anglaise* by Liam Gillick and Andrew Renton, a comprehensive book about young London artists. The exhibition in Hyde Park took place from 1st of August to 1st of September 1991 and represented the first ever occasion in an established venue for the former warehouse show contributors. The featured artists chosen by Graham Dixon, Julia Peyton Jones and Andrea Schlieker were Angela Bulloch, Ian Davenport, Damien Hirst, Gary Hume, Anya Gallaccio, Michael Landy, Sarah Staton and Rachel Whiteread – all artists in their twenties that had already found representation in a London gallery, either a rising or an established one. That same year the first comprehensive portrait of the rising London art scene was published, thanks to the outstanding work of Andrew Renton and Liam Gillick who edited *Technique Anglaise: Current Trends in British Art.* The book is a collection of more than 200 black and white pictures showing only works by authors of the upcoming generation, including Damien Hirst, Sarah Lucas and Rachel Whiteread's creations so far. Soon after in 1992, Gillick would found together with American collector and publisher Jack Wendler a book series of limited editions on rising YBA stars, which went under the name of G-W Press. These two events had revealed that the alternative scene was flourishing all over London despite economic recession – or maybe exactly because of the crisis – and that it involved far more people than Goldsmiths graduates, including even much more interesting artists other than the original *Freeze* contributors. Despite this great ferment, however, neither the British Council nor other influential institutions took the stance of this new generation, probably because they appeared to be at a premature stage compared to the long established art scene and this would have caused a huge disruption of the given art market equilibrium (Saatchi, 2009, p.57). According to Michael Craig-Martin the initial skepticism of the institutional players towards the YBAs didn't depend on the revival of conceptual theories they brought about – as opposed to neo-expressionist trend of the Eighties – but was rather caused by the rudeness of the new generation and its artworks. Indeed, Hirst and his age peers didn't stick to the austere aesthetic of former conceptual artists, instead their work appeared aggressive, vulgar and disrespectful – very little British, in a way. Enjoying the support of some newer London galleries was a good opportunity for the rising generation of artists, but at the beginning of the Nineties they had drawn much more attention abroad rather than at home (Gillick, 1991, p.56). Some early YBAs had shown their works in Cologne and New York thanks to their dealers, while others had been contacted for important international group shows, but the most relevant British institutions found it difficult to switch to this new trend. It appeared that some other event was necessary that could trigger real interest in these new British authors, both from the establishment as well as from mass media. The true first person that caused big sensation wasn't Damien Hirst, but a female artist from the Slade, Rachel Whiteread, for her work *Ghost* (1990) which was a plaster cast of a whole Victorian living room full of everyday objects. Researching the theme of empty spaces, particularly on their reversed image and on human intrusion, *Ghost* hit the nerve of dwelling conditions in times of severe recession. At least this seemed to be the interpretation to Whiteread's creations given by London lower and middle classes and which caused a vehement reaction, especially after producing an analogous work called *House* (1993). While she had had her first solo show already in 1988 at the Carlyle Gallery in Islington, *Ghost* was displayed at the Chisenhale Gallery and got her much bigger appraisal, as well as the endorsement of Charles Saatchi who immediately purchased this work. Applying the same technique of concrete casting though on a larger scale, on the occasion of *House* she installed the inside plaster cast of an entire Victorian residential building that had recently been pulled down in the heart of a densely populated area of East London, standing like a ghost on the empty original site. Produced by James Lingwood's Artangel Trust and promoted by Karsten Schubert, the concrete cast of the interior of a terrace house in the Bow neighborhood of the run-down East End was received with unusual unanimity by British critics, celebrated by Andrew Graham-Dixon as one of the most extraordinary public sculptures of the century by an English author (Roberta, 1993, p.2948). On the contrary, the Bow Standing Neighbourhood Committee overseen by one Eric Flounders vehemently opposed the installation, which was considered an insulting attack on lower and middle class housing conditions, hence voting for its immediate removal on a tight ballot. Already the uproar caused by *Ghost* granted Whiteread a shortlist nomination for the Turner Prize in 1991, while the much bigger media outcry caused by *House* in 1993 finally rewarded her with the victory at the Tate. Even though she did not belong to the Goldsmiths peers and had not participated in any of their warehouse shows, Whiteread's achievements became instrumental for the breakthrough of the YBAs, as they would by revealing of a generational desire to break free (Cooper, 2012, p.39). On her part she has always refused to be associated with the young British artists, maintaining that unlike the latter she was only ambitious for her work and not for her public persona. Nevertheless, the press has associated her name to that of the general rising art scene and the sensation caused by her works helped a whole generation of artists, making a decisive contribution to its reputation and opening to mass media attention (Stallabrass, 2006b, p.185).

Still in 1991, Transmission artists in Glasgow were going a completely different path, given that they couldn't count on structured commercial establishments nor on particular press coverage. Unlike their London peers, they tried to get in touch with older artists who had some influence in the international art system. What Gordon and his friends were really looking for at that point was the endorsement of one or more relevant mentors in the art field – chosen on the side of artists and curators rather than seeking dealers and collectors – or at least their friendship hoping to gain access to a new set of relationships. As a matter of facts, in his biennium serving on the Transmission committee, the young Glaswegian artist exploited all acquaintances he had made in London when he was attending the Slade. In particular, back then his art teacher Bruce McLean had introduced him to fellow countrymen Alan Johnston, a minimalist painter who had studied in Düsseldorf with Joseph Beuys and was renown for his public art interventions as well as wall drawings. By early 1991 the Transmission committee had established to apply a two-tire strategy: on the one side they would organize group exhibitions for young locals that were internationally informed, such as happened with *Windfall 91,* while on the other hand they should try to have solo shows of relevant artists they esteemed and thus wanted to get in touch with. Knowing Gordon from London and also Richard Wright, whom he had taught at the Edinburgh College of Arts, Alan Johnston was a true inspirational figure and Transmission invited him in March of 1991 for his personal exhibition at the artist-run gallery, which opened a set of solo shows by very important authors such as Lawrence Weiner and Thomas Lawson. Johnston took

Gordon literally under his wing and agreed to introduce the young Glaswegian to anyone he would like to meet from his personal acquaintances. Gordon expressed the wish to come across celebrated conceptual artist Weiner, whose work with language had inspired the young artist's early text-pieces. Johnston arranged for Gordon and Richardson to meet up with Weiner at the ICA in London, who then officially invited the American artist for a solo show at Transmission. The arrival of such a illustrious conceptual artist in an artist-run space was celebrated as a great event in Glasgow, followed by panels and lectures crowded with students and young artists. The visual strategy and career path adopted by Weiner, as well as by several fellow conceptualists such as Carl Andre and Joseph Kosuth, were a true inspiration for outcasts of the art system like the Glaswegian artists. Weiner spoke to the assembly about what he meant was working as an artist, arguing that this profession entailed humility and deference just as any common job. Even in the interview given to Douglas Gordon on the central pages of *Variant,* Weiner did resist flattering descriptions of his career achievements and insisted that the artist is an ordinary person, who should thus keep a kind of moral modesty that belongs to ordinary people:

> *"'Ordinary people'? I'm an ordinary person. I eat, drink, piss, shit, just like everybody else. I have the same feelings and desires that I have to quell and I have all the same other things. There is no stuff to say on this issue, it's a non-issue." (Weiner in Gordon, 1991, p.40)*

Reading through the answers of the American artist to Gordon's queries it is possible to perceive two slightly different approaches to the developments in recent art. While the young Glaswegian tried to emphasize several aspects of Weiner's career as well as the ferment on the art scene brought about by his breakthrough in the Sixties, the American artist rather minimized his personal achievements and insisted on the necessity of downplaying the artist persona. In his opinion, the most important aspect was an upright professional ethic, keeping close contact with fellow artists and acting together as a community or even as a sort of trade union. These words struck Gordon and his peers, further determining their professional disposition, which was already marked by a solid team spirit that last to this day, as Gordon asserts interviewed by Graham Fagen:

> *"[...] Because people would tell you it's special just being an artist, but on the other hand it's a job. And this goes back to when Lawrence Weiner came to Glasgow, and the kind of respect I have for his attitude, and the way that he thought he could best talk about work*

> *to people in Glasgow. [...] you're doing a job, so you get paid for it, you don't get exploited for it, or you try not to get exploited for it. That's your duty as a worker, you don't fuck around with your peers because they are workers too, it's a union agreement, even although there's no union you've got it as an ethic, especially considering the kind of culture that we're from, don't fuck over your peer group, because you don't want to fuck yourself in the end." (Gordon in Fagen, 1999, pp.85-86)*

Weiner's show at Transmission opened in November, for which he had prepared a band of black type running around the inner walls at eye-height baring the inscription "AN ARCH AFFORDED IN A WALL OF STONE WITH A KEYSTONE OF CHALK & IMPOSTS OF SLATE" (Lowndes, 2010, p.149). The text was also circulated as a sticker in the Transmission mailing and inside the *Variant* issue number 10, because in the artist's opinion it had a much more subversive quality than occupying commercial billboards. Weiner would think the latter as impositions of the dominant culture, which might eventually allow to place contents on the empty public space, while a sticker can be stuck anyplace, by anybody, anytime. Weiner and Gordon later crossed their paths several times meeting again on occasion of some exhibitions in Germany, namely in Leipzig in 1995 and then at the Skulpturprojekte Münster in 1997.

Still in 1991 the young Glaswegian artist had the opportunity to profit again twice of Alan Johnston's connections, being chosen as a contributor for a two part group shows travelling from New York to Edinburgh and curated by Johnston himself. Called *Walk On*, it was the first touring exhibition Gordon took part in and it also provided his landing in front of an American audience. This situation clearly depicts one recurring feature of the art system, which at first sight could seem incongruous or even paradoxical: the first supporters of emerging artists are indeed often older artists that find themselves at the peak of a brilliant career. Far from deterring young people or considering them as dangerous competitors, famous artists often help new entries, trying to transfer trust capital onto a younger artist by the power of endorsement that arises from their established position. It is by no means necessary to go back over the case of apprentices in the Renaissance workshops, because the 20th century affords a lot of meaningful examples in these regards, as for instance Andy Warhol's promotion and protection of some Eighties stars such as Keith Haring e Jean-Michel Basquiat which are paradigmatic. A successful artist can even decide to help a younger colleague to access his or her own network of connections in the art system, such as presenting him or her to influent collectors, curators and dealers. Such cooperation between artists of very different standing may same unnatural, because economically speaking one tends to consider new entries as menacing competitors to successful artists. Even though one may sometimes observe a hostile attitude towards young artists by famous ones, there are many cases of mutual collaboration. In fact, economist David Galenson (2005a, p.29) points out that such situations are not at all unusual and by investigating the professional biography of many successful artists, it is often the case that they found the support of older colleagues at their career kick-start and possibly did the same later on with younger artists after having reached their own success. Besides finding a plausible explanation in generosity or restitution, older artists might tend to help younger colleagues in an attempt to create a sort of legacy. Gordon's friendship with Alan Johnston fits in the picture, as do the previously mentioned relationships of Anthony Caro with Henry Moore, of Liam Gillick with Michael Craig-Martin, of the Chapman brothers with Gilbert & George or of Marc Quinn with Barry Flanagan. Back to *Walk On*, the first exhibition was held at the Jack Tilton Gallery in New York and then the second at the Fruitmarket Gallery in Edinburgh. Besides Gordon, Johnston invited five other young Scottish artists: Craig Richardson, Kevin Henderson, Karen Forbes, Graeme Todd and Angus Hood. The artists' contribution was very different from one another, except for the three Transmission members that kept a unitary conceptual style, so that several reviews deemed the outcome was too heterogeneous and blamed the curator for this uneven result[8]. In response to the critics, Johnston said that the true common ground of the chosen artists was in fact no uniformed aesthetics, but rather the public house and the evenings they spent there together debating and drinking. Even if this may seem an inadequate answer, it is useful to explain how important socializing is in the artists' milieu and in Scotland in particular. Gordon produced different works for the two *Walk On* exhibitions, but both were inspired by Minimalist and Conceptual Art. In New York he showed some canvasses like the ones for *Windfall 91*, but this time they referred to the specific context of the Jack Tilton Gallery. In fact, after gathering information on the exhibition venue, he learnt it was the place of the former Betty Parsons Gallery, where years before artists of the likes of Ad Reinhardt, Mark Rothko and Ellesworth Kelly had shown their paintings. On each canvas Gordon painted date and title of a celebrated work that had been exhibited in that room, hence the viewer was then free to reconstruct their sense in connection with the specific context. The paintings combined the title and year as follows: *Black Arrangement – 1946*, *Red Dividing – 1969*,

Yellow Whites – 1963, White Relief – 1959, Red Whites – 1963, Red Front – 1946, Korea Goes to War – 1959 e *Black City 1948*. Some old gallery visitors immediately realized the cross-reference connection that Gordon's paintings intended to create with the American author's displayed in that very room in the Fifties and Sixties. In an interview with Thomas Lawson the young Glaswegian asserted these works arose from his peculiar work method, which had always been unbound from isolated studio practice, while rooted instead in a sort of anthropological research. Hence, the choice he made of painting, as an artistic medium, should be understood as a mere tool to probe a specific context rooted in collective imagination:

> *"The paintings that you have seen have come about as a result of the attitudes and strategies that I had developed through working outside of a studio: you become steeped in a research, which isn't based on physical materials. [...] It's obvious that my interest in painting is not so much in the practical, physical side, as in the idea of it. I'm interested in the fine line between my intentions and the perceptions of others; that moment when someone encounters something and realises that there is more than meets the eye. [...] I would say that all of the work plays with recognition and expectation in this way." (Gordon in Lawson, 1995, pp.63-64)*

For the Edinburgh show, on the other hand, Gordon created a completely different work titled *1900-2000*, which was a set of equal square wood poles randomly piled up in the centre of the room, as if they were huge Shanghai sticks. On one end of each pole he marked a progressive number from 1900 to 2000, though the choice of numbers was completely arbitrary. The effect on the spectator, however, made the numbers appear as a year date because of routine thinking, but each viewer would independently determine its meaning. Indeed, if some years may mark a shared reference, for instance the beginning and end of the two World Wars, others on the contrary acquire an individual sense, evoking relevant events in the life of the specific spectator. In Katrina Brown's (2004, pp.16-17) opinion, this is one of the earliest works by means of which Gordon explicitly tried to investigate the cognitive process, as shaped by the twofold influence of social and individual conditioning. Still in 1991, he applied the same method together with Roderick Buchanan in creating the collaborative work *London Road* for the Orpheus Gallery in Belfast[9]. The procedure for this installation was clearly developed after Harding's contextualist theories, as the two artists displayed the giant photograph on canvass depicting in scale a facade section of a former poor people shelter in

Glasgow's London Road, but the image relocated in another setting made a completely different though planned effect. The Orpheus Gallery had recently opened in a building that had previously been a business facility, hence it possessed a huge full-length show window looking onto the street and the canvas for *London Road* was installed on the opposite wall, so as to fill the visual field for the people walking outside in the street. The picture corresponded only to a small fraction of facade for the homeless shelter, leaving just a few visible letters of an unspecified word – presumably "Salvation" – and under it the recognizable word "Army", hence the letterings were the remains of a sign that probably referred to the *Salvation Army*, the well known charity. However, since the word "Salvation" was almost unreadable, the term "Army" written in white block capital stood out against the red bricks background. If seen through the window from the street, the giant picture of the Glasgow building could be misleading and looked like a glimpse of the gallery's backyard. As a consequence, the word Army appeared to emerge from the very depth of Belfast's soul, as if it was an undesirable truth hidden behind the houses. In fact, no Ulster dweller could fail to think that the word referred to both factions which had been fighting for years in the country: on one hand it referred to the British Army, on the other hand to the Irish Republican Army. Gordon and Buchanan employed a simple strategy, which consisted merely in shifting locations, but it had succeeded to reveal the highly politicized context of Northern Ireland at the time.

Gordon's most important artwork of 1991, however, was probably his intervention in London that year for the *Barclays Young Artist's Award* at the Serpentine Gallery, as if he had retained his best shot for the capital – well aware of the commercial importance of the local art scene[10]. As a matter of facts, his return to Scotland didn't stop him to take part to the upcoming London wave on several occasions, because from 1991 to 1993 his Slade acquaintances gave him the chance to participate in a strain of different group shows, which allowed his name to be associated to the wider YBA circle. The *Barclays Young Artist's Award* was a very important event sponsored by the namesake insurance company and was furthermore hosted in one of the best-known venues in the city. The show also profited from an extensive coverage by critics and specialized magazines, apart being closely watched by dealers and talent scouts in search for new artists. Any young contributor to the Barclays exhibition was aware of its relevance as a beginners show, especially because the selection system was hard to access. Gordon's name was put to the attention of the admittance committee thanks to Bruce McLean, his Scottish teacher at the

Slade, as he was a close friend of one of the event promoter Mel Gooding, an influent writer and London based art critic. McLean's intervention was crucial to put the young Glaswegian among the nine nominees of the 1991 edition of the prize together with Richard Woods, Peter Doig, Nicholas May and Tania Kovats, the latter resulting then as the winner. On this occasion Gordon resorted to his text-pieces presenting two installations, the first being *Above all else....* (1991) and the second called *New Maps* (1991). The former work has been described in previous chapters, as it represents a crucial step in the artistic development of the Scottish artist: it reads the sentence 'WE ARE EVIL' written in Bembo capital typeface that was applied as a wall text on the central hall dome together with a huge blue ink stain. *New Maps* was instead a public art intervention conceived as a sort of personal memorial that took advantage of the Serpentine Gallery location in Hyde Park. Gordon put a white stripe on various trees near the gallery, on each of them writing in black block letterings the surnames of more or less renowned people – all of them important for the artist himself. While walking in the park, a visitor could come across a tree bearing the name 'CICCONE' – pop-star Madonna's real surname – or again a shrub called 'DUCHAMP'. Gordon decided to write only the surname, in order to make the person's identity ambiguous: in fact, 'PARKER' for instance could refer to a large number of historical people or even to completely unknown ones. For himself he had thought of well-known jazz saxophonist Charlie Parker, but Gordon's intention was to allow anyone to imagine their personal heroes. Although the Scottish artists didn't result the winner of the ten thousand pound award, his participation earned him the first extensive coverage in specialized magazines. As a matter of facts, the installation was incredibly photogenic, such that the photograph of the white dome with the inscription and the stain on it was printed even on the influential *Art Monthly*. Critics and experts further praised *Above all else...*, because the sentence which was featured seemed an appropriate comment – though ironical – on the friction between the rising artists generation and the art system, the latter still clinging to the art trends of the Eighties. It appeared as if this bunch of young, irreverent and ambitious artists labelled themselves as 'Evil', or at least joked about being considered as such by the establishment. Not by ay chance the installation struck a relevant gatekeeper such as Nicholas Logsdail, who asked to be introduced straight away to the Glaswegian artist on the day of the opening at the Serpentine Gallery. After a friendly talk, the influent London dealer said he intended to observe Gordon's career path and to invite him to exhibit very soon. As with Damian Hirst two years before, Logsdail proved very interested in the rising tide of young British artists, but he would keep on waiting a bit before deciding to pick some of them up, fundamentally refusing to act as a beginners gallery, because he intended to be sure about who out of the dozens would make a good start on his or her own. Nevertheless, Gordon belonged to the few ones of the YBA generation to be approached so early by Lisson Gallery, which until then had only watched the *Freeze* group and other emerging artists from safe distance. The exhibition for the Barclays Award revealed itself an important test for Gordon's career, which he successfully passed considering the media exposure as well as the connection to one of the most important London dealers: his hometown, on the contrary, definitely couldn't have afforded him such opportunities at the time.

The caution of Nicholas Logsdail in approaching the young, noisy artists of London's restless alternative scene matched the general scepticism of the art establishment towards the YBAs at this early stage in the Nineties. Although the interest for this new generation was fast growing, indeed the difficulty to break through remained and became most apparent, if one considers the outcome of three Turner Prize exhibitions that range from 1991 to 1993. As a matter of facts, throughout the decade the yearly recognition for the best British artist, awarded by the Tate, turned into a true barometer of London art market preferences. However, it soon became one of the main means for attracting public attention on contemporary art and on YBAs especially, progressively legitimating this trend (Muir, 2011, p.180). Awards in the field of contemporary art draw from mercantile tradition, which started in particular with the world fairs in the second half of the 19th century, where the best commercial products would be given a prize. Hence, awarding in the art system is apparently derived from a capitalistic logic and indeed results into an increase in the winners' exposure and quotations, which of course match the importance of the given prize. In fact, as with commercial galleries or public venues, a fundamental difference can be drawn as regards to the relevance of an award for the curriculum of an artist, as there are competitions for beginners such as the Barclays Young Artist Award or others for very established authors. Awards in the art world are now quite common, but only a few are really prestigious, because they can ordain an artist's career or persona as if it was a trade mark, rather than valuing specific artworks. Among the most important prizes worldwide one should include the Hugo Boss Prize of New York's Guggenheim, the Berlin DAAD Stipendium, Pittsburgh's Carnagie International, the Golden Lion of the Venice Biennale and of course the Turner Prize awarded by London's Tate Gallery. As far as the latter is concerned, its relevance up to now is due to the radical reform of the prize carried out in the late Eighties by the newly appointed Tate director Nicholas Serota, who had taken office in 1988. Indeed, the Turner Prize is fairly recent as a group called Patrons of New Art founded it in the early Eighties. They were a group of wealthy art lovers who intended to help the Tate in purchasing new artworks for its collection, encouraging a wider interest in contemporary creations. Among the founding group was Oliver Prenn, who in 1984 decided to establish a prize associated with the great British painter William Turner, which was to be awarded annually to anyone who had promoted the visual arts in the United Kingdom in the preceding twelve months. However, the regulations for the first six editions had proved ineffective and rather confusing, thus preventing the Turner Prize from being a true means for the promotion of new British art (Stallabrass, 2006b, p.183). Until 1989, in fact, the prize could be awarded to anyone who worked in the field of visual arts, not only to artists but virtually to every player of the art system, including dealers, critics and curators. In 1986, for instance, among the nominees there was Nicholas Serota, at the time director of London's Whitechapel Gallery. The rules of selection were utterly unclear and the criteria for the composition of the shortlist had never been defined properly, hence the number of finalists could vary at every edition. In Stuart Morgan's (1991, p.4) opinion, the true source of the described problems was the model of the competition, which had been inspired by the Booker Prize, which is a well-known British literary award. Choosing the criteria to define the book of the year appears an easier task, since one may look at the number of sold copies, and the chosen parameters are less controversial in the eyes of the general public. However, Morgan maintained that this procedure could hardly be applied to visual arts:

> *"I have insisted, against some opposition, on changing the format. It was a mistake to follow the literary Booker Prize format because art and artists work differently from writers. It is too wide a range – the public get confused." (Serota in Morgan, 1991, pp.4-5)*

As a consequence, the unresolved rules of the Turner Prize didn't make clear to public opinion who exactly was awarded – and especially what for. In the Eighties this award mirrored the London art system of that decade, which was run as an elitist activity, confined in the inner circle of a few experts, dealers and collectors (Stallabrass, 2006b, p.184). In 1987 Prenn stopped sponsoring the prize and the American company Drexel Burnham Lambert International jumped in, but eventually this corporation went bankrupt two years later causing the 1990 edition to be cancelled. That year revealed to be an *annus horribilis* for Nicholas Serota, who had to fight back harsh disapproval from critics for his general work as newly appointed director of the Tate. Even if he had previously contributed to the success of the Whitechapel Gallery, Serota was strongly opposed by many influent art experts, headed by Peter Fuller, columnist for the *Sunday Telegraph.* Originally Fuller's view on art was informed by Marxism, but he later became the most prominent advocate of conservatism, launching the review *Modern Painters* in the mid-Eighties to fight the trends emanating from Conceptual Art, performances and new media. The title of the magazines itself illustrates the reactionary attitude of Fuller and his fellow contributors such as Brian Sewell, who were all expressing total dismay for the new Tate director. The critiques to Serota were not necessarily a matter of personal dislike, since Fuller had actually criticized the Turner Prize right from its start in 1984. In fact, he considered the award a mere advertisement campaign conceived for the advantage of its patrons and other established art collectors, hence he had saluted the debut edition with a belligerent statement:

> *"[...] the Director of the Tate wants us to understand that the Turner Prize is a great publicity gimmick. And the critic of the Sunday Times thinks Turner would have enjoyed the 'genteel romp'. And the Minister for the Arts in Her Majesty's Government thinks all the `razzmatazz' and `knees up' is such fun. [...] An ageing photo-realist [Malcolm Morley] is ten grand richer. And Saatchi is laughing all the way to the bank. Shame on you. Shame on you all!" (Fuller, 1985, pp.5-6)*

In 1990 the Turner Prize was flooded with criticism and seemed to be stuck in a dead end, when Nicholas Serota decided to revolutionize the format and find a procedure that could draw mass media attention. First of all, he convinced Channel 4 to sponsor the award, hence starting a partnership with the new commercial television network. The sum awarded to the winner was doubled to twenty thousand pounds and the final announcement would be broadcasted live during a big ceremony at the Tate. Besides such media stratagems, it was defined that the prize would be awarded only to visual artists – and not anymore to other actors of the art system – but they had to be strictly under fifty years of age and reside in the United Kingdom. Even the shortlist was reduced to a fixed number of four final nominees, who had to display their works in a group show at the Tate in Autumn before the award ceremony, so that the public could judge for themselves. Furthermore, the decision of the jury would be based on the artists' creations ranging back to the last twelve months starting from 1st of June of the previous year to 31st of May of the current year. This extensive reform made the aims and procedure of the prize much clearer to the general public, while the Channel 4 partnership turned the award ceremony into a major event eagerly followed by media commentators – even by tabloids. The new course of the Turner Prize had a massive impact, though the biggest trouble with it – as again stigmatized by Stuart Morgan (1991, p.6) and agreed by Julian Stallabrass (2006b, p.184) – was the fact that the award rather confirmed an artist's fame and not so much his or her specific production. The reformed Turner Prize was indeed designed to endorse an artist's reputation, as it appeared almost impossible to judge an author for works that had been created in a limited period, keeping all others aside.

Already in the first three editions of the new course there were astonishingly many rising artists among the four finalists, though the art system didn't appear ready to acclaim this new generation and instead favoured older artists with a more established career (Muir, 2011, p.180-183). The most striking example took immediately place in 1991, when the shortlist counted internationally renowned artist Anish Kapoor opposed to three much younger authors that were rather at the kick-start of their professional path. In fact, Rachel Whiteread, Ian Davenport and Fiona Rae were all still in their twenties and had been active for little more than three years. Whiteread had recently distinguished herself for the mentioned concrete-cast of a Victorian sitting room, while Rae and Davenport had been among the original group of *Freeze* contributors, furthermore being the only ones to be picked by an influential gallery such as Waddington which definitely helped them to be nominated. The final result of the 1991 edition matched every expectation awarding the Turner Prize to Kapoor, as it would have been unlikely for any of the younger artists to challenge such an internationally established artist. The following year again there was a comparable situation, since Hirst was nominated among the four finalists for his recent exhibition at the Institute of Contemporary Arts that had been widely appreciated by critics, however he wasn't awarded the prize in the end. The YBA generation was certainly defeated in the first two editions of the reformed Turner Prize, but it had been able to take the floor on an occasion, which would grant large popularity. In addition, the nomination of numerous rising artists had started to change the face of British art, because in the Nineties Turner Prize jurors clearly favoured artists that were on the average in their 20's and 30's, instead of in their 40's as in the previous decade. Conceived as a means for the promotion of contemporary art, the new format even turned the Turner Prize into a hyper-effective marketing machine that would allow the YBAs to be quickly incorporated by the establishment (Morgan, 1991, p.5). Eventually, the extensive media coverage of the award ceremony granted contemporary art direct access into popular culture, becoming a frequent subject of tabloid articles and even of everyday conversations in the entire United Kingdom. As regards to the latter circumstance, Julian Stallabrass noted indeed that the new Turner Prize format proved ideal for the gradual rise of the YBA trend, matching the cool image of Channel 4 and placing emphasis on youth (Stallabrass, 2006b, pp.184-185).

Together with the media attention aroused by the young Turner Prize nominees, in late 1991 another influential player of the London art system was planning a major move in the game that would have decisively promoted a new generation of British artists. In the last three years, in fact, hyper-collector Charles Saatchi had started to pick several rising artists that had characterized themselves on the alternative art scene for particular capabilities, especially for the strong attraction of their presentations. In particular he had purchased Rachel Whitread's *Ghost*, as well as Marc Quinn's *Self* (1991), and he had finally commissioned a major animal installation to Damien Hirst – three pieces that would become paradigmatic for the entire decade. Hirst and his peers considered the progressive endorsement by the great collector as a premonitory symptom for their personal success, but it was in fact also the climax of a carefully planned strategy both on the collector's side and on the Goldsmiths' graduates side (Muir, 2011, p.46). Beginning with *Freeze*, these young people had consciously tried to follow, suit and imitate Saatchi's exhibition venue playing along his manifest art tastes (Stallabrass, 2006b, p.207). For his part, the collector maintained at the time that he aimed at making contemporary art popular in Great Britain by means of the country's mass media, so he chose young artists who would stir enough sensation to reach this goal. As he was used to attend graduates exhibitions in London schools, Saatchi soon realized the potential of young artists such as the recent group of former Goldsmiths' students and understood they could soon climb up the ladder of celebrity:

> *"The YBAs represented a singular moment for British art, rather like the Beatles, the Rolling Stones and the Sex Pistols created breakthroughs for British music." (Saatchi, 2009, p.44)*

However, the new authors that gained Saatchi's favour were collected on his very conditions, which were block sales of almost their entire body of works at discount rates. Besides his particular collection behaviour, Charles Saatchi represents one of the key figures of the art system, one who would spend lavishly on art. A collector is committed to art following his personal taste or the collective taste he has been informed with by experts, hence economists consider this actor as being steered from a utility perspective that draws chiefly on artistic pleasure. In theory, this would be the main difference of the collector's role from investors and speculators, who on the contrary are rather interested in the possible growth of quotations for an artwork. From an economical point of view, artworks can indeed be assimilated to investment or stock goods, as they would maintain their value throughout time and possibly increase it. The art market can thus be compared to real estate, as it holds similar traits for economic theory: scarce liquidity, high transaction costs and imperfect fungibility with other works. Like for financial market, speculators are interested in making rapid money from temporary bubbles, which in the art market may regard a specific artist or movement. Investors behave differently, since they rather aim at exploiting an artefact as an asset, which keeps or increases its value in time. The different attitudes of the two types analysed imply diverse purchase choices: if speculators earn money from hyper-promotion of new trends, investors rely on works whose value is already stable (Santagata, 1998). The collector, instead, often identifies with the artists whose works he or she buys, or at least creates a mutual intellectual relationship with them and becomes a much more upright promoter. The origins of modern collecting date back to the 16th century, when the first art amateurs appeared – as distinct from traditional Renaissance clients or patrons – because they were characterized by an almost compulsive obsession to purchase already finished works, instead of commissioning new ones (Haskell, 1980). The distinct definitions of these players appear less precise when examining the case of Charles Saatchi who, as a collector, has rather been defined by his purchasing attitude: still now he uses to buy up all he likes, but also to resell out what he does not appreciate any longer; he buys finished works but he also makes commissions for new pieces; he collects or sells off artists and also promotes or spoils their reputation. As a matter of facts, Saatchi has always been unscrupulous towards artists and pretty impertinent on the art market, as he was aware he could effectively influence the success or failure of an author or of an entire trend. Italian artist Sandro Chia experienced it to his detriment, being the most striking example of Saatchi's market conduct, though not the only one. After patronizing the Florentine painter for a long time, in the mid Eighties he decided to sell off all Chia's works he possessed, substantially triggering a chain reaction that resulted in a quotation crash for the Italian artist

(Gambillara, 2011). The British tycoon has always refused to admit he had stifled the painter's career, saying that he owned only seven paintings of his, not enough to cause such a deflation in his opinion (Saatchi, 2009, p.6). Owing to such examples, Saatchi has often been accused of not being a collector in its own right, because he behaves like a ruthless speculator. On the other hand, the publicity tycoon has always claimed that he has only been driven by his particular taste, which he maintains was always aimed at showing off and having the general public to respond to the art he collected. In truth, the Iraqui-born collector appears to mix up several roles on the buyers side of the art market, at times being a patron or client, some other times acting as an investor or even a speculator. Hence, daily reality of the art system shows that it is difficult sometime to identify the exact place of an actor in the field, which may be in fact a multiple role, so what truly counts appears to be the strength a player can put in conditioning the art market. Definitely, Saatchi's taste and choices could and still can influence the career or production of young authors, especially those who would wish to draw his attention. However, despite his undoubted power over the contemporary art market in the United Kingdom, even his patronage can't necessarily guarantee success for the artists he purchases or advocates. His support alone couldn't certainly make an artist's fortune, though his commitment to those he patronized and his obsessive keenness in collecting their works often promoted his choices on the market. Consequently, Saatchi's tastes are well identifiable and thus have encouraged a certain type of output from artists. As a matter of facts, several critics admit that Saatchi's preferences as a collector are pretty consistent and self-evident in the works he buys, so that over time a lot of young artists tried to play up to him adapting their creations to his likes. In painter Chris Ofili's opinion, who was patronized by Saatchi in the Nineties and then Turner Prize winner in 1998, the tycoon evidently preferred shocking pieces and would have bought anything by an artist he already supported:

> *"A lot of artists are producing what is known as Saatchi art... You know it's Saatchi art because it's one-off shockers. Something designed to attract his attention. And these artists are getting cynical. Some of them with works already in his collection produce half-hearted crap knowing he'll take it off their hands. And he does." (Ofili in Pitman, 1997)*

Taking the observation further back than the Nineties, however, Saatchi's choices have not been constant in time, on the contrary changing now and again thus highlighting different periods in his collecting activity. Truly, while in the early Eighties his collection included mostly renown British figurative painters such as Howard Hodgkin and Lucien Freud, since the exhibition *NY Art Now* in 1987 he definitively turned to a kind of minimalist and sensational trend in installation art, consequently selling almost all previously collected artworks. Saatchi had been collecting contemporary art since 1972, at the beginning due to the passion of then-wife Doris Lockhart, and soon became one of the most influential collectors on the international art market. Analyzing individual preferences in the case of an influential player such as Charles Saatchi reveals itself a fundamental factor to investigate how art trends may be influenced by personal choices. As exposed by British philosopher Berys Gaut (2000, p.37), in fact, considering art as a cluster-concept helps to understand the way that a specific subset of properties – depending on individual or collective taste, theories and belief – forms altogether the definition of art for a specific time and place. The focus should be placed on the possible combination of the given subset, which can explain why there is divergence of opinions among different players in the art system, tough all may be legitimate from the assessor's view. Any actor may further impose his or her own particular preferences upon the wider art system, but the success of such an action depends largely on the player's acquired position and capital, which is the reason why it is crucial to grab the settings of influent actors such as Saatchi, who was in part responsible for launching the YBA generation. His complete new collection was displayed on occasion of the blockbuster-exhibition *Sensation* at London Royal Academy in 1997, which tells a lot about the new subset of preferences that steered his purchasing choices in the Nineties. Julian Stallabrass (2006b, pp.206-207) remarks the predominance of sensational works – hence the exhibition title – wordplays or puns as well as immediately accessible images, features that could easily be attributed to his advertisement profession. However, he was also very keen on wax sculptures (by Gavin Turk, Abigail Lane or Ron Mueck), animal skin and bodies (by Damien Hirst or Thomas Grünfeld), frozen works (by Marc Quinn and Rose Finn-Kelcey) and in general every piece of art that bears a very realist mark. As a matter of facts, the British tycoon had made his shift to a new trend clear with the two-part-exhibition *New York Art Now*, which indeed showcased early collected pieces by Jeff Koons. However, the preference for young homeland artists was definitely due to recession that hit hard on Saatchi's business, forcing the resale of his previous collection and granting a much smaller budget for new purchases than in the Eighties. Owing to the financial crisis, investing on young and cheap British artists appeared to be a favourable strategy, because it didn't cost much and could be very promising as regards to growth rates, provided that it would arouse sufficient attention. In 1991, Saatchi had picked three young British authors that he thought especially capable of causing much sensation thanks to their works, being Rachel Whiteread, Damien Hirst and Marc Quinn. The latter was not a member of the original Goldsmiths group, but was soon associated by the press with the wider YBA movement particularly because of Saatchi's and Jay Jopling's patronage. In fact, at the newly opened White Cube he presented the sculpture *Self* (1991), which was the artist's self-portrait in the form of a head made from 4.5 litres of his own frozen blood, a piece that was immediately bought by Saatchi for his private collection. *Self* was meant to reflect on physical decay, but its presentation at Jopling's gallery caused a broad scandal owing to the chosen medium, being the artist's haematic fluid. Together with *Ghost* by Whiteread, this work caused huge sensation in the London art world, though it is nothing as compared to the true public outcry – both on tabloids and broadsheet papers – provoked by Hirst's new work commissioned by Saatchi. Created in 1991 and called *The physical impossibility of death in the mind of someone living* (1991), the installation was finally displayed in early 1992 for the group show *Young British Artists* at the Saatchi Gallery, the first in a number of exhibitions that would display the tycoon's new home-grown collection. The work consisted in an entire Australian tiger shark with spread jaws dipped in formaldehyde inside a transparent and minimalist looking glass case with white frames. It was the central piece of the show and to this day undoubtedly the best-known creation of Damien Hirst, at least as far as its media echo is concerned. London art world rose up against this installation as it considered the work viciously provoking: a shark inside a vitrine could not be accepted as an artwork, even if it had been exhibited in an art venue, as it would make most works in the city's galleries look instantly out of fashion. Besides, the price Saatchi had paid for it appeared outrageous even to tabloid readers, as *The Sun* headlined "£50.000 for fish without chips" (Muir, 2011, pp.44-45). For all the criticism of general press and specialist press, Hirst had hit his target earning wide media attention and an immense increase of his personal reputation, while Saatchi on his part had found a new creative vein to exploit – which, furthermore, was local and cheap, if compared to the US artists he had collected previously.

5.3. How to reach far: defining style and production

The claim aroused by Whiteread, Quinn and Hirst for one single work produced at such an early stage reveals a particular feature of the art system, which new entries should be well aware of. There is in fact an unwritten distinction that the market makes automatically between major an minor pieces of an artist, as these differ both in cultural and commercial value from one another. Sometimes such a diverse evaluation of an author's works is made considering the creative period in his or her biography to which the pieces belong to, as can for instance be read form auction returns of Pablo Picasso or Andy Warhol (Thompson, 2008, p.84). Shifting prices for one and the same author, however, may also depend on the particular kind of product and on its relative scarcity, not only on its size or timeframe. As a matter of facts, this drives to a useful distinction which can be made between iconic pieces and retail artworks, the former being sporadic masterpieces intended to contribute to the development of visual arts, while the latter are rather frequent products that carry the artist's sign but are meant to be sold in a higher number to a wider public of collectors (Graw, 2009, pp.187, 207). The production rate and quality usually differs from one artist to another, depending on his or her particular choices: to take two extreme attitudes, an author may opt for a scarce and refined type of creations or on the contrary prefer a massive as well as commercial mode of production. However, different kinds of artworks may be produced at one and the same time, since they actually respond to different needs: while iconic pieces help enhancing an artist's reputation, as they might be bought by major museums or displayed at relevant exhibitions, retail artworks aim at the direct increase of financial capital, hence they support the author's life and profession. As a consequence, besides defining stylistic choices, a young artist needs also to determine his type and scope of production, which goes together with different segments of the art market. The particular artworks a new entry decides to produce may thus be intended to foster his or her own network, artistic, financial or social capital. It is interesting how art market expectations put on new entries were starting to change in the early Nineties, since in the past established dealers or collectors would have waited for a more consistent body of works before picking a young artist, but the upcoming trend rather appeared to demand for quick burning stars which could match the euphoria of the recovering financial market (Stallabrass, 2006a, p.77). Indeed, as mentioned previously, new players on the British art scene such as Karsten Schubert and Jay Jopling asked for sensational pieces, while a long-run dealer like Nicholas Logsdail would wait for a young artist to have walked a longer path before proposing to enter Lisson Gallery. Damien Hirst makes a good example for this demanded variety of production as well as for this new market attitude, which he acquired looking at the examples of some American superstars as in the case of Andy Warhol and Jeff Koons. As a matter of facts, Hirst's animal installations were definitely meant as iconic pieces that would struck art experts and the public, while series such as the spot paintings or the medicine cabinets were rather conveyor-line-like products, which in fact were frequently created or assembled by assistants.

In the early Nineties, even Lucas, Borland and Gordon were experimenting with different sets of creations, trying several techniques and artifacts, until they appeared to have found a first stylistic and productive stage of some maturity. Sarah Lucas finally got her chance to show the results of three years of hard work at her first ever solo show, which took place at City Racing as she was still completely foreign to the London commercial inner-circle, even that of beginner galleries. *Penis Nailed to the Board* was part of the exhibitions that the artist-run space dedicated to fairly unknown artists of the local art scene and resulted in an impressive show, which had a lasting impact on her career. The central piece of the exhibition was an upside-down turned bicycle with a narrow shelve on the wheels onto which Lucas had placed several cutout-photographs of a naked man – her ex-boyfriend Gary Hume – holding a banana and various fruits in sexually-ambiguous positions. Titled *Last night I got loaded, on a bottle of whiskey, you know I feel alright* (1992), this assembled installation was meant as a sculpture and summarized the general theme of the exhibition, highlighting sexual ambiguity in gender representation and language, as well as reflecting on sexism and pornography implied in mass media culture. Other pieces in the show were some self-portraits shot by Hume, such as *Eating a Banana* (1990) and *Divine* (1991), which were the female counterpart to the male cut-outs. Furthermore, Lucas displayed two series of almost ready-mades which used sheets from tabloid papers: there were blow-ups of sexually compromising pictures mounted on cardboards – such as *Sod Your Gits* (1990), *Fat, Forty and Flabulous* (1990) and *Seven Up* (1991) – as well as cut outs from articles on disturbed sexual behaviour – like for instance *Penis Nailed to a Board* (1992). Of all the works on show, it was especially the mentioned paper collages that attracted the attention of experts and were instantly bought in a bulk by Charles Saatchi, who got most of them for a total of only £3.000. The purchase made by the great collector in a way reassured the local art market that Sarah Lucas was back on the rails – recovering at last from earlier failures – due to the acquired maturity of her recent production, style and presentation (Bonami and Robecchi, 2007, p.10).

From 1991 onwards also Christine Borland was progressively entering general attention for her latest works, having seemingly found a ripe strain of production as well as catching good opportunities. From June to August that year she travelled to Karlsruhe for a group show funded by the British Council, since curators had associated her creations with other conceptually oriented sculptors and photographers of the rising London art scene at such a crucial moment. With *Kunst, Europa* (1991) she displayed in Germany a specially devised container stacked with shattered glass sheets hit by a bullet shot, which she had elaborated from her Belfast period. Although avoiding the kind of visual opportunism that appeared predominant in the capital, her installations had found a good balance between Minimalism and Conceptual Art, history and science thus being appreciated by influent critics and curators. The sober tone of her works, as compared to some London-based artists, was likely the result of her temper as well as of the particular working-situation she had found for herself in Glasgow, which would be archetypical for many other Glaswegians throughout the Nineties. In fact, she could financially support her artistic activity thanks to a range of different sources such as research funds or scholarships, teaching income at art schools, a few commissions and private sales thus skipping the gallery system. Listing the grants and scholarships that Borland could make use of between 1987 and 1993 is helpful to understand how a Glaswegian artist would try to fund his or her career kick off, based largely on public or private support rather than the art market. In fact, Borland could get hold of ten different kinds of resources in this period, being the following in chronological order: The Governors Award (Glasgow School of Art, 1987); Peter Moores Travel Bursary (University of Ulster, Belfast, 1989); Scottish Arts Council Small Assistance Grant (1991); Hope Scott Trust Award for Travel (1991); Scottish Arts Council Major Bursary (1992); Hope Scott Trust Award (1992); British Council Visiting Artist Grant (1992); Goethe Institute Cultural Scholarship to Berlin (1992); Scottish Arts Council Small Assistance Grant (1993); Visiting Artist Grant (British Council, Scotland, 1993). Jacqueline Donachie, Julie Roberts, Simon Stirling, Claire Barclay and Gordon himself would fund the kick-start of their activity through a comparable variety of support, including some sporadic museum jobs for mounting exhibitions. The result of such diversity of sources for financial capital certainly conferred a relative market freedom to Glaswegian artists – which Londoners could only dream of – though it also encouraged a sort of research-intensive working method that could provide more mature works (Richardson, pp.164-165). Hence, while the fortunes of the city on the Clyde seemed to slowly improve, so too did the production and style of the Transmission artists, which by now were starting to be durably linked by the art system to the rising London generation, taking up the role of Scottish counterpart.

Indeed, the impact these Glasgow artists made at the beginning of the Nineties was so unexpected, that some years later many commentators maintained it was an incredible wonder. In a conference held for the Turner Prize at the Tate in 1996, for instance, Swiss star-curator Hans Ulrich Obrist labelled 'Glasgow miracle' what had happened in the Scottish city in the late Eighties and early Nineties, though encountering much critique by the direct protagonists of that renaissance. He referred to the miracle of a city that in a few years had become a dynamic art centre without big public support, but uniquely due to the effort and ambition of young artists materialized in independent shows and artist-run spaces such as Transmission (McKee, 2003). It is interesting to notice that Craig Richardson and Ross Sinclair disagreed with the concept of miracle, sharing the opinion of many other peers, since in their belief it was the straightforward result of the humble and passionate attitude of individuals focused on doing well with the dire situation they were confronted with. Sinclair even vehemently opposed the talk at the Tate, addressing the panel of curators with arguments that he referred again in a later publication, which deserves to be read in full-length:

> *"Hans Ulrich Obrist started going on about this idea 'The Glasgow Miracle', I'm still not sure exactly what he meant, but back then in '96 I really thought it sounded odd. I think he was asking, or maybe reflecting, or perhaps proposing – how could it be that so many interesting artists develop in a place which was so bereft of culture with no history of, or relation to, modern art? How could this city be hosting and generating so many important exhibitions and conferences, writers, artists etc. when there was not even a system of private galleries for the commissioning, buying and selling of contemporary art. No infrastructure, no rules, the Wild West, I guess he was thinking. [...] So, anyway, I get up and say that, amazing as it all seems, the dynamic of Glasgow was, in fact, a very tenuous proposition, a castle built on sand, if you like. A ghost – a spectre – a phantom. I tell them all that the main gallery spaces, Tramway, CCA, Transmission etc.etc., were effectively being kept going by a tiny group of individuals who put their heart and soul into carving out a space for these galleries in a very unforgiving civic climate. There was no provision within the structure of these spaces for the success to be consolidated in a longer term way – it was all about the individuals and their ambition and passion for art." (Sinclair in Lowndes, 2010, pp.234-235)*

This passage is relevant to highlight the spirit of the rising Glasgow art scene, which in fact didn't find institutional support in its hometown until the turn of the century. While Londoners were slowly conquering the favour of the local establishment, the Transmission generation was treated as an outcast in the Scottish city, thus Gordon and his colleagues worked hard to catch up with the international art world by means of a methodical search for connections. In this respect, Obrist proved to be a crucial lifeline for many Glaswegian artists in order to build their international career, as he had started very early to invite some of them to group shows all over Europe, especially Douglas Gordon. Obrist had been an assistant to influential curators such as Kasper König and Suzanne Page, quickly rising to one of the most pioneering European curators, who travelled far and wide to create exhibition chances for the artists he had met. His personal attitude towards the role of the curator has always aimed at letting artists totally free, keeping from imposing the curator's ideas on them, but rather trying to ease and stage the creativity of artists (Materassi, 2012). Obrist's personality is quite telling about the pivotal role curators have acquired in the contemporary art system in the last decades of the 20th century, even if their tasks still remain undefined and freely modifiable. This public figure appeared regularly from the Seventies onwards and has his roots in the evolution of the art world of the post-war period. As a matter of facts, it is a hybrid role between the avant-garde critic and the event organizer, whose importance has dramatically increased since exhibitions have become the focal point of the art world, as well as the basic life nourishment for contemporary art museums. Some curators got really powerful as they contributed to establish new artists and upcoming trends, though their reputation depends on how successful the artists they promote will be in the long run. The curator status is also debated by experts, because curators themselves have been showing different attitudes, which can be comprised between two opposing poles: on the one side the guru curator like Harald Szeemann, who decisively shaped the art trends he promoted, on the other side the catalyst curator represented by Obrist himself, who is less interfering and lets artists come up with their own projects. In any case curators can hardly launch a young artist on his or her own, on the contrary they also need to build consensus around all that they want to promote, making the most of relational capital and joining forces with dealers, critics, collectors and of course other curators. In 1991, still in his early twenties, Obrist was already an influential character and he soon realized what was happening up in Scotland, deciding to travel to the Glasgow School of Art to hold a lecture. Students and graduates were excited for his visit and interested in his talks, since he promoted cross-boundary projects and equality of art wherever it is displayed, be it a major museum or a private room. Gordon was struck by the conference and by Obrist's comments on the exhibition the latter had recently set in his kitchen in Sankt Gallen. Held from July to September 1991, *The Kitchen Show* was indeed the first of a number the Swiss curator set in unconventional venues. During his stay in Glasgow, Obrist met upon Gordon and they immediately made good friends, deciding soon to cooperate as they shared a common view on creating opportunities to make art. The Swiss curator was very resourceful for Gordon in the early Nineties, repeatedly inviting him to exhibit around Europe, hence making it easier for the Glaswegian artist to make his works known abroad and enter in some relevant venues or international projects. The convenient aspect of this cooperation was represented by the fact, that most opportunities created by Obrist did not imply the artist's participation in person on the spot, hence being easily affordable for Gordon's budget. At an exhibition held in Nevers in 1991, for instance, every artist had been asked to send his work to the French museum. Considering his limited financial situation, Gordon decided to work on a strategy to make the biggest possible impact without actually being there nor planning something material. This condition made him reach for the kind of relationship art that was performed by artists such as Rirkrit Tiravanija and promoted by Obrist himself. Hence, Gordon came up with the idea of sending letters, clearly exploiting a strategy, which is very dear to conceptual artists, as he thought it would be the only viable tactic to make his art known abroad and beat the non-existent infrastructures in Scotland, as he mentioned later on in an interview to Obrist:

> *"Around 1990-91 I was living in a very small flat in Glasgow and it wasn't – I don't think it was so much an ethical position like artists from the sixties. It was a much more pragmatic decision for an artist living in Glasgow, with no money and no space, no studio. There wasn't an idea of a rejection of institutions. It was just an idea that institutions and the gallery system don't exist in Scotland in the way that they do elsewhere in Europe. So I just wanted to get ideas out. And one of the ways to get ideas out was to use the postal system and the telephone." (Gordon in Obrist, 1996b, p.160)*

After receiving a list of all artists invited at the exhibition in Nevers, he realized that most of them were based in London and were fairly well known, while on the contrary he was probably unknown to them all. Thus he conceived the idea to send a letter to each of them, simply stating 'I am aware of who you are and what you do', which was the plain truth, as he actually knew the addressees and their work. This was the first of a large number of text pieces that Gordon circulated by mail to people he was somehow related to or that belonged to the art system, in order to arouse their attention and interest. As a matter of facts, besides sending the letters to friends and relatives, Gordon had cleverly decided to send them systematically to curators, critics, dealers and collectors of whom he got hold of the address. The recourse to the mail system was indeed a very conscious parallel with the postcards sent since the early Seventies by On Kawara, the renowned American conceptual artist of Japanese origins. The principal reference is of course the series *I am still alive* dating back to 1973, consisting in a telegram sent from New York, which enclosed the cited words. Compared to Gordon's communications, however, the latter lacked the kind of internalisation of Kawara. Instead of being centred on the author's mood or feelings, Gordon tried to connect with the reader keeping a forthright and personal tenor, inducing a personal reflection on the communicated content. The Scottish author's letters were addressed directly to the readers, stating for instance at the incipit 'Dear Kathrina...', and then signed as to create a certain intimacy with the addressee, thus stirring some kind of direct response to them. Furthermore, as this was an on-going project, the letters that followed had statements, which grew more and more ambiguous, as they could even appear disturbing in the eyes of the addressee. A good example is the 1992 *Letter (Number 4)* whose content sounded pretty insulting, even though it was a Bible quote, as it read: 'If only you were hot, or cold. But you are neither hot, nor cold. I am going to vomit you out of my mouth'[11]. Another interesting example is again a mail of 1992, *Letter (Number 8)*, that was sent from Dublin on occasion of the group show *Guilt by Association*, admonishing the addressees that they could not conceal any truth much longer, the full sentence reading 'Nothing can be hidden forever'. Thanks to his first collaboration with Obrist, the Scottish artist started writing letters that soon attracted the experts' attention, hence working both to define his artistic product as well as to exploit a strategy for increasing relational capital, a practice that Gordon would conveniently carry on:

> *"After this I just got into the habit of sending them out to various people, some of whom I'd met. I thought there was a nice parallel with On Kawara's postcards, and that it would be good to keep the whole thing going. [...] They are not anonymous. The idea is to project a role that is morally ambiguous [...]. There has to be some kind of relationship between me and the person receiving the letter – it might be that we met casually, or through the art world, or are*

in a show together, or sometimes it will be people who crop up on the mailing lists of galleries and museums." (Gordon in Lawson, 1995, p.59)

It appears that Gordon was well aware that this could be suitable means to reach influential gatekeepers of the art system, hence by no chance the period of most intense mailing dates from 1991 to 1994, when the Glaswegian artist was living on a low budget and still needed to make a name for himself. Indeed, this strategy proved effective, since many addresses – especially influential ones – were intrigued by the content of the letters and still remember them after many years. As an example, in a review to one of Gordon's shows in 1995, the London correspondent for *Flash Art International* Martin Maloney (1995) even quoted a letter he had received from the Scottish artist some years earlier.

Together with the definition of style and production, new entries must slowly move their way forwards climbing up the art system ladder, trying to go always a step further also in reference to exhibition venues. Entering established exhibition spaces is probably the most difficult task to accomplish for young artists, since it entails the necessity of an improved network in the art system that may grant access to museums or galleries. As regards to relationships, Transmission artists in the early Nineties were good at exchanging the reciprocal connections they had made while abroad and then capitalized them together for the sake of many. This had been the case of Gordon's acquaintance to Alan Johnston in 1991, as well as a a year later with Buchanan's connections to Ireland that proved instrumental for the initiation of the first museum show of the new Glaswegian generation. Like Christine Borland, having finished his MA in Belfast helped Roderick Buchanan making durable links with the Irish context and getting in touch with Declan McGonagle. A highly influential curator, the latter had fostered in Ireland throughout the Eighties a new sort of global-localism that was slowly emerging in the Western art scene, being informed by site-specificity and a renewed interest in representational politics. McGonagle had shown how to debate the development of contemporary art in the geographical outskirts of the art world, fuelling change in Ireland with an extensive arts program at Derry's Orchard Gallery, where in the early Eighties he had started to host international artists in a small town context. It was the exact model the Transmission committee had tried to replicate in Glasgow for the past two years, hence they wanted to get in closer contact and it was planned to have a show at the Orchard Gallery. In 1992 the same group of exhibitors of *Self Concious State* set out for Ireland to organize another exhibition, called *Guilt by Association*[12]. In the meanwhile, McGonagle had made a decisive progress, as he was called to Dublin as curator of the recently opened Irish Museum of Modern Art and maintained the invitation for the Glaswegian artists to exhibit at the new venue for the museum, being the 17th century building of the former Royal Hospital Kilmainham. Even if the venue came about by chance, this exhibition resulted in a crucial step forward for all featured contributors as well as for the entire Glasgow alternative art scene, because it finally was the first major museum show for a group of Scottish conceptual artists. Furthermore, the shift in venues caused radical change, also because the event had to be coherent to the Dublin's context and its complicated historical past, as well as to the building which housed the museum. Borland, Buchanan, Gordon, Henderson and Richardson agreed they would have to make distinctively Dublin-related works, though avoiding to be trapped by site-specificity or to get lost in the city's difficult history. As a matter of facts, the exhibition showcased the working procedure of the young Glaswegians, which is conversations and constant debate among a supportive network of peers, in order to convey a consistent and unitary meaning to all works displayed. This process and disposition among the contributors is made clear even in the exhibition title, *Guilt by Association*, and revealed in the catalogue by Gordon himself:

> *"None of the projects are collaborative as such, but we have been meeting regularly to discuss each other's works throughout the development of the show. A good deal of these discussions concern the relationships that can be nurtured between the separate ideas and objects we are considering." (Gordon in* Guilt by Association, *Cat.1992, p.3)*

The two most mature artists appeared to be Borland and Gordon, who provided interesting examples of context-specific production, which could be highly evocative in dealing with mortality, memory and identity. Christine Borland displayed the results of an on-going project called *Small Objects that Save Lives* (1991-1993), which indeed featured various items sent by friends and associates that were inspired by the title. Objects ranged from condoms to photographs and were then scientifically displayed on trestle tables alongside the name of each sender. On the contrary, Gordon decided to produce his works sticking to the museums own resources, for instance by exploiting the complete mailing list of the Irish Museum of Modern Art to send some of his text pieces to critics, journalists, dealers and curators. It was a strategy aimed at getting people involved who were already familiar with the Dublin museum and trying to project them into a psychological space – not a physical one – catalysed by the artist. Three different letters were used on the occasion: *Letter (Number 5)* had the sentence 'I forgive you'; *Letter (Number 6)* with the words 'Life or Death'; and finally *Letter (Number 8)* consisting in the phrase 'Nothing can be hidden forever'. Furthermore Gordon presented a modified version of *List of Names*, using the opposite technique as applied to the Third Eye Centre installation. On this occasion the list included the names of all the people the artist did not remember, divided into prearranged categories: 'Those I do not know. Those I cannot know. Those I will never know. Those I would like to know. Those I have forgotten but will remember. Those I have forgotten and will never remember.' The most original contribution to the Dublin show, however, was the work *Museum Keys* that featured the true copies of the Irish institution's keys, which could be bought by visitors at a small price. Interestingly this simple action implies a twofold meaning in the context of a museum, considered as an institution awarding cultural and economical value to artifacts. On one hand, it openly criticizes culture system at large, since the author takes the keys away from the deputed decision-makers of the museum and hands them over to the public. On the other hand, it challenges the visitor's trust in the pieces they are shown in a museum: as a matter of facts, it is up to viewers to decide on whether the keys are valuable and authentic, as they do for any other object displayed in such institutions. Gordon's purpose was to make the viewer responsible for constructing the meaning of an artwork, thus claiming that the viewer shouldn't be a passive receptor of the establishment's decision about what is art:

> *"The work is a mechanism for pushing that kind of responsibility onto the viewer. They have the responsibility to construct a meaning for the work. Decisions related to the construction of meaning have to be made by asking questions and weighing answers. Those answers are not to be found in gazing at the objects; they are based on an individual's thinking around moral and ethical issues. [...] The relationship that a viewer has with a work can be much the same as any other kind of relationship." (Gordon in Sinclair, 1992, p.43)*

The group show earned good reviews, especially from *Frieze* that seemed to watch closely the events promoted by the Transmission committee. Ian Connolly Hunt (1992, pp.76-77) for instance, an important contributor for the London-based magazine, argued that the Scottish spirit of the exhibition was unmistakable, showcased by the artists' genuine cooperation and their resolved decision to work on shared themes. In his opinion the five Glaswegian artists had been able to succeed in purporting the idea of addressing an active viewer, even if a deeper interpretation of their works needed a thorough analysis. Indeed, it was a constant idea of various *Frieze* authors at the time – including James Roberts – that art receivers couldn't be treated as passive, since their reaction was thought necessary in order to close the circle of meaning started by an artist (Stallabrass, 2006b, p.120). In the course of the Nineties, such an attitude of the artist towards the public had become a typical trait in the development of visual arts, with several critics and curators dealing with this theme for the past two decades. Accepting the public's active role in contemporary art arises from the belief that spectators are never quiescent or neutral as far as cultural processes are concerned, instead playing a vital role that goes far beyond growing number of museum and exhibition visitors around the world. Italian star-curator Francesco Bonami has consistently stressed the viewer's role in contemporary art, turning it into the main theme of the 2003 Venice Biennale named *Dreams and Conflicts – The Viewer's Dictatorship*. The title was obviously a provocation, so much so that some critics ironically suggested the counter-name *Curators' Dictatorship* (Cat.2003), since Bonami had called about ten international colleagues to curate the extensive Venetian exhibition. In any case, the 50th Biennale argued convincingly that art cannot exist without its public: all things considered, the viewer gives life to works by means of a response to the artwork, blending together the narration created by the artist and the personal viewing experience. Art theorist Jacques Rancière (2009) seems to follow the same line of thought, since he has contributed to define the public's role in contemporary art coining the phrase 'emancipated spectator'. The French scholar's arguments developed from the 'spectator paradox' which is derived from theatrical studies and considers that theatre cannot exist without a public, though spectatorship has negative aspects too when meaning unawareness and inertia in front of a spectacle. Still, Rancière (2009, pp.10-15) shows that this paradox relays on a pedagogical model based on the theory of ignorance, postulating that the job of a schoolteacher is to fill the gap between his or her personal knowledge and that of the pupils. According to the French critic, however, the specific knowledge of the teacher and that of the students don't consist of two different levels of learning, but they rather represent two different positions whose distance must be covered in order to weave a thread between the dividing points. Hence, every artist who wishes to educate spectators would irremediably fail, because the knowledge-gap principle this choice is based on results incorrect from Rancière's point of view. Communication between artists and spectators does not lay on cause-effect processes, but it is reached at a median point where the author's intentions and the public's life experience run upon each other. An artist should strive to stir up the spectator's awareness, capacity and energy, hence kindling the public's intellectual emancipation which art can indeed favour. In Rancière's (2009, p.22) opinion the artist only creates the conditions for performing ideas and skills, though creating a language whose meaning must be actively interpreted by the spectator. The spectator's active role was also postulated by studies concerning art of much older ages, especially following the strand of Hans Belting's *Rezeptionsgeschichte*. American scholar John Shearman (1988) gave very useful examples dating back to Italian Renaissance, demonstrating that the public did already express intellectually emancipated views on their contemporary art production. For instance, he reconstructs people's reaction when seeing new works located in public spaces, such as the case of Baccio Bandinelli's sculpture of *Hercules and Cacus* (1525-1534) in front of Palazzo Vecchio in Florence. Studying the example of this artwork commissioned by Duke Alessandro de' Medici, Shearman (1988, pp.44-58) shows that Renaissance viewers were active art receivers, sometimes even an educated and self-aware public. Even if the commissioner and the author had attached an intentional meaning to the sculpture, which was the acquired freedom of Florence from foreign rulers, the piece itself was misinterpreted and even distorted in its sense by local spectators, who linked it to the kind of political oppression preformed by the Florentine establishment, hence interpreting the work according to their life experience and expectations. *Rezeptionsgeshichte* at large helps art historians to trace back the reactions of the public, hinting at the existence in all periods of a truly emancipated spectator, though it is not easy to ponder the exact influence of the public in visual arts development. There could even be an economical explanation for the existence of an active spectator, again recurring to Mossetto's (2003) considerations for this purpose, as he maintains that a distinctive trait of art consumption from an economical point of view is addiction. In this case, it is of course meant as a positive consequence, but the behavioural model can indeed be compared to that of drug dependence: each dose of the product causes the demand for the next dose to sore. In fact, culture is a commodity people tend to overstock, therefore stimulating growing consumption and knowledge, which can be easily observed in everyday life, as a museum visitor tends to increase his cultural demand in time. The idea of art addiction delivers a powerful means against opinions that advocate the obscurity of contemporary art, since any sort of cultural product may seem difficult to appreciate, but the more a visitor attends cultural facilities or reads books and magazines, the deeper his or her competence will grow. Hence, due to increasing consumption rates of cultural products a viewer's taste and inclinations become more and more sophisticated, finally allowing the spectator to emancipate from guidelines set by opinion leaders or by the art establishment.

Back to *Guilt by Association*, besides addressing the emancipated viewer, this exhibition acquired a special meaning for the career of its contributors and for the sake of Transmission. It was in fact the last group show that the gallery committee organized together, having handed over the responsibility to younger colleagues as their two-year mandate had expired. Borland and Gordon were indeed aware that so far they had gained access to a bigger arena, distant and different from their experience as newly graduates in 1990. In two years they had considerably moved forward, being able to exhibit in prestigious venues, to contact influent gatekeepers and mentors, to be credited for their work as promising artists and to end up on the pages of influent magazines. Many Transmission members had welcomed the effectiveness of the committee's initiatives, though there was also consistent grumble by some who accused the directors of having used the artist-run space for the advancement of their personal careers (Lowndes, 2010, p.157). Gordon and Borland rejected the alleged accusations, but all in all felt they should make room for younger artists to take over Transmission activities. After the Dublin exhibition the committee members tried to progress on their own path mainly as individuals rather than as a movement, though still supporting each other at times. After two years serving on the committee, Borland felt that Glaswegian artists had together successfully broken the entrance barriers that had seemed insurmountable at the beginning, confirming that artists themselves become aware of the different career stages they proceed to:

> *"We just got on with what we wanted to do: made/shared good art, dealt with people and situations on our own terms no matter how important or awesome these people said they were. Helped each other, relied on peer-group support, pushed at what appeared to be barriers of age, experience, claims of financial status. Now it seems they weren't barriers at all, just gates waiting to be nudged open." (Borland in* Guilt by Association, *Cat.1992, p.4)*

Still in 1992 Gordon further refined his production to reach far beyond Scotland, developing new methods to spread his text pieces, hence a year after starting to send his letters he recurred to the telephone as a means for his works[13]. The first telephone conversation was devised as a so-called *Instruction* piece in 1992 for a low budget project he attended with Martin Boyce at Café Picasso, a restaurant in Rome's city centre. That same year he let other two instructions be performed as telephone works in Italy, the first at the Galleria Giò Marconi in Milan, the second again in Rome at the Museo del Folklore. Italian friendliness inspired the Scottish author, as he thought it interesting to exploit the relaxed atmosphere enjoyed by people in a cafe or restaurant, in order suddenly intrude in a person's privacy by means of an unsettling message delivered through the phone. In fact, the typical situation of these performances ran as follows: the artist advised with written instructions the dealer or curator to call a bar or other kind of public place close to the exhibition venue, of which the landlord had been previously informed about the project; when receiving the call, the landlord had to put it through to one of the regular costumer of his facility who happened to be there at the moment; when the unknowing client took the call, the caller would quickly refer the sentence devised by the artist and hang up immediately, as to avoid any reaction from the receiver. In Gordon's intentions, the resulting situation should resemble the climax of a classical thriller movie, when an unexpected phone call bursts in the character's routine. As a matter of facts, Gordon refers to a Hollywood movie of 1938, featuring James Cagney and Humphrey Bogart, which he had seen on television as a child:

> *"This situation has classic cinema 'thriller' references. There's a scene in 'Angels with dirty faces' where a similar thing happens." (Gordon in Lawson, 1995, p.62)*

The text read by the caller could be perceived as a disturbance in the receiver's life, an unsettling message that could lay one's inner feelings bare, even without recognizing to be part of an artistic performance. The artist indeed didn't spoil the artwork immediately, but rather wanted to allow the unaware spectator to later recognize the sentence at the gallery and maybe think back of what he had experienced earlier that day. The bar or restaurant chosen was usually just a few steps off the gallery, where the sentence whispered over the phone was replicated in vinyl letterings on the window or on the inner walls. Gordon set out to unsettle the chosen spectator three times: first of all intruding his or her privacy at an unexpected moment with the phone call, then leaving him or her mull over the strange message due to the sudden hanging up and finally fascinating him or her again, if and when it is acknowledged that one was part of an art project seeing the sentence in a proper art environment. In the worst case, however, the curious incident could simply become the next topic of discussion for the unaware target and his or her friends at the public house, so that art could unexpectedly become the sparkle for a conversation, as the Glaswegian artist often likes to say. According to Thomas Lawson (1995) and Stephanie Moisdon-Trembley (1996, p.120), through these telephone pieces and letters Gordon had finally succeeded in effectively addressing a theme that is particularly dear to his production, which is creating a psychological ground shared by the artist and the spectator. What is more, as noticed by Lawson (1995, p.62), the Scottish artist had been able to do so without recurring to real objects and setting site-specificity far aside, furthermore bringing the moment of art consumption into the private lives of unwary spectators.

For the first telephone piece at Cafè Picasso in Rome, titled *Instruction (Number 1)* (1992), the words spoken over the phone were 'You can't hide your love forever', while for the group show *Instructions Received* at Galleria Gio' Marconi in Milan he created *Instruction (Number 2)* (1992), speaking the sentence 'I won't breath a word (to anyone)'. The framed documentation of the latter instruction piece including two photographs of the performance was very much appreciated by Dutch curator Jan Debbaut, when he got to see it at Lisson Gallery in 1993. The work was then displayed as a small-framed picture showing the instructions on a sheet of paper together with the caller's photograph and that of the place where the phone call had been received, while the delivered sentence was also applied as a wall text. This telephone piece makes it fairly clear that the recipient's reaction might vary according to his or her personal and emotional condition, as the artist explains:

> *"I did another piece in Milan recently where the instructions were similar but the message was 'I won't breathe a word (to anyone)'. There's nothing wrong with that, unless you happen to feel guilty already." (Gordon in Lawson, 1995, p.61)*

On the contrary, the instructions created for *Molteplici culture* (Cat.1992) at the Museo del Folklore in Rome were more complex and involved Liam Gillick, who had been asked to select the British artists to be sent to Italy, but unaware of being featured in a performance. Curated by Carolyn Christov-Bakargiev and Ludovico Pratesi, it was a comprehensive group show in the rooms of the former monastery of Sant'Egidio which included a large number of young Italian and foreign artists. For the British section called *Speaker Project,* replicated later that year at the Institute of Contemporary Arts in London, besides Gordon Gillick had chosen Damien

Hirst, Willie Doherty and Margherita Sprio. The piece by the Glaswegian artist was simply titled *Instruction* (1992) and consisted in an anonymous telephone conversation that the former Glasgow based artist Gianni Piacentini was to have with Liam Gillick, even if the two had never met before. Gordon was a friend of Piacentini's since the latter's stay in Scotland in 1989, when he had been awarded a scholarship, and then invited him over again as a foreign contributor to *Windfall 91*. For *Molteplici Culture*, Gordon sent Piacentini instructions to start an anonymous telephone conversation with Gillick – the latter being completely unaware of the situation – to be recorded on a cassette and then written out. The aim of the project was to act out an intimate conversation without disclosing the caller's identity and, at the same time, creating a disturbing situation, which lingered at the edge of stalking. Whatever Gillick's reaction would be at the moment of the call, Gordon actually hoped the event would stay with the curator and induce him to think about this experience, maybe recounting the strange call to other people (Lawson, 1995, p.62). In fact, it was the same aim that the Scottish artist had seized by means of previous instruction pieces in Italy or of the numerous letters he had been sending since 1991, which clearly were trying to bring the moment of artistic consumption in the life of the unaware spectator.

As previously mentioned, *Instruction* was displayed also on occasion of *Speaker Project* curated by Liam Gillick at the Institute of Contemporary Art (ICA), which featured all artists that participated into the group show in Rome. This was a good opportunity for Gordon to be present in London again and, for the first time, in an institutional context of big relevance. Still in 1992 he had another opportunity to be featured in the capital, but this time on the side of the alternative art scene for the exhibition *A Modest Proposal* at Lawren Maben's Milch Gallery[14]. The latter show arose from the extensive cooperation of Gordon with Simon Patterson that year – whom he got acquainted with through Liam Gillick – and reached back to an artistic project that the Glaswegian artist had started at Gianni Piacentini's home back in 1989. While staying in Glasgow, the Italian artist had curated a small exhibition called *The Living Room*, which was one of the first in the Scottish city to be installed in a private home, in fact Piacentini's sitting room where twenty young Glasgow artists exhibited in turn. Gordon offered a project for the living room of his Italian friend, which consisted in applying a wide range of house paint samples on one of the walls, each colour being then labeled with an invented and curious name. In 1992, this same work was readapted by Gordon in collaboration with Patterson and then published on the pages of *Frieze*, for which the two neo-conceptual artists had re-labeled all house gloss colours in use in the United Kingdom, naming them after historical figures and quoting the price per litre after the degree of celebrity. Still in the same year Gordon e Patterson reworked this project for the reopening of Milch Gallery, on this occasion turning it into an installation composed of pyramids of paint buckets, grouped according to their colour family and named after British, Scottish and American dynasties. Housing both an exhibition space on the first floor and a club in the basement flat, Milch Gallery in Great Russell Street was a strange location with an ambiguous character, which was the direct result of its manager's own personality. A Canadian homosexual, Lawren Maben dressed like an anarchist skinhead and funded his activities with the profits from the events held in the disco – a combination of a club privet and a rave party – as well as from occasionally prostituting himself. After being closed for two years, *A Modest Proposal* celebrated the reopening of Milch Gallery in a new venue, for which Maben had asked for contribution by his great friend Simon Patterson, who in turn had extended the invitation to Gordon. Many experts considered this occasion as one of the best London underground events of 1992. Besides the collaborative work, the Scottish artist applied the words 'I forgive you' on to the gallery walls, which was drawn from *Letter (Number 5)* that had been sent for the group show in Dublin. On this occasion, Patterson presented instead *The Great Bear* (1992) for the first time, a work that would soon became his most renowned piece. It was an adaptation of the official London Underground map, but the different lines and stations had been replaced with the names of celebrities such as actors and soccer players, as well as of famous humanists and scientists. The different professional categories were given each their own tube line, for instance the Northern Line featuring Hollywood stars which included Laurence Olivier, Gina Lollobrigida, Kirk Douglas and Humphrey Bogart. Exploiting the familiarity of the viewer with the original tube map, Patterson intended to replace and overlap a different set of information. Still in 1992 Gordon resumed his connections with another London friend, since he invited Martin Creed to Transmission Gallery for the group show *Outta here.* It was one of the first shows for Creed after graduation and he was such grateful to Gordon that he introduced him to Bernhard Starkmann, an early collector of his works. As a matter of facts, the latter was one of the most important contemporary art collectors in London and the founder of an important publishing house and book distributor. Gordon immediately drew the attention of Starkmann, who soon became a great supporter of Gordon's and helped him through the kickstart of his career, de facto being his first influent buyer.

Between 1992 and 1993 Gordon contributed in various group shows also abroad, mostly in Europe – France, Norway, Germany and Austria – while others even took place across the Atlantic and in Japan. Among the many exhibitions, the following are worth mentioning, the venue's relevance considered: *5 Dialogues* at Naturhistorisches Museum in Bergen, Norway, and *240 Minuten* at the Galerie Esther Schipper in Cologne in 1992. At the beginning of the following year he was in Tokyo and Nagoya for *High Fidelity*, at the Schirn Kunsthalle in Frankfurt for *Prospekt '93*, in New York for *The Return of the Cadavre Exquis* at the Drawing Center and at the *Wiener Sezession* for Viennese Story. In 1993 Obrist called him for the project *Chambre 763*, an exhibition mounted in a room of the Carlton Palace Hotel in Paris. On all these occasions the Scottish artist sent some of his text pieces wither as letters or telephone instructions, hence they represent without doubt the defining production of his debut years. At the beginning these works had been a suitable strategy to overcome problems of low budget and lack of personal space, but after some time these products proved very rewarding for increasing relation capital and displaying wherever he could. As a matter of facts, this kind of production allowed Gordon to accept every invitation to group shows he received in that period, even if he was allotted very short time to create his contribution. The pressure under which the young artists toiled at the time is very well described by Ross Sinclair, who recalls that at after-parties for openings in Glasgow there was always the chance to meet a lot of people, often bumping into someone who was organizing an exhibition somewhere else. Quite often it happened that one was contacted in the aftermath and asked to take part in the previously discussed group show, but given a very short time, a wide distance gap and no compensation to participate. Despite any sort of geographical, financial and temporal difficulties, for a young artist these were wonderful chances to arouse international attention; therefore it was virtually impossible to refuse. The procedure and production Gordon had chosen in his early career was indeed suitable to react to such a situation. In fact, his text pieces made a great impact on experts by means of minimal action, while they could be produced and sent anywhere in a very short time at a very low rate. This is how Sinclair would describe the ingenious works that Gordon devised in his early career:

> *"In one sense these are contingency works, and they reflect and thrive on the social genesis of much art production. Say you meet someone in a bar, after an exhibition opening; you get talking with them, they're organising a show somewhere in Europe or America. Later on they phone you, and ask if you would like to contribute*

> *something to the show. But it's in two weeks time, 3000 miles away. There's no time or money to ship anything over. This is a situation familiar to many young artists and it provides a context well suited to an art practice like Gordon's. It reflects his ability to make the maximum impact with the most minimal of interventions." (Sinclair, 1993a, p.5)*

Thanks to these text pieces, employed as a very pragmatic and clever stratagem, Gordon could attract much attention on his production at a crucial point for every new entry. Furthermore, they allowed him to take part in twenty-eight group shows worldwide from 1990 to 1993, which is an average of eight per year – an impressive number for an artist in his twenties who was not sponsored by a commercial gallery. The large number of events he organized or he took part in allowed him to design a network of worldwide relationships, soon helping him to be integrated in the international art world. His friendship with Hans Ulrich Obrist was also essential, as the young Swiss curator's career was advancing considerably and he kept supporting the Scottish artist throughout the Nineties. As a matter of facts, in April 1993 Gordon's first solo show was curated by Obrist, who had recently been put in charge of the *Programme Migrateurs* at the Musée d'Art Moderne de la Ville de Paris. Having his first personal exhibition at an important venue definitely marked a new stage in Douglas Gordon's career and he could then rightly be defined a rising artist on an international scope.

Images

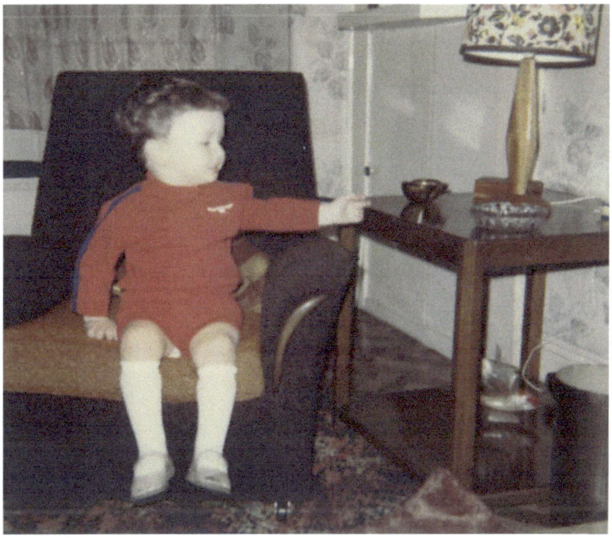

Figure 1

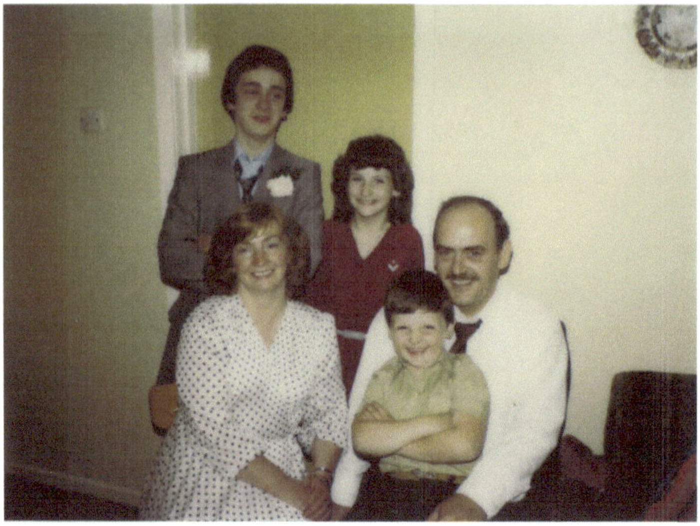

Figure 2

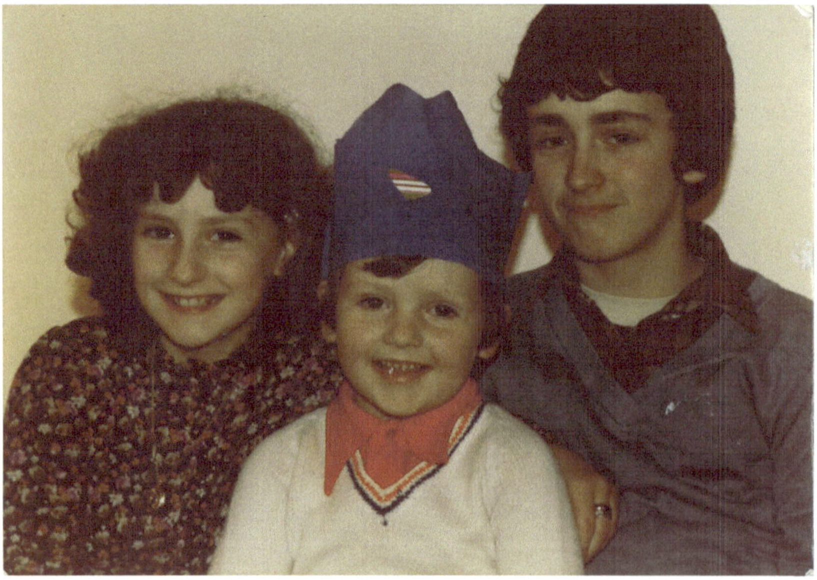

Figure 3

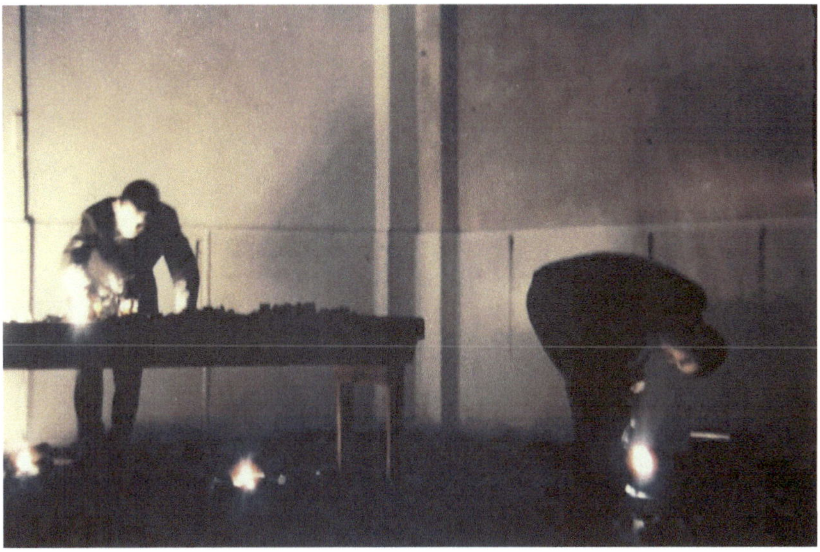

Figure 4

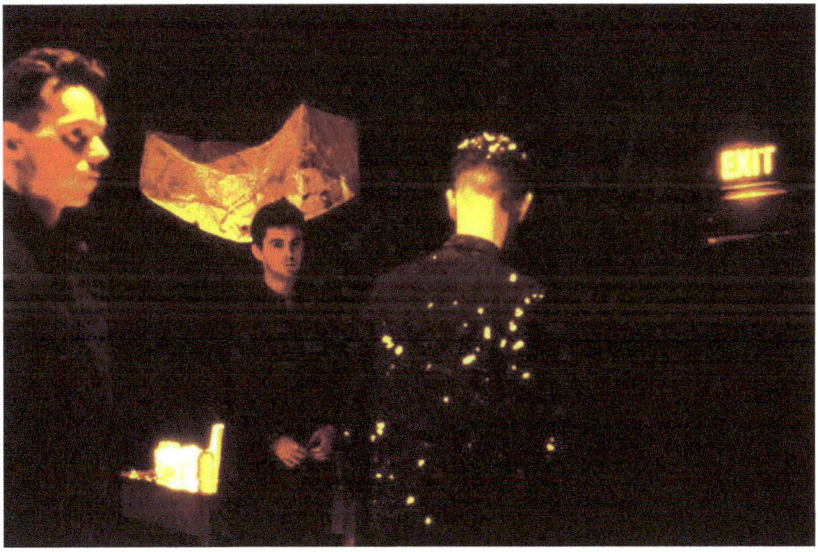

Figure 5

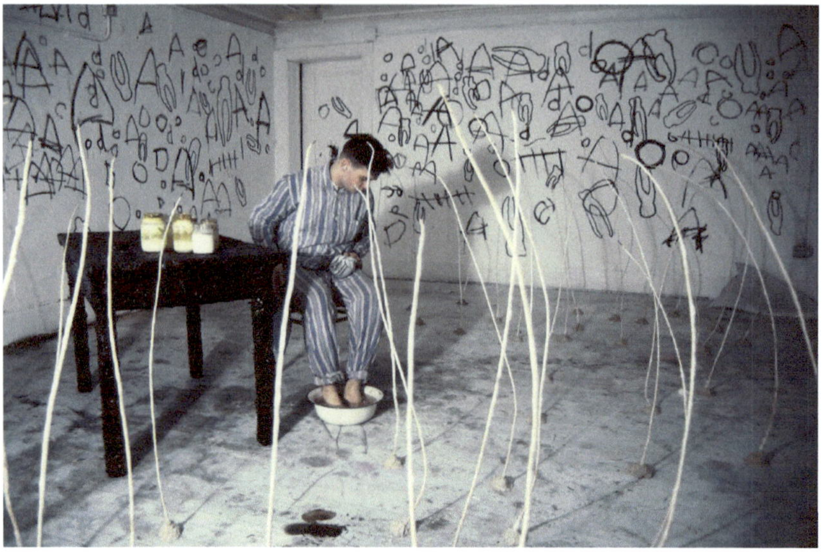

Figure 6

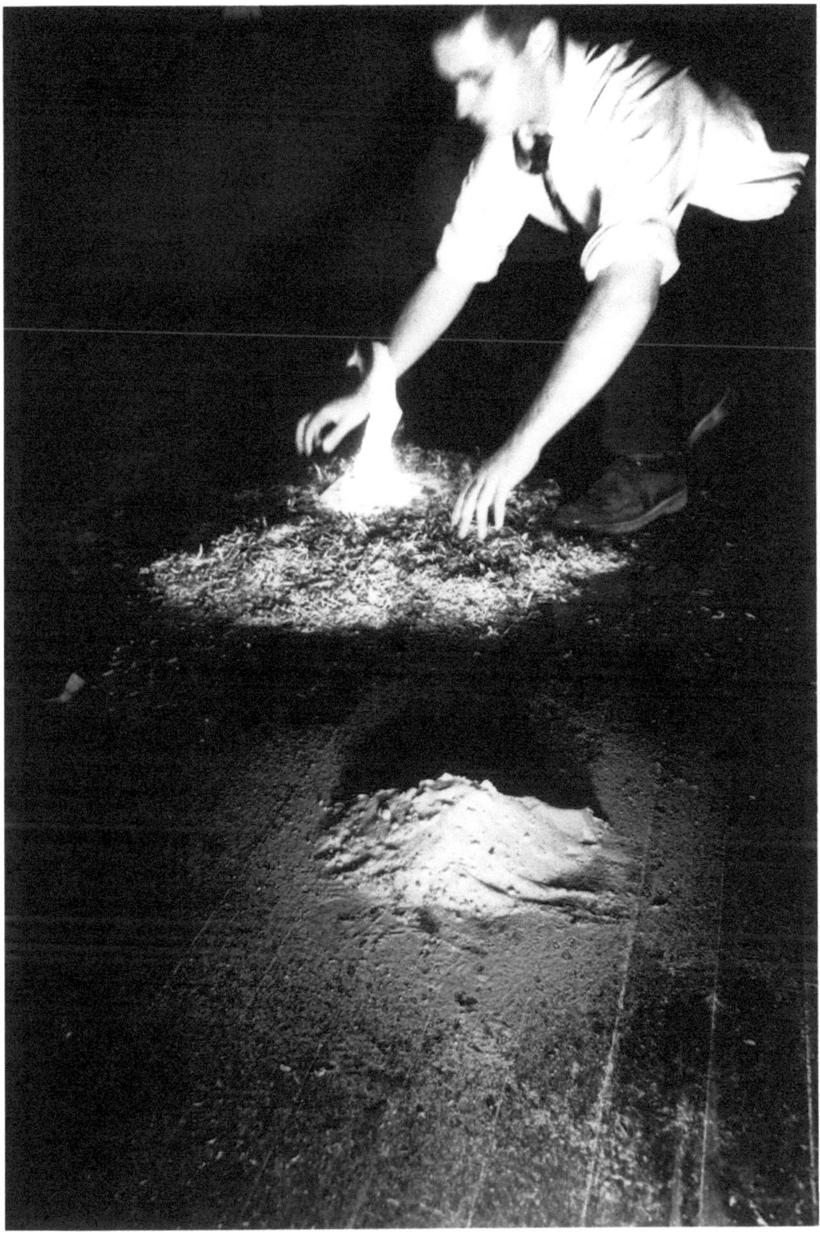

Figure 7

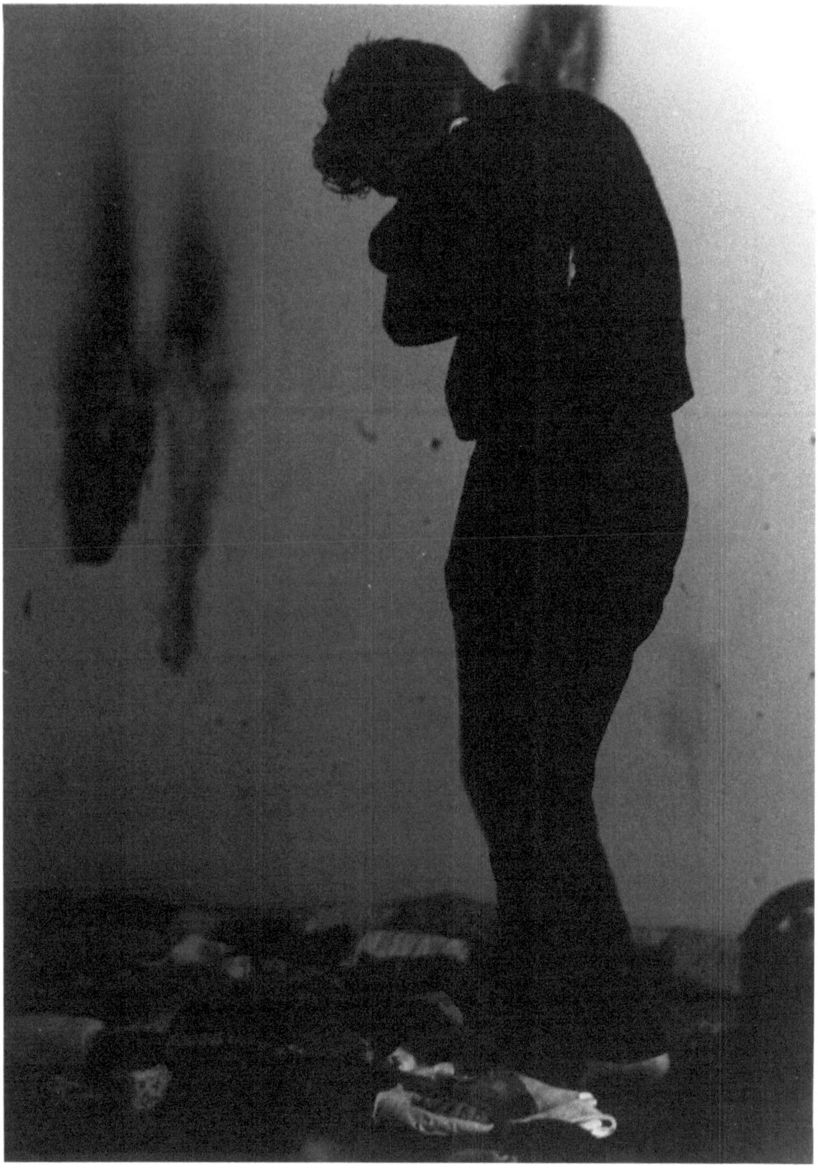

Figure 8

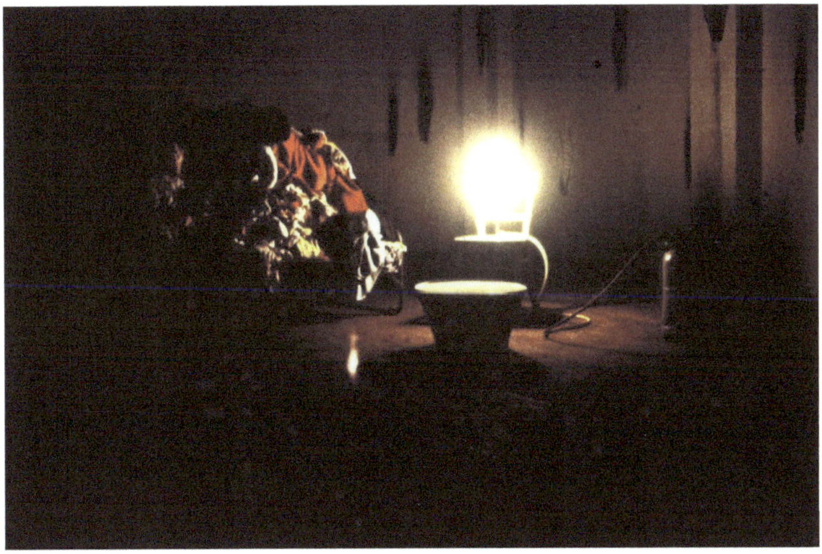

Figure 9

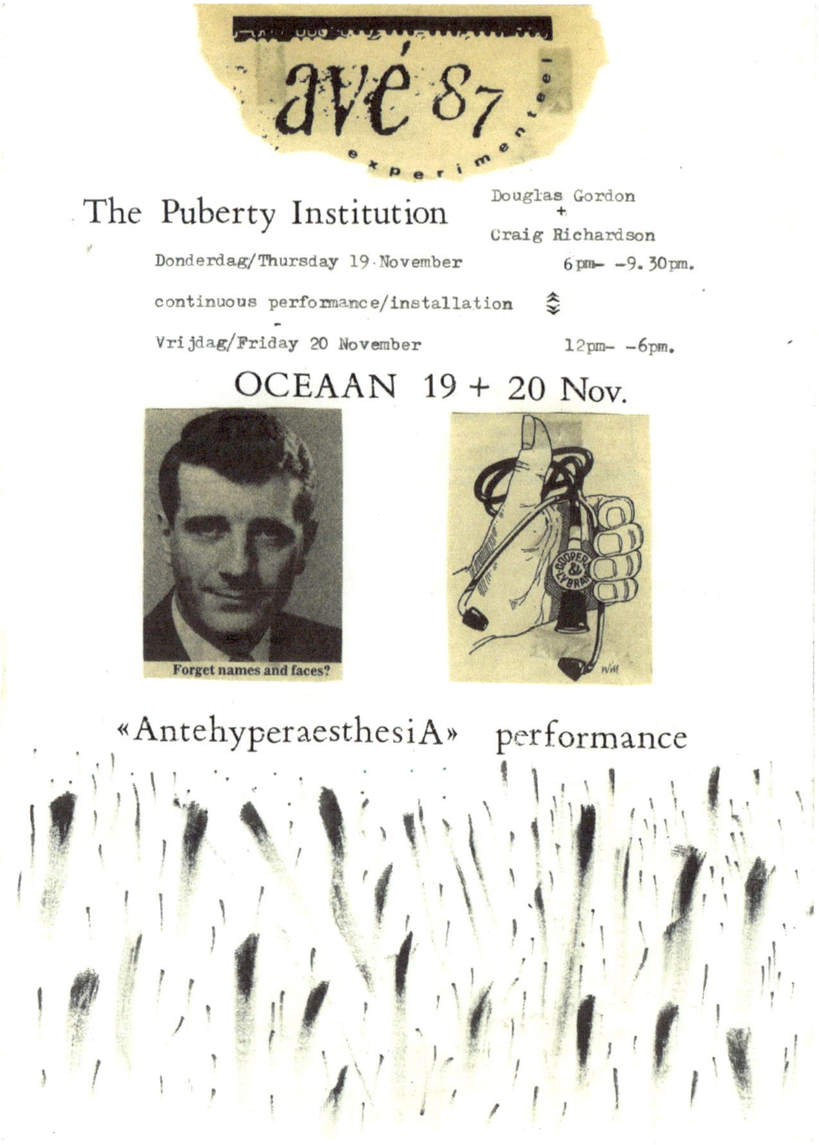
avé 87
experimenteel
The Puberty Institution
Douglas Gordon
+
Craig Richardson
Donderdag/Thursday 19 November 6pm- -9.30pm.
continuous performance/installation
Vrijdag/Friday 20 November 12pm- -6pm.
OCEAAN 19 + 20 Nov.
Forget names and faces?
«AntehyperaesthesiA» performance

Figure 10

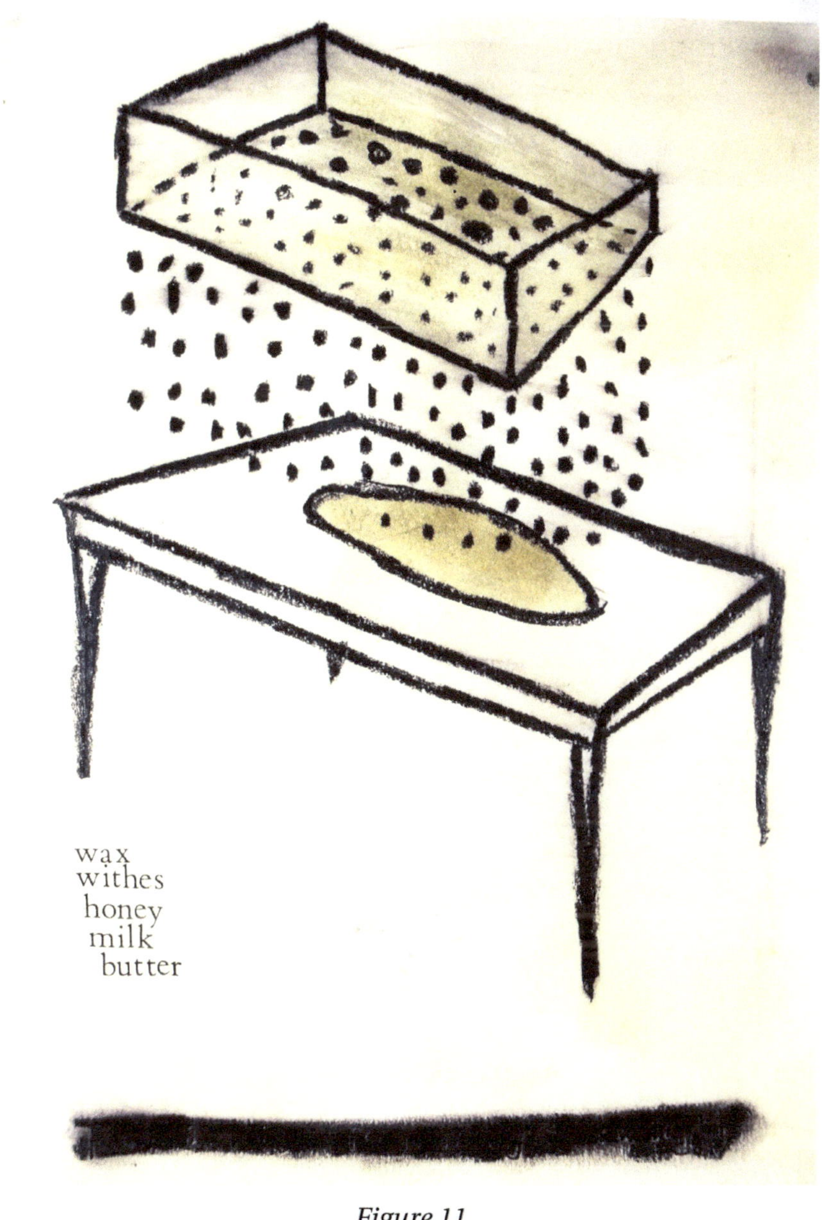

Figure 11

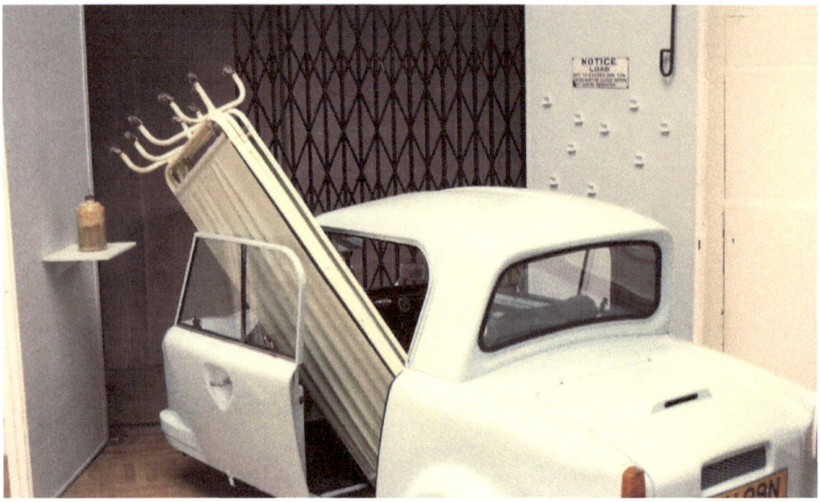

Figure 12

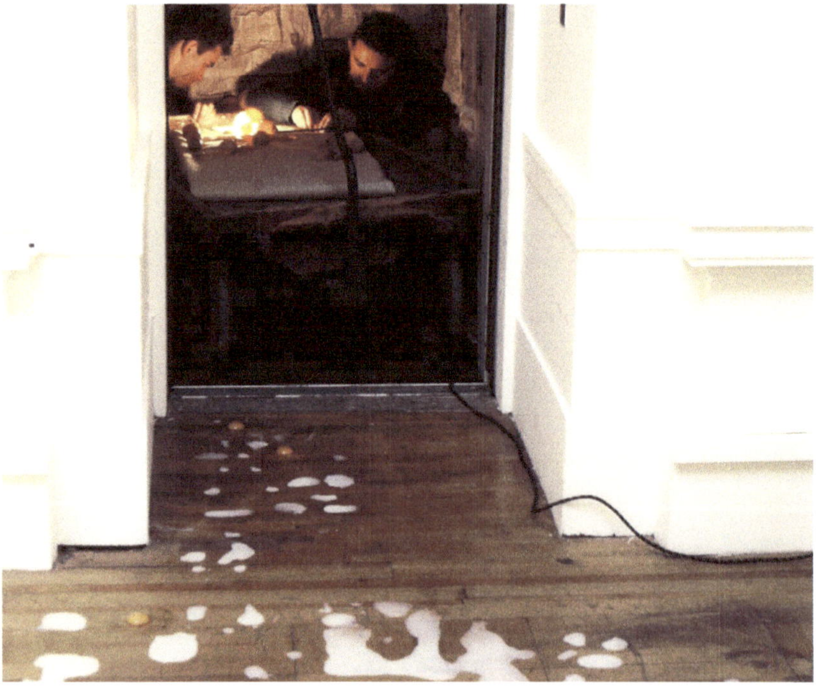

Figure 13

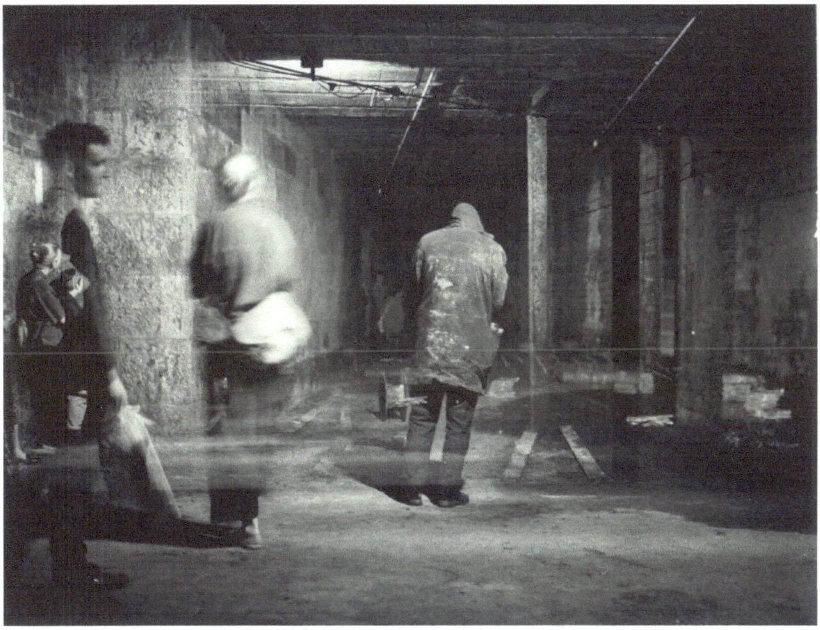

Figure 14

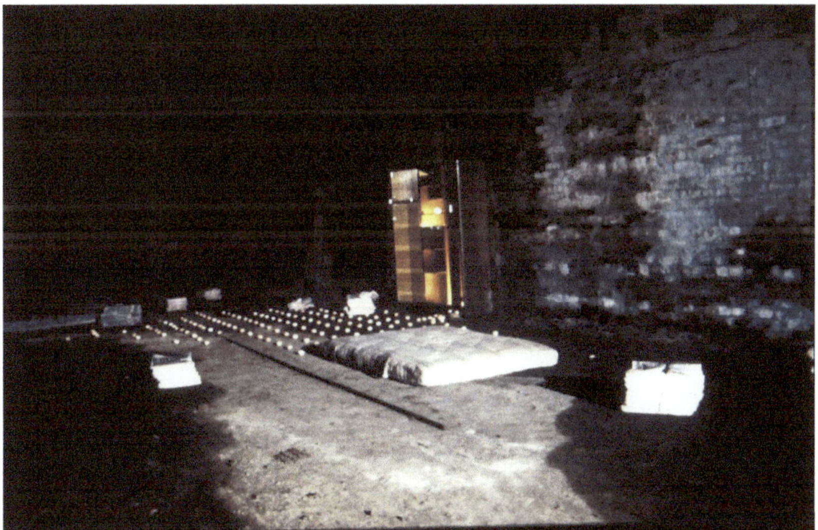

Figure 15

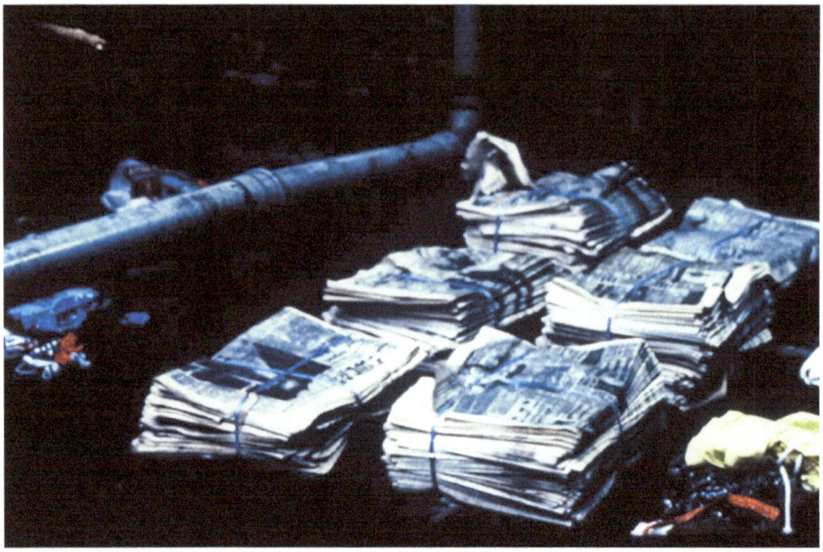

Figure 16

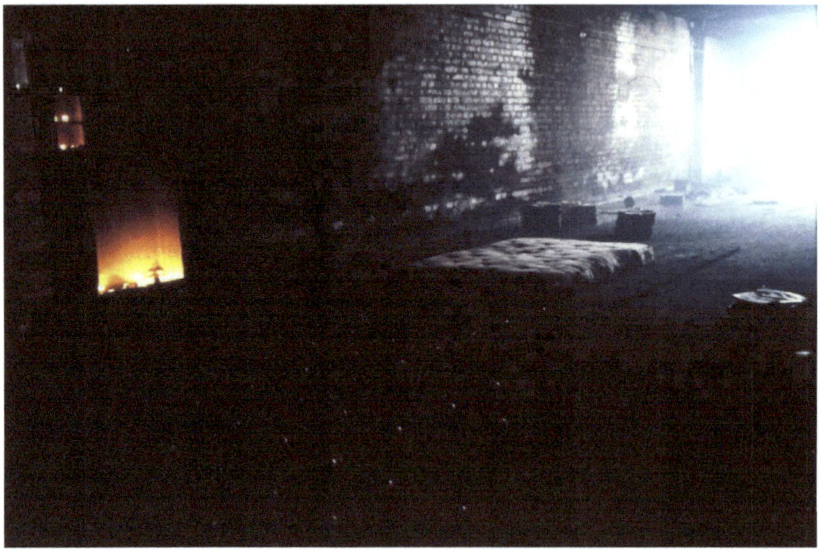

Figure 17

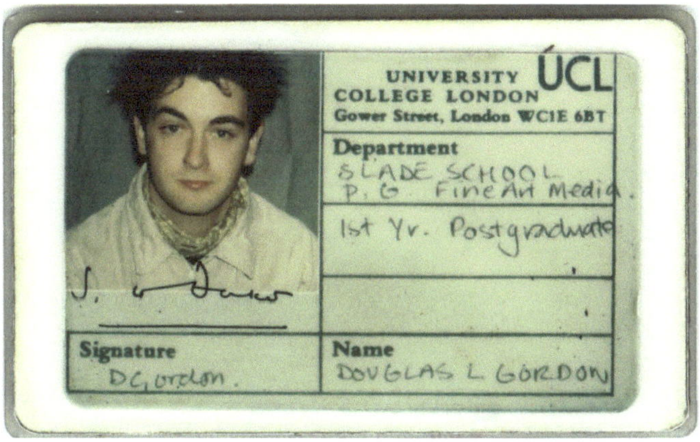

Figure 18

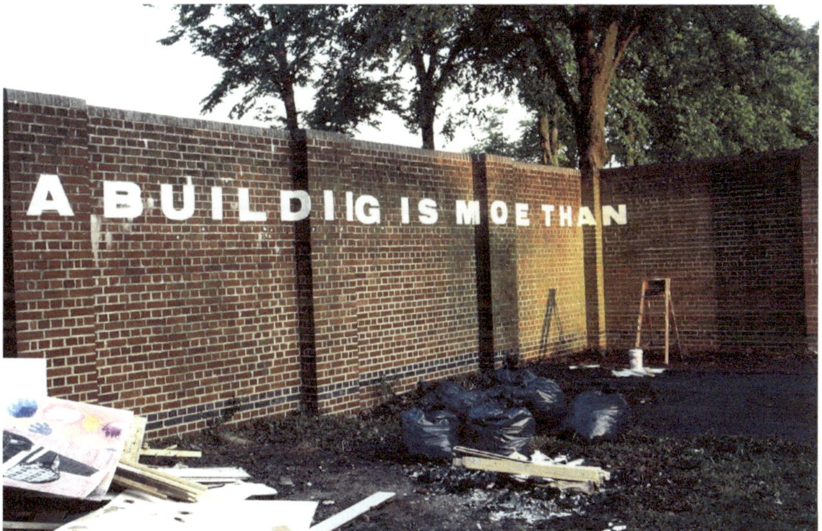

Figure 19

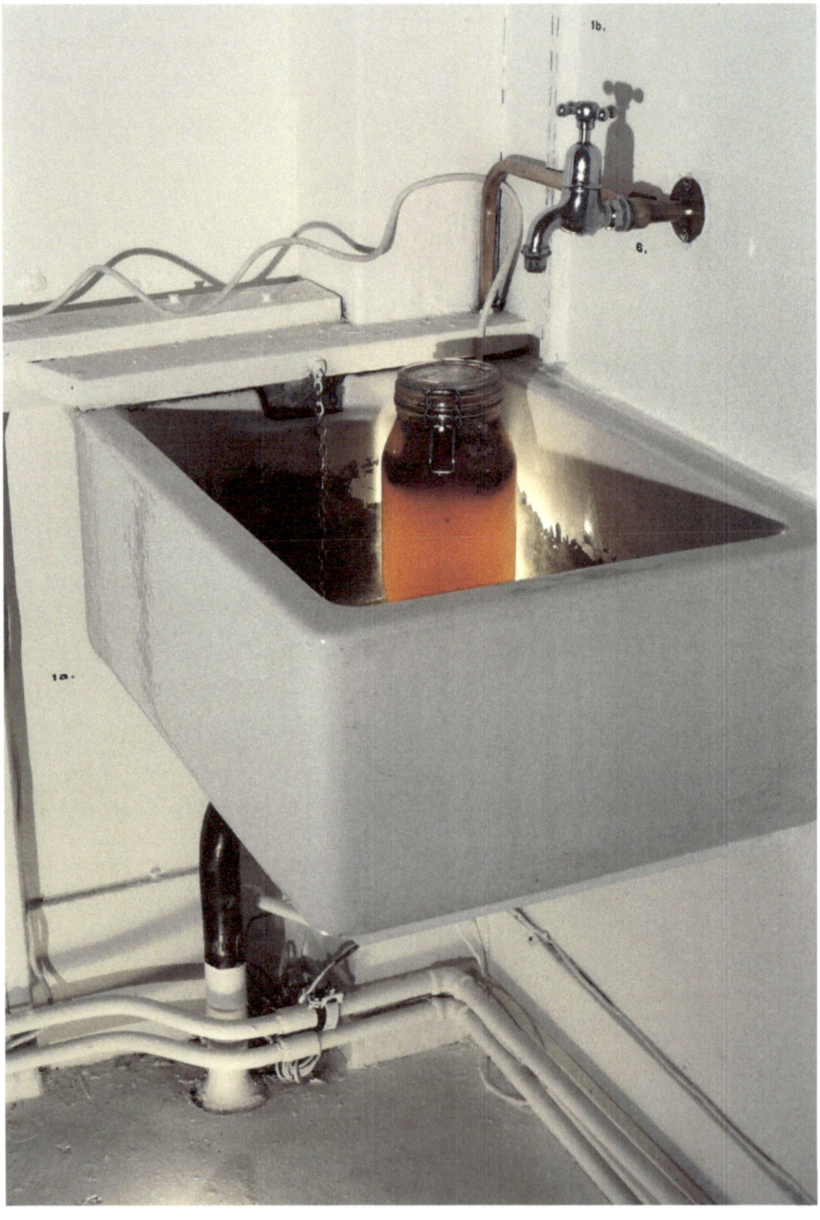

Figure 20

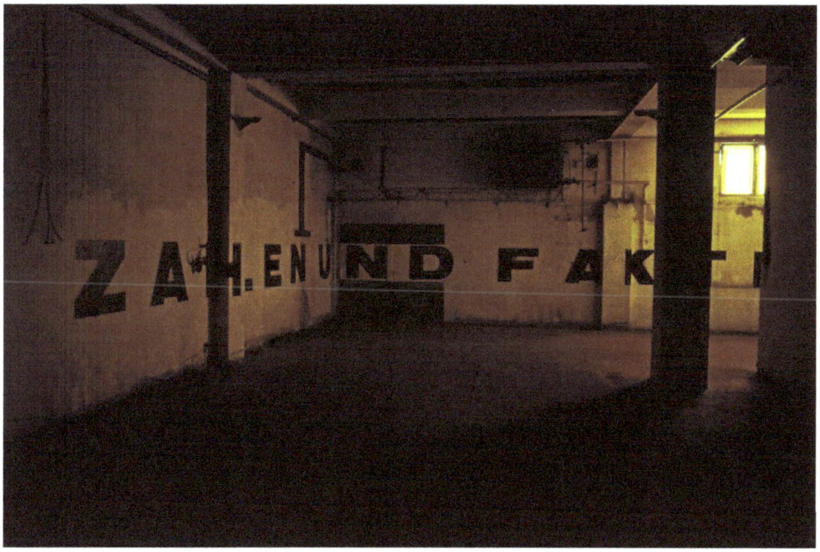

Figure 21

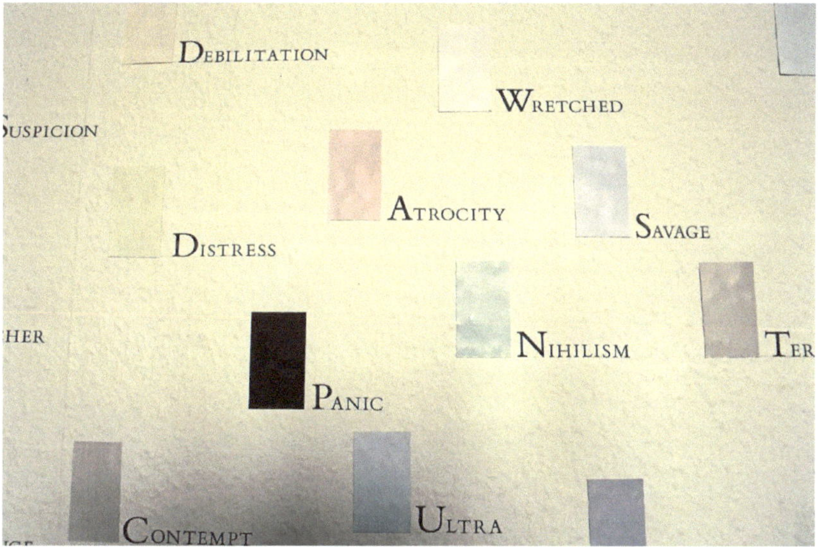

Figure 22

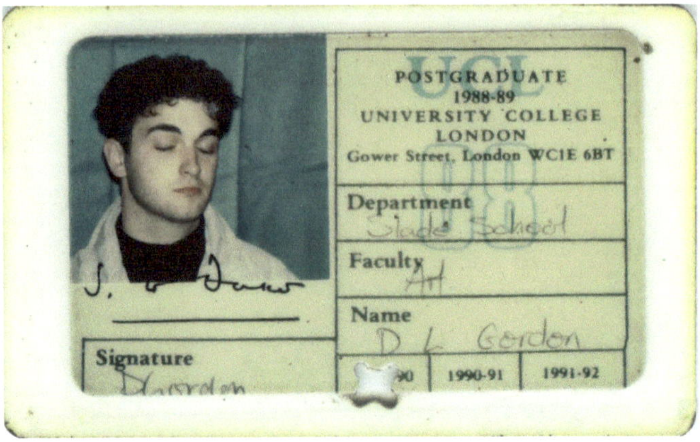
POSTGRADUATE
1988-89
UNIVERSITY COLLEGE
LONDON
Gower Street, London WC1E 6BT
Department
Slade School
Faculty
Art
Name
D L Gordon
Signature
1990-91
1991-92

Figure 23

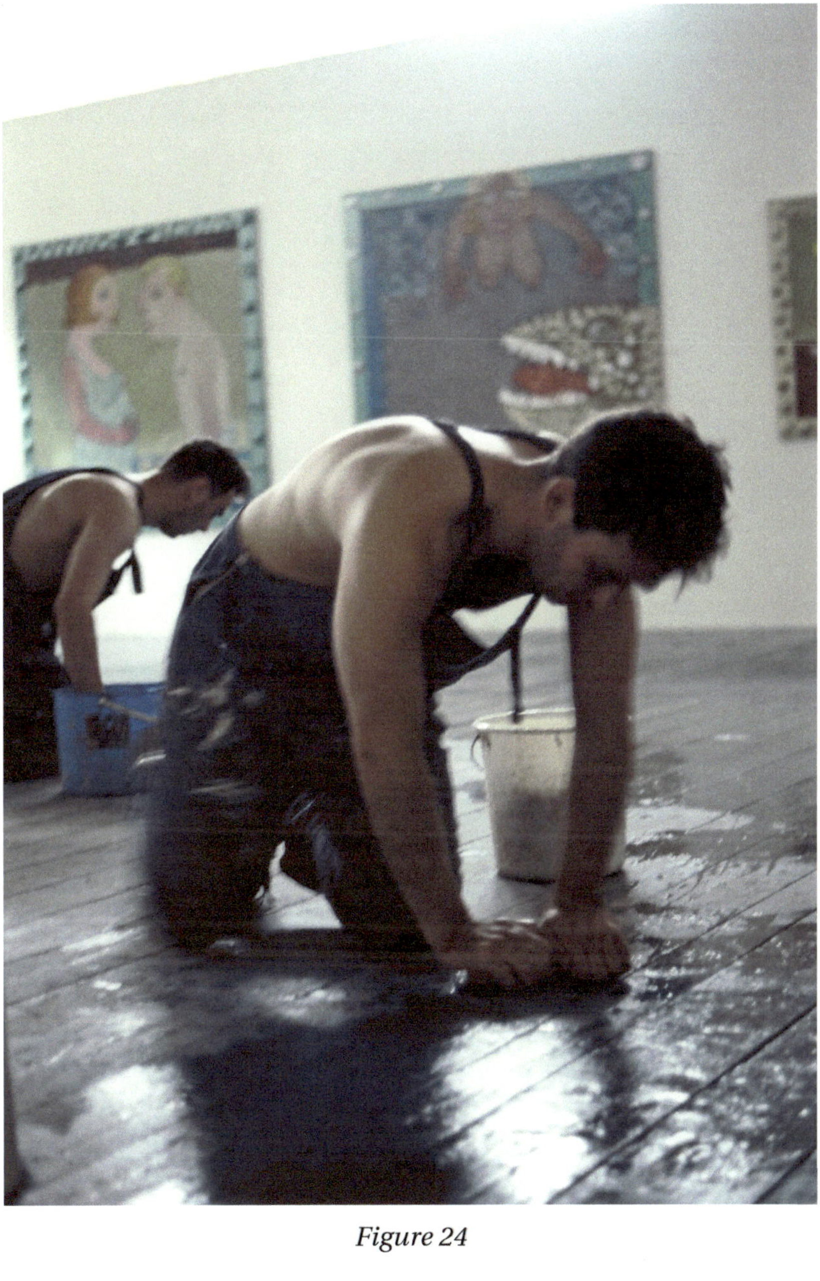

Figure 24

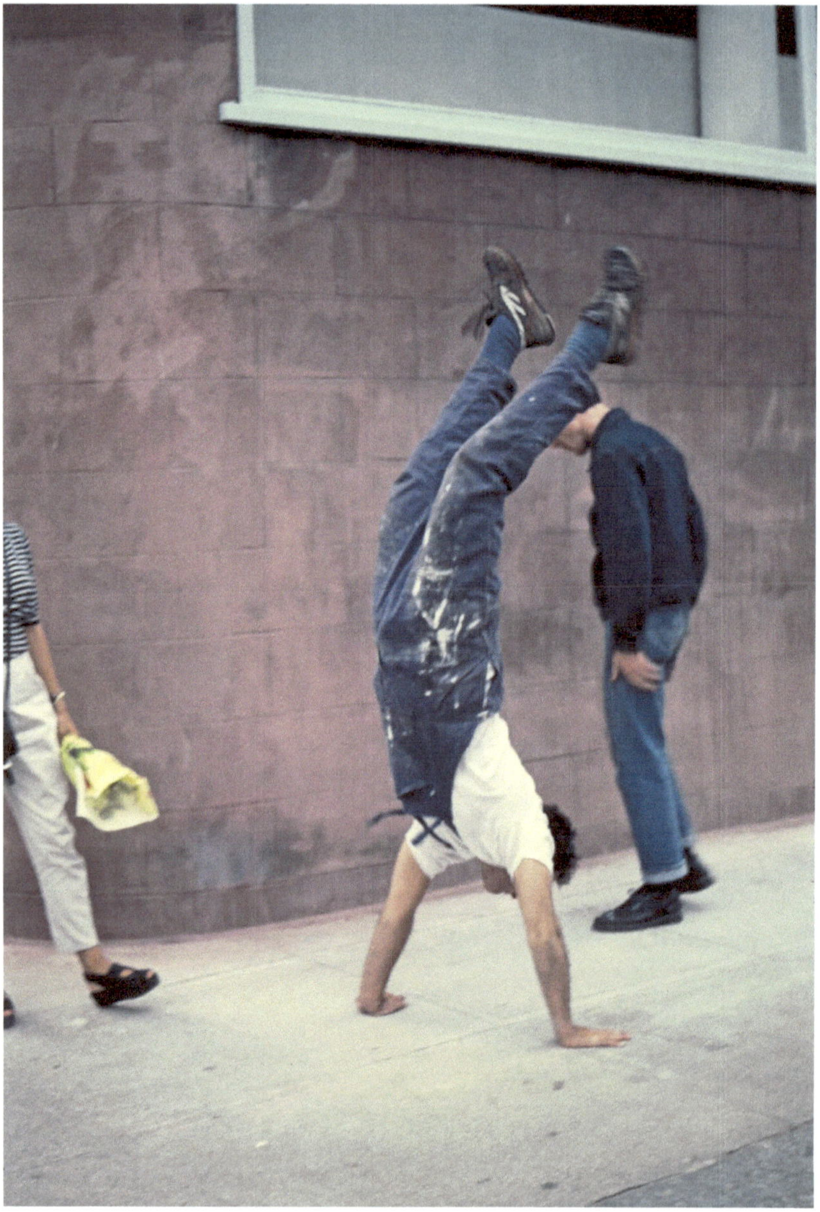

Figure 25

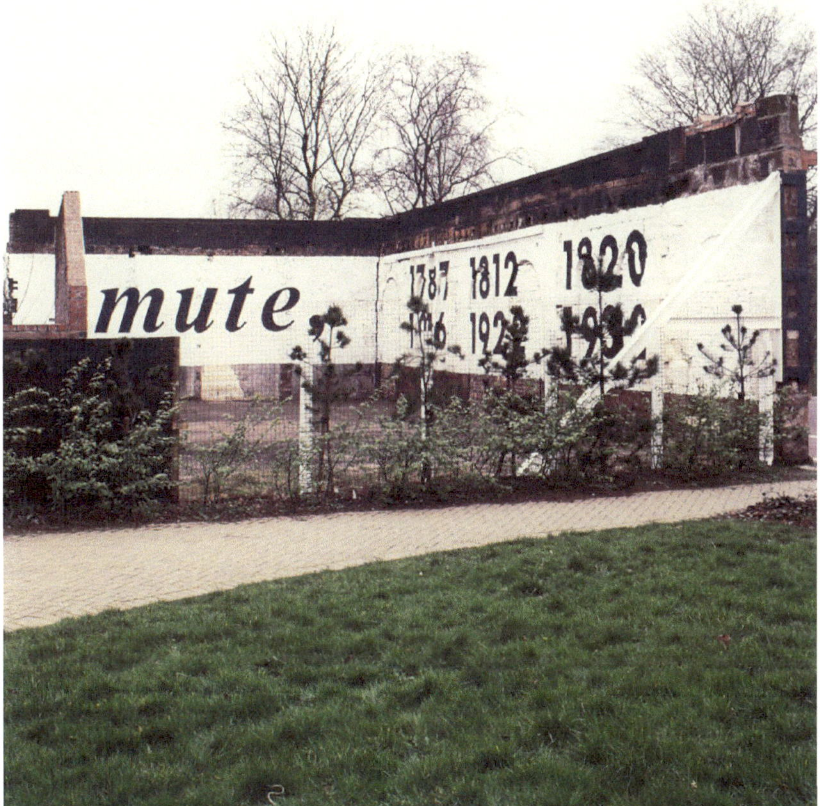

Figure 26

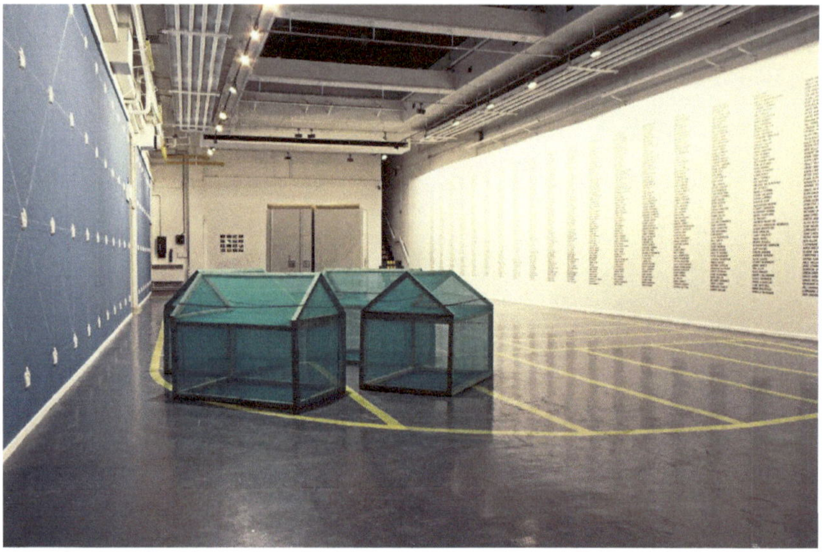

Figure 27

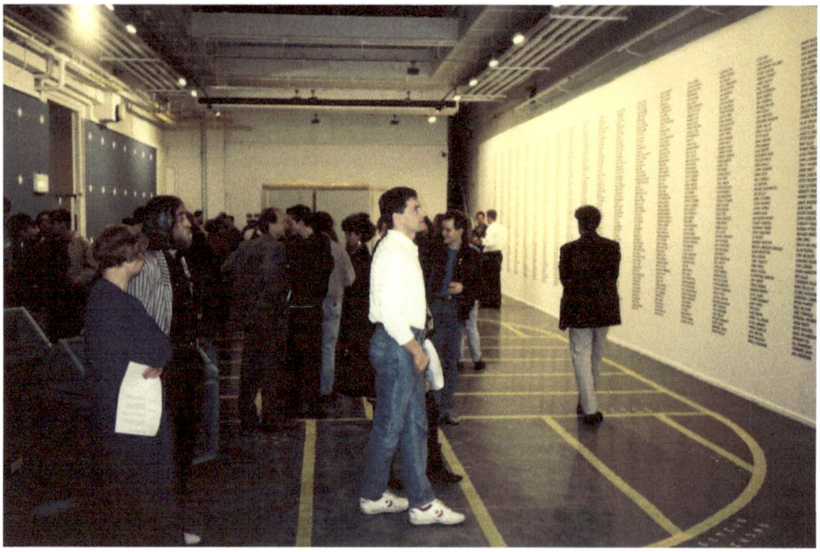

Figure 28

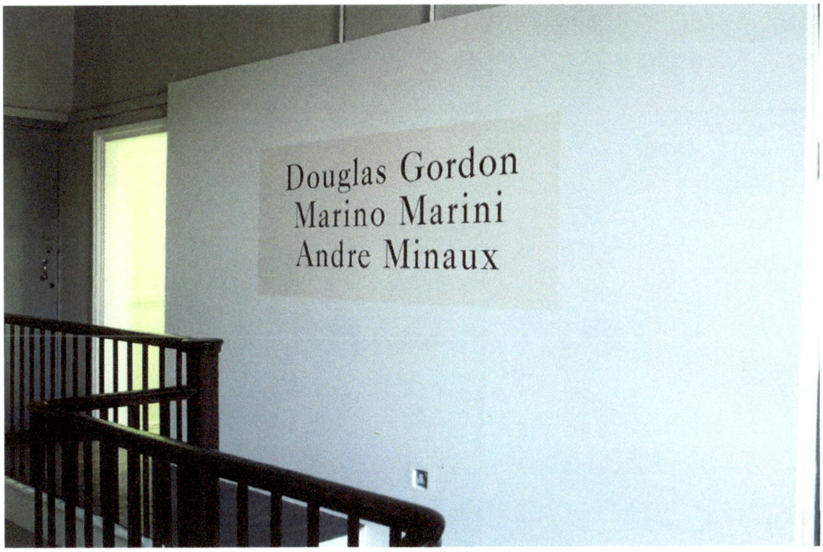

Figure 29

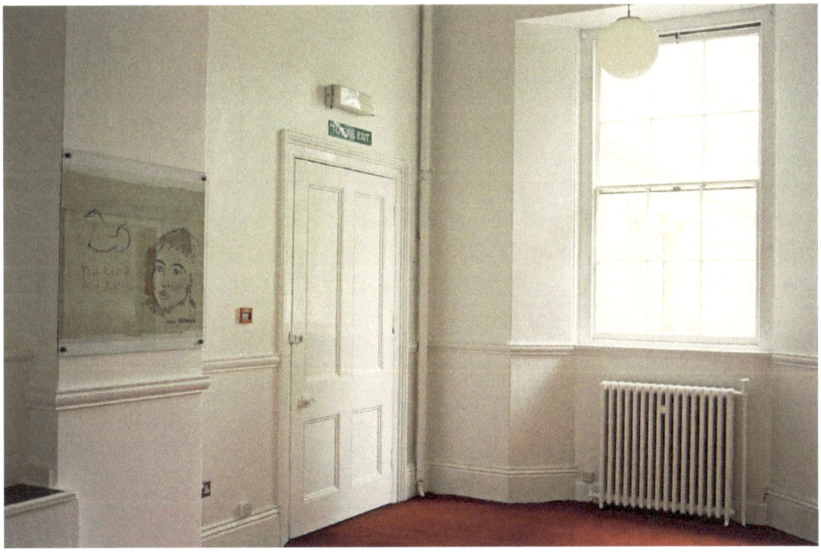

Figure 30

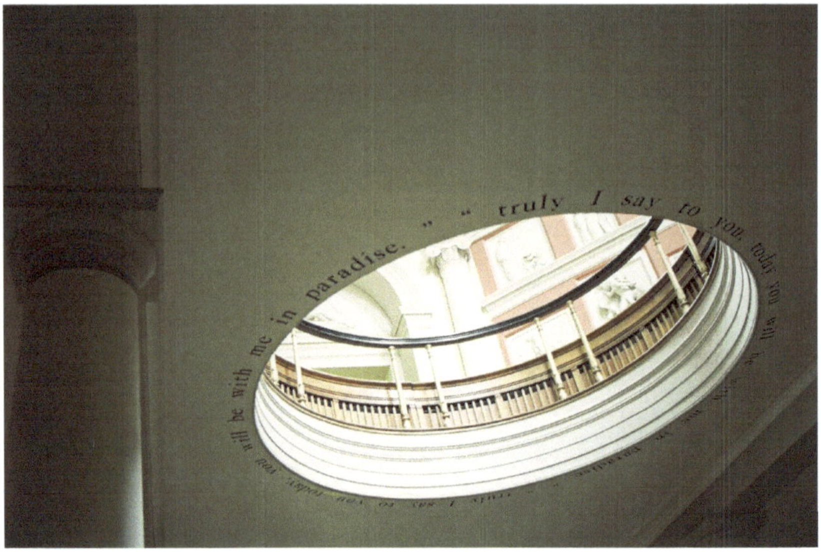

Figure 31

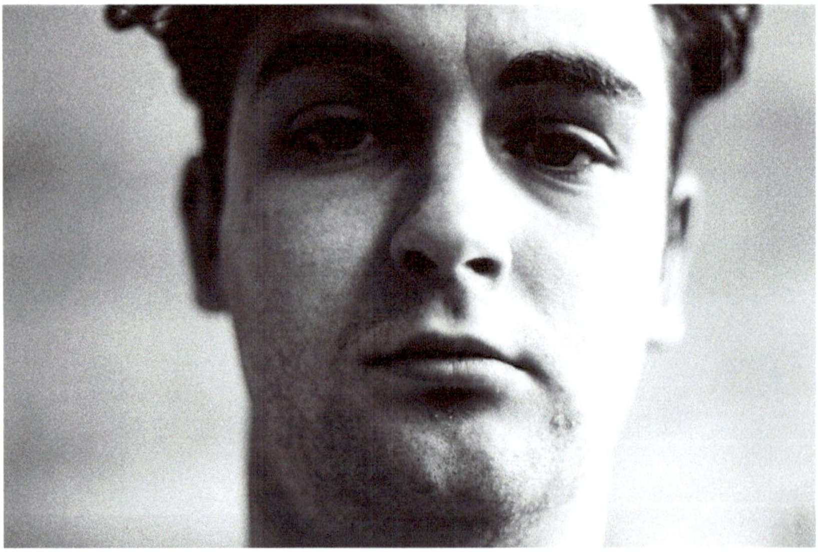

Figure 32

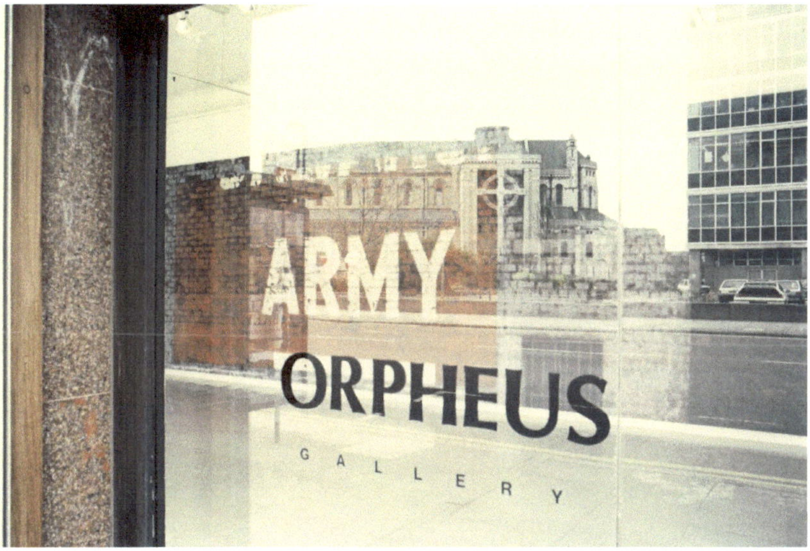

Figure 33

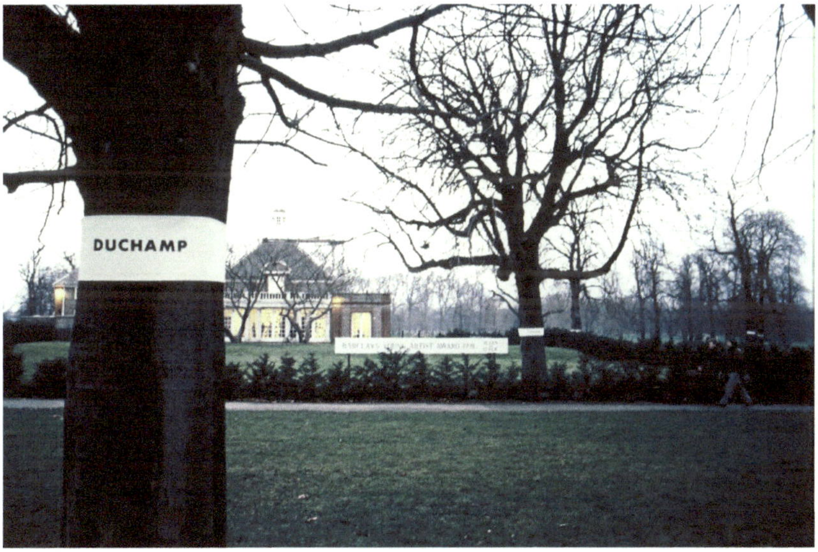

Figure 34

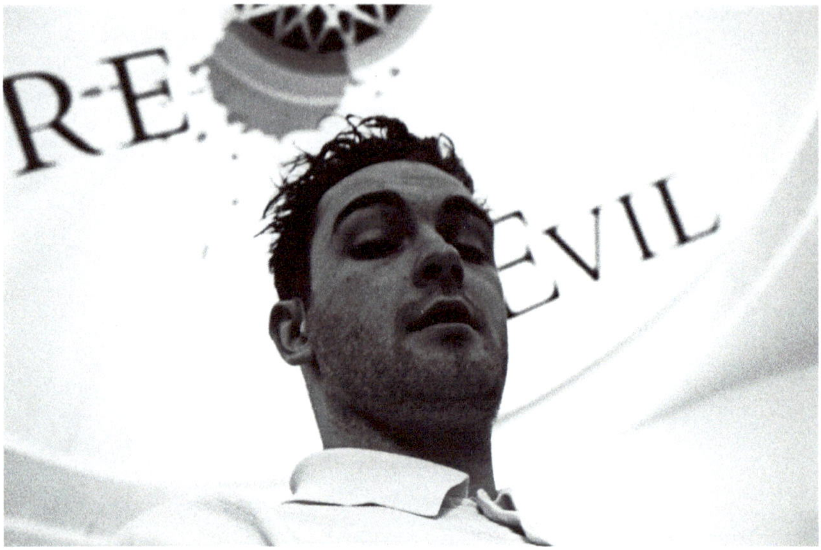

Figure 35

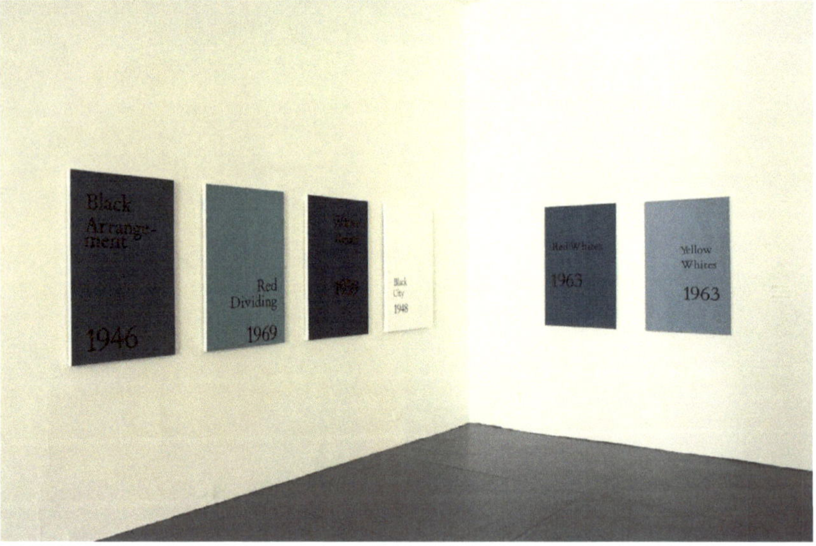

Figure 36

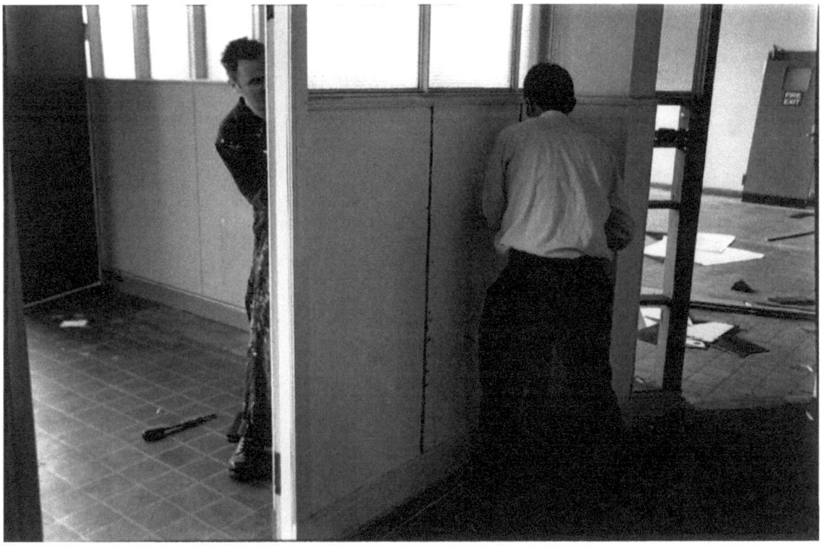

Figure 37

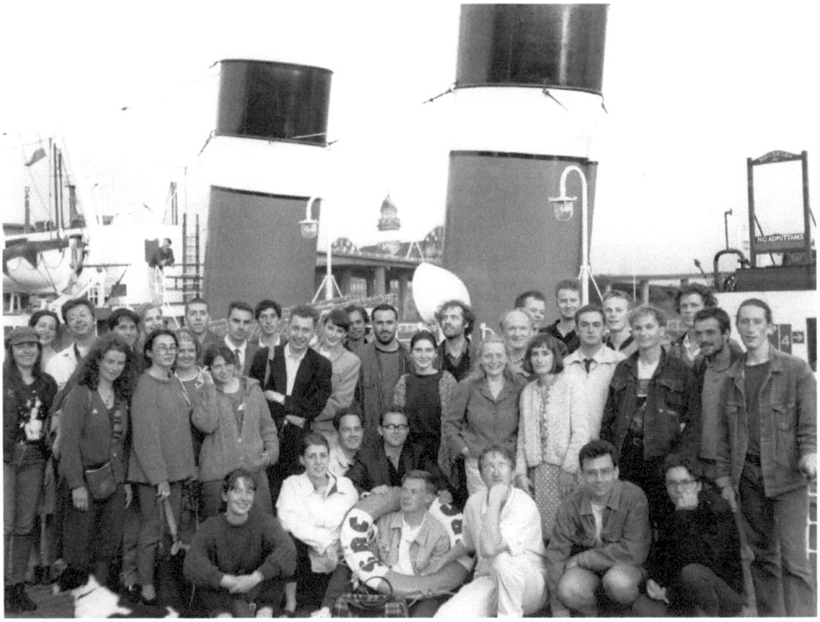

Figure 38

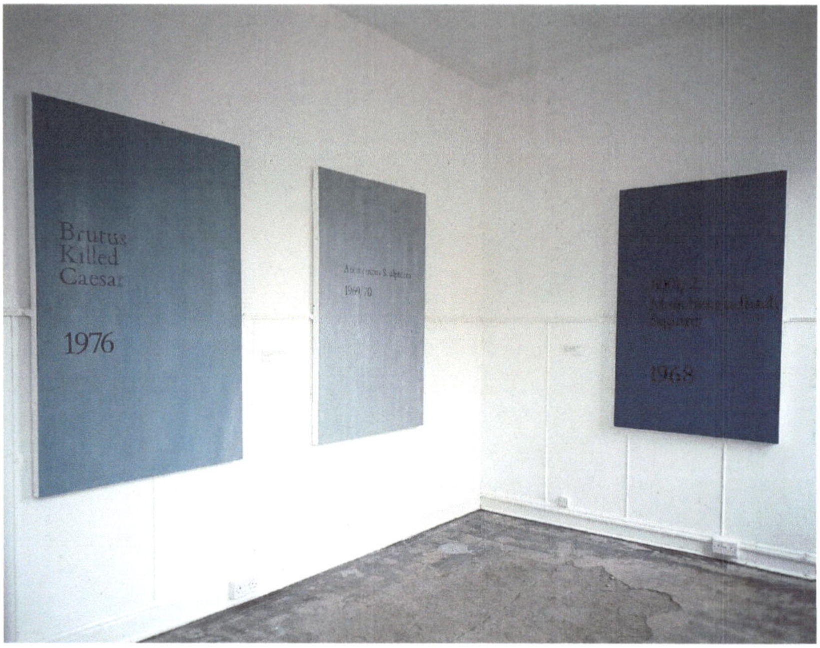

Figure 39

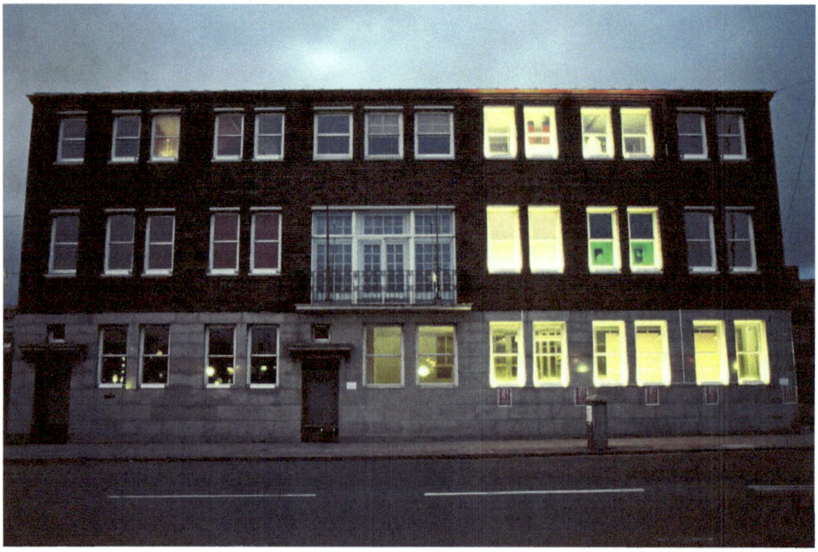

Figure 40

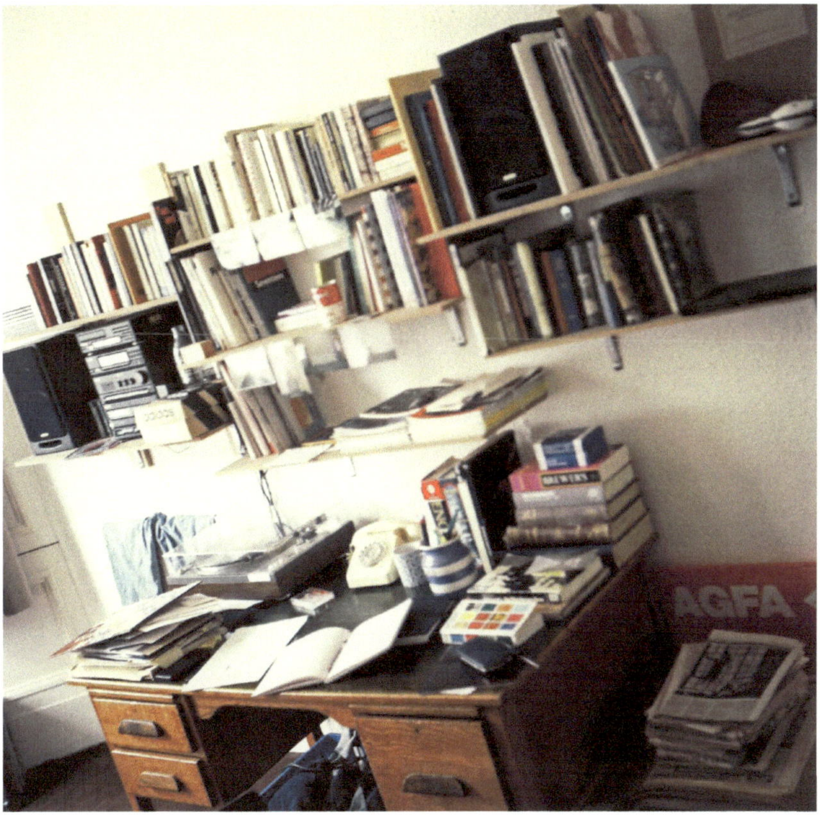

Figure 41

Instruction. (Number 1)

Location; Cafe Picasso, Rome. March, 1992.

Exhibition; L' u Di Carte. Curated by Gianni Piacentini.

On each day, for the duration of the exhibition, the curator should make at least one telephone call following the instructions below.

The success of the work depends upon collaboration between the artist and the curator/ the curator and the owner of the cafe.

(1) The curator will call to the public telephone in the cafe.

(2) The cafe owner will answer the call with prior knowledge of the instructions.

(3) The owner should choose an individual, by name, from the customers in the cafe. The owner should call the customer to the telephone, indicating that someone wishes to talk to them.

(4) The chosen customer will take the telephone and receive a spoken text, the artwork, from the curator.

(5) The text;

You can't hide your love forever.

(6) There should be no dialogue between the curator and the cafe customer. The curator should disconnect the call immediately after speaking the text.

(7) The customers chosen by the cafe owner can be male or female.

(8) For the purpose of the potential dialogue within the cafe, the owner should not be aware of the content of the telephone call.

Douglas Gordon, 1992.

Figure 42

INSTRUCTIONS FOR THE ATTENTION OF; Gianni Piacentini

On Monday, February 18th, 1992.

Telephone call to the following number, 071 240 0399.

Telephone call to be recorded.

For participation in a compilation of artists soundworks, in the exhibition 'Multiplici Culture', Rome 1992.

The identity of the caller to remain unknown.

The reciever is Liam Gillick, curator of the above exhibition.

Neither party have previously met, or spoken together.

The dialogue should be controlled by the caller.

The questions are not prescribed by the artist; the dialogue should be 'free-form', although the instructions are to question on a personal, or familiar, line of enquiry.

Call should last approx. 7 minutes.

Douglas Gordon. February 15th, 1992.

Figure 43

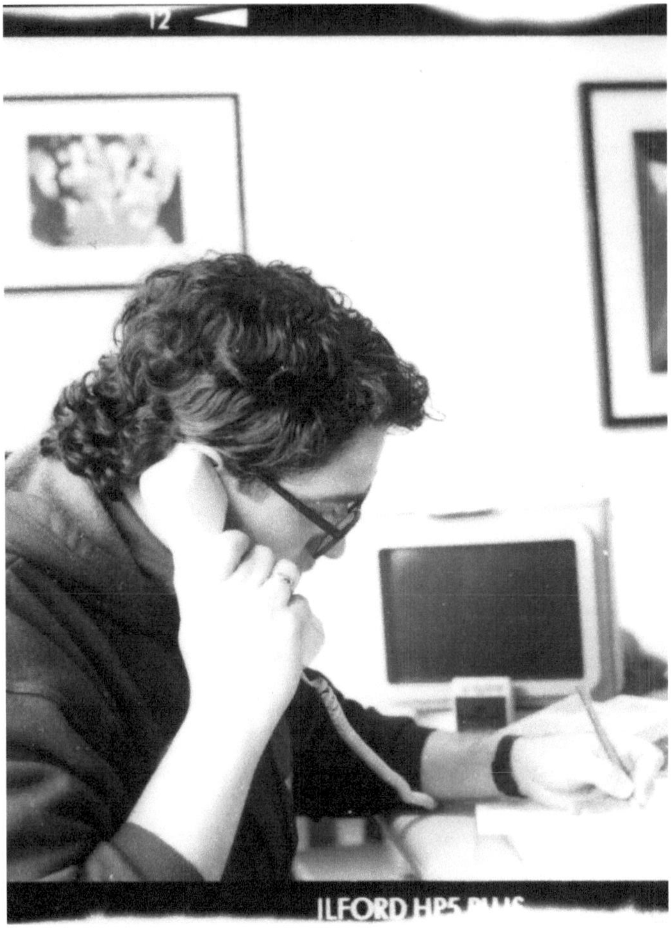

Figure 44

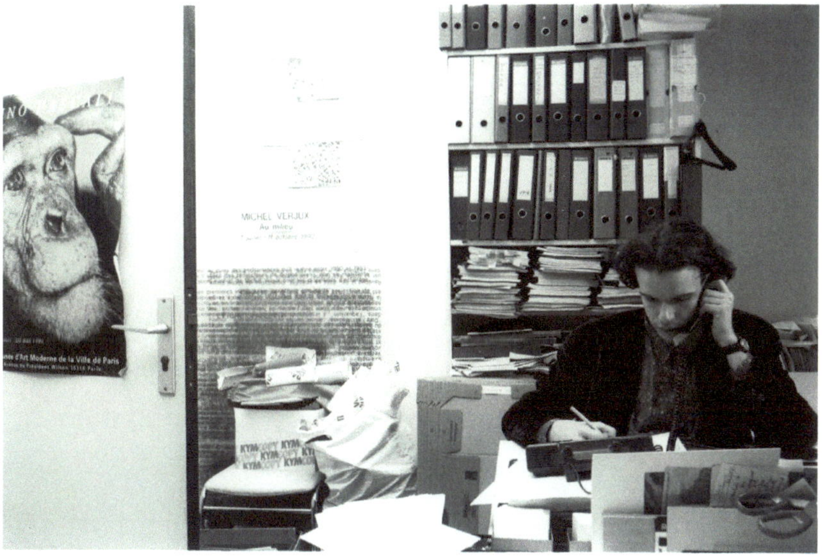

Figure 45

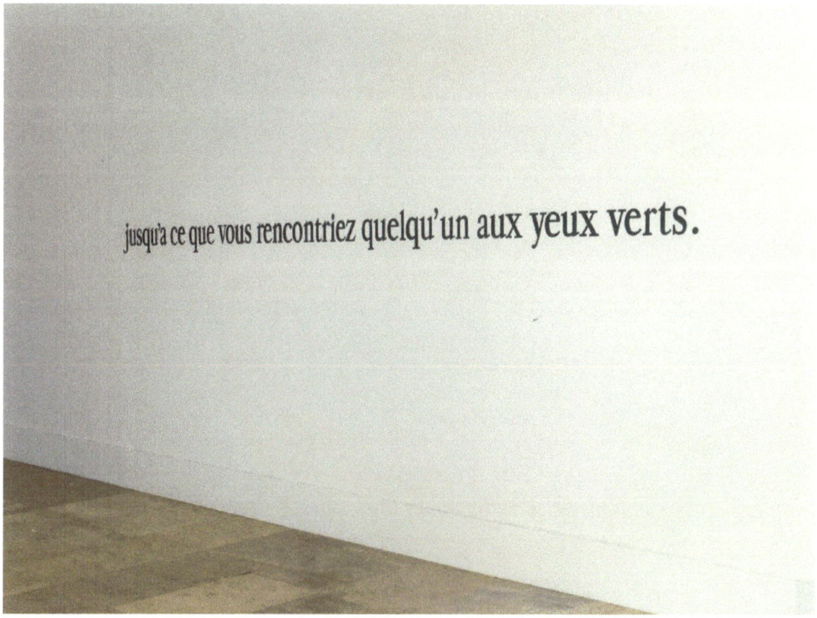

Figure 46

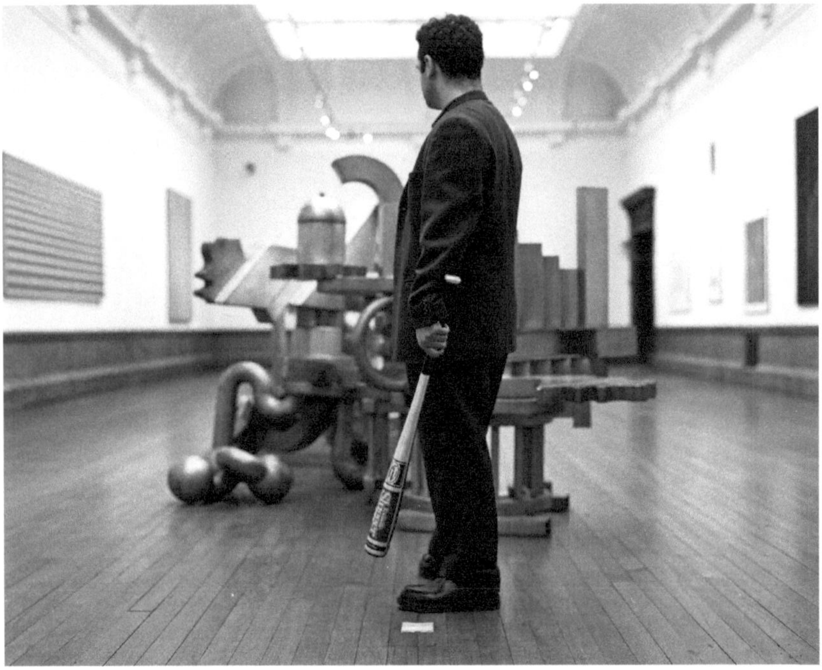

Figure 47

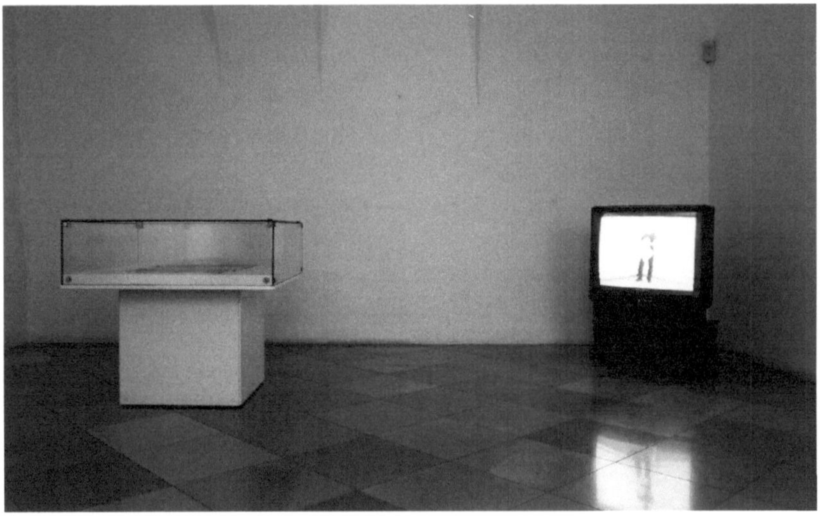

Figure 48

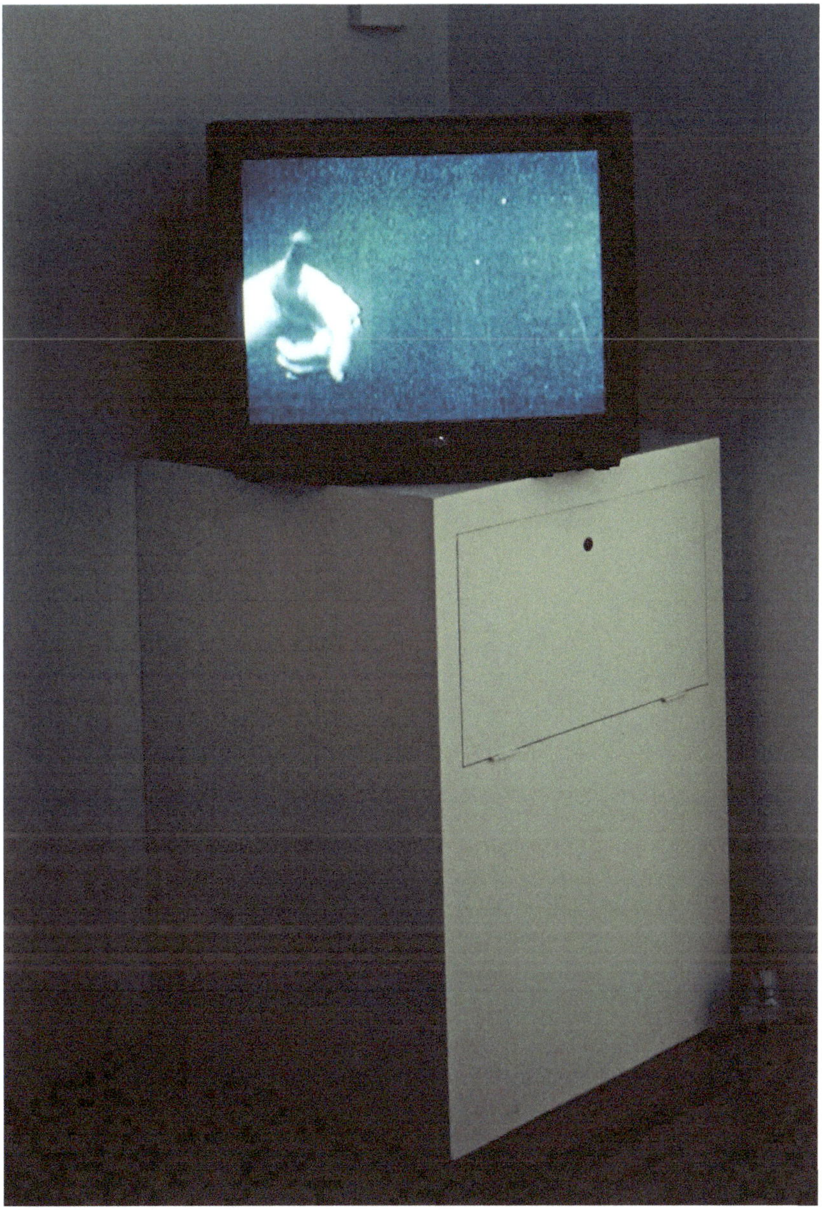

Figure 49

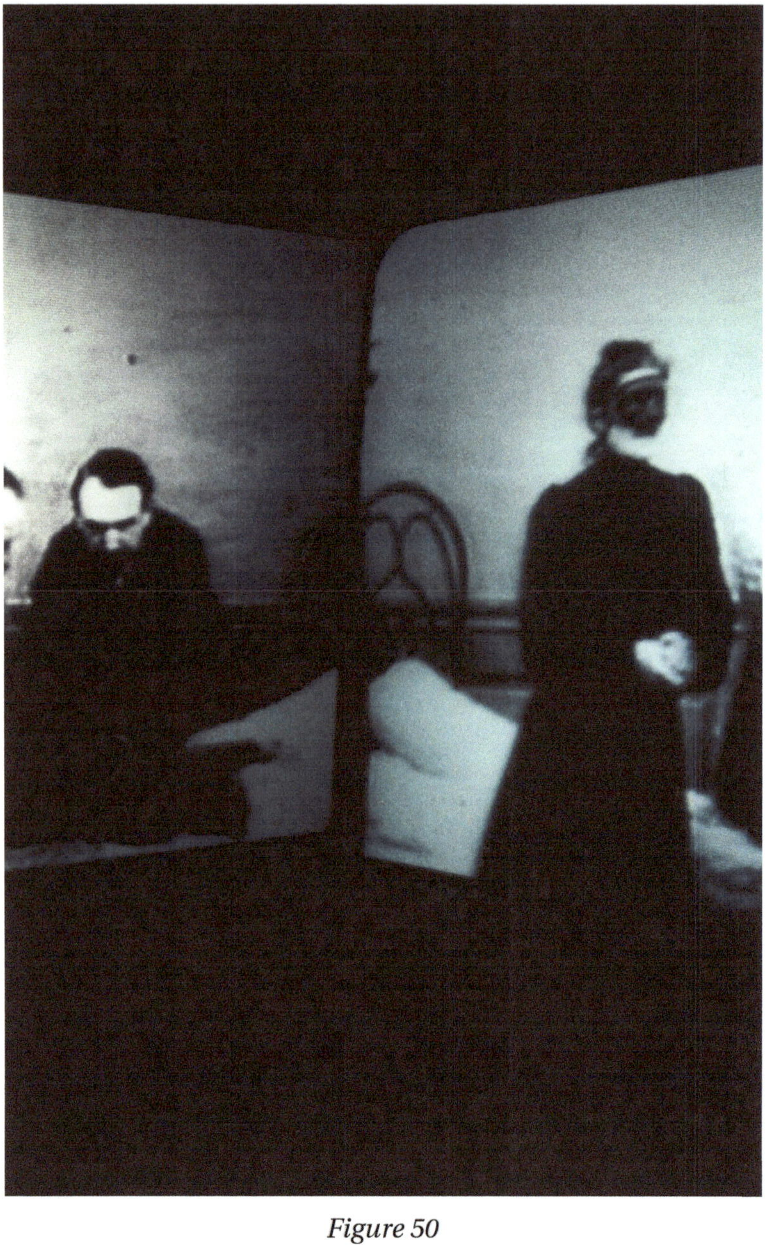

Figure 50

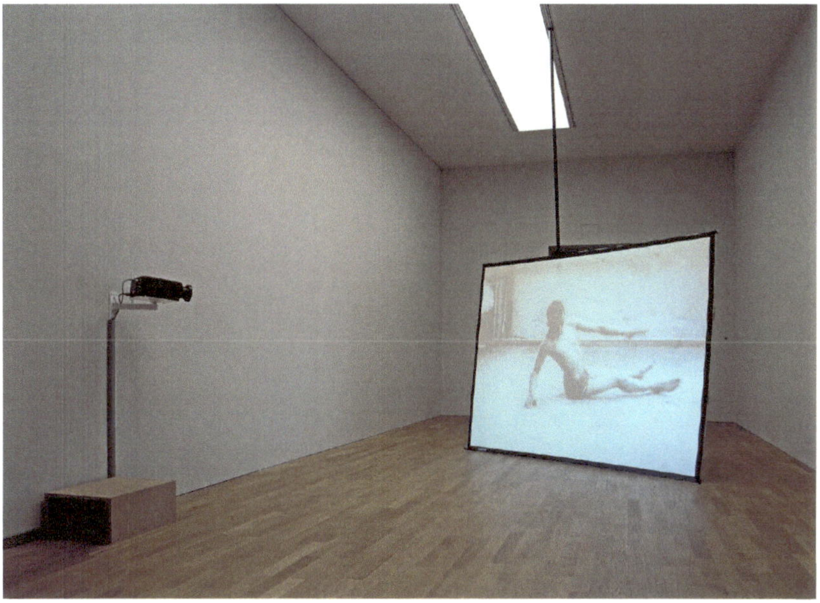

Figure 51

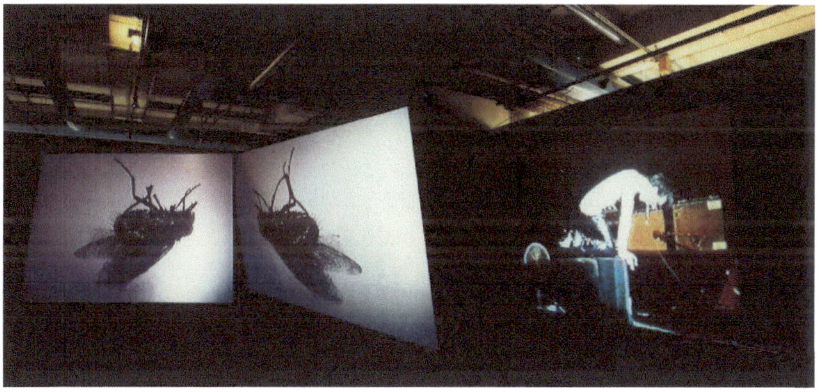

Figure 52

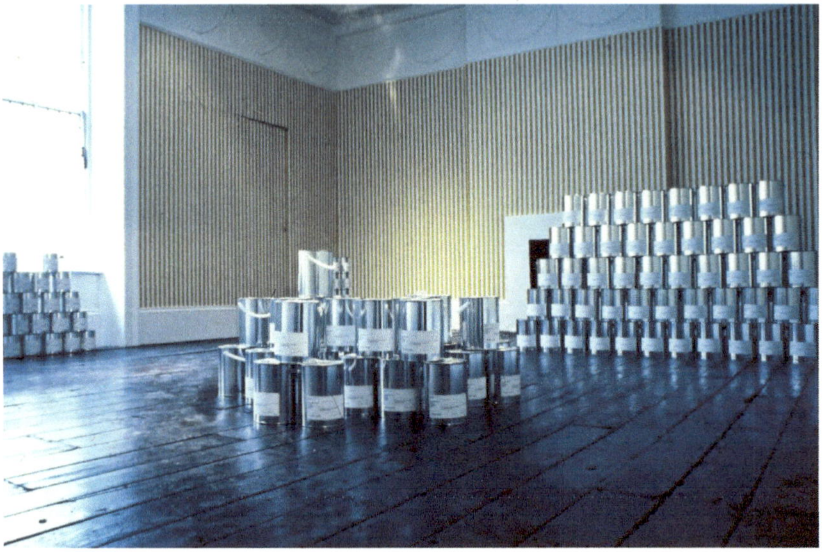

Figure 53

Chapter 6
Going for more and more, at home and abroad

6.1. All alone in the darkness: big solo smash in Glasgow

The next significant step for any new entry of the art system is obtaining a major solo show in an important city or – even better – in an established institution, be it a commercial gallery or a public venue. This is not an easy task to accomplish, of course, since admittance to relevant exhibition spaces is very selective and sometimes seemingly impenetrable, as has been shown in the previous chapters. However, such an achievement is usually possible due to the amount of relational capital a young artist has been able to gain after graduating from art school, hence exploiting any opportunity that might arise from direct or indirect contacts in the art world. The responsibility that goes with an artist's first ever solo show is huge, because it will have him or her exposed all alone in front of art experts and the general audience. The success or failure of this exhibition crucially affects the artist's future career path, deciding whether he or she will be considered a new rising author or rather having provided an unsure attempt of professional progress. As a consequence, the first solo show is always planned very carefully, both for the chosen venue as well as for the exhibited works, according to one's personal strategic awareness and attitude. If a young author is capable of arousing the attention of a commercial gallery, it is likely that he or she will exhibit in the dealer's own venue, as happened to those YBAs that had been picked early by newly founded ventures or well established art businesses. Others that couldn't get immediate representation, instead, had to struggle hard for such an opportunity, though this gave them more time and control over the planning of their first solo show. Of the four considered artists, Damien Hirst was the first to reach this goal on a double occasion in 1991, one as a self-initiated project in a temporary art space – the previously mentioned *In and Out of Love* – and the other one in a relevant institutional venue, the Institute of Contemporary Arts in London for the exhibition *Internal Affairs*. Besides showing his acquired artistic capital, which received an enthusiastic feedback, both shows were fundamental to increase Hirst's reputation in the London art system, although they didn't resolve in an immediate breakthrough. On the contrary, these exhibitions rather led to an enhanced visibility, which definitely contributed to his 1992 Turner Prize nomination and later the 1993 assignment of a DAAD Stipendium in Berlin. Whether planned or accidental, Hirst's example makes evident that even the aftermath of an artist's first solo show is fundamental.

In case of a successful debut exhibition, market pressure on a young artist accrues immediately, since he or she is expected to produce a given standard of artworks at an ever-rising speed, often hindering further research and experimentation. Rising artists who still don't have a solid reputation are usually advised by dealers to keep a steady course, avoiding abrupt changes such as conceptual or formal developments of their creativity. The latter alterations would indeed appear risky, as they may be misunderstood as an abjuration to previous artworks, hence causing its depreciation. In an essay on Gary Hume, *Frieze* critic Adrian Searle vividly described the kind of pressure that young artists were facing after an initial favour:

> *"First your friends, and then your teachers, and then your dealers, and then the collectors and critics and curators and all of the others watch as the one idea grows and flourishes and comes to be expected. And this one idea of yours ceases to be an idea and turns into a product, a waiting-list, a schedule, a production-line. [...] It was a good idea. It still is a good idea, but not the only one. There are forces at work, though, to keep things as they are. [...] If you change track now, will it wipe out the one idea?" (Searle, 1993, p.49)*

Allowing full creative freedom would seem the most adequate means to let rising artists bloom, especially if they reference Conceptual Art, but the art market is in a constant struggle to beat chronic information gap by bestowing a stable position to artists and artworks. The kind of pressure set on young artists is confirmed by another case of an early YBA star such as Fiona Rae, who was immediately picked by the much-established Waddington's. In the catalogue introduction for her solo show at her London gallery in 1995, Richard Shone expressed the challenge faced by rising artists with words that match Searle's above description:

> *"Will she sustain this level of achievement? The risks are tremendous. The tightrope is long and high, the safety net seemingly miles below [...] Rae has confidently side-stepped the trap, not so much of easy success but that of continuing to please without raising our expectations. This is rare in British art where painters of obvious*

> *gifts and youthful achievements seem to roll over into the mud of imitations or self-indulgent picture-making." (Shone in Cooper, 2012, p.137)*

An episode that involves Gary Hume may again be useful to illustrate this aspect, as he felt a kind of creative constraint while being represented by Karsten Schubert. Having reached some commercial notoriety for his *Door Paintings* in the aftermath of *Freeze*, the young painter intended to change style, though the German dealer feared this switch might turn out to be unsuccessful and asked Hume to revert to his older paintings. Faced with the artist's refusal to comply, Schubert dismissed the painter at once in 1992, the latter finding shelter in New York at Matthew Mark's and two years later back again in London at Jay Jopling's White Cube on the occasion of a new solo show held later in 1995[1]. While Hume has constantly cooperated with his dealers, resisting to enter a gallery might thus be a conscious choice made by other artists, in order to keep some distance from market pressure and stay free at a time, when his or her position is lower than that of other relevant players in the field. Given the opportunity to show at City Racing, Sarah Lucas had successfully captured Saatchi's attention thanks to the 1993 solo show *Penis Nailed to a Board*, but in the aftermath she took a year off and then repeatedly refused formal gallery representation. As a matter of facts, that same year she opened a small shop on Bethnal Green Road in East London together with Tracey Emin for a six months period, which became a sort of unattractive hangout place for the alternative art scene – completely against art market logic. The two friends sold decorated key-rings and wire penises, ashtrays with Hirst's face at the bottom, folded and pencilled cigarette packs, suspended cut-outs of Lucas' self-portraits, various hand painted T-shirts emblazoned with "Complete Arsehole", ""Sperm Counts", I'm so fucky" or "Fucking Useless". Matthew Collings (2002, p.29) described the atmosphere of *The Shop* as punk-like and rude, foolish and destructive – a sort of reversed gift shop that sold negative souvenirs rather than artworks, at the same time staging a parody of a commercial gallery in which money had almost no meaning at all. The fellowship between the two young artist women became so strong that they are still very often linked together, even though they hardly cooperated again after this experience that occurred at a necessary transitional phase for both of them, when they were just starting to take off. Furthermore, they somehow interpreted two different roles, representing quite opposite kinds of attitude towards the art system and the media. While Emin immediately entered Jay Jopling's White Cube as soon as *The Shop* was closed, starting on a hyper-exposed career path that would draw attention to her as a sort of bad girl celebrity, Lucas would rather avoid dealer representation and escape the limelight, despite the initial shock effect of some of her work. For four more years the Islington grown-up artist wouldn't opt for any gallery offer nor to play along with her persona as a product of both her reputation and creative vein. Although she could sense the effectiveness of a provocative strategy built on high media exposure and infamous works, she maintains she couldn't herself go along the same path as Hirst and Emin:

> *"[...] if you look at Damien or Tracey, obviously they were very clear about what their gift was. I think probably both Damien and Tracey really grasped the punk thing. They realised the value of being a brat and that it does actually work. And I don't think I did. I was more... proper about it, or something. And so's Sadie [Coles, her friend and dealer]. I can't imagine either of us ever wearing that sort of brattishness." (Lucas in Edamariam, 2011)*

On the contrary, Lucas would rather concentrate on deepening the work she was producing and thus cooperated with various galleries in London as well as abroad, though never embarking in a continuous partnership. In 1994 she had two important individual exhibitions in established ventures of the Capital city, which were *Got a Salmon On (Prawn)* for Anthony D'Offay Gallery and *Where's My Moss* at the White Cube. A year later she started solo shows abroad, first landing in New York for *Supersensible* at Barbara Gladstone Gallery and then in 1996 travelling to Berlin for *Is Suicide Genetic?* at Contemporary Fine Arts. It was not until she really felt ready to show the outcome of this research period that she decided to start to cooperate with her friend Sadie Coles, previously an assistant to Anthony D'Offay, who had opened her own London establishment in 1997, which was launched with Lucas' solo show *Bunny Gets Snookered.* On this occasion, the artist presented an installation piece consisting in a multiple sculpture called *Bunny,* which was made out of stuffed tights applied on the back of a chair resembling arms and legs of a naked female body wearing tights.

Sarah Lucas' choice of resisting gallery representation so far was definitely unusual for a London-based artist, given the power of the local art market, but it did serve her well in the end. The creative freedom she earned with this decision links Lucas to the experience of her Glaswegian contemporaries, which virtually stood no chance to find gallery representation at such an early stage. Since waiting to be discovered was no option at all, going for a first solo show depended uniquely on the ability to activate one's own network capital, especially getting involved with curators at public venues. Among the young Glasgow based artists, Douglas Gordon was certainly master at this kind of relationship building and indeed was the first one to be proposed an individual exhibition by an important institution. The young artist could profit from the favourable moment in his hometown arts milieu that occurred some time after the 1990 Year of Culture was over. Between 1992 and 1993, several establishments that had well operated for the programs of the European Capital of Culture were re-launched by three dynamic curators, which proved crucial for the new conceptualist generation of local artists (Lowndes, 2010, pp.164-169). The Third Eye Centre was reopened in 1992, after a one-year closure, and became the Centre for Contemporary Arts (CCA) again coordinated by Andrew Nairne, who had already helped the former Transmission committee in mounting their first group show *Self Conscious State* back in 1990. Meanwhile, even Tramway was revived after its shutdown in 1991 and Nicola White was called back to curate the visual arts program, opening her first exhibitions in May 1992 with two Glasgow based artists, *Windfall* founder David McMillan and Matthew Dalziel, who would then start a lasting artistic duo with Environmental Art graduate Louise Scullion. Given the success of *Self Conscious State*, White had originally contacted Douglas Gordon in January 1992 to hold a solo show at Tramway in May of that same year, thus launching the reopening of this venue. As a matter of facts, the Tramway curator was rather interested in promoting projects by younger talented artists and she was convinced that Gordon would have been capable of dealing with the huge empty space of the gallery, as she had previously seen some text pieces by the author installed in large surroundings. On the contrary, to her very surprise, Gordon refused this opportunity believing he did not have enough time to conceive new works suitable for this specific gallery space. However, it was a very pondered decision, as the young Glaswegian also feared that his refusal would jeopardize any future prospect of working again with Tramway. Something similar had happened in London the year before, when he had turned down the offer for a solo show at the Riverside Gallery and did not get a second chance, while his friend Simon Patterson immediately accepted to drop in as a substitute. Still Gordon's preoccupation of being unprepared to engage with the main hall at Tramway and thus fail his first big solo show was much greater than the fear of losing a good opportunity. He decided in the end to tell Nicola White about his concerns and the curator proved very understanding, agreeing to have the exhibition a year later so that he could carefully produce new works in advance. Though it might have seemed foolish to turn down another solo show, this episode demonstrates that Gordon was particularly aware of the relevance of such opportunities as well as of the fact, that at this early stage he couldn't risk a false step. Besides the spatial difficulties of the Tramway, he felt he still hadn't come up with the right strategy to tackle the exhibition venue and offer something unexpected that could finally launch his career.

For the above reasons, the first ever solo show of the Scottish artist wasn't held in his hometown, but instead in Paris for the *Migrateurs* programme ran by Hans Ulrich Obrist at the Musée d'Art Moderne de la Ville de Paris in 1992. Although this might seem an even bigger opportunity than the prospected Tramway exhibition, on the contrary it was a rather safe bet in a friendly environment. In fact, Gordon's contribution was just a little part of a broader project staged outside Britain, hence avoiding the risk of hostile judgements by homeland art players. In this regards, Gordon's first true solo show must be considered the 1993 Tramway exhibition, since the whole public gallery had then been allotted to him as an ad hoc event for the artist, rather than being part of a bigger project such as in the case of *Migrateurs*. Consequently, in Paris Gordon still felt free to create three more phone works, which matched the text pieces and instructions he had already sent for previous group shows. The three works were a part of a single project revolving around a sentence spoken on the phone and applied on to the museum wall in three different colours: *Instruction (Number 3a) (1992)* locution was 'From the moment you hear these words, until you kiss someone with blue eyes' and was attached to the wall in dull-blue letterings, while *Instruction (Number 3b)* (1992) and *Instruction (Number 3c)*(1992) consisted of the same text though with a diverse colour – both as far as the eyes and the wall inscription were concerned – being green in the first case and brown in the second one. The work was further developed as letters that followed the same colour pattern, although they were sent separately. The first two were on the occasion of the group show *Wonderful Life* at Lisson Gallery in London, though the writings *Letter (Number 10a)* (1993) e *Letter (Number 10b)* (1993) actually referred to meeting someone – and not kissing: 'From the moment you read these words, until you meet someone with blue eyes'. *Letter (Number 10c)*, on the contrary, was the same as in the telephone conversations referring to kiss a brown-eyed person and was prepared for the exhibition *Propositions* held at the Musée Dèpartemental d'Art Contemporain in the Chateu de Rochechouart in Limoges in 1993. The Paris solo show in 1992 crowned a relationship of mutual consideration between Gordon and Obrist, which would have led to other exhibitions over the years, all of them generally held in unconventional art venues such as *museum in progress* along the streets of Vienna in 1996 or the *Nano Museum* project, a pocket museum set up by several artists in turn between 1994 and 1998[2].

After the *Migrateurs* project, Gordon felt finally ready for an extensive exhibition in his hometown, although the frenzy of 1992 again didn't give him much time to reflect on what to display at Tramway. The show had been scheduled from 24th April to 23rd May of 1993 and would later result as one of that year's major events, but until the end of 1992 the young artist still had not come up with a satisfying idea to offer to Nicola White. According to Gordon's own tale, he found his inspiration on Christmas Eve, his recollections deserving to be quoted in full, as they afford a good example of the artist's story-telling skills expressed in an interview with Graham Fagen:

> *"I just kept thinking about the space, made a wee model of the space, this kind of thing, all the things that a young artist is supposed to do, so I did all that, and couldn't come up with an idea, really the architecture of the space is so dominant, and at Christmas '92 I was back home, it was Christmas Eve, the pubs were closed, my friends weren't around, I'm not used to going to bed very early, there was nothing on television, my family were all asleep, I remember lying upstairs in my wee brother's bedroom, just playing about with the video recorder, and really, honestly, whatever tapes that he happened to have and at the same time I'd been asked to do some piece for a show in Germany, I really liked the idea of speeding something up...he had a tape lying about, and it was Psycho, and when I saw it I thought, wow, five minute Psycho, that would be really brilliant. So I tried to watch Psycho really fast, and it was fair enough, and then I started just doing the opposite, like you do, so I started watching it slow, and there were specific sequences in it that I thought I wanted to watch again in slow motion, and really that's the root of where the idea came from, the more I watched in slow motion the more I realised how interesting this could be." (Gordon in Fagen, 1999, p.80)*

The above account makes it appear, as if the creative process behind the origin of *24 Hour Psycho* (1993) had been an accidental, almost unintended discovery, however Gordon had been trying to create a video work for quite some time before the Tramway show. Although the curator Nicola White was expecting him to produce a major text-piece installation, that was exactly what Gordon didn't want to come up with, in order to break any expectation and try something more audacious that could start a much more successful production of his (Lowndes, 2010, p.166). Throughout 1992 he had filmed some home set shots, mostly portraying himself performing some kind of actions like kicking the video camera around on the living room floor, but these early attempts didn't seem good enough to launch a new set of artworks at a solo show. The first video he shot is called *The magic newspaper* (1992) and shows the full-figured artist rolling up a newspaper, throwing it out of sight to his left and, a few seconds later, catching it back from the right. This video and many other cuts were hardly sufficient to be shown as single works, hence they are today often displayed by the artist within a wider installation that simultaneously repeats all his video works on dozens of monitors set on crates or on the floor of a darkened room. The installation was first mounted in 2002 for an extensive solo exhibition at the Hayward Gallery in London and goes with the title *Pretty much every film and video work from about 1992 until now. To be seen on monitors, some with headphones, others run silently, and all simultaneously* (1992-ongoing)[3]. The adoption of video marks a relevant shift in Gordon's methods and production, trying to come to terms with a technique that was literally starting to spread all over the art world. Indeed, there are several reasons why Gordon started to experiment with the video-camera in 1992, starting with the fact that it wasn't simply a newer technique as compared to painting or even performance art, but it represented an upcoming trend which appeared to allow much space for experimentation and improvement. According to Craig Richardson (2011, p.157), Gordon's switch to video art and installations was crucially influenced by his visit to Documenta 9 in Kassel curated by Jan Hoet, who had decided to avoid a constraining theoretical structure and widely embraced the display of video works. Documenta 9 took place between June 13th and September 20th 1992 being the first edition to include new venues alongside the classic locations of Fridericianum and Orangerie, turning the exhibition into an extensive and widespread event[4]. The accompanying program included jazz concerts, boxing matches and baseball games, which were part of an extended presentation concept understood as a central metaphor for art and life. Due to the variety of venues and events, this edition was celebrated for an enormous popularity, attracting for the first time in the history of the Documenta more than half a million visitors. In eluding a theoretical framework and refraining from a general thematic context, Hoet indeed broke with a general principle of previous Documenta exhibitions, as well as of other biennales around the world. The curator intended contemporary art to present real subjective experiences, such that could counter a reality that was progressively slipping into the virtual realm, hence Bruce Nauman's video installation

Anthro/Socio (1992) displayed in the entrance hall of the Fridericianum was an excellent example of this phenomenon[5]. The work by the renowned American artist consists of a video showing different takes on the head of a man and is being displayed on three projection surfaces – namely the walls of the room – and six monitors. While the head is seen swiftly revolving about his own axis, the man sings in a variety of tonalities the following sentences: «FEED ME/ EAT ME/ ANTHROPOLOGY,» «HELP ME/ HURT ME/ SOCIOLOGY,» and «FEED ME, HELP ME, EAT ME, HURT ME». Standing in the space affords a full impact of the installation, since the man's contradictory and aggressive demands are heard from different directions creating a disturbing effect together with the constant revolving of the singer's body. The kind of physical threat portrayed by the artist is transferred to the viewer who enters the room and who becomes part of an all-encompassing sensual experience.

Gordon was struck by Nauman's ability of generating anxiety, ambient threat and everyday experiences by means of a video projection, which furthermore appeared less expensive than a complex environmental installation (Richardson, 2011, p.157). As a matter of facts, the growing technological and financial availability of mass produced video cameras in the Eighties had made this technique finally accessible even for artists working on a low budget. Gordon's first experiments were all limited to everyday circumstances owing to the high professional production costs of a proper feature movie. In order to achieve a professional-looking outcome despite limited budget, soon after he maintained to have worked out a better strategy, which consisted in the re-use of existing materials, completely avoiding production problems:

> *"I got some Super-8 black and white film – because I didn't want to make colour, I wanted to make black and white film – and it turned out to be so expensive that I just stopped, so it's been well documented that one of the reasons why '24 Hour Psycho' was so appealing to me was that I could actually take an epic and do something else with it, get the same effect as if I'd spent a quarter of a million pounds." (Gordon in Fagen, 1999, p.109)*

Before deciding to use pre-existing video material, he had actually thought of re-shooting a famous movie, since the plot aroused his interest in feature films, that is the story conjured by the images rather than the frames it conveyed. Working with familiar stories slowly disclosed Gordon's original aims and paved the way to a kind of appropriation praxis he would later carry out. In fact, the essential features he meant to exploit were the development of the film narrative, on one side, and the spectators' collective and individual memory, on the other side, as the author asserts:

> *"I thought it might be interesting to take an existing film and re-make it. I wanted a picture with a story which was very familiar to a broad audience; so I started to work with 'Psycho'. What I decided to do was alter the narrative of the original by making it 24 hours long, and without sound. Although the strategy of expanding the narrative is quite simple, it is very easy to disturb the familiarity that someone might bring to a film which is that well known." (Gordon in Lawson, 1993, p.65)*

Trying to disengage the original story line would indeed allow the projected material to be contaminated with the viewer's own expectations and memories. In the artist's opinion, this result could be reached only by means of well known images – or at least very familiar ones – because they must subconsciously arouse some connections in the viewers mind, while time disruption would intervene later on to challenge the effectiveness of the projected images:

> *"[...] I was interested in allowing the micro narrative to become disengaged from the original version, and let it exist in real time alongside our memories and anticipations of what we think we are about to see. [...] the film is being projected so slowly as to deny our anticipations and undermine our memory of events. [...] That's what was interesting for me: to use a logical system that completely imploded in practice." (Gordon in De Burgerolle, 1995, p.97)*

The interference has the effect of subverting the film convention, but – most importantly – it shows how people relate to cinematic time experience, which is mistaken for a real time experience. Nancy Spector (1997, p.70) remarks that shooting 24 frames per second and projecting them at the same speed corresponds to reality in the spectator's mind, even if it is but an optical mechanics stratagem. Had not such a famous film been used, where the time factor is vital in order to render the terror and expectancy atmosphere, the artistic result might have been less powerful. Picking a Hitchcock movie certainly was no accidental choice, but rather a carefully planned strategy grounded in the public and personal relevance of the original material to be processed, as Gordon's opinions evidently imply. There were in fact two reasons in particular for choosing *Psycho*, on the one hand being a paramount noir film, while on the other hand it belonged to the author's own adolescent imagination. As explained above in the artist's own words, the reputation of the film should allow viewers to bring their own memories into play, but it was also required to help as a marketing tool for the new artwork. *Psycho* apparently possessed both qualities Gordon was looking for, being a popular movie that was deeply rooted in collective memory and, furthermore, associating his own name to a renown Hollywood feature, as well as to a celebrated film director, which would likely have caused a sounding board effect in the British media. There are no doubts about the intentionality of Gordon's maneuver, since he had already employed a similar strategy on previous occasions, such as for his graduate exhibition at the Slade in 1990, when he had announced an imaginary exhibition together with Marino Marini and Andre Minaux. This feature would seem to credit Gordon's performed action for *24 Hour Psycho* as a sort of affiliation to Hitchcock's work, rather than a mere and plain appropriation of an existing feature film, though this is definitely a slippery issue. Carefully avoiding the question about the use of ready-made material, in an interview with Stéphanie Moisdon-Trembley the Scottish author admits that the result has been obtained by means of a direct adoption, but he prefers to define this intervention as an abduction, which would imply the hostage's acceptance – up to a point:

> *"Both the works ['24 Hour Psycho' and 'Predictable incidents in unfamiliar surroundings'[6]] are using high profile and popular media icons in order to 'extort' another role with those images. [...] these works, as I see it, are not simply works of appropriation. They are more like acts of affiliation. When I was wanting to use Hitchcock's* Psycho, *it wasn't a straightforward case of abduction. [...] I wanted to maintain the authorship of Hitchcock so that when an audience would see my '24 Hour Psycho' they would think much more about Hitchcock and much less, or not at all, about me. [...] yes, there are some clear similarities with the kind of relationship that necessarily develop between a hostage and a captor; in the way that they both become dependent on one another, for all sorts of reasons [...]" (Gordon in Moisdon-Trembley, 1996, p.125)*

However, Gordon refers kidnapping not only to Hitchcock's film, but even to the prospective viewers of his work. As a matter of facts, the artist meant to turn the museum space into a sort of cinema hall, as he had experienced with Bruce Nauman's video-installation in Kassel, hence defying any expectancy or prejudice of the art public:

> *"So in social terms, I use the mechanisms of film to 'kidnap' people and bring them out of the situation they expected to find – an artistic*

> *situation – so that they are compelled to think of other spaces." (Gordon in Sheikh, 1997, p.23)*

Furthermore, there are other reasons linked directly to Gordon's personal life that drove him to the adoption of *Psycho*, because together with Hitchcock's *Birds* it was one of those movies that he had to wait until his adolescence to be allowed by his parents to see, as it was generally considered too disturbing. As a consequence, his first encounter with this and other classical Hollywood movie was on television or even as a recorded VHS cassette. Hence, his personal experience with movies was mainly connected with the video recorder in a private surrounding, which affords some control over image viewing. Manipulating film material has thus become a common practice for people of Gordon's generation thanks to VHS financial and technological accessibility. As a matter of facts, both slow motion and fast forward are features adolescents were pretty familiar with in the Eighties and Nineties, they were used as means to play compulsively with one's own favourite film, music clip or porn movie (Haase, 1999, p.141). Although being originally used by scientists to perform structural analysis, slow motion in particular operates as a means to stage sexual fantasies one might be obsessed with, therefore ceasing to be a mere detached analytical procedure and turning into a voyeuristic practice, so Gordon believes:

> *"We grew up with video recorders – maybe it's as simple as that. We had inexpensive access to movies, and we had the technological means to screw it all up. [...] any girl or guy can sit in their bedroom and run, and re-run a video of their current obsession and watch the whole thing in slow-motion. This is not an academic exercise. This is about sex. This is about a human drive of real desire to see what shouldn't be seen." (Gordon in Moisdon-Trembley, 1996, pp.128-129)*

While he was working on *24 Hour Psycho*, one of the features he found more interesting to play with was exactly this subtle ambiguity about slow motion, which lays on the crossroads between scientific methodology and teenager imagination. Pushed altogether in an alien context to both, such as a venue for contemporary art, Gordon was convinced this twofold approach would finally produce a perpetual source for thought. Talking to Graham Fagen, the Glasgow artist was absolutely aware of the potential effect that this procedure could have had, if applied as an autonomous artwork:

"If you're very lucky you might be able to go in there and know the academy idea and the bedroom idea, so you get to collide those two things, or the intentions of those two things, and end up being somewhere altogether, you're not actually masturbating, you're nor actually coming to any conclusion either. But if you think about that half-masturbation and half-conclusion, for me that is the ideal state of constant stimulation, there's no end to it in a way." (Gordon in Fagen, 1999, pp.81-82)

However, slowing down *Psycho* was just one part of the game, since Gordon wanted the spectator to enter a different dimension and put the viewer's body into direct contact with the film. In order to reach his aim, the artist decided to black out the Tramway hall completely and then suspend the projection screen in its centre at the height of two and a half metres above the ground. The projection surface allowed the image to be seen on both sides of the screen, while its height permitted the viewer to go around or pass under it. Unlike cinemas, the projector had been placed directly on the floor so that visitors could inadvertently pass in front of light beam and see their own shadow on the screen inside the movie. The viewer could thus gain physical access to Hitchcock's masterpiece, which on its part had been turned into a string of still images or a set of iconic slides (Fricke, 1998, pp.29-30). Even if he was convinced to have come up with a consistent project, the young artist had some serious qualms before presenting the idea for *24 Hour Psycho* to Nicola White. Setting apart the curator's expectations for one of his text-piece, Gordon was conscious that his new purpose could be seen as a mere act of bravado and insolence:

"I was kind of nervous of going to the Tramway with the idea, because it was a totally audacious thing to do, it still for some people is a ridiculous idea, that all you're doing is slowing something down [...]" (Gordon in Fagen, 1999, pp.81-82)

Nicola White's reaction was a bit uncertain at the beginning, as she knew Gordon had not displayed a video work before, but she believed the idea was brilliant and still recalls how things moved on:

"It took a long time to work out the practicalities of it: the display and the screen and how to slow the film down. But it was brilliant. I don't think you can beat it for a title, '24 Hour Psycho', so it becomes an iconic thing that people don't forget, it triggers a remembrance. And I think that 'Psycho' is such a shared subject matter [...]. I knew it was very successful, it was fantastic in the space. It wasn't like

> *anything anyone had done – it wasn't like anything that Douglas had done." (White in Lowndes, 2010, p.166)*

In the end, the exhibition was titled *24 Hour Psycho* and displayed one single work by Douglas Gordon plus another set of two, albeit directly related to the main video installation. Darkening the main exhibition hall, indeed, revealed itself to be a clever strategy for dominating such a difficult venue, leaving no room for other works. As a matter of facts, in addition to *24 Hour Psycho* the artist showed only an inscription on the entrance wall of Tramway, which had also been sent by post for the occasion – as he usually did by then for openings. The sentence applied to the wall and delivered as a letter seemed to refer explicitly to what the visitors were going to see in the darkened room, but it resulted almost in a prophecy as to the role played by this artwork for Gordon's future career: "Nothing will ever be the same". The poster promoting the event on specialized magazines showed the artist's black and white self-portrait as a hitchhiker on the edge of a motorway. The performance captured by the picture had been staged ad hoc for the exhibition at Tramway, since Gordon was carrying a sign with the capitalized word "Psycho" onto it, the slang word for psychopath. He had chosen to wear black trousers and a loose white jacket, together with a black cap fitted on his head, while his facial expression looked wide-eyed and gaping at the passing cars. His outfit and gaze didn't appear reassuring at all and, as in many of his works, he seemed to let the viewer decide whether to run the risk of sharing the journey with him – in the car or at the exhibition.

In the aftermath of the opening *24 Hour Psycho* was appreciated in different ways: while the popular press condemned it, the critics – especially the militant ones – heaped praise on Gordon's work. Several local newspapers censured the project for being pretentious and ridiculous, journalists wondered if that was to be considered an artwork and whatever the artist would dare to propose next. Heavy controversy on the exhibition was published on *The Herald*, the most popular Scottish newspaper, on several occasions. Gordon's video installation was thought to be obscure for an inexperienced audience as well as unnecessarily provocative, but none could deny the spectacular nature of the work on display. Right after the opening on April 30th, *The Herald* correspondent Sara Villiers wrote a merciless report:

> *"How far Gordon has put his own mark on 'Psycho' is questionable, and as with all experimental work it needs to be put in context. I do wish exhibition organisers would use common sense and give the*

public some background information and explanation. Tramway's presentation is a prime example of lack of concern for gallery goers and explains why avant-garde art has such a bad name. [...] The differing response is part of the work, for Gordon's aim is orchestration of social situations which deny expectation and engage perceptions of moral responsibility." (Villiers, 1993a)

Only a few days later, however, on May 3rd the same author had to confess she was surprised by Gordon's ability to capture the viewer's attention with a hypnotizing atmosphere:

"Gordon's treatment is surprisingly mesmeric and despite expectations of boredom I was astonished to be enthralled. My fellow spectator, however, coughed and left. [...] I feel slightly sickened, but whether it's by Gordon, Hitchcock or myself I'm not sure. Douglas Gordon's project is certainly a disturbing and provocative work." (Villiers, 1993b)

Again in December 1993, while summing up that year's major art events in Scotland, another *Herald* critic Mary Brennan confirmed that the impression made by Gordon's artwork was still vivid in the mind of the local media and the audience:

"Douglas Gordon's '24 Hour Psycho' was perplexing but made a big impression; the memory of slow-mo Hitchcock lingers on." (Brennan, 1993)

In perfect YBA style, as had happened for Hirst's formaldehyde dipped shark the year before or Whiteread's voluminous sculptures, *24 Hour Psycho* had aroused big media interest and coverage, so that the author became fairly well-known even outside the field of art. In view of this, the exhibition at Tramway can be considered as the first time, when Gordon began to enjoy media attention and to be acknowledged by the general public. Even if one should pretend that *24 Hour Psycho* did not aim directly at creating clamour in an artificial manner, the publicity – either positive or negative – that ensued was undoubtedly significant for the young Glaswegian. Local media attention also fostered the shooting in 1993 of a BBC Scotland documentary on the neo-conceptual artists active in Glasgow, titled *Out There: Conceptual Artist* and which featured Douglas Gordon, Christine Borland and Craig Richardson.

The art press criticism was mainly favourable and – what is more – the opinion was widely shared by various experts on different magazines. Of course *Frieze* supported Gordon's work: its leading journalist Stuart Morgan even wrote a short essay about the work which then became the gallery catalogue for the opening night. The influent critic praised the young artist who, in his opinion, had been able to create a monument to cinema history resorting to such simple work – that is slowing down the images and suppressing the audio – at the same time, building the perfect memorial for Alfred Hitchcock:

> *"Gordon's Psycho is complete, in a sense more "complete" than it was ever meant to be. [...] Despite being unable to determine the plot, the first-time viewer would still take away these snapshots from an event that ranks as a critical act in its own right, perhaps even the first in a series of modified appropriations which would stand as permanent comments on Gordon's other works. Criticism keeps works of art alive, talked about, current. Yet despite the element of homage implied in Gordon's action, there is also a way in which he is out to bury Hitchcock." ('24 Hour Psycho: Hitchcock's Tomb', Cat.1993, pp.7-8)*

Flash Art International defined the Tramway exhibition as one of the year's most interesting art projects in Britain, firmly rooted in Conceptual Art (Renton, 1993, p.93). A very strong opinion considering that Rachel Whiteread had recently shown her monumental installation *House*, perhaps the work that created the most vehement social and media debate over the whole YBA season and that was finally responsible for her Turner Prize victory in 1993. *Art Monthly* was also enthusiastic about Gordon's work, his friend and companion Ross Sinclair expressing that the success of *24 Hour Psycho* was to be attributed to the minimalism of its idea:

> *" '24 Hour Psycho' is a pretty good idea. And with it Gordon has generated a good deal of interest. One reason for this success was the ease with which this idea captured the imagination of a wide cross-section of the public, both inside and outside the art-world. [...] And let's be honest, I can't remember the last time I spent three hours sitting contemplating an artwork in situ. It was a refreshing experience indeed." (Sinclair, 1993b, pp.22-23)*

However, even some years later on the occasion of *24 Hour Psycho*'s inclusion in a group show at the Hayward Gallery Mark Sladen, a much more influent critic for *Art Monthly* at the time, was astonished by the power of Gordon's video installation:

> *"I expected Gordon's intervention to rid the film of any dramatic tension but the reverse is true. I expected the piece to expose Hitchcock's manipulation of the viewer, but this is almost irrelevant. I kept revisiting the work and willing it to fail, but each time found myself recreating the shock of my first encounter with the original movie." (Sladen, 1996, p.26)*

Nicholas Logsdail, the influent patron of London's Lisson Gallery, was among the earliest visitors flocking to see the work that had caused so much attention and argument. As he saw *24 Hour Psycho* by himself, he finally decided to propose Gordon to enter his gallery for stable representation and offered to organize his first solo show in a commercial establishment for the following year. Typical for Logsdail, the influent dealer had waited for Gordon to mature on his own before accepting him into his gallery. In fact, the powerful gallery patron had seized the young Glaswegian already in 1991 at the time of his contribution into the Barclays Young Artist's Award, but wouldn't dare to pick him at such an early career stage. Logsdail's resolution after viewing *24 Hour Psycho* pledges for the absolute relevance of this artwork in the career of Douglas Gordon.

Satisfied with her achievements on her first year at Tramway, though fatigued by the spatial difficulties of the exhibition venue, Nicola White decided to move back to CCA soon after the opening of Gordon's solo show. At the same time, Andrew Nairne left CCA to take the post of Head of Visual Arts at the Scottish Arts Council, while Charles Esche was appointed Visual Arts Director at Tramway. The three put together were now in crucial positions to support the independent Glasgow art scene, although not many other Scottish institutions or experts shared their sympathy for the young neo-conceptualists. Nevertheless – together with Transmission gallery, as well as thanks to Judith Findlay's regular reports on *Flash Art International* – Nairne, White and Esche wholeheartedly promoted Gordon, Borland and their companions, cooperating as a three pronged attack line to foster Glaswegian neo-Conceptual Art abroad. Shortly after Gordon's Tramway show closed, the new curator Charles Esche proposed to present the artist's work in Germany, as he had good contacts with Klaus Biesenbach, a young Berlin curator who had recently founded a centre for contemporary art in the heart of the reunited German city, which was particularly dedicated to new media and performances. Esche was especially committed to have the Tramway exhibitions to tour abroad, in order to help Glasgow based artists to get international attention (Lowndes, 2010, p.169). In January 1994, hence Gordon was invited to show his video installation at Kunstwerke, a new Berlin establishment set in an old factory in former Eastern Germany and whose premises were still in a state of neglect. The work was installed in the loft at the third floor of the industrial building, the screen hanging from one of the inner pillars. The opening of the exhibition, one of the first to be held at Kunstwerke, was very crowded and the curator decided to keep the premises open for twenty-four hours, so that the work could be seen to the full. It is reported, that one of the visitors stood in front of the screen for eleven hours and a television reporter came to film what was happening. The screening of *24 Hour Psycho* in Berlin was very successful, especially for the interest the installation aroused in the German art world. Biesenbach was fascinated by the quality of the work that literally changed space and time perception, besides evoking the mass media produced collective imagination, which in his opinion had replaced history and religion in contemporary society. The Berlin show yielded further opportunity for Gordon to exhibit in Germany: as a matter of facts, on seeing his work another Berlin based curator, Gerti Fietzek, invited him to show the work in Leipzig for the exhibition *Kopfbahnhof/Terminal* (Cat.1995) that was held in March 1995 in the city train station together with Lawrence Weiner and another young conceptual artist, Maria Eichhorn. This exhibition afforded Gordon with the opportunity to demonstrate the quality of his works had matured up to a point that he could participate into a group show together with the renowned American conceptual artist, who represented a true benchmark for the young Glaswegian. *24 Hour Psycho* was installed in an old waiting room of the station, which was completely blacked out for the occasion. Gordon's double presentation in Germany aroused German critics' growing interest in his career path, so that he was invited to install the piece again on German speaking ground. The third screening of the work was held in Austria in 1996 at the prestigious Akademie der Bildenden Künste in Vienna as a solo exhibition.

Besides earning international recognition and drawing the attention of critics, curators and dealers, *24 Hour Psycho* was Gordon's first piece to be bought by one of the most influent British art collectors. Founder of a successful London book distribution firm, Bernhard Starkmann immediately requested the video installation, but the artist was unsure as to what he could sell exactly. Although Gordon had tried to avoid an interpretation of his work restricted to the ready-made issue, the need to transform this piece into a commodity to be exchanged on the market brought out the essence of *24 Hour Psycho*, which was based on an act of appropriation. Of course Gordon couldn't sell the movie, as he wasn't the film director nor had he purchased the rights over the Hollywood movie. The collector himself suggested a viable solution to the artist, the latter being asked to issue detailed instructions on how to implement the *Psycho* slow motion vision. The economic aspect of Conceptual Art had been previously dealt with at the origin of this strain, when Seth Sieglaub had set up his enterprise to promote American artists working with mere ideas. Considering that ownership of a Conceptual Art piece didn't confer to the owner the advantage of control over the piece acquired, this kind of artworks turned back onto the question of the value of art's private appropriation. In Sieglaub's opinion, the way a collector should get hold of an idea could only be by means of its instructions:

> *"For if elements of documentary information now constituted the work, then possession of these elements became ownership, and documents became artworks." (Sieglaub in Alberro, 2003, p.74)*[7]

In view of the fact that the *24 Hour Psycho* had been reduced to a set of instructions in order to become marketable, Hans Ulrich Obrist (1996b, p.168) drew the conclusion that the work represented one of the most successful forms of *time ready-made*, already postulated by Duchamp in opposition to spatial ones, which were instead obtained by displacing and de-contextualizing common objects. Gordon appears to agree with Duchamp's classification of temporal ready-made, since he admits having been inspired by the French master's works, especially by the famous chess game performed with a naked woman during his major retrospective at the Pasadena Art Museum in 1963:

> *"[...] one of the most important things, when I was reading Duchamp, was this chess game with the naked woman in Los Angeles. To take social activity as a readymade, bring it into the museum, and almost kill people with time because of how long this was going to take." (Gordon in Obrist, 1996b, p.169)*

The praxis of appropriation applied to Conceptual Art, as well as the interaction of cinema and visual arts proved to be the key ingredients for the immediate and durable success of *24-Hour Psycho* with the critics, such that the work has entered several manuals on contemporary art history, both of educational and academic level. The work has also been able to make an original contribution to two central issues concerning the Nineties art production, on the one hand the relationship with the temporal dimension of art, on the other hand the connection with the cult of images screened on television. As far as the second of those issues is concerned, Jörg Heiser (2008, p.195) credits the Scottish artist's work for transforming everyday technology and media consumption into a source of artistic possibilities. By means of a very famous film, that was now associated to the home video scene rather than with cinema, the artist had been able to re-create in the museum that state of hypnosis and absorption typical of television as a medium. In Michael Rush's (2007, p.221) opinion with a clever stratagem Gordon had been able to outwit the first attempts by early video artists – including Nam June Paik, Aldo Tambellini and Frank Gillette – that had tried in vain to respond to the dictatorship of television. Michael Newman (2009, p.105) agrees that the strategy of the Glaswegian author had reversed roles between production and consumption of audiovisual material, so that the viewer could acquire the competence to look at the images autonomously. As regards to the pervasiveness of image marketing in contemporary world, Harald Fricke (1998, pp.23-24, 30-31) for his part believes that Gordon has found a solution for re-cycling the waste of an image-saturated society: the artist would thus be capable to show a way out of the maze of signs and icons, which are based on the fantasies of our collective memory. In his opinion, slowing down the projection would expose the structure of the narrative logic inherent in audio-visual products. However, slow motion is also related to the subject matter of time and to how it is treated as a theme in contemporary art. In this respect, Nancy Spector (1997, pp.68-69) links Gordon's work to procedural and performance art of the Seventies, because they were based on the individual experience of time endurance, as well as on ensuing a transformation of temporal perception. In fact, those artistic actions only existed for the duration of their operation time and needed the direct involvement of the spectator, which are two circumstances that clearly correspond to the conditions for the existence of *24 Hour Psycho* as well. Ursula Frohne (2008, p.365) emphasizes the psychological aspect of time experience in Gordon's work, since the visual dynamics established by the slowed down image flow appears to operate like the obsessive repetition of a traumatic event. In Frohne's opinion, this kind of video art proves emotionally effective, because it transforms the gallery from a white aseptic cube into a psychologically loaded black box, where repressed feelings can re-emerge into consciousness.

In consideration of the media outcry for *24 Hour Psycho* and of the interest it aroused across the board of art critics and experts, the Tramway solo show definitely represented the biggest achievement Douglas Gordon had reached so far. Together with the Europe-wide touring of his artwork, on the aftermath of this exhibition the young Glaswegian could finally consider himself a fast rising artist, drawing much more attention to his future career path as well as to the entire Glasgow art scene. As he had prophetically written in the letter accompanying the Tramway exhibition, after this event nothing would have ever been the same both for his professional life and – to some extent – even for his hometown.

Right after Gordon's accomplishment, in 1994 Tramway offered Christine Borland her first major solo show, which opened in October with the title *From Life* causing a huge media interest again, because of the main piece on show. In fact, it revolved around a real female skeleton the artist had purchased per mail order, which some papers felt as an insulting provocation. However, the work represented a interesting advancement in Borland's work, since it put together two different strains of research she had pursued so far: on the one side her interest in forensics and anatomical studies, like in *Supported* (1990), on the other side the collection and display of apparently found objects meant as anthropological traces of human existence, as she did for her on-going project *Small Objects that Save Lives* (1991-1993). As with Gordon's Tramway show, Borland's exhibition toured to Berlin's Kunstwerke finally introducing the two young Glaswegians to the international art scene as rising artists who quickly earned wide appreciation.

6.2. Generational breakthrough: of young rascals and old hands

While the period between 1990 and 1992 was only the starting point of new generational wave in British art, the following years were characterized by the steady assessment on the national art scene of the so called YBSs, which had by then become a definition referring to a large group of authors in their late twenties and early thirties. As a matter of facts, from 1993 on, established institutions started to appreciate the ferment originated by the alternative art scene and gradually included a selection of these young artists in relevant touring exhibitions both in Great Britain and abroad[8]. As soon as the British art world establishment realized that YBAs were finding increasing appreciation in foreign countries, various museums and galleries across the UK embraced the rising tide, comforted by the general acceptance young *rascals* like Hirst and Whiteread had found in the art market. The year 1993 can be regarded as the turning point in this respect, as there had been various signs early that year which could foretell the imminent outburst of the YBA phenomenon, both in the art world as well as in the British mass media. Together with the Tramway exhibition of Douglas Gordon, which held particular meaning for Glasgow's role on the British art stage, another set of events that took place in 1993 was clearly signaling the growing predominance of a new generation in the UK. Among the most influent moments one must count the following: Charles Saatchi's second exhibition committed to young British artists he was collecting; the first group show of YBAs at an established London dealer's venue such as Nicholas Logsdail's Lisson Gallery; the gallery opening of Jay Jopling's White Cube in Duke Street; the large number of young artists who were sent by the British Council to the Venice Biennale as UK representatives; finally, Rachel Whiteread's Turner Prize victory due to a very controversial environmental installation.

Charles Saatchi had indeed forestalled most art British dealers and collectors, starting to buy artworks by young local artists already in the early 1990s, although or maybe exactly because his business activities were starting to bounce back (Stallabrass, 2006b, p.206). Particularly 1991 may be defined his *annus horribilis,* for his advertising firm lost sixty-four million pounds, a situation that was exacerbated by problems in private life too, since he had to bear the cost of divorcing his first wife Doris Lockhart. To some extent, Saatchi could recover by selling seventy works from his private collection through Sotheby's just before the recession, which earned him about ten million pounds. Since the sold lot consisted mainly of 1980ies art stars' works that had already reached a top price, to stay on the cutting-edge side of art he employed a strategy that consisted in buying up works by young and still little known British artists, whose value could be decisively increased by means of a large scale promotion on a medium term. Considering that Saatchi was an experienced businessman, who furthermore knew how to play with the advertising clockwork, it is likely that his definitive shift towards the rising generation of local artists relied on an intentional plan to get him out of a tight corner. Collecting much cheaper British artists, whose value and prices had not been established yet but could rise immensely, was probably the best possible solution at hand. However, it is true that he had genuinely shown his appreciation for the Goldsmiths graduates gathered around Damien Hirst at a very early stage, when they were still lingering in warehouse shows scattered around the town, though many critics would nevertheless blame Saatchi for his supposed opportunism, as stressed by Chris Blackhurst and Mark Honigsbaum on *The Independent* in the aftermath of the *Sensation* exhibition of the collector's YBA collection at the London Royal Academy in 1997:

> *"Critics of Mr Saatchi point to the way in which he buys paintings and sculptures in bulk, frequently lighting on unknown artists and snapping up every single item of their output. The effect of this, they maintain, is twofold: to anoint the hitherto little-appreciated artist as a star; and to send the value of his or her works sky-high." (Blackhurst and Honigsbaum, 1997)*

As argued in previous chapters, Saatchi launched this new season in his collector's career with the opening of the St. John's Wood gallery in April 1992, hosting the exhibition *Young British Artists 1* (Cat.1992) as its very first event, which featured the shark he had commissioned to Damien Hirst. The numeration included in the title implied that other similar exhibitions would probably follow soon, which in fact happened, since the tycoon then mounted an exhibition every year until 1997. The second exhibition in 1993 proved that Saatchi was seriously resolved to launch the new British artists, hence it led the way to the crucial year for YBA's final breakthrough. As a matter of facts, *Young British Artists 2* shortly preceded the opening of Jay Jopling's new commercial gallery in London, which would soon be renowned as the White Cube, as well as the opening of the exhibition *Wonderful Life* at Lisson Gallery, the first group show at a preeminent London establishment to be entirely centred on the rising generation of artists. In 1992 he displayed works by Rachel Whiteread, John Greenwood, Alex Landrum, Langlands & Bell and Damien Hirst, while in February 1993 there were works by Rose Finn-Kalcey, Sarah Lucas, Marc Quinn e Mark Wallinger. The following year he put on show pieces by Simon Callery, Simon English and Jenny Saville, and then in April 1995 he showed John Frankland, Marcus Harvey, Brad Lochore, Marcus Taylor and Gavin Turk. This series of yearly events was a means for Saatchi to unfold an articulate strategy to promote his protégées and thus a whole new generation of artists. Although the acronym YBA wasn't used before 1995, it appears that Saatchi had effectively named a whole generation of artists due to this series of exhibitions, far beyond the few authors he actually collected (Muir, 2011, pp.121-123). The media soon enrolled in this loose grouping the Glaswegian artists who made particular impression on the London art scene, such as Borland and Gordon, although they never really felt to fall into this definition, whatever the latter might have meant. In an interview on the subject matter, Christine Borland seems very resolute about the lack of affinity with the young British artists:

> *"It's a media construct, that's all. And I know these things are useful for some people, and I've been in some very nice shows, I suppose, on the back of that, and been able to produce work on the back of that, so I'm not about to say that I think it's absolutely terrible or that I want nothing to do with it. I'm sure whatever happens with the YBA phenomenon, I'll just keep on doing the same thing; I won't have identifiably changed to fit into anything or fall out of anything." (Barclay Morgan, 1999)*

On July 17th Nicholas Logsdail opened Lisson Gallery to *Wonderful Life*, the first extensive group show that an established London dealer would grant to the upcoming wave of British artists[9]. In fact, this exhibition somehow consecrated the new trend as being finally acknowledged by crucial players of the London art market, hence reassuring also public institutions that collectors and critics would back young British artist from that moment on. However, going through the list of contributors it appears that Logsdail had chosen a mitigated and polished version of YBA, systematically avoiding such authors that might produce very provocative or crude artworks. As a matter of facts, the main artists on show were Terrence Bond, Adam Chodzko, Thomas Gidley, Douglas Gordon, Marysia Lewandowska, Jason Martin and Simon Patterson, although many more participated into the show, among those Christine Borland and Roderick Buchanan from Glasgow, Damien Hirst and Gary Hume from the original Goldsmiths grouping, as well as several friends of Gordon like Liam Gillick, Martin Creed and Graham Fagen. None of them presented groundbreaking pieces at Lisson Gallery: Simon Patterson for instance showed *The Great Bear*, while Gordon presented the documentation of his first telephone performances made in Italy a year before. A relevant aspect of this exhibition was rather represented by the chosen curator, *Frieze* critic James Roberts (1996, p.32), who counted among the biggest supporters of the YBA generation, especially because he appreciated their attack to stern post-modern theories taught in British art schools. He was also one of the most influent advocates of the Chapman brothers and tried to outline an art theory to explain the poetics of YBAs, which Julian Stallabrass plainly opposed at the time and later recapped as the vindication of popular culture on intellectual art:

> *"In the category of popular culture, Roberts [...] includes cinema, pornography, television – aspects of culture largely produced and managed by multi-billion-dollar corporations. The uses of such 'popular' forms in high art are nevertheless considered to be 'gestures*

of proletarian and philistine disaffirmation'." (Stallabrass, 2006b, p.122)

For the Scottish artists on show – Borland, Buchanan, Fagen and Gordon – it revealed itself as a good opportunity to show alongside some of London's most renown rising artists and impress an international audience that would have never come all the way up to Glasgow. Indeed, one of the visitors was the curator of Van Abbemuseum in Eindhoven, Jan Debbaut, who led one of the most prestigious contemporary art institutions in continental Europe. The Dutch curator was struck by Gordon's instruction pieces and asked immediately for his contacts, promising he would meet Gordon in Glasgow soon in order to discuss a possible solo show at the Eindhoven museum. Looking back to the year 1993, Gordon had made several decisive steps forward for his career: he had gained a good degree of public renown – both at home and abroad, sold a major piece to a big British collector, was on display at one of London's most influential galleries and got in touch with the curator of an important European museum. More in general, as regards to the entire generation of young British artists, the concurrent support by the most important British collector, Charles Saatchi, the most ambitious new dealer, Jay Jopling, and the most successful gallery patron of the previous decade, Nicholas Logsdail, implied that the British market was really willing to side with the upcoming trend. This perception was made visibly clear at the yearly Cologne Art Fair, attended by an impressive number of London galleries (Muir, p.88): ten of the best known dealers displayed in the main room, among them Victoria Miro and Lisson Gallery, while the four younger London galleries – that is Interim Art, White Cube, Cabinet Gallery and Karsten Schubert – exhibited their artist in the external section *UnFair*. In the centre of the main pavilion Charles Saatchi had mounted the exhibition *Junge Britische Kunst aus der Sammlung Saatchi*, showing the very best of the tycoon's new collection, including Hirst's shark and Whiteread's *Ghost*. The London invasion of the 1993 Cologne Art Fair made clear, that the British art system was taking off and had numerous players ready to market new artists on an international level.

The sudden turnaround of the London art market makes furthermore evident that gatekeepers in the art system may change at some point, either if established players change their mind about the artists and trends to promote – such as in the case of Saatchi who sold his past collection or of Logsdail who opened up his gallery to a new generation of artists – or otherwise when new players reach a powerful position inside the field of art

– such as new curators, new magazines and new dealers rising together with another set of authors. As a matter of facts, there aren't new entries only on the artists' side, but also in every possible role of the art system and young authors may try to catch up with rising dealers, curators, collectors or critics. Although being recently founded, Jopling's White Cube for instance became the most successful gallery of all London establishments in the Nineties, since it acted as the true and only promoter and sales representative for the new generation of British artists, as recalled by Gregor Muir:

> *"White Cube would become the defining gallery of the Nineties. [...] no other gallery could remotely claim to have the same connections with the key figures in the history of recent British art. [...] White Cube would find itself at the epicentre of YBA." (Muir, 2011, p.75)*

Indeed Jay Jopling was among the first dealers to organize solo shows for new leading artists and allowed them full creative freedom, as he sensed that their works were essentially conceptual. Unlike Karsten Schubert, he had immediately grasped that many authors of the YBA generation, especially artists from the Goldsmiths, kept close to the conceptualist approach they had been trained at during their art school education. They were rather used to place ideas before artworks, consequently demanding a marketing strategy revolving around the artist's persona, which differed from the traditional model centred on the artistic production of an author. In the Sixties and Seventies Seth Sieglaub had already been confronted with a similar situation and immediately understood the increasing relevance of the artist image to foster sales, especially since Conceptual Art had questioned the primacy of the artwork (Alberro, 2003, pp.11-12, 41-42). Right from the start Sieglaub had placed importance on working over press coverage and publicity, convinced that of the effectiveness of identity and publicity strategies, which paralleled the organization of shows. As a consequence, from 1966 on the American dealer undertook an effective advertising campaign of a selected group of artists, creating a network of connections to potential clients and trying to enhance desirability of the chosen authors, the likes of a commercial ad for a dishwashing liquid. Of course such a campaign is not sufficient in itself to launch a new artist or an entire movement, because any player of the art system must find the support of other likeminded gatekeepers and, furthermore, every artist has his or her own peculiarities. However, today the art market has finally adapted to the key feature of contemporary art, which is represented by the evaluation of an artwork as the trace of an exceptional person and not simply as an object in itself. Hence, the combination of the artist persona with the artwork becomes the piece of art in itself and creates an all-comprising aura, rather than concrete objects (Blanché, 2012, p.300). Economically speaking, this phenomenon would in fact be called branding, which is the strategy that Jay Jopling pursued by means of massive promotion capable of leveling any difference between art and life. The outcome was the art demand concentrating solely on the artist's personality and uniqueness, rather than on the produced objects, which proved an appropriate means of public visibility for authors such as Damien Hirst and Tracey Emin. Jopling himself has been frank about the decision to adopted a strategy that explicitly aimed at an enhanced media exposure for his protégés:

> *"It was a deliberate strategy to go to the tabloid newspapers to draw their attention to these works of art." (Jopling in Macdonald, 1997)*

In order to fully understand this logic, one should take a closer look at some aspects of the art market, especially those concerning the behaviour and bias that determine supply decisions by dealers. Besides selling artworks, any commercial gallery is usually concerned with promoting its represented artists, in order to stimulate market demand and possibly develop favourable trends. Given the information gap that characterizes the art market, dealers must reinforce and increase their reputation, which in turn is based on the image and value of the artists they represent. Since galleries must reassure their costumers about the stability of a specific artist's value, dealers know that this will obviously depend on the artist's future decisions – say, the types of works he or she will produce, the group shows he or she will take part into, the solo shows he or she will be granted in important venues, as well as the critics' response to his or her production. Since the number of contemporary art buyers is rather small, dealers must devise strategies to guarantee clients and foster their loyalty towards the gallery itself. As a consequence, the most frequent strategy for dealers consists in a tight control over the production of the represented artists, motivating them to pursue a consistent and distinctive profile, which may lead to easy recognizable works. In the end, the entirety of an artist's works is transformed into one specific and reliable brand that clients will readily identify. Once an artist has been successfully branded, he or she is practically allowed anything, even a complete reassessment of previous creations. In fact, what is being sold at that point is not single artworks, but the artist's persona as a trademark (Thompson, 2008, pp.68-69). Jopling's strategy for the YBAs – as well as Sieglaub's for the American conceptual artists – consisted of applying the mechanics of stardom to rising artists by arousing wide media attention, hence creating celebrities that were famous for being famous. Originally a means to overcome the information gap of the art market, the White Cube patron understood that tabloid-exposure could be used to foster the immediate rise of young artist celebrities, as if they were some kind of pop stars. As regards to the balance of forces inside the art market, Jopling had also been able to abolish the vertical differentiation between galleries, which would usually separate those for launching newcomers and others that represent already established artists (Caves, 2000, p.60). The White Cube behaved like a celebrity gallery, although it was essentially presenting artists that didn't have a solid reputation and in fact had not been picked by any other established venture. To obviate to the lack of social capital, Jopling invested financial resources in media communication and promotion, trying to put his artists in the limelight of popular press as well as of specialized magazines. In order for this marketing strategy to be profitable, in fact, the artist was requested to create at least one remarkable work based on a simple and often challenging idea, so that he or she could be spotted for quite some time. On the other hand, the author should then try to transfer this very recognizable idea on artworks suitable for a low-cost and serial production to be sold on the art market for small collectors. The logic to support this stratagem is based on the idea, that the artistic conception derives nevertheless from the author's aura, which for its part can be inserted onto an artwork like a brand on a shoe or t-shirt.

In this regards, there are a several useful examples that may be taken into account, such as Damien Hirst's *Butterfly Paintings*, a series of works that integrate dead butterflies on the canvas. These paintings were definitely an adaptation of the life and death themes dealt with in major works as *A thousand years* (1990) or *In And Out Of Love* (1991). In the case of the *Spot Paintings*, on various occasions Hirst himself was brutally clear about the fact that only the idea should matter, hence he had his collaborators to paint them serially (Muir, 2011, p.38). Even if he did not avail himself of other people's direct help, Douglas Gordon also started to resort to similar strategies, particularly when the extremely influential Gagosian Gallery offered to represent him. As soon as the New York gallery took over his promotion, the Glasgow artist needed to increase and vary his production, in order to meet the demand for a vast number of works to allocate on the market for private collectors. Hence, Gordon conceived a series of works that were based on the same concept and easy to produce, though belonging to a potentially unlimited sequence of unique pieces. In 2002 he created the *Blind Star* series and then in 2006 the *Self-Portrait of You + Me* series, both for solo shows at Gagosian Gallery[10]: the former consisted of old cinema star posters from which he had excised the eyes and substituted them with small mirrors, while the latter were also pictures of Hollywood celebrities, which on the contrary had been partially burnt and then fixed on a mirrored background. This twofold production strategy clearly divides an author's artworks into two different sets, as has been argued previously, confirming that one may separate the few iconic pieces, that might be purchased by big collectors or even museums, from so-called retail products of minor artistic relevance that represent the real cash cow, since they are sold to a broader audience of small collectors. As a matter of facts, only a few pieces by an author usually become truly famous and stand as major achievements in art history – or at least for the artist's personal career – while all remaining artworks merely support his or her professional survival. The same approach of serial production by means of easily replicable techniques applies to many other authors of Hirst's and Gordon's generation, such as Ian Davenport for a painting series he created by simply pouring paint through several syringes onto an inclined canvas, letting gravity do all the work. With regards to this procedure, the author maintained that he always tried to do very little, though at the same time to produce a lot of pieces (Davenport in *The British Art Show 3*, Cat.1990, p.50).

Minimum productive labour and maximum production achieved – this would rather seem a principle of Fordist logic rather than of an artist's work ethics, still it adequately expresses these artists' attitude to the art market, as well as to the producing and marketing of their artworks. Both are fundamental aspects to understand two distinctive features of the YBA phenomenon, that were on one hand the very young age at which many artists became successful – a feature further analysed by art economist David Galenson – and on the other one their gradual integration into the logic of neo-liberal economy – a feature examined by several art historians, among those Paul Wood (1996), Julian Stallabrass (2006a), Joseph Koerner and Lisbet Rausing (1996). In a range of essays Galenson (2001, 2005a, 2006) investigated the structural development of the art market from Modern Times up to the last century, especially concentrating on the analysis of the prevailing production system. Although his take on 20th century visual arts may be a bit loose from an art historical point of view, his considerations about the reasons for an artist's improvement in the art field appear rather consistent. Taking for granted that the art market needs constant innovation on the supply side, the American scholar maintains that until the first half of the past century – in particular up to the early Sixties – enhancement of artistic results was aimed at aesthetic features, thus the most influential artists did experiment with the visual development of their praxis. Such an approach implies a relatively long phase of artistic growth, since aesthetic developments need more time to mature, so that the great masters would usually create their best works a long time after their debut years. However, at the beginning of the 20th century some authors started to focus on the process of conceiving their works, rather than engrossing in their practical production. Celebrated artists such as Marcel Duchamp and Hans Arp, or later Piero Manzoni and Yves Klein, were among the pioneers of a new course of action in visual arts, one that implied the primacy of ideas and of conceptualization. Still, according to Galenson, the turning point was Jasper Johns' exhibition at Leo Castelli's gallery in 1958, which he believes marked the decisive transition from a kind of practical experimentation in art praxis to a rather conceptual tendency (Galenson, 2005a, pp.11-12). The latter is likely to be a quite controversial statement, since different art trends in the Sixties would appear much more relevant for the turn towards conceptualization of visual arts, such as Minimalism, performance art in the wake of Fluxus or even Conceptual Art as practised by the group of authors gathered around Seth Sieglaub. In fact, rather than going back to Jasper Johns, it appears more adequate to credit Carl Andre and Lawrence Weiner for the gradual dismantlement of artworks created for galleries in favour of more articulate exhibition venues, participatory models and production methods that directly interacted with the institutional framework of the art field. Examining the origins of Conceptual Art, Alexander Alberro (2003, pp.24,34) points attention to Joseph Kosuth as the true initiator of the definitive separation between idea and form in visual arts: further developing the idea of Dan Flavin and Carl Andre, who would provide museums and galleries with instructions to re-build their work on site, Kosuth brought this trend to the extreme point of having the propositions alone without needing to materialize the artwork. Be as it is, Galenson (2005a, p.12) is then correct in asserting that the conceptual approach to art caused another relevant shift in the art system as regards to innovation. As a matter of facts, the new idea-based praxis requires a much shorter innovation span than previous trends that relied on experimental stages, simply because Conceptual Art may skip the practical realization of artworks. Sieglaub once highlighted this achievement for visual arts in a paradigmatic way:

> *"I can have my ideas in twenty different places at once. Ideas are faster than tedious objects." (Sieglaub in Alberro, 2003, p.155)*

Furthermore, in Galenson's (2006, pp.22-23) opinion the most fertile and radical ideas are often devised by young authors, who have not been stifled by artistic conventions or restrained by common mindset. This might then be the reason why the young British artists, substantially counting on good or provocative ideas, could make it at such an early stage, when Conceptual Art praxis was again revived on the art market. Despite art historical inaccuracies, Galenson's considerations on the structural developments of the art field are useful to underline the importance of capturing the prevailing production model in visual arts of a given period. Each author who wants to establish a presence in the art system should indeed be aware of the expectations projected onto the artist persona and on the methods applied to the artist's work. In this respect, starting with Damien Hirst the YBA generation appeared fully aware of the prevailing production system in the art field, in particular acknowledging the new trends coming from the USA, and bet on the forthcoming rise of neo-conceptual practices on the art market. However, the YBAs really started to take off, only when several players around them – amongst those new and old dealers and curators, collectors and critics – agreed on the novelty of this trend and legitimated the ideas put forward. Furthermore, since dealing with a conceptualist tendency, it must be stressed that the support of magazines and journalists is crucial, since communication takes predominance over production – which altogether appears to be a general inclination of an information-based society (Alberro, 2003, pp.55-57,120). Already Sieglaub had correctly caught about Conceptual Art, that when the primary information – which is the idea – is separated from its secondary information – being its material form – a lot of surplus information must thus be dealt with to communicate the value of artworks, for instance organizing reviews and articles that explain their genesis and meaning.

It may thus be true that the conceptual drift allows a young author to achieve early recognition, as Galenson points out because of the pre-eminence of ideas, however the spotlight on frenetic innovation would also imply that an artist can easily fall from fashion, as soon as better thoughts emerge. If so, this course of action would lead to a frequent and incessant turnover of artists, but economist William Goetzman (1996, pp.71-85) has proved that survivorship bias in the painting market result in a quite small rate of obsolescence for established artists, about 3 to 4% annually. Using auction records and repeat-sales data, evidence shows that transactions may be conditioned upon previous increase in value of a specific author, not necessarily in relative valuation of the artist's present achievements. Hence, it appears that tastes and trends are more persistent on the art market then one may think, which helps especially established artists not to fall from fashion, because it would be costly also for every single collector and institution that owns his or her artworks. This is the reason, why rising artists must seek for the acquisition into the collection of an important museum or of an influential private collector, as other art field players would regard this as a sufficient guarantee of the artworks future value stability. Of course one should hope that the museum or collector wouldn't want to sell off his or her works all of a sudden, such as Charles Saatchi did with Sandro Chia's paintings in the Eighties or more recently with Damien Hirst's tiger shark. Thus the art market has proved capable of fostering artistic innovation, but once an artist has achieved a strong position in the art field, it is difficult that he or she might fall back too much. In fact, Stallabrass (2006a, p.77) argues that even on the event of an art market bubble burst – such as happened at the end of the Eighties or more recently after the Lehman Brothers bankruptcy – the damaged artists are those who may have reached high prices before the crisis, but didn't see their position stabilized in the art system on time.

One last consideration about innovation in the field of art refers to the actual concept of progress in visual arts, since Galenson appears to take it as a self-explanatory term that influences the entire development of the arts. Indeed, back in the Eighties the renown art theorist Arthur Danto (1984, p.XV) published a paradigmatic essay on the philosophical disenfranchisement of art, pointing at the fact that the constant self-revolutionizing of art was past by then, since innovation in the field of art couldn't be taken for granted. The great American scholar maintained that there would thus always be external causes for making it appear as though such a history may go on, but preeminently for reasons related to the art market's requirement to thrive on the illusion of constant novelty. Danto consistently underlines that the reason why progress in the visual arts is important depends on society's general attitude towards economics and innovation. If innovation as such is thought paradigmatic for society's expectations and mindset – such as emerges from the constant development of new technological products – then anything must always be or at least seem innovative: this is a rule which applies even to the visual arts, which generally reflect the *Zeitgeist* of a given time and place. These observations clearly put the development of visual arts in connection with the overall trends of society, but specifically with the economic forces driving its change and progress. As regards to the latter, art commodification appears to be a crucial phenomenon to have determined the arts throughout the second half of the previous century, especially in its last decade. According to Paul Wood (1996, pp.263-269), the quest for commodification would decisively attain the art world, because capitalism is considered a global production system both for objects and ideas: as a result, art could only be its mere by-product. In the scholar's opinion, the impact of commodification has brought even bodies and minds to resort to the market, where objects and values are exchanged as if they were commodities. Wood maintains that prompt consumerism and commoditized pleasure resulted from Ronald Regan's and Margaret Thatcher's policies in the Western hemisphere. Even Stallbrass (2006a, p.49) agrees with this opinion, arguing that the art system has since been transformed into a spokesman of neoliberal ideals due to the inner development of capitalism itself. As a matter of facts, economists also observe that during the Eighties a major shift towards post-Fordism had taken place, which led to a production model based on services rather than on objects. Indeed, with the rise of financial markets and service industry, art has been seized as a safe-haven asset like a bond rated on the stock exchange. As far as visual arts are concerned, the result of this development on the art market was a particular pressure on artistic innovation cycles, in order to bring about a constant rise of value and prices. While capitalism was running towards its own financial conversion, the production of commodities turned to an overt push to define signs and meanings – that is brands and trends – rather than creating real objects. Hence the production of goods, being now centred on their symbolic value instead of their material aspect, seems to have achieved almost complete affinity with art, that is supposed to be all about ideas, meanings and symbols (Koerner and Rausing, 1996, pp.302-304). As a chief consequence, the overlapping of the world of goods with the world of art has produced the trend of aesthetic commodities, because consumerism has become part of a cultural system that got used to commercialize images and meanings as plain products. It may thus be observed, that many industrial sectors have added an aesthetic feature to consumer goods, consequently fostering innovation cycles by means of fashion waves, rather than on technological progress. Many corporations have since decided to pour money into aesthetic research for product development purposes, hence financing art projects or drawing direct inspiration from visual arts. Business firms have discovered that art can be an extraordinary tool for improving their image and make their brand attractive, just like patrons and rulers did for their name's and power's sake in previous centuries. The final result appears to be an inextricable bond between art and commerce: while goods have become more cultural, art has been further commoditized, since its market has been integrated as one of the various capitalist activities (Stallabrass, 2006a, pp.51-55). The tight connection between industry and art deeply influences the latter, at times even determining its development, if one considers that investment choices follow the tastes of stakeholders. The massive involvement of industry and finance in the role of collectors and sponsors would then set off a series of specific consequences in the art system, Stallbrass (2006a, pp.92-93) highlighting some of the most relevant that emerged in the last decade of the 20th century: relevance over youth, charm and appeal, as happens with pop music; production of works that adjust to consumerism culture and become integrated with fashion or entertainment industry; understatement or even abolishment of any possible critical stance towards capitalism; improvement of spectacular and expensive installations, whose cost directly conveys the value of the artwork; finally, the acquisition of celebrity status and the exploitation of branding strategy by more and more successful artists. Stallabras (2006b, pp.193) further points out, that most of these aspects were ideally implemented by the YBA generation, who was seemingly able to turn into an efficient marketing agent of aesthetic consumerism. Wood (1996, p.276) further defines these features as an effect of a *super-commodification*, which would compel artists to follow market rules in order to seek a swift ascent, taken that failing to do so might seriously hinder their survival in the art system. In this respect, the young artists who stood out in the United Kingdom during the Nineties appear to have been able to adjust to a mode of artistic production, which became part of the larger creativity industry, halfway between luxury products and popular entertainment (Wollen, 1998, p.24).

Although the above considerations might have an excessive Marxist take on the art system, seemingly annihilating any possibility of autonomous thought by artists, it appears true that the success of rising British artists was closely linked with the economic upturn, which started in 1993. Artists such as Damien Hirst – as well as Jeff Koons and Andy Warhol way before him – had understood how to coalesce critics over consumerism with an extreme commercial attitude thanks to a good dose of irony and irreverence. As exemplified by Hirst's case – or by Rachel Whiteread's *House* or again by Gordon's *24 Hour Psycho* – the art market indeed started to pay attention to the younger generation, also because of their adequate attitude to media and consumerism society. Still, in order to sanction the final transition to the new trend, the endorsement of public institutions was needed, which means official museum shows and possibly even purchases of works into established collections. According to Stallabrass (2006b, pp.195-196), British state museums and public galleries cannot afford to act directly on the art market, given the high risk of misled acquisitions, hence they usually avoid to buy works of rising artists who don't have a stable position yet. Public institutions would rather be confined sanctioning – with some delay – the choices already made by the most authoritative dealers and collectors, thus taking commercial galleries as a sort of research and experimentation department for new artistic trends. Consequently, museums would work to confirm the balance reached on the art market and ratify official acceptance of a given artist or an entire trend. As matter of facts, Seth Sieglaub spoiled this logic maintaining that any form of art, which becomes established is turned into establishment itself (Alberro, 2003, p.151). In this perspective, the gauge of the situation would be again the Turner Prize, which by any chance awarded Rachel Whiteread in 1993, although it had previously rejected both her and Hirst in previous editions, and marked the new generation's public legitimation and unstoppable rise. As a matter of facts – except for Anthony Gormley's success in 1994 – from 1993 artists credited to belong to the YBAs won all Turner Prize editions of the Nineties. The winners were Damien Hirst in 1995, Douglas Gordon in 1996, Gillian Wearing in 1997, Chris Ofili in 1998 and Steve McQueen in 1999. Furthermore, between 1996 and 1999 all shortlisted artists for the Tate's autumn exhibition could be included in the new trend[11]. YBA's monopoly on the Turner Prize throughout the Nineties caused two main effects: on one hand the finalists' average age dropped dramatically, showing a sharp shift towards the younger generation, on the other hand visitors' attendance increased considerably, especially thanks to the media coverage of the artists and works shown[12]. It is impossible to say, who took most advantage of the media attention aroused by the Turner Prize – whether the award itself and the Tate or the YBA generation and its supporters – anyway, it produced a sensational coverage worldwide and fostered the offensive of British art abroad.

6.3. Picking the upcoming wave: video and installation art rising

The critical success of artworks like *A Thousand Years* and *In and Out of Love* by Damien Hirst, as well as *Ghost* and *House* by Rachel Whiteread or again *24 Hour Psycho* by Douglas Gordon, pointed out that in the early Nineties installation art was sprawling even in the UK. Julian Stallabrass (2006a, p.16) argued that the decisive primacy of installations in museums and exhibitions during the Nineties confirms that it had progressively become the art system's chief production mode for the decade. Agreeing with the British scholar's opinion, already in the Nineties *New York Times* critic Michael Kimmelmann had convincingly pointed out a parallel with previous praxis or strategies that had found a similar level of diffusion:

> *"Installation art is in the late 90's roughly what Abstract Expressionism was by the late 50's. I suspect the term itself will eventually come to seem too vague to be of lasting value. [...] Having exhausted their value, catchwords or phrases may then be abandoned. [...] But unlike Pop, installation art is not even a style or movement; it is a strategy, a way of working." (Kimmelmann, 1998, p.2973)*

Interestingly, despite installation art becoming mainstream in the Nineties' art system, as a praxis it is definitely rooted in rather unconventional and alternative movements typical of environmental art in the Sixties and Seventies, which were overtly contrasting the drift towards commodification. As Kimmelmann (1998, p.2974-2975) puts it, those historical examples emerged at a point when artists generally became attuned to the political or social context in which their works were displayed. Drawing awareness to the gallery as an active container of meaning, as well as considering the audience an active part in the art process, fostered formal kinship of the kind of installation art that was later to be established at the end of the century. The art market boom of the Eighties proved a difficult period for the trend in environmental art, but the sudden collapse of the art bubble due to 1989 recession unfolded previously inconceivable opportunities for articulate spatial installations. However, according to Julian Stallabrass (2006a, pp.16-18), the name shift from environmental art to installation art was vital for this praxis to spread successfully, since it obliterated any link to possible socialist or revolutionary approaches and thus appeared adequate to the new industrial organization model of museums, considering that any exhibition is to be *installed.* At the same time, referencing alternative art praxis was a way to make amends for excessive market euphoria of the previous decade, as well as for the fact that art had been gradually turned into a commodity. Apparently disappointing the art market, installation art being produced at first was usually for temporary projects and sometimes even made of ephemeral materials, hence resulting in nearly unsaleable works if compared to the traditional forms of a painting, sculpture or photography. Moreover, installation art cannot be classified as a medium, because it generally conveys a large number of media: from video to performance and often including well-established art genres such as the ones mentioned before. Despite any appearance, however, installation art proved to be very adaptable and fitted the new requirements of the global art system much better than traditional techniques. Indeed, museums and curators seem to have benefitted the most from the fact that installations are site-specific up to a point – although not in a strict sense – hence their presentation often draws international audience to a specific venue, be it for instance a recurrent group exhibition or a dedicated solo show. Consequently installation art reassured institutions that need to compete on a global scenario between one another and, furthermore, with other products of mass culture. As a matter of facts, contemporary art museums and exhibitions had and still have to struggle hard with the endless entertainment options available for the general public. Technical reproduction systems have afforded many opportunities, but couldn't yet reproduce the multiplicity of sensations and feelings given by the corporal presence of the audience in the case of installation art. The latter is capable of shaping the stage on which the work appears, such as in the case of video and film installations by artists like Bruce Naumann, Diana Thater, Douglas Gordon and Sam Taylor-Wood, whose works depend on a sort of physical interaction with spectators. The involvement of the viewer together with the spectacular quality of its display were certainly reasons enough for installation art to rise quickly into prominence and create a stable link with mass media culture and business corporations (Stallabrass, 2006a, pp.17-18).

In the aftermath of his solo show at Tramway, Gordon became one of the leading figures of the rising British artists' generation, but foremost he had successfully experimented with video and installation art, hence understanding that this strategy fitted his artistic purposes (Sans, 1996). Nevertheless, the Glasgow born author was well aware he needed to avoid any sort of self-repetition that would make his future artworks seem predictable. He was also conscious that critics were watching him closely to catch him out should he make false steps or revert to trite ideas. After *24 Hour Psycho*, many in the establishment expected him to produce another slowed down Hollywood movie, but slow motion could hardly become Gordon's brand, if he intended to keep arousing interest. In this regards, as Harald Fricke (1998, pp.30-31) pointed out, it is important to emphasize again that the Scottish artist meant to exploit the logical structure of filmed material in order to create situations that could possibly foster altered perception. Video as such – that is as a medium to convey a narrative – wasn't so much Gordon's aim, but rather the means to influence the viewer's psychological state of mind. Hence, soon after the presentation of

24 Hour Psycho, the young Glaswegian author chose to further apply the manipulation of filmed material, being convinced that it would provide valuable results for the psychological effect on the audience, as well as create spectacular artworks of high visual impact. However, he felt an experimentation stage was necessary, both to search for new video sources to exploit – which couldn't be solely Hollywood movies anymore – and to test feasible methods of image alteration. In order to unsettle expectations that lay on him, Gordon decided to avoid popular culture products, hence avoiding that his intentions and authorship over the final work would eventually fall in the background when weighed against the images he had used. Consequently he opted for found footage, especially amateur shots and medical clips he could find in archives or accidentally discover at flea markets, a he recalls in conversation with Graham Fagen:

> *"One thing that I wanted to do was that when '24 Hour Psycho' got so much attention everyone was waiting for the next slowed down Hollywood thing and I wanted to try and confound that, so I used the medical things, for all sorts of reasons, but that suited the idea of confounding people's expectations. [...] but also I didn't want to only work with high culture, and artists are some of the few people who can still drag objects or images or ideas out of the gutter and put them in a museum [...]. It could be completely experimental, it doesn't have to be always worked out, but it's very important that it happens." (Gordon in Fagen, 1999, pp.105-106)*

In summer 1993 the artist started to travel different places to seek for filmed materials, such as in London's Camden Town, where he searched the stalls for colour bootleg records or other shootings of live rock concerts dating back to the Sixties and Seventies. At the archives of the Wellcome Institute, again in the Capital, he further viewed hundreds of black and white clips of clinical studies related to the consequences of the First World War. In particular, his interest was aroused by cases of schizophrenia and other mental disorders, where external forces appeared to take control over the patient's body. The latter choice in favour of psychological disturbance seems to be a resilient theme of interest for Gordon, since it is linked to the villain character of *Psycho*, but it also represents the result of a conversation he had with art historian Francis McKee in 1993, who had compared watching *24 Hour Psycho* to a schizophrenic experience (Brown, 2004, p.40). In the same period he took part in a group exhibition at the Real Art Ways, the Institute of Contemporary Art in Hartford Connecticut, which was entitled *Purpose-Built: Long Distance Information* and curated by

Michael Corris. He took advantage of his American stay to search flea markets for a third possible source of found footage, that is vintage or black and white porn movies which possibly had to be shot by amateurs. After completing this period of thorough survey, he then carefully analysed what he had collected and tried different ways of viewing the source material: in slow motion or fast forward, soundless or loud, on monitors or projected onto a widescreen. Many of the records were of poor quality or in bad conditions, though this was exactly the reason why the artist believed blowing them up would render a new aesthetic quality, so that the images be watched and considered from a different perspective:

> *"[...] when I'd been looking at some of these again I slowed them down, really just to see what was happening in them, and as a kind of deconstruction of the performance aspect of it, then I projected them large, and all of a sudden the lack of quality became an incredibly beautiful quality, and I liked that idea as well, that you could again take in something form the gutter basically, something that is probably about fifth generation copy, all of a sudden you have it four metres by three metres in a museum, and it's undeniably beautiful, it's absolutely incredibly beautiful, and the amateurisms of it have their value, so you begin to establish a different kind of vocabulary in terms of ways of looking at something [...]." (Gordon in Fagen, 1999, pp.106-107)*

His research on found footage resulted in three series of large spatial installations that were divided into multiple projections on 4:3 size screens. The processed video material constitutes his main production in the period between 1994 and 1996, as it was the core of the four most significant solo shows held in those years, as well as of some group exhibitions promoted by the British Council and which will be discussed later on. These are the four mentioned solo exhibitions in chronological order[13]: the exhibition at Lisson Gallery in London in 1994, which also marked the official start of Nicholas Logsdail's representation of the Scottish artist; *Entr'Acte 3* curated by Jan Debbaut at the Van Abbemuseum in Eindhoven in 1995, being the first major museum show for Gordon to be housed in an important European institution; *Fuzzy Logic* curated by Christine Van Assche at the Centre Gorges Pompidou in Paris, again in 1995; finally, a comprehensive exhibition – almost a retrospective – curated by Rein Wolfs in 1996 at Migros in Zurich, the Museum für Gegenwartskunst of the Swiss city.

His solo show at the prestigious Lisson Gallery was seen as an important event in the artistic life of the Capital, as it was his first one after the success of *24 Hour Psycho*. As argued above, Gordon avoided reviving a Hollywood movie and instead presented different works, among those an ex-novo environmental installation and one of his textual works. However, he also took the chance to finally introduce two new types of works that would become part of his lasting production throughout the Nineties along with text-pieces, which are portrayed tattoos and articulate video installations. The textual work he had created on the occasion read "From someone lost, to someone found" and was mailed as usual to all guests for the opening, as well as applied onto a wall of the gallery[14]. The environmental installation, on the contrary, bore no title and consisted of a high voltage cable pulled across the gallery upper floor room at man's height with a photograph of Niagara Falls hanging on the side. Critics and audience were quite puzzled by this installation, because they found it hard to grasp its meaning – probably referring to the danger of imminent catastrophe looming onto the artist, whose reputation was in a sense hanging by a thread over a precipice. In any case, this work hardly made impression on critics, since it markedly seemed to owe its inspiration to conceptual tradition, hence being almost obsolete in the view of Martin Maloney on the pages of *Flash Art International*:

> *"[... Gordon's] philosophical speculation is obscured as the style is so closely associated with phenomenological speculation of relevance in art twenty-five years ago." (Maloney, 1995)*

Perhaps this environmental installation constituted a sort of distraction devised to protect the true new works Gordon was presenting to the London audience, which consisted of two video installations showed as a preview on the ground floor of Lisson[15]. Inside a darkened room the viewer could experience *Trigger Finger* and *10ms-1*, both created in 1994, which displayed the very first outcome of Gordon's research on manipulated clinical frames. The two video installations were made of two separate sets of black and white footage, each projected onto a screen of three metres by four put on the floor instead of being hung on the ceiling. All footage belongs to medical studies dating back to the First World War and show the bodily effects of psychological traumas caused by war experience. *Trigger Finger* shows a person's stretched forearm, probably a young man's, whose hand seems to mimic the act of shooting with a gun. For a few seconds the image seems still frame, but all of a sudden the hand shakes as if a shot had been fired and twists towards the camera focus. *10ms-1* instead shows a full shot of a young man wearing knickers who lies flat on the floor and repeatedly tries to get up. Despite appearing perfectly healthy, the man seems to fight hard against gravity and never actually succeeds in rising up completely. Both sequences last only a few seconds, but they are set to run in loop on the screens, hence their obsessive repetition suggests that the viewer can imagine no interruption. Gordon appears to emphasize how mind conditioning is able to influence the body, as well as how mental disorders are expressed by physical behaviour. Katrina Brown (2004, p.40) has convincingly described the twitching movement of the hand in *Trigger Finger* as if it was the physical recollection of an unknown trauma, like an indelible tattoo inscribed on the body. This concept of unforgettable memory acquisitions, albeit produced by actions, leads to the last two works on display at Lisson, that is two black and white photographs of the artist's tattooed arm. Entitled *Tattoo I* and *Tattoo II* (1994), they show two shots in which the artist's left arm seems to float against a white background, in the first picture from the top downwards and vice versa in the second. Halfway between the biceps and triceps the tattooed words "TRUST ME" can be read, obviously written in Bembo font that was by then identified as Gordon's primary script style. The stretched arm together with the featured words evoke thoughts of betrayal and forgiveness, trust and sentimental interdependence, but they also appear to credit the spectator with an invitation to share a psychological situation. The two photos taken in 1994 show some of many tattoos that Gordon would later have inscribed on his own skin, which appear to suspend any distinction between his art and his life. Hence, the artist becomes a living expression of his art, his body being used as a talisman for magical rites, as Gordon once expressed to Oscar Van den Boogard, before the latter would have one of the artist's tattoos made:

> *"[...] I view myself differently – you know the stories from the Middle Ages about people who came to the village and sold drugs, some substance or other, like the elixir of life. There are people for whom art is something like that. I believe in a new kind of medievalism. It's an obsession for me. A little shamanistic – but I would never claim to be a shaman." (Gordon in Van den Boogard, 1997, p.40)*

Indeed, the artist didn't only subject himself to this practice, but made projects over the years for other people to wear his textual works on their own skin, such as in the case of *Tattoo (for reflection)* (1997), which was presented at the Guggenheim in New York on the occasion of the exhibition for the Hugo Boss Prize in 1998. For this work Gordon convinced Dutch writer and dealer Oscar van den Boogaard to have a tattoo made on his left shoulder, which consisted in the word "GUILTY" written backwards, so that it could be read correctly only when seen in a mirror. The artist later took a colour picture of the tattoo showing Van den Boogaard's bare back together with its mirror reflection, hence allowing to read the inscribed word both backwards and correctly on the dealer's shoulder. Beyond the subtle irony of gashing and blaming an art dealer for indelible guilt, this project can also be openly related to physical manifestation of mental disorders, such as an ineradicable conscience burden. Yet the mirror, as well as the reflected image, was intended to lead to further considerations on the theme of the double self and split personality, hence dealing with the contemporary presence of positive qualities and their opposites in one and the same person, as stressed by Gordon:

> *"A tattoo like that has something Lacanian about it. To look in a mirror for the first time, see your own reflection, and that reflection shows your guilt... I wish I were getting the tattoo myself." (Gordon in Van den Boogard, 1997, p.39)*

The issue concerning the double self and the methodical use of mirrored images to evoke this represent a natural continuation towards investigating schizophrenia and other mental disorders, themes that were comprehensively developed by Gordon since 1995. In fact, the Lisson Gallery show just hinted at these issues, rather aiming at the psychological involvement of the viewer in a state of psychic suffering. As far as to the two video installations are concerned, on a comparison between *Trigger Finger* and *10ms1* the latter appears to have one more peculiarity that clearly characterizes this project as a true environmental installation, rather than a mere video-work. In fact, the screen on which the frames are projected is slightly tilted backwards – about fifteen degrees from a perpendicular position – so that it fails to recreate the typical cinematic experience of a parallel vision from the spectator's eye to the screen. This choice shows that the artist was by no means indifferent to the conditions of the work's display – quite the opposite, the installation was designed to interfere with the viewer's perception significantly. The screen arrangement seems to be intended to convey a sense of precarious stability, as well as irresistible downward pull, which are the precise feelings experienced by the young patient in the clinical footage. It comes then with no surprise that the title of the work refers to the approximate unit of measurement of the force of gravity, that is earth attraction at a speed of ten metres per second. Furthermore, it seems now clear that the artist intended to emotionally involve the viewer, starting with a careful consideration on the origin of the projected images. When watching the footage, one is instinctively drawn to think about its authenticity, as it is difficult to place the shooting in a specific context. When awareness emerges that the images might actually document a real patients' physical suffering, the viewers' perspective changes radically, as the audience is challenged to react to the obsessively repeated clips, as Gordon pointed out in conversation with Nancy Spector:

> *"One of the details that engaged me most with these works, was how people were able to pick up on the distress of the films – both physically and metaphorically. This was the point at which I started to talk less about voyeurism and more about sadism – because these films were so extreme in some ways." (Gordon in Spector, 1997, p.75)*

As a matter of facts, watching these video installations is hard to endure in the long run, unlike *24 Hour Psycho*, where the spectator is hypnotized by the images. Consequently, the viewer is intentionally transformed from the voyeur into the sadist, from the Peeping Tom who is still able to keep some distance from the desired images into the fully possessed and obsessed individual who can't resist psychological involvement, as expressed by Gordon himself:

> *"In the theatre usually you keep a distance. And the metaphor for distance is the metaphor of voyeurism. But when you get closer and closer you could actually take the sadist's part, if you are close enough to get involved." (Gordon in Haase, 1999, p.143)*

The result of Gordon's experimentation with found footage appeared to have reached with moving images that sort of disturbance, which the Glaswegian artist had already achieved by means of letters and telephone conversations in the early Nineties (Verzotti, 2006, p.18). With these two video installations he had proved capable of turning a comfortable situation such as film watching into an alienating experience, which compelled the audience to face a disturbing truth: the irresistible appeal that originates from the clash of comedy and cruelty – such as was the case of the young man constantly falling though conditioned by a mental illness – is a feature often exploited by the entertainment industry. Thus, the audience can be attracted to the spectacle of cinema while watching something absolutely repulsive.

Gordon's work with found footage, especially clinical material, allows one to set up a consistent parallel to the themes of research which Christine Borland was exploring around the same time on forensic methods, as they both tried to show what would have otherwise remained unseen (Richardson, 2011, p.164). Still working on collections and subsequent display of found objects, indeed in 1993 she went a step further calling in forensic scientists to do a project for the 2nd Tyne International exhibition in Newcastle-upon-Tyne. Down by the city docks, she roped off a piece of derelict land used as a car park and brought in police officers to gather the kind of samples that would have been collected in the course of a criminal investigation. Nothing very spectacular or glamorous was discovered in this improvised quest, though the laid out samples looked like ghostly traces of human life drawn from a geographic spot. Between 1994 an 1995 she was then working in France on anatomical representations for a solo show that would later be held at Galerie d'Eole, FRAC Languedoc-Rouissilon in Montpellier in 1997. Her repeated visits to a very famous local anatomy museum, which she struggled to gain access to, were meant to reference the collection in the same way she had done before in the case of anthropological or medical museums in Scotland and Ireland (Barclay Morgan, 1999). However, since she had been allowed neither to take any item from the museum nor to shoot pictures, the show was a presentation of a duality between her traced drawings and the photographs taken covertly with a spy camera. As argued before, the true shift in her practice occurred with her celebrated project *From Life* (1994-1997), first presented for her solo show at Tramway in 1994 and then brought to Berlin's Kunstwerke in 1996, as well as displayed at her first solo show for Lisson Gallery in 1997 along with another new skeleton piece[16]. The latter exhibition took place from April 12th to May 10th and was crucial for her later inclusion in that year's Turner Prize shortlist. In *From Life* forensic methods met casual obtained objects, when Borland set out to purchase a skeleton – as one would do with any commercial commodity – and then offered it to crime scientists to reveal the identity of the bones' person. What she did was recording each moment of the project: from ordering the bones to shooting their arrival, from unpacking them in her bedroom to having them examined by an osteologist. Borland recalls that the involved forensic scientist was absorbed by the project's aim, fully grasping the meaning the artist bestowed to her intervention:

> *"To her [the osteologist] they were not just a pile of old bones, and she felt what I was doing was a gesture to mark this life that had fallen through the net." (Borland in Bredin, 1997)*

Embarking on articulate research projects appears likely to be a feature that both Gordon and Borland acquired during their training at the

Environmental Art Department. Thus the growing opportunities they faced between 1993 and 1995, when both were to be considered rising artists, allowed them to unfold new and more thorough strategies, finally being able to refine their artistic production with a bit more serenity. Therefore, the solo show at Lisson Gallery in December 1994 proved crucial to understand the new course in Gordon's creativity, which was by then characterized by the predominance of video installations that tackled the audience's response. Furthermore, he also appeared to have found a fertile strain of themes to concentrate on with several rather unconventional media he found appropriate, in particular dealing with schizophrenia, split personality and altered mental states. In Autumn 1995 he was given another pivotal opportunity to pursue research on found footage thanks to Van Abbemuseum curator in Eindhoven, who offered him the first comprehensive solo show in a relevant European museum. The young Glasgow artist had raised Debbaut's interest already in 1993, when the latter appreciated Gordon's instruction pieces displayed at Lisson Gallery for the group exhibition *Wonderful Life*. The solo show *Entr'Acte* at the museum in Eindhoven also started a tight professional partnership between Gordon and the Dutch curator, that would later bear other relevant possibilities, such as the publication of a retrospective catalogue[17]. Titled *Kidnapping* (Cat.1998), the catalogue was published by Van Abbemuseum and consists of a long conversation between Debbaut and Gordon, in an attempt to retrace the origin of the artist's works and ideas – placed somewhere in-between reality and fiction. For *Entr'Acte* the Scottish author continued to experiment with medical clips, trying to further challenge the psychological endurance of the audience, although he didn't pursue plain provocation or shock effect. On this occasion he visited a medical archive in Utrecht to obtain new material for an ad hoc installation consisting of six separate black and white clips titled *Film Noir* (1995). Altogether they were presented as a single articulate installation and projected onto six three by four metre screens placed in the darkened main hall of the museum. Five videos showed extracts from one and the same clinical footage, which dated back to the Second World War and documented a patient's response to insulin-coma therapy. The five screens showed different parts of the man's body shortly after receiving this treatment, that at the time was very common to relieve pain caused by psychological trauma. For this therapy the patient would be induced in a comatose state by means of insulin injections, in order to be awakened later with high doses of sugar. The five videos running showed details of the patient's physical reactions while awakening: *Film Noir (Hand)* focused on the finger movements; *Film Noir (Perspire)* showed sweat running down the man's eyebrow; *Film Noir (Fear)* was a close range cut of the patient's face, clearly conveying high anxiety; finally, *Film Noir (Twins)* consisted of two screens set side by side – one in vertical position and the other horizontally – both of which displayed full images of the man's head. The sixth video was located in the centre of the hall and displayed a different footage, instead: *Film Noir (Fly)* was indeed abstracted from supposedly scientific clips found in a flea market that showed a blow up of a dying fly lying on its wings. The inclusion of this shooting created a clear parallel with the kind of medical footage of the patient's pain, as if both the latter and the fly were the victims of cruelty, resulting in a dual drive of fascination and yet repulsion for the helpless viewer. A few months later Gordon reprised a modified version of the installation conceived for the Van Abbemuseum, in order to display it on the occasion of his solo show *Fuzzy Logic* at the Centre Gorges Pompidou in Paris, which was curated by Christine Van Assche. Titled *Fuzzy Logic* (1995), the piece maintained the same environmental structure, which was six screens installed in a large darkened room for visitors to walk among them, sometimes coming between the light beams and the screens. However, the only footage remaining from the original installation was *Film Noir (Fly)*, which Gordon repeated on all six screens, though the projections were not synchronized. Due to this latter visual strategy, looking at the frames of the magnified insect would soon induce disorientation onto the viewer because of a kind of sensory overload.

In autumn 1996 Gordon finally presented in Zurich the results of his research on bootleg records filmed during rock concerts of the Sixties and Seventies, which were the first colour footage series he used for an installation, though still keeping it soundless[18]. The occasion was an extensive solo exhibition organized by Rein Wolfs at Migros, the Museum of Contemporary Art in the Swiss city, marking the second important solo show in a relevant European institution. Among other works, the Glasgow artist presented three new video installation in the main hall, where they were displayed onto 4:3 projections screens together with two earlier clinical clips, that is *10ms-1* and *Hysterical* (1995). The three new works were titled *Bootleg (Bigmouth)*, *Bootleg (Cramped)* and *Bootleg (Stoned)*, each one of them processing a clip from a different rock concert which showed in a loop respectively the front-men of The Smiths, of The Cramps and finally Mike Jagger of the Rolling Stones, while they were mimicking a state of insanity on stage. Using these frames, Gordon displayed socially unacceptable behaviour originated through drug abuse, a fundamental feature of rock music that created a bond between the stars and their audience. Hence, the title of Gordon's installations referred both to the fact that the shootings had been taken illegally, as well as to the illicit behaviour displayed by the singers. However, the intended effect for Gordon was to combine the clips of raving rock stars – rolling half naked on the stage because of their distressed state of mind – together with the screening of authentic mental illness displayed in clinical clips, which were hard to separate from the bootleg records:

> *"What interested me about the show in Zurich, where I showed three bootleg pieces and two medical pieces all together in the same room was that it was very difficult to tell the difference between them." (Gordon in Fagen, 1999, p.107)*

The three videos of the Bootleg series take insanity on a very different meaning, if compared with the medical pieces. In fact, they rather seemed to explore the origin of behaviours that society associates to madness or bestiality, thus being considered undesirable. With the Migros exhibition Gordon had accomplished the strain of experiments he had begun at Lisson Gallery in 1994, trying to reach sensational effects with video installations that dealt with mental disorder. All pieces belonging to this period were characterized by their physical presences, which was intended to impress viewers and affect their psychological perception. As highlighted by art historian Rein Wolfs (1996, p.8), Gordon's video projections are meant to pay impression on the spectator fostering mental confusion due to the environmental conditions of the work's fruition.

Although almost completely absorbed with the use of found footage in this period, still Gordon did not forsake the strain of Hollywood movies altogether. Despite the risk of repeating the pattern of *24 Hour Psycho,* in 1995 the artist worked on a new slow motion project, which was fully realized only in 2001. The purpose was to take to the extreme the proceedings he had exploited for Hitchcock's movie, which meant he intended to expand the projection time until finally overlapping with the time span referred to in the storyline of the featured film. Specifically, Gordon intended to work on another renowned movie belonging to his childhood imagery, but this time he had chosen a Western, thus exploiting a different type of iconic entertainment category[19]. The film was *The Searchers,* shot in 1956 by John Ford with legendary John Wayne in the title role, revolving around a father's desperate search for his daughter who was kidnapped by Indians. Gordon's ambitious project meant to crush narrative time into real time by slowing the film down to five years, which was the time span of Wayne's original quest in the movie:

> *"The five-year project has to do with how one movie of less than two hours' duration can possibly portray the misery of this man's waiting. The notion of so-called 'real' time is dependent on whether you're sitting outside or inside [...]" (Gordon in Rosengarten, 1999, p.17)*

In order to do so, he needed to turn down the projecting speed to only four frames per hour, since the film lasted one hundred and thirteen minutes run in real time lapse. The idea behind this work was in a sense to present the artist's personal tribute to the theme of time flow that was the subject matter of this epic tale. However, Gordon was aware of the extreme difficulties to put this project into effect, still he tirelessly strived to spread this idea. The original plan was to organize a sort of open-air cinema such as a drive-in, though it would more likely have been a drive-by, that is to say a screen set beside a main road to be seen from the passing cars. He called the project *5 Year Drive-By* and planned to mount the installation in the desert of Utah, an archetypal landscape for Western fictions. According to Nancy Spector, *5 Year Drive-By* fully stands in the tradition of formal conceptual art, as Gordon admitted that the project didn't need to be realized in order to express the chosen research theme:

> *"Sure, the piece need not be made. But in some ways, the struggle necessary to realize it and situate it where I want it runs parallel to the narrative of the original film." (Gordon in Spector, 1997, p.72)*

However, he repeatedly tried to translate the project into reality, the first attempt of which took place at the Kunstverein in Hannover in 1997, when the film was shown outdoors in front of the museum for 9 consecutive hours from dusk to dawn. The viewers who resisted the whole night experienced physical and mental exhaustion, as the extreme use of slow motion lead to the explosion of cinematic storytelling, which in the opinion of the artist caused the movie and the viewers to exchange their roles and power relation:

> *"[...] I know that the relationship between viewer and image is rarely fair, but this five-year project is almost a complete switch in roles. Where the viewer/voyeur is always assumed to be in the commanding position in relation to cinema/ television/video, the simple alteration of speed, and the explosion of traditional cinematic narrative makes this relationship no longer viable. The viewer becomes a slave to the image." (Gordon in Spector, 1997, p.74)*

In 1999 the work was shown again in Germany for a few months at the Neue Nationalgalerie in Berlin, where the work on display could be seen from the outside of the transparent building designed by Mies van der Rohe. Walking along Potsdamer Straße in front of the Nationalgalerie any pedestrian or driver could see the almost frozen images at any time of day and night. The project was fully produced only six years after being conceived, on occasion of the artist's first American solo show at the Los Angeles Museum of Contemporary Art, MoCA, when the screen for Gordon's projection was set up at the roadside in Twentynine Palms, against a semi-desert background as he had originally intended.

Gordon's massive use of ready material for his video installations obtained by means of appropriation and then processed through different manipulation techniques, can be related to the general development of visual arts in the late 20th century, which again has been convincingly summed up by Hal Foster (1996). In his writings on the *return of the real*, the American scholar drew interesting conclusions about the concept of the real, which in his opinion had permeated artistic praxis and methods of the last few decades. Foster (1996, pp.1-71) argued that the true distinctive trait of the period under consideration was a shift from a kind of art focusing on formal aspects towards another trend that was rather concentrating on conceptual issues. However, the latter change did not lead – as may be expected – to forsaking figurative art in favour of abstract art, or realism in favour of pure imagination. Quite the contrary, the American scholar demonstrated that the transition from form to idea actually gave rise to two separate trends, of which only one was rejecting realism, such as in the case of minimal art and early Conceptual Art. The concurrent trend, instead, would start from realism itself to achieve a new concept of reality, one that didn't result from its formal representation, but which was rather meant to render the traumatic experience of reality as such. According to Foster (1996, pp.132-146), the latter tendency included Pop Art as well as Hyper-Realism and was overtly aimed at interpreting life experience in terms of historical trauma: art no longer wished to soften the clash with reality by means of a comforting delusion. The critic further described two main strategies for the return of the real that had been adopted by artists in the last decades of the 20th century. First comes illusionism, where the recreation of reality could be brought to its extreme limit, which is represented by the use of real objects, though distorted in appearance or in scale as in the case of Jeff Koons' works. The second strategy would instead consist in absolutely rejecting illusionism, such as was done by Abject Art, which intended to reach reality by abusing the human body. So while the first of the two strategies meant to discover the real by means of its objects, the second was up at performing a sort of de-constructivist analysis. In both cases, however, the artist presided over the artistic procedure with absolute authority, since the real he or she was investigating referred to cognitive and traumatic experiences on an individual level. As regards both Gordon's video installations and his previous works, provided that his procedures are seen in the light of Foster's (1996, pp.152-168) above considerations, one may argue that the Scottish artist recurred to different approaches towards the real. While it is true that the author most rigorously used the methods of Conceptual Art for his instructions and text pieces, he also made systematic use of appropriation of real products such as Hollywood films or found footage. Furthermore, considering the realist strain, while Foster divided realism into two opposing trends, even in this case Gordon appears to have made use of both given possibilities. Indeed, taking possession of Hollywood movies such as *24 Hour Psycho*, albeit altered in its projection time, can be considered typical of extreme illusionism. At the same time, the way the artist manipulated the filmed material resulted in a de-constructivist process, almost sectioning the real material consisting of show business leftovers. These considerations appear to emphasize that in the years from 1993 to 1995 Gordon had reached a more complete thematic and stylistic maturation that coincided with the more general developments in contemporary art. Furthermore, he also seemed to have acquired the skill to turn his artistic purposes into consistent projects by mastering the different media he had chosen, in particular text-pieces and video installations. The events of the year 1996 would finally demonstrate he had truly reached a level of full maturity, as he proved able to propose the right projects for crucial events in his career.

6.4. British art sprawl and export: patronized touring, inland and abroad

When considering the possible drivers of an artist's strategy to success, a key issue is to be raised about the specific location, where an artist has settled to thrive and work. In order to enhance individual visibility and foster its own career path, the case of creative industries has demonstrated the importance of both concentration – that means living close to other artists – and localization, which should preferably be in relevant cities for the art system (Caves, 1998, pp.33-35). The same is true for all artistic disciplines, since innovation of subjects and techniques is bound to distinct geographical areas set in a specific time. It has been argued before, that

London and Glasgow held very different positions inside the United Kingdom at the beginning of the Nineties: while the first was at the heart of Britain's art system and only needed to reactivate its functions, the latter lingered at its periphery with no supporting infrastructure of museums and galleries that had to be invented anew. Laying aside the differences between specific cities, as the case of Douglas Gordon and various other Glaswegians has shown so far, the question of location is not centred on the chosen city alone. In fact, the Transmission generation found ways to go far beyond their hometown boarders and display works across Britain and Europe, exploiting every opportunity at home and abroad to enhance their network capital and share it then among the other local artists. Indeed, many occasions that the Glasgow based artists were able to take advantage of were originated thanks to their individual mobility, such as by means of Gordon's plentiful London connections. The issue with location must therefore be extended to the entire nation under consideration, since most assuredly an artist's primary strength is represented by the general country system that is backing him or her. As a matter of facts, it is probably undeniable that the level of economic and cultural development of a nation is crucial even for an artist, since both the state's general wealth standard and its art system are likely to influence an author's career path. The capability of spreading cultural products – both at home and abroad – is definitely dependent on the industrial strength of a country, as well as to the depth and articulation of the nation's art system, which includes the specific number, size and role of different players. At least since the late 19th century, high on the heels of universal expositions, international exhibitions and fairs proved that each nation displays itself to the world also through the art it produces. Of course, economic power easily makes the difference, because art trends are most likely to conform to the production of dominant countries. One can hardly deny the economic predominance of the United States worldwide, which is paralleled by its power in the art field, since their industrial and political authority is matched by the capability to steer the global art system by means of galleries and collectors, magazines and publishing houses, universities and academies, museums and foundations. Hence, the general principle according to which a strong country is able to foster its art production worldwide appears to be still in force, because a nation's best cultural products become very effective promotion tools for the country at large (Vettese, 2007, p.50). As far as the foreign art market is concerned, Stallabrass (2006b, pp.196-203) argues that public establishments function as a means of spreading national creativity, thus even supporting the commodity industry at an international level. As a matter of facts, it can be observed that immediately after recession Great

Britain tried to improve its national economy worldwide, the arts becoming an advertisement driver that could improve the country's image. In a way the sensation caused by the YBA generation internationally could be exploited and further amplified to bestow the nation with an innovative and fashionable reputation. Both John Major's conservative government and especially Toni Blair's new course would indeed highly praise the British visual arts, patronizing events and allocating more funds for touring exhibitions. In 1997 Secretary of Cultural Virginia Bottomley even expressed her firm belief that British art was the most stimulating and innovative in the world (Walden, 1997, p.10). Though the latter might seem a roughly exaggerated statement, it clearly indicates that the British establishment was convinced that the arts – amongst them young British artists, as well as fashion, music and cinema – represented a valuable asset to strengthen the national image. Promoting the visual arts abroad would thus help to redefine *Britishness* in such a way that would prove much more effective on the art market and for the UK's general economy.

The start of public institutions' massive and systematic promotion of British art abroad can be tracked down to the group of young artists who contributed to the *Aperto* section of the forty-fifth Biennale in Venice, curated by Achille Bonito Oliva in the summer of 1993. *Aperto* was dedicated to rising artists under-forty years of age from each participating nation and was organized in temporary premises at the Magazzini del Sale, the historical salt warehouse of the once Venetian Republic. This section had been launched already in 1980 by Bonito Oliva himself, whose purpose was to overcome the Biennale's ingrained oversight towards art produced by younger artists of little renown (Vecco, 2002, p.33). Hence, each national delegation traditionally present in Venice was asked to have commissioners selecting at their discretion a group of under-forty artists to send along for the *Aperto* section. In 1993 the chosen delegation for Britain included eight artists, all of them ascribable at large to the rising alternative scene: Christine Borland, Henry Bond, Angela Bulloch, Mat Collishaw, Damien Hirst, Simon Patterson, Julie Roberts and Georgina Starr. Sending along this group of artists proved that the British Council, which was responsible for the choice, had rested the future of British Art on the YBA generation. In fact, the selection was by no means a matter of pure chance, since the British Council had summoned Matthew Slotover and Benjamin Weill to curate the British delegation, the former being co-founder of *Frieze* magazine and the latter one of its leading journalists. The choice in favour of the new generation of artists had thus been made even before picking the specific contributors, since the British Council would trust two people openly linked to the YBA generation. The establishment's stance in favour of curators belonging to the rising art scene was further confirmed both at home and abroad on various relevant occasions, such as for the following delegation sent to Venice for the Hundredth Anniversary of the Biennale in 1995 and for the fourth British Art Show in November of that same year. The recurring names among the new curators were for instance Liam Gillick, Gregor Muir, Graham Fagen and James Roberts, revealing that a transition towards a new generation of curators was being endorsed the same way that the YBA shift was established (Muir, 2011, p.125). Indeed, young artists and curators, as well as new critics and journalists appeared to support one another as a sort of unitary faction against the older established groupings, in order to achieve a common advancement of their position in the art field (Vettese, 2007, p.21). The approach can be roughly described as a sort of roped party: whenever a curator sponsoring the YBA faction was appointed for an important exhibition – such as *Wonderful Life* at Lisson Gallery or the *Aperto* section in Venice – he or she would invite artists belonging to the same grouping, while supportive press and critics bestowed great praise on the chosen authors, as well as on the artworks displayed. Although the rising generation of British artists, curators and critics didn't share a unitary programme or common style, as argued in previous chapters, still they acted as a homogeneous faction, including several players set in different roles of the art system which offered reciprocal support, in order to establish their hold on contemporary art. As a matter of facts, mutual endorsement is a general feature of the art system, since even the critics and curators become successful only if they have discovered new talents, their job being that of offering a unitary theory capable of summing up several artists and supplying it to museum directors. This attitude clearly reveals that the art world, like any specific field or sector, is shaped by factions that share common values or interests in its inner circle and try to sprawl them by prevailing over other groups or forming alliances with one another to enhance their position. For this reason it was crucial that together with the rising tide of artists there were new players also among the other roles of the system – such as new curators, critics and dealers – that engaged this collective struggle. The new players were often former artist candidates that had studied together with the rising authors, but didn't make it so far, hence switched over to different roles in the field of art giving support to their previous colleagues.

Indeed the art world appears to be divided into factions, each with its gatekeepers who adopt their own criteria for determining what art should look like and who the most influential artists are supposed to be. Every grouping in the art system can't help but rely on its own theory of art, claiming its internal consistency and objectivity, as argued by art philosopher Joseph Margolis (2000, pp.126-127). Hence, as further suggested by Arthur Danto (2008), in order to grasp the internal development of the visual arts it is necessary to concentrate on art narratives, criteria and preferences adopted by the different factions in the system and by means of which they describe art. Julian Stallabrass maintains that the period in which the YBA emerged was characterized by the clash between two conflicting art trends, which were neo-expressionism of the Eighties versus a neo-conceptual strain, drawn towards the return to realism described by Hal Foster. These opposing views are well represented for instance by two renown curators of that period, Frenchman Jean Clair (2005, 2011) and Italian Francesco Bonami (2009, 2010), whose opinions are useful to analyse the conflicting parties in the art field. While the former condemned almost all art created in the Nineties, the latter proved to be an enthusiastic supporter of that decade's rising trends. Clair's (2005, p.74) strain of thought can be considered decisively conservative, since he still held up 19th century's traditional categories – that is painting and sculpture – and romantically conceived art's aim as being a "harmonic representation of our idea of the world, its inhabitants and its gods". In his view, any attempt other than idealising life and respecting life's sacredness shouldn't be considered as art, albeit he was well aware of a massive push towards a tautological and material kind of art, which seemed to renounce to the past and manufacture artworks as on an assembly line. In many of his writings Clair pinpointed American culture supremacy, which in his opinion had led to the hyper-evaluation of the artist's role, as well as to the financial drift of the art system. Clair (2011, pp.14-25) claimed that this situation was stigmatized by a different conception of the role of contemporary art museums in Europe and in the US. While in the former case they were meant to reinforce historical awareness, America's establishments appeared unconcerned with history, playing an active role on the art market and therefore ready to dispose of their collections. The French curator believed that the world's financial oligarchy – though represented by few institutions and galleries he does not care to mention – was in full control of the art's sake, having replaced the refined and educated bourgeoisie of the early 20th century. Consequently, in Clair's opinion the result couldn't be anything but a sort of immaterial, banal and meaningless production, which had turned its back on true art that should rather be centred on physical objects of rational and moral value[20]. Jean Clair blamed artists such as Marcel Duchamp and Joseph Beuys, Andy Warhol and Jeff Koons – but also curators like Harald

Szeemann – for causing a fatal disruption, which diverted attention from the art work onto the artist[21]. In his view, the author's acquired centrality would have been originated by the rise of a kind of neo-paganism in contemporary art, which turned the artist into a true messiah that could even found a new personal mythology. In contrast, Francesco Bonami embraced the upcoming trends of the Nineties as well as the new instances and media arising in contemporary production, of which the YBAs were chief representatives (*Sogni e conflitti*, Cat.2003, pp.XXII-XXIII). Persuaded that there is no such thing as objective truth in art, but only different opinions and stances that should be dealt with, the Italian curator values art as a "crucial expression of our world in the attempt to understand it" (Bonami, 2009, pp.5-6). In several writings, he identified artists as those who are able to transform their lives into art pieces, feeling the urge to talk to mankind and being able to produce works that the general audience would appreciate as inevitable or unforgettable. The aim of visual arts would thus lay in the ideas and meanings conveyed by the artists into their works, rather than in the chosen technique or tangible form. This difference in perspectives between Clair and Bonami clearly leads the to a divergent opinion on specific artists, so if Jean Clair disapproves of Duchamp, Bonami credits the French author for relieving artists of the burden of tradition (2009, pp.27-32, 87-90). As regards more recent authors, while the French critic condemns Koons for transforming art into a commodity and behaving like an unscrupulous Wall Street trader, conversely the Italian curator thinks the American artist would have fully grasped the spirit of his time, as he had proved capable of transforming consumerism into art. Although both positions are debatable and account just for two relevant players of the Nineties' art system, they appear to possess an inner consistency and adequately represent clashing positions in the art field of that period.

Considering the arduous rise of the YBA generation, the struggle between these and other positions was pretty tough, since the predominance in the art system was at stake. The appointment of Slotover and Weill as curators of the *Aperto* exhibition in 1993 needs thus to be seen as a major achievement for the emerging generation of artists and curators, who could fully profit from this endorsement. As regards to the specific artists picked for Venice, besides the obvious selection of Damien Hirst and many other authors belonging to the original Goldsmiths grouping, the true development appeared to be the inclusion of Christine Borland and Julie Roberts as the only non-London-based artists. In the words of *Frieze* editor Slotover it seemed that the only mention-worthy art events outside of the capital would be referred to the Glasgow scene that had caused much excitement in the previous two years:

> *"I certainly felt that there should be some artists from Glasgow in the selection to reflect the significance of the activity there." (Slotover in Lowndes, 2010, p.179)*

Consequently, Borland and Roberts were the first Glaswegian artists to be picked by the upcoming tide of touring exhibitions, which were prompted by the British Council. For the Venice Biennale, Borland displayed *A Lifetime of Love* (1993) that attracted a great deal of attention: it consisted of a stack of woollen blankets that dealt wit the masculine-feminine juxtaposition, presenting comforting items that could also become suffocating. From the 1993 *Aperto* section on, a number of Glasgow based conceptual artists – amongst whom Gordon and Borland on a permanent basis – managed to constantly travel abroad as they were featured by relevant YBA shows the British Council and other institutions would organize to promote the rising art scene. The durable inclusion of this group of artists finally succeed in linking Scotland to the European visual arts and turned Glasgow into the junction between homeland and global art world (Richardson, 2011, p.156). However, these artists kept a relatively low profile in their hometown, given the parochialism of the Glasgow art establishment until the late Nineties, and thus avoided the intense media exposure of their London counterparts, which helped the Glaswegians to better survive the later downfall of the YBA frenzy (Lowndes, 2010, p.234).

The 1993 *Aperto* edition was the last one of its series, as the following Biennale curator, the French critic Jean Clair, would finally abolish this section in 1995. Heedless of this abolition, the British Council decided to carry on independently by renting the so-called Scuola di San Pasquale set amid the cloisters of the monastery of San Francesco della Vigna (Di Martino, 2003). There the UK intended to allocate a pavilion to under-forty British Artists in Venice, thus supporting the systematic spread abroad of Britain's young artists. In the autumn preceding the 46th Biennale, Ann Gallagher was appointed new director of the visual arts for the British Council and proved crucial for focussing the public establishment's attention on the rising trends (Muir, 2011, pp.122-125). In fact, in sight of the 1995 Venice Biennale she called for collaboration Gregor Muir and James Roberts, who were still both *Frieze* columnists and had been curators of some important YBA shows in London, belonging to the same age group and cultural background as the rising artists (Rose, 1995, p.7). According to Muir, the acronym YBA would have been coined at the first preparatory meeting for the Venice exhibition, which was later titled *General Release*, although he appears to underestimate the importance of Saatchi's group shows of the same period:

> *"It was during this meeting, towards the end of 1994, that we stopped saying 'young British artists' and started saying 'YBA'. In truth, we'd simply given up stumbling through the unabridged version and 'YBA' made for easy shorthand, but this was the first time I'd ever heard the term used in regular discussion. [...] YBA was not the result of the 'Young British Artists' shows taking place at the Saatchi Gallery. Instead, the term referred to an all-encompassing phenomenon that included a number of different artists from a variety of backgrounds." (Muir, 2011, pp.122-123)*

Nine individual artists plus three pairs were invited to exhibit in Venice and they were all first-time participants in the Biennale, even though they already had drawn attention in past years both at home and abroad. Besides Douglas Gordon, there were Fiona Banner, Adam Chodzko, Ceal Floyer, Tom Gidley, Gary Hume, Jaki Irvine, Elizabeth Wright and Cerith Wyn Evans, together with the brothers Dinos and Jake Chapman, Matthew Dalziel and Louise Scullion, the twin sisters Jane e Louise Wilson. More than half of the artists listed – including Gordon – had participated in the exhibition *Wonderful Life* at Lisson Gallery two years before, curated by James Roberts himself. The centre of gravity of the delegation was clearly set in the British capital, since twelve of the fifteen artists had studied in London academies. However, only seven had graduated at Goldsmiths, which marked the end of the group's hegemony over the general YBA generation. The remaining non London based artists – that is Gordon, Dalziel and Scullion – were again all Glaswegians and had furthermore attended the Glasgow School of Art, confirming that the city's alternative scene was the only grouping who could keep pace with the artistic events in the capital. Muir and Roberts made further capital of this opportunity by publishing an exhibition catalogue that detailed an extensive chronology of significant events related to the YBA in the years comprised between 1990 and 1995 (*General Release*, Cat.1995, pp.72-103). The timeline included two main works by Douglas Gordon, which were *Above all else...* shown at Barclays Young Artist's Award in 1991 and, of course, *24 Hour Psycho* displayed at Tramway in 1993. The curators' essay attempted to set the development of young British artists in their original context, explaining that these authors had been able to stand out by means of their marked resourcefulness: according to Muir and Roberts (1995, p.49), right from the start these young people could stand the severe recession thanks to self-promotion and to autonomously initiated exhibitions. The catalogue essay was definitely an early bid to submit an official history of the YBAs – as seen from insiders of this generation – marking crucial milestones of their evolution towards establishment. However, it was probably the overdue enthusiasm for the rising artists that fed several inaccuracies in the story told by Muir and Roberts, since they appeared to depict the young authors as knight-errants who had fought all alone against the evil establishment. The two curators obviously favoured their own generation and intended to exploit this opportunity to finally ordain the YBAs as a mainstream trend, since it was the first exhibition explicitly dedicated to these artists and entirely sponsored by state institutions.

This attempt apparently proved successful, since the Venice show in 1995 was but one of a number of experiences supported by the British Council abroad and started a season of touring group exhibitions that were promoted all over the world. This strategy was effectively implemented, such that Friedrich Meschede (1998, p.175) exposed the activity of the British institutions, deemed too aggressive and often intrusive with regards to foreign countries. According to the German critic's calculation, the British Council had promoted as many as seventy projects and twelve group shows in Germany over the biennium 1997-1998 involving a hundred-and-fifty-three British artists, while only ten German artists had shown their works in the United Kingdom in the same period due to government funding. Stallabrass (2006b, p.196) agrees that the export effort of the British institutions was consistent and quite extraordinary, successfully riding on the back of US cultural hegemony and exploiting the global ascendency of the English language, in order to favour the penetration of young artists from Britain. Indeed, when the 1995 Biennale closed, *General Release* was shown in several other locations, including the exhibition *Artisti britannici a Roma* from 22nd May to 29th June 1996, curated by Mario Codognato (*Artisti Britannici*, Cat.1996). In this period Gordon also took part in further group shows organised by the British Council, such as *Arte inglese d'oggi* at Galleria Civica in Modena in 1995; *The Scottish Autumn* at Ludwig Museum in Cologne and at Kortars Muvesti Museu in Budapest later that year; *Full House – Young British Art* at Wolfsburg Kunstmuseum in 1996; *Swan-off* at Uppsala Konstmuseum still in the same year; finally, *Emotion: Young British and American Art from the Sammlung Goetz* at Hamburg Deichtorhallen in 1998.

In all of the above occasions Gordon displayed his new video installation *Hysterical*, which he had originally devised for *General Release* in Venice and that belonged to his research output on early 20th century psychiatric clips[22]. Two new features of video manipulation proved relevant in the case of this piece and influenced the later production of the Glasgow artist: on the one hand the employment of two screens hanging side by side, while on the other hand the footage shown on the second screen was reversed from right to left as to create a mirror image. Both screens were standing on the floor and were slightly inclined, while the projectors were as usual lying on the floor, so that the viewer could eventually interpose between the projectors and the screens. As with previous works, the mentioned features made the viewer aware of the environmental quality of the work, hence it clearly represents a video installation rather than a mere video projection. The footage shown in constant loop on the two screens was a kind of medical black and white short film, starring two doctors and a woman apparently suffering from some mental illness. In the course of the action she seems often seized with convulsions and hysteria attacks, causing a severely disturbed behaviour. The scene appears to be set in bedroom with a window on the background, but upon closer observation it appears as if it may be a carefully planned film stage. The woman is wearing a long black dress and a Carnival-like mask on her face, while the two men look like doctors dressed in early 20th century style. After an initial chat that the viewer can't hear, the doctors suddenly prevent the patient from falling down repeatedly and in the end they appear to placate her with some sort of treatment, finally forcing her to lay down on the bed. The last frame shows the two men quickly turning towards the camera with an unnatural smile, as if they had been aware of being filmed. For the video installation, Gordon chose to show the sequence in real time on the first screen, while the mirror image on the second one was projected in slow motion. Consequently, the events displayed at the original pace seemed very quick for the spectator to realize what exactly was going on in the film, though the slowed down frames on the second screen weren't of much help either, since they created a sense of alienation and seemed to suggest the footage was but a piece of skilful acting. The viewers found themselves caught by the ambiguity of the filmed actions and soaked up the almost comic and – at the same time – dismal atmosphere. Gordon aimed indeed at creating this sort of uneasiness, which he achieved by means of the contrast between the comedy effect of the footage – almost like a silent movie sketch – and the seriousness of the medical observation documented in the clip. Furthermore, the constant repetition of the projection turned the public's original curiosity into a sort of perverse sadism, allowing no escape from the display of the recorded trauma. In addition to the touring exhibitions promoted by the British Council, *Hysterical* was displayed on other occasions in this period, the most relevant being *Am Rande der Malerei*, curated by Ulrich Loock at the Kunsthalle in Bern in Autumn 1995, which featured other two UK artists, Angela Bulloch and Jessica Diamond.

After numerous exhibitions abroad, Gordon profited also from the activities of other British institutions inside the UK, which also turned to the promotion of these emerging artists. *The British Art Show 4* held in 1995 was one of these opportunities that was meant to foster publicity for new British artists at home, being a large group show organized every five years by the Hayward Gallery at the South Bank Centre in London. For the first time in the story of this event, the 1995 edition was set up as a touring exhibition, thus travelling from London to Edinburgh, from Cardiff to Manchester. Richard Cork, Rose Finn-Kelcey and Thomas Lawson were asked to curate the exhibition and select the participating artists, albeit the latter two were also esteemed artists other than curators, Lawson in particular being even a renowned columnist for *Frieze*. In the curators' opinion, the 1995 edition should do justice the YBA generation, which had proved resourceful enough to rise up gradually into prominence (Cork, 1995, p.13). The exhibition featured twenty-six young artists, among whom many that had made the headlines of specialized magazines in the past five years, such as Damien Hirst, Tacita Dean, Mat Collishaw, the Wilson twins, Steve McQueen, Chris Ofili, Sam Taylor-Wood, Gillian Wearing, Gary Hume and Mark Wallinger. Their presence provided a fairly accurate idea of the emerging trends on the British art scene, confirming the centripetal feature of the London art market over the UK, since most of the contributors were active in the Capital city or had at least good connections to local establishment. In his catalogue essay, Lawson was very clear about the scope of the *British Art Show 4*, as well as on the infrastructure of Britain's art system:

> *"The show could not hope to be a survey of national trends but a selection of what we three could agree was the most challenging work made in Britain during the past five years. […] Contemporary art is a complex business in which artists/producers attempt to circulate their images and ideas through various international markets. To do this successfully, they need access to distribution systems […]. London, with its network of galleries, magazines, art schools and other artists, provides this in a way no other city in the country can. So, inevitably, the most ambitious artists gravitate there, at least for the years it takes to establish their careers. This truth is very clearly borne out by a glance at the biographies of the artists in this show." (Lawson, 1995, p.90)*

Albeit London artists appeared to have set the standard, the curators were well aware that the consistency of the body of artworks displayed was not to be found in style, but rather in the background and ambitions, themes and procedures which distinguished the new generation of artists. Indeed, the artists on show seemed to share that sort of 'high art lite' approach as described by Julian Stallabrass, which resulted in the use of everyday objects and in the creation of spectacular installations, which attracted both popular audience and media attention. In Lawson's opinion, sensationalism was a common quality that would thus trigger mixed reactions, challenging morality and sense of responsibility:

> *"I think it is clear that the work in this exhibition is not content to sit quietly on the wall; it is attention-grabbing, eye-popping, ear-bending. [...] the artists insist that we each think through the implications of what we see." (Lawson, 1995, p.94)*

The 1995 edition of the *British Art Show*, however, set the stage also to show further developments of the so-called YBA trend, that is primarily the use of new media technologies, which had finally become reasonably priced and easy to master. Many contributors displayed works created by means of computer graphics, large format photography, film and video, but they generally avoided setting the focus on the media themselves. According to James Roberts, who tried to provide YBAs with a consistent art theory, these media would have allowed a new break with the stagnant production of the earlier decade:

> *"[...] domestic video technology has simultaneously undergone a radical increase in quality and drop price, resulting in video-based work rising significantly in prominence. [...] Artists are producing work that involves print, photography, film, video and computer-based media [...], but are able to do so without drawing unnecessary attention to the medium itself. [...] This opening up of language has, inevitably, moved art away from static categories and many artists have looked back to Conceptual art practices from the late 1960s and early 1970s." (Roberts, 1995, p.51)*

Lawson (1995, p.94) agreed that technological means had been so gracefully and efficiently employed by the new generation of artists, that the primacy and importance of traditional artistic categories had been finally questioned. Concerning the themes and issues dealt with by these young authors, the curators noticed a particular engagement over existential anguish, psychological anxiety and identity disorders, which were addressed with a marked subjectivity and often irreverent humour. The above considerations of the curators obviously aimed at finding a unitary explanation and backing for the selected contributors, as well as for the general curatorial choices. Most of these reflections might even be consistent, though their explanatory nature falls rather short when artists other than the Londoners of the time are taken into consideration. The only non-London-based artists featured in the the *British Art Show 4* were four Glaswegians, once again proving the absolute relevance of the Glasgow art scene on a national and international level. Furthermore, three of the Glaswegians had attended the Glasgow School of Art – being Christine Borland, Douglas Gordon and Julie Roberts – while the fourth author, Kerry Stewart, had studied in Edinburgh and London, albeit living and working in Glasgow. The link to Glasgow was made over Thomas Lawson, who was well acquainted with Nicola White and Charles Esche, as well as with Pavel Büchler who was a teacher at the local art school (*The British Art Show 4*, Cat.1995, p.8). Furthermore, Lawson was even familiar with Gordon's work because of a long interview with the young artist about the latter's instruction pieces and telephone performances, which was published on *Frieze* in April 1993. Hence, Gordon was invited to display two recent video installations, being *10ms-1* and *Hysterical*, which needed some time for the audience to be fully absorbed as compared to some instant-jokes-artworks by his London based counterparts. Indeed, the Glasgow based artists in the exhibition were used to produce a very different kind of art projects, which were frequently immaterial and opposed complex and time-intensive works to the much more consumable and media friendly pieces of the Londoners. Far from demonstrating the existence of a unitary movement among the new generation of artists, the *British Art Show 4* finally highlighted further differences between the London art scene and the one in Glasgow.

The exhibition *Swan Off* in 1996, curated by Maria Lind in different Swedish locations, was a slight exception to the other group shows sponsored by the British Council, because it toured only Glaswegian artists – hence being a good opportunity to draw a distinction to the London art scene[23]. In fact, the six chosen contributors on show all belonged to the Transmission generation: works by Dave Allen, Christine Borland and Nathan Coley were exhibited in Stockholm, those by Jacqueline Donachie in Norrtälje, Julie Roberts' pieces in Solna and Gordon's installation in Uppsala. Surrounded by his old fellows and art school mates, Gordon did not present any of his previous video works, but decided to base his intervention partially on the principles of contextualism, that had been crucial for his studies at the Environmental Art Department[24]. He was inspired by his preparatory visit to the prospective venue housed in Uppsala castle, but also used some vintage footing found at the Wellcome Trust in London. The historic building in Uppsala had recently been renovated for adaptation as a museum, albeit the original structure and decorations of the castle had not been fully respected. In the first room of the venue, where Gordon's exhibition was to be held, the artist noticed a stucco bas-relief of an angel whose head had disappeared due to the lowering of the upper floor:

> *"At a certain point there was the relief of an angel. They just cut his head off. That was very strange: the image of an angel without a head. I was shocked that they would be that cruel to such a beautiful piece of decoration."* (Gordon in Haase, 1999, pp.144-145)

The headless image deeply impressed him and led him to connect the venue with his previous considerations on the violence implied in the act of beheading, which he had scrutinized by means of archive material found at the Wellcome Trust. In the course of his research on the subject, Gordon had further found out about the cruel scientific experiments conducted by a certain Dr. Baurieux in Montpellier around 1905. At the turn of the century, the French doctor had repeatedly tried to talk to decapitate heads, in order to measure the time-lapse between beheading and death. According to Baurieux's opinion, a severed head still reacted for thirty seconds on average, before the spark of life went out definitively. Gordon's original plan for Uppsala was to break in the ceiling above the angel bas-relief and liberate its head, a violent act that would have countered the fierce thirst for knowledge expressed by the French doctor's experiments in 1905. The artist was discouraged to cause any damage to the castle, hence the thought of a text that summarized the experiments of Dr. Baurieux, which should take exactly thirty seconds to be read. The final project for Uppsale was titled *...head* (1996) and consisted of three parts set in three different rooms of the museum: in the first room *30 Seconds Text* was shown at the foot of the angel's bas-relief by means of a simple overhead projector, while the next two rooms were darkened for a video projection to be displayed on a three-by-four metre screen. Again using black and white medical footage of the first half of the 20th century, the first video featured the recovery of a severed head, while the second sequence was extremely blurred, but clearly gave a glimpse of the decapitated body lying on the ground. Both critics and audience were quite shocked by the grisly outcome of the project, which caused deep anxiety even for the artist himself:

> *"I showed ...head only once, in Uppsala; I showed it never again, because I was too shocked by the images. [...] I think it worked, but it was very hard." (Gordon in Haase, 1999, pp.144-145)*

Although the Glasgow artist didn't display the complete installation ever again, he made *30 Seconds Text* into an environmental installation housed in a dark room with a time-lit bulb. The viewer was invited to enter a pitch-black room and could read the text in white letterings onto the wall, while the lights went out exactly after thirty seconds. Gordon installed this new piece for the first time at the Musée d'art moderne de la Ville of Paris in 1996, on the occasion of the group show *life/live* curated by Hans Ulrich Obrist, and then again at Venice Biennale in 1997 which earned him the prize as best young artist.

The numerous group shows that Gordon participated in between 1993 and 1996 helped the young author to practice a very important ability for a rising artist, which is in fact learning to make the right choice of pieces to display on which occasion. Besides producing interesting works, this appears to be a crucial feature for any artist who is given good chances in relevant venues or exhibitions.

Chapter 7
Exploiting each favourable opportunity

7.1. Catching the high-speed train: celebrations for one-hundred years of cinema

As trivial as it may sound, finding oneself in the right place at the right time isn't just a question of mere luck, on the contrary it is more likely to be the outcome of intentional behaviour, if not directly of a planned strategy. Indeed, even visual artists must be apt to operate creative choices and activate influent connections that might lead to crucial career opportunities, instead of waiting to be blessed with fortune and fame. Especially for emerging artists, who need to make their position stable within the art field, it is important to have a good reputation based on a consistent body of works and also to be able to leverage their network capital, in order to be granted access to more and more relevant venues. Albeit still present, financial concerns don't appear to be of superior importance anymore, since the first barriers of the art system have been broken, for instance by means of the continuous support of a dealer, a curator, a major collector or a public institution. While a rising artist's curriculum and contacts may be fundamental to increase the number and prestige of occasions to display or create new works, once a new opportunity arises it is crucial to have the adequate artistic project ready to respond immediately. Unlike one could do before being considered an emerging author – such was the case of Gordon's first refusal for his Tramway solo show back in 1992 – at this career stage it is truly decisive to seize every opportunity one is presented with, as occasions might not happen again. It appears indeed difficult to determine precisely, when an emerging artist becomes established, but there are several features that could be seen as tangible clues. Seth Sieglaub's significant statement about established art soon becoming establishment seems explanatory in this regards, because it stresses the fact that once an artist or a specific trend has been legitimized by various gatekeepers, it is very difficult to loose the acquired position as that would affect also the balance of other players (Alberro, 2003, p.151). Having succeeded in finding representation at a respected gallery is for instance an essential backing to find collectors and increase an artist's financial capital, while participating in bigger and bigger group shows can help to foster one's connections with other relevant players of the art system. Being granted solo shows in relevant museums or even having an artwork purchased by an important collection are two more key features that may suggest, whether an emerging artist has finally assembled a sufficient artistic capital to be recognized as established. Furthermore, constant coverage by specialized media or even some considerations by academic papers are fundamental to reinforce an artist's professional reputation and international renown in the eyes of the art system. It can be argued, that each of the above features on its own may not suffice to gain access to the establishment, though their joint occurrence in all probability would foster and stabilize an artist's position. However, there is one further element that could signal the definitive acquisition of an established status, since it is being regarded as such by most players of the system. As a matter of facts, winning an important award or at least being shortlisted for a prize is an unmistakable sign that would be interpreted as a final reassurance and validation of an artist's career by the art market and other players of the art field. Such an achievement and the resulting enhanced visibility could indeed trigger the relevant dealers' interest or museum acquisitions, as well as extensive media coverage and proposals for solo shows. Although winning an important prize doesn't necessarily confer real celebrity status, it grants access to a new arena and it is likely to offer consideration as an established artist. Provided that the specific prize itself has the correct reputation to mark the acquisition of a stable position in the art field, awards such as the Turner Prize in the Nineties are perfect devices to corroborate an emerging artist's first career moves. Of course one may acquire an established position even without winning awards – or even refusing to be shortlisted, as Sarah Lucas did repeatedly with the Turner Prize – but their importance for career progress can hardly be denied. For this reason, as argued in previous chapters, art prizes are today quite common, although only a few are really prestigious and can make a fundamental difference for an artist's career.

Following this strain of thought, it appears that a rising artist who wishes to enter establishment should seek opportunities that can enhance the above discussed features and be prepared to exploit them as well as he or she is able to. In the specific case of Douglas Gordon, the year 1996 proved to be a momentous period, which delivered several chances to enhance his personal career status, especially by means of his acquired ability to create captivating video installations and for his clever re-use of filmed material. As a matter of facts, that year was worldwide dedicated to the celebrations for cinema's centennial jubilee, as it coincided with the anniversary of

Lumière brothers' first public screening in Britain. Although not all the projects carried out by Gordon in 1996 had to do with cinematic appropriation, the official centennial of motion picture afforded several opportunities to participate in important group shows around the world and be appreciated on an international level. Hence, it is no coincidence that this was the year, which would grant him the Turner Prize nomination first and then its victory, on the contrary it can rather be considered as a direct consequence of the way he could exploit various opportunities related to cinema's centennial in the course of 1996. This leads to a careful consideration on Gordon's approach to cinema, which is useful to explain the origin and thought underlying the process of appropriation and alteration the Scottish artist has practiced from *24 Hour Psycho* on. First it must be observed that the young Glaswegian didn't chose cinema as a medium per se, nor did he focus on its history as an art form in a mere celebratory way. As argued before, right from his starting experiments he appeared rather interested in cinema as communication tool, that is a means by which to get in touch with people's everyday reality and individual memories due to collective imagination, as the artist maintains:

> *"Film for me is just a channel, a way to reach people, real life and real time, memories of something." (Gordon in Haase, 1999, p.138)*

This is the reason why Gordon chose films that held a specific meaning in his personal recollections, not so much for the movie itself but for the original viewing context at home as a child or teenager, thus revealing a rather innocent desire towards cinema and by no means a scientific purpose. In fact, this relationship to cinema seems to reflect that of Gordon's wider generation, which grew up with television and video recorders, de facto limiting cinema to a lower-ranking position. Defeated by home entertainment technologies, in the eyes of Gordon and his generation the original requisites of cinematic experience had expired by then, thus jeopardising cinema's further resistance as a medium (Moisdon-Trembley, 1996, pp.127-128). In the artist's own words, it is the acquired distance from the original medium that allowed him to dispose of cinematic materials and icons:

> *"I think that my generation are in a good position, or we will be soon, to say what cinema is. I think that my generation have the necessary distance from the phenomenon to be able to look at it with some clarity that was not affordable for the audience or the film-maker before now. [...] I think that cinema, as a progressive medium, is over. It's not quite dead, and maybe it will never die [...].*

But it's over, as far as I am concerned. [...] The visual world is accelerating towards a completely digitised synthesis of images and this slowly allowing cinema to a secondary medium. [...] The way in which I tray to use the medium, as a ready-made, is a position of some luxury, afforded by the distance we've just been talking about." (Gordon in Van Assche, 1995, p.85)

Following Gordon's strain of thought, his method of appropriation was not intended to consecrate a memorial to cinema, thus mourning this or that Hollywood movie. Quite the contrary, his experiments aimed at reviving this medium by transferring films on VHS, such as to induce a state of artificial life for a deep coma patient. In conversation with Nancy Spector, the Scottish artist explained his view and actions as a kind of resuscitation process:

"I don't think that what I'm doing is making 'memento mori'. [...] If we say cinema is dead, then working with it and temporarily re-animating some of its limbs is a much more appealing image to me. It also makes me think of the traditional Haitian method of Zombie-making." (Gordon in Spector, 1997, p.77)

This rather profane idea of reanimating corpses, as if the artist were a medieval necromancer, inspired another work that Gordon showed in Vienna in 1996 on the occasion of a series of public art presentations curated by Hans Ulrich Obrist. The general structure of this event was decided by *museum in progress,* an association founded by Kathrin Messner and Josef Ortner in 1990, which was involved in public art and in the attempt to find new ways of exhibiting works in the Austrian capital (*10 Jahre museum in progress,* Cat.2000). They called Obrist to curate an exhibition that required all contributors to show a large-scale mural painting to be applied outdoors opposite the Wiener Sezession building. Gordon's original idea was to draw the words "Cinema is dead" with spray paint, but given the above considerations on his approach towards the motion picture he decided to keep it as the title of his work, while the applied text would assert "raise the dead". These words were written on a brick wall in Glasgow with red paint, while in Vienna he showed its enlarged black and white photography. In an interview with Obrist on the very occasion of this text piece, Gordon himself referred again to the idea of zombie-making as a prohibited social convention:

"And I liked this idea that [...] if cinema is dead then, well, let's 'raise the dead'. Let's bring it back to life because the idea of raising

> *the dead is absolutely taboo in every culture on every level. When they're dead you're supposed to acknowledge the dead and let them be, and by raising the dead you bring in lots of other ideas of zombiism and ghosts and doppelgangers – and that to me was very interesting when I started to think about it more." (Gordon in Obrist, 1996b, p.162)*

Gordon's intention was to de-contextualize the statement, which was originally related to cinema, and create a supposedly hyper-realist work that inserted such a disruptive statement in the heart of Vienna, which stood as the depiction of what is acceptable social belief and behaviour. *Cinema is dead* (1996) reached back to his word pieces set in public spaces of the late Eighties and early Nineties, but – referring to cinema – this work shows the centrality of the motion picture as a major research theme for Gordon's career in the year 1996. As a matter of facts, that year he would exploit his acquaintance with the cinematic medium on several occasions which proved crucial for establishing his position in the art field. Among the most important international exhibitions for the anniversary of cinema was *Hall of Mirrors: Art and Film since 1945* staged at the Museum of Contemporary Art (MoCA) in Los Angeles, which was the only visual arts show to be included in the official programme for the *Motion Picture Centennial* sponsored by the Academy of Motion Picture, Arts and Sciences (Cat.1996). The exhibition was held at the MoCA from March 17th to July 28th 1996 and showcased as many as 175 works, sixty films or clips, fifteen video-installations and film screenings. A true blockbuster show, it was later moved to three other important venues[1]: the Wexner Center for the Arts in Columbus, the Palazzo delle Esposizioni in Rome and the Museum of Contemporary Art in Chicago. Curated by Kerry Brougher, this exhibition intended to analyse the complex and profound relationship between cinema and visual arts after World War II, examining on the one hand how art had approached film and video, on the other how cinema had been influenced by visual arts. The overall output was a fandango that meant to illustrate how these two art categories had often blended to produce new means of expression, staging works by more than ninety filmmakers and artists. Some featured artists were big celebrities such as Alfred Hitchcock and Stan Douglas, Richard Hamilton and Michelangelo Antonioni, Jean-Luc Godard and Andy Warhol, Cindy Sherman and Akira Kurosawa, while other contributors – like Gordon himself – were far less renowned, but very cheerful to be associated with these absolute stars on such an important occasion. Unsurprisingly the young Scottish artist – who had not turned thirty, yet – had deserved an invitation to the MoCA for his de-constructivist approach to cinema, especially thanks to *24 Hour Psycho* as well as to the project for *5 Year Drive-By*, which proved a powerful lure for international attention.

Albeit in recent years he had chiefly experimented with video installations that focused on found footage, the impact of the Tramway work and the idea for a slow-motion screening of *The Searchers* had meanwhile succeeded in linking his name durably with motion picture celebrities. Gordon's appropriation strategy finally turned out to be very effective and perfectly fitted the occasion of group shows committed to investigate the relationship between cinema and visual arts, moreover delivering an evocative and dramatic quality by means of carefully devised installations. However, by then the Glasgow artist was used to bewilder expectations, thus in Los Angeles he presented *Hysterical* instead of *24 Hour Psycho*, which was currently on display on another group show in London, while another video-installation featuring bootleg records was currently being exhibited at another touring exhibition. All of these shows celebrated cinema's anniversary and Gordon could not afford to participate at each of them with the same artwork, or he would have risked his full and varied artistic capital to go unnoticed. The other two mentioned exhibitions were *Spellbound* (Cat.1996) at the Hayward Gallery in London, which took place from February 22nd to May 6th in collaboration with the British Film Institute, and *Scream and Scream Again: Film in Art* (Cat.1996) at the Museum of Modern Art in Oxford from July 14th to September 22nd, later travelling to the Irish Museum of Modern Art in Dublin and to the Museum of Contemporary Art in Helsinki. Both group shows were way smaller than the Los Angeles event, but proved equally crucial for Gordon's career path, as they obtained a wide media coverage in the UK. For *Spellbound* ten artists had been invited, among whom important film directors of international renown, while the Oxford show was dedicated to six younger visual artists. As will be discussed in the next paragraph, Gordon decided to display *24 Hour Psycho* in London, because it would have been the first time for the British capital and he was further granted the opportunity to choose the exact location for its installation inside the Hayward Gallery. On the contrary, the organizers of *Scream and Scream Again* had commissioned a new work to the Scottish artist, which gave him the opportunity to present the outcome of his experiments with amateur pornographic footage he had found in the United States some years before[2]. The fact that he had been commissioned a new work for an international touring exhibition is proof enough that Gordon was progressively establishing his position in the art system, since public institutions besides the art market were asking him to create new works. The Oxford exhibition featured five other young American and British artists working with video and film installations: Marijke van Warmerdam, Sadie Benning, Tony Oursler, Liisa Roberts and Isaac Julien. Curator Chrissie Iles' aim was to present the ideas and procedures of these artists, which should demonstrate how the use of new video technology by the younger generation had increased the power of conventional cinema to convey new meanings, despite detractors' claims that it was an outdated medium. Also Roberts and Julien had been commissioned new works to respond to the curator's purpose, while the remaining contributors displayed pieces they had already shown. Isaac Julien's work *Trussed* was a double projection that explored gay love scenes in cinema and the mourning for an AIDS deceased. The video installation *Trap Door* by Liisa Roberts featured four shootings, the first three showing a sequence of rambling images – human limbs, landscapes, words – which frustrated the viewer's attempts to find any logic in the narrative, while the fourth video was the take of a statue of three dancers in a public park. Gordon's piece was a video-installation of the kind he had created in the last few years featuring a double projection in a darkened room, though this time he resorted to erotic bootleg records of the 1960s. The title for this new commission was *Black and White (Babylon)* and it showcased a brief sequence of a busty stripper secretly caught on 16mm film, probably for home pornography or private club screening purposes. The black and white take was again slowed down and projected on two 4:3 screens hanging side by side, the first one displaying the correct version, while the second screen showed the exact same frames though flipped upside down. The blow-up projection of the originally poor-quality film – together with the usual slowed down pace and the sound removal – rendered an aesthetic result that gave the clip a spellbinding attraction, completely removing it from its hardcore context and intended voyeuristic goal. The work's title referred to the black and white film, but it also implied two opposite principles, which are usually identified with these contrary colours, speak good and evil. The subtitle *Babylon* would confirm this possible interpretation, since in biblical tradition the sinful city of Babylon or Babel was antipodal to hallowed Jerusalem and often characterized as a great whore. Albeit Gordon's work possessed the by now usual environmental quality that would pay impression on the audience, the newspaper reviewers had conflicting opinions. A great supporter of this commissioned piece was *Times* critic Richard Cork (1995), while among the skeptics were William Feaver for *The Observer* and Matt Seaton who reviewed on *The New Statesman*. In their account on the exhibition, Feaver (1996a) and Seaton (1996) particularly targeted the Scottish artist, probably because he had recently been included in the Turner Prize shortlist. *The Observer* critic censured Gordon, because he felt the Scottish artist had fallen short of new ideas, recurring to older tricks of his previous production such as slow motion, dual screen projection and image distortion. Apparently not a big fan of video installations, Feaver further noticed that the general approach of *Scream and Scream Again* was self-referring and overindulgent, as was true in his opinion for so many other exhibitions based on video art:

> *"Like 'Spellbound', recently at the Hayward, 'Scream & Scream Again', at the Museum of Modern Art, Oxford, is a multiplex of filmic art settings. The presumption is that the time spent watching a film loop run its course once or twice is bound to be far more rewarding, for a photo-attuned modern audience, than spending time on a painting. Darkness, of course, adds to the sense of occasion. There is anticipation before the eyes adjust, and the tendency to linger on, through longueurs that would not be tolerated in a painting, for fear of missing a good moment." (Feaver, 1996a)*

Matt Seaton also criticized Gordon denouncing the supposed arrogance and triviality of his conceptualist approach, an opinion that reveals to be symmetrical to the typical conservative attitude of critics like Brian Sewell, the renown *London Evening Standard* columnist who was among the most vehement detractors of the YBA generation:

> *"Whether he [Douglas Gordon] has anything particular to say about film and spectatorship, his work at least displays a sense of humour. In fact, this is its saving grace. The problem with much conceptual art is that its manifestos turn out to be so banal. Conceptualism may proclaim the primacy of the artist's intellect; but in its bossy didacticism it often treats the intellect of the beholder with contempt. Do we need to be confronted by arrangements of whirring projections to understand that film is artifice, mechanically conveyed?" (Seaton, 1996)*

Despite harsh criticism from tabloid press and broadsheet papers, Gordon's cinematic projects seemed instead to be appreciated by various international players of the art system, as he was further invited to important group shows. Still in 1996, the artist embarked on another project related to cinema together with Rirkrit Tiravanija, whom he had been introduced to by Liam Gillick in New York a few years earlier. From January 19th to March 2nd the two artists created an event called *Cinema Liberte/Bar Lounge* in the rooms of the FRAC Languedoc-Roussillon in

Montpellier. For this intervention they had set up two adjacent rooms, the first as a small projection room with cushions to sit on the floor, the other one as a small pub with a bar-counter and a TV. In the first room they had arranged the screening of a series of films that the spectators could choose from. Gordon had previously selected these among movies that had been censored by French authorities in the past. The films included classics such as *Nuit* and *Brouillard* by Alan Resnais (1955), as well as *Et Dieu crea la femme* by Roger Vadim (1956). The neighboring bar instead had been designed by Tiravanija to allow the public to discuss in a friendly environment what they had just seen, while the TV showed what was currently being screened in the projection room. This was the first time that the two artists worked together and their project was installed again on several other occasions with only small changes, as for example at the first edition of Manifesta I in Rotterdam still in 1996, which included films censored by the Dutch authorities[3]. The use of censored films was meant to expose the ambiguous frontier of social and cultural suitability, as well as the violent situation produced by authoritarian decisions. The project met on divisive opinions by the critics: while Stuart Morgan (1996) on *Frieze* praised this collaborative work for it succeeded in reinventing psychological space by means of revising old structures, the Swedish curator Daniel Birnbaum highlighted the self-referential stance of the project on the pages of *Artforum International*:

> "Cinema Liberté, *1996, a collaborative project by Rirkrit Tiravanija and Douglas Gordon, the young art stars of the exhibition, was actually pretty dull. [...] I am sure the party on opening night was fun, but a couple of days later the small cinema was completely empty. Which comes as no surprise. Why would anyone want to sit alone on a beanbag and watch a bad projection of* Ben Hur *(inexplicably targeted by Dutch censors) while drinking a lukewarm Dutch beer?" (Birnbaum, 1996)*

Birnbaum's critique appears to focus on the fact that much relational art, as performed by Tiravanija and Gordon, may work for the inner circle of art initiates rather than for the general public. In his review, however, the curator implicitly acknowledges that the Scottish artist was by then to be considered a main character of the international art system, not far from being definitively an established author. In fact, going through the list of contributors to the first edition of this new European contemporary art event, which was held in the Netherlands from June 9th to August 19th, his name stood out together with Tiravanija's and Olafur Eliasson's above many others[4]. Despite Birnbaum's disapproval, being defined as the *young star* on show by *Artforum International* in the Summer of 1996 most certainly seemed to label that year as the true turning point for Gordon's career, even before the Turner Prize victory.

7.2. A burst on the passing-lane: an unexpected overtaking?

While the mentioned group shows abroad fostered Gordon's international renown, the official cinema celebration event at London's Hayward Gallery proved particularly important for the Scotsman, given the media coverage the group show deserved in the UK. This event was planned to open the anniversary of the first film screening in Britain and promised to be the blockbuster exhibition of the year at the South Bank Centre[5]. Borne out of the partnership among the Hayward Gallery and the British Film Institute, this group show was meant to emphasize proximity between visual arts and cinema throughout the 20th century, as well as their mutual contamination. The title itself referred directly to one of the most famous collaborations among artists of the two genres, that is Hitchcock's 1945 film *Spellbound*[6], whose scenes were designed by Salvador Dalí. The British film director involved the Spanish artist to conceive the set for the dream-state of the main character. Despite historical references implied in the exhibition title, the two curators Ian Christie and Philip Dodd didn't intend to present a retrospective on genre fusion between art and cinema. In their opinion, the new perspective to be shown was the massive use of video made by the new generation of British artists:

> *"Most disheartening is the fact that the new generation of artists working in Britain, and enjoying recognition here and abroad, have taken to film and video not as light relief from their 'real' work but as a central and absorbing activity. It is the air they breathe. This is as true of Jane and Louise Wilson and Sam Taylor Wood (not in the show) as of Fiona Banner, Steve McQueen and Damien Hirst." (Dodd, 1996, p.33)*

Surprisingly, Hirst was included by the curators in the list of those young British artists who were used to work with video installations and film production, which actually rather sounded like a new development in his career. In fact, by then he had only directed the music clip for *Country House* by the celebrated British rock group *Blur*, which was nominated best video clip at the Brit Awards in 1996. Hence, his only resort to the moving image had been on a mere commercial occasion, which appears too weak a motive to include the artist in an exhibition focussing on art and cinema. Albeit Hirst's alleged cinematic experience was quite farfetched, it was a sufficient justification to have the young art star and fresh-winner of the last Turner Prize on board of the Hayward Gallery's forthcoming exhibition, as noticed by the *Sunday Telegraph* reviewer John McEwan:

> *"Spellbound opened last week at the Hayward Gallery, 100 years to the day from the first film screening in Britain. Damien Hirst, the art world's current milch cow, is inevitably one of the artists invited to commemorate this historic event." (McEwan, 1996a)*

The inclusion of the Leeds born artist was also meant to support the organizers, since *Spellbound* was intended as a blockbuster event and Hirst was certainly in the position to ensure wide mass media coverage. The press release offered on the opening day leaves no doubt that the organizers had consciously planned this effect:

> *"First there was Britpop. Now Britart along with Britfilm are talking the world by storm. [...] Hot on the heels of his pop video for Blur, Damien Hirst presents his first ever narrative film." (Press Release in Feaver, 1996a)*

As a consequence, Hirst's commissioned short film inevitably drew most attention and a lot of information was leaked in advance to promote the entire exhibition. For instance, prior to the opening the organizers had already disclosed that the original title of Hirst's contribution was likely to be *Is Mister Death in?*, being the anagram of author's name, and especially that it would feature pop star Keith Allen and actor Eddie Izzard. Evidence of this half-concealed advertising strategy finds further confirmation in Kevin Jackson's ironical opinion on *The Independen*t:

> *"Much of the publicity for 'Spellbound' has been centred on one of the short films commissioned by its curators, Ian Christie and Philip Dodd – a Tales of the Unexpected-style piece originally titled 'Is Mr. Death in?', an anagram for the name of its director, Damien Hirst, of whom you may have heard." (Jackson, 1996)*

Besides Hirst, *Spellbound* included nine more British artists and film directors, since curators Christie and Dodd were eager to demonstrate that the relationship between visual arts and film constituted a great opportunity rather than a lurking risk even for the three cinema celebrities they invited, which were Ridley Scott, Terry Gilliam and Peter Greenaway. Indeed, the three famous film directors were commissioned an installation each, while the other contributors were pure visual artists of different generations. There were four artists who were to produce short films or video installations – Douglas Gordon, Steve McQueen, Boyd Webb and Damien Hirst – and three more authors who usually engaged with cinema fiction and narratives – Eduardo Paolozzi, Paula Rego and Fiona Banner. Given the different professional background as well as age group and career stage, the works presented at the Hayward couldn't be seen as a coherent selection, but were rather supposed to mix up cinema and art in a cheerful way. The catalogue of the exhibition, on the contrary, appeared to have the ambition of being understood as an almost anthological book on the history of cinema in Great Britain. However, the featured essays seemed to overemphasize the troubled relationship of motion picture with visual arts, venturing to find by any means connections and parallels between the recent generation of British artists and cinema celebrities of long past times. According to John McEwan *(1996a)* in his *Telegraph* review, the result was an all-comprehensive tale of cinema over the last century, seen from a perspective that meant to accentuate how visual arts of the last few decades had supposedly affected the motion picture industry. Altogether, cinema was the sole theme of the catalogue – almost forgetting about the works of the contributors – which can be seen as a consequence of the centennial celebrations, but perhaps it depended also on the curators' background. Both were in fact cinema historians who were provisionally curating an art exhibition: Christie had been in charge of the special projects at the Hayward Gallery, while Dodd directed the research department at the British Film Institute. Unsurprisingly, arts critics did not appreciate the exhibition, as it simply showed a great variety of possible art and cinema fusion patterns lacking any sort of theoretical consistency. The general impression of reviewers was twofold: some of the visual artists had committed themselves to cinema, in order to share its power to attract the public, while the filmmakers on show ventured in the domain of visual arts, as they probably intended to be considered more than mere entertainers. Mark Sladen's harsh comment on *Art Monthly* rejected without appeal the work of the two curators:

> *"This formal diversity isn't a problem in itself, but it becomes one when you realise that it isn't backed up by any conceptual coherence. The closest the organisers come to a polemical statement about their show is to say it demonstrates 'that the internationalism and*

> *pervasiveness of cinema [...] can generate a wide range of personal and critical responses. Group shows in contested territories need stronger curation than this if they're to hold together, and in the absence of any real theme it is actually the divisions between participants that emerge as the exhibition's most interesting subject." (Sladen, 1996, p.26)*

In order to fully grasp the reasons for such an adverse position, it might be useful to go over the featured works in *Spellbound*, since the curators had left absolute freedom to both artists and film directors in the show. Given he was free to choose the exact setting for his contribution, Gordon didn't hesitate an instant to install *24 Hour Psycho* in the gallery entrance atrium. The location he found was very appropriate, because to enter the exhibition visitors had to pass under the projection screen hanging slantwise in the centre of a darkened room, while the images were even reflected on the huge mirror at the bottom of the hall. The Scottish artist risked a lot with this choice, which could have drawn much criticism, as he was the only contributor who didn't produce an original work for the event. However, Gordon was so sure about the power of his piece for this particular opportunity that he argued it was the first installation of *24 Hour Psycho* in London – a choice that would later prove very effective. Going along in the gallery, the first room on the right housed a giant and rather distracting installation created by seventy-year-old Scottish sculptor Eduardo Paolozzi, titled *The Jesus Works and Stores*. Basically the room had been packed with objects of cinematic reminiscence: most were junk materials of his sculptures that Paolozzi jumbled with Hollywood props and souvenirs of various sizes, which the artist meant as references to the dreams and desires one may find in mass culture. Among the many objects one could recognize the Tin Man from *The Wizard of Oz* or a statue from *Robocop*, the rats of Murnau's *Nosferatu* or again the robot from Fritz Lang's *Metropolis*. Proceeding in the visit, a series of large figurative oil pastels by Paula Rego were hung on the walls, which had been inspired by three classic Disney films: *Fantasia*, *Snow White* and *Pinocchio*. The painter presented some of the most significant scenes of these three cartoons, though she had portrayed human actors mimicking still frames, for instance some plump ballerinas wearing grey tutus had interpreted the stout birds of the *Hour Dance*. Born in Portugal in 1935, Rego also belonged to a much older generation than the YBAs and, like Paolozzi, appeared to have just fitted some film quotations in her usual works. Their gap to the younger artists was self-evident at a glance, when viewing the next work on show, which was *Apocalypse Now* by Fiona Banner. A former Goldsmiths student that graduated in 1993 and took part in *General Release* at the Venice Biennale, she also didn't display a video work, but drew from Conceptual Art giving it an intimate interpretation. The piece consisted of a huge sheet of paper – the approximate size and proportion of a film projection screen, that is 16:9 – hanging on the wall and showing a handwritten text spanning the whole surface with no word breaks. Banner had in fact written down his individual impressions on the famous film by Francis Ford Coppola in a long description, which spanned from the first to the last shot, thus rendering the substantial subjectivity of any cinematic experience. The next featured pieces were finally some short films by Damien Hirst, Steve McQueen and Boyd Webb. In the end, the recent Turner Prize winner had titled his piece *Hanging Around*, whose main character Marcus was played by Keith Allen and resembled a kind of polygamist drug dealer, caught while wandering around London parties and apparently causing death outbursts wherever he dropped by. The clip had been partly shot in the private residence of two collectors of Damien Hirst, being Richard and Judith Greer, and was accompanied by a fashionable Britpop soundtrack. The plot simply consisted of a multitude of horrific deaths soaked in constant quotes of Hirstian symbols, like raw meat, electrocuted insects and a beautiful woman wearing a colourful spot-dress. Steve McQueen's video *Stage* was a black and white feature film of an African man – the artist himself – and a Caucasian woman performing a silent choreography that would never allow them to touch each other. The shots had a sculptural impact as the concentrated on the movements and details of the two bodies, as well as on the light and shadow effects of the whirling masses. Photographer Boyd Webb had shot a short clip titled *Love* Story with the collaboration of *Spitting Image*, a very popular series of satirical puppets in Britain. Halfway between comedy and romance, this short film told the bizarre affection between two popcorn grains which had fallen onto the floor of a movie theatre. The upper floor the Hayward Gallery had been transformed into a huge arena, in order to make room for the work by Peter Greenaway, one of the Eighties' best-known British filmmakers and a prolific author of movies such as *The Draughtsman's Contract* (1982) and *The Cook, the Thief, his Wife & her Lover* (1989). The project was called *In the dark* and consisted of an installation that conceptually seemed similar to Paolozzi's, in some respects. In fact, Greenaway had organized a huge cluster of objects, locations, characters and references from the cinematic world, as if they were stereotypes drawn from collective imagination. The film director presented all the elements necessary to shoot a film movie, such as actors and actresses, lights and projectors, fragments of scripts and amplifiers delivering sounds and noises, as well as numerous props including a pig's head in a bucket. Every day the set was reorganized to stage new imaginary shots, though the plot was absolutely random or even depended on the reactions of the gathered audience. Greenaway appeared to challenge the viewer with the scrappy ingredients, which crowd a film director's mind before sorting out a meaningful narrative. The remaining two filmmakers in the exhibition prepared similar installations to the above by Greenaway, but avoided to pressure the public's imagination. Ridley Scott simply assembled a video that featured sketches and screenplay excerpts from two of his most famous films, *Alien* and *Blade Runner*, resulting in a sort of backstage clip one would find in the special contents for home entertainment. Most inconveniently, Terry Gilliam's work was not ready for the opening, since the director was still promoting his latest Hollywood success, *The Twelve Monkeys* (1995) starring Brad Pitt and Bruce Willis. A few days after the vernissage he showed *Road to Monkey Heaven*, a room lined with floor to ceiling grey cabinets on every wall, onto which scenes of his recent film were projected. Inside the cabinets spectators could again find various props, the director's notes, small monitors and telephones that told about the making of the film.

Having described the variety and diversity of works on show, it rather seems appropriate to consider *Spellbound* a blockbuster exhibition that meant to entertain the audience with popular and spectacular installations, rather than paying attention to its conceptual coherence. It goes then without surprise that the reviews by art critics on top national newspapers and specialized magazines generally disapproved of the outcome, blaming the curators for blowing the event. However, the opinions on the single contributors varied a lot, especially for the most controversial pieces on show as well as for the more renown artists or film directors. Going over the accounts of several columnists is useful to understand the feeling for this momentous exhibition, as well as the specific assessments by art experts on the featured artists. Hence, it appears crucial to scrutinize the most important reviews on *Spellbound*, in order to fully grasp the seemingly unanimous appraisal, which celebrated Gordon's contribution. The articles taken into consideration include William Feaver's on *The Observer*, Kevin Jackson's for *The Independent*, Richard Dorment's on *The Daily Telegraph* and John McEwan's for *The Sunday Telegraph*, Mark Sladen's in *Art Monthly*, Jonathan Romney's and Adrian Searle's for *The Guardian*. Paolozzi and Greenaway found themselves under crossfire, deserving harsh criticism and delighted humour:

"By far the most disappointing piece here is an installation created by the sculptor Eduardo Paolozzi [...]." (Dorment, 1996a); "Paolozzi has the measure of Spellbound: multi-reference stacked high." (Feaver, 1996a); "For many visitors, though, the most beguiling project in Spellbound will be Eduardo Paolozzi's Jesus Works and Stores." (Jackson, 1996); "Paolozzi and Greenaway hide behind excess, chaos and mess, and are really only interested in their own over-blown solipsistic narcissism." (Romney, 1996); "Greenaway's complicatedness (not complexity) lacks give and feel." (Feaver, 1996a); "Greenaway's work is more ambitious but also more annoying." (Sladen, 1996); "As with Greenaway's films, I found the whole exercise pretentious and enjoyable equal measure." (Dorment, 1996a).

Funny and light-hearted, Boyd Webb's animated clip on the two popcorns wasn't criticized, but neither was it taken very seriously:

"Boyd Webb [...] claims intermission time as his own, bringing popcorn to life in a short but sweet film about love sprouting underfoot." (Feaver, 1996a); "The artist Boyd Webb's film of the life and times of a lovelorn popcorn that didn't pop is funny, weightless and momentarily satisfying." (Searle, 1996a); "[...] a slick and funny animated film about the lives and loves of two kernels of popcorn. It may not belong in an art gallery, but it certainly deserves an Oscar." (Dorment, 1996a).

Ridley Scott and Terry Gilliam were deemed inconclusive by many critics, as regards the latter not least because of the absence of his work on the opening day. General opinion on their projects hold that they might have been suitable for a museum of the moving image, but hardly sufficed for an art exhibition:

"To my mind the least successful parts of the show are the installations by Scott, Gilliam and Greenaway. [...] Their installations have an air of self-justification." (Sladen, 1996); "But Ridley Scott alone, with a derisory video assemblage of script and storyboard snippets, seems to have missed the point." (Romney, 1996); "I can't say how good Terry Gilliam's contribution is, because his installation wasn't ready last week." (Feaver, 1996a).

Paula Rego's paintings inspired by Disney cartoons were commonly appreciated, even if they were not considered very original works. They were thought to be some of her best creations so far, but certainly couldn't influence the development of visual arts in any way:

> *"Paula Rego, in large pastel drawings [...] keeps the cinematic references to a minimum. She runs no risk [...]." (Feaver, 1996a); "Finally, Paula Rego's large-scale pastel drawings inspired by Walt Disney characters are the strongest works she's ever done." (Dorment, 1996a); "Rego is the star of the show, with a superb selection of large pastels inspired by three Walt Disney classics [...]. They give full rein to her talent and represent an important advance [...] in her work." (McEwan, 1996a); "[...] there are too many walk-on parts – like Paula Rego', whose presence seems entirely arbitrary." (Searle, 1996a).*

While Paolozzi or the featured film directors could well outlive criticism – just as Hirst, who was now considered a new star – the critics' opinion was crucial for the younger artists on show. Gordon, Banner and McQueen all made a very good impression, especially when compared to the rather unconvincing projects of older contributors. Indeed, reviewers agreed on the fact that their works resulted the most significant of the show, especially since they appeared appropriate for the exhibition theme. In the critics' opinions, their contribution demonstrated the better ability of the younger generation to engage with cinema in the visual arts in a more cogent and inventive way:

> *"It is the younger artists in the exhibition who provide more complex takes upon cinematic spectacle." (Sladen, 1996); "The triumvirate Banner, McQueen and Gordon – all artists, first and foremost – have produced the most compelling works here." (Searle, 1996a).*

Despite general appreciation, however, neither Fiona Banner nor Steve McQueen seemed to have unanimously persuaded the critics. Although interesting, in fact, Mark Sladen deemed their works not to be fresh enough, but rather connected to outdated art trends, while Richard Dorment didn't even bother to comment:

> *"Both McQueen and Banner address the issue of power-relations within cinema – between on-screen characters and between the viewer and society. This is important territory, but has been quite heavily explored in the wake of the film studies movement and, although both these artists are interesting, their pieces in Spellbound*

don't seem particularly fresh." (Sladen, 1996); "I won't bore you with my reservations about the submissions of Ridley Scott, Steve McQueen and Fiona Banner [...]." (Dorment, 1996aa)

Remarkably, the only work on which the critics were apparently undivided was *24 Hour Psycho*, no doubt having surprised most experts and lay spectators for its striking atmosphere despite its formal simplicity. To the various columnists, the Glaswegian artist had made a consistent point: by blending cinema with analytical rigor drawn from a decidedly conceptualist practice, he had been able to create a piece that was both visceral and mesmerizing. A unanimous hail of appraisal seems to rise from the statements of all six considered critics on Gordon's video installation at the Hayward Gallery:

"The best things in 'Spellbound' – Paolozzi's cyber-bouncers, Douglas Gordon's yawning silent screams and Boyd Webb's popcorn embrace – come from the heart of film, a location unknown to Greenaway." (Feaver, 1996a); "Douglas Gordon makes the point by playing Hitchcock's 'Psycho' in slow motion.! (McEwan, 1996a); "But 'Spellbound' does have its moments. Douglas [Gordon] on a screen floating over the spectators' heads in a darkened, empty space, generates an all-pervasive atmosphere of narcoleptic menace." (Searle, 1996a); "From a distance, the slow motion is ecstatically voluptuous; up close, frame follows frame in nervy, spasmodic leaps. Either way, it makes you feel as unsettled as Norman Bates." (Romney, 1996); "Douglas Gordon's '24 Hour Psycho' is one of the most impressive works by a young artist I've come across in recent years. [...] He does not expect us to sit through the whole thing, but let me assure you that after 10 minutes in front of it, you'll be hooked." (Dorment, 1996a); "[...] one reason I find Gordon's appropriation of it so fascinating is that he seems to sidestep the discourse. His piece relies heavily on the iconic status of 'Psycho' and yet it isn't about that film. Likewise the piece makes you aware of the insidiousness and durability of cinema and yet doesn't really encourage critical distance. '24 Hour Psycho' is an amazing piece of spectacle, and one which justifies itself." (Sladen, 1996).

The tremendous appeal and exceptional success of *24 Hour Psycho* can hardly be underestimated, instead it is further confirmed when considering the bad reviews Damien Hirst received on the same occasion. Indeed, the curators' and critics' anticipation had been all for the Leeds star, but

Hanging Around had to face the negative barrage of newspapers and magazines, finally disappointing even Hirst's loyal fans. True enough, many critics and experts were eager for the Leeds artist to fail in his first major public appearance after the Turner Prize victory, because of his overexposed persona and provocative behaviour, but it suffices to go over the various accounts to realize that he had really missed the target this time:

> *"But when it comes to defeating expectations there's no one like Damien Hirst. [...] The work is in no sense an 'artist's film', and says nothing about the interface between the two media. It's just another play in Hirst's protracted end game. (Mark Sladen, 1996); "By MTV standard, Hirst could be the next Francis Ford Coppola." (Feaver, 1996a); "Again, context is all: in a film festival, it would be shrugged off as lazy cod cockney Lynch; here it functions as 'the latest Damien Hirst'". (Romney, 1996); "Damien Hirst's first short film [...] is by no means bad, but it's still the work of an amteur. The thing about artists who make films is that they never seem to make films that sustain the interest for long." (Dorment, 1996a); "Hirst's is a particular let-down: a self-reverential and indulgent slice-of-life ramble, crammed with banal images of violence, no better than the average film-school student standard." (McEwan, 1996a); "The movie might not be art – though it has art in it, by Man Ray, Meret Oppenheim and Hirst himself – but it is unashamed in terms of entertainment values." (Searle, 1996a); "[...] this remarkably conventional drama is still possessed by death, and the artist's admirers will be pleased to hear that many of his leading motifs, from raw meat to insect electrocutions, are present and correct." (Jackson, 1996).*

Hanging Around was literally torn to shreds, at best being considered pretentious and self-referential, trivial and amateurish, mundane and boring, nothing but a bundle of hirstian imagery set on the background of a fake *Swinging London* and complemented with a glamorous soundtrack. Some critics even refused to define it an artwork or a commercial video, as they blamed Hirst to lack any substance and mastery in video-making, failing to deal with the exhibition's subject matter and presenting the result of a mere video-art-beginner. To Julian Stallabrass (2006b, p.99) the short film was indeed negligible apart from Hirst's ubiquitous symbolism, though *New York Times* critic Michael Kimmelmann (1996, p.2962) maintained that he had only done what publicity-hound artists did at the time – so for instance Julian Schnabel and David Salle – which is trying to jump over to new business sectors in order to expand their personal brand. As a matter of facts, after directing the Blur music clip, *Hanging Around* was supposed to launch his filmmaker career and Hirst had planned to direct a real movie in order to plunge into the field of cinema. Unpredictably, Hirst's shortcomings in the use of video even met upon the disappointment of his usual supporters, as recalled by Gregor Muir in his memories about the YBA decade:

> *"He was eager to work for bigger projects, such as pop promos, that in turn might lead to full-blown film productions. But Hirst's attempts to extend his credentials in this field were thwarted soon after he screened his short film 'Hanging Around' at the Hayward's 'Spellbound' exhibition in 1996. Shot in Richard and Judith Greer's home in Notting Hill, the film starred Eddie Izzard and Keith Allen and was universally panned. It was the first time that people, who might otherwise claim to be fans of Hirst, appeared visibly let down." (Muir, 2011, p.187)*

Curiously, it would be another contributor to *Spellbound* and 1999 Turner Prize winner who successfully start a career in cinema later, namely Steve McQueen. Indeed, the latter succeeded in jumping over to proper filmmaking by means of his acquired ability to work with video art, which Hirst had seemingly lacked. The Leeds artist's failure of his ambitions as a filmmaker, irrevocably decreed at the Hayward Gallery, induced him to try luxury catering instead, which he did by opening in 1998 for five years a trendy restaurant called *Pharmacy* in London's Notting Hill, finally auctioning all the furniture for eleven million pounds. Even on the short run, Hirst's video clip flop didn't affect his career that much, since in 1996 he was about to provide his first solo show at New York's Gagosian, the temple gallery of the most powerful art dealer in the world, which is probably also the reason why he didn't put too much effort in *Hanging Around* and rather worked for his success in the USA. Ironically, while it had been Hirst's announced participation to turn *Spellbound* into an eagerly anticipated event, it was in the end Douglas Gordon who enjoyed the critic's spotlight. The first screening of *24 Hour Psycho* in London – included in a heterogeneous but highly publicized group show – obtained unanimous admiration of art experts and general audience, celebrating the twenty-nine-year-old Glaswegian as a true master in the use of video in the art field. In the darkened entrance hall at the Hayward Gallery, looming underneath the still image sequence of *Psycho*, a real noir drama had taken place, as a new art celebrity's trip had been immediately exploited by a less renown competitor. Indeed, Gordon ended up as the real *Spellbound* attraction, as Richard Dorment clearly suggested in his comprehensive review on *The Daily Telegraph*:

> *"'Spellbound' is far from perfect [...] but there is enough of interest in it to merit a visit. And by the way, the knife first slashes through that shower curtain every day at 3.30pm precisely." (Dorment, 1996a)*

7.3. Finish line and a new start: the Turner Prize goes to Glasgow

At the end of 1995, as soon as a sensational edition of the Turner Prize exhibition had closed and Damien Hirst had finally been awarded on his second candidacy as expected, Douglas Gordon got word that his name might have been taken into account for the forthcoming shortlist. At the time, the Scottish artist wasn't struck by the news, as he feared to be annoyed by the media overexposure that a nomination would have implied. As a matter of facts, since the award ceremony had been put on live broadcast on Channel Four commencing with the 1991 edition, the Turner Prize had become a major event, eagerly covered by tabloids as well as by specialized magazines. As argued in previous chapters, Nicholas Serota had been able to put the award in the limelight, helping visual arts to gain immense popularity in Britain's Nineties, which for the finalists of each edition entailed an excessive media attention. Winning at her second nomination in 1993, Rachel Whiteread was a blatant example of the kind of media fever that one could attract. The artist had suffered harsh critic for her public sculpture *House* by area residents, finally leading to its demolishment, while the K Foundation – a quite debatable art organization led by two retired British pop stars – conferred her the title of *worst artist of the year*. Indeed, the K Foundation had been set up by Bill Drummond and Jimmy Cauty who decided to award Rachel Whiteread their £40,000 prize – double the sum offered by the Tate – and made the announcement on the same evening as the Turner Prize ceremony[7]. Whiteread initially refused to accept the prize of the K Foundation, but accepted when she learnt the money would have been incinerated and so she decided to fund scholarships for young artists with three quarters of the money, while donating the remaining sum to a housing charity called Shelter. Considering the media impact of the Turner Prize, anyone who was shortlisted was well aware that big popularity would also result in an unyielding press scrutiny, as Gordon maintained in conversation with Graham Fagen a few years later:

> *"You do actually have to endure quite a lot to go through the nomination, and there's probably worse to come from it. I remember being on a panel talking about the Turner Prize, the year Rachel Whiteread won it, and I remember saying, that wasn't a lot of money, twenty thousand quid, and I stand by that, it's not worth the amount of distress that people have to go through to win it, it's certainly not worth the amount of distress to go through it and not win it." (Gordon in Fagen, 1999, pp.89-90)*

The same opinion appears to be shared by another 1996 finalist, Simon Patterson, who was admittedly worried when he was told of his nomination:

> *"The Turner Prize is always good fun, I'll just have to see how to cope with the attention." (Patterson in Glaister, 1996a)*

In early June 1996 the artist was finally called back by the Tate, as he was invited to participate in the exhibition for the four Turner Prize nominees to be held in November that year. In that particular moment, Gordon recalls he was holding exams at the Glasgow School of Art and found himself annoyed by the call, so he answered on the spot he wouldn't probably be able to attend the Turner Prize. As a matter of facts, he knew in the same period he would be working for his major solo show at the Migros in Zurich and feared he might be pressed on working for the Tate. Meanwhile he had learned from the Tate that his dear friend Simon Patterson and further acquaintance Gary Hume – both original *Freeze* contributors and by then well known in London – had already accepted the nomination. Although he believed not to be in the best position to win the award, he had immediate afterthoughts and finally convinced himself that this opportunity shouldn't be let down.

After accepting he was required to send his photo-portrait to be included in the Tate's press kit, so he sent a passport photo accidentally taken while trying to wear a blonde wig in the attempt to disguise himself as Myra Hindley, the notorious Yorkshire children-killer. This work has been previously described, though it seems important to stress that apparently the artist didn't ponder much over sending this picture to the Tate. However, Katrina Brown (2004, p.70) believes it could be interpreted as an attempt to conceal his true identity – at least to some extent – and hinted at the artist's current research on schizophrenia and split personality, hence the three works on display at the Tate in Autumn would indeed be based on these topics. Myra Hindley was intended as Norman Bates' living counterpart, the psychopathic killer in *Psycho,* since she too looked harmless and innocent but had revealed an insane and murderous nature. Gordon reported about the puzzled reactions of friends and acquaintances at the sight of this portray published in the newspapers, which was later developed into an autonomous piece:

> *"That photo was taken by chance. I hadn't thought much about it. A lot of people thought I wanted to disguise myself as Kurt Cobain, others thought of Marilyn Monroe or Andy Warhol. For me it was more Myra Hindley, the child murderer from Yorkshire." (Gordon in Van den Boogard, 1997, p.45)*

On June 19th Nicholas Serota, who had been the president of the Turner Prize jury since 1991, proclaimed the nominees for the 1996 edition dividing them into four schematic categories: 46-year-old photographer Craigie Horsfield, 34-year-old painter Gary Hume, 29-year-old conceptual artist Simon Patterson and video artist Douglas Gordon[8]. Even if the distinction between painting, photography, conceptual and video art suggested by the Tate organizers was slightly inaccurate – at least it was only partly consistent with Gordon's body of work – the press immediately acknowledged those four art genres to make communication easier. The selection committee had chosen the artists out of a hundred candidates and would also serve as the prize jury in autumn after the opening of the finalists' exhibition. Besides Nicholas Serota as the host, there were four more jurors out of influent art experts and curators such as the director of Artangel Trust foundation James Lingwood, art writer and curator Mel Gooding, Edward Lee representing the Patrons of New Art and one woman, *Parkett Magazine* editor Bice Curiger. As usual, the finalists had been selected on the basis of their production in the twelve months prior to May 31st, 1996 and the jury was also to consider external recommendations, besides relying on their own assessment. At the Tate press conference the jurors explained the reasons for their shortlist, which were then reported and commented in various newspapers, since the committee appeared to stress the overall poetics of the selected artists rather than pinpointing specific achievements of the four artists in the previous year. As regards Horsfield, jurors merely highlighted the importance of his option for photography:

"Craigie Horsfield turned to film and photography following his 'dissatisfaction with contemporary painting's lack of engagement with reality'." (Lister, 1996a); "Edward Lee [...] described the work as highly charged, exploring 'urban life and decay, human fragility and isolation'." (Alberge, 1996a).

Gary Hume had just witnessed a career revival thanks to an impressive solo show at Jay Jopling's White Cube the previous year, where he had shown a new series of paintings after abandoning hospital doors for good. However, the committee underlined his care for an object so unusual for visual arts as swing doors, but also praised his recent decision of shifting style to better grasp British pop culture sprawl of notoriety abroad:

"Hume had also recognised the potential of a subject hardly explored before in painting, and one not without resonance – to pass through the swing doors in a hospital may as well be to pass from life to death..." (Lister, 1996a)

For his part, the painter himself believed his friend and companion Damien Hirst would have deserved another nomination:

"Gary Hume said he thought Damien Hirst should have been nominated for a second time 'for doing what he does'. "(Glaister, 1996a)

Bookmakers initially favoured Simon Patterson, having deserved a nomination for his dedication to information systems, although the jurors could mention only his older conceptual work *The Great Bear*, which dated back to 1992:

"William Hill bookmakers yesterday declared Patterson the 6-4 favourite for the prize." (Lister, 1996b); "Mr Gooding called him [Simon Patterson] a 'passionate artist, concerned about how we think about the world'." (Alberge, 1996a).

According to the selection committee, Gordon had instead been chosen out of his work on human psychology and reception systems, but he was the only one for which the jurors referred to a specific event in the last twelve months. In fact, the jury specifically mentioned the presentation of *24 Hour Psycho* at the Hayward Gallery, which London journalists and critics had still vividly in mind, as can be understood from their reports:

"Douglas Gordon, aged 29, gained attention this year for his slowed-down version of the film 'Psycho', screened as part of the Hayward Gallery's 'Spellbound' exhibition. Il lasted 24 hours." (Glaister, 1996a); "With one artist whose work includes a 24-hour showing of Hitchcock's Psycho slowed down to two frames a second [...] this year's Turner Prize shortlist clings to its usual arena of controversy." (Lister, 1996b)

In the habitual way, British critics targeted the 1996 shortlist, labelling it as flat, dull and absolutely uninteresting. Curiously these were opposite reasons to those that had set the previous edition on fire, since the 1995 Turner Prize selection had caused considerable scandal for some of the works included, such as Damien Hirst's *Mother and Child Divided* (1995) – a cow and calf cut in half and preserved in formaldehyde – or Mona Hatoum's eye endoscopy titled *Corpes étranger* (1994). Although it seemed objectively difficult to keep up with Hirst's voluntary provocations and acquired popularity, many correspondents simply considered the four finalists as almost unheard-of artists, accusing the Tate to have run out of fresh air. Nicholas Serota rejected such critique answering that the candidates had deserved their nominations, even if they didn't enjoy mass media celebrity yet. Opinions on the 1996 shortlist should be weighed against the general media attention that the Turner Prize had called since its 1991 reform. In a way, the competition was affected by its own success and couldn't resist being constantly targeted by critics for opposing motives, not unlike any important event covered by the media. Reports of the press conference reveal the kind of criticism expressed by various experts:

"David Lee, editor of Art Review magazine, was surprised the jury had chosen a shortlist lacking in notoriety." (Glaister, 1996a); "The shortlist was denounced by Brian Sewell, art critic of the London Evening Standard. He said: '[...] These four are nobodies. They are not outrageous or slap-in-the-face or whatever [...] they're plain damned dull and boring.'" (Lister, 1996b); Last year's entrants, who included Damien Hirst with his severed cow and calf and Mona Hatoum with her video trip into her body, are hard acts to follow. And so it has proved." (Stringer, 1996); "Mr Serota said the jury had been surprised at the absence of women on the shortlist. "Maybe there is no single manifestation by a woman that really caught the eye.'" (Glaister, 1996a).

While much critique was debatable, the latter comment was but the undeniable truth and appeared to set jurors in a tight spot, since journalists stigmatized the absolute absence of women artists in the 1996 shortlist. Serota's explanation on this point didn't seem satisfying; hence many critics pressed the jury, wondering why artists such as Tracy Emin and Georgina Starr had not been taken into account. To commentators' great surprise had come the exclusion of Cornelia Parker, who had shown *The Maybe* at the Serpentine Gallery in the previous year earning much media attention. It was a quite sensational vitrine installation showcasing relics of famous historical figures and featuring actress Tilda Swinton who lay apparently asleep in a transparent box. The jury didn't admit any error in assembling the all-male shortlist, but the exclusion of women artists would definitely burden the 1996 edition. Indeed, the months spent from the shortlist announcement to the finalists' exhibition opening were marked by this feminist controversy. The jury had even been considering an afterthought of its choice, for instance by adding a woman artist or substituting one of the selected finalists. However, the Tate feared that any change would undermine the authority of the final verdict and weaken the four shortlisted candidates, hence resolved not to make any amendments. As a matter of facts, the dilemma was solved only in the following year, as the jury selected four women artists to counter the previous shortlist (Stallabrass, 2006b, p.185). The 1997 selection may partly have been a mere compensation for the fault on women artists of the previous year, but it made clear that the male-female debate in art had finally come to a turning point in the Western world. Provided that it hopefully was a definitive achievement, the Nineties had witnessed a real boom of women artists on an international level, especially from Great Britain, Japan and Northern Europe (Vettese, 1998, pp.103-105). It seemed, as if the younger generation of women artists had finally reached some balance as to their professional chances when opposed to male counterparts. According to New York Times critic Roberta Smith (1992, p.2939), women had used particularly conceptual rigour to create more robust artworks that had successfully questioned the meaning and power of male art. Complete equality of opportunities was probably still to achieve, but the public outcry for the all-male shortlist of the 1996 Turner Prize had shown at least that there finally was a breach in the masculine art system for women to exploit. Things had not changed radically, since women artists still had to fight hard to keep notoriety, but there definitely was a growing sense of need to consider their fundamental role in the art world. Questioned about her feeling for the nomination among an all-female shortlist in 1997[9], Christine Borland confirms that it could possibly represent an important stance in favour of women artists:

> *"I really hoped that this meant that things were not going to regress. I hoped it was something which meant that it will never be unquestioningly for men again; that was what I would like to feel is the most positive thing that came out of this. I genuinely think that it was representative of the field—there are a lot more women artists out there working now—and that it might be one of the results of all the women who did struggle through art, during the '70s and '80s, and that maybe my generation is the one that finally is achieving the numbers, in terms of people who have been able to keep going long enough to get some acknowledgment. But no one was asked the previous year (in 1996) how they felt being four men; it just wouldn't happen." (Barclay Morgan, 1999)*

In spite of the negative comments of the press, Tate's expectations for the Turner Prize show were still optimistic, as the award was claiming growing media and audience attention after its reorganization five years earlier. Indeed, attendance rates had increased from 500,000 visitors in 1994 to 700,000 the following year, such that the organizers decided to prolong the exhibition period of one whole month than previous editions, commencing on October 28th 1996 and finishing on January 12th 1997.

The 1996 exhibition was organized by Tate head curator Virginia Button together with Serota, whom the nominated artists had to submit their projects to, in order to get leave[10]. Indeed Gordon's first proposal was rejected, which should have been a slow motion screening of *The Exorcist* (1974) inside a darkened room furnished with bean bags, like he had recently done for *Cinema Liberté* in Montpellier and Rotterdam. The curators persuaded the artist to renounce this project, as the renowned horror movie would have prevented younger visitors to attend the exhibition, albeit the projection was slowed down. Gordon had thus to reassess his propositions for the Tate show, but maintains he wasn't really obsessed with the Turner Prize, as he was already very occupied that year with other relevant projects which have been mentioned before:

> *"I took the show seriously, I wanted to do the best possible show within the circumstances, but, you know, it was another show, and I was very busy around that time, which made it difficult but on the other hand actually made it quite good, because while I was doing*

that show I had to have one eye on something else all the time [...].” (Gordon in Fagen, 1999, p.90)

In the end, the Glasgow born artist decided to present three pieces, which should highlight the range of different media and artistic processes he had employed so far in his career path. In fact, his plan was to engage the same subject matter with three different strategies: a video installation, a short film and a text piece. The latter was applied on the corner of a black wall, while a great double screen video projection stood in the centre of the room and TV monitors played a pair of videos. They had all been conceived for the Turner Prize show and were respectively *Untitled Text (for someplace else than this)* (1996), *Confessions of a justified sinner* (1996) and *A divided self I and II* (1996). As regards to the chosen theme, he opted for different aspects of schizophrenia and split personality, though dealing more in general with the problem of duality and ambiguity of opposites, hence carrying on his research on disturbed human psychology.

Untitled Text is a sequence of word pairs that the artist equates, even if they would be opposite according to reason, thus challenging the supposed consistency of the entire text. The text piece was applied as a white letter vinyl text on to the corner of two black walls, so that the angle made the text appear convergent. The first line of the text for instance read “...hot is cold, day is night, lost is found, everywhere is nowhere”. The second half of the text presented the same word pairs as in its first part, such that the last line confirmed the same mentioned equivalence, though inverting the terms as if they were a mirror image: “nowhere is everywhere, found is lost, night is day, cold is hot...”. The whole text had 29 lines, so the central line was not repeated and further featured a word pair whose inversion hopelessly failed, hence breaking down the equation of the opposites on which the text apparently abided by: “(desire is) fulfillment, I am you, you are me, fulfillment (is desire)”. When reading the text from the beginning to the end the viewers took a two-way journey between antithetical words, whereas at its turning point they collide with an impossible reversal: the I can't be you and vice versa. Gordon was apparently suggesting that fulfillment is possible only through another person, but the failure of language inversion also stressed the ambiguity of oppositions on which human reason is based upon[11].

The video installation *Confessions of a justified sinner* resorted instead to the most celebrated Scottish novels of the 19th century, so that the artist could draw from his own cultural background and ironically feed the press with national stereotypes. The title of the work refers to the already mentioned novel by James Hogg *The private memoirs and confessions of a justified sinner* published in 1824, while the images projected on the double screen were excerpts from an early screen adaptation of *The Strange Case of Doctor Jekyll and Mister Hyde* by Robert Louis Stevenson printed in 1886. The film was directed by Rouben Mamoulin in 1932 featuring Frederick March in the title role, who in Gordon's piece was seen repeatedly transforming from Dr. Jekyll into monstrous Mr. Hyde. The installation reproduced the display mode tested for *Hysterical*, that is two screens of three metres by four set at an obtuse angle with each other and standing on the floor, but slightly leaning backwards. The chosen clip showed details of the expanding teeth and claws, while the hands and head had grown hairy – then all of a sudden a hand reached for the neck, as if one of the split personalities was trying to suppress the other. The twenty-minute loop sequence was projected in slow motion and synchronized on both screens, though the images of the left side had been flipped from left to right and transformed into photographic negatives. The final impression was that of an endless struggle between good and evil, where positive and negative would endlessly alternate. Considering the literary reference in the title, the images should also reflect human's double sided conscience, as Gordon himself put it in conversation with Nancy Spector:

> *"The work must be firmly ambiguous, moral and amoral, self-righteous in intent and self-denying in stature, communicating in tandem a desire for confession and a denial of responsibility, ethical but disruptive [...]." (Gordon in Spector, 1997, p.81)*

Gordon's last work for the exhibition was a series of two videos, *A Divided Self I and II*, shot by the artist himself and transmitted on two monitors, hence proving Gordon's acquired ability to work even without found footage or borrowed records. Both screens show a pair of forearms – one hairless, the second very hairy – fiercely fighting on a bed sheet, whereas on one video the right arm seems to prevail and on the other one the left arm appears predominant. Given their different exterior appearance, at first glance the arms seem to belong to two different people struggling against one another, perhaps a man and a woman. However, at a closer look one understands they belong to the same person, in fact being a perfectly identical pair of forearms, except for the hairs. Indeed, they are Gordon's forearms who had one shaved and then filmed this seemingly endless struggle between two opposite but similar entities confined in one and the same body. This piece appeared to address the physical concepts of left and right, as well as the psychological issue of duality or sexual opposites such as male and female, in order to challenge supposedly antithetical categories in human belief. Gordon's video piece made viewers aware of how two things could be equal and not coincident at the same time, the same and the contrary in one piece, the same way as a person's right arm looks like the left one, although being its opposite. Even this work referred to Scottish culture, because the title *A divided self* had been borrowed by an important book published by renowned Glasgow psychiatrist Ronald David Laing in 1960, who had been a pioneer in studying and treating schizophrenia. In fact, the doctor had suffered from this disease and tried to understand the rationale of that experience, thus experimenting a revolutionary therapy already in the Fifties. He decided to deal with schizophrenic people simply talking to them and their multiples, instead of cancelling by means of rational denial one or more of the personalities expressed by patients. Consequently, the psychiatric ward of Glasgow hospital was transformed into a community space, in which patients, nurses and doctors interacted without any hierarchic structure, leading to significant results that allowed schizophrenia treatment without the use of psychotropic drugs[12]. Laing's book title perfectly fitted Gordon's interpretation of schizophrenia and human soul duality as featured by the two videos, which favourably integrated his contributions for the Turner Prize show that were all about the notion of difference and equivalence of opposites, as well as of duplicity and double representation.

Every finalist had received his own spot to install his works and Gary Hume had filled his with numerous paintings, some of which had been created purposely for the Tate show. Since 1994 the celebrated *Freeze* painter had forsaken the geometrical pattern of *Door Paintings* and started to produce simplified sketch duplicates of images drawn from glossy magazines with bright home paint applied onto polished aluminum panels, portraying celebrities or banal subjects such as dogs and teddy bears. He exhibited four new paintings to which he added three completed in previous years, which were two celebs portrays of 1994 depicting DJ Tony Blackburn and actress Patsy Kensit, as well as a Renaissance portrait cut-out from painter Petrus Christus made in 1995. In order to understand the kind of aesthetic results of his new production, *Tony* (1994) looked like a grey clover topped by a black semi-circle on a yellow and pink background, hence acquiring a shiny and cool look. Among the new paintings were *Whistler* (1996), *Innocence and Stupidity* (1996) and *Snowman* (1996): the first was the sketch of a whistling person, the second depicted the cut-out of a rabbit from the well-known series of French tapestry *La Dame à la Licorne* housed at the Musée de Cluny in Paris, the third showed two simple overlapping red circles on a pink background. Perhaps the most interesting of the seven paintings on display was *Kate* (1996), which was supposed to be the portrait of British supermodel Kate Moss, whose face Hume hadn't apparently been capable to render in abstract style because of her stunning beauty.

Craige Horsfield, the oldest among the shortlisted artists, had graduated from St. Martin's College in London, but then stopped painting at the end of the Sixties. During the following decade he had moved to Communist Poland, where he had started using photography as his primary medium to portray landscapes, still lives and nudes trying to delve into the surrounding environment. When he went back to England at the end of the Eighties, his photos dating to the Polish period were soon credited for their good quality, but surprisingly his career was later associated with the YBA movement even though he belonged to a completely different background and personal history. For the Turner Prize exhibition he presented a wide range of black and white photographs taken during his recent three-year stay in Barcelona, which included both individual and group portraits of the Catalonian citizens. All photos were printed in large format with a black frame and were then displayed in several rows on the walls of his room, the first being dedicated to close-ups of middle-aged Catalan people, while the second depicted market scenes and dance halls crowded with people. Some pictures documented the so-called *midnight dance*, during which it is believed that no one can refuse being invited to dance. Tate curator Virginia Button even ventured to compare these particular shots to the joyful dance scenes painted by Flemish master Pieter Bruegel the Elder in the 16th century.

Being the youngest artist on show and yet indicated by bookmakers as the winning horse, Simon Patterson submitted three works, two of them expressly made for the Tate exhibition, while the third one was his well-known *The Great Bear* of 1992. The latter could have been the first public art work on display at a Turner Prize exhibition, since Patterson was determined to persuade the London Underground company to post copies of his altered tube map in various stations around town. However, London authorities unfortunately rejected the idea, fearing that passengers could get confused by the artist's poster, who had changed the names of all tube lines and stations. *The Great Bear* was exhibited together with two other works, again focusing on the subversion of standard information systems, as well as on the reversal of signifier and signified. A wall of the room dedicated to Patterson was taken up by *The First Circle* (1996), a reproduction of the solar system pictured against a background painted with the colours of the light spectrum that can be detected by human eye. The planets' orbits were drawn as white ellipses revolving around the sun, which was represented by a large circle outlined in white. In place of the nine planets, however, Patterson had inserted the names that in various cultures and traditions hold the meaning for heavenly places or conditions, such as Cockagne, Nirvana, Xanadu and Cloud 9. His last work on show, *Untitled* (1996), was installed in the main gallery room, as it consisted of three racing yacht sails, each of them inscribed with the name of a famous writer, as well as with their date of birth and death: Raymond Chandler (1886-1959), Currer Bell (1816-1855) and Laurence Sterne (1713-1768). The artist had chosen these writers simply because their names could by chance be associated with a shipping item: *stern* is the rear of a boat, *bell* can signify the alarm signal on a ship and *chandler* was called a dealer or trader in maritime supplies. *Untitled* openly referred to a boat race and could be understood as a comment on the Turner Prize exhibition itself, as the latter was indeed a fierce competition and not a friendly group show. While for the three sails in the main hall an underlying logic could be found, Patterson claimed that in the remaining two works he had not implied any specific associations of ideas, as in much of his previous works:

> *"I'm not really interested in mystification. There is no code to be cracked in any of my work." (Patterson in Burdon, 1996)*

Superficially the works displayed by the four finalists belonged to different genres, as announced by the Tate in June, which appeared to be painting, video art, photography and conceptual art. This simplistic categorization is indeed to be found in most reports on the 1996 Turner Prize exhibition, such that Adrian Searle on *The Guardian* maintained it would be impossible to compare different artistic categories, not to mention the range of topics covered:

> *"And as ever, the current contenders are dealing with issues so divergent, and working in such utterly different ways, as to make a nonsense of comparative judgements. Do you prefer bananas or Ford Fiestas, the Cairngorms or Persil?" (Searle, 1996b)*

Skipping any methodological consideration, *Art Review* editor David Lee judged the show as incredibly boring, while hyper-critic Brian Sewell was reported to have sarcastically wished for Hirst's return:

> *"I'm almost tempted to say 'Come back Damien Hirst, all is forgiven'. It was pitiful." (Sewell in Glaister, 1996b)*

Albeit Sewell's statement was only partly serious, it was indeed a strong opinion on the supposed failure of the 1996 show, though opposite to what *The Sun* critic Norman Tebbit had commented on the opening of the previous Turner Prize edition, confirming that the press was hardly ever satisfied with Tate's decisions:

> *"Have they gone stark raving mad? [...] The works of the 'artist' are lumps of dead animals. There are thousands of young artists who didn't get a look in, presumably because their work was too attractive to some people. Modern art experts never learn." (Tebbit in Beckett, 1996)*

Hence, while in 1995 the exhibited works had shocked much of the critics, one year later it appeared that the lack of outrageous contributions would anyway arouse criticism. Comparing the two editions, much of the press believed that in 1996 the Tate had consciously tried to avoid scandal at all costs, turning to a more gracious and milder version of the YBA generation (Stallabrass, 2006b, pp.185-187). This opinion found such a widespread acceptance that the K Foundation decided not to award the prize for the worst artist of the year. More reasonable and detailed comments were to be found on national newspapers, such as John McEwan's (1996b) review on *The Telegraph* who noticed the ascendancy of certain commercial galleries on the Turner Prize, which was probably related to Nicholas Serota's permanent presidency of the jury and to his personal connections to various London dealers. Indeed, many of the finalists and winners in the Nineties were represented by a small number of establishments, especially Logsdail's Lisson Gallery and Jopling's White Cube, the latter confirming its rapid ascent into prominence in the London art market chiefly thanks to Damien Hirst. In the 1996 edition, three of the shortlisted artists were linked to the above galleries, Hume to White Cube, while Patterson and Gordon were being represented by Lisson Gallery. Renowned *Independent* critic Andrew Graham Dixon, instead, disapproved of the considerable presence of brochures and captions, as well as audio guides and video interviews with the artists, as they rather seemed to highlight the inaccessible nature of much contemporary production:

> *"The abundance of explanatory material – the presence, indeed, of an entire gallery consecrated to explanation, is presumably meant to sugar the difficult pill of contemporary art." (Graham-Dixon, 1996)*

Apart from such art-critical stances, it is interesting to follow out the progress of forecasts on the likely winner made throughout the exhibition period, as they appeared to rely on popularity symptoms rather than artistic motivations. At the announcement of the shortlist in June bookmakers favoured Simon Patterson, while after the opening of the exhibition quotations were supportive of Gary Hume's probable victory. As a matter of facts, at the end of October the largest British bookmaker company William Hill ranked the four finalists in the following order as regards to probability: Gary Hume first with 6 to 4; Simon Patterson followed high on the heels with 7 to 4; Craigie Horsfield arrived third with 7 to 2; last came Douglas Gordon with 4 to 1 (Vv.Aa., 1996a). Two weeks before the award ceremony, the assumptions made by bookmakers had slightly changed, but the classification remained unvaried: Hume was given 7 to 4, Patterson 9 to 4, Horsfield 2 to 1 and Gordon still last with 9 to 2 (Shepherd, 1996). Professional betters seemed to leave little room for doubt, so that Patterson bet money on himself, hoping to unsaddle Hume on the last mile, while Jopling had already organized a celebration party for the latter to be held on the evening of the award ceremony (Glaister, 1996b). Still, these placements did not reflect the opinions expressed by some of the most influential critics and experts: with the exception of John McEwen, who supported Gary Hume, William Feaver and Adrian Searle were undecided between Gordon and Horsfield, while Richard Dorment overtly supported the Scottish artist and Andrew Graham-Dixon rejected all four finalists. Going over some of the arguments stated by critics it appears easier to understand, why the Glasgow author could in the end beat all the odds. John McEwen on *The Telegraph* thoroughly analysed the works by Horsfield, Gordon and Patterson to expose their weaknesses and concluded that Hume was the only one left, who was worth taking into consideration:

> *"Most of his [Horsfiled's] photographs are self-consciously humdrum. It shows him tarred with the puritan brush of the post-1968 generation. [...] He [Gordon] asserts his Scottishness by linking himself to his famous countrymen. [...] "black is white", "bad is good". The presumption of comparing this with the devilish dichotomy of the self explored by Hogg only adds to the irritation. [...] [Patterson's] gigantic mural of a planetary chart and a floor-piece of three windsurfing sails, which make the same point using different sets of associative names, only repeat and weaken the joke. [...] But someone's got to win and Hume at least has a bit of vim and vigour." (McEwen, 1996b)*

The Observer critic William Feaver (1996c) criticized Patterson's works with roughly the same arguments as McEwen's, maintaining that substituting names with no clear-cut logic seemed rather meaningless, the same way that Hume's paintings looked brilliant but vacuous. He didn't object much to Gordon's and Horsfield's works, except for the fact that a gallery directed by juror James Lingwood's wife supported him. On the pages of *The Guardian*, Dan Glaister (1996b) also thought that the only prospective winners could be either Gordon or Horsfield, because their works could at least address topics of some moral relevance: the photographer demonstrated awareness to social issues, while the Glaswegian showcased the ambiguity of human soul. Likewise McEwen (1996b) and Feaver, in Glaister's opinion Patterson had revealed himself the worst of the four finalists, as he kept repeating an old student's joke. Again on *The Guardian*, Adrian Searle (1996b) totally agreed on the latter instance – as well as on the possibilities for Gordon and Horsfield – and believed that Hume had produced noticeable paintings for their formal complexity, but far to weak for Tate's current standards of spectacular display:

> *"Horsfield and Gordon are undoubtedly the favourites in this year's show. In a sense, both artists deal with moral issues. [...] Patterson, I feel, is the outsider this year. He has only one captivating idea, and that came to him while he was still a student at Goldsmiths in the late eighties." (Searle, 1996b)*

In his column on the *The Independent*, Andrew Graham Dixon (1996) found fault with all four artists, so that later that year he wouldn't comment on the final results of the 1996 Turner Prize edition. Of Hume's painting he thought they were heading for a blind alley, as he thought had been the case of German Pop painter Sigmar Polke. As regards the remaining three finalists, he almost didn't consider their contributions as real art:

> *"This [Hume's] is not a kind of pictorial language that contains much possibility for growth. [...] Craige Horsfield's black and white pictures of people in Barcelona look like competent but hardly outstanding instances of social documentary photography. [...] The fragile nature of his [Patteron's] conceits and his briefly funny jokes makes the ambition to render them permanent, as Art, seem somewhat perverse. [...] Gordon has hit upon a device around which it might be fun to theme a chain of restaurants, not one upon which to build a career as an artist." (Graham-Dixon, 1996)*

Fascinated with Gordon's works since the times of *Spellbound*, Richard Dorment (1996b) took on the challenge posed by Searle, who had wondered how one could compare such different work genres. *The Daily Telegraph* critic responded to *the Guardian* columnist assuming that contemporary art should prove capable of dealing with complex and varied issues, in order to create works with strong narrative and psychological features. From that point of view, neither Hume nor Patterson could fulfill the critic's requisites, indeed Dorment believed Hume's paintings were mere decorative objects and Patterson's word puns only weak jokes, while Horsfield's photos seemed aesthetically dry. In his opinion, only Gordon had successfully produced hypnotic, ambitious and complex works, hence Dorment pledged for the Glaswegian to be awarded:

> *"Whether or not you are as fascinated by what Gordon does as I am, unless you recognise modern art's ranging from literature to psychology you won't understand what a young painter like Gary Hume is up against. For any artist in the Nineties must ask himself how a painted image can possibly compete with a complex video installation such as Gordon's. [...] If not exactly beautiful, I find [his] works hypnotic, ambitious and complex. It gives the viewer a lot to think about." (Dorment, 1996b)*

On the evening of November 28th 1996 the award ceremony at the Tate was broadcasted live on Channel Four, as usual, but contrary to the bookmakers' expectations the underdog Douglas Gordon was called on stage to be awarded the Turner Prize by Virginia Button. The Scottish artist was himself bewildered, since several other incidents on that evening had led him to think he didn't stand a chance[13]. Resorting to his habitual storytelling attitude, in private conversations the Scottish artist recalls he had been kept waiting for long in front of the Tate entrance with his family and then-girlfriend Tanya Leighton, while the other finalists were immediately let in. Furthermore, he had been the only one of the four shortlisted artists not to be pinned in Serota's office before the ceremony. Finally, during the dinner a cleaner in the Tate's bathroom had apparently confused the Glaswegian artist with Gary Hume and told him she had heard he – that is Hume – would be awarded. Slightly depressed and annoyed, after the unexpected announcement the cameras of Channel Four caught the astonished artist being shaken by Nicholas Logsdail before climbing up the stage[14]. It took Gordon several seconds to recollect himself from the surprise and start a concise acceptance speech with much aplomb. Besides thanking the organizers and Lisson Gallery, he didn't forget to thank the

Scotia nostra, by which he meant the group of friends, colleagues, teachers and curators back in Glasgow who had supported him over the years (Harding, 2001a). As regards to the £ 20,000 award, he was immediately determined to use the money for his project of *5 Year Dirve-By*, which he still hadn't been able to accomplish. The jury's official motivation, as reported by *The Daily Telegraph*, left no doubt about jurors remaining impressed by the works Gordon had created for the Tate show:

> *"[...] the jury last night praised 'his engagement with profound issues of memory, psychological division, and moral ambiguity and for his use of a wide range of media with consistent wit, intelligence and creative insight'." (Raynolds, 1996)*

Whether his victory was truly unexpected or not, Gordon's achievement was seen as an important event by various correspondents and critics, in particular for a set of three different reasons[15]. First of all, he was the first Scotsman to win the Turner Prize, thus breaking the tradition that had lasted for the past five editions, whereas only London-based authors had been awarded. Secondly, Gordon was also the first artist to triumph thanks to works that drew from video and moving image as artistic media. Finally, his success had brought the entire Glasgow alternative art scene under the spotlight, which had dwelt for years without any mass media attention, almost unnoticed by the broad audience. Richard Dorment (1996c), the only expert who had guessed Gordon's victory, rejoiced for the Glaswegian artist's success, convinced that it marked a durable turning point in British art. In fact, he maintained that a new generation had finally mastered video technique as a cognitive process, rather than applying it to a mere reproduction of human sight, as the first video artists had done in the Sixties. Dorment's final comments made it clear, that Gordon received this prize after an impressive contribution to the Tate show, but it also concluded a year of unique achievements:

> *"It is symptomatic of the way British art is changing that Douglas Gordon, the winner, makes dramatic video installations which drew on film, literature and psychology to investigate a range of emotion and experience. [...] I don't see how a painter stood a chance against the work Gordon has shown this year." (Dorment, 1996c)*

Adrian Searle (1996c), who had suggested a possible victory for Gordon or Horsfield, agreed on the pages of *The Guardian* on the fact that the young Glaswegian had well deserved the Turner Prize, finally unfolding the British art system towards the application of new media and delivering an international role to Glasgow art scene:

> *"This is the Turner Prize's first vindication of film, video and installation art. [...] Gordon's award is also a welcome acknowledgement of the vital artistic scene in Glasgow, despite the absence of commercial galleries and, more importantly, despite the invisibility." (Searle, 1996c)*

John McEwen (1996c), who would have preferred Gary Hume to succeed, sarcastically remarked that Gordon was the fifth artist linked to Lisson Gallery who had won one of the last nine editions. Consequently, the critic maintained that the Turner Prize needed some adjustment and suggested changing the jury president every year, in order to prevent the Tate director from being too influential on the final choice.

Be it a major event in recent British art history, Douglas Gordon's victory marked a decisive turning point in his career, as he could be finally considered a truly established artist. As a matter of facts, this success consecrated him on the national art scene and made him very popular with the national media, besides paving the way to further international achievements. The Turner Prize was definitely crucial for Douglas Gordon's artistic career, though he didn't consider it its arrival point – quite the contrary in several conversations and interviews he tended to minimize its relevance:

> *"It's like a band who wins something at the Brit Awards. Next year they could be nowhere." (Gordon in Henry, 1996)*

This sort of understatement fitted Gordon's temper very well, as he proved to be aware that he needed to move forward, in order to keep the position he had reached in the art field:

> *"I'm always busy with projects, people don't want to sit down and talk to me as a Turner Prize winner, they want to know what the next work is." (Gordon in Fagen, 1999, p.90)*

To be ahead in the game, Gordon resorted to his preferred strategy that is being again unpredictable and risk something new, rather than remaining stuck in clichés. A few months after the Turner Prize ceremony, Gordon was granted the honor of a DAAD Stipendium for established artists in 1997 – another clear signal for his newly acquired status in the art system – and thus got the chance to step out of the limelight moving to Germany later that year. In Gordon's opinion, getting away and starting all over again seemed the best option to foster his creativity and conceive new projects:

> *"It just feels like the right time to duck out of things for a wee while, and if I go to Hanover and Berlin then automatically that's going to cut off say forty or fifty percent of people who could contact me in Glasgow, and it's time to do that, in a way. [...] By taking myself away physically from a certain situation of support that might mean that I have to support myself, it might mean that I have to confront some aspects of the way I think in isolation. But that's part of the job again, that when the job becomes very comfortable then you have to fuck up a bit more, because I don't think that great or challenging ideas come out of a comfortable situation." (Gordon in Fagen, 1999, pp.91-92)*

He spent the following two years rambling in Hanover, Cologne and Berlin, where he got in touch with the German art system and had the chance to accomplish several projects. Among the most important ones there is the installation of *Between Darkness and Light* at Skulptur Projekte in Münster in 1997, a work, which was later purchased by the MoMA in New York granting him a stable place in one of the most important collections worldwide. Furthermore, in 1998 he was awarded the Central Kunstpreis at the Kölnischer Kunstverein in Cologne and could consequently shoot his first full-length movie, *Feature Film* (1999), which was produced by James Lingwood's Artangel Foundation. Even before, in 1997 he had won the Premio 2000 for the best young artist at the Venice Biennale, where he had installed his new version of *30 Seconds Text*. Again in 1998 he was also awarded the prestigious Hugo Boss Prize at the Guggenheim in New York, which finally convinced the powerful Larry Gagosian to include the Glasgow artist in his gallery.

Apparently, the three years immediately following Gordon's Turner Prize victory account for a different story from the one that has been written so far. Indeed, they seem to tell about an established artist seeking to score some points in the major league – such as entering a superstar gallery, achieving the purchase of an iconic work by a major museum, holding retrospective solo shows in some of the most relevant international venues – which implies a completely different set of strategies from those useful to climb up from the basement to the top floor of the art system. Hence, the Turner Prize definitely marked the end of Gordon's rise into prominence, which may be defined as his early career. What followed would be a consolidation phase of his international standing and a further climb amongst the renowned authors of today's contemporary art, thus the aim and scope of this study seem to have reached their outer limit. While he was weaving the envelope with the check of 20 grands, Gordon's own final words at the Turner Prize acceptance speech demonstrate full awareness of having reached a defining moment in his career – as well as the goal of this research so far:

> *"Yeah, I think I am at the bar. I am at the bar, definitely. Thanks!" (Gordon: see note 14)*

Conclusion

Rise of the enterprising artist

Far from discovering ontological truth, provided such a thing exists in art historical matters, the previous pages have attempted to outline some answers to the fundamental questions that opened this research. Seen from the perspective of an aspiring artist, the analysis tried to understand what makes a good career start in the art world, who are considered influential players in the field and what might be valuable strategies to apply. The study case to Douglas Gordon and the wider generation of British artists that rose into prominence in the 1990s, thus, should have partially enhanced academic understanding of the factors that allow a young artist to enter the arena of contemporary art, further becoming a recognized author at national or even international level. Foremost, the analysis showed that artists – especially when at the kick-start of their career – truly interrogate themselves as to how become successful, which resources to gather along the path and whether to turn decisions about their profession into a precise career plan. Indeed, the foregoing chapters have highlighted several features and strategies – be them planned or subconscious – that were applied by the Scottish artist and several other peers, thus revealing to be crucial for their swift affirmation and probably more in general for any artist who wishes to become established in today's art field. Allan Bowness maintains there are several conditions for success in the art world, which he sums up in four subsequent steps towards recognition: first comes peer acceptance, then legitimation by critics followed by market success, finally celebrity among the wider public (Vettese, 1998, p.119). Albeit these four stages are indeed fundamental for an artist's affirmation, they don't tell what an aspiring artist is exactly supposed to do and further appear to separate the ideal career path in several sealed-up compartments. On the contrary, evidence emerging from the chosen research topic rather suggests that a young artist might seize on all above stages at the same time and should even simultaneously interact with several players of the art system to be effective. As a matter of facts, participating into group shows, getting dealers and curators interested, finding a mentor or collector, obtaining a museum show or purchase, being constantly reviewed by art magazines and winning a prize are likely to be interlaced events. Hence, career progress is closely related to the overall attitude and activities that an artist performs in the field he or she intends to approach, not just by the artworks he or she creates. Consequently, the initial assumption concerning the artist's role model has depicted the latter as a self-conscious player, who is or should be aware of the art system's structure and mechanics. This hypothesis was tested covering the professional career of Douglas Gordon as compered to other relevant artists of his generation, inescapably resulting in a heightened awareness of the artistic field of their time. Aspiring artists thus appear to be conscious of the existence of entry barriers to the art system, which of course are not insurmountable, but that can hardly be overcome relying on mere luck. Be it or not part of an intentional plan, young authors need to recognize the various players of the field and their specific position in the arena, as well as understand their peculiar preferences and which network of relationships they are linked to. At the heart of this work lays the purpose of identifying and classifying the various strategies that lay at hand for artists to start a successful career, though among the most important findings of this research one should count the necessity for an artist's enhanced attitude towards those resources that are crucial for the acceptance into the art system. Indeed, opportunities seem to arise quicker, when artists are conscious of what features they should possess and how to foster their development, gradually getting involved in the dynamics of the art world.

The research showed that explicit strategy awareness might not be necessary for visual artists, but acting strategically appears instead to be a fundamental feature to aim at a rapid ascent. Although it could seem audacious to credit artists with a business-like engagement, they are indeed professionals of a specific field in which the level of competition is extreme. As for any other business sector, the number and pugnacity of competitors in the market – be them aspiring or already established – determines the necessity of an intentional action plan in order to gain access or keep one's position in the arena. As a matter of facts, the specific study case demonstrated that bursting enrolment figures at British art schools together with self-aware working class kids and women students decidedly put enormous pressure on aspiring artists of the late Eighties and early Nineties in the UK. On balance, the number of artist candidates in the country grew at such a rate as to exacerbate competition, while the situation was even worsened by the consequences due to the harsh economic recession of 1989. Having said this, it is unimportant whether artists are fully aware of a strategy or if they carry it out completely, as that is hardly the point. What really counts is that artists understand they must consciously distinguish their own persona and production from their competitors, in order to be characterized and seek for unique recognition in the art field. In summary, the general question concerning artists' strategies should thus be about the possible options the latter can have at their disposal to gain or leverage capital stock in the art field, rather then if they are at all conscious of acting strategically, since any plan could also fail in the end or may even have been originally mistaken. Furthermore, the crucial aspect is about choosing the right timing for strategies to be employed: although there might not be such thing as *the* perfect moment for a specific decision to be taken or action to be performed, the discussed study case has certainly provided insight in different career stages. Indeed, for each level of the art system there seem to be peculiar features that are responsive to specific action schemes, hence baring better fruits if artists understand when and how to play their cards. This feature would seem consistent with other fields, such as with any further business sector where one may recognize different strategies for different enterprises, which depend on the company's level of development and competitive position in the given sector. All of this points to the fact that recognizing different career stages is useful for research purpose, as well as for artists to understand what they should better be doing to foster their success chances. However, one must constantly keep in mind that career stages are not steadfast categories, but rather helpful devices to organize a thorough research scheme or an effective action plan. As regards social science, theoretic clarification usually relays on the observed phenomenon, hence describing what groups or individuals are already doing. In fact, artists may act strategically even without formalizing or performing an intended action plan and they can also disrupt or innovate the art system's structure and dynamics that was previously accepted by the field's members. Evidence emerging from the case of YBA, for instance, has demonstrated that vertical differentiation in the art system may be helpful to distinguish the varied career stages an artist might be at, but boundaries can be broken at one's own advantage. Indeed, artists such as Damien Hirst and dealers like Jay Jopling appear to have been careless of the separated levels in the British art system, employing aggressive media strategies and exploiting celebrity status for rising artists who would have been previously expected to walk a long path towards establishment. Whether to play by the rules or rather think out of the box is only a matter of personal disposition, both can be viable strategies, so the true key to gain access to the art system is being aware of the field's current state.

The chosen research topic has proved that entrance was rather granted to those aspiring artists who possessed a vast amount of information on the trends and force relations inside the art field, thus one should better be familiar with the field's past, comprehend its present condition and be capable of anticipating its future development. In order to do so, artists must get hold of specific resources that define their position in the art system, which has been argued are artistic capital, network capital, social capital and financial capital. Truly, the previous chapters showed that artists do in fact think about production, connections, reputation and money, which must be considered the four leverages they must activate to make a career in visual arts. Hence, the possible options for artists to take can be divided into four subsequent categories, though strategies and actions may also involve more than one featured asset.

To start with artistic capital, the foregoing discussion proved that artists must take decisions concerning the adopted media or technique, the chosen research topics or contents, the style and sources of reference, the targeted reference group and finally the production model, although not necessarily in this order. So for instance one may resort to a more traditional and marketable technique such as painting or instead to a far less commercial though sensational media like installation art. Artists may further choose to walk the path of outraging provocation or rely on a few catchy but reputable ideas, as well as side for tradition or rather prefer to go for cutting edge styles. They should also decide whether to produce serial and repetitive artworks or prefer to create very innovative though sporadic pieces, which drives to a distinction between retail artworks and iconic ones. Of course artists can choose to put their artistic capital somewhere in-between these options, sometimes even making recourse to varied or even opposing strategies. What they should keep in mind, however, is an understanding of the art field as a system based on trust and self-validation that inevitably leads aspiring artists to choose which gatekeepers to target or which other influent players to reference, in order to find admittance in the system or in one of its subparts due to their legitimation. The first step in this perspective is definitely to speak a global language, one that may be understood further than the mere local art scene, as is exemplified by both the London and the Glasgow artists who were attempting to draw attention in the early Nineties. As a matter of facts, the previous chapters proved that employing international paradigms was fundamental to connect with the broader art system and get out of a tight spot. All in all, three appear to be the different means which have been – and still are – adopted most frequently in order to conform to established styles or to acquire the basis of upcoming trends. Some artists may choose to go for *back-up-artworks*, such that directly refer to already celebrated authors or recognized international trends, although one risks to produce mere copies of the *original* art. A safer pick is represented by a sort of *appropriation game* which rather aims at replicating the poetics and methods of successful artists, which isn't of course an easy task and could however be seen as an act of following the referenced style. Finally, artists can opt for a *critical parody* of the author or trend they wish to be related to, but this choice could be regarded as an uncertain attempt or even a mere prank. Obviously these hypotheses have a restricted validity, as they should be tested on the case of further artists and maybe even of different art historical periods, nevertheless they appear to sum up appropriately the basic choices with which Gordon and his generation were confronted with. Moreover, such kind of appropriation or reception strategies seem consistent with behavioural models that have been described by social scientists and institutional theorists in the instance of organizational innovation spreading in the industrial system. Far from diminishing the importance of individual creativity and talent – which are of course necessary features for every aspiring artist – the above considerations rather reflect on the relevance to inform oneself about the development of artistic discourse in the art system. Indeed, to foster artistic capital it is crucial to recognize dominant positions in the field and identify new market opportunities, whether by following established trends or pursuing an innovative path. Artist should better be aware that they have to decide whether aspire to be among the trendsetters for upcoming styles – which could eventually never become established – or if they prefer to follow the flock of already branded art and possibly score fast – though stylistic obsolescence might catch up even faster. The chosen case study has further proved that artistic decisions are conditioned by various factors, foremost by art education which acts as the primal entry barrier to the art system and deeply affects the art concept of aspiring artists, as well as of other players that may have gone through art school – like for instance critics, curators and dealers.

Referencing established art or upcoming trends is an issue that touches also upon an artist's network capital, since the present research has demonstrated the relevance of building connections in the art field and getting in touch with influent gatekeepers. Indeed, artists appear to focus on network capital as a means to break the rigid access barriers set by the cultural establishment and they usually begin in art school by picking up every valuable contact, since this environment gives direct or indirect access to some players of the art system who might otherwise be difficult to intercept. During art education, as well as immediately after graduation, collectiveness seems the best viable solution for new entries to find early support and to arouse the attention of influent gatekeepers, such as critics and dealers. In a way, artists resort to this basic social strategy, because groups can provide shelter against adversities and foster communal chances of breakthrough. Be it a peer group, an ideological movement, a style collective or an artist union, each of these options resolve in an enhanced capability for the individual to access the art system. The analysis of the wider YBA generation showed that it is rather secondary, whether a group shares ideas or even style, since the fundamental trait is to act as a recognizable cluster within or against the establishment. Often such collective solutions are born out of loose groupings of art schoolmates that keep hanging out together and support each other for friendship. Artist-run spaces and warehouse shows emerged as two crucial means for artists to take advantage of collective strength and try to interact with the art system. Acting as a group may further help to get in touch with relevant players and gatekeepers, but even if left alone an artist needs to explicitly address dealers and collectors, critics and curators or look for mentors among established artists, for instance serving as an assistant. Network capital emerges as a crucial asset and being capable of leveraging relationships among other players of the art system appears to be a key factor for acceptance into the field, as well as to be granted growing opportunities.

Another central feature of today's art system is represented by social capital, as the chosen study case proved that artworks don't necessarily speak for themselves. Quite the contrary, the artist persona is now crucial for the art system to thrive on, thus individual reputation becomes a crucial aspect artists must pay attention to and possibly attempt to shape at their freewill, such as to characterize one's own position in the field. Concerning the YBA phenomenon, several critics argued that it was all about advertising, though this opinion would grossly exaggerate the influence of media exposure on the art system. Although referencing Conceptual Art apparently demands for a marketing strategy, which revolves around the artist persona, publicity may indeed be insufficient to foster artistic success. In fact, the previous research showed that a real breakthrough is only possible, if there are other likeminded players struggling for the same cause, or when several influent gatekeepers of the art system decide to embrace an upcoming trend. Hence media exposure is one of several options to foster an artist's reputation, while other equally effective strategies exist such as resorting to self-entrepreneurship, exploiting celebrity status or creating an individual mythology that appeals to other art system players. Among the many ways, branding is likely to be regarded as the most efficient one the art market has found to vouch for cultural appreciation of a specific author, such that successful branding in the art field may even spill over to different cultural arenas or even business sectors.

One last factor, which determines the peculiar path an aspiring artist decides to walk, is doubtless financial capital, as confirmed by the research carried out in the previous chapters. A career in the visual arts – as well as in various other cultural fields – is a risky and hardly remunerative choice, especially at the beginning thus compelling an aspiring artist to find financial drivers besides artistic production. The problem presents itself particularly after finishing art education, at a time when family support has usually expired due to the accomplished graduation and one is set alone to seek access into the art system. At this point artist candidates must prove to be extremely motivated, taking the high risk of failure and accepting to find ways to fund their career otherwise, frequently resorting to non-artistic jobs or art-related jobs. One may try to find the immediate backing of a dealer or a collector, but depending on social and geographic circumstances both aspiring and rising artists largely resort to public or private support outside the art market, such as in the case of scholarships, paid residencies and monetary awards. Whatever the financial sources artists choose to employ, unless they have a scheme of action to sustain their career kick-start, it appears difficult they may endure for long at the borders of the art system.

The thesis this research is based on seems to be consistent, since there are a number of factors which artists can get hold of – to some extent – in order to turn their professional aspirations into a real career in the art field. Evidence shows indeed that talent is only one feature to be possessed, because artists should simultaneously leverage network capital, reputation and financial opportunities. The analysis conducted on the early years of Douglas Gordon is useful to highlight the structure and dynamics of today's art system, arguing that artists should better be aware of the various players in the field, of the necessary resources to emerge and of some strategies to foster one's position. These findings may be tested on the career of other successful artists and movements or even on completely different periods in art history. Besides general and theoretical results, however, the contribution of this research rests on an area also regarding the specific case study, which is the British art scene of the 1990s. To be more specific, it appears there are three useful conclusions that may be drawn from the study of the wider YBA generation, which concern the centre-periphery duality between London and Glasgow, the male-female opposition among emerging artists and the gradual predominance of the more resourceful young authors over the British art system. Clearly, some of the propositions that will be offered may not be entirely unique, but they give rather congruous answers to some issues of the subject matter, which had since caused much debate and diverging opinions among art historians and critics.

As regards the centre-periphery discourse, previous studies on the young British artists have disclosed a tendency to unify the Glasgow scene to the events and influent characters in London, while only Scottish scholars have pledged for their diversity. As a matter of facts, the outcome of this research should have definitely stressed the structural difference of trends and approaches between young artists of the two cities during the period under examination. National newspapers, radio and television were captivated by the YBA phenomenon and the Turner Prize, hence mounting a London-centric perspective that helped many young artists to come into prominence, but which decidedly distorted the picture. On the contrary, following the opinions expressed by critics and experts within the UK art scene in the Nineties it was possible to find plurality, divisiveness and argument which revolved in particular around the duality between London and Glasgow artists. As a matter of facts, the two cities possessed completely different art systems, which aspiring artists were well aware of, though at the end of the 1980s circumstances young art school graduates were confronted with appeared absolutely comparable. It is indeed the divergent response to similar challenges that confirms the diversity of approaches and groups within the wider range of artists credited as YBAs. To start with art education, the rediscovery of Conceptual Art in London went together with the re-appropriation of its methods in Glasgow, though for different reasons and with different aims. While Londoners appeared to exploit conceptualist practices as a way to reference high art, hence without a formal unity of style among young graduates, in Glasgow conceptualism became part of a proper working method that connected various authors into a coherent grouping and somehow could even be understood as a specific movement or regional class of artists. A further difference between the two cities' rising artists consists in a decidedly varied approach to the art system, which certainly originated from the specific geographic conditions. Although the London art market had lost its influence on the global art scene during the Eighties, there were all various gatekeepers such as dealers, collectors and curators that young artists could attempt to intercept to start a career in the art field. On the contrary, commercial concerns were completely irrelevant for Glaswegian artists, simply because there was no access to structured facilities in their hometown. Not by any chance, these divergent situations have fostered different responses as regards actions to enter the art system: in London aspiring artists were seeking dealers and patrons to access the local art market, while their peers in Glasgow watched out for mentors and godfathers to create a link with the international art scene. An effective strategy in the British capital would thus be warehouse shows, who had a sporadic character and were organized to attract immediate attention of influent players. In reverse, artist-run spaces such as Transmission proved long lasting, unfolding various activities on a wider period of time and building a network of international relationships that would prove a useful asset later on. These varied approaches give also a sound explanation for the fact that new entries in London tended to build their personal reputation by shaping their self-image and producing impressive artworks with an eye for media attention, while in Glasgow the best strategy to run for appeared to be offering ideas and a solid body of works to an extended network of connections which could then provide endorsement.

Another crucial aspect emerging from the observed case study further seems to be the breakthrough and sustained presence of a considerable number of women in the artists milieu, which constitutes an important shift in Western art tradition. Consequently, the YBA generation placed the UK in front of many other countries concerning the affirmation of women artists on the international art scene, although female authors still appear to have to fight harder than male colleagues to rise into prominence and – especially – to keep notoriety. However, the massive access of women into higher education during the Eighties has proved disruptive – much more than the increased participation of working class students – clearly causing the following decade's surge of women artists against the male-dominated art system, further determining the rise of gender related issues, as well as affecting trends and themes expressed by artists.

Finally, this study may have served as a window to an understanding of the way a new generation of artists approached the art system in the UK during the 1990s and brought about a generational shift over a few years only, demonstrating a particular awareness and heightened sensibility for the dynamics and key players of the art field. Indeed, self-promotion and entrepreneurship have emerged as distinctive features for many rising artists of the broader YBA generation, which were turned from basic means to outlive the economic crisis or the nonexistence of a solid art market into a coherent strategy to arouse attention. Mastering their career start with growing competence and true entrepreneurial inclination, several young artists of this decade have been able to contrive a vast amount of contacts and media attention, instead of concentrating merely on their artistic output. Understanding that exhibitions rather than artworks were becoming the true drive of the art system, this generation focused on the organization of events as means to access networks of influent players and to strengthen individual or collective reputation. As a matter of facts, most iconic pieces of the 1990s in the UK were created expressly on the occasion of self-initiated projects or for shows at independent spaces. The case of Douglas Gordon and his generation proved that their acceptance by the UK art system was dependent also on a transformation of the field's balance, since it is evident that gatekeepers in the art system may shift at some point, either if established players change their mind about artists and trends to promote or, otherwise, when new actors reach a powerful position. Indeed, the swift rise of a new generation of artists wouldn't have been possible without the simultaneous ascent of new players who entered the arena, such as recently opened commercial galleries, newly founded art magazines, young curators and receptive critics, since they all had a comparable urgency to gain resources that could help them to become established. However, even some already influent actors took advantage of the situation and improved their position considerably in the art field by means of the rising tide. As it appears, tastes and trends are more persistent on the art market than one may think, because falling out of fashion affects the overall balance of the system. Hence, public institutions sanctioned the final transition to the new trend when they decided to grant their endorsement by means of official museum shows, touring exhibitions and possibly even purchases of works into important collections. Furthermore, UK establishment turned a profit on the rising generation of artists to progress the country's position on the global art scene and even strengthen national economy. As a matter of facts, the massive export of the nation's supposedly best cultural products became a very effective promotion tool for the country at large, which also put London – and even Glasgow, to some extents – back at the very heart of global art system, mainly at the expense of Continental Europe.

Naturally, some of the propositions that have been offered so far may still be questioned or could make good use of further analysis, but it appears they rightly highlight artist's awareness – especially of the generation of Douglas Gordon's – concerning the field of art, its players and the relative position of each, as well as the ways and strategies to acquire resources useful for rising into prominence. Hal Foster correctly recognized the conversion of the artist into an anthropologist, which gradually prevailed during the 1980s, postulating a new approach to visual arts that compares to ethnography. The study case on Douglas Gordon and the broader YBA generation further seems to stress a new attitude also towards the art system at large, which came about in the 1990s bestowing success to such authors that could manage their career with growing proficiency. A true entrepreneurial turn is evident, which grants acceptance in the art system and improvement of the individual position to those artists that prove most resourceful. At a much higher point, celebrity artists even become real entrepreneurs, controlling studios with dozens of assistants likewise an architectural firm or design industry, though this is a stage that has intentionally been left out by the present book and could be a convenient subject for further research. What appears to have been settled is the rise of the *enterprising artist* at the end of the 20th century, which became an attitude already manifest at an early stage in an author's career in order to enter Parnassus as quickly as possible.

Notes

Chapter 1
Unveiling successful artist strategies

1. The referenced definition of economics as a social science bound to the examination of human interaction is borrowed from the writings of economist Nicholas Gregory Mankiw, especially his *Principles of Economics*.

2. The definition "Glasgow Miracle" was coined by curator Hans Ulrich Obrist at a conference held at the Tate in London in 1996. As will be discussed in later chapters, this term was immediately picked up by art specialists, but at times vehemently opposed by local artists who were the actual protagonists of the city's art scene explosion.

3. Goldsmiths College is part of the University of London and specializes in the arts, humanities and social sciences.

4. The author, who has re-organized the archive of the Douglas Gordon setting a standard to the latter work and exhibition catalogue, has calculated the numbers of exhibitions Gordon participated into.

5. One should consider Gordon winning especially the Premio 2000 in 1997 at the Venice Biennale and the Hugo Boss Prize in 1998 at the Guggenheim in New York.

6. One might consider the shooting of *Feature Film* (1999) in Cologne with Artangel Production.

7. In 1998 Gagosian Gallery picks Gordon for official representation.

8. Gordon's archive is set in Berlin, nowadays in his Schöneberg studio. Before it travelled over from his apartment in Glasgow and was set in several locations of the German capital following the route of his studio from Charlottenburg (Herderstraße) to Kreuzberg (Blücherstraße and then Gneisenaustraße) and now in Schöneberg (Kurfürstenstraße).

Chapter 2
A cultural producer in the art system

1. The longe durée was particularly claimed and proved by the *Annales* School of Ernst Bloch.

2. Gaut proposes a list of possible criteria to define an artwork: 1) possess aesthetic properties such as beauty; 2) express emotions; 3) be intellectually challenging; 4) show formal complexity and coherence; 5) having the capability of conveying an articulate meaning; 6) express a personal opinion; 7) employ imagination and creativity; 8) result out of the adoption of high competences; 9) be part of an already prominent art category; 10) be the product of artistic intention (Gaut, 2000, p.28).

3. The Top World Artist Ranking by *Rank Art Facts*, which considers both living and recently deceased artists, places Douglas Gordon at number 21 in the top list of 2012 and at number 20 for 2013, being at place number 12 of the living artists. *Art Report*, which has developed a segmented artist ranking, places the Scottish artist at number 28 of the overall contemporary artists, while at number 18 of living artists. In 2015 the renowned German ranking system Kunstkompass places Douglas Gordon at number 17 of best living artists worldwide, being the first among authors from the YBA generation. See: http://rankartfacts.net/ and http://www.art-report.com/de/ranking/top-30-lebend (03/07/2014).

4. Reference is made to *24 Hour Psycho Back and Forth and To and Fro* (2008), which was purchased with the Max Geldner-Foundation.

5. These are takes of a friend of Gordon who had his index finger tattooed, for the artist wanted to display the measure that physically gets to the human heart, being exactly three inches. Photo dimensions 80,5 per 105 cm.

6. They are takes of the artist's newborn nephew who grabs his own foot to bite it gently, as the undertakers used to do in France to be sure a man was dead before burial. Photo dimensions 94,6 per 137,2 cm.

7. Ref. Gordon: "I work with whatever is necessary and available [...] I'm not in the medium, I work with it, alongside it. [...] For me the idea comes first." (Van Assche, 1996, pp.137-138)

8. Giorgio Verzotti has coined an appropriate phrase for Gordon's style: 'poetica del perturbante', meaning a poetics of unsettlement, an art that points at unsettling (Verzotti, 2006, p.18).

9. Such a definition of art system is clearly derived from art theorist Gorge Dickie's early version of the institutional theory of art.

10. Both George Dickie and sociologist Howard Becker support this view (Becker, 1984).

11. The first version of the institutional theory by George Dickie sets the artist, on one side, and the public, on the opposite side, at the two poles of the art system (Dickie, 2000, p.107).

12. Working on an art historical interpretation which takes into account the whole range of different social classes, Arnold Hauser identifies even three divergent types of art: one deriving from popular culture, one aiming at broad entertainment (later mass culture) and one of the dominant elite, which may be defined high culture (Hauser, 1987, p.581).

13. Expounding his institutional theory of art, George Dickie maintains that the fundamental actors are the artist and the public, while all the others in-between would in fact be parasitic compared to the fundamental relation between an artist and his public (Dickie, 2000, p.107).

14. In economics, adverse selection and moral hazard are two possible consequences of information asymmetry. While the former is a situation, in which one party could make a wrong decision, since it doesn't know the information the other party is hold of, moral hazard stems from the possible risk-taking nature of one of the two parties that is delegated to take decisions in a principal-agent problem.

15. "Art works are generally unique products and there are non perfect substitutes that can replace them. The dealers and auction houses compete to acquire major art works within the field of their product specialization." (Jyrämä, 2008, p.73)

16. Mintzberg and Waters identify a strain of different strategies with peculiar features according to the origin of the strategy itself: (i) planned strategy, its origin is a formal plan; (ii) entrepreneurial strategy, originated in a central vision; (iii) ideological strategy, growing out of shared beliefs; (iv) Umbrella strategy, born out of constraints; (v) process strategy, based on the method rather then contents, (vi)

Unconnected strategy, originated in conclaves; (vii) consensus strategy, grown out of convergence; (viii) imposed strategy, originated in environment (Mintzberg and Waters, 1985, p.270).

Chapter 3
Family, society, religion in the Scottish Sixties

1. After a major review of government social classification, in 2001 the Office for National Statistics introduced a new socio-economic classification that divides society as follows: 1) Higher managerial and professional; 2) Lower managerial and professional; 3) intermediate; 4) Small employers and own account workers; 5) Lower supervisory and technical; 6) semi routine; 7) routine (Bolton, 2010, p.3).
2. It is a series of photographic portraits taken of amateur footballers in Glasgow's outskirt wearing the t-shirts of the famous soccer teams AC Milan and Inter Milan.
3. It is a series of photographic portraits taken of passer-bys in South London, who were asked to write down their deepest fears and feelings on a small white sign.
4. Roderick Buchanan at Transmission Gallery in Glasgow, both Sarah Lucas and Gillian Wearing at City Racing in London.
5. Of the four characters the title refers to, the only infamous one is Myra Hindley, who was found a British serial killer together with her husband assassinating dozens of children and burying them in their backyard.
6. A copy of the letter has been preserved in the private archive of Douglas Gordon in Berlin among the documents dating back between 1987-1991.
7. The exhibition at Hayward Gallery was held from November 1st 2002 to January 5th 2003. (*What have I done,* Cat.2002)
8. Years later the work was lost in a fire that burnt down the warehouse of collector Charles Saatchi together with many other pieces of the young British artists.

Chapter 4
Art education between Glasgow and London

1. The reference is to the performance piece *Spit and Chew/Art and Culture* (1966-67).
2. The catalogue *Pretty much every word written, spoken, heard, overheard from 1989* for the solo show at Mart Rovereto in 2006 includes some of the pictures taken during that holiday in the Summer of 1985 (*Prettymucheverywordwritten,* Cat.2006).
3. Following sources are useful to analyse the early performative works by Douglas Gordon: (Bain, 1987), (Dickson, 1989, p.7), (Fagen, 1999, pp.72-74), (Lowndes, 2010, pp.109-112), (Richardson, 2011, pp.138-146), (Sinclair, 1993a).
4. Following sources are useful to analyse the works by *Freeze* exhibitors: (Bonami and Robecchi, 2007, pp.8-9), (Cooper, 2012, pp.25-26), (Fortnum, 2007, p.2-3), (Lack, 2008), (Morton, 2006), (Muir, 2011, pp.21-22), (Serota, 2011, p.93), (Sooke, 2008), (Watson, 2012).
5. The group exhibition was ironically titled *Dependants* (Lowndes, 2010, p.131).
6. Following sources are useful to analyse the early text pieces by Douglas Gordon: (Brown, 2004, p.11), (Lowndes, 2010, pp.118-127), (Richardson, 2011, p.147), (Sinclair, 1993a, pp.10-11).
7. *Untitled,* 1989 – Medium: wall text, typeface Akzidenz Grotesk and Bembo, white gloss, dimensions variable – First installation: Reading (UK), 1989
8. For a complete overview on the text-pieces by Douglas Gordon see the catalogue for the 2006 exhibition held at MART in Rovereto, Italy (*Prettymucheverywordwritten,* Cat.2006, pp.97-101).
9. Following sources are useful to analyse the works for Gordon's graduate show at the Slade: (Brown, 2004, pp.8-10), (Sheikh, 1997, p.16), (Sinclair, 1993a, pp.10-14).
10. Marino Marini (Pistoia 1901 – Viareggio 1980), André Minaux (Parigi 1923 – Toquin 1986).

Chapter 5
Southern flames and Northern lights

1. Following sources are useful to analyse the origin and development of Transmission: (*Guilt by Association*, Cat.1992), (Lowndes, 2010, pp.117-139), (Richardson, 2011, pp.133-156), (Slotover, 1991).

2. Following sources are useful to analyse the group exhibition *Self Conscious State*: (Fagen, 1999, p.75), (Fortnum, 2007, pp.10-11), (*Guilt by Association*, Cat.1992, p.9), (Harding, 2001a), (Lawson, 1995, p.57), (Lowndes, 2010, pp.140-141), (Moisdon-Tremblay, 1996, p.121), (Richardson, 2011, pp.148-149), (Sheikh, 1997, p.16).

3. This piece was reproduced for Borland's extensive retrospective show at the Fruitmarket Gallery in Edinburgh held from December 2nd 2006 to January 28th 2007 (*Christine Borland: Preserves*, Cat.2006).

4. Following source is useful to analyse the geographic and historic background of the artist run spaces in the London former Docklands: (http://southwarknotes.wordpress.com/art-and-regeneration/art-empty-southwark-industrial-buildings/).

5. This appears to be true, for instance, as regards to the statements of Michael Landy, Adam Chodzko and Angus Fairhurst (Cooper, 2012, p.42).

6. Following sources are useful to analyse the group exhibition *Windfall 91*: (*Guilt by Association*, Cat.1992, p.8), (Lowndes, 2010, pp., 63, 146), (Sinclair, 1993a, p.18), (Slotover, 1991, pp.36-46).

7. Following source is useful to analyse the reputation strategy adopted by several YBAs: (Stallabrass, 2006b, pp.42-43,130-132).

8. Following sources are useful to analyse the group exhibition *Walk On*: (Castle, 1991), (Lawson, 1995, p.63), (Sinclair, 1993a, p.20).

9. Following sources are useful to analyse the group exhibition *London Road*: (Brown, 2004, p.11), (Sinclair, 1993a, pp.14-15).

10. Following sources are useful to analyse the group exhibition *Barclays Young Artist's Award*: (Brown, 2004, p.11), (Castle, 1991, p.16), (Gillick, 1991, p.58), (Stallabrass, 2006b, p.130).

11. *Letter (Number 4)* was mailed from London on 6th of April 1992.

12. Following sources are useful to analyse the group exhibition *Guilt by Association*: (*Guilt by Association*, Cat.1992), (Lowndes, 2010, p.150), (Richardson, 2011, p.156), (Sinclair, pp.40-43).
13. Following sources are useful to analyse Gordon's early *Instruction* pieces: (Lawson, 1995, pp.61-62), (Moisdon-Tremblay, 1996, pp.120, 128), (Obrist, 1996b, p.169), (Prettymucheverywordwritten, Cat.2006, pp. 50-53), (Sheikh, 1997, p.16), (Sinclair, 1993a, pp.3-5).
14. Following sources are useful to analyse the group exhibition *A Modest Proposal*: (Brandtzaeg, 2008), (Dingle, 2010), (Muir, 2011, p.118), (Obrist, 1996b, p.173), (Sinclair, 1993a, pp.14-15).

Chapter 6
Going for more and more, at home and abroad

1. This was the exhibition *Gary Hume: New paintings* held at White Cube, April 7th – May 13th 1995, London (Muir, 2011, pp.80-81).
2. The project curiously came to an end when Gordon lost the model miniature in a Glasgow pub and couldn't retrace it.
3. Reference is made to the solo show *What have I done*, curated by Fiona Bradley and James Lingwood, which took place at the London Hayward Gallery from November 1st 2002 to January 5th 2003.
4. The Neue Galerie, the staircase of the AOK health insurance company and the Ottoneum, as well as temporary buildings in the Karlsaue Park and the newly erected Documenta Hall.
5. Source: D9 1992 on http://archiv.documenta12.de/d9.html?&L=1; accessed on 18/06/2014.
6. The mentioned work is a video installation, with variable dimensions, that projects some slow motion clips of the popular sci-fi TV series *Star Trek*. Its creation began in 1992, but it was completed in 1995 and first displayed on the occasion of the group show *Chez l'un, l'autre* organized in the garden of Isabelle Suret's gallery at 5 Rue des Ursulines, Paris.
7. Sieglaub once even declared "[...] the information about the work would function as a certificate of authenticity for the patron." (Seth Sieglaub form Letter dated 8 July 1968, in SSARCH, Box 5, File 118)

8. Reference is made to the group shows *The British Art Show 4* (Cat.1995) and *General Release* (Cat.1995).

9. The exhibition ran from July 17th until October 16th 1993.

10. Reference is made to the solo show *Douglas Gordon: self-portrait of you + me, after the factory* (Cat.2007).

11. Besides Gordon, the shortlisted artists in 1996 were Craigie Horsfield, Gary Hume and Simon Patterson. In 1997 four women were chosen: Christine Borland, Angela Bulloch, Cornelia Parker and Gillian Wearing. In 1998 Tacita Dean, Cathy de Monchaux, Chris Ofili and Sam Taylor-Wood. In 1999 Tracey Emin, Steve McQueen, Steven Pippin, Jane and Louise Wilson.
    In this regards, official data may be useful:
    Avarage age of Turner Prize shortlisted artists
    Year (Δ age): 1984 (44); 1985 (46); 1986 (43); 1987 (39); 1988 (45); 1989 (50); 1991 (30); 1992 (27); 1993 (37); 1994 (38); 1995 (36); 1996 (35); 1997 (35); 1998 (33)
    Attendance rates at the Tate Gallery in London
    (Year:Visitors) 1980: 1.330.937; 1981: 885.168; 1982: 1.219.102; 1983: 1.270.925; 1984: 1.265.605; 1985: 980.105; 1986: 1.137.070; 1987: 1.725.084; 1988: 1.581.467; 1989: 1.234.281; 1990: 1.562.431; 1991: 1.816.421; 1992: 1.575.637; 1993: 1.760.091; 1994: 2.226.399; 1995: 1.769.662; 1996: 2.203.001; 1997: 1.757.735
    Source: data drawn from www.tate.co.org processed by the author

12. These are the exact dates for the mentioned exhibitions: Lisson Gallery, London, from December 9th 1994 to January 21st 1995; *Entr'Acte 3* at Van Abbemuseum, Eindhoven, from September 16th to November 12th 1995; *Fuzzy Logic* at Centre Gorges Pompidou, Paris, from December 6th 1995 to January 22nd 1996; Migros, Zurich, from October 12th 1996 to January 19th 1997.

13. The referred work is *Letter (Number 17)* (1994).

14. Following source is useful to analyse the solo show at Lisson Gallery: (Brown, 2004, pp.39-44).

15. The referenced artwork is *Skull. Upper extremities, right. Upper extremities, left. Breastbone. Collarbones. Shoulder blades. Ribs. Spine. Sacrum. Pelvis. Lower extremities, right. Lower extremities, left* (1997).

16. Following sources are useful to analyse the solo exhibition *Entr'Acte*: (Brown, 2004, pp.48-51), (*Entr'Acte*, Cat.1995), (*Kidnapping*, Cat.1998), (Sans, 1996, p.110).
17. Following sources are useful to analyse the solo exhibition at Migros, Zurich: (Brown, 2004, pp.56-58), (Fagen, 1999, pp.107-108), (Sheikh, 1997, p.20).
18. Following sources are useful to analyse the work *5 Years Drive-By*: (Brown, 2004, p.53), (Heiser, 2008, p.195), (Spector, 1997, p.72), (Van den Boogard, 1997, p.43).
19. In Clair's opinion, painters such as Lucien Freud and hence other neo-expressionist artists were still able to meet the criteria dear to the French curator (Clair, 2011, pp.104-105).
20. Clair indicates precisely the exhibition curated by Szeemann at Kunsthalle Bern in 1969, titled *When attitudes become form*.
21. Following sources are useful to analyse the work *Hysterical*: (Am Rande der Malerei, Cat.1995), (Brown, 2004, p.47-48), (Cork, 1995, p.32), (Newman, 1995, p.33).
22. The exhibition *Swan Off* ran from March 9th to April 14th 1996.
23. Following sources are useful to analyse the group exhibition *Swan Off*: (Arrhenius, 1996, p.37-38), (Brown, 1996, pp.40,60).

Chapter 7
Exploiting each favourable opportunity

1. These were the exhibition running dates: in Columbus from September 1996 to January 1997; at the Palazzo delle Esposizioni in Rome from June to September 1997; in Chicago from October 1997 to January 1998.
2. Following sources are useful to analyse the group exhibition *Scream and Scream Again*: (*Babylon*, Cat.2008), (Brown, 2004, p.51), (Cork, 1995), (Feaver, 1996a), (*Scream and scream again*, Cat.1996).
3. More recently the piece was displayed for the group show *theanyspacewhatever* (Cat.2009)at the Guggenheim Museum in New York in 2011.
4. Among the remaining participants, the only British artists on show were Mat Collishaw and Sam Taylor-Wood.

5. Following sources are useful to analyse the group exhibition Spellbound: (Dorment, 1996a), (Feaver, 1996a), (Houghton, 1996), (Jackson, 1996), (McEwan, 1996a), (McQuay, 2005), (Meyeric Hughes and Hilty, 1996, p.8), (Romney, 1996), (Searle, 1996a), (Sladen, 1996, pp.25-26).

6. The movie *Spellbound* by Alfred Hitchcock revolves on the case of a woman doctor who administrates a psychoanalytic therapy to her lover in order to reveal his true identity, fearing he might actually be a murderer.

7. Further reference on the subject is to be found under Three 30-second K Foundation TV advertisements on www.libraryofmu.org

8. Following sources are useful to analyse the nomination of the 1996 Turner Prize shortlist: (Alberge, 1996a), (Barclay Morgan, 1999), (Glaister, 1996a), (Lister, 1996a), (Stringer, 1996).

9. At the Turner Prize show in 1997 Borland displayed two major works, the first called *Phantom Twins*, which consisted of two medical baby dolls made of hand-sewn leather, as they were based on 18th-century models. The new piece expressly created for the Turner show was titled *After a true story - Giant and Fairy Tales* and was again based on things she had seen in anatomy collections as regards to deformity and freaks (Barclay Morgan, 1999).

10. Following sources are useful to analyse the exhibition of the 1996 Turner Prize shortlist: (Alberge, 1996b), (Beckett, 1996), (Brown, 2004, pp.64-67), (Burdon, 1996), (Dorment, 1996b), (Feaver, 1996c), (Glaister, 1996b), (Graham-Dixon, 1996), (Lebovici, 2000, pp.165-166), (Lister, 1996b), (McEwen, 1996b), (Muir, 2011, p.83), (Searle, 1996b), (Shepherd, 1996), (Spector, 1997, p.81), (Van den Boogard, 1997, p.37).

11. Katrina Brown (2004, p.64) underlines that this work masterfully illustrates George Bataille's paradox: the French anthropologist wrote that sexual intercourse implies that two otherwise separate individuals become indistinguishable.

12. Further reference on the subject is to be found in BURSTON, D. (1996) *The wing of madness. The life and work of R.D.Laing.* Cambridge: Harvard University Press.

13. The author has recollected the accounts on the incidents involving Douglas Gordon at the Turner Prize ceremony in 1996 in the course of a private conversation with the artist in late Autumn 2009.

14. A clip of the award ceremony and acceptance speech of 1996 can be found on youtube.com at the following address: https://www.youtube.com/watch?v=uof0N5JHH4Y

15. Following sources are useful to analyse the Gordon's victory of the 1996 Turner Prize: (Fagen, 1999, pp.91-92), (Glaister, 1996c), (Henry, 1996), (Raynolds, 1996), (Dorment, 1996c), (Searle, 1996c).

Table of images

The images shown in chronological order on the central pages of the book all stem from artist Douglas Gordon's personal archive, which is located at his studio in Berlin's Kurfürstenstrasse. They were chosen among several archival boxes that account for the years of his early career, dating from 1987 to 1996. Particular attention was put on selection criteria, which were set to portray the progression of Gordon's professional path as well as his artistic evolution. Foremost, the explicit intention was to avoid photos of Gordon's major artworks, which have been already displayed in numerous publications and catalogues. Indeed, none of the pictures has ever been published before, thus offering an unprecedented insight to the Glaswegian artist's biography. As a result, the images chosen portray the life and deeds of Douglas Gordon in his career kick-start, focusing on unreleased material that illustrates the sources of inspiration and the early attempts of one of the world's most successful living artists. It is important to notice, however, that when no photographer is mentioned for a picture, the author is either unknown or likely to be Gordon himself or some assistant and friend who documented the installation process at an exhibition or the finished artwork.

All images are a courtesy of *Lost but found*, Douglas Gordon's studio, and were digitalized thanks to archivist Katharina Kiebacher. The author wishes to express all his gratitude for this generous concession and for the support.

List of illustrations

Fig.1. (1968?) *Douglas Gordon as a child (probably 2 years old) sitting on the armchair in the living room* [Digitalized photograph] In possession of: Lost but found, Berlin.

Fig.2. (1980-1981?) *Douglas Gordon (probably 14 or 15 years old) with his entire family* [Digitalized Polaroid] In possession of: Lost but found, Berlin.

Fig.3. (1980-1981?) *Douglas Gordon (probably 14 or 15 years old) with his younger sister and brother* [Digitalized photograph] In possession of: Lost but found, Berlin.

Fig.24. (1989-1990?) *Douglas Gordon and friends refurbishing the inner part of Transmission Gallery in Glasgow* [Diapositive, box folder year 1990] In possession of: Lost but found, Berlin.

Fig.25. (1989-1990?) *Douglas Gordon armstanding and friends in front of Transmission Gallery in Glasgow* [Diapositive, box folder year 1990] In possession of: Lost but found, Berlin.

Fig.26. (1990) *Installation view of 'Proof' for the exhibition* Sites/Position *in Glasgow* [Diapositive, box folder year 1990] In possession of: Lost but found, Berlin.

Fig.27. (1990) *Installation view of the exhibition* Self Conscious *State at the Third Eye Centre in Glasgow with Gordon's 'List of Names' on the background* [Diapositive, box folder year 1990] In possession of: Lost but found, Berlin.

Fig.28. (1990) *Installation view at opening night of the exhibition* Self Conscious *State at the Third Eye Centre in Glasgow with Gordon's 'List of Names' on the background* [Diapositive, box folder year 1990] In possession of: Lost but found, Berlin.

Fig.29. (1990) *Entrance of the* Archive Room *at the Slade School in London with a supposed collaboration with Marino Marini and André Minaux* [Diapositive, box folder year 1990] In possession of: Lost but found, Berlin.

Fig.30. (1990) *Installation view of the* Archive Room *at the Slade School in London with the supposed wall drawings by Marino Marini and André Minaux in the foreground* [Diapositive, box folder year 1990] In possession of: Lost but found, Berlin.

Fig.31. (1990) *Installation view of 'Meaning and Location' at the Octagon of the Slade School in London* [Diapositive, box folder year 1990] In possession of: Lost but found, Berlin.

Fig.32. (1990) *Self-portrait of Douglas Gordon at the age of 24* [Diapositive, box folder year 1990] In possession of: Lost but found, Berlin.

Fig.33. (1991) *Installation view of 'London Road' from the shop window of the Orpheus Gallery in Belfast* [Diapositive, box folder year 1991] In possession of: Lost but found, Berlin.

Fig.34. (1991) *Installation view of 'New Maps' in London's Hyde Park with the Serpentine Gallery on the rear for* Barclays Young Artist Award

Fig.45. (1993) *Hans Ulrich Obrist on the phone performing 'Instruction (Number 3b)'* [Diapositive, box folder year 1993] In possession of: Lost but found, Berlin.

Fig.46. (1993) *Installation view of 'Instruction (Number 3b)' for the exhibition* Migrateurs at *ARC Musée d'Art Moderne de la Ville de Paris* [Diapositive, box folder year 1993] In possession of: Lost but found, Berlin.

Fig.47. (1993) *'Potential for Violence' showing Douglas Gordon with a baseball bat standing in front of a sculpture by Eduardo Paolozzi* [Diapositive, box folder year 1993] In possession of: Lost but found, Berlin.

Fig.48. (1993) *Installation view of 'The Magic Newspaper' for the group exhibition* Übergänge *at the Museum Moderner Kunst in Passau* [Diapositive, box folder year 1993] In possession of: Lost but found, Berlin.

Fig.49. Ridely, J. (1994) *Installation view of 'Trigger finger' for the solo show* Douglas Gordon: Recent Works *at Lisson Gallery in London* [Diapositive, box folder year 1993] In possession of: Lost but found, Berlin.

Fig.50. (1995) *Installation view of 'Hysterical' for the group* show General Release *at the Scuola di San Pasquale on the occasion of 1995 Venice Biennale* [Diapositive, box folder year 1993] In possession of: Lost but found, Berlin.

Fig.51. Ridely, J. (1994) *Installation view of '10ms-1' for the solo show* Douglas Gordon: Recent Works *at Lisson Gallery in London* [Diapositive, box folder year 1993] In possession of: Lost but found, Berlin.

Fig.52. (1996) *Installation view of 'Fuzzy Logic' and 'Bootlegd' for the solo exhibition* Close your eyes *at MIGROS in Zurich* [Diapositive, box folder year 1995] In possession of: Lost but found, Berlin.

Fig.53. White, S. (1997) *Installation view with replica of the piece for the exhibition* A Modest Proposal *at Milch Gallery showing created in collaboration with Simon Patterson, then titled 'Framework for Colour Co-ordination for Building Purposes (House of Windsor & House of Stuart)' and here installed at the exhibition* Material Culture. The Object in British art of 1980's and 90's *at Hayward*

Gallery in London (April 3rd 1997) [Diapositive, box folder year 1992] In possession of: Lost but found, Berlin.

Index of names

L

M

N

O

P

R

Index of exhibitions

Following is a complete list of exhibitions in which Douglas Gordon participated to in the considered period, set in strict chronological order from 1987 to 1996 and divided between solo and group shows.

1987

SOLO SHOWS: *Experiments under Nostalgia's Umbrella* (with Richardson), Third Eye Centre, Glasgow (UK); *tradition:dehabilitation, National Review of Live Art* (with Craig Richardson and Euan Sutherland), Riverside Studios, London (UK); *Puberty Institution: AntehyperaesthesiA*, Transmission Gallery, Glasgow (UK); *Puberty Institution: AntehyperaesthesiA* (with Craig Richardson), *4th Avé Festival* (with Craig Richardson), Arnhem (The Netherlands).

1988

SOLO SHOWS: *40 Years from Cradle to Grave* (with Craig Richardson), Royal Scottish Academy, Edinburgh (UK); *The Puberty Institution: The Arches* (with Craig Richardson), Midland Street Car Park, Glasgow (UK); *The Puberty Institution: Refuse-consumption-decay-survival* (with Craig Richardson), Third Eye Centre, Glasgow (UK).

1989

GROUP SHOWS: *Festival of Plagiarism*, Transmission Gallery, Glasgow (UK); *Glasgow Group*, Tramway, Glasgow (UK); *Smith Biennial*, Smith Art Gallery and Museum, Stirling (UK); *Information*, Paisley Museum and Galleries, Scotland (UK); *Live Art at the Keep*, Open-Eland Studios, England (UK); *Windfall '89*, A.G. Weser and Kommunale Galerie, Bremen (Germany); *The Living Room*, in Gianni Piacentini's flat, Glasgow (UK); *Untitled #1* (wall text), Reading (UK); *The Unite Room*, Slade School of Fine Arts, London (UK).

1990

GROUP SHOWS: *Archive Room*, Slade School of Fine Art, London (UK); *Meaning and Location*, Octagon Gallery, University of London, London (UK); *Self concious State*, Third Eye Centre, Glasgow (UK) curator: Andrew Nairne; *Sites/Positions*; several open-air venues in Glasgow (UK).

1991

GROUP SHOWS: *Archive Project*, APAC Centre d'Art contemporain, Nevers (France) curator: Hans Ulrich Obrist; *Barclays Young Artist Award*, Serpentine Gallery, London (UK) curator: Mel Gooding; *The Bellgrove Station Billboard Project* , Bellgrove Station, Glasgow (UK); *London Road (with Roderick Buchanan)*, Orpheus Gallery, Belfast (UK); *Walk On*, Jack Tilton Gallery, New York (USA) Fruitmarket Gallery, Edinburgh (UK) curator: Alan Johnston; *Windfall '91*, Seaman's Mission, Glasgow (UK) curators: Douglas Gordon, Joseph Beuys, Nathan Coley; *Speed*, Transmission Gallery, Glasgow (UK).

1992

GROUP SHOWS: *And what do you represent?*, Anthony Reynolds Gallery, London (UK); *Anomie*, Patent House, London (UK); *L'U di carte*, Café Picasso, Rome (Italy); *Il mistero die 100 dollari scomparsi: Instructions Received*, Galleria Gio' Marconi, Milan (Italy); *Molteplici Culture*, Museo del Folklore, Rome (Italy) curators: Carolyn Christov Bakargiev and Ludovico Pratesi; *The Speaker Project*, Institute of contemporary Arts, London (UK) curator: Liam Gillick; *5 Dialogues*, Natuurhistorish Samlinger, Bergen (Norway); *Guilt by Association*, Museum of Modern Art, Dublino (Ireland) curator: Declan McGonagle; *240 Minuten*, Galerie Esther Schipper, Colonia (Germany); *A modest proposal (with Simon Patterson)*, Milch Gallery, London (UK); *Love at first sight*, The Showroom, London (UK).

1993

SOLO SHOWS: *24 Hour Psycho*, Tramway, Glasgow (UK) curators: Nicola White, Neil Wallace, John Clark KunstWerke, Berlin (Germany) curator:

Klaus Biesenbach; *Migrateurs*, ARC Musée d'Art Moderne de la Ville de Paris, Paris (France) curator: Hans Ulrich Obrist.

GROUP SHOWS: *Before the Sound of the Beep*, audio works at several venues, Paris (France); *Chambre 763*, Hotel Carlton Palace, Paris (France) curator: Hans Ulrich Obrist; *Douglas Gordon/Simon Patterson*, Galerie Gruppe Grün, Bremen (Germany); *Moving into View: Recent British Painting*, Royal Festival Hall, London (UK); *Prospekt '93*, Schim Kunsthalle Frankfurt and Frankfurter Kunstverein, Frankfurt (Germany); *Purpose Built New England: Long Distance Information*, Real Art Ways, Hartford, Connecticut (USA) curator: Michael Corris; *The Return of the Cadavre Exquis*, The Drawing Center, New York (USA); *Übergänge*, Museum Moderner Kunst, Passau (Germany); *Viennese Story*, Wiener Seccession, Vienna (Austria) curator: Jerome Sans; *Walter Benjamin's Briefcase*, Oportos Festival of contemporary Art, Porto (Portugal) curator: Andrew Renton; *Wonderful Life* , Lisson Gallery, London (UK) curator: James Roberts; *High Fidelity*, Kohji Ogura Gallery, Nagoya (Japan) Röntgen Kunst Institut, Tokyo (Japan) curator: James Roberts; *Left Luggage/Rencontres dans un couloir*, Maison Hanru, Paris (France); *Propositions*, Musée Départmental d'Art contemporain, Chateau de Rochechoouart, Limoges (France).

1994

SOLO SHOWS: *Douglas Gordon: Recent Works*, Lisson Gallery, London (UK).

GROUP SHOWS: *Something between my mouth and your ear*, Dolphin Gallery, Oxford (UK) installation for *The Reading Room*, a project by Bookworks London; *conceptual Living*, Rhizome, Amsterdam (The Netherlands); *Europa '94*, First European Gallerist congress, Munich (Germany); *Gaze: L'impossible transparence*, Carré des Art du Parc Floral de Paris, Paris (France); *Minima Media*, Media Biennale Leipzig, Leipzig (Germany); *Modern Art*, Transmission Gallery, Glasgow (UK); *New Painting*, Chapter, Cardiff (UK) Oriel Gallery, Mold (UK); *Points de vue: Images d'Europe*, Centre national d'art et de culture Georges Pompidou, Paris (France); *Rue des Marins*, Galerie Air de Paris, Nice (France); *Some of my friends*, Gallerie Campbells Occasionally, Copenhagen (Denmark); *Stain in Reality: Stan Douglas, Douglas Gordon, Joachim Koester*, Galerie Nicolai Wallner, Copenhagen (Denmark); *The Institute of Cultural Anxiety: Works from the Collection*, Institution of contemporary Arts,

London (UK) curator: Jeremy Millar; *Übergänge/Atjaras*, Galeria Kiaallitohazaba, Budapest (Hungary) curator: Hans Knoll; *Wall to Wall: South Bank Touring Exhibition* (touring exhibition) South Bank Centre, London (UK) Leeds City Art Gallery, Leeds (UK) Southampton City Art Centre, Southampton (UK), curator: Maureen Paley; *WATT*, Witte de With & Kunsthal, Rotterdam (The Netherlands); *Fiction Non-Fiction*, Galleria Bonomo, Rome (Italy).

1995

SOLO SHOWS: *Bad Faith*, Künstlerhaus Stuttgart, Stuttgart (Germany); *The End*, Jack Tilton Gallery, New York (USA), Café Rooseum Espresso, Malmö (Sweden); *Jukebox – Douglas Gordon/Graham Gussin: a collaboration*, The Agency, London (UK); *Fuzzy Logic*, Centre Gorges Pompidou, Paris (France) curator: Christine Van Assche; *Entr'Acte 3*, Stedelijk Van Abbemuseum, Eindhoven (The Netherlands) curator: Jan Debbaut.

GROUP SHOWS: *Am Rande der Malerei*, Kunsthalle Bern, Bern (Switzerland) curators: Ulrich Loock, Rein Wolfs; *Aperto '95*, FRAC Languedoc-Roussillon, Montepellier (France); *Arte inglese d'oggi*, Galleria Civica, Modena (Italy) curators: Flaminio Gualdoni and Gail Cochrane; *Beyond the Borders: Kwangju Biennale*, Kwangju Biennale, Kwangju (South Korea); *Chez l'un, L'AUTRE*, Galerie Anton Weller, Paris (France); *Eigen + Art at the Independent Art Space*, Independent Art Space, London (UK); *Every Time I See You*, Galleri Nicolai Wallner, Malmö (Sweden); *General Release: British Council Selection of Young British Artists*, at the 46th Venice Biennale, Venice (Italy) curator: Andrea Rose; *Projected Images*, 46th International Art Exhibition, Venice (Italy) curator: Jean Clair; *On Board: Riva San Biagio* , at the 46th Venice Biennale, Venice (Italy); *Installation, cinema, video, informatique: Lyon Biennale*, Biennale di Lione, Lyon (France); *Kopfbahnhof/Terminal*, Förderkreis der Leipziger Galerie für Zeitgenössische Kunst, Leipzig (Germany) curator: Gerti Fietzek; *L'Effet Cinéma:Quand l'image raconte*, Musée d'Art contemporain, Montreal (Canada); *Over de melancholie*, Galerie Donia Cieremans, Rotterdam (The Netherlands); *Perfect Speed*, Macdonald Stewart Art Centre, Ontario (Canada) Southern Florida contemporary Art Museum, Tempa (USA) curator: Catsou Roberts; *Pulp Fact*, Photographer's Gallery, London (UK); *Scottish Autumn*, Ludwig Muzeum e Kortars Muveszti Museum, Budapest (Hungary); *Seeing Things*, Galeria Antoni Estrani, Barcelona (Spain); *Shift*, De Appel Centrum voor Beeldende Kunst, Amsterdam (The Netherlands); *Shopping*, CAPC Musee d'art contemporain de Bordeaux, Bordeaux (France); *Take me (I'm yours)*, Serpentine Gallery, London (UK) Kunsthalle Nürnberg, Nuremberg (Germany) curator: Hans Ulrich Obrist; *The British Art Show 4: South Bank Touring Exhibition* (touring exhibition) South Bank Centre, London (UK) part of a touring exhibition in Manchester, Cardiff, Edinburgh curators: Vicky Lewis, Thomas Lawson and Katrina Crookall; *Transitions*, National Gallery for Foreign Art, Sofia (Bulgaria); *Wild Walls*, Stedelijk Museum, Amsterdam (The Netherlands) curators: Martijn Nieuwenhuyzen and Leontine Coelewij; *You Show*, Knoll Galéria, Budapest (Hungary).

1996

SOLO SHOWS: *British Art Festival*, Galleria Bonomo, Rome (Italy); *Douglas Gordon*, Canberra contemporary Art Space, Canberra (Australia); *24 Hour Psycho*, Akademie der Bildenden Künste, Vienna (Austria); *Cinéma is dead*, Museum in Progress, Vienna (Austria) curator: Hans Ulrich Obrist; *Cinéma Liberté-Bar Lounge (with Rikrit Tiravanija)*, FRAC Languedoc-Rousillon, Montpellier (France); *Close your eyes*, MIGROS Museum für Gegenwartskunst, Zurich (Switzerland) curator: Rein Wolfs; *...head* (nell'ambito di *Swan-Off*) Uppsala Konstmuseum, Uppsala (Sweden) curator: Maria Lind; *Douglas Gordon*, Galerie Walcheturm, Zurich (Switzerland), Institut d'art contemporain de Villeurbanne, Lyon (France).

GROUP SHOWS: *21 Days of Darkness*, Transmission Gallery, Glasgow (UK); *33 1/3*, Canberra contemporary Art Space, Canberra (Australia); *Artisti britannici a Roma*, Galleria Bonomo, Rome (Italy) curator: Andrea Rose; *Auto reverse 2*, Le Magasin, Grenoble (France); *By Night*, Fondation Cartier pour l'art contemporain, Paris (France) curator: Herve Chandes; *controfigura*, Studio Guenzani, Milan (Italy); *Entre-deux*, Galerie Mot & van den Boogaard, Bruxelles (Belgium); *Found Footage: Kunst über Film*, Klemens Gasser & Tanja Grünert, Cologne (Germany); *Full House: Young British Art*, Kunstmuseum Wolfsburg, Wolfsburg (Germany); *Girls High*, Glasgow School of Art, Glasgow (UK) The Fruitmarket Gallery, Edinburgh (UK) curators: David Harding and Rebecca Gordon-Nesbitt; *Hall of Mirrors: Art and Film since 1945*, MOCA Museum of contemporary Art, Los Angeles (USA) The Wexner Centre for the Arts, Columbus, Ohio (USA) Palazzo delle Esposizioni, Rome (Italy) Museum of contemporary Art, Chicago (USA) curator: Kerry Brougher; *Host*, OB Projects, Amsterdam (The Netherlands); *ID*, Stedelijk Van Abbemuseum, Eindhoven (The

Netherlands); *Itinerant Texts*, Camden Arts Centre, London (UK); *Jurassic Technologies Revenant: 10th Biennale*, Art Gallery of New South Wales, Sydney (Australia) curator: Lynee Cooke; *Life/live*, Musée d'Art Moderne de la Ville de Paris, Paris (France) Centro Cultural de Belem, Lisbon (Portugal) curator: Hans Ulrich Obrist; *Looking Away*, Ambasciata del Brasile, Paris (France); *Manifesta 1 (with Rikrit Tiravanija)*, Rotterdam (The Netherlands) curators: Rosa Martinez, Viktor Misiano, Katalin Neray, Hans Ulrich Obrist, Andrew Renton; *Nach Weimar*, Kunstsammlungen zu Weimar, Weimar (Germany) curators: Klaus Biesenbach, Nicolaus Schafhausen; *Out of Space*, Cole and Cole, Oxford (UK); *Propositions*, Musée départemental d'art contemporain de Rochechouart, Rochechouart (France) curator: Jean-Marc Prevost; *Scream and Scream Again: Film in Art*, Museum of Modern Art Oxford, Oxford (UK) Irish Museum of Modern Art, Dublin (Ireland) Museum of contemporary Art, Helsinki (Finland) curator: Chrissie Iles; *Spellbound: art and film*, Hayward Gallery, London (UK) curators: Ian Christie and Philip Dodd; *The Turner Prize 1996*, Tate Gallery, London (UK) curator: Virginia Button; *Traffic*, CAPC Musée d'art contemporain de Bordeaux, Bordeaux (France); *Travaux Publics (Public Works)*, Stedelijk Van Abbemuseum, Eindhoven (The Netherlands).

Index of works

Following is a list of Douglas Gordon's main oeuvre in the considered period, set in strict chronological order from 1987 to 1996.

tradition:dehabilitation, 1987 (with Craig Richardson and Euan Sutherland) – medium: performance; first at: Riverside Studios, London (UK), 1987.

Experiments under Nostalgia's Umbrella, 1987 (with Craig Richardson) – medium: performance and environmental installation; first at: Third Eye Centre, Glasgow (UK), 1987.

AntehyperaesthesiA, 1987 (with Craig Richardson) – medium: performance and environmental installation; first at: Transmission Gallery, Glasgow (UK), 1987.

40 Years from Cradle to Grave, 1988 (with Craig Richardson) – medium: performance and environmental installation Royal Scottish; first at: Academy, Edinburgh (UK), 1988.

Refuse-consumption-decay-survival, 1988 (with Craig Richardson) – medium: performance and environmental installation; first at: Third Eye Centre, Glasgow (UK), 1988.

Untitled performance, 1988 (underneath The Arches with Craig Richardson) – medium: performance and environmental installation; first at: Midland Street Car Park, Glasgow (UK), 1988.

Untitled (#1), 1989: 'A BUILDING IS MORE THAN a dwelling place,... AND HAS INFLUENCE in the emotions OF HUMAN BEINGS' – medium: wall text, typeface Akzidenz Grotesk and Bembo, white gloss, dimensions variable; first at: Reading (UK), 1989.

Now time, 1989: 'JETZTZEIT 1946' - medium: wall text, typeface Akzidenz Grotesk, black opaque, dimensions variable; first at: *Windfall '89*, A.G. Weser Industries and Kommunale Galerie, Bremen (Germany), 1989.

Forget Facts and Figures, 1989: 'ZAHLEN UND FAKTEN VERGESSEN' – medium: wall text, typeface Akzidenz Grotesk, black opaque, dimensions variable; first at: *Windfall '89*, A.G. Weser Industries and Kommunale Galerie, Bremen (Germany), 1989.

Rotting from the Inside Out, 1989: 'ROTTING FROM THE INSIDE OUT' – medium: wall text, typeface Akzidenz Grotesk, black opaque, dimensions variable; first at: *Smith Biennial*, Smith Art Gallery and Museum, Stirling (UK), 1989.

Untitled (#2), 1989 – medium: colour samples on the wall and wall text, typeface Akzidenz Grotesk, black opaque, dimensions variable; first at: *The Living Room*, in Gianni Piacentini's living room, Glasgow (UK), 1989.

Proof, 1990: 'mute 1787 1812 1829 1916 1922 1932' – medium: wall text, typeface Times Italic and Futura Bold, black opaque, dimensions variable; public work for *Sites/Positions*, Green Station and London Road, Glasgow (UK), 1990.

Meaning and Location, 1990: 'truly I say to you today, you will be with me in paradise' 'truly I say to you, today you will be with me in paradise' – medium: wall text for ceiling, typeface Palatino, black opaque, dimensions variable; first at: *Meaning and Location*, Octagon Gallery, University of London, London (UK), 1990.

The Archive Room, 1990 – medium: environmental installation, refurbished room, framing glass boxes on the wall, wall drawings by Marino Marini and André Minaux; first at: *Archive Room*, Slade School of Fine Art, London (UK), 1990.

List of Names 1990 – open end, 1990 – medium: list of names, wall text, typeface Akzidenz Grotesk, black opaque, dimensions variable; first at: *Self Concious State*, Third Eye Centre, Glasgow (UK), 1990.

Installation for the spine of a book, 1991: 'READ THE WORD ... HEAR THE VOICE' – medium: installation for the spine of a book, typeface Bembo, black opaque, dimensions variable text; published on the spine of the book *The Missing Text Sight Works: Volume Two*, Chance Books, London, 1991.

Installation for a wall in a room in a private house, 1991: 'LUDWIG WITTGENSTEIN - you'll never walk alone' – medium: wall text for ceiling, typeface Bembo, black opaque, dimensions variable; text published on *The Missing Text Sight Works: Volume Two*, Chance Books, London, 1991.

Walk a million miles, 1991: 'WALK A MILLION MILES' – medium: wall text, typeface Bembo, black opaque, dimensions variable; first at: *The Bellgrove Station Billboard Project*, Bellgrove Station, Glasgow (UK), 1991.

Above all else..., 1991: 'WE ARE EVIL' – medium: wall text for ceiling, typeface Bembo, black opaque, blue paint stain, dimensions variable; first at: *Barclays Young Artist Award*, Serpentine Gallery, London (UK), 1991.

New Maps, 1991 – medium: white wrappers with text, typeface Akzidenz Grotesk, black opaque, dimensions variable; first at: *Barclays Young Artist Award*, Serpentine Gallery, London (UK), 1991.

Letter (Number 1), 1991: 'I am aware of who you are & what you do' – medium: letter and wall text, typeface Bembo, green opaque, dimensions variable; sent for: *Archive Project*, APAC Centre d'Art Contemporain, Nevers (France), 1991.

Letter (Number 2), 1991: 'I am aware of what you have done' – medium: letter and wall text, typeface Bembo, green opaque, dimensions variable; sent for: *Speed*, Transmission Gallery, Glasgow (UK), 1991.

Letter (Number 3), 1991: 'I have discovered the truth' – medium: letter and wall text, typeface Bembo, green opaque, dimensions variable; sent for: *Walk On*, Jack Tilton Gallery, New York (USA) and Fruitmarket Gallery, Edinburgh (UK), 1991.

Untitled (Series of 8 paintings for the old Betty Parsons Gallery), 1991: 'Black Arrangement – 1946', 'Red Dividing – 1969', 'Yellow Whites – 1963', 'White Relief – 1959', 'Red Whites – 1963', 'Red Front – 1946', 'Korea Goes to War – 1959', 'Balck City 1948' – medium: print on canvas; first at: *Walk On*, Jack Tilton Gallery, New York (USA), 1991.

1900 – 2000, 1991 – medium: installation, 101 wood poles; first at: Fruitmarket Gallery, Edinburgh (UK), 1991.

London Road, 1991 (with Roderick Buchanan) – medium: Print on canvas; first at: *London Road*, Orpheus Gallery, Belfast (UK), 1991.

Painting Carl Andre (Series), 1991 – medium: Black polish 18c39 or acrylic 18c35 on canvas, 166 x 100 cm; first at: *Windfall '91*, Seaman's Mission, Glasgow (UK), 1991.

Painting Christo (Series), 1991 – medium: Black polish over acrylic 14c39 on canvas, 100 c 166 cm; first at: *Windfall '91*, Seaman's Mission, Glasgow (UK), 1991.

'Columbo – Prescription Murder!', 1992: 'MORALS ARE CONDITIONED LIEUTNANT, THEY ARE RELATIVE, LIKE EVERYTHING ELSE IS TODAY' – medium: letter and wall text, typeface Bembo, black opaque, dimensions variable; planned for an independent television broadcast.

Instruction (Number 1), 1992: 'You can't hide your love forever' – medium: phone call and wall text, typeface Bembo, green opaque, dimensions variable; first at: *L'U di carte*, Café Picasso, Rome (Italy), 1992.

Instruction (Number 2), 1992: 'I won't breathe a word (to anyone)' – medium: phone call and wall text, typeface Bembo, blue opaque, dimensions variable; first at: *Il mistero dei 100 dollari scomparsi: Instructions Received*, Galleria Gio' Marconi, Milan (Italy), 1992.

Instruction, 1992: 'It doesn't matter who I am, I just want to talk to you' – medium: phone call and documentation, typeface Bembo, black opaque, dimensions variable, 7 min; first at: *Molteplici Culture*, Museo del Folklore, Rome (Italy), 1992.

Letter (Number 4), 1992: 'If only you were hot, or cold. But you are neither hot, nor cold. I'm going to vomit you out of my mouth.' – medium: letter and wall text, typeface Courier, black opaque, dimensions variable; letter sent from London on 6th of April 1992.

Untitled, 1992: 'THOSE I WILL NEVER KNOW', 'THOSE I HAVE FORGOTTEN BUT WILL NEVER REMEMBER', 'THOSE I WOULD LIKE TO KNOW', 'THOSE I DO NOT KNOW', 'THOSE I CANNOT KNOW', 'THOSE I WOULD NOT LIKE TO KNOW', 'THOSE I HAVE FORGOTTEN BUT WILL REMEMBER' – medium: wall text, typeface Bembo, black opaque, dimensions variable; first at: *Guilt by Association*, Museum of Modern Art, Dublin (Ireland), 1992.

Museum Keys, 1992 – medium: Museum keys duplicate; first at: *Guilt by Association*, Museum of Modern Art, Dublin (Ireland), 1992.

Letter (Number 5), 1992: 'I forgive you' – medium: letter and wall text, typeface Courier, black opaque, dimensions variable; sent for: *Guilt by Association*, Museum of Modern Art, Dublin (Ireland), 1992.

Letter (Number 6), 1992: 'I know the place for you' – medium: letter and wall text, typeface Bembo, blue opaque, dimensions variable; sent for: *A modest proposal*, Milch Gallery, London (UK), 1992.

Letter (Number 8), 1992: 'Nothing can be hidden forever' – medium: letter and wall text, typeface Bembo, green opaque, dimensions variable; first at: *Guilt by Association*, Museum of Modern Art, Dublin (Ireland), 1992.

Untitled, 1991-92 – medium: advertising pages, reclassification of standard interior paint colours and pricing in respect of the assigned celebrity; published on *Frieze Magazine*, between 1991 and 1992.

Untitled, 1992 – medium: sculpture with paint pots, reclassification of standard interior paint colours in respect of the colour range and naming after several royal dynasties; first at: *A modest proposal*, Milch Gallery, London (UK), 1992.

Silence in the museum, 1992: 'SILENCE IN THE MUSEUM' – medium: letter and wall text, typeface Bembo, black opaque, dimensions variable; first at: *5 Dialogues*, Natuurhistorish Samlinger, Bergen (Norway), 1992.

Letter (Number 9), 1992: 'I remember more than you know' – medium: letter and wall text, typeface Bembo, blue opaque, dimensions variable; sent for: *Entr'Acte 3*, Stedelijk Van Abbemuseum, Eindhoven (The Netherlands), 1992.

Faust, 1992: 'Faust 1224 – 1237' – medium: neon sign.

Letter (Number 10a), 1993: 'From the moment you read these words, until you meet someone with blue eyes' – medium: letter and wall text, typeface Bembo, blue opaque, dimensions variable; sent for: *Wonderful Life*, Lisson Gallery, London (UK), 1993.

Letter (Number 10b), 1993: 'From the moment you read these words, until you meet someone with green eyes' – medium: letter and wall text, typeface Bembo, green opaque, dimensions variable; sent for: *Wonderful Life*, Lisson Gallery, London (UK), 1993.

Letter (Number 10c), 1993: 'From the moment you read these words, until you kiss someone with brown eyes' – medium: letter and wall text, typeface Bembo, blue opaque, dimensions variable; sent for: *Propositions*, Musée Départmental d'Art Contemporain, Chateau de Rochechoouart, Limoges (France), 1993.

Chambre, 1993: 'From this moment, until next time' – medium: certificate and wall text, typeface Bembo, blue opaque, dimensions variable; first at: *Chambre 763*, Hotel Carlton Palace, Paris (France), 1993.

Instruction (Number 3a), 1993: 'From the moment you hear these words, until you kiss someone with blue eyes' – medium: phone call and wall text, typeface Bembo, blue opaque, dimensions variable; first at: *Migrateurs*, ARC Musée d'Art Moderne de la Ville de Paris, Paris (France), 1993.

Instruction (Number 3b), 1993: 'From the moment you hear these words, until you kiss someone with green eyes' – medium: phone call and wall text, typeface Bembo, green opaque, dimensions variable; first at: *Migrateurs*, ARC Musée d'Art Moderne de la Ville de Paris, Paris (France), 1993.

Instruction (Number 3c), 1993: 'From the moment you hear these words, until you kiss someone with brown eyes' – medium: phone call and wall text, typeface Bembo, brown opaque, dimensions variable; first at: *Migrateurs*, ARC Musée d'Art Moderne de la Ville de Paris, Paris (France), 1993.

Instruction (Number 4), 1993: 'It's only just begun' – medium: phone call and wall text, typeface Bembo, blue opaque, dimensions variable; first at: *Douglas Gordon/Simon Patterson*, Galerie Gruppe Grün, Bremen (Germany), 1993.

Instruction (Number 5), 1993: 'Everything is going to be alright' – medium: phone call and wall text, typeface Bembo, green opaque, dimensions variable; first at: *Purpose Built New England: Long Distance Information*, Real Art Ways, Hartford, Connecticut (USA), 1993.

Instruction (Number 6), 1993: 'Nothing will ever be the same' – medium: phone call and wall text, typeface Bembo, blue opaque, dimensions variable; first at: *24 Hour Psycho*, Tramway, Glasgow (UK), 1993.

Psycho Hitchhiker, 1993 – medium: black and white photography, 46 x 59.5 cm; first at: *24 Hour Psycho*, Tramway, Glasgow (UK), 1998.

24 Hour Psycho, 1993 – medium: black and white video installation, mute, single screen (300 x 400 cm), VHS of *Psycho*, 24 hours; first at: *24 Hour Psycho*, Tramway, Glasgow (UK), 1993.

I cannot remember anything, 1993: 'I CANNOT REMEMBER ANYTHING' – medium: wall text, typeface Bembo, black opaque, dimensions variable; first at: *Prospekt '93*, Schirn Kunsthalle Frankfurt and Frankfurter Kunstverein, Frankfurt (Germany), 1993.

...by way of an introduction, 1993 – medium: short story; originally published as "In love in Vienna" for *Viennese Story*, Wiener Seccession, Vienna (Austria), 1993.

Potential for Violence, 1993 – medium: black and white photography of a sculpture by Eduardo Paolozzi and a baseball bat.

Trust Me, 1993 – medium: photographic documentation; first at: *Walter Benjamin's Briefcase*, Oportos Festival of Contemporary Art, Oporto (Portugal), 1993.

A Souvenir of Non-Existence, 1993 – medium: letter, envelope and framed black and white photographies, 64 x 120 cm.

The Magic Newspaper, 1993 – medium: colour video to be shown on TV screen or monitor; first at: *Übergänge*, Museum Moderner Kunst, Passau (Germany).

I have forgotten everything, 1994: 'I HAVE FORGOTTEN EVERYTHING' – medium: wall text, typeface Bembo, black opaque, dimensions variable; first at: *Übergänge/Atjaras*, Galeria Kiaallitohazaba, Budapest (Hungary), 1994.

I remember nothing, 1994: 'I REMEMBER NOTHING' – medium: wall text, typeface Bembo, black opaque, dimensions variable; first at: *WATT*, Witte de With & Kunsthal, Rotterdam (The Netherlands), 1994.

Letter (Number 13), 1994: 'What have I done' – medium: letter and wall text, typeface Bembo, blue opaque, dimensions variable; letter sent from Tokyo, 17th of March 1994.

Letter (Number 14), 1994: 'There is something you should know' – medium: letter and wall text, typeface Bembo, green opaque, dimensions variable; letter sent from Glasgow, 25th of April 1994.

Letter (Number 15), 1994: 'I have not forgotten, because I cannot forget' – medium: letter and wall text, typeface Bembo, blue opaque, dimensions variable; sent for: *Fiction Non-Fiction*, Galleria Bonomo, Rome (Italy), 1994.

Letter (Number 16), 1994: 'Someone is looking' – medium: letter and wall text, typeface Bembo, blue opaque, dimensions variable; sent for: *Gaze: L'impossible transparence*, Carré des Art du Parc Floral de Paris, Paris (France), 1994.

Instruction (Number 7), 1994: 'I believe in miracles' – medium: phone call and wall text, typeface Bembo, blue opaque, dimensions variable; first at: *Stain in Reality: Stan Douglas, Douglas Gordon, Joachim Koester*, Galerie Nicolai Wallner, Kopenhagen (Denmark), 1994.

Instruction (Number 8), 1994: 'I know what you are thinking' – medium: phone call and wall text, typeface Bembo, green opaque, dimensions variable; first at: *Fiction Non-Fiction*, Galleria Bonomo, Rome (Italy), 1994.

Instruction (Number 9), 1994: 'The simple things you see are all complicated' – medium: phone call and wall text, typeface Bembo, green opaque, dimensions variable; first at: *Rue des Marins*, Galerie Air de Paris, Nice (France), 1994.

Instruction (Number 10), 1994: 'Someone is listening' – medium: phone call and wall text, typeface Bembo, blue opaque, dimensions variable; first at: *Gaze: L'impossible transparence*, Carré des Art du Parc Floral de Paris, Paris (France), 1994.

Postcard, 1994: 'I know you are not there' – medium: postcard and wall text, black gloss spray.

Letter (Number 17), 1994: 'From someone lost, to someone found' – medium: letter and wall text, typeface Bembo, green opaque, dimensions variable; sent for: *Douglas Gordon: Recent Works*, Lisson Gallery, London (UK), 1994.

Trigger Finger, 1994 – medium: black and white video installation, mute, single screen or monitor, dimensions variable, transferred on Betacam from 16mm, loop 10min 05sec; first at: *Douglas Gordon: Recent Works*, Lisson Gallery, London (UK), 1994.

10ms^{-1}, 1994 – medium: black and white video installation, mute, single screen (228.5 x 306 cm), transferred on Betacam from 16mm, loop 10min 37sec; first at: *Douglas Gordon: Recent Works*, Lisson Gallery, London (UK), 1994.

Douglas Gordon sings "The Best of Lou Reed and The Velvet Underground" (for Bas Jan Ader), 1994 – medium: Colour video installation, monitor, transferred on Betacam from VHS shooting, 84min 56sec; carpet; first at: *Aperto '95*, FRAC Languedoc-Roussillon, Montepellier (France), 1995.

Tattoo (I) and ***Tattoo (II)***, 1994 – medium: Black and white photographies, 134.5 x 88 cm; first at: *Douglas Gordon: Recent Works*, Lisson Gallery, London (UK), 1994.

Kissing with Sodium Pentathol, 1994 – medium: Slide presentation in 35mm, dimensions variable, first at: *Take me (I'm yours)*, Serpentine Gallery, London (UK), 1995.

Self-portrait (Kissing with Scopolamine), 1994 – medium: Slide presentation in 35mm, dimensions variable, first at: *Take me (I'm yours)*, Serpentine Gallery, London (UK), 1995.

Something between my mouth and your ear, 1994 – medium: Audio tape playing constantly, booster, blue room, dimensions variable first at *Something between my mouth and your ear*, Dolphin Gallery, Oxford (UK), 1994.

...lost, then found, then lost again; a true story, after samuel beckett, 1994 – medium: short story; originally published in Witte de With Cahier, No. 2 (June), 1994.

Kissing with Amobarbital, 1995 – medium: Slide presentation in 35mm, dimensions variable; first at: *Take me (I'm yours)*, Serpentine Gallery, London (UK), 1995.

Untitled-in lieu of being found, 1995: 'I'm not laughing, I'm crying' – medium: screen saver and wall text, typeface Bembo, black opaque, dimensions variable; first at: *Entr'Acte 3*, Stedelijk Van Abbemuseum, Eindhoven (The Netherlands), 1995.

Pocket Telepathy, 1995 – medium: 35mm slide, image still from a VJS copy originally filmed in 16mm.

Film Noir (Sleeper), 1995 – medium: wall projection, dimensions variable, transferred on Betacam from 16mm, loop 16sec; first at: *Entr'Acte 3*, Stedelijk Van Abbemuseum, Eindhoven (The Netherlands), 1995.

Film Noir (Twins), 1995 – medium: black and white video installation, double screen (300 x 400 cm), transferred on Betacam from VHS, loop 35min 40sec; first at: *Entr'Acte 3*, Stedelijk Van Abbemuseum, Eindhoven (The Netherlands), 1995.

Film Noir (Fear), 1995 – medium: wall projection, dimensions variable, transferred on Betacam from 16mm, loop 9min 4sec; first at: *Entr'Acte 3*, Stedelijk Van Abbemuseum, Eindhoven (The Netherlands), 1995.

Film Noir (Fly), 1995 – medium: black and white video installation, screens, dimensions variable, transferred on Betacam from 16mm, loop 11min 40sec right screen, loop 11min 50sec left screen; first at: *Entr'Acte 3*, Stedelijk Van Abbemuseum, Eindhoven (The Netherlands), 1995.

Film Noir (Fear), 1995 – medium: black and white video installation, single screen, dimensions variable, transferred on Betacam da 16mm, loop 10min 14sec; first at: *Entr'Acte 3*, Stedelijk Van Abbemuseum, Eindhoven (The Netherlands), 1995.

Film Noir (Hand), 1995 – medium: Wall projection, dimensions variable, transferred on Betacam from 16mm, loop 10min 9sec; first at: *Entr'Acte 3*, Stedelijk Van Abbemuseum, Eindhoven (The Netherlands), 1995.

Hysterical, 1994-95 – medium: black and white video installation, mute, two screens(300 x 400 cm), transferred on Betacam da 16mm, slow motion loop 29min 12sec, real time loop 29min 14sec; first at: *General Release: British Council Selection of Young British Artists*, Venice (Italy), 1995.

Fuzzy Logic, 1995 – medium: black and white video installation, mute, two screens (300 x 400 cm), dimensions variable, transferred on Betacam from VHS, loop 51min 5sec; first at: *Fuzzy Logic*, Centre Gorges Pompidou, Paris (France), 1995.

...by way of statement on the artist's behalf, 1995 – medium: letter sent to Martijn Nieuwenhuyzen and Leontine Coelewij from David Gordon, the artist's brother; published on the cataolgue *Wild Walls*, Stedelijk Museum, Amsterdam (The Netherlands), 1995.

Remote Viewing, 13.05.94 (Horror Movie), 1995 – medium: colour video installation, single screen (300 x 400 cm), radio, red walls, loop 13min 28sec; first at: *Wild Walls*, Stedelijk Museum, Amsterdam (The Netherlands), 1995.

...an apology as a short story/a short story as an apology, 1995 – medium: letter sent to the curator of the Lyon Biennial, in order to justify the delay of a project; first at: *Installation, cinema, video, informatique: Lyon Biennale*, Lyon (France), 1995.

Predictable Incidents in Unfamiliar Surroundings, 1992-95 – medium: colour video projection, dimensions variable, VHS tape of television broadcast, variable running time; beer; first at: *Chez l'un, L'AUTRE*, Galerie Anton Weller, Paris (France), 1995.

5 Year Drive-By, 1995 – medium: Colour video projection, dimensions variable, VHS copy of *The Searchers*, 5 years; first at: *Over Night #1*, Hannover Kunstverein, Hannover (Germany), 1997.

The End (Split-Second Configuration), 1995 – medium: 2 scanned photographs printed on canvas,180 x 240 x 3 cm e 240 x 180 x 3 cm; first at: *The End*, Jack Tilton Gallery, New York (USA), 1995.

Bootleg (Cramped), 1995 – medium: colour wall projection, dimensions variable, transferred on Betacam from VHS, loop 48min 21sec; first at: *Close your eyes*, MIGROS Museum für Gegenwartskunst, Zurich (Switzerland), 1996.

Bootleg (Stoned), 1996 – medium: black and white video installation, two screens (300 x 400 cm), transferred on Betacam da 16mm, loop 30min; first at: *Close your eyes*, MIGROS Museum für Gegenwartskunst, Zurich (Switzerland), 1996.

Bootleg (Bigmouth), 1996 – medium: colour wall projection, dimensions variable, transferred on Betacam from VHS, loop 19min 44sec; first at: *Close your eyes*, MIGROS Museum für Gegenwartskunst, Zurich (Switzerland), 1996.

A Few Words on the Nature of Relationships, 1996: 'Close your eyes, open your mouth' – medium: wall text for a corner, typeface Bembo, black opaque, dimensions variable; first at: *Artisti britannici a Rome*, Galleria Bonomo, Rome (Italy), 1996.

Untitled, 1996: 'I've changed, You've changed' – medium: wall text, typeface Courier, black opaque, dimensions variable; first at: *what have I done*, Hayward Gallery, London (UK), 2002.

Cinema is dead, 1996: 'raise the dead' – medium: wall text, red spray, dimensions variable; black and white photography, first at: *Cinema is dead*, Museum in Progress, Vienna (Austria), 1996.

Dance Practice, 1996 (together with David Allen e Jonathan Monk) – medium: VHS video on monitor.

entre-deux, 1996 – medium: 7 balck and white photographies.

Unintentional, Sustained, Never-Ending, Always Changing, 1996 – medium: 12 LP records (*Great Tenor Arias*) and sound equipment; first at: *Entre-deux*, Galerie Mot & van den Boogaard, Brussels (Belgium), 1996.

head..., 1996 – medium: projected wall text, typeface Bembo and Helvetica, two screens (300 x 400 cm); first at: *...head* (part of *Swan-Off*), Uppsala Konstmuseum, Uppsala (Sweden), 1996.

Words and Pictures (Part I and Part II), 1996 – medium: beanbags, audiovisual equipment, neon lights; first at: *Douglas Gordon*, Galerie Walcheturm, Zurich (Switzerland), 1994.

Cinéma Liberté Bar Lounge, 1996 (together with Rikrit Tiravanija) – medium: beanbags, video projection and bar; first at: *Cinéma Liberté-Bar Lounge (with Rikrit Tiravanija)*, FRAC Languedoc-Rousillon, Montpellier (France), 1996.

Hand and Foot (Left) and Hand and Foot (Right), 1995-96 – medium: colour wall projection; Hand and Foot (Left), original size, loop 30min 39sec; Hand and Foot (Right), dimensions variable, loop 32min 8sec; VHS tape.

From God to Nothing, 1996 – medium: environmental installation, wall text, typeface Bembo, 3 light bulbs at several hights (of the head, of the heart and of the genitals), dimensions variable; first at: *Légende*, Centre Régional d'Art Contemporain, Sète (France), 1997.

Untitled Text (for someplace other than this), 1996 – medium: wall text for a corner, typeface Bembo, black opaque, dimensions 125pt, first at: *The Turner Prize 1996*, Tate Gallery, London (UK), 1996.

Confessions of a Justified Sinner, 1995-96 – medium: black and white video installation, two screens (300 x 400 cm), transferred on Betacam from VHS tape of television broadcast, loop 25min 50sec; first at: *The Turner Prize 1996*, Tate Gallery, London (UK), 1996.

Selfportrait as Kurt Cobain, as Andy Warhol, as Myra Hindley, as Marilyn Monroe, 1996 – medium: C-Print, passport photo dimensions; first at: The Turner Prize 1996, Tate Gallery, London (UK), 1996.

A Divided Self I and II, 1996 – medium: colour video installation, two monitors, transferred on Betacam from VHS, loop 14min (I), loop 15min (II); first at: *The Turner Prize 1996*, Tate Gallery, London (UK), 1996.

Bibliography

Books and essays

ALBERRO, A. [2003] Conceptual Art an the policy of publicity. Boston: MIT press.

ANDERSON, J.C. [2000] "Aesthetic concepts of art". In Carrol, N. (ed.), pp.65-92.

ARRHENIUS, S. [1996] "The headless angel". In *Swan-Off* (Cat.), pp.37-39.

BECKER, H.S. [1984] "Les professions artistiques: Mondes de l'art et type sociaux". In *Sociologie du travail.* No.4.

BENHAMOU, F. [2000] *L'economie de la culture.* Paris: La Decouverte.

BERGER, D. [2011] "Julian Schnabels self-fashioning Intermediale Selbstinszenierungen als Maler". In FASTEN, S. JOACHIMIDES, A. and KRIEGER, V., pp.73-88.

BERGER, R. [2011] "Aufstand gegen die sekundäre Welt - Die Biografik zwischen fact und fiction". In FASTEN, S. JOACHIMIDES, A. and KRIEGER, V., pp.293-302.

BLANCHÉ, U. [2012] Konsumkunst: Kultur und Kommerz bei Banksy und Damien Hirst. Bielefeld: transcript Verlag.

BOLTON, P. [2010] "Higher Education and Social Class". In *Social & General Statistics* on 18/06/2010. London: House of Commons Library.

BOLTON, P. [2012] "Education: Historical statistics". In *Social & General Statistics* on 27/11/2012. London: Library House of Commons Library.

BONAMI, F. AND ROBECCHI, M. [2007] *Sarah Lucas.* Milan: Electa.

BONAMI, F. [2009] Lo potevo fare anch'io. Perché l'arte contemporanea è davvero arte. Milan: Mondadori.

BONAMI, F. [2010] Si crede Picasso. Come distinguere un vero artista contemporaneo da uno che non lo è. Milan: Mondadori.

BOURDIEU, P. [1993] *The Field of Cultural Production.* Cambridge: Polity Press.

BOURDIEU, P. [2013] "The Intellectual Field: A World Apart (1990)". In KOCUR, Z. AND LEUNG, S. (ed.) *Theory in contemporary art since 1985.* Malden: John Wiley & Sons.

BRADEN, S. [1978] *Artists and People.* London: Routledge and Kegan Paul.

BRANDTZAEG, K.J. [2008] Glasgow: A presentation of the art scene in the 90's. Glasgow: ForArt.

BRATTI, M. [2006] Social Class and Undergraduate Degree Subject in the UK. *Discussion Paper.* Econstor.eu: N.1979, February.

BRODIE, C. [2011] "The outlook is bad but not desperate". In *Glasgow Economic Review.* July.

BROWN, K. [2004] *DG: Douglas Gordon.* London: Tate Publishing.

BURGES, J., COVENTRY, K., HALE, M., NOBLE, P. AND OWEN, P. [2002] *City Racing: The Life and Times of an Artist-Run Gallery.* London: Black Dog Publishing.

BURKE, P. [1998] The European Renaissance: Centres and Peripheries. Oxford: Blackwell Publishers.

BURKE, P. [2009] *La storia culturale.* Bologna: Il Mulino.

GORDON, B. and HIRST, D. [2004] *Manuale per Giovani Artisti* (transl.: *On the Way to Work*). Milan: Postmediabooks.

BURROWS, D. (ed.) [1998] Who's afraid o red white & blue: attitudes to popular and mass culture, celebrity, alternative & critical practice & Identity politics in recent British Art. Birmingham: University of Central England/ARTicle Press.

CARROL, N. (ed.) [2000] *Theories of art today.* Madison: The University of Wisconsin Press.

CASEY, B., DUNLOP R. AND SELWOOD, S. [1996] *Culture as Commodity? the economics of the arts and built heritage in the UK.* London: Policy Studies Institute.

CAVES, R.E. [2000] Creative Industries: Contracts between Art and Commerce. Boston: Harvard University Press.

CHANDLER, A.D. [1969] Strategy and Structure: Chapters in the History of the Industrial Enterprise. Cambridge: M.I.T. Press.

CHRISTIE, I. [1996] "The odd couple". In *Spellbound* (Cat.), pp.42-75.

CLAIR, J. [2005] *De Immundo.* Milan: Abscondita Srl.

CLAIR, J. [2011] *L'hiver de la culture.* Paris: Café Voltaire – Flammarion.

CLIFFORD, J. AND MARCUS, G.E. [1986] *Writing Culture: Poetics and Politics of Ethnography.* Los Angeles: University of California Press.

COLLINGS, M. [1997] Blimey! From Bohemia to Britpop: the London artworld from Francis Bacon to Damien Hirst. London: 21 Publishing Ltd.

COLLINGS, M. [2002] *SL: Sarah Lucas.* London: Tate Publishing.

COMER, S. (ed.) [2009] *Film and video art.* London: Tate Publishing.

CONNOR, H. and DEWSON, S. [2001] "Social Class and Higher Education: Issues Affecting Decisions on Participation by Lower Social Class Groups". In *Research Brief.* No.267, March. Sheffield: Department for Education and Employment.

COOPER, J. [2012] *Growing up: the Young British Artists at 50.* Munich: Prestel Publishing.

CORK, R. [1995] "Injury Time". In *The British Art Show 4* (Cat.), pp.12-34.

CRAIG-MARTIN, M. [2012] "Damian Hirst: The Early Years". In *Damien Hirst* (Cat.), pp.38-39.

DANTINI, M. [2012] Geopolitiche dell'arte. Arte e critica d'arte italiana nel contesto internazionale dalle neoavanguerdie a oggi. Milan: Marinotti Edizioni.

DANTO, A.C. [1984] *The Philosophical Disenfranchisement of Art.* New York: Columbia University Press.

DANTO, A.C. [2000] "Art and meaning". In CARROL, N. (ed.), pp.130-140.

DANTO, A.C. [2008] *L'abuso della bellezza.* Milan: Postmedia books.

D'ARGENZIO, M. [2004] "Like People, Like Flies: Damien Hirst Interviewed". In *The Agony and the Ecstasy: Selected Works from 1989–2004* (Cat.). Napoli: Electa.

D'ARGENZIO, M. [2006], "Le anime morte, le anime vive". In *prettymucheverywordwritten, spoken, heard, overheard from 1989...* [Cat.], pp.21-42.

DEBBAUT, J. [1998] "Excerpt:... Jan Debbaut in conversation with Douglas Gordon". In GORDON, D. (ed.) [2000b], pp.85-126.

DE BURGEROLLE, M. [1995] "Seing is believing". In GORDON, D. (ed.) [2000a], pp.89-102.

DETHERIDGE, A. and VETTESE, A. (ed.) [1991] Guardare l'arte. Cultura visiva contemporanea: le recensioni, i temi e gli appuntamenti 1997-1999. Milan: Edizioni Il Sole 24 Ore S.p.A.

DICKIE, G. [2000] "The institutional theory of art". In Carrol, N. (ed.), pp.93-108

DICKSON, M. [2002] "Letter 6". In Vv.Aa., *Justified Sinners.* Edinburgh: Pocketbooks.

DI MARTINO, E. [2003] *Storia della Biennale di Venezia 1985-2003.* Enna: Papiro Arte.

DINGLE, R. [2010] "Interview with Simon Patterson". In *The Gathering: Building the Arts Council Collection* [Cat.].

DODD, P. [1996] "Modern Stories". In *Spellbound* [Cat], pp.33-41.

DOUGLAS, S. and EAMON, C. (ed.) [2009], *Art of projection.* Ostfildern: Hatje Cantz Verlag.

FAGEN, G. [1999] "The exact vague history". In Gordon D. (ed.) [2000b], pp.21-126.

FASTEN, S., JOACHIMIDES, A. and KRIEGER, V. (ed.) [2011] Die Wiederkehr des Künstlers. Themen und Positionen der aktuellen Künsrler/innenforschung. Vol.2. Köln: Böhlau Verlag.

FILLIS, I. [2004] "The theory and practice of visual arts marketing". In KERRING, F., FRASER, P. and ÖZBILGIN, M. (ed.), pp.119-138.

FINN-KELCEY, R. [1995] "Questionnaire". In Gordon D. (ed.) [2000a], pp.103-110.

FOGLIO, A. [2005] Il marketing dell'arte : strategia di marketing per artisti, musei, gallerie, case d'asta, show art. Milan: Franco Angeli.

FORTNUM, R. [2007] Contemporary British Women Artists: In Their Own Words. Tauris: I.B..

FOSTER, A. [2003] *Susan Hiller.* London: Tate Publishing.

FOSTER, H. [1996] The return of the real: the avant-garde at the end of the Century. Cambridge: The MIT Press.

FOSTER, H. and KRAUSS, R. (ed.) [2004] *Art since 1900: modernism, antimodernism, postmodernism.* London: Thames & Hudson.

FOSTER, H. (ed.) [2006] Arte dal 1900: modernismo, antimodernismo, postmodernismo. Bologna: Zanichelli.

FOUCAULT, M. [2004] *L'ordine del discorso,* Einaudi, Torino

FREY, B.S. [2000] Arts & economics: analysis & cultural policy. Berlin: Springer.

FRICKE, H. [1998] "Introduction: Confusion in noir". In Gordon, D. (ed.) [2000a], pp.13-32

FRICKE, H. [2000] "As beautiful as a Barnett Newman". In Gordon, D. (ed.) [2000b], pp.127-137

FRIED, M. [2008] *Why photography matters as art as never before.* New Haven: Yale University Press.

FROHNE, U. [2008] "Dissolution of the frame: immersion and participation in video installations". In Leighton, T. (ed.), pp.355-370

GALENSON, D.W. [2001] Young geniuses and old masters: the life cycles of great artists from Masaccio to Jasper Johns. Cambridge: NBER working paper series, July.

GALENSON, D.W. [2005a] *Who are the greatest living artists? The view from the auction market.* Cambridge: NBER working paper series, September.

GALENSON, D.W. [2005b] Do the young British artists rule? (or: has London stolen the idea of postmodern art from New York?): evidence from the auction market. Cambridge: NBER working paper series, October.

GALENSON, D.W. [2006] A conceptual world: why the art of the Twentieth-Century is so different from the art of all earlier centuries. Cambridge: NBER working paper series, August.

GALENSON, D.W. [2007] Artists and the market: from Leonardo and Titian to Andy Warhol and Damien Hirst. Cambridge: NBER working paper series, September.

GALENSON, D.W. [2008] *The back story of Twentieth-Century art.* Cambridge: NBER working paper series, June.

GALENSON, D.W. [2009] *Conceptual revolutions in Twentieth-Century art.* Cambridge: NBER working paper series, June.

GALLAGHER, T. [1987] Glasgow, The Uneasy Peace: Religious Tension in Modern Scotland, 1819-1914. Manchester: Manchester University Press.

GAUT, B. [2000] “Art as a cluster concept”. In Carrol, N. (ed.), pp.25-44.

GILLICK, L. and RENTON, A. (ed.) [1989] *Technique Anglaise: Current Trends in British Art.* London: Karsten Schubert & Thames and Hudson.

GINSBURGH, V.A. and MENGER, P.M. (ed.) [1996] *Economics of the arts, selected essays.* Amsterdam: Elsevier.

GOETZMAN, W. [1996] “How costly is the fall from fashion? Survivorship bias in the painting market”. In GINSBURGH, V.A. and MENGER, P.M. (ed.), pp.71-85

GORDON, D. (ed.) [2000a] *Déjà-vu: questions & answers. Volume 1. 1992-1996.* Paris: MARC Musée d'art moderne de la ville de Paris.

GORDON, D. (ed.) [2000b] *Déjà-vu: questions & answers. Volume 2. 1997-1998.* Paris: MARC Musée d'art moderne de la ville de Paris.

GORDON, D. (ed.) [2000c] *Déjà-vu: questions & answers. Volume 3. 1999-2000.* Paris: MARC Musée d'art moderne de la ville de Paris.

GOTTDANG, A. [2011], “Durchschnitt ist überall gleich spießig. George Grosz' Selbstinszenierung in der Weimarer Republik”. In FASTEN, S., JOACHIMIDES, A. and KRIEGER, V. (ed.), pp.43-56.

GRAW, I. [2009] High Price - Art Between The Market And Celebrity Culture. Berlin: Sternberg Press.

HAASE, A. [1999] “On the other side of the mirror”. In GORDON, D. (ed.) [2000b], pp.127-148.

HATT, M. and KLONK, C. [2006] *Art history. A critical introduction to its methods.* Manchester: Manchester University Press.

HATTON, R. and WALKER, J.A. [2010] *Supercollector: A critique of Charles Saatchi.* Esher: The Institute of Artology.

HARDING, D. [1995] “Another History. Memories and Vagaries: the development of social art practices in Scotland from the 60s to the 90s”. In DICKSON, M. (ed.) *Art with people.* Sunderland: AN Publication.

HARDING, D. [2001a] “Friendship, socialisation and networking among Glasgow artists 1985-2001. The Scotia Nostra – Myth and Truth”. In the exhibition catalogue *Circles.* Karlsruhe: Galerie ZKM.

HARDING, D. [2001b] "Who took the (he)art out of art schools?". Essay written on occasion of his resignation from Glasgow School of Art. Available from: www.davidharding.net. [Accessed: 20th October 2011].

HASKELL, F. [1980] *Patrons and painters.* New Haven: Yale University Press.

HAUSER, A. [1958] *Philosophie der Kunstgeschichte.* Munich: Beck.

HAUSER, A. [1983] *Soziologie der Kunst.* Munich: Deutscher Taschenbuch Verlag.

HAUSER, A. [1987] *Sozialgeschichte der Kunst und Literatur.* Vol.2. Dresden: Fundus-Bücher.

HEINICH, N. [1999] "Objets, problematique, terrains, methodes: pour un pluralisme methodique". In *Sociologie de l'art,* Moulin, R. (ed.). Paris: L'Harmattan, pp.11-28.

HEINICH, N. [2001] Art contemporain, dérision, et sociologie". In *HERMES.* No.29, pp.121-130.

HEISER, J. [2008] All of a sudden: Things that matter in contemporary Art. New York: Sternberg Press.

HICKS, J. and ALLEN, G. [1999] "A Century of Change: Trends in UK Statistics since 1900". In *Social & General Statistics* on 21/12/1999. London: House of Commons Library.

JENSEN, U. [2010] "*The pack (das Rudel)".* In ACKERMANN, M. (ed.), *Joseph Beuys. Parallelprozesse.* Düsseldorf: Kunstsammlung Nordrhein-Westfalen.

JYRÄMÄ, A. [2008a] "Conceptual analysis of the art market". In UUSITALO, L. (ed.), pp.72-90.

JYRÄMÄ, A. [2008b] "Identifying organizational fields in the art market – an institutional approach". In UUSITALO, L. (ed.), pp.91-110.

KERRING, F., FRASER, P. and ÖZBILGIN, M. (ed.) [2004] *Arts marketing.* Amsterdam: Elsevier.

KLAMER, A. (ed.) [1996] The value of culture : on the relationship between economics and arts. Amsterdam: Amsterdam University Press.

KOERNER, J.L. and RAUSING, L. [1996] "Value". In NELSON, R.S. and SHIFF, R. (ed.), pp.419-435.

KOTZ, L. [2008] "Video projection: the space between screens". In LEIGHTON, T. (ed.); pp.371-385.

LEIGHTON, T. (ed.) [2008] *Art and the moving image: a critical reader.* London: Tate Publishing in association with Afterall.

LAWSON, T. [1993] "Hello, it's me". In GORDON, D. (ed.) [2000a], pp.47-68.

LAWSON, T. [1995] "Unrelating Jet Lag and Iron-Hard Jets". In *The British Art Show 4* (Cat.), pp.88-95.

LOWNDES, S. [2010] Social Sculpture: The Rise of the Glasgow Art Scene. Glasgow: Lutah Press.

LEBOVICI, E. [2000] "Thinking twice". In GORDON, D. (ed.) [2000b], pp.149-167.

LUSINI, V. [2011] "Arte contemporanea e cultura dell'alterità". In *Studi culturali.* Year 8, April.

MACINNES, J. [2010] "The deindustrialisation of Glasgow". In *Scottish Affairs.* No.11, pp.73-95.

MANDELBAUM, M. [1962] "Philosophy Science, and Sense-Perception". In *Proceedings and Addresses of The American Philosophical Association.* Vol.36, pp.5-20.

MANKIW, N.G. [2009] *Principles of Economics.* Mason: South-Western Cengage Learning.

MANTOAN, D. [2012] Vita e carriera di Douglas Gordon dal 1966 al 1996: La via al successo di un artista visivo scozzese fra gli anni Ottanta e Novanta del XX secolo. Trento: Università di Trento (MA thesis).

MARCONE, M. [1998] *L'artista, il potere, la società.* Lanciano: Rivista di politica e cultura.

MARGOLIS, J. [2000] "The deviant ontology of artworks". In CARROL, N. (ed.), pp.109-129.

MCCORQUODALE, D., SIDERFIN, N. and STALLABRASS, J. [1998] *Occupational hazard: critical writing on recent British art.* London: Black Dog.

MCDONOUGH, T. [2009] "Production/projection: notes on the capitalist fairy tale". In DOUGLAS, S. and EAMON, C. (ed.), pp.124-140.

MCKEAN, J. [2004] Charles Rennie Mackintosh: architect, artist, icon. London: Lomond Books.

MCKEE, F. [2003] “Irrelevant Information”. Available from: *www.francismckee.org*. [Accessed: 26th February 2014]

MCMANUS, I.C. and FURNHAM, A. [2006] “Aesthetic activities and aesthetic attitudes: Influences of education, background and personality on interest and involvement in the arts”. In *British Journal of Psychology*. No.97. The British Psychological Society, p.555–587

MCQUAY, M.A. [2005] “Spellbound: art into film, film into art”. Available from: *www.luxonline.org.uk/ history/1990-1999/spellbound.html.* [Accessed: 26th June 2014]

MESCHEDE, F. [1998] “Emotion and Sensation”. In Emotion: Young British and American Art from the Goetz Collection (Cat.).

MEYERIC HUGHES, H. and MALBERT, R. [1995] “Foreword”. In *The British Art Show 4* (Cat.), pp.8-11.

MEYERIC HUGHES, H. and HILTY, G. [1996] “Preface”. In *Spellbound* (Cat.), pp.8-9.

MINTZBERG, H. and WATERS, J.A. [1985] “Of strategies, deliberate and emergent”. In *Strategic Management Journal*, Vol.6, No.3. Chicago: John Wiley & Sons, pp.257-272.

MOISDON-TREMBLEY, S. [1996] “Attraction-répulsion”. In GORDON, D. (ed.) [2000a], pp.111-130.

MORGAN, S. [1997] “Damien Hirst: The Butterfly Effect”. In I want to spend the rest of my life everywhere, with everyone, one to one, always, forever, now / Damien Hirst (Cat.), pp.68-73.

MOSSETTO, G. [1993] *Aesthetics and Economics*. Dordrecht: Kluewer Academic publishers.

MOSSETTO, G. [2003] *Aesthetics and Economics*. Berlin: Springer.

MUIR, G. [1995] “Daddy's Speeding”. In *General Release* (Cat.), pp.10-22

MUIR, G. [2011] Lucky Kunst. The rise and fall of Young British Art. London: Artum Press.

MULHOLLAND, N. [2003] The Cultural Devolution: Art in Britain in the Late Twentieth Century (British Art & Visual Culture Since 1750: New Readings). Aldershot: Ashgate Publishing.

NELSON, R.S. and SHIFF, R. (ed.) [1996] *Critical terms for art history.* Chicago: The University of Chicago Press.

NEWMAN, M. [1995] "Deckerinnerungen: Das Trauma der Zeit". In *Am Rande der Malerei* (Cat.), pp.29-34.

NEWMAN, M. [2009] "Moving the image in the gallery since the 1990s". In COMER, S. (ed.), pp.86-121.

OBRIST, H.U. [1996a] *Delta X. Der Kurator als Katalysator.* Regendburg: Lindinger & Schmid Verlag GdbR.

OBRIST, H.U. [1996b] "(P)ars pro toto". In GORDON, D. (ed.) [2000a], pp.143-176.

OBRIST, H.U. [2003] *Interviews. Volume I.* Florence: Fondazione Pitti Immagine Discovery.

OLVA VELTHUIS, O. [2009] Imaginary Economics: quando l'arte sfida il capitalism. Milan: Johan & Levi.

PAGE, S. [2000] "Preface". In GORDON, D. (ed.) [2000a], pp.5-7.

PREVITALI, G. [1979] *Storia dell'arte italiana.* Vol.II. Torino: Einaudi.

PÜTZ, S. [2010] *Conference Report of Die Wiederkehr des Künstlers. H-ArtHist,* 14th July. Wien: Universität für angewandte Kunst. Available from: http://arthist.net/reviews/369. [Accessed: 29th January 2014].

RAFFE, D., CROXFORD, L., IANNELLI, C., SHAPIRA, M. and HOWIESON, C. [2006] "Social-Class Inequalities in Education in England and Scotland. Special CES Briefing". No.40, May. Edinburgh: Centre for Educational Sociology.

RANCIÈRE, J. [2009] *The emancipated spectator* (transl. Elliot G.). London: Verso.

RECKHENRICH, J., ANDERSON, J. and KUPP, M. [2009] "The Shark is Dead: How to Build Yourself a New Market". In *Business Strategy Review.* Winter. London: London Business School.

RICHARDSON, C. [2011] Scottish Art since 1960: Historical Reflections and Contemporary Overviews. Farnham: Ashgate Publishing.

ROBERTS, J. [1995] "Never had it so good...". In *General Release* (Cat.), pp.48-71.

ROLFE, N. [1991] "Foreword". In *Bellgrove* (Cat.), p.6.

ROSE, A. [1995] "Foreword". In *General Release* (Cat.), pp.6-7.

ROSENGARTEN, R. [1999] "He loves you". In GORDON, D. (ed.) [2000b], pp.7-20.

RUSH, M. [2007] *Video art: revised edition.* London: Thames & Hudson.

SACCO, P.L. [1998] "La selezione dei giovani artisti nei mercati delle arti visive". In Santagata, W. (ed.); pp.43-75.

SANTAGATA, W. (ed.) [1998], Economia dell'arte. Istituzioni e mercati dell'arte e della cultura. Torino: Utet.

SANTAGATA, W. [1999] Produrre culture: note di economia sulle istituzioni e sui mercati culturali. Torino: CELID.

SAATCHI, C. [2009] My name is Charles Saatchi and I am an artoholic. London: Phaidon Press.

SCHUMACHER, R. [2002] Die Wohltat der Kunst : post-feministische Positionen der neunziger Jahre aus der Sammlung Goetz. Cologne: Verlag der Buchhandlung König.

SEROTA, N. [2011] "Nicholas Serota interviews Damien Hirst". In *Damien Hirst* (Cat.), pp.91-99.

SHEARMAN, J. [1988] Only connect... Art and the spectator in the Italian Renaissance: The A. W. Mellon Lectures in the fine arts. Princeton: Princeton University Press.

SHEIKH, S. [1997] "Art is merely an excuse for communicating". In GORDON, D. (ed.) [2000b], pp.7-24.

26. Sega P.B., Tolomeo M.G. [2002], Ultime generazioni e new media: l'arte europea alla fine del XX secolo, Clueb, Bologna

SINCLAIR, R. [1992] "Museum keys". In GORDON, D. (ed.) [2000a], pp.33-46.

SINCLAIR, R. [1993] It doesn't matter who I am, I just want to talk to you. The sociable art of Douglas Gordon. Glasgow: Tramway.

SNOWMAN N. and STEVENSON W. [1996] "Foreword". In *Spellbound* (Cat.), p.7.

SPECTOR, N. [1997] "This is all true, and contradictory, if not hysterical". In GORDON, D. (ed.) [2000b], pp.49-84.

STALLABRASS, J. [2004] *Art incorporated: the story of contemporary art.* Oxford: Oxford University Press.

STALLABRASS, J. [2006a] *Contemporary Art. A very short introduction.* Oxford: Oxford University Press.

STALLABRASS, J. [2006b] High Art Lite. The rise and fall of Young British Art. London: Verso.

STECKER, R. [2000] "Is it reasonable to define art?". In CARROL, N. (ed.), pp.45-66.

STEMMRICH, G. [1995] "Kopfbahnhof" in *Kopfbahnhof/Terminal* (Cat.), pp.8-26.

STEMMRICH, G. [2005] "The area between the image and the visual". In *Videonale 10* (Cat.).

STEMMRICH, G. [2008] *Dan Graham.* Cologne: DuMont Buchverlag.

STRASSOLDO, R. [2001] Forma e funzione : introduzione alla sociologia dell'arte. Udine: Forum.

THOMPSON, D. [2008] The 12 Million Dollars Stuffed Shark: The Curious Economics of Contemporary Art. London: Aurum Press,

THROSBY, D. [1996] "Disaggregated Functions for artists". In GINSBURGH, V.A. and MENGER, P.M. (ed.), pp.331-346.

THROSBY, D. [2005] *Economia e Cultura.* Bologna: Il Mulino.

TOWSE, R. [1996a] "Economics of training artists". In GINSBURGH, V.A. and MENGER, P.M. (ed.), pp.303-330.

TOWSE, R. [1996b] "Market a Value and Artists' Earnings". In KLAMER, A. (ed.), pp.96-107.

TRIMARCHI, M. [1993] Economia e cultura, Organizzazione e finanziamento delle istitutioni culturali. Milan: Franco Angeli.

TZANAKIS, M. [2011] "Bourdieu's Social Reproduction Thesis and The Role of Cultural Capital in Educational Attainment: A Critical Review of Key Empirical Studies". In *Educate.* Vol.11, No.1, pp.76-90.

UUSITALO, L. (ed.) [2008], *Museum and visual art marketing.* Helsinki: Helsingin kauppakorkeaoulu.

VAN ASSCHE, C. [1995] "Entretien". In GORDON, D. (ed.) [2000a], pp.69-88.

VAN ASSCHE, C. [1996] "Six questions to Douglas Gordon". In GORDON, D. (ed.) [2000a], pp.131-142.

VAN DEN BOOGARD, O. [1997] "Oscar van den Boogard talks with Douglas Gordon" . In GORDON, D. (ed.) [2000b], pp.25-48.

VECCO, M. [2002] La Biennale di Venezia – Documenta di Kassel: Esposizione, vendita, pubblicizzazione dell'arte contemporanea. Milan: Franco Angeli.

VERZOTTI, G. [2006] "Douglas Gordon". In prettymucheverywordwritten, spoken, heard, overheard from 1989... (Cat.), pp.15-20.

VETTESE, A. [1998] *Artisti si diventa.* Rome: Carocci Editore

VETTESE, A. [2007] Ma questo è un quadro? Il valore nell'arte contemporanea. Rome: Carocci.

VON BISMARCK, B. [2011] "Effizienz und Verschwendung Paradoxien des Künstlerbildes im 21. Jahrhundert". In FASTEN, S., JOACHIMIDES, A. and KRIEGER, V., pp.147-156.

VV.AA. [2002] *The New York Times guide to the arts of the 20th Century.* Vol.4, 1980-1999. London: Fitzroy Dearborn Publishers.

VV.AA. [2010] Active aging and universities: engaging older learners. February. London: Universities UK.

WAKELING, P.B.J. [2009] Social Class and Access to Postgraduate Education in the UK: a Sociological Analysis (PhD thesis). Manchester: University of Manchester.

WOLFF, J. [1981] *The Social Production of Art.* London: The MacMillan Press.

WOLFF, J. [1999] "Cultural Studies and the Sociology of Culture". In *Invisible Culture: An electronic journal for visual studies.* Available from: https://www.rochester.edu/in_visible_culture/issue1/wolff/wolff.html

[Accessed: 15th November 2013]

WOLFS, R. [1996] "Die Suche nach einer Perspektive". In *Douglas Gordon* (Cat.), pp.8-10.

WOLLEN, P. [1998] "London Swings". In BURROWS, D. (ed.).

WOOD, P. [1996] "Commodity". In NELSON, R.S. and SHIFF, R. (ed.), pp.382-406.

Exhibition catalogues (solo shows of Douglas Gordon)

24 Hour Psycho: Hitchcok's Tomb [Cat.1993]. Writings by Stuart Morgan. Glasgow: Tramway.

Double vision: Stan Douglas and Douglas Gordon [Cat.2000]. Writings by Michael Govan, Lynne Cooke, Sianne Nagai, Nancy Shaw and Neville Wakefield. New York: Dia Center for the Arts.

Douglas Gordon [Cat.1996]. Writings by Francis McKee and Rein Wolfs. Zurich: MIGROS Museum für Gegenwartskunst Zürich.

Douglas Gordon [Cat.1999]. Writings by Christine van Assche, Raymond Bellour, Oscar van den Boogaard, Jeremy Millar and Pavel Büchler. Lisbon: Centro Cultural de Belém.

Douglas Gordon [Cat.2001]. Writings by Russel Ferguson, Michael Darling, Francis McKee, Nancy Spector and David Sylvester. Los Angeles: MOCA. The MIT Press, Boston.

Douglas Gordon: Between darkness and light [Cat. 2007]. Writings by Markus Brüderlin, Holger Broeker, Keith Hartley, Ian Rankin, Jaroslav Andel and Michael Fried. Wolfsburg: Kunstmuseum Wolfsburg.

Douglas Gordon: Black Spot [Cat.2000]. Writings by Douglas Gordon e Mark Francis. London: Tate Gallery Publishing.

Douglas Gordon: blood, sweat, tears [Cat.2009]. Writings by Jaroslav Andel, Keith Hartley and Israel Rosenfield. Prague: DOX Centre for Contemporary Art.

Douglas Gordon: kidnapping [Cat.1998]. Writings by Douglas Gordon, Jan Debbaute and Francis McKee. Eindhoven: Stedelijk Van Abbemuseum.

Douglas Gordon: self-portrait of you + me, after the factory [Cat. 2007]. Writings by Mark Francis, Francis McKee and Lynne Cooke. New York: Gagosian Gallery.

Douglas Gordon: superhumanatural [Cat.2006]. Writings by Ian Rankin, Keith Hartley, Holger Broeker, Michael Fried and Jaroslav Andel. Edinburgh: National Galleries of Scotland.

Douglas Gordon's The Vanity of Allegory [Cat.2005]. Writings by Nancy Spector and Francis McKee. Deutsche Guggenheim Berlin. New York: Guggenheim Museum Publications.

Douglas Gordon: Timeline [Cat.2006]. Writings by Klaus Biesenbach. New York: The Museum of Modern Art.

Douglas Gordon: What you want me to say...I'm already dead. [Cat. 2006]. Writings by Rosa Maria Malet, Barry Barker and Frédéric Hermel. Barcellona, Fundació Joan Miró.

Douglas Gordon: Words [Cat.1998]. Writings by Eckhard Schneider, Lynne Cooke, Friedrich Meschede and Charles Esche. Hannover: Kunstverein Hannover.

Entr'acte editie #3: Douglas Gordon [Cat.1995]. Writings by Jan Debbaut and Selma Klein Essink. Eindhoven: Stedelijk Van Abbemuseum.

Migrateurs: Douglas Gordon [Cat.1993]. Writings by Hans Ulrich Obrist. Paris: ARC Musée d'Art Moderne de la Ville de Paris.

Moderna Museet Projekt: Douglas Gordon [Cat.2001]. Writings by Maria Lind and Jonas Ekeberg. Stockholm: Moderna Museet.

Oú se trouvent les clefs? Unnaturalhistoire [Cat.2008]. Writings by Eric Mézil, Jacques Chiffoleau, Rudolf Sagmeister and Corinne Rondeau. Avignon: Collection Yvon Lambert. Paris: Edition Gallimar,.

prettymucheverywordwritten, spoken, heard, overheard from 1989... [Cat.2006]. Writings by Mirta D'Argenzio and Giorgio Verzotti. Rovereto: MART. Milan: Skira Editore.

What have I done: Douglas Gordon [Cat.2002]. Writings by Caroline Wetherilt and Jonathan Jones. London: Hayward Gallery Publishing.

Exhibition catalogues (group shows of Douglas Gordon)

10 Jahre museum in progress – Modularer Katalog [Cat.2000]. Vol.3. Vienna: museum in progress.

Am Rande der Malerei [Cat.1995]. Writings by Ulrich Loock. Bern: Kunsthalle Bern.

Art from the UK: Angela Bulloch, Willie Doherty, Tracey Emin, Mona Hatoum, Douglas Gordon, Abigail Lane, Sarah Lucas, Sam Taylor-Wood, Rachel Whiteread [Cat.1998]. Munich: Sammlung Goetz.

Artisti Britannici a Roma [Cat.1996]. Writings by Mario Codognato. Rome: Galleria Bonomo. Torino: Umberto Allemandi.

Babylon: Mythos und Wahrheit [Cat.2008]. Writings by Moritz Wullen (ed.). , Berlin: Pergamonmuseum. Munich: Hirmer Verlag.

Bellgrove [Cat.1991]. Writings by Alan Dunn and Lindsay Litho. Glasgow: The Bellgrove Station.

Desire Lines – Art on Campus [Cat.2009]. University of Edinburgh: Talbot Rice Gallery.

Emotion: Young British and American Art from the Goetz Collection [Cat. 1998]. Hamburg: Deichtorhallen. Ostfildern: Hatjie Cantz.

General Release [Cat.1995]. Writings by Andrea Rose, Gregor Muir and James Roberts. Venice: Young British Artists at Scuola di San Pasquale. London: The British Council.

Guilt by Association [Cat.1992]. Writings by Thomas Lawson. Dublin: The Irish Museum of Modern Art.

Hall of Mirrors: Art and Film since 1945 [Cat.1996]. Writings by Kerry Brougher, Russel Ferguson and Jonathan Crary. Los Angeles, MOCA.

Kopfbahnhof/Terminal [Cat.1995]. Writings by Klaus Werner, Gerti Fietzek and Gregor Stemmrich. Leipzig: Förderkreis der Leipziger Galerie für Zeitgenössische Kunst.

Michael Craig-Martin: Landscapes [Cat.2001]. Dublin: Douglas Hyde Gallery.

Molteplici Culture: Arte Critica 92 [Cat.1992]. Rome, Museo del Folklore. Rome: Edizioni Carte Segrete.

Nach Weimar [Cat.1996]. Writings by Kalus Biesenbach and Nicolau Schafhausen. Weimar: Kunstsammlungen zu Weimar.

Nettverk - Glasgow : Richard Wright, Ross Sinclair, Julie Robert, Louise Hopkins, Douglas Gordon, Nathan Coley, Roderick Buchanan, Martin Boyce, Christine Borland, Claire Barclay [Cat.1998]. Oslo: Museet for Samtidskunst.

Out in the open: public art in Scotland past and present [Cat.1990]. Writings by Anne Millar. St.Andrews: University of St.Andrews.

Scream and scream again: Film in art [Cat.1996]. Writings by David Elliott and Chrissie Iles. Oxford: Museum of Modern Art.

Spellbound [Cat.1996]. Writings by Ian Christie and Philip Dodd. London: Hayward Gallery. London: The South Bank Centre.

Swan-Off [Cat.1996]. Writings by Maria Lind. Uppsala: Uppsala Castle.

theanyspacewhatever [Cat.2009]. Writings by Nancy Spector. New York: Guggenheim Museum.

The British Art Show 4 [Cat.1995]. Writings by Richard Cork, Rose Finn-Kelcey and Thomas Lawson. London: The South Bank Centre.

The Gathering: Building the Arts Council Collection [Cat.2010]. Longside Gallery, Yorkshire Sculpture Park.

The Turner Prize [Cat.1996]. Writings by Virginia Button. London: The Tate Gallery. London: Tate Gallery Publishing.

Exhibition catalogues (solo and group shows of other artists)

Christine Borland: progressive disorder [Cat.2001]. Sundee: Dundee Contemporary Arts. London: Book Works.

Christine Borland: Preserves [Cat.2006]. Writings by Katrina Brown, Charles Esche, Greg Hilty, Ian Hunt, Maria Lind, Ruth Richardson, Craig Richardson. Edinburgh: Fruitmarket Gallery.

Christine Borland: the dead teach the living: selected works 1990-1999 [Cat.2000]. Zurich: Migros Museum.

Damien Hirst [Cat.2012]. Writings by Anna Gallagher. London:

Tate Modern. London: Tate Publishing.

In-A-Gadda-Da-Vida: Angus Fairhurst, Damien Hirst, Sarah Lucas [Cat.2004]. Writings by Gregor Muir. London: Tate Britain. London: Tate Publishing.

I want to spend the rest of my life everywhere, with everyone, one to one, always, forever, now / Damien Hirst [Cat.1997]. Writings by Robert Violette. London: Booth-Clibborn Editions.

Sarah Lucas : exhibitions and catalogue raisonné : 1989-2005 [Cat.2005]. Touring exhibition: Kunstahalle Zürich, Kunstverein Hamburg, Tate Liverpool. Ostfildern: Hatje Cantz.

Sensation. Young British Artists from the Saatchi collection [Cat.1997]. Writings by Brooks Adams, Lisa Jardine, Martin Maloney, Norman Rosenthal, Richard Shone. London: Royal Academy of Arts. London: Thames & Hudson.

Sogni e conflitti. La dittatura dello spettatore [Cat.2003], Writings by Francesco Bonami. La Biennale di Venezia: 50th International Art Exhibition. Venice: Marsilio.

The British Art Show 3 [Cat.1990]. London: The South Bank Centre.

The Gap SHOW: junge zeitkritische Kunst aus Grossbritannien / young critical art from Great Britain [Cat.2002]. Writings by Rosemarie E. Pahlke. Dortmund: Museum am Ostwall.

Videonale 10 [Cat.2005]. Writings by Florian Matzner. Bonn: Kunstmuseum Bonn. Cologne: Walther König.

Young British Artists [Cat.1992]. London: Saatchi Gallery.

Articles and essays in art magazines

AKMAN, K. [2009] “Flashing Emin: critical analysis of 'spectacular' contemporary arts”. *Ctrl+P Journal of Contemporary Art.* No.15, October, pp.28-32.

BARCLAY MORGAN, A. [1999] “Memorial for Anonymous: An Interview with Christine Borland”. *Sculpture Magazine.* Vol.18, No.8, October.

BARRETT, D. [1997] “Christine Borland: Lisson Gallery”. *Frieze.* Is.35, June-August.

BELLINGHAM, D. and SINCLAIR, R. [2007] “Art & The Political Seminar: Part 2 Democracy and Its Discontents”. *Art&Research. Journal of ideas, contexts and methods.* Vol.1, No.2, Summer.

BHABHA, H.K. [1992] “Double Visions”. *ArtForum.* January.

BIRNBAUM, D. [1996] “Manifesta I: Rotterdam”. *ArtForum.* Vol.35, No.1, September.

BROWN, K. [1996] “Swan Off”. *Art Monthly.* No.196, May, pp.40-43.

BUSH, K. [2004] “Young British Art: Kate Bush on the YBA sensation”. *ArtForum.* October.

CAMPUS, P. [2008] “The expensive lens: interview with Douglas Gordon and David A. Ross”. *Tate etc.* No.14, October.

CASTLE, F.T. [1991] “A letter from New York. Visual philosophy in practice”. *Art Monthly.* No.151, November, pp.12-16.

CHAPMAN, P. [2003] "New Glasgow Boys". *The Independent.* 4th January.

COHEN, D. [1997] "Letter from London: Sensation". *artnet.com.* 24th October.

CONNOLLY HUNT, I. [1992] "Guilt by Associaction". *Frieze.* No.7, December.

CRICKMAY, C. [2003] "Art and social context: contextual art practice in education". *Journal of Visual Art Practice.* No.2, Vol.3.

DICKSON, M. [1989] "Underneath the Arches". *Projects UK.* Vol.10, Is.1, March.

FOX, D. [2013] "Then and Now, British Art and the 1990s". *Frieze.* Is.159.

FULLER, P. [1985] "The Lady's Not for Turner". *Art Monthly.* No.82, December 1984-January 1985, pp.5-6.

GAMBILLARA, M. [2011] "Charles Saatchi: lo specullector". *Artribune.* 23th July.

GILLICK, L. [1991] "The Placebo Effect. Some Art in Britain". *Arts Magazine.* May, pp.56-59.

GORDON, D. [1991], "Lawrence Weiner". *Variant.* Is.10, pp.36-41.

GRANT, S. [2009] "Cultural propaganda?". *Apollo.* 27th March.

GRAVANO, V. [2007] "Il critico come etnografo? Il posizionamento nella scrittura da Santa Fé ad Hal Foster". *Art'O.* Year 10, No.24, Autumn-Winter.

HADEN GUEST, A. [2008] "Damien Hirst - fresh from auctioning more than 200 pieces of his work". *Interview Magazine.* December. pp.155-157.

HERBERT, M. [2009] "Dematerialised: Jack Wendler Gallery 1971-1974". *Art Monthly.* June.

HOLMES, P. [2007] "The Branding of Damien Hirst". New York: ARTnews LLC. Available from: *artnews.com.* [Accessed: 16th January 2013]

HOUGHTON, G. [1996] "Spellbound Review". *The Edge.* February.

HUNT, A. [2005] "Art & Language". *Frieze.* No.94, October.

LUSINI, V. [2011] "Arte contemporanea a cultura dellalterità". *Studi Culturali.* Year 8, No.1, April.

MALONEY, M. [1995] "Douglas Gordon: Lisson". *Flash Art International.* Vol.28, No.182.

MATERASSI, L. [2012] "Intervista a Hans Ulrich Obrist". *Il Giornale dell'arte.* No.316, January.

MORGAN, S. [1991] "The Turner Prize". *Frieze.* No.1, September, pp.4-12.

MORGAN, S. [1996] "Manifesta: Looking back". *Frieze.* No.30, September-October.

MORGAN, S.J. [2001] "Contextualism: the development of a postmodern practice in higher education in the UK". *Kunst, Kontext, Vermittlung.* Conference Papers.

MORGAN, S.J. [2003] "Beautiful Impurity: British contextualism as processual postmodern practice". *Journal of Visual Art Practice.* No.2, Vol.3.

MORTON, T. [2002] "Art & Language". *Frieze.* No.66, April.

MORTON, T. [2006] "Definitely, Maybe". *Frieze.* No.98, April.

RENTON, A. [1991] "A new internationalism: interview with Karsten Schubert and Michael Craig-Martin". *Frieze.* Pilot Issue, Summer, pp. 16-20.

RENTON, A. [1993] "Douglas Gordon: Tramway". *Flash Art International.* Vol.26, No.172, October, p.92.

ROBERTS, J. [1996] "Mad for it!". *Third Text.* No.35, Summer.

SANS, J. [1996] "Douglas Gordon: Centre Georges Pompidou". *Artforum.* April, pp.169-170.

SEARLE, A. [1993] "Shut that door". *Frieze.* No.11, Summer.

SHERWIN, B. [2007] "Interview with Michael Craig-Martin". *Art Space Talk.* 16th August.

SINCLAIR, R. [1993] "Douglas Gordon". *Art Monthly.* No.167, June, pp.22-23.

SLADEN, M. [1996] "Spellbound: Art and Film". *Art Monthly.* No.195, April, pp.25-27.

SLOTOVER, M. [1991] "Windfall: Northern Lights". *Frieze.* No.1, September, pp.36-41.

STALLABRASS, J. [1994] "Success and failure of Peter Fuller". *New Left Review.* No.207.

STALLABRASS, J. [1996] "In and out of love with Damien Hirst". *New Left Review.* No.216.

TIMMINS, N. [1995] "A powerful indictment of the Eighties". *The Independent.* 10th February.

WALDEN, G. [1997] "Leave your weapons at the door. Democracy, State modernism and the official embrace of the arts". *London Review of Books.* 26th September.

Articles and reviews in newspapers

ALBERGE, D. [1996a] "Tate excludes shock factor from Turner Prize". *The Times.* 20th June.

ALBERGE, D. [1996b] "Turner contenders crave open mind as well as open eyes". *The Times.* 29th October.

BAIN, A. [1987] "Third Eye Centre, Glasgow: Experiments under nostalgia's umbrella". *The Herald.* 22th October.

BECKETT, A. [1996] "Is there life after the dead cow?". *Independent on Sunday.* 27th October, pp.18-22.

BERENS, J. [2008] "Freeze: 20 years on". *The Observer.* 1st June.

BLACK, C. [2006] "Interview with Christine Borland". *Sunday Herald.* 19th November. Available from: artandphilosophy.com. [Accessed: 22nd March 2014]

BLACKHURST, C. and HONIGSBAUM, M. [1997] "Royal Academy warned of acting as a dealer for Saatchi". *Independent on Sunday.* 14th September.

BORDEN, S. [2012] "Dissolving Scotland's Old Firm". *New York Times.* 8th August.

BREDIN, L. [1997] "Tie a knot in that bone". *The Telegraph.* 12 April. Available from: telegraph.co.uk. [Accessed: 22nd March 2014].

BRENNAN, M.[1993] "Re-runs of heaven and hell". *The Herald Scotland.* 30th December.

BRUCE, K. [1996] "Turner Prize goes to Glasgow artist". *The Herald.* 29th November.

BURDON, J. [1996] "Turner prize is hit by a lack of controversy". *The Scotsman*, 29th October.

COLIN, B. [1996] "The man they couldn't hang". *The Scotsman: Weekend.* 17th August.

COLLINGS, M. [1996] "The Hirst effect". *Telegraph Magazine.* 21st September.

CONNOLLY, C. [2007] "Michael Craig-Martin: out of the ordinary". *The Telegraph.* 24th November.

CORK, R. [1996] "Life and death in the glow of magic lanterns". *The Times*, 6th August.

DETHERIDGE, A. [1997] "Iniezione di sangue per la Royal Academy – Londra, Sensation". *Il Sole 24 Ore.* 21st September.

DORMENT, R. [1996a] "Mixed media caught on camera". *The Daily Telegraph.* 28th February.

DORMENT, R. [1996b] "How do you measure modern art". *The Daily Telegraph.* 6th November.

DORMENT, R. [1996c] "Artists find a new frame of reference". *The Daily Telegraph.* 29th November.

EASTON, M. [2011] "Britain's mysterious baby boom". *BBC News UK.* 17th June.

EDAMARIAM, A. [2009] "All the fun of the fair". *The Guardian.* 3rd October.

EDAMARIAM, A. [2011] "The Saturday interview: Sarah Lucas". *The Guardian.* 27th May. Available from: theguardian.co.uk. [Accessed: 12th March 2014].

FEAVER, W. [1996a] "Primal screen". *The Observer Review.* 25th February.

FEAVER, W. [1996b] "Plight of the paper people". *The Observer.* 21st July.

FEAVER, W. [1996c] "Forget the fat ladies. Rubens was also big on trees and cows". *The Observer.* 3rd November.

GARNER, L. [1996] "Turning art on its head". *The Express.* 29th October.

GLAISTER, D. [1996a] "Turner shortlist fails to shock". *The Guardian.* 20th June.

GLAISTER, D. [1996b] "Turner show will turn no heads". *The Guardian.* 29th October.

GLAISTER, D. [1996c] "Slow motion movies help outsider to take £20,000". *The Guardian,* 29th November.

GRAHAM-DIXON, A. [1990] "The Midas Touch? Graduates of Goldsmiths School of Art dominate the current British art scene". *The Independent,* 31st July, p.13.

GRAHAM-DIXON, A. [1996] "Spreading the word". *The Independent Tabloid.* 12th November.

HENRY, C. [1996] "The very moving image of success". *The Herald.* 11th December.

HIGGINS, C. [2007] "Rachel Whiteread Turner Prize winner 1993". *The Guardian.* 8th September.

HIGGINS, C. [2011a] "Glasgow's Turner connection. Why does Glasgow keep producing so many Turner prize winners? Could it be all down to this man?". *The Guardian.* 17th October.

HIGGINS, C. [2011b] "Turner prize winner Martin Boyce: triumph of a slowburner". *The Guardian.* 6th December.

HILL, P. [1996] "Get the slow down on film". *The Herald.* 18th November.

KIMMELMANN, M. [1996] "Cows, Pigs, Cigarettes: All Dead". *New York Times.* 10th May. In VV.AA. [2002], pp.2961-2962.

KIMMELMANN, M. [1998] "Installation art moves on, moves in" . *New York Times.* 9th August. In VV.AA. [2002], pp.2973-2975.

JACKSON, K. [1996] "The eye of the beholder". *Independent on Sunday.* 25th February.

JAMIESON, T. [2008] "Connected: They have inspired the biggest names in scottish art. Meet the mentors". *The Herald Magazine.* 18th October, pp.18-21.

LACK, J. [2008] "Artist of the week no 1: Mat Collishaw". *The Guardian.* 23rd July.

LAPPIN, T. [1996] "What's your name". *Scotland on Sunday.* 17th November.

LILLINGTON, D. [1990] "The East Country Yard Show". *Time Out.* 18th June, p.55.

LISTER, D. [1996a] "Boys' own club occupies shortlist for the Turner Prize". *The Independent.* 20th June.

LISTER, D. [1996b] "Turner judges reject politically correct shortlist". *The Independent.* 29th October.

MACDONALD, M. [1997] "Shark operator". *Observer Life Magazine.* 31st August.

MANSFIELD, S. [2012] "Loyalist and Republican bands march to very different tunes, so how did Roddy Buchanan splice the two sides of the sectarian divide?". *Scotland on Sunday.* 8th July. Available from: *scotsman.com.* [Accessed: 12th March 2014].

MCALPINE, J. [1996] "Away goals of an artist abroad". *The Sunday Times.* 17th November.

MCEWAN, J. [1996a] "To the beat of a poptastical drum". *The Sunday Telegraph: The Sunday Review.* 25th February.

MCEWAN, J. [1996b] "It may swing but it don't mean a thing". *The Sunday Telegraph.* 3rd November.

MCEWAN, J. [1996c] "The Turner Prize". *The Telegraph.* 7th December.

PITMAN, J. [1997] "Art Breaker". *The Times.* 13th September.

RAYNOLDS, N. [1996] "Scottish artist captures the Turner Prize on video". *The Daily Telegraph.* 29th November.

ROMNEY, J. [1996] "Popcorn, Britpop and pop art. Does it work? Yes, says film critic Jonathan Romney". *The Guardian: Outlook.* 24th February.

ROSS, A. [1996] "Patrick Bristle". *The Sun.* 14th November.

SEARLE, A. [1996a] "Popcorn, Britpop and pop art. Does it work? No, says critic Adrian Searle". *The Guardian: Outlook.* 24th February.

SEARLE, A. [1996b], "Bananas". *The Guardian: G2.* 29th October.

SEARLE, A. [1996c] "Winning game of good and evil: Guardian art critic Adrian Searle on the vindication of film installations". *The Guardian.* 29th November.

SEATON, M. [1996] "Film in art: How to make the Turner shortlist". *New Statesman.* 19th July.

SHEPHERD, F. [1996] “Trust in me”. *The List.* 15th November.

SIMON, E. [2011] “Baby boomers are very privileged human beings”. *The Telegraph.* 22th October.

SMITH, R. [1992] “Women artists engage the enemy”. *New York Times.* 16th August. In VV.AA. [2002], pp.2938-2940

SMITH, R. [1993] “The best of sculptors, the worst of sculptors”. *New York Times.* 30th November. In VV.AA. [2002], pp.2947-2949.

SMITH, R. [2004] “Art Reviews: Good, Evil And Life, Head-On”. *The New York Times.* 20th February.

SOOKE, A. [2008] “Gary Hume: the doors that unhinged the establishment”. *The Telegraph.* 14th June.

STRINGER, R. [1996] “Photograpghs and technology vie for GBP20,000 Turner Prize”. *Evening Standard.* 19th June.

VILLIERS, S. [1993a] “Burgeoning in Spring”. *The Herald Scotland.* 30th April.

VILLIERS, S. [1993b] “Psycho with surreal touch for fast-frame generation”. *The Herald Scotland.* 3rd May.

VV.AA. [1996a] “Turner Prize is hit by a lack of controversy”. *The Post.* 28th October.

VV.AA. [1996b] “Hitchcock classic made name for artist” in *The Herald,* 29 November 1996

WASER, G. [1996] “Kunst im Zeitlupentempo: Douglas Gordon - Turner Prize Träger”. *Neue Zürcher Zeitung Feuilleton.* 30th November.

WATSON, L. [2012] “Spot the difference: Damien Hirst painted only five of the 300 'spot paintings' in his latest collection”. *The Daily Mail.* 13th January.

www.ingramcontent.com/pod-product-compliance
Ingram Content Group UK Ltd.
Pitfield, Milton Keynes, MK11 3LW, UK
UKHW061545051026
15625UKWH00025B/693/J
* 9 7 8 1 6 2 2 7 3 0 2 9 2 *